THE BLACK
BOOK

THE BLACK BOOK

The Ruthless Murder of Jews
by German-Fascist Invaders
Throughout the Temporarily-Occupied
Regions of The Soviet Union
and in the Death Camps of Poland
During the War of 1941-1945

Prepared under the editorship of
Ilya Ehrenburg & Vasily Grossman

Translated from the Russian by
John Glad and James S. Levine

HOLOCAUST LIBRARY
New York

Library of Congress Catalog Card No. 81-81517
ISBN 0-89604-031-3 Cloth
ISBN 0-89604-032-1 Paper

Cover Design by Michael Meyerowitz
Printed in the United States

Contents

1. Material listed under this title is absent from the manuscript, and the title itself was carefully crossed out of the table of contents. (The title was restored with the aid of infrared rays.)

2. See preceding note. Maria Mikhailovna Shkapsky Andreevsky (1891-1952) was a poetess and essay writer. In 1942 she published a book, "This Really Happened," in which she told of the Nazi atrocities in the U.S.S.R.

3. Material listed under this title is absent from the manuscript, and the title itself was carefully crossed out of the table of contents. (The title was restored with the aid of infrared rays.) Hersh Smolyar was a Jewish journalist and author who wrote a book of memoirs about the struggle and resistance in the Minsk ghetto: *Avengers of the Ghetto* (translated from the Yiddish by M. Shambadal), *Der Emes*, Moscow, 1947. English translation available.

4. Material absent from manuscript. See preceding footnote.

5. Mention is made of the massacre of the Jews in the village of Gory in Ehrenburg's book *Murderers of Peoples*, Volume II, publication of *Der Emes*, Moscow, 1945, pp. 136-37.

6. Material listed under this title is absent from the manuscript, and the title itself was carefully crossed out of the table of contents. (The title was restored with the aid of infrared rays.)

7. Sutskever, Abram (Abram Gertsevich, b. 1913), poet writes in Yiddish. During the Second World War he participated in the resistance movement in the Vilnius Ghetto and also in a Jewish partisan group. He became a member of the Jewish Anti-Fascist Committee in 1944, and wrote for the newspaper *Einikeit*. He testified as a witness at the Nuremberg Trials. Since 1947 he has lived in Israel. At the present time he edits the Yiddish quarterly "Di goldene Keyt" (The Golden Chain), Tel Aviv.

8. Meyer Yelin (b. 1910), prose writer, writes in Yiddish and Lithuanian. While in the Kaunas Ghetto during the war years, he participated in the resistance movement and kept a chronicle of the ghetto. In 1973 he repatriated to Israel.

9. Yakov Iosade (1911), prose writer, playwright; writes mainly in Lithuanian. During World War II years he fought in the ranks of the Sixteenth Lithuanian Division; wrote for army publications.

10. Material listed under this title is absent from the manuscript, and the title itself was carefully crossed out of the table of contents. (The title was re-established with the aid of infrared rays.) The full title of this commission was: The Extraordinary Commission to Ascertain and Investigate the War Crimes of the German-Fascist Invaders and Their Accomplices.

11. Chapter not included in the English edition.

12. See footnote no. 10 for full title.

From the Editors of *The Black Book*

The Black Book is the story of the mass murder of Soviet Jewish citizens perpetrated by the German-Fascist authorities throughout the temporarily-occupied areas of Russia, The Ukraine, Byelorussia, Latvia, Lithuania, and Estonia.*

In those instances where the description touches upon the fate of Soviet Jewish citizens transported to death camps on the territory of Poland (Oswiecim, Treblinka, Sobibor), the editors considered it essential to include in the book a description of those camps, even though they were on Polish, and not Soviet territory.

All the materials which have been included in *The Black Book* are strictly documentary. These materials can be divided into three categories:

1) Letters, diaries, stenograms of stories and testimony by witnesses and victims of Fascist violence who escaped death. Many of the letters were penned by persons who were executed by the Germans and have been given to the editors of *The Black Book* by their relatives and acquaintances.

2) Articles written by Soviet authors. These articles were written on the basis of testimony, letters, diaries, stenograms of stories which were made available to the editors of *The Black Book*. Everything discussed in these articles corresponds precisely to the materials upon which they were based. In some instances the writers talked personally with witnesses, examined the sites of mass execution and the areas upon which the ghettos and death camps were situated, or were present at the openings of mass graves and the writing of official records.

3) Materials presented to the editors of *The Black Book* by the extraordinary commission to ascertain and investigate the war crimes of the Fascist German invaders and their accomplices. These materials consist of testimony given to the official investigators by persons who directly organized and carried out the murders, and also of testimony given by witnesses.

*Moldavia is not mentioned among the occupied Soviet territories. The material on Moldavia (L. Bazarov, "German-Rumanian Atrocities in Kishinev") formed part of the original variation of the manuscript, but is not present in the final version. In 1945 Ehrenburg published in Yiddish "Letters from Orphans" (*Murderers of Peoples*, vol. II, Moscow, 1945). Of these letters, only those of children in the Ukraine were included in *The Black Book*. Letters from children in Bessarabia were excluded.

In preparing *The Black Book* for publication, the editors have set themselves the following goals:

The Black Book should become a memorial placed over the innumerable graves of Soviet people viciously murdered by the German Fascists.

The Black Book is intended to serve as material for the prosecution of the Fascist villains who organized and participated in the murder of millions of old men, women, and children.

* * *

The Russian-language edition of this book was prepared by *Yad Vashem* (Martyrs' and Heroes' Remembrance Authority, Jerusalem), the Israeli Research Institute of Contemporary Society, and the Tarbut Publishing House. The book was printed from the manuscript of a collection compiled by Vasily Grossman and Ilya Ehrenburg in 1944-1946. *The Black Book* was prepared for publication in the U.S.S.R., but never came out. The printing plates were destroyed.

This edition also includes materials from *The Black Book* which were published in the Soviet press but were absent from the manuscript received in Israel. The Israeli editors have supplemented the text with notes, brief biographical data about the contributors, an index of names, and a geographical index. Some of the pages which were absent in the manuscript were retranslated into Russian from the Rumanian edition, "Ilya Ehrenburg, Vasilii Grossman, Lew Ozerow, Vladimir Lidin . . . *Cartea Neagra*, Bucharest (1946)." In comparing the manuscript with the collections MERDER FUN FELKER, by Ilya Ehrenburg, "Der Emes," Moscow, Vol. I-1944, Vol. II-1945, a few minor omissions have been noted. These omitted passages have been restored by retranslation from the Yiddish. The unclear lines and cut passages in V. Grossman's essay, "Treblinka," have been restored on the basis of his book, "The Hell of Treblinka" (Moscow, 1945). The unclear parts in the letter of P. Fradis-Milner have been clarified by the author herself, who now lives in Israel.

The manuscript of *The Black Book* was prepared for publication and provided with indexes by the researchers, Mark Kipnis and Khaya Lifshits.

The chief editor of the edition was Felix Dektor.

We wish to express our gratitude to Susan Ashe for her fine style editing of the text and also to Carol Pearce and Cynthia Rosenberger for their work on the index.

CONTRIBUTORS:

Margarita ALIGER
Pavel ANTOKOLSKY
Vagram APRESIAN
Osip CHERNY
Abraham DERMAN
Ilya EHRENBURG
Ruvim FRAYERMAN
Yefim GEKHTMAN
Valery GERASIMOV
Leyb GOLDBERG
Vasily GROSSMAN
Vasily ILYENKOV
Vera INBER
Yakov IOSADE
Vsevolod IVANOV
Veniamin KAVERIN
Lev KVITKO
Rakhil KOVNATOR
Vladimir LIDIN
Bernard MARK
Georgy MUNBLIT
Girsh OSHEROVICH
Lev OZEROV
Ovady SAVICH
Lidia SEIFULLIN
Viktor SHKLOVSKY
Abram SUTSKEVER
Ilya TRAININ
Meyer YELIN

The Destruction of the Jewish Population on German-Occupied Soviet Territory

During the Second World War the Nazis murdered six million Jews, among them one and one half million Jews on occupied Soviet territory.

The policies of Nazi Germany with regard to the Jews were characterized by a gradually increasing brutality. From January, 1933, when Hitler came to power, until the beginning of the Second World War, Nazi policies regarding the Jews were aimed at depriving them of their civil rights, forcing them to abandon Germany, and confiscating their property. With the beginning of the Second World War and the German occupation of the territories of western and central Poland, Nazi policies entered a new, more vicious stage. Jews were forced into the ghettos, where they were subjected to all sorts of humiliations, starved, forced to wear distinguishing signs, used for heavy forced labor, and made to pay impossible war indemnities. Jews were subjected to collective punishments, and many were killed for the slightest rule violations or refusals to submit.

The physical destruction of the Jews in Europe began after Germany attacked the U.S.S.R. in June, 1941. Soviet Jews were the first to be marked for death.

The decision to totally liquidate the Jews precisely after the attack on the Soviet Union resulted from Hitler's conception of the role of Jews in the U.S.S.R. and the connection between Bolshevism and Jewry. Hitler viewed the Soviet government and communist ideology as an instrument utilized by Jews to control the world.

The physical destruction of the Jews on the territory of the Soviet Union was part of the so-called "Final Solution of the Jewish Question." It was also viewed as a means of destroying the Soviet state and of preparing the territories of the Soviet Union for German colonization.

The directives of the plan "Barbarossa" (the code for the attack on the Soviet Union), approved by the Wehrmacht on March 13, 1941, state: "In order to prepare for the political control of the territory on which the army will be operating, the SS *Reichsführer* [Himmler] receives special instructions from the *Führer*. These instructions are determined by the decisive struggle taking place between two opposing political systems."

In practice, the *Führer's* "special instructions" amounted to destroying all Jews and communist activists on occupied territories.

The "Orders on Courts Martial and Commissars" issued by the high command of the *Wehrmacht* in May and June 1941 stressed that all citizens suspected of hostile activity — communists, military commissars, and political activists — were to be executed without investigation or trial.

These orders contain no direct mention of Jews, but they had been defined earlier as communists and enemies of the *Reich*. Many documents of the *Wehrmacht* refer to Jews as a principal hostile force. These orders were thus used by the German army as a justification for the mass destruction of Jews on occupied territory.

Four SS operative groups (*Einsatzgruppen*) were formed to carry out the immediate task of destroying Jews and commissars. To achieve maximum secrecy these groups were issued oral instructions on the destruction of the Jews. The heads of the *Einsatzgruppen* stressed this fact during the trials which took place after the war.

Einsatzgruppe A was active in the Baltic republics and in the direction of Leningrad; *Einsatzgruppe B* was responsible for Byelorussia and the territories leading to Moscow; *Einsatzgruppe C* raged in the Ukraine; *Einsatzgruppe D* was assigned the southern Ukraine, the Crimea, and the northern Caucasus.

They left behind them only carelessly filled-in ravines — the mass graves of those barbarously murdered in Rumbuli (near Riga), the Ninth Fort (Kaunas), Ponary (near Vilnius), Babi Yar (in Kiev), the Travitsk Valley (near Kharkov), and many other places.

The occupied area of the Soviet Union was divided into two zones. A military administration was established in the one immediately adjoining the line of the front. The second zone, which comprised the rear, was administered by a German civil administration headed by the Minister of Eastern Territories, Alfred Rosenberg. This zone included Estonia, Latvia, Lithuania, western Byelorussia along with its capital, Minsk, and that part of the Ukraine which extended to the Dnieper.

In territories placed under military administration, the *Wehrmacht* gave a free hand to the *Einsatzgruppen*, and the Jews were almost totally eradicated in the very first months of the occupation.

Due to an inadequate work force, and in particular a shortage of technicians, the German civil administration ordered that the ghettos and labor-camps be preserved in Vilnius, Kaunas, Minsk, Lvov, Transnistria, and certain other places.

Life in the ghettos has been described in sufficient detail: hunger, fear, unbearable living conditions. The Germans regularly carried out "aktions," during which they destroyed all those incapable of work — the children, the sick, and the elderly.

The prisoners of the ghettos were forbidden all forms of social activity, the observance of religious rituals, even love. Before dying, Jews had to admit that they were an inferior people; it was the intent of the Germans to torment, degrade, crush them to the maximum extent, and only afterwards — to kill them.

The Jews of the ghettos bravely resisted the Nazis' barbaric actions. Ignoring German orders, they organized medical aid, carried on cultural and religious activities, assisted each other in a social sense. Synagogues functioned, and there were illegal deliveries of food. Concealed radio receivers brought the ghetto prisoners information on the defeats of the German armies, and forbidden publications were smuggled into the ghettos through the barbed wire. Some of the ghettos had underground archives intended to preserve written testimony about these terrible times, and the story of the struggle and death of the Jews.

All this was fraught with great risk, and thousands of Jews paid with their lives to preserve their human dignity in these unbearable conditions.

In the course of 1943 the ghettos and forced-labor camps were liquidated. Most of the inhabitants of the ghettos were destroyed within those areas where they resided, and the rest were transported to death camps: Sobibor, Treblinka, Belżec, Majdanek. The very last labor camps were eliminated just before the German retreat in 1944.

Those few Jews who were saved from the ghettos and the camps searched for refuge, but they were frequently unable to find support among the local population. A significant proportion of the local inhabitants — particularly in the Baltic republics and in the Western Ukraine — actively collaborated with the Germans in destroying the Jews. Some of these people were totally indifferent to the fate of their former neighbors and acquaintances, who were now doomed to die. The motives for such an attitude varied — fear of German reprisals, anti-Semitism, greed, etc. People willing to risk their lives to save Jews were few in number.

The Jews who remained on occupied territory attempted to resist

Hitler's troops. A Jewish underground force was formed in the ghettos and the camps. This underground force included representatives of differing political persuasions. Jews of the Vilnius, Kaunas, Bialystok, Minsk, and other ghettos undertook a brave but unequal fight with the dark forces of Nazism.

The members of these underground organizations formed resistance groups and carried on subversive activity in the rear. Many Jews who had managed to escape the camps — both individuals and groups — joined the partisans. Tens of thousands of Jews fought in Jewish and multi-national detachments in the forests of Byelorussia, the Ukraine, and Eastern Lithuania. They attacked German troops, organized ambushes along the roads, set mines, and derailed trains. Thousands of Jews sacrificed their lives in ghetto uprisings and in the partisan war. There were nearly a half million Jews in the Red Army during the (Great) Patriotic War, and many died bravely on the front. The Jews of the U.S.S.R. distinguished themselves in this war, and more than 150 of them received the highest award — the Gold Medal and the title of Hero of the Soviet Union.

When Soviet troops liberated the occupied territories, there were no Jews left in these areas. The handful that survived had found refuge among the local population or had fought with the partisans. Approximately one and one half million Jews were brutally murdered by Hitler's troops.

The lasting testimony of these events has been set down in the pages of *The Black Book*, which is intended to serve as a reminder and a warning to the entire world.

Yitzhak Arad

The History of the Manuscript
of *The Black Book*

Before *The Black Book* could appear in print, the manuscript received in 1965 by the archives of *Yad Vashem*, The Institute to Honor the Memory of the Victims of Nazism and the Heroes of the Resistance, needed lengthy preparation.

I first heard about this monumental collection of materials and documents a few weeks after the end of World War Two. The collection was compiled mainly by I. Ehrenburg and is dedicated to the fate of the Jews during World War Two. The well-known New York publicist, Ben-Zion Goldberg, visited the Central Jewish Historical Commission in Poland and told us he had been invited by Ehrenburg to visit Moscow to discuss the possibility of publishing in English a collection of materials dedicated to the Jewish resistance movement and the destruction of Soviet Jewry.

Jewish researchers of liberated Poland had long awaited the appearance of such a publication. Such a publication was also awaited by the Jews who had survived, many of whom had handed over documents they had preserved not only to the Historical Commission, created in 1944, but also directly to Ilya Ehrenburg. At the time Ehrenburg was the most popular (Soviet) writer and publicist who as is well known had furthered the victory over Nazism by writing articles full of anger from the moment Nazi Germany attacked the Soviet Union. His articles were read avidly by soldiers of the Red Army, and he himself was idolized by young people in the universities.

From the very first days of the war, Ehrenburg began to gather documents and materials on German war crimes, the national tragedy of the Jewish people, its resistance and heroism. Red-Army soldiers brought him their diaries, wills, photographs, songs, and documents found in destroyed towns and villages. Many of the documents and materials testifying as to the Nazi crimes were given to him by the partisans. Among them were documents of testimony by witnesses of Jewish heroism in those terrible years.

The poet and partisan, Abram Sutskever, recalls that, when he met with Ehrenburg and told him of the tragedy of Lithuanian Jewry, Ehrenburg jotted down the most important facts in pencil. "Ehrenburg fell in love with those heroic Jewish partisans," Sutskever writes. Later Ehrenburg was actually to write a story,

"Death of a Hero," about the tragic death of Itsik Vittenberg, a partisan commander in the Vilnius ghetto. As for the poet-partisan, Abram Sutskever, Ehrenburg dedicated an article to him entitled "Victory of a Man" (*Pravda*, 4/29 1944).

During the war, Ehrenburg collected an enormous amount of material on the mass destruction of the Jewish population. This collection included, among other documents, a Greek-language prose work on the tragedy of Greek Jewry, a long poem written in French on cigarette paper in a death camp, an approximately two-hundred page drama written in Hebrew, the diaries of several Jewish children who had found refuge in Catholic churches, and poems and notes in Yiddish. All these materials were gathered by Ehrenburg in three enormous albums. There is reason to believe that Ehrenburg hoped to donate these unique materials to the Jewish University in Jerusalem. During a visit to the Jewish Museum in Vilnius, he gave the materials to the museum under the condition that they would be returned to him in the event that the museum should ever be closed. (Ehrenburg already foresaw such a possibility.) In fact, when the museum was closed, the albums (manuscripts) were returned to Ehrenburg.

* * *

By the beginning of 1943 Ehrenburg had worked out a plan for publishing three books. The first was to tell of the murder of Jews on Soviet territory. (Later this book was given the tentative title "The Black Book.") The theme of the second book was formulated by Ehrenburg at a plenary meeting of the Jewish Anti-Fascist Committee in March, 1943; his speech was published under the title, "The Need for an Anthology about Jewish Heroes Who Participated in The Great Patriotic War." He proposed that the third book be dedicated to Jewish partisans who fought on German-occupied Soviet territories.

To carry out this grandiose plan, the Jewish Anti-Fascist Committee formed The Literary Committee, whose primary task was to prepare the first volume for publication. The well-known Soviet writer, Vasily Grossman, took an active part in this work. Ehrenburg invited a number of authors, Jews and non-Jews, to collaborate in this task. These were people who possessed materials received from survivors and also memoirs of how they themselves had survived the war years. Abram Sutskever, for example, wrote about two hundred pages of memoirs on the destruction of the

Jews of Vilnius. (The manuscript was translated into the Russian by Rakhil Kovnator.)

The first version of *The Black Book* was completed in the beginning of 1944, and excerpts from it were published in the magazine *Znamya* (The Banner) with a preface by Ehrenburg entitled "Murderers of Peoples." In the same year, the publishing house "Der Emes" published in Yiddish the first part of the book under the editorship of Ehrenburg: *Murderers of Peoples*. The second part appeared in 1945. Ehrenburg wrote a separate preface to each part of the book. Ehrenburg included a number of documents on Nazi crimes and testimony by witnesses in these two small publications. Ehrenburg had himself questioned high-ranking captured German officers, and in these instances his first words were: "I am a Jew." This always had a terrifying effect on the Nazis. Aside from testimony by witnesses, communications, documents, and fragments from diaries written in the ghettos, this collection contained many letters written by Jewish soldiers and officers from recaptured cities and villages. These persons also sent to Ehrenburg letters that they had found from Jews who had perished. Each letter repeated the words: "This must not be forgotten."

In the same year Ehrenburg compiled a collection in Russian and French entitled "One Hundred Letters." These were selected letters sent to him during the Second World War. Among them are letters describing the Jewish tragedy. The French text of this collection appeared in Moscow in 1944, but the publication of the Russian text was stopped. The only copy of the proofs still extant is in Ehrenburg's personal archive.

Ehrenburg invariably answered the hundreds of letters sent to him by Jews from all corners of the Soviet Union, asking about the fate of their friends and relatives. He would do everything possible to find these people or at least learn their fate.

The Black Book edited by Ehrenburg and Grossman represents, in its published form, the work of more than forty writers and journalists. Approximately one third of the testimony contained in the book was edited directly by Ehrenburg himself. He said of the book: "This is not literature, but true stories told without any embellishment."

Of great significance are little-known facts testifying to the heroism and national pride of the Jews and demonstrating how unarmed Jews attempted to resist their persecutors and heroically met their death.

Among the authors were Jewish writers now living in Israel: Abram Sutskever, Meyer Yelin, Hersh Smolyar. Some authors became victims of the Stalin regime's repressions. Leyb (Lev) Kvitko was shot together with other representatives of Jewish culture in the beginning of the fifties. Girsh Osherovich was another such victim, having spent seven years in Soviet prisons and camps. (Osherovich now lives in Israel.)

Other famous writers and journalists — Jews and non-Jews — took part in preparing *The Black Book*: M. Aliger, V. Ivanov, R. Frayerman, V. Inber, V. Shklovsky, O. Savich, A. Derman, and others. The work continued from 1944 to 1946.

Ehrenburg's original intent was to immediately translate *The Black Book* into several languages — first of all into English. Ben-Zion Goldberg, who met with him in 1945, spoke of this. Goldberg was one of the leaders of the American committee of Jewish writers, artists, and scientists who organized the trip to the United States of the Moscow Jewish Anti-Fascist Committee — Solomon (Shloyme) Mikhoels and Itsik Fefer.

The preparation of *The Black Book* for publication had reached its peak when the Literary Commission of the Jewish Anti-Fascist Committee received instructions to stop work on the edition and hand over directly to the Jewish Committee all materials pertaining to *The Black Book*. The instructions came from S. Lozovsky, head of the Soviet Information Bureau (Sovinformbureau) and also official head of the Jewish Anti-Fascist Committee.

After the dissolution of the Literary Commission, there appeared in *Pravda* an article by G. Aleksandrov: "Comrade Ehrenburg is Simplifying." The article contained severe criticism of Ehrenburg for supposedly not distinguishing clearly between Fascist Germans and Democratic Germans.

Ehrenburg wrote the following letter to Sutskever about the dissolution of the Literary Commission:

Dear Abram Gertsevich,

S.A. Lozovsky had decided to entrust the publication of the Black Book *directly to the Jewish Anti-Fascist Committee. Therefore the Literary Commission which I created to prepare this book for publication is ceasing its activity.*

You may have the materials which you have edited and dispose of them as you see fit and publish them.

I thank you, Abram Gertsevich, from the bottom of my heart for your participation in the work of the commission. I am deeply convinced that the work which you have accomplished will not be lost to history.

Respectfully yours,
Ilya Ehrenburg

There is no doubt that after the Literary Commission was dissolved, the Jewish Anti-Fascist Committee reduced the size of the book and made certain changes in the text. This is evident from the changes made in the textual content of the copy sent to Eretz-Israel.

Copies of the corrected version of the manuscript of *The Black Book* were distributed for publication to various Jewish organizations in the U.S.A., Rumania, Eretz-Israel (Palestine).

The version of *The Black Book* published in Israel also relates of events which took place in the middle and end of 1944, of the victories of the Allies over Germany (May 1945), and of the Nuremberg Trials (end of 1945). Therefore the manuscript could not have been completed earlier than 1946.

In the words of Ehrenburg, who continued to do everything in his power to get it published, the *Black Book* was printed in Russian in the publishing house, "Der Emes." Ehrenburg writes: "When the Jewish Anti-Fascist Committee was shut down at the end of 1948, the book was destroyed."

The Black Book of Jewish death and heroism and of German evil deeds during the Second World War had become a hindrance in the postwar politics of the Soviet Union.

In those years the Soviet Union did a sharp about-face with regard to Germany: East Germany had entered into the orbit of the Soviet Union and this signified a certain rapprochement with the Germans. Stalin ordered the dissolution of the Extraordinary Commission to Ascertain and Investigate the War Crimes of the Fascist-German Invaders and Their Accomplices. All cases were ordered closed which had to do with German crimes — among them, those related to the destruction of the Jews.

It was only in the sixties that the investigation of Nazi crimes became topical and the trials of war criminals were renewed.

As early as 1944, another of Ehrenburg's important projects was "buried": the publication of a so-called "Red Book" about the participation of Jews in the Great Patriotic War. Ehrenburg mentions this indirectly: "That summer the Soviet Information Bureau asked me to compose a message to American Jews about the crimes of Hitler's legions and about the necessity of destroying the Third Reich as quickly as possible. One of A. S. Shcherbakov's assistants, Kondakov, rejected my text on the grounds that there was no need to dwell on the feats of Jewish soldiers in the Red Army: "That is bragging."

Nevertheless, on the eve of the dissolution of the anti-Fascist committee, the book, "Partisan Friendship," was published about the participation of Jewish partisans in the Great Patriotic War, their heroism, and feats in battle.

Thanks to the efforts of Benjamin West and Yad Vashem, this book was published in a Hebrew translation in Israel in 1968.

As stated above, the publication of *The Black Book* was stopped in Moscow, but the first section was published in Rumania in 1946 by The Democratic Organization of the Rumanian Jewish Union together with the Rumanian Institute of Documentation.

In the same year, a *Black Book* appeared in English in New York, published by the "Jewish Committee for the Publication of *The Black Book*." Member organizations of this committee included the World Jewish Congress, the Jewish Anti-Fascist Committee of the USSR, Va'ad Leumi (The National Committee of Eretz-Israel), and The American Committee of Jewish Writers, Artists, and Scientists. This book is a collection of materials about the destruction of Jews on European territory. The sections devoted to the destruction of the Jews and their resistance in Soviet Russia, the Ukraine, Byelorussia, Lithuania, Latvia, and Estonia contain large excerpts from the basic source — the Russian text of *The Black Book*, although there is no mention of the source from which these texts were taken. Only the notes sometimes make mention of writers who participated in the compilation of the basic material of *The Black Book* — Ilya Ehrenburg, Abram Sutskever, and others.

According to Abram Sutskever, who brought the text of *The Black Book* to Yad Vashem in 1965, the book had been sent to Eretz-Israel in 1946. Aside from the testimony of witnesses, the book contained documents from the State Archives of the U.S.S.R., collected by I. Trainin. The manuscript also contained thirty-six photographs found among the belongings of captured and dead Germans.

Researchers of the Yad Vashem archives immediately took measures to restore the manuscript, which was in extremely bad condition. The corrections made by hand on the yellowed, partially ruined pages of typescript could barely be read. Unfortunately, attempts to locate the lost part of the manuscript, "Lithuania," have thus far remained unsuccessful. Hopefully, this part of the manuscript will yet be discovered and will become part of later editions of the book.

The text of *The Black Book* possessed by Yad Vashem was prepared for publication by the researchers, Khaya Lifshits and Mark Kipnis (Research Institute of Contemporary Society). They identified all the existing and missing parts, located different variations and fragments of *The Black Book* which were published in various years in different editions and in magazines in Russian, Yiddish, English, and Rumanian. Thus, a large number of the pages that had been lost or destroyed by time were restored. In the course of the work, texts were found which had not been included in the copy sent to Eretz-Israel.

Contacts with living witnesses of the Holocaust proved fruitful. These were people who had earlier sent their memoirs and documents to Ehrenburg and also those authors who are now living in Israel and who helped Ehrenburg and Grossman collect and prepare the materials of *The Black Book*.

* * *

Ilya Ehrenburg explained his point of view with regard to the fate of the Jews in the war in an article published on June 25, 1943 in the Soviet Jewish newspaper *Einikeit*: "The Jews were never entirely wiped out in Egypt, in Rome, or by the fanatics of the Inquisition. Neither can Hitler wipe out the Jews, although history has never witnessed such a massive destruction of an entire people. . . . The degenerate Hitler does not understand that it is impossible to destroy a people. There are fewer Jews now than before, but each Jew has become greater than he was."

Ehrenburg's viewpoint is clearly reflected in *The Black Book*, and Ehrenburg was proud of the heroic efforts of Jews on all fronts of the Patriotic War.

The Black Book contains hundreds of testimonial documents — particularly about the interior of the U.S.S.R. such as the Crimea and the Northern Caucasus. The book does contain certain inaccuracies of the sort sometimes encountered in primary historical documents, and it does reveal on occasion a one-sided and subjective perception of individual facts. There are, for example, virtually no data on the participation of the local populations in the murder of Jews throughout the Soviet Union while, at the same time, a large amount of space is devoted to how Soviet citizens saved Jews. In spite of these inadequacies, however, this book is the document of an epoch and, with all its merits and flaws, is one of the fundamental sources for the study of Soviet Jewry during the years of the Second World War.

The publication of *The Black Book* is no less topical today than it was thirty-four years ago, when this monumental work was forbidden. The appearance of such a book in Stalin's time would undoubtedly have been in conflict with the entire (foreign) policy of the Soviet state which was then avoiding the Jewish topic and making every effort to ignore it. *The Black Book* is the last word of Soviet Jewry, which has been condemned to silence.

The publication of *The Black Book* also realizes the dream of the keeper of the Israeli manuscript, Solomon Tsiriulnikov, who believed that the appearance of the book would smash the Soviet conspiracy of silence with regard to the destruction of the Jews.

We also wish to mention and thank all of those who were not indifferent to the fate of this book and who, both in the press and on radio, demanded that *The Black Book* appear as soon as possible. Among them were the writer and publicist S.L. Shneiderman, the journalist Schor, a member of the Knesset (Parliament), Kh. Grossman, the pedagogue. L. Lourié, the writer K. Segal, and others. We express our special gratitude to Shimon Daich, who established the fund for the publication of *The Black Book* in Yiddish.

Joseph Kermish

Preface

During the years of its dominion, German Fascism transformed entire regions into desert, devastated hundreds of cities and the capitals of many European countries, put to the torch tens of thousands of villages and destroyed many millions of lives. If we cast our minds back to all the European countries where Hitler's legions ruled, if we acquaint ourselves with the atrocities committed in those countries, if we measure the enormity of the destruction of cultural values held dear by all of humanity, it might appear to us that all that happened was an act of madness, the consequence of insanity. It might appear that the forces of nature, the forces of a chaos tantamount to an uncontrollable hurricane ruled Europe in those years. Such a thought is inevitable, so inhuman are the crimes, so vast and wanton the destruction. It seems that human intelligence had nothing to do with this, could not — by its very nature — have been a participant. Such, however, is not the case. The whirlwind which swept over Europe did not arise spontaneously. This whirlwind had its organizers. Atrocities hitherto unknown to mankind were given a theoretical foundation. The necessity for mass murder and enslavement was justified by lengthy deliberations on the part of the proponents of the racial theory of living space (*Lebensraum*) for the Germanic people. This theory was preached and developed by the leaders of German Fascism — Hitler, Goering, Rosenberg, Streicher, Goebbels, and many others. Hundreds of books were written, research centers were created, university departments were organized — all to justify this racial theory. Ancient and modern history, jurisprudence, the laws of economic development, the history of philosophy, the history of culture, religious beliefs, and the ethical and moral precepts of mankind were reexamined by the proponents of racism. The peoples of the world now know the meaning of this racial theory and the theory of *Lebensraum* for the German people. They know about fascist law, ethics, etc., etc. The ruins of Europe and innumerable mass graves give testimony.

The principles devised by Nazi theoreticians were realized by German legislation, in the activity of "Reichsführer SS" Himmler, of his second-in-charge, Kaltenbrunner, of their deputies Koch, Frank, Seyss-Inquart, who ruled foreign countries, of the hundreds, the thousands, the tens of thousands of Gestapo officials, of the SS officers, of the SA and SD leaders, of the gendarmes, the police battalions and regiments, the commandment offices, innumerable "Brigadenführers," "Obersturmbannführers," "Rottenführers," "Oberscharführers," "Unterscharführers," "Sonderführers," etc.

The mass murder and enslavement of millions of people had a schedule, standards to be observed, monthly and quarterly deadlines. The transportation of millions of people doomed either to death or slavery required train schedules. The construction of gas chambers and crematoriums required the participation of chemists, furnace specialists, engineers, specialists in construction. These structures were designed, and the designs were discussed and approved. The technology of mass murder was worked out for individual operations — as for any other construction process. The valuables and money of the murdered became part of government funds; furniture, belongings, clothing, and footwear were sorted, accumulated in warehouses, and later distributed. Agricultural and military soapworks applied for, received, and distributed women's hair, ashes, and the crushed bones of the murdered. No, this was no whirlwind that swept over Europe. This was the theory and practice of racism. This was a matter of intent and the carrying out of that intent, of an idea and the realization of that idea. This was a blueprint, and the edifice was constructed according to it.

The stubborn bloody struggle of the freedom-loving peoples of the world, above all of the Soviet people, demanded enormous sacrifices, but it was that struggle alone that destroyed the edifice erected by the German fascists. It was that struggle alone that smashed the executioner's block erected by Hitler in the center of Europe.

Hitler, his headquarters, his field marshals and advisors considered the Red Army and the Soviet state their chief enemies. In preparing his *Blitzkrieg* against the Soviet Union, Hitler mobilized the military strength of Germany and her satellites to crush the resistance of the Red Army with their superior power.

In the throes of this deadly struggle, the Red Army displayed an unmatched spirit of self-sacrifice and heroism. The Red Army resisted the German military machine with the military technology created by young Soviet industry. The Soviet people and their Red Army resisted the black ideas of racism with the ideas of Soviet humanism in which Red-Army soldiers, officers, and generals were raised. The Red Army resisted the dull, treacherous German-fascist strategy with remarkable farseeing Stalinist strategy that revealed a deep understanding of the moving forces of struggle.

The Soviet people has been and will continue to be the bearer of the great ideas of progress, democracy, national equality, and the friendship of peoples, and it is these ideas that achieved victory on the fields of battle.

* * *

From their very first days in power, and even during their struggle for power, the Nazis declared the Jews to be the chief cause of all the evils that have afflicted mankind.

Proponents of this racial theory mobilized all resources: lies, wild senseless, slander, long-forgotten superstitions from the Middle Ages, provocative conclusions of a Jesuitic pseudo-science — in a word, the entire ancient arsenal of reactionaries, obscurantists, and political bandits seeking to hide from the people their true goals and the true reasons for the villainous game that they had concocted. Why has reaction made its play under the banner of anti-Semitism? The explanation is that reaction never defends the true interests of the broad masses of the people. Reaction always supports the interests of individual, privileged groups, comes out against the interests of the people, against the objective laws of social development, against truth. In such a struggle it is impossible to turn to society with an appeal to logic, to a sense of justice, to the laws of humanity, to democracy. In such a struggle there is an inborn need to appeal to prejudice, to lie, to pander to base instincts, to deceive, to engage in unrestrained demagoguery. This is why German fascism, in its plan to hurl the peoples of Europe into a carnage where each man would turn upon his brother, resorted to fanning the coals of racial hatred, to resurrecting anti-Semitic prejudices and ravings, to deceiving the masses of the people. This was done to cloud the consciousness of the broad masses of the people of Germany, to strengthen them in their belief in a false superiority over the other peoples of the world, to heighten their feelings of cruelty and contempt, to undermine the idea of the brotherhood of all working people. Without all of this the predatory war of conquest was unthinkable. The demagogic principle of racial schism, racial hatred, racial superiority, and racial privileges was accepted by Hitler as the foundation of the party and the governmental policy of Nazism. The German race was declared to form the apex of this pyramid — a master race. They were followed by the Anglo-Saxon races, which were recognized as inferior and then by the Latin races, which were considered still lower.

The foundation of the pyramid was formed by Slaves — a race of slaves. The fascists placed the Jews in opposition to all peoples inhabitating the world. Jews were accused by the fascists of absolutely fantastic crimes — of striving toward world domination and enslavement of all the peoples of the world. The Fascists declared themselves to be the defenders of mankind against the Jews. Racial distinctions, distinctions of blood were declared to be the decisive elements of the historical process. History, according to Hitlerism, consists in the struggle of races, and the laws of history lead to the triumph of the highest over the inferior, to the destruction and disappearance of the lower races.

It is appropriate here that we recall the words of Stalin, written in response to a request from the Jewish Telegraphic Agency in America:

"I am responding to your question. National and racial chauvinism is a vestige of the misanthropic mores characteristic of the period of cannibalism. Anti-Semitism, like any form of racial chauvinism, is the most dangerous vestige of cannibalism. Anti-Semitism is advantageous to the exploiters — it acts like a lightning rod deflecting the blow of the working people away from capitalism, just as a false path diverts the working people and leads them into the jungle. It is for this reason that communists, as true internationalists, cannot but be implacable and sworn foes of anti-Semitism. In the U.S.S.R., anti-Semitism is severely prosecuted as phenomenon deeply antithetical to the Soviet system. Active anti-Semites are, in accordance with Soviet law, executed in the U.S.S.R.

J. Stalin."

These words were written by Comrade Stalin on January 12, 1931 — precisely at the time when the German Fascists were preparing to seize power and were furiously fanning the coals of racial hatred. History has shown which side was right. The Fascists always attempted to make their attitude toward the Jews a special plank in their racial platform. Everywhere and in everything they did, the Fascists attempted to stir up anti-Semitism as their primary goal, regardless of whatever other causes they were pursuing — whether it was attacking the working people, the intelligentsia, progressive tendencies in science, literature, and art, or even re-examining school programs. Jews were inevitably declared the universal source of evil — in the unions, in government institutions, in factory shops, in the editorial offices of newspapers and magazines, in commerce, in philosophy, in music, in legal societies, in medical science, in the railroads, etc.

Masquerading under the flag of struggle with the Jews, the Nazis attacked, destroyed, burned out the spirit of resistance and protest. On territories occupied by German-Fascist troops, the Jews were persistently contrasted with other nationalities. Why was this done? These violent acts were committed with the purpose of creating the impression that German Fascism set as its primary goal the destruction of Jews, thus supposedly deflecting the blow from the other peoples.

In the greatest act of provocation known to history, Fascism attempted to conceal its true face from the people of the world. Fascism wanted to cross out the concept "Man" from human consciousness.

In 1935 the Union of National-Socialist Lawyers proposed eliminating the concept "Man" from the German legal codex on the grounds that it "blurred and distorted the distinctions between tribal member, imperial citizen, foreigner, Jew, etc." Such was the opinion of the German-Fascist lawyers.

Fascism, however, did not succeed in obliterating the concept "Man."

* * *

The consistency of the German-Fascist government's activities leaves no shadow of a doubt that the murder of millions of people was prepared gradually, step by step, by Hitler and his clique. On September 15, 1935, the law of imperial citizenship was published, signed by the imperial chancellor, Hitler, and the Reich minister of internal affairs, Frick. The second point in this law reads: "Only those citizens who are of German or German-related blood and who demonstrate by their conduct that they desire and are capable of faithfully serving the German people and the Reich are imperial citizens." This law deprived of German citizenship German Jews, foreigners, and — simultaneously — all Germans hostile to Hitler's regime.

Point four of Hitler's program reads: "Only those who have German blood in their veins can be citizens of the state. Jews, therefore, cannot belong to the German people."

Simultaneous with the law on German citizenship of September 15, 1935, the law on preserving German blood and German honor was published. This law was signed by Hitler (Chancellor), Frick (Minister of Internal Affairs), Gürtner (Minister of Justice), and Hess (the Führer's second-in-charge and minister without portfolio). Paragraph one of the law forbade marriages between Jews and citizens of German and German-related blood. Paragraph five reads: "Persons violating the contents of paragraph one are to be published by hard labor." In a different paragraph it was declared: "Jews are forbidden to display the imperial and national flag, or to use the imperial colors."

From that point on, laws, regulations, and explanations flowed as if from a cornucopia. The press and legal publications glittered with expressions such as "full Jew," "half-Jew," "three fourth-Jew," "one fourth-Jew," "pure-blooded German," "German-related blood." An enactment of November 14, 1935, decreed that Jews were deprived of citizenship and that Jews were forbidden to occupy government positions. After December 31, 1935, all Jewish employees of government offices were declared retired. The ancestry of persons born of mixed marriages was traced back to determine the percentage of Jewish blood. Their parents' ancestry was researched back to 1800. All grandfathers, great-grandfathers, and great-great-grandfathers of persons desiring to enter into marriage were studied in detail. New labor prohibitions followed. Jewish doctors were forbidden to treat "Aryans." Injunctions against working in the universities, printing books, giving lectures, exhibiting pictures, and giving concerts rained down on the heads of Jewish scientists, writers, and painters.

This was the initial period of legislative and administrative limitations, a period of isolating the Jews, of expelling them from all areas of social life, science, industry.

At the same time, Hitler's government and the Nazi Party organized and provoked, in ever increasing frequency, open acts of violence — pogroms, beatings, the looting of stores and homes. The pogroms washed over Germany, wave after wave. They were organized and carried out by members of the Gestapo — the activists of the Nazi Party.

At the same time, concealed by the black fog of racial hatred and of demagogic wails about the defense of blood, state, and German honor, all democratic organizations and the German people's forces for resistance were smashed and destroyed. Tens of thousands of progressive social figures were imprisoned in concentration camps, accused of high treason, and executed. The Fascist takeover of the unions, government and private organizations, science, art, secondary schools and universities, and all areas of social life, without exception, paralleled the pogroms and anti-Semitic activity of the German government.

Probably at no time in history has the connection between racism and anti-Semitism been so specific and obvious, and never was it so clear that an anti-Semitic campaign had been initiated to disguise a general attack on the rights and freedoms of the working classes of Germany.

The second period of Nazi policies with regard to the Jews corresponded with the beginning of World War II and the successful invasion of Poland, France, Norway, Belgium, and a number of other European countries. German imperialism had commenced to openly carry out its aggressive plans. During this period, the concepts of "living space," "the superior German race," and "the master race" were revealed in concrete actions. German imperialism was striving toward world-wide hegemony.

The freedom of the peoples of the world was under attack, and they had to be convinced that German Fascism had resolved to apply any and all terroristic methods and would not hesitate to use any sort of force to achieve its goals. This resolve was demonstrated.

The German axe hung over the peoples of Europe.

True to their tactics, the Fascists quietly prepared a bloody massacre of the enslaved peoples and loudly proclaimed their implacable struggle against the Jews. This was a provocation of unheard-of proportions. If the initial period of Jewish persecution was reminiscent of the anti-Semitic activities of the "Black Hundred" in tsarist Russia during the difficult period of reaction (but was several times worse), the new era restored to life the darkest days of the Middle Ages. On the territory of the eastern lands ghettos were organized into which the millions of Jews inhabiting Poland were driven. The Germans began to transport the Jews of Germany, Austria, and Czechoslovakia to these Polish ghettos. The Jewish populations of small towns and villages were concentrated in these large ghettos.

More than one half million people lived in the Warsaw Ghetto. The Lodz Ghetto had two hundred and fifty thousand.* There

*The Lodz Ghetto contained 164,000 Jews.

were tens of thousands of people in the ghettos of Radom, Lublin, and Czestochowa. The ghettos were surrounded by stone walls bristling with broken glass. Barbed wire ran along the walls, and in some areas high-voltage current was passed through it. SS guard posts were located at the gates of the ghettos. All Jews living in the ghettos were forced to wear six-pointed stars sewn to the back and front of their clothing, or white armbands with blue stars of David.

Millions of people lived in conditions of unheard-of deprivation. Horrifying as was the suffering from cold and hunger, no less terrible were the moral torments of people totally deprived of all rights, excluded from social life and industry, marked as convicts, and actually undefended by any law. The first winter in the ghetto brought epidemics and mass starvation. At that time, persons who believed that the ghettos would last for a long time were considered pessimists. The majority of people assumed that the ghettos were a temporary, "special" measure taken because of the war.

Even the most gloomy pessimists, however, did not guess the true intents of the Hitlerites. The concentration of people in the ghettos was only a preliminary stage in the total extermination of the Jewish population. This was a link in a chain of premeditated measures, a step on the ladder that would lead millions to the places of execution. In the occupied territories the Fascists were reusing devices that they had already tried out within Germany. Concealing their actions under the roll of anti-Semitic drums, the clamor of misanthropic slander, and the poisonous fog of senseless lies about the Jews, they methodically murdered hundreds and thousands of Polish intellectuals and people who believed in democracy. While shouting about settling scores with the Jews, they simultaneously shackled the peoples of Poland and Czechoslovakia. They printed descriptions and photographs of the Warsaw Ghetto, and quietly went on murdering Poles and Czechs.

At the same time, in the quiet of Berlin offices, detailed plans were being worked out for the final, concluding stage of the slaughter, and locations were being approved for the construction of camps of destruction, factories of death. The methodology of mass murder and the burial of bodies was undergoing final approval, and the plans for gas chambers and crematoriums were being examined.

On June 22, 1941, German-Fascist troops invaded the land of the Soviets.

This was the major effort of Fascist Germany's struggle to rule the world. Hitler declared that this would be a *Blitzkrieg* and that the U.S.S.R. would cease to exist by the end of 1941. Any resistance by England and America after the defeat of the Soviet Union seemed senseless. The Fascists assumed that the war had entered its final, decisive stage. Fascism linked the culmination of its racial politics with this last, decisive phase of the *Blitzkrieg*. Fascist racial propaganda was never as massive as at this time. Armed to the teeth and carefully instructed in advance, SS bands awaited the order to murder.

In June of 1941 Hitler gave the order, and there began a slaughter hitherto unknown in the history of mankind of Soviet citizens, primarily Jews.

This slaughter was a link in the chain of terrorist measures by means of which the German Fascists hoped to paralyze the will and resistance of the freedom-loving Soviet people. The Fascists planned to astound Soviet people with their unheard-of cruelty. Blood flowed in streams as the Fascists slaughtered hundreds and thousands of Russians, Byelorussians, and Ukrainians.

A secret order issued by Hitler before the invasion of the Soviet Union permitted any and all punitive measures to be taken against the population of Soviet villages and towns. In accordance with this order, military tribunals received instructions not to examine complaints by the Russian, Byelorussian, or Ukrainian population with regard to lawless acts committed by soldiers or officers of the German army. Looting, murder, arson, harassment, and rape committed by German soldiers on Soviet territory were not considered crimes, for such acts had the sanction and blessing of Hitler, his field marshals, and his generals. Hundreds and thousands of villages were put to the torch. Entire regions were transformed into "desert zones." The Germans leveled almost all the villages in the area between the Desna and Dnieper Rivers. Vast areas in the Smolensk Region and the Orlov *oblast* were turned into wasteland. The intention was to condemn the people of these areas to enormous sufferings and to death from starvation and the winter cold.

Deprived of housing, millions of people took to the forests, living in earthen shelters and abandoned dugouts. German economic policies in the villages and towns were unparalleled in their brutality. Work became convict labor — a curse hanging over the peasantry. Armed with all manner of whips and sticks, German overseers and police agricultural overseers rained down dozens of the cruelest reprisals on the peasantry for the slightest violations of the rules of forced labor.

Vigorous industrial regions were laid waste, beautiful cities were destroyed, and the people — doomed to starvation — flooded into the villages in search of food. But the villages were also almost totally looted. Day and night, trains loaded with stolen grain, factory equipment, household utensils, historic relics, and works of art left for Germany. The conditions under which captured Red-Army soldiers were kept were infinitely cruel. Thousands of people died of hunger and epidemics in the camps, and mass executions of unarmed prisoners of war were periodically organized, during which hundreds of thousands of people perished — near Vyazma, in Minsk, in the Kholm Region.

The Germans viewed this murderous work as a preliminary stage in the preparation for settlement of the "eastern areas." Hitler was merely taking the first steps in his plan to destroy the Slavic peoples. The main action was still to come, and the Germans were delaying carrying out their program for the destruction of the slaves until the war had been successfully brought to a conclusion. As far as the Jews were concerned, however, the Fascists were carrying out their plans immediately. The entire Jewish population found on territories occupied by the Germans was to be destroyed. Both old men and children were to be executed without exception. Children not yet able to walk, paralytics, and elderly who were unable to move because of their age were carried to the places of execution in sheets or transported in trucks and carts.

Executions were carried out in identical fashion in places separated from each other by hundreds and even thousands of kilometers. Such total uniformity is evidence of secret instructions worked out in advance. The henchmen obeyed these instructions. The form and depth of the pits, guard procedures for bringing people to the sites of execution, explanations given to the people about to be executed (often ignorant of their fate until the last minutes) were identical in thousands of incidents. Imprisonment in the ghettos immediately organized by the Germans in the occupied territories of the Soviet Union was brief; it immediately preceded the slaughter. The ghettos were areas for collecting those condemned to death. It was more convenient to lead people to their execution from the ghettos; within the ghettos it was easier to control all strata of the population; and within the ghettos those capable of resistance could be separated from helpless children and the elderly. Only in the western areas of the Soviet Union were there organized ghettos that lasted for a year or two — in the cities of Minsk, Kaunas (Kovno), Vilnius (Vilno), Shaulyai (Shavli), and others. In the eastern areas of the occupied part of the Soviet Union, people were usually murdered soon after German civil authorities, the Gestapo, the police, the S.D., and the S.A. arrived in the occupied city. Normally, a period of two to two-and-one-half months would pass between the taking of a city and the mass executions. This period consisted of several stages: first of all, eight to ten days would pass before the Gestapo arrived. Himmler's hyenas preferred not to expose themselves to danger in areas where military success had not yet been insured. After that, a certain amount of time was required to organize the work of the Gestapo, the police, and the commandant's office. Immediately after the organization of a punitive and investigatory network, an order would be issued about the resettlement of the Jews to the ghetto. The resettlement would take two to three days, sometimes a week. After that, the Germans would begin secret preparations for the murders and select a convenient place for the execution. Sometimes anti-tank trenches would serve for the mass burials; on other occasions natural ravines were selected. In the majority of cases, however, the graves were actually dug. In form and size the graves looked like wide deep trenches. Peasants from nearby villages, captured Red-Army soldiers, or Jews from the ghetto did the work. None of those working ever guessed the true purpose of these trenches. People assumed that this was a normal military activity. Once the preparation had been completed, the execution could be delayed for one reason only — if the SS regiments, the storm troopers, and the guard detachments were not capable of handling such an enormous number of murders. After all, millions of children, women, men, and old people had to be killed simultaneously.

In certain instances mass murders took place in still shorter periods of time. In Kiev, for example, many tens of thousands of people were killed with unparalleled cruelty nine days after the taking of the city by German bands.

There is no doubt that in the entire history of humanity there has never been committed a crime comparable to this one. This was an unheard-of fusion of sadistic violence on the part of criminals and murderers, on the one hand, and of premeditated measures of government magnitude on the other. The population of the occupied regions was dumbfounded at the monstrosity of these crimes. Frequently the victims themselves did not believe that they were being led to their deaths — so outrageous and meaningless did the sudden murder of millions of innocent people appear.

The Black Book contains the story of a German officer who tells how Himmler personally checked to insure that the planned rate of murders was being maintained and how he severely criticized a representative of the SS who had fallen somewhat behind schedule.

The Germans attempted to keep the doomed people ignorant until the last minute of the fate awaiting them. There existed a single, precisely worked out system of deception. Rumors were circulated among the doomed people that they had been concentrated in one area to be exchanged for German prisoners-of-war, or that they were to be shipped off to do agricultural work, or that they would be transported to camps located in the western areas. Often, a day or two before the mass execution, the Germans would begin building bathhouses or other public structures in the ghetto in order to lull any suspicions. People being led to their execution were told to bring warm clothing and a two-week supply of food, even though they had only a few hours left to live. The doomed people were formed into columns and told a fictitious itinerary: they would have to march to the nearest railroad station to travel farther by train. Columns of people with warm clothing and food would set off along the highway, only to change directions suddenly and find themselves in the forest, standing before their own freshly dug graves.

If the doomed persons were taken by train to their execution, they never knew until the last minute where they were going. They were assured that they were being sent to new jobs — either in agriculture or at a factory.

The Treblinka camp of destruction had a fake train station complete with ticket windows, train schedules, etc., so that the fresh arrivals would not be able to orient themselves immediately and realize that they had been brought to a remote place. In some instances people were forced to write letters to their relatives before dying; this had the effect of lulling suspicion and nervousness.

The logic of this system was absolutely clear. The Hitlerites wished to avoid resistance or uprisings.

In the eastern regions of the occupied Soviet areas, where the murders were carried out immediately after the arrival of the invaders, the Hitlerites often succeeded with this system of deception. Completely unaware of the monstrous act that was about to bring them to their deaths, the people were unable to organize themselves to resist their murderers. This was the case in Kiev, Dnepropetrovsk, Mariupol, and a number of towns and villages on the left bank of the Dnieper. The Hitlerites were also aided by the fact that those members of the Jewish population in the eastern Soviet regions capable of fighting were already in the ranks of the Red Army, and those capable of work had been evacuated together with plants, factories, and Soviet offices. Thus, the brunt of the blow of these villains fell upon the weakest, the most helpless, and least organized: old people, the sick, invalids, minors, and women burdened with large families consisting of persons incapable of work or ill. It was on these helpless and unarmed people that the motorized SS regiments, police regiments, Gestapo groups, Storm troopers, and guard detachments plied their murderous trade, using the most modern automatic weapons. The disparity between the strength of these bullies armed with all manner of the military technology and the weakness of the victims was horrifying. The organized Fascist armies, which had prepared their murder plans down to the last detail, could not possibly have been opposed by those unprepared persons who suddenly found themselves at the edge of a mass grave together with their children and elders.

In spite of these hopeless conditions, however, the doomed people attempted to fight, resist, and carry out acts of vengeance. Women defending their children attacked armed SS soldiers, struggled with them, and perished from bayonet thrusts, their bodies pierced with bullets. In the western areas where the ghettos existed longer than just a few days or weeks, the struggle of the Jews with the occupants took on an organized character of major proportions. Underground fighting organizations were created in many towns. This occurred in Minsk, Vilnius, Bialystok, Kaunas, and many other towns. Underground fighters in the ghettos established contacts with resistance organizations beyond the borders of the ghettos and created organizations for fighting and sabotage. In the face of immense difficulties, members of the underground smuggled pistols, hand grenades, and machine guns into the ghettos. In some cases the production of weapons and explosives was arranged within the ghettos. Members of the ghetto underground took part in sabotage at factories and on railroads, organized explosions, committed arson, disabled plants which serviced the German army. In many instances members of the ghetto underground established contact with partisan detachments, sent them fighters, weapons, and medications.

Within the underground, people set up secret radio stations, received bulletins of the Soviet Information Bureau, and published illegal flyers, newspapers, and calls-to-arms. Jews who had managed to escape the ghettos joined partisan detachments; there is considerable evidence of their having worked together with the partisans of Byelorussia, Lithuania, many areas of the Ukraine, and the forests of Bryansk and Smolensk.

The organization of the underground in such inhumanly difficult conditions, the obtainment of weapons, and the establishment of military contact demanded enormous efforts and vast amounts of time, experience, and skill.

Within the borders of the ghettos the struggle with the invaders varied considerably from place to place.

Ideological struggle must be considered the primary form of protest. The German-Fascist authorities deprived the Jews incarcerated in the ghettos of all human rights, equated them with animals, and forced them into conditions in which neither domestic livestock nor the beasts in the forest would have survived.

The fact that culture survived in the ghettos was an expression of ideological protest against reducing human beings to a bestial level of existence. Within the ghettos, underground lectures were given, theatrical presentations were put on, schools were established for children dying from hunger. All this was an affirmation of human dignity and the spiritual right of the insulted and the injured to remain human beings right up to their last breath. A number of pages in *The Black Book* are dedicated to a description of underground cultural life in the Vilnius Ghetto. It might appear senseless to have organized schools and lectures for doomed people, but this was not so. The spiritual and intellectual life maintained in these inhuman conditions by persons of culture served as a sort of foundation and precondition for the organization of partisan resistance.

The next stage of resistance was the manifold sabotage of German orders, the concealment and destruction of valuables liable to confiscation, the concealment by the workers of skills that might be useful to the invaders, the damage to or destruction of machine tools, equipment, raw material, and manufactured goods at the factories.

The third, culminating stage was the preparation for armed struggle and the struggle itself. This preparation took various forms: agitation through underground flyers and calls-to-arms, recruitment of members of combat detachments, military training, preparation within the ghettos of explosives for grenades, bombs, mines, procurement of pistols, automatic rifles, mortars, and machine guns from outside the ghettos. Armed struggle manifested itself in two forms, the first consisting of the departure of armed individuals and organized groups to join forces with the partisans. This form of struggle was practiced in the ghettos of Minsk, Kaunas, and other towns and cities. Hundreds of people left to join the partisans, and partisan warfare took on major proportions. Simultaneously, members of the underground were able to render aid to the partisans not only by contributing to their ranks, but also by sending medication, clothing, and food.

Uprisings within the ghettos were the second form of struggle. Usually these uprisings coincided with the periods during which the Fascists prepared and carried out their mass murders or "aktions."

The Black Book contains stories about uprisings in various ghettos and camps: Bialystok, Warsaw, Treblinka, Sobibor, and others. The descriptions cannot, of course, provide a full picture of the armed struggle. Rebellions numbered, not in tens, but in hundreds. The course and duration of the uprisings varied, beginning with fierce one-day battles involving hand grenades and revolvers (as in Lutsk, for example) and running the whole gamut to the battles in the Kremenets area, where the Jews managed to break free to the mountains and hold out for many days. The Warsaw Ghetto uprising was a conflict of major proportions; it developed into a forty-day battle of Jews with German tank, artillery, infantry, and aviation units. The results of ghetto uprisings were, for the most part, identical: the deaths of these heroes. The tragic outcome of these uprisings, known in advance by those who took part in them, only stresses the grandeur of their struggle.

By the end of 1943 the German-Fascist authorities had almost entirely destroyed the Jewish population of the eastern areas of the occupied territories, and by the end of 1944 the destruction of Jews in the western areas was already drawing to a conclusion.

Simultaneous with the murders of the Jews, the German-Fascist authorities remained faithful to the methods they had established and committed the most monstrous acts of violence on the Russian, Ukrainian, and Byelorussian population of the occupied Soviet lands. Hundreds of thousands of prisoners-of-war were viciously murdered. Hundreds of thousands of peasants, workers, and intellectuals who were suspected of either participating in the partisan movement or of sympathizing with it were subjected to incredible torture and then executed. The concept of a "partisan village" appeared. There were many hundred such villages, and the Germans burned them to the ground. Four million people were driven off into slavery, experienced incredible humiliations, torments, and hunger. Many were beaten and tortured. In this last stage of its existence German Fascism again and again attempted to use its pogroms to camouflage its terroristic measures against the peoples living in the occupied territories.

One of the sections of *The Black Book* contains a number of documents testifying as to how Russians, Byelorussians, and Lithuanians rendered fraternal aid to Jews in the worst days of racial terror. The wise mind of the people realized why the Fascists had undertaken this monstrous, bloody provocation, and the pure heart of the people shuddered when rivers of innocent blood began to flow. Old peasant women, young *Kolkhoz* girls, workers, teachers, professors, priests often risked their lives and the lives of their family members to save these innocent doomed people. (The occupants equated the concealment of Jews with the concealment of active partisans.) Hundreds of Jewish children were saved by Russians, Byelorussians, and Ukrainians who claimed that they were their own children and hid them for long months and even years. Among the black clouds of racial insanity and the poisonous fog of misanthropy, the eternal undying stars of rationality, good, and humanitarianism continued to sparkle. They proclaimed the doom of the terrible kingdom of darkness and the glimmerings of a near dawn. The Fascists were unable to extinguish, to drown in seas of blood the forces of good and reason which live in the soul of the people. Only the moral rabble, the scum of humanity, pitiful bands of criminals and sadists heeded the criminal call of Hitler's propagandists.

Today the forces of darkness have been destroyed. The armies of the freedom-loving peoples have crushed Hitler's hordes. This was an unparalleled feat of the Red Army, which passed from the Volga to the Elba rivers in a series of bloody battles that dealt the death blow to the German-Fascist troops. The Red Army stormed the capital of world obscurantism and world reaction, Berlin, and this feat will be etched on the golden tables of humanity. As long as there are people left on earth, this feat will not be forgotten.

The victory over Fascism was not just a military victory. This was a victory of the powers of progress over the powers of reaction. This was a victory for democracy and humanitarianism, a victory of the concept of justice. The defeat of Fascist Germany in the war was not only the military defeat of Fascism; it was the defeat of the entire ideology of Hitlerism. This was a defeat of the ideas of racial terrorism, of the concept of a race of masters dominating the peoples of the world.

The day of justice, the day of retribution came.

Those who planned, organized, and carried out crimes against humanity were brought before the tribunal of peoples in Nuremberg.

Before the eyes of the world the court unfolded an endless scroll of monstrous crimes. The court demonstrated that the whirlwind that raged over Europe had its organizers, that the murder of millions was conceived, prepared, and carried out in cold-blooded fashion.

Millions of murdered innocent people, whose ashes are buried in the earth or scattered over the fields and roads, believed that the hour of punishment would come. Standing on the edge of a mass grave, crossing the threshold of the gas chamber, or approaching the bonfire in their last minutes, the doomed people hurled down curses upon their executioners, reminding them of an inescapable vengeance.

And vengeance came. The victory of justice after the terrible years of Hitler's rule allows us to look into the future with hope and faith.

Fascism murdered millions of innocent people, but Fascism did not succeed in murdering truth, good, and justice. May hatred for the terrible ideas of racism always live in the hearts of mankind.

May the memory of the sufferings and fearful deaths of millions of murdered children, women, and old people never be wiped out. May the radiant memory of those brutally murdered people become a terrifying guardian of good. May the ashes of the crematoriums flow in the hearts of the living, calling for a brotherhood of people and peoples.

Vasily Grossman

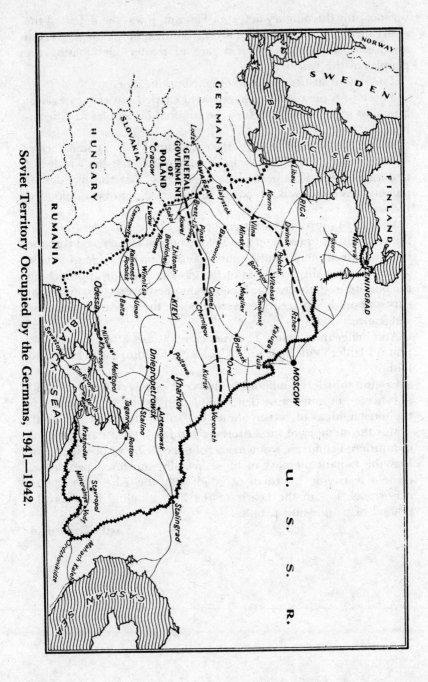

Soviet Territory Occupied by the Germans, 1941—1942.

THE UKRAINE

Kiev, Babi Yar

German troops entered Kiev on the nineteenth of September, 1941. On that same day the Hitlerites began to loot stores on Bessarabka Street. Jews were detained, beaten, and hauled away in trucks.

Residents of Kiev watched Germans on Lenin Street beat male Jews on the legs with rifle butts, forcing them to dance. These cruelly beaten people were then forced to load heavy crates onto trucks. When people collapsed from the unbearable loads, they were again beaten with rubber truncheons.

On September 22 an enormously powerful explosion awakened Kievans. Smoke and a smell of burning were coming from the direction of Kreshchatik Street. People on the streets abutting Kreshchatik Street were driven by the Germans to move straight into the fire.

On that same day a newspaper in Ukrainian was affixed to the walls of city buildings. It stated that Jews, communists, commissars, and partisans would be destroyed. A reward of two hundred rubles was promised for each partisan or communist. Such papers were to be seen on Saksagansky Street, Red Army Street, and many other streets in the city.

Life in Kiev became increasingly unbearable. Germans barged into homes and abducted the inhabitants. These people never returned home.

On September 22 a mass beating of Jews took place on the streets, near the water towers, and in the parks.

Gestapo men checked the documents of people on the streets, beat Jews, and took them away to the police station or to the Gestapo. These people were shot at night.

Many residents of Kiev, particularly of the Podol and Slobodka districts, saw the bloated corpses of tortured old people and children float down the Dnieper River as early as the second or third day of German occupation. On September 26-27 (Friday-Saturday), Jews who had gone to the synagogue disappeared. Yevgenia Litoshchenko, a resident of Kiev, testified that her neighbors — an elderly man named Schneider and a couple by the name of Rosenblat — did not return from the synagogue. Later she saw their corpses in the Dnieper. Her testimony was supported by T. Mikhasev. German machine gunners and policemen surrounded the synagogues and took away those who had been praying there.

In several spots near Kiev the river current washed ashore bags containing articles of worship.

On the fifth day after the arrival of the Germans in Kiev, V. Liberman left his house, walked down Korolenko Street, and turned onto Tolstoy Square. He was stopped by a tall man in a cap and black overcoat who ordered him to show his passport. Liberman did not have his passport with him, and the police agent ordered Liberman to follow him. Walking down Kreshchatik Street, Liberman saw a car making frequent stops along the street. From it, someone with an enormous megaphone was shouting in a thunderous voice: "Inform the Gestapo and the police of the whereabouts of Communists, partisans, and Jews. Report them."

The agent took Liberman to a movie theater on Kreshchatik, not far from Proreznaya Street. The Gestapo man struck him on the back and shoved him into the theater foyer. Liberman passed through the foyer into the theater itself, where more than three hundred Jews were sitting. Most of them were gray-bearded old men. They were all absolutely silent. Liberman sat down next to a young Jew who whispered to him: "We're to be taken to Syrets, where we'll be shot at night."

Liberman walked up to an open window in the theater foyer and watched the passers-by as they hurried back and forth along Kreshchatik Street. Suddenly he caught sight of a man who lived in his building and called to him. When the man approached the window, Liberman asked him to tell his wife that he had been detained and that he was in the theater.

Soon Liberman's wife Valentina Berezlev arrived at the theater. She approached the Gestapo men and implored them to release her husband, but one of them pushed her as hard as he could. The unfortunate woman fell down the steps of the theater and hit her head against the sidewalk.

It was clear that all those being held in the theater were to be murdered, but chance saved them. At two o'clock in the afternoon there occurred a powerful explosion near the theater. Panic-stricken people, among them a woman smeared with blood, ran madly down Kreshchatik Street. Thick yellow clouds of smoke billowed down the street, and a second explosion soon followed the first. Shouting "Feuer!" (Fire!), the Gestapo men abandoned their posts. At that point the prisoners fled to freedom.

In the evenings the crimson reflection of an enormous fire tinted the sky. Put to the torch, Kreshchatik Street blazed for six days.

On September 27-28, 1941, a week after the Germans had arrived in Kiev, announcements in bold Ukrainian and Russian script on a crude dark-blue paper were displayed around town: "Kikes of the city of Kiev and surroundings! On Monday, September 29, you are to appear by 7:00 A.M. with your possessions, money, documents, valuables, and warm clothing at Dorogozhitskaya Street, next to the Jewish cemetery. Failure to appear is punishable by death. Hiding kikes is punishable by death. Occupying kike apartments is punishable by death."

There was no signature on this terrible order, which condemned seventy thousand people to death.* These Gestapo excesses continued on the streets and in apartments until September 29.

The head of a large and distinguished family which counted among its members many engineers, doctors, pharmacists, and teachers, the seventy-five-year-old Gersh Abovich Grinberg (22 Volodarskaya Street) was detained by the Germans at the Galitsky Market on September 28. He was robbed, stripped, and tortured to death in animal fashion. Grinberg's wife, an elderly woman, Telya Osipovna, never saw her husband again and herself perished in Babi Yar the next day, September 29.

The engineer I. L. Edelman, brother of the famous pianist and professor of the Kiev Conservatory, A. L. Edelman, was seized by the Germans on Zhelyanskaya Street. He was drowned in a barrel which stood beside a drain pipe.

B. A. Libman told of one Jewish family which hid for several days in a basement. The mother decided to take her two children and leave for the countryside. Drunken Germans stopped them at Galitsky Market and murdered them all cruelly. Before the mother's eyes, they decapitated one child and then killed the second. Insane with grief, the woman clasped the two dead children to her body and began to dance. When they had sated themselves with this spectacle, the Germans killed her as well. At this point the father of the family arrived on the spot where his family had just perished. He shared their fate.

Many Kievans knew the lawyer Tsiperovich, who lived at 41 Pushkin Street. He and his wife were shot.

The young writer Mark Chudnovsky was not able to leave Kiev,

*More than 100,000 people, mainly Jews, were killed in Babi Yar during the German occupation.

5

because he was ill. His wife, a Russian, would not permit her husband to go alone to the cemetery, since she knew what fate awaited him there. "We were together in days of joy, and I won't abandon you now," she said. They left for the cemetery together and perished together.

S. U. Satanovsky, a professor of the Kiev Conservatory, was shot together with his family by the Germans.

The Germans dragged Sophia Goldovsky, a paralyzed old woman, from her apartment at 27 Saksagansky Street and killed her. She was the mother of ten children.

An old woman, Sarra Maksimovna Evenson, had been — in the pre-revolutionary period — a political activist, organized discussion groups, and edited the newspaper "Volyn" in Zhitomir. An author of numerous articles (under the pen name "S. Maksimov"), she was also the first Russian translator of Feuchtwanger and a number of other contemporary foreign writers. She had an excellent command of foreign languages and maintained a correspondence with prominent figures in the world of art and literature.

Sarra Evenson's advanced age and bad health did not permit her to be evacuated from Kiev. She had not left the house for two years. This great-grandmother was thrown from a third-floor window at 14 Gorky Street.

Regina Lazarevna Magat (10 Gorky Street), the mother of a professor of medicine and biology who had died at the front, was murdered by the Germans. The well-known lawyer Ilya Lvovich Bagat died from a German bullet along with his two granddaughters, Polina and Malvina. Moisey Grigorievich Benyash, a professor of bacteriology known throughout the Soviet Union and Europe, also perished in those days together with his sister and niece.

But all this was merely a prelude to later events which unfolded in the cruelest and most treacherous fashion in Babi Yar.

At dawn of September 29 Kiev's Jews were moving slowly along the streets in the direction of the Jewish Cemetery on Lukyanovka from various parts of the city. Many of them thought they were to be sent to provincial towns, but others realized that Babi Yar meant death. There were many suicides on that day.

Families baked bread for the journey, sewed knapsacks, rented wagons and two-wheeled carts. Old men and women supported each other while mothers carried their babies in their arms or pushed baby carriages. People were carrying sacks, packages, suitcases, boxes. Children were at their parents' side. Young people took nothing along, but elderly people tried to take as much with them from home as possible. Pale sighing old women were led by their grandchildren. The paralyzed and ill were borne on stretchers, blankets, and sheets.

Streams of people flowed into the endless human current on Lvov Street, while German patrols stood on the sidewalks. So enormous was the mass of people moving along the pavement from early morning until late at night that it was difficult to cross from one side of the street to the other. This procession of death continued for three days and three nights. People walked, stopping once in a while, embraced each other without words, said good-bye, and prayed. The town fell silent. Crowds of people flowed from Pavlovskaya Street, Dmitrievskaya Street, Volodarskaya and Nekrasovskaya Streets into Lvov Street, like streams into a river. Lvov Street led to Melnik Street, which led to a barren road through naked hills to the sheer ravines of Babi Yar. As the people approached Babi Yar the din of angry voices, groans and sobs grew louder.

Dmitry Orlov, an old resident of Kiev, watched the execution from the area of the Cable Factory. He was unable to look at the terrible picture more than for a few minutes and fled, overcome by dizziness.

An entire office operation with desks had been set up in an open area. The crowd waiting at the barriers erected by the Germans at the end of the street could not see the desks. Thirty to forty persons at a time were separated from the crowd and led under armed guard for "registration." Documents and valuables were taken away. The documents were immediately thrown to the ground, and witnesses have testified that the square was covered with a thick layer of discarded papers, torn passports, and union identification cards. Then the Germans forced everyone to strip naked: girls, women, children, old men. No exceptions were made. Their clothing was gathered up and carefully folded. Rings were ripped from the fingers of the naked men and women, and these doomed people were forced to stand at the edge of a deep ravine, where the executioners shot them at pointblank range. The bodies fell over the cliff, and small children were thrown in alive. Many went insane when they reached the place of execution.

Many Kievans did not know until the last minute what the Germans were doing in Babi Yar. Some said that this was a labor mobilization. Others believed that it was a resettlement. Still others claimed that the German High Command had arranged an exchange with a Soviet commission: one Jewish family for each captured German.

Tamara Mikhasev, a young Russian woman whose Jewish husband was a commander in the Red Army, also went to Babi Yar, planning to pass herself off as Jewish. She hoped to be exchanged and find her husband on free Soviet territory.

Tamara came to her senses only after she had passed through the fence. First she got into line to hand in her belongings and then in another line to be registered. Next to her stood a tall woman with an ostrich plume in her hat, a young woman with a boy, and a tall broad-shouldered man.

The man picked up the boy.

Mikhasev walked up to them, and the man looked at her and asked:

"Are you a Jew?"

"My husband is Jewish."

"You should leave if you're not Jewish," he said. "Wait here and we'll leave together."

He picked up the boy again, kissed his eyes, and said farewell to his wife and mother-in-law. Then he said something abrupt and commanding in German, and the guard moved aside the board. The man was a Russified German and had accompanied his wife, son, and mother-in-law to Babi Yar. Mrs. Mikhasev left with him.

From the direction of Babi Yar could be heard the barking of many dogs, the crackle of automatic-rifle fire, and the cries of the dying. The crowd moved toward them, and the road was packed. Loud speakers bellowed dance melodies which drowned out the screams of the victims.

The following is the testimony of those who miraculously escaped: Nesya Elgort (40 Saksagansky Street) was moving toward the ravine pressing her trembling son Ilya to her naked body. Carrying her son in her arms, she walked up to the edge of the ravine. In only partial control of her senses, she heard the shooting and the death cries, and she fell. Untouched by the bullets, she lay under a heap of warm bloody bodies. All around hundreds and thousands of bodies lay piled on top of each other. The bodies of old men rested on the bodies of children who lay on the bodies of their dead mothers.

"It is now difficult for me to understand how I got out of that ravine of death," Nesya Elgort recalled, "but I crawled out, driven by an instinct for self-preservation. That evening I found myself in the Podol district with my son Ilya beside me. Truly, I cannot understand what miracle saved my son. It was as if he became part of me and didn't leave me for one second. I was taken in for the night by a Russian woman in Podol. I don't remember her surname, but her first name and patronymic was Marya Grigorievna. She helped me reach Saksagansky Street in the morning."

Another woman who was saved from death in Babi Yar was Yelena Yefimovna Borodyansky-Knysh. She arrived at Babi Yar carrying her child in her arms. It was already dark: "Along the way they added about one hundred and fifty people to our group — maybe more. I'll never forget one girl, Sara; she was about fifteen years old. I can't describe how beautiful she was. Her mother was pulling her own hair and screaming in a heart-rending voice: 'Kill us together. . . .' The mother was killed with a rifle butt, but they weren't in any hurry with the girl. Five or six Germans stripped her naked, but I didn't see what happened after that. I didn't see.

"They took our clothing, confiscating all our possessions, and led us about fifty meters away, where they took our documents, money, rings, earrings. They wanted to remove the gold teeth of one old man, and he tried to resist. Then one of the Germans grabbed him by the beard and threw him on the ground. There were tufts of beard in the German's hand, and the old man was covered with blood. When my child saw that, she started to cry.

"'Don't take me there, Mama. Look, they're killing the old man.'

"'Don't shout, sweety, because if you shout, we won't be able to run away, and the Germans will kill us.'

"She was a patient child, so she kept quiet, but she was shaking all over. She was four years old then. Everyone was stripped naked, but since I wore only old underwear, I didn't have to take it off.

"At about midnight the command was given in German for us to line up. I didn't wait for the next command, but threw my girl into the ditch and fell on top of her. A second later bodies started falling on me. Then everything fell silent. There were more shots, and again bloody dying and dead people began falling into the pit.

"I sensed that my daughter wasn't moving. I leaned up against her, covering her with my body. To keep her from suffocating, I made fists out of my hands and put them under her chin. She stirred. I tried to raise my body to keep from crushing her. The execution had been going on since 9:00 A.M. and there was blood all over the place. We were sandwiched between bodies.

"I felt someone walk across the bodies and swear in German. A

German soldier was checking with a bayonet to make sure no one was still alive. By chance he was standing on me, so the bayonet blow passed me.

"When he left, I raised my head. The Germans were quarrelling over the booty.

"I freed myself, got up, and took my unconscious daughter in my arms. I walked along the ravine. When I had put a kilometer between us and the execution spot, I sensed that my daughter was barely breathing. There was no water anywhere, so I wet her lips with my own saliva. I walked another kilometer and began to gather dew from the grass to moisten the child's mouth. Little by little she started to regain consciousness.

"I rested and moved on. Crawling my way over the ravines, I made my way to the village of Babi Yar. I entered the yard of the brick factory and hid in the basement. I remained there four days without any food or clothing. I would come out into the yard only at night to forage in the garbage can.

"My child and I both started to swell. I was no longer able to understand what was happening. Machine guns were firing somewhere. On the night of the fifth day I crept into an attic where I found a very worn knit skirt and two old blouses. I used one of the blouses as a dress for my little girl. I went then to Litoshenko, an acquaintance of mine. She was petrified when she saw me. She gave me a skirt and a dress and hid both me and my girl. I spent a week locked up in her house. She gave me some money to take with me, and I went to another acquaintance, Fenya Pliuyko, who also helped me a lot. Her husband had died at the front. I spent a month at her apartment. Her neighbors didn't know me, and when they asked about me, Fenya said I was her sister-in-law from the village. After that I moved in with Shkuropadsky and I spent two weeks with her. But since everyone in the Podol district knew me, I couldn't go out in the daytime."

Dmitry Pasichny hid behind a gravestone at the Jewish Cemetery and saw the Germans shoot the Jews.

Pasichny's wife, Polina, and her mother, Yevgeniya Abramovna Shevelev, were Jewish. He hid both of them in a closet and spread the rumor that they had gone to the cemetery. Then both women were taken into the priest's house of the Pokrovskaya Church in Podol. The priest of that church, Glagolev, was the son of the priest who testified in the Beylis Trial.* Glagolev permitted Pasichny's

*Mendel Beylis was a Kievan Jew who was falsely accused of having murdered a Russian boy in 1913 for a religious ritual. He was acquitted. (J.G.)

wife to live in the rectory until August of 1942, and then he took her to Kamenets-Podolsk. Father Glagolev also saved many other Jews who turned to him for help.

The Germans and their (Ukrainian) policemen combed the countryside for new victims. Hundreds of Jews who had succeeded in avoiding execution in Babi Yar perished in their apartments, in the waters of the Dnieper, in the ravines of Pechersk and Demievka, on the city streets. The Germans were suspicious of anyone who looked like a Jew, and the documents of such persons were carefully checked. A single denunciation was sufficient to have anyone under suspicion shot. The Germans not only searched apartments, but also inspected cellars and caves, and even used explosives to blast open floors, suspicious walls, attics, and chimneys.

A handful of Kiev's Jews survived Babi Yar and have been preserved by fate so that mankind could hear the truth from the lips of the victims and witnesses.

Two years later, when the Red Army was approaching the Dnieper, an order came from Berlin to destroy the bodies of the Jews buried in Babi Yar.

Vladimir Davydov, a prisoner in the Syrets Camp, related how the Germans realized they would have to give up Kiev and how, in fall of 1943, they frantically covered up the evidence of the mass executions in Babi Yar.

On August 18, 1943, the Germans took three hundred prisoners from the Syrets Camp and shackled them in leg irons. Everyone in camp realized that some particularly important job lay ahead. This group of prisoners was accompanied only by regular officers and non-commissioned officers of the SS. The prisoners were taken from camp and transported to dark earthen bunkers surrounded by barbed wire. Germans stood duty day and night in machine-gun towers next to the bunkers. On August 19 the prisoners were led from the bunkers and taken under heavy guard to Babi Yar. There they were issued shovels. It was only then that the prisoners realized that they had been assigned the terrible job of digging up the bodies of the Jews shot by the Germans at the end of September, 1941.

When the prisoners stripped off the upper layer of earth, they saw tens of thousands of bodies. The prisoner Gayevsky went mad. Since the bodies had been lying in the ground for a long time, they had fused together and had to be separated with poles. From 4:00 A.M. till late at night Vladimir Davydov and his comrades labored in Babi Yar. The Germans forced the prisoners to burn what was left of the bodies. Thousands of bodies were heaped on stacks of firewood and soaked with petrol. Enormous fires burned day and night. More than seventy thousand bodies were fed to the fire. The Germans forced the prisoners to grind up the remaining bones with large rollers, mix them with sand, and scatter them in the surrounding areas. During this terrible labor Himmler, the head of the Gestapo, came to inspect the quality of the work.

On September 28, 1943, when the destruction of the evidence was almost completed, the Germans ordered the prisoners to heat up the ovens again. The prisoners realized that they themselves were to be murdered. The Germans wanted to kill and then burn up the last living witnesses. Davydov had found a pair of rusty scissors in the pocket of a dead woman, and he used them to unlock his leg irons. The other prisoners followed suit. At dawn on September 29, 1943 — exactly two years after the mass murder of Kiev's Jews — Germany's new victims rushed from their earthen bunkers toward the cemetery wall with a shout of "Hurrah!" Caught totally by surprise by the sudden escape, the SS men failed to open fire immediately with their machine guns. They did kill 280 persons. Vladimir Davydov and eleven other persons managed to climb the wall and escape. They were harbored by residents of Kiev's suburbs. Later Davydov was able to leave Kiev and lived in the village of Varovichi.

* * *

Not all the bodies were burned, and not all the bones were ground up; there were too many of them. Anyone who comes to Babi Yar — even now — will see fragments of skulls, bones mixed with coals. He might find a shoe with a decayed human foot, slippers, galoshes, rags, scarves, children's toys. And he will see the castiron grates ripped from the cemetery fence. It was this fence that provided the grates on which the exhumed bodies of the murdered were heaped for burning in those terrible September days of 1941.

This article is based on documental materials and testimony of Kievans.
Prepared for publication by **Lev Ozerov**.

The Murder of the Jews in Berdichev

Before the War, approximately thirty thousand Jews lived in Berdichev, where they comprised half of the total population. Although Jews made up no less than sixty percent of the total population in many villages and towns in the south-west areas (the former Jewish Pale) and thus comprised a greater percentage than in Berdichev, for some reason Berdichev was considered the most Jewish town in the Ukraine. Even before the revolution, anti-Semites and members of the "Black Hundred"[1] called it the "Jewish capital." The German Fascists, who had studied the distribution of Jews in the Ukraine preliminary to their mass murders, took special note of Berdichev.

The Jewish population lived in harmony with the Russian, Ukrainian, and Polish population of the towns and neighboring villages. There had never been any sort of nationalistic excesses in the entire history of Berdichev.

The Jewish population was employed in the factories: the Ilyich Leather-Curing Factory (one of the largest in the Soviet Union), the Progress Machine-Tool Factory, the Berdichev Sugar Refinery, and tens and hundreds of factories and shops that produced shoes, leather, hats, cardboard, and metal products. Even before the revolution, "chuvyaki" — the soft slippers produced by the craftsmen of Berdichev — were well-known and were shipped to Tashkent, Samarkand, and other towns in Central Asia. The fashionable shoes of Berdichev's craftsmen were also widely known, as was the production of colored paper. Thousands of Berdichev's Jews worked as stone masons, stove builders, carpenters, jewelers, watch repairmen, opticians, bakers, barbers, porters at the railroad station, glaziers, electricians, locksmiths, plumbers, loaders, etc.

There was a large number of educated Jewish people in the town: dozens of senior, experienced doctors — therapeutists, surgeons, pediatricians, obstetricians, dentists. There were bacteriologists, chemists, druggists, engineers, technicians, bookkeepers, teachers in the numerous technical schools and high schools. There were teachers of foreign languages, teachers of music, women who worked in the nurseries, kindergartens, and playgrounds.

The Germans made their appearance in Berdichev unexpectedly: German tank troops had broken through to the town. Only a third of the Jewish population managed to evacuate. The Germans entered the town on July 7, 1941, at 7:00 in the evening. The soldiers shouted from their vehicles: "Juden kaput!" They waved their hands and laughed; they knew that almost the entire Jewish population had remained in town.

It is difficult to reproduce the mental state of the twenty thousand people who had suddenly been declared outside the law and deprived of any rights whatsoever. Even the terrible laws laid down by the Germans for the inhabitants of the occupied territories seemed an unattainable bliss to the Jews.

First of all, an indemnity was imposed upon the Jewish population. The military commandant demanded that fifteen pairs of patent-leather shoes, six oriental carpets, and one hundred thousand rubles be delivered within three days. (Considering the small size of this indemnity, it would appear that this was an act of simple theft on the part of the military commandant.) When encountering a German, Jews were required to take off their hats. Those who did not comply with this regulation were beaten, forced to crawl on the sidewalk on their stomachs, collect garbage with their hands, pick up manure from the pavement. If it was an old man, his beard was cut off. The cabinet maker Gersh Geterman, who managed to escape on the sixth day after Berdichev was occupied and make his way through the front line, told of the first crimes committed against the Jews by the Germans. German soldiers drove a group of Jews from their homes on Glinishchi Street, Greater Zhitomir Street, and Stein Street. All these streets were close to the Zhitomir Highway, next to which was located the leather-curing shop. These people were taken to the factory curing shop and forced to jump into enormous pits filled with an acidic extract used to cure leather. Those who resisted were shot on the spot, and their bodies were also thrown into the pits. The Germans participating in this execution considered it a "joke"; they were, so to speak, curing human hides. The same "joking" execution was carried out in the old section of the city — that part of Berdichev which was located between the Zhitomir Highway and the Gnilopyat River. The Germans ordered the old men to put on their *tallis* and *tefillin*[2] and to conduct a service in the Old Synagogue: "Pray to God to forgive the sins committed against the Germans." The doors of the synagogue were locked, and the building was set on fire.

The third "joking" execution was conducted near the old mill.

They seized several dozen women, ordered them to undress, and declared to these unfortunates that those who managed to swim to the other shore would be allowed to live. Because of the stone dam, the river was very wide at this point. Most of the women drowned before reaching the opposite shore. Those who did manage to swim to the west shore were forced to swim back. The Germans amused themselves by watching the drowning women lose their strength and go to the bottom. The amusement continued until the last woman was drowned.

Another such German "joke" was the story of the death of Aron Mizor, an elderly butcher who lived on Belopolsky Street.

A German officer robbed Mizor's apartment and ordered his soldiers to carry off the stolen articles. He himself remained with two soldiers for some amusement. He had found the knife the butcher used on domestic fowl and thus had learned of Mizor's profession.

"I want to see how you work," he said and ordered the soldiers to bring in the small children of the neighbor women.

"Butcher them!" the officer ordered.

Mizor thought the officer was joking until the officer punched the old man in the face and repeated: "Butcher!"

His wife and daughter-in-law began to cry and to entreat the officer. At that point the officer said: "You'll have to butcher not only the children, but these two women as well!"

Mizor fainted and fell to the floor. The officer took the knife and struck him with it in the face.

Mizor's daughter-in-law, Lia Bazikhes, ran out into the street, begging passers-by to save the old people. When the people entered Mizor's apartment, they saw the dead bodies of the butcher and his wife in a pool of blood. The officer himself had demonstrated the use of the knife.

The population assumed that the harassment and murders of the first days were not the results of orders and attempted to appeal to German authorities for help against such arbitrary violence.

The conscious minds of thousands of people could not reconcile themselves with the terrible truth — that the authorities themselves, Hitler's government itself approved of these monstrous acts of violence. The inhuman fact that Jews had been declared outside the law, that torture, violence, murder, and arson were considered natural when applied to the Jews was totally unacceptable to the

15

human people. They came to the military commandant who was responsible for city government. Representatives of the German authorities cursed these petitioners and drove them away.

Horror hung above the town, entered every home, hovered above the beds of the sleeping, rose with the sun, and stalked the streets at the night. The hearts of thousands of old women and children fell silent when they heard the thud of soldiers' boots in the night or when they heard German spoken. Both the dark overcast nights and the nights of the full moon were terrible, but early mornings, bright middays, and peaceful evenings in their home town also became terrible. This lasted for fifty days.

On the twenty-sixth of August, the Germans began preparations for a general "aktion." Announcements were pasted up all over town, ordering Jews to move into the ghetto set up in the region of the Yatki City Bazaar. Those making the move were forbidden to take furniture with them.

Yatki was the poorest area of town, an area of unpaved streets and puddles that never dried up. The neighborhood consisted of ancient shacks, tiny single-storied houses, and crumbling brick buildings. Weeds grew in the yards, and everywhere were piles of junk, garbage, manure.

The resettlement lasted three days. People loaded down with packages and suitcases moved slowly down Belopolskaya, Maxnov, Grecheskaya, Pushkin, Greater Yuridika, Lesser Yuridika, Semyonov, and Danilov Streets. Teenagers and children supported feeble old people and the infirm. Those who were paralyzed or who had no legs were carried on blankets and stretchers. From the opposite direction came a stream of people from the Zagrebalny area of the town, which was located on the opposite bank of the Gnilopyat River.

People were settled five and six to a room. Tiny hovels were made to accommodate many dozens of people — mothers nursing babies, the bedridden, the elderly blind. Tiny rooms were packed with household belongings, feather beds, pillows, dishes.

Ghetto laws were announced. People were forbidden, on pain of severe punishment, to leave the borders of the ghetto. Food could be bought at the bazaar only after six o'clock, that is, when the bazaar was already empty and there was no food left to buy.

It never occurred, however, to any of those who had been moved to the ghetto, that this was only the first stage of a plan that had already been worked out, a plan to murder the twenty thousand Jews remaining in Berdichev.

A resident of Berdichev, the bookkeeper Nikolay Vasilievich Nemolovsky, visited the family of his friend Nuzhny in the ghetto. Nuzhny was an engineer and had worked at the Progress Factory. Nemolovsky related how Nuzhny's wife cried a great deal and was very upset that her ten-year-old son Garik could not continue studying in the Russian school.

The bishop of the Berdichev Cathedral, Father Nikolay, and the old priest, Gurin, maintained contact with the doctors, Vurnarg, Baraban, Blank (a woman), and also with other members of the educated Jewish community. The German authorities in Zhitomir declared to the bishop that the slightest attempt to save the Jews would be punished in the severest of fashions — including death.

According to the priests the elderly doctors of Berdichev lived in constant hope that the Red Army would return. On one occasion they were encouraged by the news, supposedly picked up by someone on the radio, that the German government had been handed a note demanding that it cease mistreating the Jews.

By that time, however, prisoners-of-war brought by the Germans from Lysaya Gora had begun to dig five deep trenches. The trenches were located in a field near the airport, close to where Brodsky Street ended and the paved road to the village of Romanovka began.

On September the fourth, one week after the ghetto was organized, the Germans and traitors who had joined their police force ordered 1,500 young people to leave for agricultural work. The young people made bundles of bread and food, said goodbye to their relatives, and set out. On that very day they were shot between Lysaya Gora and the village of Khanzhin. The henchmen prepared the execution carefully — so carefully that none of the doomed people suspected until the very last minutes that there was a massacre in the offing. The victims were given detailed instructions as to where they would work, how they would be broken up into groups, when and where they would be issued shovels and other tools. It was even hinted that, when the work was completed, they would each be permitted to take a few potatoes for the elderly who had remained in the ghetto.

In the few days of life left to them, those who remained in the ghetto never learned the fate of those young people.

"Where is your son?" someone would ask one of the old men.

"He went to dig potatoes," the old people would reply.

The shooting of the young people was the first link in a chain of planned murders of the Berdichev Jews. This execution removed from the ghetto all the young people capable of resistance. There remained in Yatki mainly old folks, women, school children, and babies. In this fashion, the Germans were able to insure themselves total impunity in carrying out the mass execution.

The preparation for the "aktion" was completed. The pits at the end of Brodsky Street were dug. The German commandant acquainted the mayor, Reder (a Russified German who had been a prisoner during the First World War), and the chief of police, Koroliuk (a traitor), with the plan of the operation. These persons — Reder and Koroliuk — took an active part in organizing and conducting the execution. On the fourteenth of September, units of an SS regiment arrived in Berdichev, and the entire city police was mobilized. On the night of the fourteenth the entire ghetto area was surrounded by troops. At four in the morning, upon command, the SS troops and policemen began to rush into the apartments, wake people, and drive them out into the bazaar square.

Many of those who could not walk — feeble old people and cripples — were killed by the executioners on the spot. The terrible wails of women and the crying of children wakened the entire town. People living on the most distant streets woke up and listened in horror to the groans of thousands of people — groans that fused into a single wail and shook the soul.

Soon the bazaar square was filled. Surrounded by guards, Reder and Koroliuk stood on a small hill. Groups of people were led up to them, and they selected from each group two or three people known to possess certain skills. Those selected were led to the side, to that part of the square which abutted Greater Zhitomir Street.

The doomed people were formed into columns and led away under heavy guard down Brodsky Street through the old city, in the direction of the airport. Before forming the people into columns, the SS men and police ordered that they leave their valuables and documents on the ground.

The spot where Reder and Koroliuk stood became white with paper — identification cards, passports, certificates, union cards.

Four hundred people were separated from the group — among them the elderly doctors, Vurnarg, Baraban, Liberman, the woman doctor, Blank, artisans and skilled workers well known in town, including Epelfeld, an electrician and radio repairman, the photographer Nuzhny, the shoe repairman Milmeister, the elderly Pekelis and his two sons, Mikhl and Vulf (all of whom were masons), the tailors, shoe repairmen, and locksmiths known for their skills, and a few barbers. Those selected were permitted to take their families with them. Many were unable to find their wives and children, who had gotten lost in the enormous crowd. Witnesses tell of terrible scenes. People, attempting to make themselves heard in the fear-crazed crowd,shouted the names of their wives and children, and hundreds of doomed mothers stretched out their own sons and daughters to them, begging them to pass them off as their own and thus save them from death.

"You won't find your own family in this crowd anyway!" the women shouted.

Along with the columns of people on foot, trucks also moved down Brodsky Street, carrying feeble old persons, small children, and all those who were unable to walk the four kilometers separating Yatki from the place of execution. The picture presented by those thousands of women, children, and old people walking to their own execution was so terrible that even today witnesses grow pale and cry when they remember or tell it. The wife of the priest, Gurin, lived on the street along which the people were sent to their death. When she saw those thousands of women and children calling for help, she became deranged and was in a state of deep depression for several months.

At the same time, however, there were also vicious criminals who derived material benefits from this great tragedy. Greedy for profit, these people were eager to enrich themselves at the expense of their innocent victims. Policemen, members of their families, and the mistresses of German soldiers rushed to loot the vacated apartments. Before the eyes of the living dead, the looters carried off scarves, pillows, feather mattresses. Some walked past the guards and took scarves and knitted woolen sweaters from women and girls who were awaiting their death. By now the head of the column had reached the airport. Half-drunk SS men led the first group of forty people to the edge of the pit, and the first burst of automatic-rifle fire resounded. The execution place was fifty or sixty meters from the road along which the doomed people had been led. Thousands of eyes watched the murdered old people and children fall. New groups were led up to the airport hangars to await their turn to go to the place of execution and receive their death.

Groups of forty people were led from the airport hangars to the pits. They had to walk about eight hundred meters along the uneven tussocky field. While the SS men were killing one group, the second group of people had already taken off their outer clothing and were awaiting their turn a few dozen meters from the pits, and a third group was being brought up from behind the hangars.

Even though the overwhelming majority of those murdered on that day were totally enfeebled old people, children, and women carrying babies, the SS men nevertheless were worried that they might resist. The massacre was organized in such a way that there were more murderers with automatic rifles at the place of execution than there were unarmed victims.

This monstrous slaughter of the innocent and the helpless, this spilling of blood continued the entire day. The pits were filled with blood since the clayey soil could no longer absorb any more, and the blood spilled over the edges, forming enomous puddles and flowing in rivulets into low-lying areas. When the wounded fell into the pits, they did not die from the SS bullets, but by drowning in the blood that filled the pits. The boots of the executioners were soaked in blood. The victims walked through blood to get to their graves. The terrified screams of those being murdered hung in the air the entire day. Peasants from nearby farms fled their fields so as not to hear wails of suffering unendurable to the human heart. All day people moved in endless columns past the place of execution, where they could see their own mothers and children standing at the edge of the pit which they themselves were fated to approach in an hour or two. All day the air rang with farewells:

"Good-bye! Good-bye! We'll soon meet again," people shouted from the highway.

"Farewell!" answered those who were already standing at the edge of the pit.

Terrible wails rent the air: people screamed the names of relatives; last words of instruction and comfort rang out.

Old men prayed loudly, clinging to their faith in God even in these terrible hours marked by the rule of Satan. On that day, September 15, 1941, in a field next to the Berdichev airport, twelve thousand people were murdered. The overwhelming majority of them were women, girls, children, and old people.

All five pits were filled to the brim, and mounds of earth were heaped above them to cover the bodies. The ground moved as if in shuddering breath. That night many dug themselves out from under these burial mounds. Fresh air penetrated the loose soil of the upper layers and lent strength to those who were only wounded, whose hearts were still beating, but who had been lying unconscious. They crawled in different directions along the field, instinctively attempting to get as far away as possible from the pits. Exhausted, and streaming blood, most of them died right there in the field, a few yards from the place of execution.

Peasants driving at dawn from Romanovka to town saw that the entire field covered with the bodies of the dead. In the morning the Germans and the police removed the bodies, killed all of those who were still breathing, and buried them again.

Three times in a short period the soil above the graves cracked open from pressure inside, and a bloody fluid spilled over the edges of the pits and flowed across the field. Three times the Germans forced the peasants to heap up new hills above the enormous graves.

We have information about two children who actually stood at the edge of these open graves and were miraculously saved.

One of them was a ten-year-old boy by the name of Garik; he was the son of the engineer Nuzhny. His father, mother, and six-year-old sister were executed. When Garik was brought together with his mother and sister to the edge of the pit, his mother, wanting to save him, shouted:

"This boy is Russian. He's my neighbor's son. He's Russian, Russian!"

An SS man shoved the boy aside, and he lay hiding in the bushes until darkness. He went to town, to the house on Belopolskaya Street where he had lived his little life.

He entered the apartment of Nikolay Vasilievich Nemolovsky, a friend of his father. As soon as he saw familiar faces, he fainted, choking in tears.

He told how his father, mother, and sister were killed and how his mother had saved him. He sobbed all night, jumping up out of bed and wanting to return to the place of execution.

The Nemolovskys hid him for ten days. On the tenth day Nemolovsky learned that engineer Nuzhny's brother was among the four hundred artisans and technicians who had been left alive. He went to the photographic studio where Nuzhny worked and told him his nephew was alive.

That night Nuzhny came to see his nephew. When Nemolovsky described the meeting of the nephew with Nuzhny, who had lost his entire family, to the author of these lines, Nemolovsky burst into sobs and said: "It's impossible to describe."

In a few days Nuzhny came for his nephew and took him to live with him. Their fate is a tragic one: both nephew and uncle were shot at the next execution.

The second person to leave the place of execution was ten-year-old Khaim Roitman. His father, mother, and younger brother, Boris, were killed before his very eyes. When the German raised his submachine gun Khaim, who was already standing at the edge of the pit, said to him: "Look, a watch!" He pointed at a piece of glass that was glistening not far away. When the German bent down to pick up the object, Khaim took off at a run. The bullets of the German gun struck his cap, but the boy was not wounded. He ran until he fell unconscious. He was picked up, hidden, and adopted by Gerasim Prokofievich Ostapchuk. Thus, he was probably the only one of those taken to be shot on September 15, 1941, who was still alive when the Red Army returned.

After this mass execution, Jews who had fled from the town into the villages sought shelter in the empty ghetto. Residents of nearby villages where the Jewish population was being wiped out also fled to the ghetto. Someone had told them that they could escape death on the special streets set aside especially for the Jews. Soon, however, the Germans and the police returned, and new bloody deeds were committed.

The heads of small children were crushed against the stones of the pavement; women's breasts were cut off. Fifteen-year-old Leva Milmeister was a witness to this slaughter. Although wounded in the leg by a German bullet, he escaped from the place of execution.

Between the twentieth and the thirtieth of October, 1941, searches were conducted for all those secretly living in areas of town forbidden to Jews. Not only Germans, but also police abetted by volunteer members of the "Black Hundred" participated in these searches. By the third of November, two thousand people had been herded inside the ancient monastery of the Discalced (Barefooted) Carmelites. The monastery was located on a bluff above the river and was surrounded by a thick, tall fortress wall. The four hundred artisans and technicians (and their families) selected by Reder and Koroliuk during the execution of September 15, 1941, were also taken there. On November third these people were ordered to put their valuables and money within the area of a circle drawn on the ground. A German officer announced that anyone who concealed valuables would not be shot, but would be buried alive.

22

After that, people were led out in groups of 150 to be shot. They were formed into a paired column and loaded on trucks. The men were taken first — about eight hundred persons — then the women and children. Some of those who had been imprisoned in the monastery looked upon death as a relief after their terrible beatings, torments, hunger, thirst, and four months of German brigandry. People joined this line of death without attempting to delay the moment of death even for a few hours.

One man pushed his way to the entrance and shouted:

"Jews, let me go first! Five minutes and everything will be over. What is there to be afraid of?"

That day two thousand people were shot, among them Dr. Vurnarg, Dr. Baraban, Dr. Liberman, Dr. Blank (a dentist), and the family of Dr. Rubinstein (also a dentist). This execution took place outside of town, in the area of the collective farm, Sakulino.

At this new execution, before the very pits, 150 of the best artisans and technicians were again selected. They were taken to the camp at Lysaya Gora. Gradually the best artisans and technicians were brought to this camp from other areas. All together, there were about 500 people in the camp.

On April 27, 1942, all registered Jewish women married to Russians were shot, as were also children born of mixed marriages. There were about seventy such persons.

The camp at Lysaya Gora existed until June of 1942; at dawn on June 15 the last artisans and technicians, together with their families, were executed by machine gun, and the camp was closed. Again, at the very place of execution, the Germans and police selected sixty of the most skilled tailors, shoemakers, electricians, and masons. These people were imprisoned and forced to serve the personal needs of members of the Gestapo and of the Ukrainian police.

The fate of these last sixty Jews was resolved somewhat later. They were shot by the Germans during the first advance of the Red Army on Zhitomir. Thus, following plan, the Germans executed Berdichev's entire Jewish population — from feeble old people to new-born babies.

Out of twenty thousand only ten or fifteen survived, among them the fifteen-year-old Leva Milmeister, the ten-year-old Khaim Roitman, and Vulf and Mikhel Pekelis[3] — sons of the Berdichev mason and stove maker.

In conclusion we present the following lines from the Red-Army newspaper, *Za chest' rodiny* (For the Honor of the Motherland), January 13, 1944:

"Senior Lieutenant Bashkatov's company was among the first to break through to Berdichev. Private Isaak Speer,[4] a native of Berdichev, served in that company. By the time he reached Belopolsky Street he had killed three German submachine gunners. This Red-Army soldier looked around with quivering heart. Before him lay the ruins of a street he had known since childhood. He went to his family home on Shevchenko Street. The walls, the roof, and shutters were undamaged. Speer learned from the neighbors that the Germans had killed his father, mother, and little Boris and Dora.

"The Germans were still fighting at Lysaya Gora. In the morning the soldiers crossed the ice of the Golopyat River and stormed Lysaya Gora. Isaak Speer was in the front ranks. He crawled up to a machine gun and killed the two gunners with grenades. Speer's leg was ripped open by a mine fragment, but he continued fighting. Speer shot one other German and was killed by a hollow-point bullet at Lysaya Gora, where the Germans had killed his mother. Private Speer was buried in his home town, on Belopolsky Street."

Vasily Grossman

1. An extreme right-wing organization in the early twentieth century that supported anti-Semitism, absolutism, and nationalism, and carried out pogroms against Jews and students. (J.G.)

2. Prayer shawls and phylacteries.

3. The details of how the Pekelis Brothers survived are given in the collection, *Murderers of Peoples*, vol. II, pg. 129.

"Approximately thirty thousands Jews were killed in Berdichev. Only the Pekelis brothers, Mikhl and Vulf, escaped: their family was known in town for their work as stove builders. The father and five sons built houses in Berdichev, factories in Kiev, and even participated in the building of the Moscow Subway. Mikhl and Vulf managed to escape from the ghetto. They had built solid, beautiful stoves for the local peasants, and now they hid behind those stoves. Somehow the brothers managed to dig a pit under one of the German offices on Sverdlov Street. There they spent 145 days. They were fed by the Russian engineer, Evgeny Osipovich. Later the brothers went into the forests, found the partisans, and took part in the liberation of Berdichev."

4. Information on the heroic death of I. Speer is given in the collection, *Murderers of Peoples*, vol. II, pg. 140.

●

Talnoye

Anyone walking along the high railroad embankment of the city of Talnoye could see the solitary building of the slaughterhouse situated on a gradual slope next to the city. It was here that the greatest tragedy of Talnoye was to occur — the murder of many thousands of innocent people by the Germans. Talnoye is a city in the Kiev *oblast*, more than half of whose inhabitants were Jews. Of the entire Jewish population only one man remained alive — Yulin, the butcher at the slaughterhouse.

On September 19, 1941, the German commandant of Talnoye issued an order that all Jews residing in the city be registered. When the Jews gathered in front of the commandant's office, they were told that they would be sent in several groups to Uman. Old men incapable of work were separated from the group and taken to the movie theater and the club; they were shot on the following day.

The village of Belashki is located on the other side of the Kulbid Forest, a few kilometers from the town. It was near Belashki that a large group of Talnoye's Jews — more than a thousand people — who had been brought from the city, were stopped and machinegunned.

Maria Fyodorovna Rosenfeld, who is now chief bookkeeper and Deputy of the Regional Committee of the Young Communist League in Talnoye, is married to a Jew. She is Ukrainian, and her maiden name is Moskalenko.

Russian and Ukrainian women who were married to Jews and had children were forced into a house with three apartments. Aside from the women with children, some old men were also there. The approximately one hundred people forced into these rooms awaited the hour of their death.

At 5:00 A.M. on April 17, 1942 (before Hitler's birthday), everyone in the house was led out into the yard. Children whose fathers were Jews were taken from their mothers. The Moskalenko-Rosenfeld boy was five years old; the girl was three. The punishment of the mothers was crueler than mere murder. The children were flung like logs into a truck, and in landing they struck the floor with a dull thump. Then they were taken away. Next to the city slaughterhouses, on that same terrible and cursed spot which can be seen from the high railroad embankment, all the children

25

were snot. The mothers were left alive; they had already been spiritually murdered, and the Germans were confident that they would never recover.

The Russian photographer Pogoretsky was married to a Jewish woman. His son was shot together with the mother; in a gesture of vengeful mockery the father was left alive. In the village of Glybochek the village elder was killed by partisans. The next day the Germans totally destroyed two Jewish families — the Sigalovsky family and the Khersonsky family. Next to the building which housed the office of the commandant, the body of the hanged Jewish woman, Ratushny, hung for a long time. An empty bottle was tied to her neck; one of the Germans to whom Ratushny was to deliver milk decided that the milk did not have enough butterfat. SS men killed Jewish children in the following fashion: one SS man would hold the Jewish child by his hair with one hand, and another would shoot the child in the ear with a pistol. One SS man attempted to pick up by the ear a boy with ringworm on his head. The trick did not work, and the boy fell to the ground. The German ripped off the boy's pants and in his hatred crushed his genitals with his heel. "Try reproducing now," he said to the laughter of the other soldiers.

Vladimir Lidin

Resistance in Yarmolitsy*

[In Ostrog Jews greeted their executioners with bursts of submachine-gun fire. In Proskurovo the shooting lasted several hours. Jews killed three SS men and five policemen recruited from the local population. Several young people succeeded in breaking through to the forest and escaping.]

In Yarmolitsy the Jews resisted for two days. Weapons had been brought along with household items and had been prepared in advance. The following events took place in the cantonment: Jews killed the first policeman who came in to select a group of victims and threw his body through the window. An exchange of fire took place in the course of which several other policemen were killed.

*This material is entitled "Resistance" in the collection, *Murderers of Peoples*, vol. II, pp. 128-129. The manuscript of *The Black Book* does not indicate the name of the person who provided this information, and the beginning of the text is missing.

The next day trucks arrived with policemen from the nearby areas. They were not able to get into the cantonment until evening, when the Jews' supply of ammunition gave out. The execution lasted three days; sixteen policemen were killed during this resistance, among them the chief of police and five Germans.

There were instances of suicide in other buildings of the cantonment. A father threw his two children from the window, and then he and his wife plunged to their deaths together. One girl stood in the window and shouted: "Long live the Red Army! Long live Stalin!"

Information provided by **E. Lantsman**
Prepared for publication by **Ilya Ehrenburg**.

How Doctor Lyubov Langman Died

(Sorochitsy)

Lyubov Mikhailovna Langman, a gynecologist, lived in Sorochitsy. She was loved by the local people, and the peasant women concealed her from the Germans for a long time. Her eleven-year-old daughter was in hiding with her.

While Langman was in the village of Mikhailiki, a midwife came to her and told her that the wife of the village elder was having difficulty delivering. Langman explained to the midwife what to do, but the condition of the mother got worse with every hour. Faithful to her duty, Langman went to the elder's house and saved both mother and child. After that the elder reported to the Germans that a Jewess was in his hut. The Germans took the woman and her daughter to shoot them. At first Langman begged them: "Don't kill the child." But then she clasped her daughter to herself and said: "Shoot! I don't want her to live with you." Both mother and daughter were shot.

Prepared for publication by **Ilya Ehrenburg**.

In the Vinnitsa Region

1. In the City of Khmelnik

Before the war, ten thousand Jews lived in the small town of Khmelnik in the Vinnitsa Region. They comprised more than half the population of Khmelnik. Jews had lived there for decades, for generations, and they were bound to their Ukrainian and Russian neighbors by feelings of friendship and love.

During the Soviet period the town grew rapidly and developed both in an economic and in a cultural sense.

Khmelnik boasted a textile factory, a furniture factory, a furrier factory, a machine-parts factory, a brickyard, two sugar refineries, and numerous artisan cooperatives. Together with people of other nationalities, Jews worked in those institutions as laborers, technicians, engineers.

The town knew and respected those Jews who were the best Stakhanovites, inventors, and conscientious workers.

The town had a movie, a theater, three high schools, two seven-year elementary schools, and a large, beautifully organized hospital which provided free health care to the entire population.

This whole rational way of life collapsed on June 22, 1941. Almost none of the Jews managed to evacuate, and their consternation and grief were great when the Germans entered their home town.

July days in the Ukraine are blissful, for there nature shares its wealth and beauty with man. But on that date nature understood what terrible days had ensued on earth.

The Germans burst into town, and the streets rang with their pirate-like shouts: "Juden kaput! Juden kaput!"

Beginning on the twenty-first of July, 1941, all Jews — men, women, and children over the age of five — were required to wear a white, fifteen-centimeter-wide band on their right arm with a blue Star of David embroidered on it.

Orders aimed at the Jews showered down as from a cornucopia. The first order forbade Jews to buy anything at the market except potatoes and peas. Soon a second order declared that any Jew caught at the market would receive twenty-five to fifty lashes. In this fashion, the Jewish population was doomed to starvation.

A special order categorically forbade the peasants to have any business or personal relations whatsoever with Jews. A peasant who entered the house of a Jew received from twenty-five to fifty lashes, and this sentence was always carried out.

The Jewish population was totally stripped of its property: all Jews were obliged to turn in bicycles, sewing machines, record players, and records in twenty-four hours.

Of a still more pillaging nature was the categorical order that all dishes, spoons, forks, soap, etc. be surrendered totally. Such marauding was not limited to "organized" measures. Policemen burst into houses, broke windows and doors, and hauled off everything that caught their eye. Objects that they were not able to carry away were broken and destroyed.

The Germans and the police entered every house and led off all the Jews to work. They were sent to repair destroyed bridges, wash floors, dig gardens. Some forms of work were debasing: Jews were forced to clean cesspools, shine the boots of policemen, etc., etc. Jews were even forced into such jobs as filling leaking tanks with water. Such "work" was senseless and fruitless, and the Jews were kicked and beaten.

On August 18, 1941, the Gestapo arrived in town; a new stage had begun in the life of the Jews.

One evening three Jewish boys were sitting in the street. One of them was Musya Gorbonos. He was a quiet, good boy and an excellent pupil in the eighth grade. A policeman walked up to the boys and asked Musya for a smoke. The boy responded that he did not smoke and that he didn't have, and never had had, any tobacco.

The German looked carefully at the boy and calmly shot him. Musya Gorbonos was the first victim. Horror and fear seized the population.

The Jews were ordered to be registered, and on the very first day 367 men and 2 women were separated from the crowd.

A monument to Lenin stood on a boulevard in the center of Khmelnik. There was a beautiful view of the city, and it was a favorite gathering place for young people. On holidays such as the Day of the October Revolution or the First of May a triumphant crowd of demonstrators always gathered here. It seemed that Lenin with his outstretched hand and wise squinting eyes was blessing the people.

This was the precise spot chosen by the Germans to abuse publicly these unfortunate people. The selected 367 Jews were herded onto the boulevard, beaten with rifle butts, and forced to join hands, dance, and sing the "International." The beards of old men were cut off, and the young people were forced to eat the hair of these beards.

After the "first" rehearsal, everyone was taken to the building of the regional consumers' cooperative. There, Jews were forced into the glass warehouse and made to dance barefoot on broken glass and specially prepared boards from which nails protruded. In this terrifying and base fashion the Germans tortured these people before killing them. At six o'clock in the evening these tormented people were taken out of town to pits which had been prepared along Ulyanov Road. The executioners forced the Jews to strip naked and dance again.

Before their death some of them still had the strength and courage to shout: "Long live Stalin! He'll win the war anyway. May Hitler rot!"   On that day the Gestapo and their vile helpers murdered 367 Jews and 40 Ukrainian Party members. Khmelnik was assigned to the Litin *Gebietskommissariat*. Its General Commissar was a well-known murderer of Jews, named Koch, who resided in the city of Zhitomir. With the formation of the Litin *Gebietskommissariat*, persecution of the Jews became more systematic in nature.

First of all, an order was issued that all Jews living in the center of town were to move to the outskirts within a three-day period.

On December twenty-fifth all residents were ordered to turn in all warm items of clothing for the German army. The German police demonstrated on that very day just how it regarded Jewish aid.

The Germans seized ten women and one man, brought them to the police station, stripped them naked, and threw them into a punishment cell. From nine o'clock until six o'clock in the evening policemen would come into the cell to beat these unfortunate people. At 6:00 P.M. each prisoner was dragged into a separate room and given fifteen blows with a ramrod. The women screamed and therefore received twenty-five blows. After that the miserable victims were thrown out into the cold.

"Collections" for the German army continued. . . .

All these actions, however, were only precursors of the total destruction that awaited the Jewish population. A sick man, named Abramovich, was reported to be in possession of a weapon. He was dragged from his home, and a gallows was erected on a central street. Before dying, he was ordered to say a last word. This was done with the intent of mocking him.

Barely alive after the beatings, this terribly sick old man found within himself the strength to say in a loud crisp voice: "May the Fascists and their 'ober-bandit' be wiped from the face of the earth."

The policeman pulled stronger on the rope, and Abramovich fell silent.

On January 2, 1942, the Litin Regional Commissar Witzermann came speeding into town in his car. He was notorious as an inhuman murderer.

He summoned the Jewish elder and demanded a large new contribution. Immediately after that, he gave the order that elderly Jews were to move from the new section of the city to the old area, where a ghetto was being set up. This order caused a great deal of bustling about in town. Some dragged their goods on sleighs, others on a few boards; still others carried their belongings on their shoulders. The Gestapo men and the police confiscated anything that caught their eye.

A categorical order was issued: all Russians and Ukrainians were to draw a cross on their doors; anyone who let a Jew into his house would be cruelly punished.

The ghetto had existed for several days when the inevitable German "aktion" took place.

It was 5:00 A.M. There were deep snowdrifts, a snowstorm, and it was piercing cold. As if sensing the horrors and grief the new day would bring them, people were afraid to leave their huts.

Commanded by *Gebietskommissar* Witzermann, the Gestapo men, their assistants, and the police from Litin and the village surrounded the streets. They seemed only to be waiting for the first signal. A few people appeared who had gone early for water; among them was Breitman, a member of the Jewish Council.

They were killed on the spot and the bloody "aktion" began. Sleepy people were dragged from their beds without even being permitted to dress. The old and the sick were shot on the spot.

The temperature dropped to forty below zero, but everyone was driven out pitilessly into the streets. Some were naked, barefoot, wearing only galoshes without shoes, wrapped in a blanket or only a shirt. Many attempted to escape, but were overtaken by bullets. A. Bender, who survived this terrible act of violence, tells: "I heard shooting at six o'clock. When I opened the door, a policeman was already standing in front of it with a rifle in his hands and shouting: 'Come on out!' I begged to be allowed to go with my family to make it easier for my wife to lead the children to their deaths, but

31

they simply beat me with rifle butts. I was forcibly torn away from my wife and my three beloved children in the most terrible hour of my life. I succeeded in escaping from the column and hiding in the attic of a house which had already been emptied. Everything was smashed. Screams, cries, and groans shook the air. The children were herded past by the German wife of the chairman of the city council. She pushed them along, saying: 'Keep quiet, children. Keep quiet.'"

When the square was filled with people, the *Gebietskommissar* read the list of skilled workers who were permitted to live. The rest were herded to a pine forest about three kilometers from the city. Pits had already been prepared there. Along the way, the Gestapo men pitilessly beat and tormented the people. Mrs. Goldman, an elderly woman, fell. The police picked her up and viciously hacked her body to pieces.

One Gestapo man hurried the young Lerner sisters along by poking them in the back with a dagger.

May, a four-year-old fatherless boy whose mother had been killed by the Germans, walked like an adult in the column moving toward the pit. . . .

At the pit people were lined up and forced, through beatings and threats, to undress themselves and the children. It was terribly cold, and the children shouted: "Mama, why are you undressing me when it's so cold outside?"

Every fifteen or twenty minutes, carts with the clothing of the murdered people set out for the warehouse.

In this fashion, 5,800 Jews were murdered on Friday, January 9, 1942.

On January 16, 1,240 more people were killed. The cruelty of the Gestapo men and the police was limitless. The mother of Doctor Abramson, a deaf old woman of sixty years, did not hear the order to immediately come out of the cellar where she had taken refuge. A Gestapo man seized her by her gray hair and chopped off her head with a saber.

He stood in front of the people, holding the old woman's grayed head. . . .

Some of the victims succeeded in hiding in the cellars and attics of the peasants. Many wandered in the fields with no place to take refuge. Others froze to death and were found only in the spring, when the snow melted.

Among those who managed to hide were the Goldman children.

They lay under the bed for several hours. Finally, the oldest boy, who was eighteen, said he would go to the attic to see if their father was there. At that moment a policeman entered the room; he stabbed him with a dagger, and the boy only managed to exclaim "Oh!" before he died.

When darkness fell, the little girl took her five-year-old brother and ran to acquaintances in the village.

Only a small percentage of the Jews living on Yevreiskaya (Jewish) Street escaped the first German "aktions." The head of the German gendarmerie appointed an elder, named Elson, from among those left alive. He ordered Elson to tell all Jews to come to the police station for documents. Jews, he claimed, would no longer be harassed. If an unregistered Jew were caught, the elder and three other Jews from Yevreiskaya Street would be shot. People were frightened and went. They received blue documents which had to be stamped at the police station every day at 8:00 A.M.

Naturally, these promises were meaningless. The wild and arbitrary harassment of Jews continued.

On January 25, 1942, a Gestapo man came upon the Khmelnik rabbi Shapiro and dragged him from his refuge to demand gold. Finally, he pulled him out onto the street and plunged a knife in his throat. Shapiro's body lay there several days; the Germans would not permit it to be buried.

On February fifth the Jewish elder was ordered to send twenty-four women to clear the stadium of snow. The girls who came to do the work began to remove the snow with shovels. This did not suit the policeman, and he said he would force them to work in a fashion more agreeable to him.

Soon after that, he ordered the women to dance in the deep snow and then lie down on their stomachs and crawl in the snow. When these unfortunate women lay down in the snow, the police began to kick them with their metal-tipped boots.

In the course of the next months, the Jews were constantly aware of the sword of Damocles hanging over their heads.

At 5:00 A.M. on Friday, June twelfth, Hungarian soldiers, who had arrived the previous night, surrounded Yevreiskaya Street and began to herd everyone to the police station — supposedly for reregistration. Next to the station, the men were separated from the women and children. The men were led away, and the women, children, and elderly were put on trucks and taken to the forest. It was a clear sunny day. The children were oblivious of what was about to happen and ran around the pit, playing, picking flowers. . . .

On that bloody Friday, 360 people were murdered. The German-Hungarian bandits tore the children to shreds and threw them into the pit.

In the beginning of 1943 the Germans decided to totally liquidate the ghetto.

At 7:00 A.M. on the fifth of March the policeman Schur ordered the guards not to permit any Jews to cross the bridges. People were herded out onto the streets, and the houses were surrounded by policemen with guns and axes in their hands.

On that day 1,300 people were killed. Yevreiskaya Street presented a terrible sight; it was flowing with blood and covered with broken dishes and furniture — all that was left of the senseless and vile destruction of human life and human labor. . . . After this massacre 127 men and 8 women were left alive to work in the shops and factories.

These skilled workers were taken to a school which was being used as a camp. The camp was carefully guarded day and night, and the windows were crisscrossed with barbed wire. In spite of this heavy guard, however, sixty-seven people managed to escape in the course of two weeks. Some fled to Rumanian territory, that is, to territory which the Germans had temporarily permitted the Rumanians to control.

Four persons escaped to join a partisan detachment. Khmelnik's Jews fought in the ranks of the people's avengers without regard for their own safety. Formerly an active participant in Khmelnik's social organizations, Weissman resolved not to submit to the German invaders under any circumstances.

Weissman had hidden in the village of Krylovka until October, 1943. He obtained weapons and gathered around him eleven reliable and staunch men who were ready to take any risk. On October twenty-fifth Weissman went into the forest, taking with him and his group a girl from Litin by the name of Kalerman.

Weissman was assigned his first fighting mission in a partisan detachment named in honor of Khrushchev. He was to derail military trains on the Zhmerinka section of the track.

This fearless partisan derailed three enemy military trains. Soon Weissman and his group received an important operative assignment: to supply the detachment with food. They had to demonstrate a considerable amount of resourcefulness and courage, and

Weissman was able to operate under the Germans' very noses without being captured.

Izya Reznik and Leva Knelgoiz were magnificent Jewish fighters from Khmelnik. They fought in the Lenin Partisan Detachment.

The German bandits tormented and physically destroyed the Jewish population, but they were powerless to alter the honor and soul of the people.

Two Jewish women, Sima Mazovsky and Rakhil Portnov, fought in the Menshikov Partisan Detachment. They took vengeance on the enemy for all the sufferings and torments of their country, their people, their home town.

In Khmelnik, the small group of Jews still alive was subjected to further acts of violence, and their lives became extremely difficult. At dawn on June 26, a Saturday, the Gestapo arrived. Everyone was herded out onto the street. Fourteen persons were separated from the group, and the rest were taken away in trucks. Although the people knew that they were being taken to their deaths, they did not shout or cry, but silently said goodbye to each other in a last brotherly embrace.

In the forest the pits were already dug.

Thirteen persons fled the place of execution. Four of them managed to conceal themselves. The rest were shot during the attempt. On that day fifty people were killed.

The four who had escaped the execution came to the village that night. The peasants fed, clothed, and concealed them. The peasants were threatened with death for simply talking to a Jew, let alone actively assisting him. In spite of this, however, there were wonderful people who ignored these threats and the danger. They despised the cannibalistic orders of the Germans and attempted to help the Jews in a brotherly fashion. A. Bender, who on the third of March escaped his second "aktion," related the following: "From March third to the twenty-fourth of June 1943 my brother and I hid in the village of Kurilovka, where we were born. The Ukrainians, Ivan Tsisar, Yemelyan Shevchuk, Trofim Orel, Nina Kirnitsky, Sergei Bratsiuk, Viktor Bezvoliuk, and Marko Sichenko ignored the danger and saved our lives. They were ready to share our fate. The peasants often went to town and brought back various pieces of news. On April fifteenth, Yarina Tsisar arrived and said that our uncle was in the camp. We were overjoyed and decided to save him. On June twentieth, Marko Sichenko went to Khmelnik, abducted our uncle from the camp while he was being taken to work, and brought him back to us. We decided to join the partisans."

The refugees did not, however, succeed in finding the partisans and joining them. After many trials and tribulations they ended up in Zhmerinka, where they lived in the ghetto and performed the hardest work. Such work was always done at night.

On March 16, 1944, the Rumanians left Zhmerinka, and the Germans arrived. The very next day an order was issued to the effect that the entire Jewish population from sixteen to sixty years of age was to be reregistered. Everyone who came was murdered. The bloody German "New Order" was beginning. Horror and fear reigned in the ghetto, for everyone understood that the end was near.

This time true salvation arrived. Soldiers of the Red Army approached Zhmerinka, and the Germans fled on March 21.

Again we quote the words of A. Bender: "On March 21 we heard the singing of our brothers. When the Red-Army soldiers saw the barbed wire around the ghetto, they asked: 'What is that for?' The answer was: 'The ghetto.' 'What sort of ghetto?' they asked. Then it was explained to them that this was where the Jews lived. The barbed wire was immediately torn down."

Fighting was still going on in town. The Jews, liberated from their dungeons, immediately joined the struggle.

Together with the Red-Army soldiers, they liberated the railroad station, where the Germans had dug in, and the krauts turned tail. Jews helped carry wounded Red-Army soldiers out of battle. Doctor Malkin and Jewish nurses took up their posts and did not leave the hospital.

The shooting stopped. Zhmerinka had been freed from the invaders, and the town took on a holiday atmosphere. Everyone competed to invite the Red-Army soldiers. The tormented, exhausted people stared with love at their saviors. According to A. Bender, "The company commander made a speech and said words that we had not heard for two years and nine months." He spoke of the unbreakable friendship of peoples, of equality, and brotherhood — the great law of Soviet life.

Information supplied by **I. Bekker**
Prepared for publication by **R. Kovnator**

2. In the Village of Yaryshevo

Yaryshevo is a small village which used to have a Jewish collective farm. There were artisans' guilds and a ten-grade school. People lived happily and peacefully.

On July 15, 1941, Germans and Rumanians broke through to the town. On the very first day they executed twenty-five people.

But the most terrible events began later. When the Jews were led to work, they were ordered to lie down, get up, and again lie down. Anyone who did not lie down immediately was shot on the spot. Six months later the Jews were herded into the ghetto — a ghetto of hunger, cold, and tears. On August 21, 1942, a punitive detachment arrived in Yaryshevo. The Jews were assembled and told: "You are going to be sent to work; take everything of value with you." They were taken along the Zhukov highway — as if to catch a train. There is a crossroads there; the left fork leads to the cemetery. When the command was given to take the left fork, the mathematics teacher Gitya Yakovlevna Teleisnin turned to the doomed people and made a speech: "Our brothers are still at the front. They will return. There is the Soviet government. It is immortal. There is Stalin. He will not forget this."

She was killed together with her six-year-old boy Lyova. Then the Germans killed the rest — more than five hundred people. Eight escaped, and they will never forget Gitya Yakovlevna's last words.

Information supplied by **O. Yakhot** and **M. Brekhman**
Prepared for publication by **Ilya Ehrenburg**

3. In the Village of Tsybulevo

Approximately three hundred Jewish families lived in Tsybulevo, in the Vinnitsa *oblast*. Although the winter of 1941-1942 was severe, the Germans herded unclothed women and barefoot old men to work. On one occasion they selected one hundred children and took them to a field. After a short time the policemen returned and announced to the mothers: "Go and pick up your pups. ...." The mothers rushed screaming to the field. In the ravine they found the corpses of their children.

In the spring of 1942 all the Jews were killed. The Germans took them just outside the village, stripped them, and shot them. The children were put in cages and hauled away on carts. They were buried alive.

Tamara Arkadievna Rozanov hid a Jew in her cellar. The Germans burned down her house, and she survived only by chance.

Nadya Rozanov told the following: "Dusya Kapitovsky was being taken to be executed with her baby. Dusya's husband was an officer at the front, and the baby was eight months old. Dusya threw her son over the heads of the Germans to passers-by and shouted: 'Dear people, save my son! At least let him live!'

"The baby fell on the road. A German walked up, picked the baby up by the leg, and smashed his head against the side of a car. . . ."

Lyusya Sapozhnikov was a nineteen-year-old student. When they undressed her before the execution, even the Germans were embarrassed at her beauty. But she shouted: "Shoot me, you murderers! But know that Stalin will come. . . ." She died with these words on her lips.

Prepared for publication by **Ilya Ehrenburg**

4. In the Small Town of Yaltushkovo

I asked the neighbors, who miraculously survived, and I know the whole truth. They were tortured for a long time. The ghetto was set up next to the marketplace and surrounded by a tall barbed-wire fence. The people there were starving.

On August 20, 1942, everyone was herded off to the railroad station. They had to walk about four kilometers, and rifle butts were used to hurry the children and feeble old people. Everyone was ordered to undress. . . .

I saw the scraps of clothing and underwear.

The Germans were economizing on bullets; they stood people four deep and then shot. The living were buried alive. Before being thrown into the pit, small children were ripped to shreds. That's how they killed my little Niusenka. A group of children, among them my own daughter, was shoved into the pit and covered up with earth.

Two months later my wife Manya was taken away with some other people to the village of Yakushintsy, where there was a concentration camp. There they were all tormented and then killed.

There are two graves there side by side. They contain 1,500 people — adults, old folks, children.

There is only one thing left for me: vengeance.

Information supplied by Second-Lieutenant **Kravtsov**, Hero of the Soviet Union.

Prepared for publication by **Ilya Ehrenburg**.

5. In My Hometown
(Brailov)

One warm spring day about seven years ago I went to see my parents. I had been sent by my factory to the city of Kirovgrad. I concluded my business there and was about to return to Moscow when it occurred to me to drop in on my family for a few hours and see the place where I had grown up.

The next day I had dinner at home. My unexpected visit pleased my elderly parents, and all my relatives, neighbors, and friends came by to see me. My mother rushed around the house and fussed in the kitchen for a long time, preparing me a sweet-and-sour meat dish. She said I had loved it as a child. To tell the truth, I did not remember it.

I was interrogated on how I lived, what was happening in the big world, and — among other things — had I seen anyone from our town. While we were chatting, the postman arrived and brought two letters. One of them was from me; I wrote that I had been sent to the Ukraine and that I didn't know if I would be able to stop by. The other letter was from America. The title of the sender was printed on the large envelope: "The Committee of the Brailov Landsmanshaft," in the United States of America.

The lengthy letter was signed by the president and general secretary of the association and informed us that a general meeting had listened to letters and reports from Brailov and that it had been decided to greet us former neighbors and congratulate us on the approaching Passover. The committee was sending twelve hundred dollars to Brailov, of which two hundred were to be given to Rabbi David Liberman and one hundred dollars were to be used to buy a wedding present for a certain girl. My father was authorized to distribute the money among the orphans and poorest people by Passover so that everyone could properly celebrate the holiday.

I admit, the letter struck me as amusing. Forty years had passed since its authors had left Brailov, and they were living and prospering in distant America. Even though they must have had enough of their own affairs to keep them busy, they nevertheless found time to gather together from various cities for annual conferences, to remember the leaking bathhouse roof, to keep track of fiancées, and in noisy New York to display a naive interest in all the details of the life of a small *shtetl*. But then I caught myself thinking that I myself had rushed here from several hundred kilometers away and taken three trains just to spend a few hours in the place where I had grown up. . . .

During the war, on more than one occasion, I recalled that letter from America. I had not received any mail from Brailov for almost three years, and I could not travel there. There were Germans in my hometown. Many times, however, I recalled the small *shtetl* in the Vinnitsa *oblast* where I had spent my childhood. I thought of my father, my mother, and my sister, all of whom had remained there. No matter what front of the war I was on — the forest of the North-West, the streets of Stalingrad, the Donets steppes — no matter in the liberation of what city I participated — my thoughts were of my native *shtetl*. I thought about the day when I would return home, throw open the familiar doors, and say:

"Anyone home? Come on out to say hello. . . ."

* * *

On March 23, 1944, I saw Brailov in the evening twilight. It was difficult for me to walk because of recent wounds; my right foot was swollen, and I could barely pull it out of the sticky black earth. Finally I reached the roadpost with a single word on its sign: "Brailov." It was a cherished combination of letters connected for me with so many memories.

I had covered three hundred kilometers, getting from one area of the front to the other. My car had gotten stuck in the mud, and I had covered the last ten kilometers on foot. I knew that the Bug River formed the border between the German-administered territories and the Rumanian-administered territory of Transnistria* and that there were a few ghettos left in Transnistria. At Vinnitsa, however, the border ran somewhere west of the Bug. Was Brailov on German territory or in Transnistria? Up till then, no one had been able to give me an answer to that question. I now had only several hundred meters to reach the village, and I would learn everything for sure.

A few minutes later, however, a different roadpost with a tablet caught my eye. It announced in German and Ukrainian:

"NO KIKES IN TOWN."

Everything immediately fell into place. There was no need to hurry.

I called to a bright-looking teenager who had peeked out of his

*Transnistria governorship was established during World War II by the Rumanian Antonescu government on the territory of the Ukraine between the Bug and Dniester rivers.

hut and told him to bring an ax to chop down the post with the sign.

"Is it really all right to do that, sir?"

"It's not only all right, but it's absolutely necessary," I said. "Aside from everything else, the sign doesn't correspond to the truth. You see, I've come to Brailov, and that means that there is already one Jew here."

I had entered newly liberated towns more than once, and I knew well the sweet excitement of entering a town wrested from enemy clutches and returned to the homeland. Never, however, had my nerves so betrayed me as on that occasion. Here I knew the history of virtually every house and each of their inhabitants. This was Yakov Vladimir's house. I had been a guest there many times, prepared for my exams there, enjoyed myself there. Now the house was empty and dark. In this house lived Aizik Kulik, my schoolmate who later became a railroad engineer. I peered in the window; half rotten fragments of furniture were scattered on the floor; obviously, there had not been anyone there for a long time. The next house was that of the watchmaker, Shakhno Shapiro; not a soul was there. The tailor, Shneiko Prilutsky, had lived across the street; it was the same picture there as well. . . .

I had traveled with the Red Army from the Volga River to the Carpathian Mountains; Stalingrad was destroyed before my eyes; I had seen the ruins of Rzhev and Velikie Luki, the ashes of Poltava and Kremenchug. Ruins held nothing new for me, but what I saw in my native town left me shaken. From Mirgorod to the Dnieper, a strip 100 kilometers wide, the Germans had burned all the villages to the ground. In that summer of 1943 not a single hut was left standing; the Hitlerites had created a "desert zone." But from among the debris of these burned Ukrainian huts a peaceful wisp of smoke inevitably made its way upward from somewhere beneath the earth. People set up housekeeping in abandoned bunkers, and children scampered around the clay pots in which supper was being prepared. One had to believe that life would return here. What if all the huts were burned to the ground, and the beehives and kolkhoz barns were reduced to splinters? The people had remained, and that was the best guarantee that life would return.

Here, however, I was walking through a village that had been only slightly damaged. Many of the houses even had panes in the windows, but I did not encounter a single living person. My footsteps echoed as if in a desert. To understand what this meant, one must know the customs of the towns and villages of our south.

The main street had always been a meeting place. But now I was the only passer-by. Only cats, gone wild, scampered across the empty street from time to time.

I walked on, afraid to look to the right, where the house in which I was born was standing and where the most precious people to me in the world had lived. There it was — externally almost undamaged. I walked up the windows and examined the walls, which still bore traces of blood, at the scattered down of feather pillows. There was no need for me to ask any questions. Even if there had been, there was no one to ask. Joseph Sukonnik had lived next door to us, then the hatter Grutskin; then came the apartments of Lerner, Goldman, Lumer, Kharnak. Nowhere were there any traces of life.

For one half hour I walked alone through the once noisy village. It began to get dark, and I went to the neighboring village to spend the night. The peasant woman who took me in for the night told me in brief how Brailov perished. I asked about the fates of the families that I had known, named names.

"How do you know them? Have you been in Brailov before?" she asked me.

"Yes, I have — a number of times. You used to have a paramedic in Brailov named Gekhtman. Did you know him?"

"Of course, everyone did."

"Where is he now?"

"Killed."

"Did you hear anything about his wife?"

"They cut her throat. . . ."

"How about his daughter, the student?"

"The same as the others. . . ."

I could not go on questioning her. She looked at me for a long time and then said quietly:

"Forgive me, but are you the son of our paramedic?"

"Yes, my name is Gekhtman."

"How you resemble your father!"

I don't know how, but soon the entire village learned of my arrival. Many people came to the hut where I had stopped. Many I knew, and many remembered me. We talked all night about the war, about people caught up in war, about our future victory.

In the morning, I went back to the village once more. Suddenly, someone called to me in Yiddish.

"Comrade Gekhtman."

42

Five people were running toward me — three men, a woman, and a teenage girl. They all rushed to hug and kiss me, and suddenly they all burst out crying and pressing up against me. For them I was not only an officer of the Red Army, but also a close, dear friend. Our parents had been buried in the same terrible common pit.

I immediately recognized the tailor, Abraham Tsigelman; I had been in the same class in grade school with his older daughter, Sonya, and later I had often been a guest in their home. As for the second man, I simply could not recognize him. He realized this, shook his head bitterly, and asked:

"Don't you recognize me, Gekhtman? Yes, it's hard. My name is Bas — Moses Bas, the barber. How many times did I cut your hair?"

I would never have thought that a man could change so much in three years. He stood there with bent back and gaze cast down. Before me was a man who had lost his support in life, his confidence in his own strength, in his right to exist on the earth.

"You're looking at my rags? Yes, I was once considered a dandy, but I haven't changed my underwear for the last half year."

These were virtually the only residents of Brailov who remained alive. We counted the people of the village on our fingers, and it turned out that only a few had survived.

. . . For several years my father used to describe the affairs and events of Brailov to the "Brailov Association in the United States." The Germans shot my father. He will never write anything ever again, and I, his son, have voluntarily taken it upon myself to describe how the village of Brailov perished. I have neither invented nor added anything here; I am telling exactly what the witnesses told me.

* * *

The Germans entered Brailov on July 17, 1941. It transpired that a significant portion of the population of Brailov had not evacuated and had remained at home. I often ask myself: why did so many remain behind and not get as far away as possible from this brown plague? Why did my family not leave for the east? Evidently, there were many reasons — among them the fact that my mother was seriously ill. My father and sister would not leave her alone in her sick and helpless state, and they decided to share her fate.

43

On the day the Germans entered Brailov, approximately fifteen people perished — Joseph Sukonnik, Ilya Paltin, Isaak Kopzon, and others. In passing by, the Germans tested the state of their rifles, using people as targets. They destroyed fifteen lives simply in passing. The village immediately became alert to the new danger, and everyone realized that a storm cloud had gathered over them.

Soon after that, the German commandant arrived with the police, and the "New Order" was established. In the context of a Jewish village, the "New Order" meant that the Jews had to wear a large Star of David on the back and chest. No one could leave the village or have any contact with the Ukrainian population of the neighboring villages. Although there had been a marketplace in Brailov since time immemorial, no Jew could appear there for fear of receiving a German bullet.

Jews were allowed to run to the bazaar for ten minutes a day — at the signal of a police whistle. The German commandant Kraft took great pleasure in the spectacle of Jews running to the bazaar, and he made a point of being present. After three or four minutes, the policeman would whistle a second time, and everyone had to abandon his purchases and flee the bazaar. Then it was announced that the second whistle was a mistake, and everything was repeated. Commandant Kraft was amusing himself.

Every day more than a thousand of Brailov's Jewish inhabitants were sent by the commandant to perform heavy physical labor. On no day did everyone return home from work. Either German soldiers driving past would begin to "hunt," or the police would kill those who were too exhausted. Once a month the population of Brailov received the order to deliver specific items to the local commandant's office. If these items were not brought by the date indicated, everyone was under threat of being shot.

I saw one of these "orders" — for November. In the long list there were . . . ten women's watches, twelve gold bracelets, a grand piano for the officers' club, two automobiles, three tons of gasoline.

The "orders" for November and December were filled. To this very day I cannot understand how the community, forbidden to leave the borders of the village, was able to obtain automobiles and gasoline during the war. The head of the community, Joseph Kulik, and his assistants are no longer among the living, and there is no one to ask. Khana Kulik, a student, was the only member of her family. According to her, her father told no one how he managed to obtain things to fill the German "orders."

"Don't ask, Khana," he once said to her. "It is enough that I alone go insane. Why should you worry about this?"

On a cold February day Brailov was surrounded by policemen and Gestapo men. The massacre began just before the dawn. In the words of one policeman whom I interrogated, this was the "first aktion." Each policeman was instructed to make the rounds of two or three Jewish homes, herd the people out onto the square to the meeting area, and — if anyone should resist — kill him on the spot. This was to be done silently — with bayonets, rifle butts, and knives.

At 6:00 A.M. my father was awakened by the blows of rifle butts against the door. He had slept without getting undressed that night, and he opened the door quickly. Two policemen pushed their way into the room.

"Quick! To the square! Everyone!"

"My wife is sick and can't get up."

"It's up to us to decide what to do with the healthy and what to do with the sick."

Using the butts of their rifles, they drove my father out into the street. My sister Rosa began to dress hurriedly. At that moment she saw one of the policeman raise his knife to our mother. She rushed to her assistance, but was struck on the head and driven, barefoot and in a light dress, out into the street. Father picked up Rosa and helped her reach the gathering place at the trade square opposite the Catholic Church.

The residents of Brailov had been concentrated there. But not all of them had appeared. Many, like our mother, had been murdered at home. For a bet, a policeman had lined up the grocer's family and shot them all with a single submachine-gun blast.

After an hour-and-a-half check, the policemen declared that three hundred people would be retained to serve the German army. These were mainly tailors, cobblers, furriers and their families. The rest would be shot. Under heavy guard, the procession set out. It developed that my father and sister were in the head of the column. Behind them was Oskar Shmaryan, a sixteen-year-old relative of ours from Kiev who had come to Brailov to spend the holidays. The column was halted at the drugstore; the chief of police remembered that they had forgotten Joseph Schwartz, who lived just outside the village, next to the Orthodox cemetery. They sent a policeman for him. In a few minutes Schwartz appeared with his wife, and they found themselves at the head of this sad procession.

Everyone walked silently, in heavy concentration and casting a last farewell glance at his native village and life. Suddenly a song rang out above the column. A resonant girl's voice sang of her native land, its wide spaces, its forests, seas and rivers, of how free the air was. It was my sister Rosa. In a few minutes her song was choked off. . . .

I asked several witnesses and rechecked this fact as scrupulously and carefully as possible. Everything was exactly as I have described it. My sister was never considered to have any special talent as a singer. She had spent about two hours barefoot and virtually unclothed in the cold. Her feet must have been frostbitten by then. How did she manage to break out suddenly in song? Where did she get the strength for this last feat?

A policeman ordered her to stop, but she went on singing. Two shots rang out, and everything fell silent. My father picked up the body of his own daughter and carried this burden, so precious and sacred to him, in his arms to the place of his own execution. He carried her for another kilometer and a half on this his last journey. . . .

When the column reached the pit, the first group of people was ordered to strip naked, put all their clothing in one heap, and lie down on the bottom of the pit. My father carefully put my sister's body in the pit and began to undress. About a dozen peasant sleighs had been brought up from the direction of the village to take the clothing of the executed people to police warehouses. At that moment a small delay occurred: a young girl by the name of Liza Perkel had refused to undress and was demanding that she be shot in her clothing. She was beaten with rifle butts and stabbed with bayonets, but she refused to give in. She lunged at the throat of a Gestapo soldier and, when he tried to push her away from him, she bit his hand. The man squealed in a frightened voice, and the other executioners came to his assistance. There were many of them — all armed to the teeth— but she would not submit to the enemy.

The executioners threw Liza Perkel to the ground and attempted to tear off her dress, but she would not surrender. She managed to free her leg for a moment and kicked one of the Gestapo men in the face. Commandant Kraft decided to restore "order" himself and walked up closer, giving commands along the way. The girl rose to her feet, blood pouring from her mouth, and her dress ripped to shreds. Calmly she met the gaze of the commandant, who had just came up to her, and spat in his face.

"Fire!" the commandant shouted.

A volley of shots rang out. Liza Perkel died on her feet, meeting her death in battle. What could this young unarmed girl have done confronted with this army of executioners? The Germans did not succeed in crushing her will. They had the weapons and they were able to kill her, but they could not touch her honor and will.

My father made use of the fact that the attention of the commandant and the Gestapo men was distracted by the "incident." He had seen a woman from the collective farm whom he had once treated, and he pushed Oskar Shmaryan into the pile of clothing with a whisper: "Garpina, hide the boy." The woman quickly threw someone's overcoat on him and put him in the sleigh together with the clothing. The boy lay there for about fifteen minutes, and then the string of carts set out. The peasant woman concealed Shmaryan for several days, dressed him, and he soon joined a partisan detachment. He is still alive today. It was from him that I learned how my family died. Oskar Shmaryan saw my father in his last minute. . . . My father did what he could right up to the end. He saved for our people one more avenger — young, implacable, merciless.

When about two hundred people had been executed, it was the turn of the elder of the community, Joseph Kulik. The police and the Gestapo men held a small conference, and then the chief of police said:

"Kulik, you can take your family and go back to the village. You'll stay on as elder of the community."

Kulik's wife took her shawl from the heap of clothing and began to wrap herself in it with trembling hands. It seemed to her that salvation had miraculously arrived while they were already standing at the very edge of the pit.

"Basya, drop the shawl," her husband said quietly but in a strict voice. Turning to the policeman, he said: "When you shoot two thousand of my people, there is nothing left for me as elder of the community to do in this world."

"So you don't want to save your own life?"

"I have been elected by the people as elder of the community, and I will remain with the majority."

"We're asking you for the last time, Kulik. Will you go back to the village or not?"

"Only if you let the Jews live."

. . . Joseph Kulik was shot together with his wife. The last elder of Brailov's Jewish community, he was the father of four sons who became engineers and are now soldiers in the Red Army.

The tailor, Yakov Vladimir, approached the place of execution. The police hunted in their lists and consulted among themselves for a long time.

"Vladimir, you were told to stay in the village. We don't have any more women's tailors."

"I'll stay if you'll leave my family with me."

"We'll leave them with you."

"And my daughter, Sonya? And my grandchildren?"

"No, that's not your family. She has a husband in Leningrad."

"She is my daughter, flesh of my flesh, and I won't stay without her."

The quarrel between Yakov Vladimir and the policemen continued for five minutes. They needed a highly skilled tailor, since they had stolen a large amount of clothing, and the policemen wanted to send it to their wives and whores. But the thirst for blood was stronger even than their insatiable greed. Yakov Vladimir was shot together with his wife, children, and grandchildren.

The "aktion" was coming to an end. Suddenly an eighty-year-old man, Khaim-Arn, approached the place of execution with a scroll of the Torah in his hands. It turned out that the police had not found him at home, and he had remained in his cellar until noon.

Then he went out into the street, but it was empty.

"Where are all the people?" he asked Dr. Yanitsky's son, who was just passing.

"What do you mean — where? They're being shot behind the mill."

"That means I'm left alone. No I won't be left all by myself."

He picked up a scroll of the Torah and ran to the mill. The only thing he asked of the policeman was to be able to lie down in the pit together with the Torah. Thus how this old village *balagole**
Khaim-Arn, was shot embracing his Torah.

All together, more than two thousand people were shot on that day, Thursday, February 12, 1942, the twenty-sixth day of Shebat (the 5702nd year according to the Jewish calendar).

The pit was not filled in. The Germans were expecting the guards to return from the neighboring village of Mezhurov with more Jews, and two policemen were left to guard the pit. On the next morning a woman smeared with blood crawled from the pit. She had lain under the corpses for twenty hours but, wounded as she was, she found the strength to get out and crawl off to the side. She was Cheselnitsky's daughter-in-law. She was a doctor and had

*Coachman, wagon driver.

48

come to Brailov from Kiev to visit a day before the war began. She begged the policemen to give her the opportunity to reach the village, but they threw her in the grave and then shot her.

... According to the local residents, the pits stirred for three days, and groans and wheezing could be heard coming from them. ...

Aside from the three hundred who had been left in Brailov by the Gestapo, another two hundred people emerged from cellars and secret hiding places by evening. A ghetto was set up for them. The "laws" laid down for the ghettos could only have arisen in the heads of the Germans: the dead could not be removed from the ghetto but were to be buried deep in the ground and the earth above leveled. If a baby was born, the entire family was shot. If even a few grams of butter or meat, or so much as a chicken egg were found in the house, the entire family was shot.

A month and a half later, the second "aktion" took place. This time, of the fifteen tailors, five were allowed to live, of eighteen shoemakers — six. And so it went. Anyone able to flee Brailov did so. The Rov River, which runs through the village, served as a border with Transnistria. Nearly three hundred people crossed it. The majority of them found refuge in the Zhmerinka Ghetto. In April, Brailov's last Jews were shot. A month later the Rumanian gendarmerie of Zhmerinka handed over to the German police 270 residents of Brailov; they were marched to Brailov and shot next to that same steep granite slope.

... In July 1942 the Germans put up the sign at the entrance to Brailov which read: "TOWN FREE OF KIKES."

* * *

It was time for me to leave.

"I want to ask a big favor of you," the tailor, Abram Tsigelman, said to me. "You were a friend of our children and knew our entire family well. I can open my heart to you. You know, it is terrible for me to remain in the world. I am already sixty years old. I am alone in my old age — without family, without friends, without relatives. There is no one to live for. But rage is boiling in my soul. Brailov produced twenty-five doctors, twenty engineers, Lord only knows how many lawyers, artists, journalists, officers. Can it be that Brailov has turned into a desert? You were right when you ordered that the sign 'TOWN FREE OF KIKES' be chopped down, but you are leaving. I don't want Brailov to remain without Jews, and I will stay here — even if I'm alone at first. I only ask you for one thing: help me get back my sewing machine. I saw it in the house of one of the former policemen. Don't worry about me. Tsigelman the tailor will always earn his living. And in my free hours I will sit next to the mill, by the pit. Everything I had, and all of your family too, is buried there. . . ."

In a few hours the sewing machine was returned to Tsigelman's house. When I left, I could hear its impetuous thumping. Brailov's last tailor had returned to work. . . .

Yefim Gekhtman, author

What I Lived Through In Kharkov

On October 24, 1941, the Germans entered Kharkov. It is difficult to describe the horror I felt. I had been forced by a hopeless situation to remain in the city.

The Fascists showed their true selves on the very first day. Bodies hung from gallows on the squares. Next day looting started. It was impossible to remain in one's apartment, since the Germans kept knocking at the door: "Open up!" They took all the clothing and anything that could be worn. Then they began to take hostages. The Hotel International was filled with unfortunate victims. The windows were broken, and the rooms were so packed that there was no place to sit or lie down. During the interrogations those who had been arrested were beaten. They were held for ten days, and then these half-dead people were shot.

On one occasion some people had gathered in front of the Regional Council Headquarters, where there was a radio. I happened to be passing by on the way to get water. Suddenly we saw a young man descending by a rope from the upper balcony. At first we did not understand what was happening, but then we heard a heart-rending scream: "Help!" The unfortunate man was hanged from the balcony. The crowd disappeared as the people went in horror to their homes.

This happened the morning after I had had a nightmare.

It was as if I had sensed the future in my dream: our building was ordered to present ten Jews for work. I was not among them. After work, these people were sent to the Hotel International as hostages. I began to wait my turn.

On December 15, 1941, all the Jews in our building were ordered to present themselves as hostages. I resolved not to end up in the hands of these monsters and to commit suicide. I had no poison, but I found a razor blade. I cut away at myself for ten minutes but because of inexperience was unable to locate a vein. Then I fainted from loss of blood. I regained consciousness at a knock on the door. I was told that today, the fifteenth of December, 1941, all the Jews were required to leave the town and go to the barracks behind the tractor factory which was twelve kilometers from Kharkov. Blood was flowing from my wound, and I could not think clearly. I set off for Golgotha.

It is difficult to describe the scene I encountered — fifteen thousand people, perhaps more, were walking down Old Moscow Street to the tractor factory. Many were carrying things with them. There were sick people, and even paralytics, who were carried in the arms of others. The road from Old Moscow Street to the tractor factory was littered with the bodies of children, old people, the ill.

By nightfall we had reached our new residence. Instead of windows, there were slits without panes for light, and the doors did not close. A cold wind was blowing, and there was nothing to sit on. I was so weakened from loss of blood that I collapsed unconscious on the ground. I regained consciousness at the screams of a mother and child. More and more people kept arriving, and in the crowded darkness someone fell on a mother and new baby. The baby cried out, and the mother, realizing that her child had stopped moving, began to scream: "Help! She is all I have left. My husband and son were hanged." But what could be done? Lights were forbidden and the baby died.

I was in a bad barracks. Of the fifty of us, some lucky ones had brought beds which accommodated five or six people. It became colder and colder. I slept on the floor, and my hands and legs stiffened from the cold. A new tribulation lay ahead of me. My only sister had been christened about thirty years prior to these events, and her passport showed her as "Russian." I was lying on the floor and recalling the past when someone suddenly pushed me. I looked around and saw my only, my beloved sister. She spent four days in the barracks with me. Some good people helped her escape. She had a "Russian" passport,* and it was easier to help her than me. In order not to attract attention, she and I did not say goodbye. I simply looked at her, attempting to tell her everything with my gaze.

The wound on my hand would not heal, and I was suffering from cold and hunger. The Germans would let us go to the market or for water if we gave them things. Sometimes the Germans would murder people. Once I saw a German call to a boy: "Hey, little kike!" When the boy approached, the German threw him in the pit, held him down with his foot, and shot him. Until the order came for the general execution, they killed about fifty people a day. Once they announced: "If there are any children crying tonight, we will shoot everyone." How could anyone expect babies not to cry? There was no way to change their diapers, and they lay, wet in the

*Soviet passports indicate nationality (J.G.).

freezing cold. After all these experiences, their mothers had no milk, and there was nothing to feed them.

I succeeded in transferring to a different barracks — No. 9. This was a lucky barracks; its inhabitants were to be shot last.

The Germans intended to take us to our execution by means of a trick. During the third week they announced that anyone who wanted to go to Poland, Lubny, or Romny should step forward. I felt a needle-like pain in my heart, and I recalled my sinister dream. Eight hundred people signed up. I saw them get in the trucks. They were not permitted to take their possessions with them.

Soon we heard shots. The next day no one asked who wanted to go away. Women were seized, separated from their children, and flung into vans. The men were herded on foot.

Gathering my strength, I went to the last barracks. It was hell there. Everything was in a confused mass — corpses, dishes, pillow down, clothing, food, feces. The corpse of a woman lay in one corner on her bed, and a baby was sucking her dead finger. An old man lay dead in another corner.

I don't remember how I ran to my barracks. I very much wanted to live then. I envied dogs and cats that had the right to live, while I, a Jew, had to die.

We sat there each day from early morning in the expectation of death. Once we enjoyed a moment of brief relief. The rumble of artillery could be heard from the direction of Saltov. The doomed people thought that our troops were approaching. They said: "We will be saved." They deceived each other and cried. I must have had strong nerves to have withstood all of this.

Finally, the next-to-last day arrived. In the evening a young pregnant woman was brought to our barracks. The next morning she went into labor. I could not fall asleep because of her screams. That night I decided to escape.

I got ready early in the morning, put a cloth in my coat pocket to bind my wound, and set out. Gestapo men stood on every corner. What could be done? Where was there to go? They would kill everyone. . . . There was little time for thinking, and every second was precious. At one point an officer summoned the soldiers to sort confiscated items heaped on a truck. I lay down on the ground and crawled to the ravine. When the Germans returned, I crawled into the snow and covered myself with a sheet. I lay that way in the freezing cold until morning. As soon as it began to get light, I crawled to the opposite side of the ravine. With difficulty I crawled to the top. It was bitterly cold, and there were no guards next to the ravine. I walked through the village with my heart in my mouth. I was terrified of every glance of everyone who saw me.

Where could I go? Everyone would be afraid to give me shelter; the penalty for that was death. My closest friends were the family of Kirill Arsentievich Redko. At the risk of their own lives, they hid Jews. Someone had denounced them, and they themselves had almost perished. I knew of this, and I did not want to get them into trouble. I went to friends who had lived in my home before the Germans came. They had told me that they would help me if anything happened, but now they pitilessly drove me out even though I said it was late and I could be arrested.

Where could I go? It would soon be night. I did not have time to get out of town. I found an outhouse with three sections, and I spent three days and three nights there. It is difficult to describe all my trials. It was bitterly cold, and the wind seemed to pass right through me. Without so much as a scrap of bread or a drop of water, I became stiff from the cold. I could be found any minute. On the fourth day I began to freeze to death.

Suddenly I felt warm. I heard myself saying: "Water! A drop of water. . . ." I do not know how I lasted until morning. I forced myself to get up from the dirty floor and go out. Falling at every step, I went to Kirill Arsentievich's house. Fortunately, they lived close to the spot where I had hidden. They received me warmly, and I spent three days there. I rested spiritually, for I felt at home in their house. They gave me some food and said goodbye with pain in their voices.

My legs hardly supported me; they were like logs. I set off in the direction of Liubotino, since it was terrifying to walk without knowing where I was going. Who would take me in? Who needed me? As for a passport. . . .

Somehow I made my way to Korotich. I had decided to find a place where no one would notice me and there freeze to death. But before that I wanted to try my luck in the farthest hut. And it was there that I found my luck. The family let me spend the night with them, and a heavy snowstorm began in the morning, so the woman took pity on me and let me stay. I spent three weeks there. Germans often came to the hut in search of partisans, but — miraculously — never found me.

I had to leave this home, but I could not walk, since my feet were two charred masses of flesh seeping pus. When I was leaving, the old woman said: "Wait." She took me to a hut which had been converted by a doctor into a laboratory. When he had examined me, the doctor said: "Your feet are done for." His words were the equivalent of a death sentence; in my situation, what could I do without my feet? I would like to tell more about the doctor, but, unfortunately, I don't know his surname. His first name was Petro. He sent me to the Liubotino Hospital, and he came there to rebandage my legs. He was a wonderful Soviet man. He guessed who I was when the nurse who was taking down my name whispered something to him. He responded: "That's no business of ours, our duty is to help this woman."

In this fashion I ended up in the Liubotino Hospital. I lay on a soft bed, and no one forced me to leave. I was fed twice a day. Even if it was only swill, it was nevertheless warm. In this fashion I lay there for five months — from February 7, 1942, until July 2, 1942.

It is terrible to remember how the toes on both my feet were amputated and how the bones were sawed. For a month I had a temperature of –40° centigrade. I could lie only on my back, but I could not fall asleep because of the pain. I wanted only one thing — to die in the hospital. If I were forced to check out, where could I go? I envied every woman in my ward who died. I realized then what a joy it was to die a natural death.

When patients were brought from Kharkov, I hid under the blanket and peered out with only one eye. What if I encountered a familiar face? The hospital personnel treated me very well, and the surgeon also took an interest in me.

Once a sick woman was brought in from Kharkov in a terminal state and died soon thereafter. She was thirty-eight years old. I kept thinking that her passport could save me. I got that passport.

When I checked out of the hospital, I spent two weeks in the house of a nurse. Then I set out on the road. I decided to try to find my sister, and I had an inkling of where she was. Now I could travel in any direction; I had a "Russian passport."

The journey was not an easy one; the wounds on my feet had not yet healed, and I had to go by foot and on an empty stomach. When I reached Merchik, I realized I could not go any farther; I was too weak. I tried to catch a train, but a German asked me if I had a pass. He threw me out of the car, and a policeman advised me to ask for a pass from the commandant. But the commandant turned out to be an animal and, without even hearing me out, shouted: "Get the hell out of here!"

I sat at the station until evening and then went to a house where the railroad workers lived. There I met a good woman who fed me and let me stay the night. She helped me get a pass.

I could not even conceive of the happiness of soon seeing my only sister, whom I loved so much. What if these animals had killed her? The train had set off from Kharkov, and I hid in the corner out of fear of being recognized. At two o'clock we arrived in the village of Smorodino. I wandered down the streets and suddenly realized I would not find my sister. After all, I could not ask about her, since that would give rise to suspicion.

A woman noticed my distracted appearance and asked: "What's the matter?" I answered that I was hungry and tired. She took me home with her. Food, bread was placed in front of me, and I ate so voraciously that I was ashamed. I said: "Please forgive me; I'll only eat this way once, and never again." I spent a month and a half there, cooking, cleaning the house. This woman played a large role in my fate: it turned out that she knew my sister.

How can I tell of our meeting? I wanted to hug my sister, kiss her. We had each believed that the other had died, but our conversation was a cold one. We pretended we did not know each other, and we both needed a lot of will power.

I lived in Smorodino for a year and three months. I was a cook, nurse, and beggar seeking shelter in the corner of any hut that would take me in.

I saw Germans abduct the young people. Immediately after an examination, they were locked in a special building and not allowed to say goodbye to their families. Their relatives ran after them, but were shot at by the villains. There were many instances when teenagers maimed themselves or committed suicide so as not to have to go to Germany. It was terrible to see the trains leave. The entire station groaned, and the unfortunate youngsters shouted: "Where are you taking us, you murderers?" Relatives were not allowed to approach the cars.

The front line drew nearer, and we spent two weeks in the cellar. Two artillery shells struck our house. Finally, our troops entered Smorodino. My heart leapt with joy. Our troops!

I am now back in my home town of Kharkov. I can walk down the streets freely and look everyone in the eye. . . .

A letter of **Maria Markovna Sokol**,
Prepared for publication by **Ilya Ehrenburg**

Pyotr Chepurenko, Witness of the Piryatin Massacre*

On April 6, 1942, the second day of Passover, the Germans murdered 1,600 Jews of the city of Piryatin in the Poltava *oblast*. These were old men, women, and children who were not able to go east.

The Jews were led out of the town along Greben Road to Pirogovskaya Levada three kilometers from town. There, capacious pits had been dug. The Jews were stripped, and the policemen and Germans divided their belongings on the spot. The doomed people were forced into the pit, five at a time, and shot with submachine guns.

Three hundred residents of Piryatin were brought to Pirogovskaya Levada to fill in the pit. Among them was Pyotr Chepurenko. He gave the following information:

"I saw them do the killing. At 5:00 P.M. they gave the command, 'Fill in the pits.' Screams and groans were coming from the pits. Suddenly I saw my neighbor, Ruderman, rise from under the soil. He had been a driver in a felt factory. His eyes were bloody, and he was screaming: 'Finish me off!' Someone behind him also screamed. It was our cabinet maker Sima who had been wounded but not killed. The Germans and policemen began to kill them. A murdered woman lay at my feet. A boy of about five years crawled out from under her body and began to scream desperately: 'Mommy!' That was all I saw since I fell unconscious."

Prepared for publication by **Ilya Ehrenburg**

*This material was published with certain changes under the title, "The Land of Piryatin," in *The War* (April 1943-March 1944), by Ilya Ehrenburg, Moscow, 1944, pp. 117–18.

The Death of the Jewish Collective Farm Workers of Zelenopolye*

[Zelenopolye is an old Jewish agricultural colony. At one time it was the site of the rich and flourishing collective farm "Emes." Before the war, Jews, Russians, and Ukrainians worked at "Emes." The people there were well-to-do. I traveled there every year to see this blissful friendly family.

When the Germans arrived in Zelenopolye, they found that a significant portion of the Jewish population had evacuated. Only a few families and a handful of old folks remained who did not want to leave the place where they were born and had grown up. These were feeble old people: Idl Kalmanovich, Girsh-Leib Kozlovsky and his wife, Shloyma Kamsoryuk and his wife, and others.

As soon as the Germans occupied the colony, they decided to "clean the earth and the air" of Jews. Murder was not enough for them. According to their plan, the people had to pass through all the circles of hell. Idl Kalmanovich was an old, respected, religious Jew. The Germans spread his *tallis* on the ground and ordered the old man to kneel on it before the bandits. The old man refused. Then the Germans shaved off his snow-white beard. But even that was not enough for them. With a razor, they scrapped the skin from his face, cut his face in many places, and cut off his ears. In spite of his terrible pain, Kalmanovich did not ask the Germans for mercy.

Shloyma Kamsoryuk was an invalid and an honest worker. The villains tortured him mercilessly. They cut Shloyma into pieces and cast the dismembered body to the dogs.

The other Jews remaining in the colony hid in the rain and the cold for a long time, but the same fate overtook them as well.

Khana Patursky's family was murdered in a vicious fashion. Her sixteen-year-old daughter Rakhil was raped and shot. Her other two children and her mother were also shot. The oldest daughter, Tanya, was hanged before her mother's eyes.

---

*This material was lost from the Israeli copy of the text of *The Black Book*. It has been restored by a reverse translation from the Rumanian edition: Ilya Ehrenburg, Vasilii Grosman, Lew Ozerow, Wladimir Lidin. . . . *Cartea Neagra*, Bucharest (1946), pp. 76–77.

All in all, seventy-four local residents and fourteen prisoners of war were killed in Zelenopolye. There were very many victims in this region, since it was a national Jewish district.]

Prepared for publication by **Ilya Ehrenburg**

Letters from Dnepropetrovsk

1. The Letters of the Indikt Spouses

I was born in 1895. Before the war I lived in Dnepropetrovsk, where I worked in the shop of the food cooperative. When the Germans approached, I was entrusted with saving the shop's equipment, and I loaded it onto a train car. The car was not attached to the rest of the train, and I remained with the equipment.

On August 25, 1941, Germans entered the town. I did not go out onto the street, since Jews were being arrested. My wife is Russian, and she was able to move about town and keep me informed as to what was happening.

On August 26 I decided to go to the food cooperative, where I worked. There I met the cleaning woman, who told me a seventeen-year-old Jewish girl had been raped and then killed in the courtyard. She said: "If you like, you can see for yourself." I went home and did not leave the house any more after that.

On September 25 the city commandant issued an order: the Jews were to pay a thirty-million ruble contribution. The Jewish community was to collect the money. My wife wanted to go to the Jewish community, but I said that it was useless and they would kill us whether we gave the money or not.

My wife found me a job at the other end of town. My surname is Indikt, but I became Indiktenko.

On October 12 my supervisor told me to leave. I left with my wife. It was dark, and we heard terrible screams. On the morning of the thirteenth it was still dark when they knocked on the door and shouted: "Come on out." The policemen were surprised that my wife was not on the list. I answered that she was Russian. I knew I was being taken to be shot. I was taken to the department store, where there were already a lot of Jews.

The first group consisted of 1,500-2,000 people. I ended up in the second group. When we approached the Jewish cemetery, we

59

heard shots and screams. We decided to try to escape, and many people were shot in the attempt, but I got away.

For two days I wandered in the steppes, but then I despaired and returned home. I came at night and knocked at the window. I spent a month in the attic. Then we decided that we had to leave the house, since the owner was suspicious.

My wife obtained a work identification booklet in which I was able to change the name and nationality.

Then she got me a passport with the name of Stupki; the date of birth was listed as 1905. Sometimes my age seemed suspicious.

I worked for three months in one place, and then the supervisor told me to leave. By that time my wife had found an isolated house near town. There was no floor in the house, but she made a floor. Three boards could be raised under the bed, and there was room for me to crawl under them. To keep anyone from moving into the second room, we changed it into a shed and kept the chickens, the dog, and the cat there. I want to say a few words about the dog since she helped save my life. Her name was "Alma," and she was extremely vicious. No one would dare to come into the house until the dog was tied up, and that would give me time to crawl under the floor.

A policeman lived next to us. Seeing that his neighbor lived alone, he would get drunk, visit my wife, and make advances, cursing when he was refused. I was forced to sit under the floor and listen to him tell my wife: "Listen, you whore, when are you going to quit playing the role of an honest woman? How long are you going to lead me around by the nose?"

Once my wife lost her patience and told him: "Get the hell out of here." He called her an "ugly Jew," and left. I crawled out from under the floor and began to laugh.

I spent two and one half years in that hole waiting for our troops to come. During the last months my nerves were giving out. My wife frequently suggested that we take poison, but I dissuaded her, and eventually our troops arrived.

Mikhail Petrovich Indikt

Dnepropetrovsk, July, 1944

My name is Nadezhda Ivanovna Indikt. When the Germans came, I was thirty-four years old, but in those circumstances I looked terrible; I did not wash, and walked around in torn clothing, expecting to die any minute.

When I lived with my husband in the hut, the neighbor, who was a policeman, came and said: "Listen, I heard your husband is a kike and that you have a kike son hiding in Odessa." I grabbed him by the sleeve and began to shout hysterically: "Let's go to the Gestapo" and dragged him along with me. Then he said: "Let me go, you louse," and left.

When our fliers attacked Dnepropetrovsk, I prayed to God that a bomb fall directly on us.

I often went out for groceries, and my husband stayed in the hole. Once, during a severe winter cold spell, I went to the village. No one would let anyone spend the night without special permission. Finally, someone did take me in; I was shivering from the cold and slept on the Russian stove, where I got carbon monoxide poisoning. When I left the hut, I realized I was very ill. I could not go on, but I had to; I had no right to die. I began to pray: "Dear God, save me for Misha! What is happening to him? How he must be waiting for me!" At that moment a cart stopped and gave me a lift.

What could I do? Just cry and cry. In Kamenskoye I had seen a notice that Russian families hiding Jews would be shot — even newborn babies. I walked on with only one thought in my head: "Is Misha still alive?" I thought of how happy he would be to see me, but he only felt my face and looked at me like a madman with tears streaming down his cheeks. My face was frostbitten.

They were searching for Jews, and I never went out unless it was for money or food. To get the money I sold our things at the bazaar and worked.

Once I was walking down the street with a neighbor woman, Varya. I trusted her. I saw a young man looking around, and I told Varya: "Wait, I think he's a Jew." He asked me where the commandant's office was. I realized from his accent that he was Jewish. He said he was from the Crimea and that he had been told he would need a pass from the commandant's office when he reached this point. I begged him not to go there, because Jews were being shot. I gave him one hundred rubles and beseeched him to avoid the main roads. When I went home, I burst out crying: "My God, why are people suffering?"

My husband had a hard time of it. I was gone the entire day, the house was locked, and he listened for the slightest noise. I would not open even the smallest window, so there was no fresh air in the house. Still, it was hardest for me: I walked around town and saw everything. I visited my aunt who lived at 84 Boulevard. There was a German unit stationed there. They took Jews to work. My aunt and I would feed them when no one was watching; we gave them bread, fat, tomatoes. The German officer was very cruel; there could not have been anyone else like him in the whole world.

What the Germans didn't do to the Jews! They would hitch them to pull large carts. Sometimes they would pour soup into a trough and make the Jews lick it up on all fours.

I went to all the camps. Once a German shot at me, and three bullets passed over my head. There was a camp next to the prison, and I saw many carts there. When I asked where they were from, I was told that they had been brought from far away. There were only men there, since their families had been shot. I gave them food, and the Germans noticed. I told them I was selling tobacco, since I had small children. A German struck me, and I ran away. When I came home, I would always tell my husband how wretched the people were.

Among the Jewish prisoners was a fifteen-year-old boy. His mother had long since died, and his father was at the front. He and his sister had been living with their grandmother, who was Russian. When the Germans arrived, someone turned them in, and the boy was taken away. When they were going to work, the boy saw the old woman on the street and rushed to her, calling "Granny!" They began to beat him, and the old woman fainted.

An old woman lived on Kherson Street together with her daughter and two grandchildren. I helped them. Once the old woman started to thank me and cry. I kissed her. People saw that and started shouting. I had to run away. I hid at the cemetery and did not dare to come home until late at night. At the cemetery I kept saying to myself: "I didn't do anything bad, and you Germans can't harm me."

At home my husband said: "You'll ruin yourself, and your kisses won't do them any good." But I said that my kisses were worth more than money, because everyone had turned his back on these people, as if they were lepers.

I took food to one family — an old man, his daughter, and two grandchildren. I also brought food to Gershon.

I obtained a passport for my husband, but I needed a photograph. I found one man on the outskirts of town who said he could do anything. I told him some collective-farm workers were coming to see me and that I needed photographs to get German documents. We agreed that I would bring people to him and he would take five hundred grams of fat for three pictures, of which I would get two hundred. When no one was around, I brought my husband to the photographer. He took his picture, and I gave him the fat. In this fashion I brought Gershon and Vera Yakovlevna to him as well.

My husband began to learn engraving. He made the first stamp for Gershon. Then he made a metal stamp for a residence permit and used it for anyone who needed it. I went everywhere looking for Jews.

The Gestapo often conducted searches on our street. I would hang the lock on the door through the window and pray to God. When the Gestapo reached the neighbors, the neighbors would tell them that I lived alone and worked. And they would go away.

I often said to my husband: "Let's die calmly. I can't go on living if I have to see this." My husband answered that we would survive and live with our people. I always had to buy the German newspaper for him. If I did not bring it home, he would look at me with reproach: "You didn't bring it?"

I told him there was nothing interesting in it — just lies. But he learned to read it and gave every word a special interpretation. He would say: "See, the next issue will say that the front is being shortened and this or that town will be abandoned." And that was exactly what would happen. He would say to me: "It doesn't matter, our troops will come back."

I learned that a certain German needed a cleaning woman, and I got the job. This German had a chemical factory. It turned out that he had blank government forms and a metal stamp. There was also a German typewriter. It was difficult for me to type, and I spoiled a lot of blanks before I got everything right. Then I quit the job.

I had to go to the police station once a week to fill out a form and have my residence permit stamped. The first question that they asked me was the nationality of my husband. I answered that he was a Bulgarian of Rumanian nationality. The official said to me: "That can't be. I myself am a Bulgarian." Then I said: "In that case, you don't know the history of your own people very well. Bulgaria has a common border with Turkey, and when the Turks were slaughtering the Bulgarians — just as the Jews are being killed now — the Bulgarians fled to Rumania and took Rumanian citizenship." The policeman said: "Thanks for the lecture." He stamped my residence permit.

Our offensive began. We prepared to go underground, and we dug a tunnel from the cellar to the well.

My husband stayed there, and I brought him food. Toward the end my husband started to mumble over and over again: "We'll survive, we'll survive." Then he lost consciousness.

It is impossible to describe everything. We went through this enormous horror, but we were there when our troops arrived.

N. Indikt

August 2, 1944

2. The Thirteenth Day of October, 1941.
The Story of Ms. A. M. Burtsev

I did not manage to evacuate from Dnepropetrovsk before the arrival of the Germans, because my daughter was dangerously ill at the time. My mother, father, and thirteen-year-old brother stayed with me. They would not leave without me.

When the Germans entered the town, they immediately ordered that the Jews wear white armbands with a six-cornered star on their sleeves. Some refused to wear this armband, and I myself saw a German bandit kill a young girl on the street for refusing to do so.

Later a contribution of thirty million rubles was demanded of the Jews. Harassment and robbery became commonplace. At one point SS men broke into our apartment and took my father and mother to the police station. There they were beaten and, when their valuables had been taken, they were released. After that my father and mother were afraid to go out of the house.

In this fashion we lived in fear for our lives and the lives of our children until October 13, 1941.

By that time my husband, who was Russian, had found a room where no one knew us and to which he planned to move us. We did not have the time, however, to carry out this plan. At 6:00 A.M. there was a knock at the door, and we were told to go to the department store on Marx Street. Supposedly all the Jews were being gathered to force them to pay the contribution.

When we arrived at the store, the enormous four-story building was already filled with people. There was a particularly large number of the elderly and women with children. At the entrance everyone's possessions were being taken. Since I had brought nothing with me, I was not allowed into the store, but had to stand in the crowd on the street. There were several thousand people in the crowd. After a while all those who were in the store were all

64

brought out onto the street. I found my mother and brother, but we lost track of father, and I never saw him again. We were formed in a column of six people abreast and led away under armed escort. My mother tried to persuade me to give my little girl to one of our acquaintances on the street so she could somehow be sent on to my husband. I began to peer into the faces of the people coming toward us and soon saw our neighbor, who was looking for his own wife (a Jew) and child. I gave Lenochka to him and soon saw my husband walking along with the column and leading Lenochka by the hand. A few minutes later an acquaintance of my husband was able to approach me, since I was walking at the edge of the column. He began to persuade me to remove the cloth strip from my arm and flee. He said we were being taken to be slaughtered. Then my mother, who had overheard our conversation, began to plead with me to escape. "You can't help us anyway,"she said, "and you have to do it for Lenochka."

At that point, a truck with old people and children drove past. Suddenly one of the people sitting in the truck jumped to his feet and slit his throat with a razor. A German shoved him into the cab to keep anyone from seeing him, and the truck drove on.

At Yuriev Street I took off the cloth strip, slipped out of the column, and went to the address that my husband's acquaintance had given me. I lived there for two weeks, and my husband was able to visit me only infrequently, since we were afraid that he might be followed. Then he brought me home, and I stayed in the room for two months, hiding behind the cupboard every time I heard steps on the stairway. But Lenochka fell ill, and I was forced to begin going out to obtain food for her. I was saved by the fact that I do not look Jewish and also by the fact that our neighbors were good people who helped us as much as they could.

In this fashion, expecting death every day, I lived two years. This life had its effect on the child as well. Whenever I was late coming home, Lenochka would become hysterical and scream: "They killed my mommy." At times, it seemed to us that we would not be able to endure all of this.

The fate of all those who were in the column with me is terrible. They were all shot in an antitank ditch outside of town. The same fate befell my family.

3. The Story of Ms. E. A. Revensky

To my great sorrow I was not able to evacuate with my family from Dnepropetrovsk in 1941. On the day when the Germans entered the town I was in my nephew's apartment. On that same evening several Germans and Hungarians came to our apartment and announced that they had been given the right to take everything in the Jewish apartments.

A few days later a census was carried out of the Jews living in Dnepropetrovsk, and the Germans began to make us do work that could not be called anything other than convict labor. Those unable to work were beaten to death by the Germans.

Finally the fatal day arrived when the Jews were ordered to come to the "Lux" Store with belongings and food for three days.

The weather that day was fall-like; the rain was mixed with snow, and the wind was so strong it actually knocked people off their feet.

As we approached the store building, I saw that it was cordoned off by police. I decided I would rather take poison than turn myself over to the Germans.

I returned home, and my neighbor, P. I. Kravchenko, advised me to leave town and gave me a letter to show to a woman he knew in the village of Krasnopolye, about eight kilometers from Dnepropetrovsk. I spent two days in Krasnopolye and then had to flee, since the Germans were missing eight hundred Jews and were searching for them in the nearby villages.

When I returned to town, I learned that all the Jews who had come to the store on that day had been shot. There was no place for me to go, and I could not return home, so I wandered the streets, wondering what to do. I could think of nothing, and I decided to die. I managed to obtain a bottle of liquid ammonia, went to the city park, sat on a bench, and drank it down in one gulp.

Evidently I was groaning, because some Germans came up to me. First of all, they asked if I was a Jew. I could no longer speak and only shook my head. Then they sent me to the hospital.

I spent one day in the hospital. In the morning a nurse came and said the German doctors would be making the rounds and that I should leave right away.

Again I found myself on the street with nowhere to go. I had not eaten anything for twenty-four hours, since my throat was burned and they would not let me eat in the hospital.

Wandering down the street, I met a group of Red-Army soldiers who had escaped captivity. They planned to go to their villages and permitted me to join them.

And I went with them; later I walked six hundred kilometers to Nikolayev, where I had once lived for nineteen years.

Friends hid me there, obtained a false passport for me, and — in a word — did everything they could to save my life.

In all that time I saw so much grief that it would take a long time to describe. I am not much of a writer, and how could I transmit to paper the things I experienced and saw? How can I describe how two Gestapo men took away through the snow a young woman carrying a baby and dressed only in a light slip? How can I describe how they threw Nikolayev's four best doctors in a truck and took them away to be shot?

4. The Story of Mrs. B. Ya. Tartakovsky

The Germans entered Dnepropetrovsk on August 24, 1941. Torture, robbery, and murders began on the very first day. The Jews, ordered under pain of death to wear a white cloth armband with a six-cornered star, could not get water from the municipal faucet and were afraid even to come out for bread.

Then all the Jews were ordered to gather at the "Lux" store. I was told that this was being done to organize a ghetto. I collected a few things and went with my two children to the store. There we were formed into a column and led away. When asked where we were being taken, the Germans answered: "To camp." When we had passed the Jewish cemetery and come to the empty lot next to the railroad, we heard shooting. It was at that point that we realized why we had been brought here. Our turn did not come immediately, however, since it began to get dark. A crowd of several thousand people was driven up against a fence and surrounded on all sides. It was cold, and the people were standing shoulder to shoulder in the icy mud. The sick and dying were simply lying in the mud. My youngest boy sat on my back, and the older boy (he was two) stood, leaning his face against my knees. In this fashion we passed the long autumn night.

When dawn broke, German soldiers appeared on the lot with cases of bullets. They showed us these cases and guffawed. Then they started forcing us toward the pits at the end of the lot. The crowd lurched to one side, the sick fell under the feet of horror-crazed people, and everywhere screams, shots, and the cries of children could be heard. The Germans dragged old people who had been crushed by the crowd to the pits and buried them together with those who had been shot. I fell to my knees, embraced my two children, and it seemed to me that I was losing my mind.

At that moment a man came up to me and said he would take me and the children out of the crowd. I still do not understand how he managed that, but in a few minutes we found ourselves with him next to a road which ran past the cemetery. We saw a cart being driven by a young peasant. We did not ask him for anything, but he himself stopped and offered to take me and the children to town. I said goodbye to my savior, and we left.

When I arrived home, I found my husband in tears. He had been told that we had been taken, not to the camp, but to be shot. My husband is Ukrainian, and we had hoped he would be able to help me and the children escape from the camp.

The next morning we all left the town to Sumy, where my husband had relatives. We had no money or documents, and the trip took one and a half months. In Sumy we managed to obtain a false passport for me, and we were not bothered for a while. Then we learned that we had been denounced. We again fled and for a long time wandered from village to village.

How can I describe our joy when we encountered a forward detachment of the Red Army in one of the villages?

Now my husband is in the army, and I am working in the hospital. I am twenty-seven, but I am an old woman. I live only for the children and to see the German beasts punished. No, they are not beasts, because anyone who could throw living children into a grave is unworthy of the title of beast.

Prepared for publication by **G. Munblit.**

68

The Letter of the Military Officer Granovsky

(Yekaterinopol)

Save this letter. All that is left of our beloved Yekaterinopol is this letter, some ruins, the graves of our countrymen, and the girl Sonya. Only grass grows on the spot where we grew up, studied, loved; our families are in the ground.

Yekaterinopol no longer exists; it was destroyed by the Germans. Only the girl Sonya is left.

When I arrived in our village on May 9, 1944, I did not find my home. The earth was bare. . . . I walked among the ruins, searching for people, but found no one. Everyone had been shot. No one met me, no one shook my hand, no one congratulated me on our victory.

Then I met Sonya Diamant. She is now fifteen years old. She survived miraculously; the Germans led her to her death three times. It was she who told me of the tragedy of Yekaterinopol.

When the SS soldiers arrived, searching, looting, and pogroms began. All the Jews were herded into special camps. In Zvenigorodka there was a camp for those incapable of work. There they locked up the old people, the ill, women with babies, and children under the age of fourteen.

Everyone capable of working ended up in the camp next to the railroad station.

On October 6, 1941, Yekaterinopol's first execution took place — communists, collective-farm leaders, many Jews.

Everyone in the Zvenigorodka camp was killed in April of 1942. They killed eighty-year-old Khana Lerner for being too old and Manya Finenberg's month-old-baby for being too young.

At the camp next to the railroad station many were tortured and forced to work eighteen and twenty hours a day. The girls were raped. Old men were beaten with birch rods. Finally everyone from Yekaterinopol, Shpola, and Zvenigorodka was shot (about 2,000 people).

Do you remember the old barber, Azril Pritsman? He was seventy years old. Before he died, he shouted: "Shoot me! My sons will avenge me." He had five sons at the front. Golikov, the cooper, was eighty. They wounded him, but he got up all bloody and shouted: "Shoot again, you swine! You won't get me with one bullet!" Golikov had twenty-eight relatives at the front — sons, grandsons, sons-in-law, nephews.

The first member of our collective farm, old Mendel Inger, met the enemy proudly. That was on the first day of the German occupation. Mendel was seventy years old, and he refused to talk to them. They shot him right away.

I stood next to the graves and it seemed to me that I saw my relatives and neighbors; they called to me from under the earth: "Vengeance!" I promised to avenge them. Twice in my life I swore an oath of loyalty to my people: once when I was entrusted with a formidable military machine and a second time at the graves of Yekaterinopol.

Abram Granovsky

Prepared for publication by **Ilya Ehrenburg**

The Diary of Sarra Gleykh*

(Mariupol)

October 8. The Germans are in town. Everyone is at home except Fanya, who is at the factory. She went to work in the morning. Is she alive? And if she is alive, how will she get here? The streetcars aren't running. Basya is at Ganya's, who is sick with typhoid. Fanya returned from the factory on foot. The Germans got there at two o'clock, and the employees were in the bomb shelter. The factory director tried to organize a fighting unit, and weapons were issued, but nothing seems to have come of that. They say that the Germans killed Gurber, the secretary of the Molotov Regional Soviet, right in his office. The chairman of the city council, Ushkats, managed to escape.

*In his memoirs, "People, Years, Life," Ehrenburg writes the following about this diary and its author: "The diary of Sarra Gleykh was a pink school notebook. It is amazing how she hurriedly and disjointedly wrote down everything from day to day. The first notes indicate that she went to work at the telegraph office on September 17 — a month after she had evacuated from Kharkov to Mariupol, where her parents lived. On September 1, her sisters, Fanya and Raya, had gone to military headquarters to ask that they be evacuated as wives of military personnel. They were told that 'evacuation would take place no earlier than spring.' On October eight she wrote: 'Melnikov, the head of the office, told me this morning that we would be evacuated tomorrow and that our documents should be ready. We can take the family, so our departure is guaranteed. . . .' On that same evening she continued: 'Germans entered the town at noon. The town was surrendered without a fight. . . .'" (I. Ehrenburg, *Collected Writings in 9 Volumes*, Moscow, 1967, vol. 9, pp. 413–414).

October 9. There is absolutely nothing to eat at home. The bakeries in the city have been destroyed, and there is no electricity or water. The bakery in the port is functioning, but it is only for the German army. The Germans have pasted announcements requiring all Jews to wear a white six-cornered star on the left sleeve. It's forbidden to go out without one. Jews are forbidden to change apartments. Fanya and her maid, Tanya, are bringing their things from the factory apartment to Mama's anyway.

October 10. The Jewish population has been ordered to elect a group of thirty persons to be in charge of the community. This committee will, according to the order, answer with their lives for "the good conduct of the Jewish population." The head of the community is Dr. Erber. I don't know any of the members of the community except for Fain. The Jewish population is supposed to register at points set up in the community. (All together 9,000 Jews have been registered.) Each "point" unites several streets. Our point is on 64 Pushkin Street. Boru, the bookkeeper, Zegelman, the lawyer, and Tomshinsky are in charge of it. Fanya has to go specially to the factory to be registered. The chairman of the factory point is Dr. Belopolsky; Slivakov is a member of the community. There have not yet been any mass repressions, but our neighbor Trievsky says that the Gestapo detachment has not yet arrived and that things will change after that.

October 13. The Germans were at our house in the night. At nine o'clock there was antiaircraft fire. We were all dressed. Vladya was asleep, and papa went outside to see if there was anyone in the bomb shelter and came upon three Germans. They were in the yard looking for Jews. Papa's appearance resolved the question; papa brought them to the apartment. They pointed a revolver in our faces and asked where the sugar and meat were. Then they began to smash the doors of the armoire, even though it was not locked. They took everything that Basya had; she was at Ganya's place. After that, the Germans shifted to our belongings. Two of them looted non-stop. They took everything — even the meat grinder.

They tied their loot in a tablecloth and left. Everything in the house was scattered and broken. We decided not to clean up the mess. If any more were to come, they would see right away that there was nothing left to take. In the morning we learned that looting had gone on all over town during the night. It continued during the day. They took everything — pillows, blankets, groceries, clothing. They move in groups of three to five men. You can hear them from far away, since their boots make so much noise.

After the Germans left, mama cried and said: "They don't consider us people; we're doomed."

October 14. Raiders came again during the night. Tanya, Fanya's maid, saved the things that were left by claiming they were hers. The Germans left empty-handed. They were at the Schwartz's and took their blankets and pillows.

The Gestapo is already in town.

The community was given two hours to collect two kilos of hot peppers, 2,500 boxes of black ointment, and 70 kilos of sugar. They went from house to house, and everybody gave what they could. After all, the committee is responsible for the "good conduct of the Jewish population."

Nine thousand Jews have registered at the committee points. The rest of the Jewish population has left town or is in hiding.

October 17. It was announced today that everyone who has registered must appear at the points and bring his valuables with him.

October 18. Today Mama, Papa, Basya, and I went to the point and turned in three silver soup spoons and a ring. After that, they did not let us leave the yard. When the entire population of the region had turned in their valuables, it was announced to us that we had to leave the city within two hours. We will have to walk to the nearest collective farm, where we will be settled. We have to take enough food and warm clothing for four days. We are to present ourselves together with our things in two hours. There will be trucks for the elderly and women with babies.

All Jewish women married to Russians or Ukrainians can stay in town, provided their husbands are with them. If the husband is in the army or absent for any reason, the wife and children have to leave town. If a Russian woman is married to a Jew, she can choose to remain or go with her husband. The children may remain with her.

The Royanovs asked Fanya to give them her grandson. Papa insisted that Fanya take Vladya to the Royanovs. Fanya categorically refused, cried, and begged Papa not to throw her out and make her go to the Royanovs. She said: "Without you, I'll lay hands on myself anyway. I won't survive, so I'll go with you." She would not give up Vladya and decided to take him with her.

Fanya's maid, Tanya, walked behind us, begging her to give Vladya to the Royanovs. She said she would take care of him, but Fanya would not even hear of this.

We stood out on the street until evening. Everyone was herded into a building for the night; we got a corner in the basement. It was dark, wet, and dirty.

October 19. It was announced that we would leave the following morning, it was Sunday and the Gestapo was resting. Tanya, Fedya Belousov and Ulyana came and brought a food package. In yesterday's confusion Fanya had left her watch on the table. They gave Tanya the spare key to the apartment; keys were not turned in at the point.

The Gestapo pasted specially printed announcements stating "No Admittance" on all Jewish apartments, and it was difficult, therefore, even to enter an apartment secretly.

Friends and acquaintances brought food packages to everyone, and many received permission to take other things from their apartments. The number of people kept increasing.

The police permitted the committee to organize the preparation of hot food.

Permission was also granted to acquire horses and carts. Regulations required that all sacks and packages clearly indicate in Russian and German the name of the owner. One member of the family would travel with the possessions, and the others would go on foot.

Vladya can't stand being here any longer, and he is begging to go home. Papa, Schwartz, and Niusya Karpilovsky's stepfather pooled their money and bought a horse and cart. We are not permitted to go beyond the gates, and the purchase was made by Fedya Belousov. Nyusya succeeded in slipping through the gates, and she was very upset when she returned. She said we should never have come here and that many people had remained in town. She said she even met them on the street.

Tomorrow at 7:00 A.M. we are to leave our last haven in town.

October 20. It rained all night, and the morning was overcast and damp, but not cold.

The whole committee left at 7:00 A.M., then the trucks with the elderly and trucks with women and babies. We had to go 9-10 kilometers, and the road was terrible. Judging by how the Germans treated those who came to say goodbye to us and brought packages, the future holds nothing good. The Germans beat all the passersby with clubs and chased them a block away from the building. The time came for mama, papa, Fanya, and Vladya to get in the truck.

Mama and papa left at 9:00 A.M. Fanya and Vladya were not ready and will leave with the next truck. V. Osovets and Reizins are

73

in charge of the truck. There are fewer and fewer people outside. Only those are left who are, according to the explanation of the Germans, to accompany possessions. Shmukler, Weiner, and R. and L. Koldobsky came up to us. I expressed my concern for my parents. It was rumored that the trucks were taking the elderly out of town to be destroyed.

Weiner looks terrible; he was released by the Gestapo only yesterday. Several Germans came into the yards and began to chase everyone out of the house with nightsticks. We could hear the screams of those being beaten in the building. Basya and I came out, and Fanya was already standing next to the truck with Vladya. V. Osovets helped her get in, and she left. We went on foot. The road was terrible and had been washed away by the rain. It was impossible to walk, difficult to raise a foot. If you stopped, you were struck with a club. People were beaten without regard to age.

I. Reichelson walked next to me and then disappeared somewhere. Shmerok, F. Gurevich and his father, and D. Polunov were walking somewhere next to us. It was about two o'clock when we approached the Petrovsky Agricultural Station. There were many people there. I rushed off to search for my sister Fanya and my parents. Fanya called to me. She had been searching for our parents before my arrival and had not found them. Probably they were already in the barn to which people were being taken in group of forty or fifty.

Vladya was hungry, and it was a good thing that I had some apples and toasted bread in my pocket. That would suffice the boy for a day. That was all we had anyway, and it was forbidden to take food with us. The Germans had confiscated everything when we left — even food.

Our turn arrived, and the horrible image of a senseless, a wildly senseless and meek death was before our eyes as we set off behind the barns. The bodies of Father and Mother were already there somewhere. By sending them by truck, I had shortened their lives by a few hours. We were herded toward the trenches which had been dug for the defense of the city. These trenches served no other function than as receptacles for the death of nine thousand Jews. We were ordered to undress to our underwear, and they searched for money and documents. Then we were herded along the edge of the ditch, but there was no longer any real edge, since the trench was filled with people for a half kilometer. Many were still alive and were begging for another bullet to finish them off. We walked over the corpses, and it seemed to me that I recognized my mother in one gray-haired woman. I rushed to her and Basya followed me, but we were driven back with clubs. At one point I thought that an old man with his brains bashed out was Papa, but I could not approach him any closer. We began to say goodbye, and we managed to kiss. We remembered Dora. Fanya did not believe that this was the end: "Can it be that I will never again see the sun and the light?", she said. Her face was blue-gray, and Vladya kept asking: "Are we going to swim? Why are we undressed?" Fanya took him in her arms, since it was difficult for him to walk in the wet clay. Basya would not stop whispering: "Vladya, Vladya, why should this happen to you too? No one even knows what they have done to us." Fanya turned around and answered: "I am dying calmly with him, because I know I am not leaving him an orphan." These were Fanya's last words. I could not stand it any longer, and I held my head and began to scream in a wild voice. I seem to remember that Fanya had time to turn around and say: "Be quiet, Sarra, be quiet." At that point everything breaks off.

When I regained consciousness, it was already twilight. The bodies lying on top of me were still shuddering; the Germans were shooting them again to make doubly sure that the wounded would not be able to leave. At any rate, I understood the Germans to say that. They were afraid that there were many who had not been finished off, and they were right; there were many like that. These people were buried alive, since no one could help them even though they screamed and called for help. Somewhere above the corpses babies were crying. Most of them had been carried by their mothers and, since we were shot in the backs, they had fallen, protected by their mothers' bodies. Not wounded by the bullets, they were covered up and buried alive under the corpses.

I began to crawl out from underneath the corpses. (I had torn the nails from the toes of one foot, but I learned of this only when I ended up at the Royanovs on October 24.) When I had crawled out, I looked around: the wounded were writhing, groaning, attempting to get up, and falling again. I began to call to Fanya in the hope that she would hear me, and a man next to me ordered me to be silent. It was Grodzinsky. His mother had been killed, and he was afraid that my shouts would attract the attention of the Germans. A small group of people were resourceful enough to jump into the trench when the first shots rang out, and they were unharmed — Vera Kulman, Shmaevsky, Pilya (I do not remember Pilya's surname). They kept pleading with me to be silent, and I begged everyone who was leaving to help me find Fanya. Grodzinsky, who was wounded in the legs and could not walk, advised me to leave. I tried to help him, but I could do nothing alone. He fell after two steps and refused to go on. He advised me to catch up with those who had left. I sat there and listened. An old woman called out in a singsong voice: "Leitenakh, Leitenakh,"* there was so much horror in this endlessly repeating word! From somewhere down below, someone shouted: "Panochku,** don't kill me. . . ." By chance I overtook V. Kulman. She had been separated from her group. The two of us, undressed except for our slips and smeared with blood from head to toe, set off to seek refuge for the night, starting in the direction from which we could hear dogs barking. We knocked at one hut, but no one answered. Then we knocked at another, and we were driven away. At a third, we were given some rags with which to cover ourselves and advised to go into the steppe. We did precisely that. In the darkness we found a haystack and sat in it until dawn. In the morning we returned to the farmstead which turned out to be named in honor of the Ukrainian writer, Shevchenko. It was not far from the trench, but on the far side. We could hear the screams of women and children until the end of the day.

October 23. We have now been in the steppe for two days and do not know the road. In moving from one haystack to another, V. Kulman accidentally came upon a group of men. Shmaevsky was among them. Naked and bloody, they had been there the entire time. We decided to set out for the Ilyich Factory during the day, since we could not find the road at night. Along the way we met a group of teenage boys who appeared to be from the collective farm. One of them advised us to stay in the steppe until evening and then left. A second boy warned us that his comrade had deceived us with his advice and that he would bring the Germans. We left hurriedly. On the morning of October twenty-fourth we knocked at the door of the Royanov home. They let me in and were horrified when they learned that everyone had died. They helped me get cleaned up, fed me, and put me to bed.***

Prepared for publication by **Ilya Ehrenburg**.

*Lieutenant (corrupted form — German). J.G.
**Sir (corrupted form — Ukrainian). J.G.
***Ehrenburg tells of the subsequent fate of S. Gleykh in his memoirs: "On November 27, after a month of wandering in the steppe, S. Gleykh learned that our troops were five kilometers from Bolshoy Log, where she had arrived by then. She succeeded in reaching a Red-Army detachment (*Ibid.*, p. 414).

Odessa

I

A broad plain spreads out near Odessa. From time to time, a low hill appears with a green grove of specially planted trees followed by more of the Black-Sea steppe separating the sea, the estuaries, and the Bug River.

Here everything is open to the eye. It is difficult in these parts for a man to hide if he is being sought by death in the image of a Rumanian or German soldier.

If you were to fly over this territory, you would see scattered settlements, state collective farms, and the villages of Dalniki, Sortirovochnaya, Sukhie Balki, and farther on — closer to the Bug — are the villages of Beryozovka, Akmechetka, Domanevka, Bogdanovka.

There was a time when these names had a peaceful sound to them and inspired fear in no one. Now, however, it is impossible to pronounce them in a calm voice, for each name speaks of murder and torture.

Camps of death were here. Here people were tortured, ripped to pieces. Children's heads were smashed, and people were buried alive — people crazed with suffering, horror, and unendurable pain.

Of tens of thousands, only dozens survived. It was from them that we learned the details of this beastly act of violence.

In all the oral and written accounts of those witnesses who survived, in their letters and memoirs, we meet the same statement — that they are incapable of describing their experience.

"Without the brush of an artist, it is impossible to describe the horrible scenes which transpired in Domanevka." These are the words of Yelizaveta Pikarmer, a woman from Odessa. "Here the best workers and the best scientists perished. The insane delirium of these people, the expressions on their faces and in their eyes shook even those who possessed the greatest spiritual strength. At one point the twenty-year-old Manya Tkach gave birth on a dung heap, next to corpses. By evening this woman died."

We read the following statement written by V. Ya. Rabinovich, the technical editor of an Odessa publisher: "A great deal could be written, but I am not a writer, and I have no strength left. The pen and paper do not exist that could describe the inhuman suffering endured by us Soviet people."

But they cannot be silent, and they write, and there is nothing left to be added to that which they have told.

An old Odessa doctor, Israel Borisovich Adesman, dictated his memoirs to his wife, Rakhil Iosifovna Goldental, who was also a doctor.

Lev Rozhetsky, a pupil in seventh grade of Odessa school No. 47, described in essay form life in the death camps, from Odessa to Bogdanovka.

"We lived in Odessa," V. Ya. Rabinovich writes, "and it was a life we both knew and understood. To us living meant working and creating artifacts of culture. And we worked. As a technical editor, I published hundreds of books. In my free time I could travel with my wife and children to Arkadia, to the sea, where we enjoyed boating, fishing, swimming. In my free time, I could read a little or go to the theater. We lived simply — as did millions of people in our great Soviet Union. We did not know the meaning of national oppression, and we enjoyed equal rights in our multinational homeland!

The tragic dates of Odessa are: October 16, 1941 — the day Rumanian troops occupied Odessa; October 17 — the day the Rumanians announced the registration of the Jewish population; October 24 — the day Jews were sent to the ghetto in the village of Slobodka. This last act led to the camps of destruction located in the valley of death outside of town. The Jews were driven there at a somewhat later date.

The night of October 16 was horrible for those Jews who had not managed to evacuate. It was terrible for the old men and women who had not been able to leave, for mothers whose children could not yet walk, for pregnant women, for the bedridden.

This was a terrible night for the paralyzed professor of mathematics, Fudim. He was dragged from his bed out onto the street and hanged. Professor Ya. S. Rabinovich, a neuropathologist, threw himself out a window, but — unfortunately — survived. Although he was seriously injured, he was still conscious and breathing. An armed guard stood next to his broken body. They spat in his face and threw stones at him.

Once they had occupied Odessa, the Hitlerites began first of all to eliminate the doctors. These professional murderers hated those whose calling was to lengthen the lives of people and spare them suffering.

In the very first days sixty-one doctors and their families were murdered.

The death list includes medical names of long standing, names known to every Odessite from childhood: Rabinovich, Rubinstein, Varshavsky, Chatsky, Polyakov, Brodsky. . . . Dr. Adesman was saved only thanks to the circumstance that he was listed as a consultant in the Slobodka Ghetto. Before that, however, he was forced to endure all the harassment and torture connected with registration and later to live through all the horrors of Domanevka, one of the most terrible death camps on the Black-Sea plain.

On October 17, 1941 — the day after the Rumanians took Odessa — registration of the Jews began.

There were several registration points. From them, the people were taken to the gallows or to the burial trenches. Some were sent to prison. A minority was permitted to return to their looted apartments. This was only a delay of death — nothing more.

"The point to which my wife and I were taken," Dr. Adesman tells, "was located in the cold dark school building. There were more than 500 of us gathered there. Denied even room to sit down, we spent the night standing, crowded up against each other. We were exhausted, hungry, thirsty, and demoralized by ignorance of our situation. All night we heard the cries of children and the groans of the adults.

"In the morning a column of three or four thousand people was formed from groups such as ours, and we were herded off to prison. Among us were very old people, cripples on crutches, and women with small babies. In prison many died from exhaustion and beatings. Many committed suicide."

On October 23, 1941, partisans blew up the Rumanian head-quarters building, and several dozen Rumanian soldiers and officers died. In response the invaders flushed the city with Jewish blood.

An announcement was hung up on the walls saying that three hundred Russians or five hundred Jews would be hanged for every officer killed. In fact, however, this "estimate" was exceeded by multiples of tens and hundreds.

On October 23, 1941, ten thousand Jews were taken from the prison. Many were mown down outside of town by machine guns. . . . On October 25 several thousand more Jews were taken out of prison to a barn, which was then blown up with dynamite.

V. Ya. Rabinovich, the technical editor who had formerly taken his children to Arkadia (How monstrous this idyllic name now sounds!) described the town in the first weeks of the occupation: "On October 23 and 24 no matter in which direction you looked you could see gallows. There were thousands of them. At the feet of the hanged lay the bodies of those who had been tortured, mutilated, and shot. Our town was a terrible sight: a town of the hanged. They led us around the streets for a long time to show us off. The Germans and the Rumanians explained: 'All these Jews, these old men, women, and children are the instigators of this war. They are the ones who attacked Germany, and they must be destroyed.' People were shot even as they were led along. The dead would fall to the ground, and the wounded would attempt to crawl away. When the group reached the New Arkadian Highway to the sea (and the famous resorts), they were led up to a deep pit. The order was given: 'Strip naked! . . . Quick, quick!' Some screamed, others said goodbye to each other. Many tore the clothes on their backs, and were bayonetted for this; the murderers wanted their clothes.

"The Rumanians and Germans tried out the strength of their bayonets on small children. A mother was breast feeding her baby when a Rumanian soldier ripped it away from her with his bayonet and flung it into the pit of the dead."

Two other female-witnesses, Bolshov and Spichenko, have also testified that there were fewer and fewer Jews in town. Every day groups of ragged people would be led down the streets. The hellish machine of destruction churned reliably on:

"In the crowd we saw a short man whose head was pulled into his shoulders. He had a high protruding forehead and thoughtful eyes. Who was he? A barbarian, a murderer, a criminal? No, it was Doctor Blank, an important scientist and neuropathologist who had dedicated himself to science, his patients, his clinic. He had ignored the impending danger and had remained with his patients to discharge the duty of a doctor. Another doctor with a Red-Cross band on his sleeve walked beside Doctor Blank. He was an older, heavy-set man, short of breath and with a bad heart. Gradually he began to fall behind, and a Rumanian gendarme beat him on the head with a stick. The doctor strained himself to walk faster, but he soon fell. They beat him on the eyes with a stick. 'Kill me!' he screamed. Two bullets pierced his skull.

"Another man was walking in the crowd. He was old, tall, and thin. The Russian women wiped their eyes and watched as he passed. He was Doctor Petrushkin, a pediatrician."

The Rumanians did not hesitate to heap the most nonsensical

slander on the Jews. Anna Margulis, a former stenographer at the Marty Ship Factory, has related the following:

"On October 29, 1941, my dying father attempted to light a lamp. The burning match fell from his weak hand, and the blanket caught fire. I put it out in a second. That very evening my Rumanian neighbor reported to the police that I had attempted to burn down the house. I was arrested in the morning and thrown into a prison with thirty other women. During the interrogation I was beaten with clubs, rifle butts, and rubber hoses. I lost consciousness.

"That night, in pitch blackness, a crowd of Rumanian soldiers broke into our cell. They threw their coats on the wet floor and began to rape the girls. We older women (I was fifty-four) sat there and cried. Many of the girls went mad."

But all of this was only the first step on the road leading to the ghetto, while the ghetto itself led to the plain of death.

"The Jews who died in the first days of the occupation were the fortunate ones." This statement of an Odessa Jew requires no explanations.

"Everyone had to go to the ghetto in Slobodka — even the paralyzed, the crippled, the feeble-minded, those ill with contagious diseases, women about to give birth. Some walked by themselves, others were led by their relatives, and still others were carried. Only a few were fortunate enough to die in their own beds. On the very first day in Slobodka the people realized that there could be no 'living' in the ghetto." There were not enough buildings, and the people crowded into the streets. The sick moaned and fell down in the snow, where the Rumanians trampled them with their horses. Everywhere were heard screams of horror, the crying of freezing children, pleas for mercy.

By evening the frozen bodies were already accumulating on the streets of Slobodka. Slobodka had been transformed into a giant trap, from which it was impossible to escape. The Rumanian gendarmerie and police were everywhere.

Dr. Adesman was a consultant in the ghetto hospital. The hospital was an assembly of the dying. When the Jews were removed from Odessa, all those who had not yet died were sent to the water-transport workers' hospital and put to death there. Doctor Adesman himself was sent with the last train on February 11, 1942. He recalls: "At Sortirovochnaya Station we were transferred to boxcars which took us to Berezovka. With our packages on our shoulders, we walked twenty-five kilometers on that cold dark night down a road covered with snow and ice. Our brief halts cost us dearly, since we had to buy them from gendarmes with our last belongings. We arrived in Domanevka as beggars."

In Domanevka they were assigned to half-decayed houses without windows or doors, to sheds, cow barns, and pigsties.

People began to fall ill with dysentery, typhus, gangrene, scabies, furunculosis. Delirious and miserable typhus victims lay unexamined in the barns, and no one paid any attention to the corpses.

We read in other memoirs: "We got on the train at Sortirovochnaya Station. They stuffed so many people in the cars that it was possible only to stand motionless, pressed against one another. The cars were shut and locked with a heavy latch, and the people inside remained in total darkness. Gradually, however, we began to make out frightened eyes and the tear-streamed faces of children and women. The train began to move, and the people's faces lit up with hope. The old women exclaimed: 'God will help us!' People began to hope that they were actually being taken to a place where they would be able to live and work. The train moved slowly, and no one knew where it was heading. Each lurch, each stop was frightening. What if the train were to be derailed? What if it were to be burned? Our only hope was that they would be unwilling to destroy the train. But where was it going? The people became stiffer and stiffer from the cold and lack of movement. The children cried and begged for something to drink and eat. First the children and then the adults began to empty their bowels.

"Suddenly groans and pleas for mercy were heard. A woman was writhing in heavy birth pains, but no one could help her. Finally the latch squeaked, and the living were driven from the car. They went on foot, beaten by the clubs of the gendarmes, who dealt out blow after blow to the weakened and frozen children. The people wanted only one thing — to reach the ghetto, to stop, not to move any longer. But now they were falling, falling. . . .

"The roads were thickly sown with bones and suggested a recent battle scene, except that these were not the bodies of soldiers, but the pitiful tiny bodies of babies and the bent figures of old people."

The plan for driving all the Jews from Odessa was conceived with the goal of having as many people as possible die a "natural death."

The group that reached the Berezov region was led through a steppe snow storm for three days although the villages intended for use as ghettos were only eighteen kilometers from the station.

The report made up by the lawyer, I. M. Leenzon, who had been in Odessa in May, 1944, states that the number of murdered Jews from the city of Odessa was approximately 100,000.

Lev Rozhetsky, a pupil in the seventh grade of the forty-seventh Odessa school, mentally composed essays, songs, and poems, but he wrote some of them down on scraps of paper, boards, and plywood. "I could, of course, have been killed for this, but I wrote two anti-Fascist songs: 'The sky soared high,' and 'Nina' (about a woman who lost her mind). Sometimes I managed to read my poems to my comrades in misery. It was a joy to me amidst those tears and groans to hear my songs sung and my verse recited."

Rozhetsky relates that he was beaten half to death when he was discovered to have some poems by Pushkin: "They wanted to kill me, but they didn't."

A youth, little more than a boy, he had been in many death camps, and he described them in detail. His essays give us a clear picture of the hell of this chain of camps that stretched from the Black Sea to the Bug River: Sortirovochnaya, Berezovka, Sirotskoye, Domanevka, and Bogdanovka. Rozhetsky wrote: "I want each letter of these names to be burned into our brains. These names must not be forgotten. These were death camps, where the Fascists destroyed innocent people simply because they were Jews."

The number of those killed in Domanevka reached fifteen thousand, while in Bogdanovka fifty-four thousand Jews were killed. This act was officially documented by representatives of the Red Army, the Soviet government, and the population on March 27, 1944.

"On January 11, 1942, my mother, my little brother Anatoly, who was just recovering from typhus, and I were herded off to Slobodka. We were called for at 3:00 A.M.

"It was terribly cold, and the snow was knee-deep. Many of the elderly and the children died in this howling blizzard while still in town, at the outskirts, or in Peresyp. The Germans laughed and took pictures of us with their cameras. The survivors finally reached Sortirovochnaya Station. A dam had been blown up in our path, and an entire river had formed. The people were soaked and freezing.

"A train was waiting at Sortirovochnaya Station. I will never forget the scene of pillows, blankets, coats, felt boots, pots, and other things scattered all over the platform.

"Frozen, the older people were unable to get up and were groaning quietly and pitifully. Mothers were losing their children, and the children were looking for their mothers. There was some shooting as well as shouting and crying. One mother was wringing her hands and tearing her hair: 'Daughter, where are you?' The child was rushing about the platform and screaming: 'Mama!'

"In Berezovka the doors opened with a squeak, and we were blinded by the bonfires. I saw people running, engulfed in flame. There was a distinct smell of gasoline; they were burning people alive.

"This slaughter took place at Beryozovka Station.

"Suddenly the train lurched violently and moved slowly on — past the bonfires. We were being taken to die in a different place."

Rozhetsky said of Domanevka that it occupied a "respectable" position among the death camps. He has provided a detailed description:

"Domanevka is a black and bloody word, for Domanevka was a center for murder and death. Thousands of groups were brought there to their deaths, arriving steadily one after the other. Three thousand people left Odessa, of whom only a handful reached Domanevka. Although only a small village, Domanevka was a regional center. The village is situated among hilly fields and next to a beautiful, small forest. Rags and fragments of clothing still cling to the bushes. There is a grave underneath each tree, and human skeletons are visible."

There were two nearly destroyed stables in the middle of Domanevka which were called "the hills." Even in the Domanevka ghetto these were terrible places. The people were not permitted to leave the barracks, the mud was knee-deep, and there were accumulations of excrement. The corpses lay there as in a morgue, and typhus, dysentery, gangrene, and death were everywhere.

"The corpses gradually formed mountains of such proportions that they were terrifying to see. Old men and women were stacked in the most varied of poses. A dead mother embraced a dead baby, and the breeze stirred the beards of the old men.

"Now I wonder if I had not lost my mind. Dogs came there day and night from all directions. Domanevka's dogs grew as fat as sheep. The stench was unbearable. One of the policemen petted a dog and said: 'Well, old boy, got your fill of kikes?'"

Bogdanovka was located on the shore of the Bug River, twenty-five kilometers from Domanevka. The lanes of a beautiful park led to a pit where tens of thousands of people found their graves.

"Those intended for death were stripped naked, led to the pit, and made to kneel down facing the Bug River. The executioners used only hollow-head bullets, which they fired into the back of the skull. The bodies were thrown into the pit. Wives were murdered before their husbands' eyes, and then the husbands were murdered."

The pig farm "Stavki" was, in the expression of Rozhetsky, "like an island in the desert of the steppe." Those who served in "the hills" met their death in Stavki.

People were herded into pigsties and kept in these filthy cages until merciful death relieved them of their misery.

"The camp was surrounded by a ditch. Anyone who dared to cross it was shot on the spot. Ten people were allowed to go for water. Once, seeing that eleven people had gone and that the 'order' had been violated, the police shot the eleventh person. It was a girl, and she screamed: 'Mama, they killed me!' A policeman walked up to her and finished her off with a bayonet."

Those who managed to survive were sent to perform the most difficult and torturous work.

"I remember how we used to go to the barracks. I would lead the horse by the reins, and Mama would push the cart from behind. We would pick up the corpses by the arms and legs and throw them onto the cart. When the cart was full, we would take our load to the pit and dump it."

Yelizaveta Pikarmer tells the following:

"A woman and baby who lived in my building and I were the first in the pit, although there had been a hundred people ahead of us in the crowd. At the last minute, however, a Rumanian horseman galloped up with a slip of paper which he showed to the guards. The prisoners were then led away, to new torments. The next day we were all thrown in the river. By giving our tormenters our last things, we bought ourselves the right to come out of the water. Many died later from pneumonia."

In Domanevka the Rumanians ripped the babies in half or grabbed them by the feet and smashed their heads against the stones. The women had their breasts chopped off, and many whole families were either buried alive or burned in the bonfires. Old Mr. Furman and eighteen-year-old Sonya Katz were given the opportunity to prolong their lives by dancing, but they were hanged two hours later anyway.

Doomed to death, people moved like automatons, went mad, raved, and hallucinated.

Lupescu and Plutoner Sandu, the commandants of the village of Gulyaevka, nightly sent their assistants to the camp to bring back pretty girls. They always derived a particular pleasure from watching the death agonies of these girls on the morning of the next day.

There was no one to look after the typhus victims. Death mowed people down by the hundreds, and it was difficult to distinguish the living from the dead, the healthy from the sick.

Tanya Rekochinsky wrote to her brother in the active army: "During the terribly cold winter weather my husband and I were driven from our apartment together with our two children. We were taken on foot to the Bug River, 180 kilometers from Odessa. My little girl, who was still nursing, died along the way. The boy was shot along with the other children in the group. It was my lot to live through all of this."

Even these horrors were insufficient. The silence, previously broken only by the groans and wheezing of the dying, was shattered by an anxious scream: "The village is surrounded. Rumanians and German colonists from the village of Kartakayevo have arrived with machine guns."

Policemen on horseback drove all the Jews into a barn, and from there to the death trenches. Some decided to die proudly and not to beg for mercy or show any fear of death to their executioners. Others tried to drown themselves. The men attempted to calm the women, and the women attempted to calm the children. Some of the smallest children were laughing, and their childish laughter was eerie in the atmosphere of this bloody slaughter.

"Mommy, where are they taking us?" a six-year-old girl asked in a clear, ringing voice.

"They're taking us to a new apartment, sweetie," the mother said to calm her. . . . Yes, the apartment would be deep and damp, and her daughter would never see either the sun or the blue sky from its windows.

When they reached the trenches, the human slaughter was performed with German precision and thoroughness. Like surgeons before an operation, the Germans and Rumanians put on white hospital gowns and rolled up their sleeves. The doomed people were stripped naked and then lined up alongside the trenches. They stood naked and trembling before their tormenters and waited for death.

No lead was wasted on the children. Their heads were crushed against posts and trees, and they were thrown alive into the bonfires which had been prepared specifically for this purpose. The mothers were not killed immediately but were pushed aside so that their maternal hearts could bleed at the sight of their children dying.

One German woman, a colonist who had been declared a *kulak* and whose farm in the village of Kartakayevo had been confiscated, was unusually vicious. "She seemed to be intoxicated by her own cruelty, and she crushed the children's skulls with a rifle butt so that the brains splattered a great distance."

In the summer of 1942 the residents of Domanevka had such a terrible appearance that, on the day the governor of Transnistria was expected, all Jews were ordered to leave the village limits by five or six kilometers and not to return until evening.

Before being destroyed in the death camps, the people were first robbed. The Rumanians and policemen took money for everything — a gulp of soup, an hour of life, each sigh and each step. In March of 1942, Yelizaveta Pikarmer fell ill with typhus and was sent with other typhus victims to the typhus storage area. Six others who were not able to rise were shot. Pikarmer relates: "I also fell in the mud, but for 20 marks a policeman dragged me up a small hill, using an iron rod."

On May 7, 1943, the order was issued that all those still alive be sent to do agricultural work. "At that time our situation improved somewhat, since we were able to wash daily in the Bug River, and once a week we could boil our rags. We used hemp to make skirts, blouses, and shoes. . . ."

This proximity to the Bug River gave the people much satisfaction, but eventually it brought them new horrors.

"On March 23, 1944, a punitive detachment of SS soldiers crossed the Bug, and we Jews were doomed to death. Everywhere along the road we encountered groups of prisoners who were being taken to Tiraspol. Hands and faces were swollen from hunger and cold. We did not have the strength to continue the journey, and we begged to be shot on the spot. The women and children were loaded onto trucks and taken away. I was among the twenty people left with a German non-commissioned officer to continue the journey. We ate nothing for two days and suffered from the cold. We were losing our minds."

II

The village of Gradovka is located in the steppes of the Odessa *oblast*, not far from the railroad station Kolosovka. Lieutenant-Colonel Shabanov was there in the summer of 1944. At the edge of the village he saw three ovens used by the peasants to burn limestone. The ovens were overgrown with weeds and thistles. Within the oven shafts Shabanov found charred forearms, shoulder blades, and vertebrae. Tiny fragments of skulls crunched under his feet; the ground was covered with such a thick layer that it was like shells on the seashore.

This was all that remained of the people who had been burned there.

The murderers had not needed any complex, specially equipped crematory ovens with "Cyclon" vortex exhausts. They had managed to accomplish their bloody task using only these simple peasant ovens.

The chief executioners were the German colonists. There were many of them in the area; the names of Russian villages alternated here with German names: München, Radstadt, etc. Aside from the names, the German colonists had also brought to Russia the bloody cruelty characteristic of all these "Aryans." These people splashed innocent blood over the land that had taken them in. They came to the ovens in the steppe as if to a holiday; they robbed with pleasure and murdered with passion. People condemned to death were not kept long in Gradovka. A "conveyor" method had been established there, and the schedule for burning people depended on the oven's capacity to consume. Each "batch" required approximately three days. While one stove was in use, executions were taking place at the others.

People were stripped naked before the ovens, lined up at the very edge of the shaft, and shot at point-blank range with submachine guns. The executioners aimed mainly at the head, and fragments of fragile skull bones flew in all directions without being picked up later. The bodies fell into the oven shafts.

When a shaft was full to the brim, kerosene was poured into it. Bundles of straw had been placed in the corners in advance. Fat melted from the bodies and fed the flame. The entire area was filled with smoke and poisoned with the stench of burning human flesh. The belongings of the executed were taken to the railroad station, where they were sorted and loaded onto cars. All this was done methodically and with expertise. People in Rumania and Germany were probably pleased with the things that had been sent to them. Their only disadvantage was that they smelled of smoke.

Approximately 7,000 people were burned in the three ovens. In Radstadt and Sukhie Balki the murdered numbered as high as 20,000. Lieutenant Colonel Shabanov concluded his report as follows: "I have seen many things during the war, but I cannot describe what I experienced in visiting these ovens. If I, a simple witness, was so profoundly affected, then what must the doomed people themselves have felt before having their skulls crushed and then falling into the fire of the ovens? One woman is said to have grabbed an executioner and pulled him into the mouth of the oven along with her."

Barges loaded with Jewish women and children returned empty a half hour after leaving for the open sea. They would take new groups and again return.

Mine sweeping was also the obligation of interned Jews, not one of whom survived. What eyewitness testimony, what official documents, what report can describe all this? Who can depict the stuffed sealed boxcars that stood for days on sidetracks? The corpses were thrown out into the steppe and burned in open fires. The entire plain from the Black Sea to the Bug River was illuminated by the flames of those bonfires.

Death from fire, from cold, from hunger, from thirst, from torture, by shooting, by hanging. . . . All manner of death, the entire bloody arsenal of torture was used on these unarmed, helpless old men, women, and children.

III

Odessa was transformed into a dungeon, terrorized, washed with blood, and festooned with gallows. The Odessa newspapers, edited by the Rumanians, were filled with fanatical ravings about the "Jewish danger." In the words of Hitler, the skeleton of a Jew was to be a rarity in the New Europe and would be found only in the archeological museum of antiquities.

In these circumstances any word of sympathy for the Jews, any compassionate look, a single glass of water or crust of bread given to a Jewish child was enough to place a Ukrainian or Russian in danger. Even so, Russians and Ukrainians risked their lives to help Jews; entire families were hidden in cellars, fed, clothed, and rendered medical aid.

"I want only to thank you, Shura, and you, Comrade Chmir, for hiding us. You were our protectors. Daily you read the orders of those animals, the Germans and the Rumanians, and you knew how dangerous this was for you. Thank you." This was written by Rabinovich, who also wrote unforgettable pages condemning the outrages of the Rumanian-German invaders in his home town.

Yelizaveta Pikarmer was saved from death only by the fact that she was accidentally seen by a Russian woman who had been a patient in the sanatorium where Pikarmer had worked as a nurse and hostess.

The Ukrainian Leonid Suvorovsky was an engineer at one of the Odessa factories and had become extremely well known among the Jewish population of Odessa. Suvorovsky not only warned his Jewish acquaintances not to take part in the registration announced by the Rumanians, but also took many of them into his apartment, which he transformed into a true headquarters where false Russian passports for dozens of Jewish families were prepared. With the help of his Russian and Ukrainian friends, Suvorovsky concealed and fed twenty-two Jewish families. To do this, he sold newspapers and even his own clothing. Finally, Suvorovsky was arrested by the German-Rumanian authorities and sentenced by a military court to seven years hard labor. On the very eve of his arrest, Suvorovsky managed to provide refuge for the Jewish families that he had saved by placing them with his friends.

Yakov Ivanovich Polishchuk, together with a group of trusted people, dug a large cellar in an uncompleted building in the very center of town where he concealed 16 Jewish families. With risk to his own life, Polishchuk brought food there. All 16 families were saved.

Andrey Ivanovich Lapin and Varvara Andreyevna Lapin were old people who hid Jewish children in their rooms. When the danger became too obvious, Mrs. Lapin sent the children to a safe place in the country. Arrested, Varvara Andreyevna Lapin refused to reveal their location and was shot.

The steppe is too level to serve as a reliable defense for partisans, but its bowels concealed them. Abandoned stone quarries, the famous Odessa catacombs, were transformed into partisan networks interconnected by underground tunnels.

The Rumanians and Germans fearfully sensed the danger threatening them from beneath the ground. From under the earth people blew up buildings, attacked prisons, and took vengeance.

The two Kantorovich sisters, Yelena and Olga, formed a resistance group together with their brother, his friend Ukuli (a Greek who worked at the post office) and several other persons. "Accused of being Jews," they were arrested twice and escaped both times. The Kantorovich sisters had connections with partisan detachments in near and distant catacombs. In the basement of their city apartment, Yelena and Olga concealed a radio receiver and a typewriter. Summaries of broadcasts of the Soviet Information Bureau circulated about the city in a fashion that the invaders were unable to uncover.

These bulletins found their way into the streetcars, the bakeries, the movie theaters, and were even smuggled into the prison in baked bread and the folds of clothing. In this dangerous work Jewish girls and boys worked shoulder to shoulder with their Russian and Ukrainian comrades. . . .

Lev Rozhetsky, a schoolboy who passed through every circle of the Fascist hell, "imagined a monument" above the infamous Bogdanovka pit, just one pit in one of the many death camps. . . . It was to this monument that he dedicated the following verse:

> Stop, noble traveller,
> And approach this cold and twilit grave.
> In a vale of sadness
> Look around you in rage,
> And let no tear cloud your eye,
> But bend your knee in silence
> To the ashes that once were men.

The Germans and Rumanians spared no effort to transform Soviet Odessa into the city of Antonescu, the capital of the notorious Transnistria. But the city refused to submit; it lived on, struggled, and shared in the victory of the entire country.

Written by **Vera Inber** on the basis of materials
and testimony of residents of Odessa.

Chernovitsy During the Rumanian-German Occupation

On July 4, 1941 the first German-Rumanian military units entered North Bukovina from various directions; on July 6 they were already in Chernovitsy. One of the first steps of Hitler's General Staff was to declare the Jewish population of Bukovina to be outside the protection of the law, and a wave of unheard-of pogroms swept over the villages and small towns. The town of Gzudak, for example, contained approximately 470 Jewish families; with the exception of three persons who succeeded in escaping, they were all killed. In many villages not a single person was left alive. Approximately 6,000 people were murdered in Chernovitsy.

The Rumanian peasant, Nikola Korda, who worked at the Chernovitsy rubber factory "Cadrom" during the Rumanian occupation, testified that not a single Jew was left alive in his native village of Voloka.

In some of the villages individual Jews managed to survive thanks to their neighbors who hid them in cellars and haystacks.

When a few representatives from the civil authorities finally arrived in Bukovina, those Jews who had not yet been killed were taken away — some to the small town of Storozhinets and some to Bayukany. From there they were transported to nearby camps, where they remained for several days (11 days in Storozhinets) and were subjected to inhuman torments. Then the camps were disbanded, and the Jews were herded off to the ghetto.

In Chernovitsy, which contained approximately 60,000 Jews,* men and women were seized on the streets, dragged from their homes, and led off to the police station. From there they were taken in groups of from 50 to 300 people under armed guard to various work sites. Rumanian women, who had gradually flooded the town and had occupied the Jewish apartments, came to the police station, where they were each allocated twenty to thirty Jewish men and women each to clean their apartments of the "filth left after the Bolsheviks." Very many Jews were handed over to the

*42,932 Jews lived in Chernovitsy before the war. See the *Black Book of Localities Whose Jewish Population Was Exterminated by the Nazis*, Yad Vashem, Jerusalem, 1965, p. 307. During the war a ghetto was created in Chernovitsy. Jews were moved to the town from nearby small towns and villages, and this increased the Jewish population.

German commandant who used them to build a railroad bridge across the Prut River. Many perished in the waters of this turbulent river, but many more died from inhuman treatment, exhaustion, and emaciation. There were no stores in town — only some bread shops which refused to sell to Jews.

One of the Rumanian National Bank's first directives was that Soviet money be exchanged at a specified rate. When Jews came to exchange their money, however, their money was simply confiscated.

Jews going to work in the morning were detained by police patrols in spite of identification cards issued to them at work. They were cruelly beaten, hauled off to the police station, and only then taken to work — under guard.

A few weeks later all Jews were required to wear a patch on the left side of the chest with the Star of David on it. In point of fact, this star actually placed Jews outside the protection of the law; attacks on Jews increased markedly, since the criminals knew they would not be punished. Jews found not to be wearing the star or to be wearing it in a different place were taken off to concentration camps. . . . General Galatescu, who was then governor of Bukovina, even issued a special order which was widely distributed and published in the local press. The general demanded that the star be sewn firmly at all six points to the appropriate area, since it had been observed that certain Jews were walking in a bent-over position so as to make the star less noticeable and that they even removed it from time to time.

Poverty among the Jewish population kept increasing, and the majority was literally starving. Their only food came in the form of handouts from their more compassionate neighbors. . . . The Jews were required to work without remuneration. Some of the doctors were permitted to practice medicine, but the word "Jew" had to be clearly indicated on their signs. Jewish doctors were strictly forbidden to treat non-Jews. Services were forbidden in the synagogues, and the municipal synagogue was burned down as soon as the German-Rumanian troops arrived in town.

Posters warning against "acts of Bolshevist sabotage" were pasted up all over town, and it was threatened that 20 Jewish hostages and 5 non-Jews would be shot if there were any sabotage. The prisons were filled to bursting. . . . The number of persons taken hostage was quite large, and most of them were murdered.

Among them were the chief rabbi of Chernovitsy, Mark, and the chief cantor, Gurman. After a short period of time, the authorities established the so-called "Jewish Committee," headed by Doctor Neiburg. The committee, consisting mainly of former Zionist leaders, was ordered to play the role of spokesman for the invaders in their relations with the Jews. The primary achievement of the committee was the preservation of five Jewish institutions — the Jewish hospital, the maternity home, the home for the aged, a home for the feeble-minded, and an orphanage. Even so, the conditions under which these institutions were allowed to function were extremely difficult.

On the basis of a decree, all Jewish real estate was confiscated. Jewish home owners were required to pay rent to live in their own houses. Any Rumanian could seize any Jewish apartment that happened to catch his eye and confiscate the furniture as well.

This situation continued until October 10, 1941, when the Jewish Committee was instructed to inform all Jews that they were to move to the ghetto, which was located in the area where only the poorest Jews had previously lived. In the early morning of October 11 crowds of people set out for the ghetto. Everyone carried in his arms or on his back bundles of clothing and bedding. Some moved their things in wheelbarrows, on dollies, or in baby carriages. To frighten the population, the military authorities had a few tanks rumble up and down the streets.

No orders were published on the creation of the ghetto, but a few days later the Bucharest newspaper *Curentul* produced a brief article stating that the "necessary measures" had been carried out "in the most humane fashion."

Some of the Jews attempted to remain in their apartments, justifying their refusal to move by the absence of an official order. On 6:00 P.M. of October 11, however, when the ghetto had already been surrounded by a tall board fence, the gendarmes removed these Jews from their apartments and took them under guard to the ghetto. As a punishment, they were not permitted to take anything with them.

The conditions in the ghetto were unbearable: small rooms held 5-8 families. The entrances to the ghetto were strictly guarded, and none of the Jews were permitted to leave.

Two days later one of the members of the Jewish Committee appeared and announced the authorities' decision to move all the Jews of Bukovina, including South Bukovina, to so-called Transnistria, that is, the area between the Dniester and Bug rivers which had been occupied by the Rumanians. The move was to be accomplished mainly by railroad, but since many regions were deprived of rail service and no other means of transportation were available, part of the journey would have to be made on foot. It was recommended that persons being moved take no more hand luggage than they could personally carry. So-called group leaders were appointed to organize the "move" and oversee preparations for the departure.

The next morning the Jews were required under pain of death to turn in all valuables: gold, jewels, foreign currency. On that same day, transports of Jews from other areas passed through Chernovitsy. The long columns of physically and emotionally exhausted people, about whom there hung an aura of death, moved slowly down the streets of the town to the freight station. Reporters from the Rumanian and German newspapers photographed this "event" and later lauded in their papers the "wise solution of the Jewish problem" in Bukovina.

The first groups of transported Jews arrived on October 14, 1941, and the next came on the following day. In the evening of October 15 the mayor of Chernovitsy, Doctor Traian Popovici, came to the building housing the Jewish Committee and announced that permission had been received from Bucharest to leave several thousand Jews in Chernovitsy. In accordance with the mayor's instructions, long lists of the Jewish population were made up according to profession and age. As a result, approximately 17,000 Jews remained in the city. These included representatives of various professions. Moreover, persons older than sixty years of age, women more than six months pregnant, mothers nursing children, persons receiving state pensions, and former reserve officers were also allowed to remain behind.

In point of fact, permission to remain in Chernovitsy was usually sold for fantastic sums. Persons who should have remained according to the instructions (because of their profession or for other reasons) but who did not possess sufficient financial means were not permitted to remain.

In the Jewish hospital, for example, the nurses were women from Bessarabia who had worked there for a long time — from ten to fifteen years. By the time the ghetto was created, the hospital was so overcrowded that there were patients in the corridors and even in the garden.

At that time several women from Chernovitsy and even several

95

"socialites" dedicated themselves to this work so as to be able personally to care for sick relatives.

When the question arose as to permission to stay, almost all the women from Chernovitsy received the appropriate documents, but the women from Bessarabia were turned down under the pretext that all Bessarabian women were communists and thus undeserving of such mercy.

What was the fate of the remaining inhabitants of Chernovitsy? It is important to take into account that the Rumanian authorities were faced with the task of restoring trade and industry in the city. To lure Rumanians to the city, a decree was issued freeing from military service all Rumanian managers of commercial enterprises. This lure proved effective, and a very large number of stores soon opened their doors in Chernovitsy. These were primarily stores which had belonged to Jews, who were now deprived of the right to own such businesses. The same was true of industry: all factories which had formerly belonged to Jews were now declared to be state property and were immediately sold for ridiculously low prices or leased to Rumanians. The new Rumanian owners, however, were not able to cope with their new tasks without the assistance of skilled workers who could be found only among the Jewish community. Each Rumanian businessman was given the opportunity to keep his "own" Jews on the job.

People who received permission to remain in Chernovitsy could keep their families with them, that is, underage children, wives, and — in certain instances — parents. All other Jews were gradually sent away. Their departure dragged on until the middle of November, when a transport problem halted it altogether. Thus, approximately 5,000 Jews remained in Chernovitsy without permission. Some of these were persons in hiding or evading the move, and others were invalids who could not be moved.

People who had permission to leave the ghetto were allowed to return to their totally looted homes. A commission was immediately set up to see that permits were properly issued. This commission met in city hall's largest chamber. It was chaired by the governor, who was assisted by representatives of the military and civilian authorities, and also by the *Siguranţă* (the secret police). The commission cancelled a number of permits which were declared to be improper. Their owners were immediately deported to Transnistria. The same fate befell those whose names were in the "black lists" of the *Siguranţă*.

This revision had not yet been completed when a new registration was announced for all Jews remaining in Chernovitsy without official permission. Later such persons were issued permits of a different type, signed not by the governor, but by the mayor, Traian Popovici (which is why they were called "Popovici permits"). This second census established that there were approximately 21,000 Jews residing in Chernovitsy, of whom roughly 16,000 had so-called "Galatescu permits" and about 5,000 had "Popovici permits." The liquidation of the ghetto was in no way an act of mercy, but simply the result of an order of the Sanitary Commission aimed at preventing epidemics.

For two and one half years there was a constant succession of revisions, each of which involved new persecutions. Each Jew was required to have a large number of identification cards and permits. In Bucharest a special department of Jewish affairs was established whose chief administrator had a portfolio in the government. One must not forget that these documents were sold for enormous sums; all these endless petitions had to be stamped — a policy designed to extort more and more money. In addition to all of this, "surtaxes" were levied on each document.

Aside from physicians, no one had permission to be self-employed. Many hundreds of Jews were forced to work without wages in various military and civil institutions. Frequently they even had to pay in addition to make their superiors treat them in an even slightly human fashion.

The following rules were established for persons employed in trade and industry: it was forbidden to employ a Jew in trade or industry without special permission from the labor exchange. In order to receive such permission, an enormous amount of formalities had to be observed. It had to be proven that the Jew in question was "irreplaceable" and that the employer could not find a Rumanian for his job. After this, the permit required the approval of the Siguranţă. Each Jew had to have a Rumanian double whom the Jew was required to train in as short a period as possible and thus prepare his own replacement. All Jews of draftable age (19-55 years) were required to pay a military tax of from 2,000 to 12,000 lei. Men not working at the factories were placed in workers' battalions and sent to work in the center of the country. They were required to provide themselves with food and clothing at their own expense.

Such was the situation of Jews up until June of 1942. By that time the governor-general Marinescu succeeded in removing the mayor, Popovici. An order was immediately issued that all persons possessing permits signed by Popovici be sent to Transnistria. At the same time all persons whose work permits had been confiscated were deported, as were also invalids who had not ended up in the work battalions. Altogether, approximately 6,000 Jews were deported in June, 1942.

That same year a small group of Jewish refugees from Poland (about 60-80 people) arrived in Chernovitsy. Although Polish citizens were originally under the protection of Chili and then of Switzerland, Marinescu handed these Polish Jews over to the Germans, who immediately sent them back to Poland. Even the police official who accompanied these unfortunate people to the Polish border said he had never in his life seen people treated so cruelly. He said that if he were ever to be given another such assignment, he would prefer to commit suicide.

Thus, by August of 1942, there remained about 16,000 Jews in Chernovitsy . At the same time the limitations on Jews continued to increase. Jews were forbidden to be on the street at specific hours — from 1:00 P.M. until 10:00 A.M. of the following day. Only workers were issued special passes which permitted them to go to work and return. Jews did not have permission to leave the city limits. In April, 1942, a Jewish religious committee was organized whose obligation it was to carry out the orders of the authorities.

Among the functions of the committee was the mobilization of Jews into workers' battalions. Numerous financial contributions were levied on the Jews: such contributions were collected through the committee. In spring of 1943 a new governor-general was appointed in Chernovitsy — Dragalin. This Dragalin was in the list of the ten most prominent war criminals published by the Soviet government. He was appointed governor of Chernovitsy when it had already become apparent that Germany would lose the war and that the day of reckoning would come for those who had caused the war. For this reason, Dragalin refrained from worsening the regimen established for the Jews. During an inspection of the concentration camps he even released those Jews who had been sent there for refusing to wear the yellow star. In January, 1944, he finally ordered that the yellow patches be removed.

When in March of 1944 the front came quite close to Bukovina, the Jews began to fear that the Germans would destroy the town and its inhabitants, as they had all the other Ukrainian towns.

Dragalin promised to evacuate the Jews, but in fact issued very few passes, distributing them primarily among members of the committee. When, however, the Red Army forced the Dniester, several hundred Jewish families managed to escape the town amid the general panic. That same day control of the town passed into German hands. On March 26 advance units of the Red Army entered the outskirts of Chernovitsy. After a three-day battle which took place outside the city, the Germans retreated without having had time to harm the population. . . . Destruction in town was not very great. The Germans had burned down two factories, the telephone exchange, the police station, and two residential dwellings in the center of town. The day before the retreat they also burned down the residence of the archbishop — a provocative act intended to stir up hatred for the Jews. The watchman, however, managed to contain the fire and discover the criminals.

An illegal communist organization of approximately 80 Jews, Poles, and Ukrainians existed in Chernovitsy during the German-Rumanian occupation.

Information supplied by **E. Grosberg**
Prepared for publication by **L. Goldberg.**

The Letter of Rakhil Fradis-Milner*

(Chernovitsy)

We lived in Chernovitsy. The enemy arrived on July 6, and we were not able to evacuate, since my husband worked in a military garage, and my baby was sick.

Jews were concentrated in the ghetto and taken from there to Transnistria. [After 50,000 people** had been deported, the deportations were temporarily halted. On June 7, 1942, they started up again.]*** We were among the first members of this last group.

The gendarmes came at night. We knew that death awaited us, but our three-year-old child slept peacefully. I woke him, gave him a toy bear, and told him we were going to visit his second cousin.

We were taken to a stone quarry in the Tulchin region. There we spent ten days without food and had to resort to cooking soup from grass. The insane from the Jewish hospital were sent with us, and they were strangling each other. Then we were transferred to Chetvertinovka, since a new group of Jews from Chernovitsy had arrived at the quarry.

We were lodged in stables and pigsties in the villages of the Tulchin county. We were beaten and tormented. The Germans arrived in the middle of August; they summoned us and asked if we wanted to work. They said they would give us jobs and feed us well.

Trucks were sent on August 13, and two automobiles with German officers also arrived. The old, the sick, and mothers nursing babies or with small children were herded off on foot.

We crossed the Bug River, and it was there that people were separated forever. Many husbands were separated from their wives, and children were taken from their mothers. . . . We were lucky in that we all remained together — my husband, Shura, and I. We arrived in Nemirov. There was a camp there for local Jews — about 200 or 300. They were all young and healthy (the others had already been killed). We were taken to their yard, where we spent the night. At dawn Nemirov's Jews appeared, dressed in rags and with wounds on their bare feet. When they saw our children, they

*Rakhil Fradis-Milner has lived with her family in Israel since 1960. Alexander (Shura) Fradis graduated from the Technion in Haifa and is employed as an engineer.

**See footnote to p. 92.

***This paragraph was restored by R. Fradis-Milner in Israel.

began to shout and cry. Mothers remembered their own children who had been tortured to death. It was difficult for us to believe their stories. One man told us that his wife and three children had been killed. Another said that his parents, brothers, and sisters had been murdered. A third man said that his pregnant wife had been viciously killed.

By morning some Ukrainians began to gather next to the camp. My child stood out with his blond hair and blue eyes. Everyone liked him, and one Ukrainian woman offered to adopt him: "They'll kill you anyway, and it would be a shame for the child to die. Give him to me." But I could not give up Shura.

At 3:00 P.M. we were transferred to our camp. When we approached it, I was seized by an even greater horror. It was our old synagogue.

Everywhere were feathers from pillows that had been ripped open. There were also blouses, children shoes, and old dishes scattered around, but, more than anything else, there were feathers. It turned out that the Germans had brought Nemirov's Jews here before taking them to be executed. They took the good things, and left the old. The pillows had been ripped apart, since they were searching for gold. We were surrounded by barbed wire and locked up. The chief of police Henig came with his assistant, "Peewee."

In the evening they brought in the old people, the sick, and the children, whom the Rumanians had refused to leave on their territory. It was a terrible sight. . . .

On August 20 a headcount was made. Those capable of working (about 200) were separated from the old and the sick (100) and the children (60). Henig, the chief of police, smiled and said: "One more immodest question: which of the women are pregnant?" Mrs. Blau, who was eight months pregnant and was the mother of a five-year-old child, gave her name. He wrote it down and then ordered everyone to come together and leave for work without the children. Only mothers nursing children were permitted to remain behind. I decided I would not abandon Shura even if they threatened to shoot me, and I stood with him. A young woman came up to me with tears in her eyes and said: "I have a ten-month baby, and I'm afraid to stay behind, because they might shoot me." I suggested that she leave the baby with me.

I remained in the camp. The others left to work in the road gang and returned when it was already becoming dark. Any contact with the local population was forbidden. Once a day a thin unsalted pea soup and 100 grams (about ¼ pound) of bread was distributed. The children were dying from hunger. Fortunately some of the Ukrainian women threw a little fruit and bread to the children. As a pharmacist, I was the only one who knew anything about medicine, so I was appointed camp doctor and thus sometimes had the opportunity to go to the drugstore and secretly bring back a little food to the children. This was a drop in the ocean. People worked like slaves and could not even wash themselves. They were beaten with sticks for the most petty reasons. The guards got drunk at night and would beat everyone. The German authorities confiscated all items that were of any use. On September 6 an adjutant of the chief of police was checking us. He called for me to help him read the names. Shura started to cry, and I gestured to him with my hand that he should not stand next to me. The German noticed this and said: "Let the child come to his mother."

At 2:00 P.M. on September 13 a car drove up. It was Henig, "Peewee," and his assistant, whom everyone called Willy. They announced that on September 14 all children and those incapable of working would be sent to a different camp so that they "would not interfere with the work." They made up a list of the sick, the old, and the children. The rest were examined like horses. Anyone who did not walk in a spritely enough fashion or did not please them for any reason ended up on the black list. We understood everything. My husband grabbed Shura, put his hand over his mouth, and climbed over the wire. They would not let him in the house but permitted him to stay in the garden.

On the night of September 13 there was no light in the large two-story synagogue. A few people had candle ends and lit them. Each mother held her children in her arms and said goodbye to them. Everyone realized that this was death, but no one wanted to believe it. An old rabbi from Poland began to read the prayer "About Children," and the old men and women assisted him. The cries and screams were heartrending; the older children attempted to console their parents. It was such a horrible scene that even our crude guards were silent.

On September 14 the people were awakened before dawn and herded off to work so that they would not interfere. . . . I also went. I did not know what had happened to my husband and child — whether they were alive or had fallen into the clutches of the murderers.

102

A few of the women took their children to work with them, and a few old women put on their best clothes and also left for work in an attempt to avoid death.

The SS soldiers carefully examined our ranks and removed all the children. Six mothers went to their deaths with their children, since they wanted to lighten their last minutes. Sura Katz from Chernovitsy (her husband was at the front) went to her death with her six boys. Mrs. Weiner went with her sick little girl. Mrs. Leger, a young woman from Lipkany, begged the executioners to allow her to die with her beautiful twelve-year-old daughter Tamara.

On the way to work we met trucks bringing old folks and children from the camps in Chukov and Voronovitsy. From a distance we saw the trucks stop, and we could see the shooting. Later the executioners told how they forced the doomed people to strip naked and how they threw the babies alive into the graves. Mothers were forced to watch their children being murdered.

A friend of ours from Yedintsy, the lawyer David Lerner, was in the Chukov camp together with his wife, six-year-old daughter, and his wife's parents — the Axelrods. When the children were being killed in September, the Lerners managed to hide their daughter in a sack. The girl was quiet and intelligent, and she was saved. For three weeks the father took his daughter with him to work, and the child stayed in the sack. Three weeks later the animal "Peewee" came to confiscate items that might be of any value. He walked up to the sack and kicked it with his foot. The girl cried out and was discovered. The executioner was seized by a wild rage, and he beat both the father and child and took all their possessions, leaving the family virtually without any clothing. He did not, however, kill the girl, and she lived through the winter fearing for her life every day. On February 5, during the second "aktion," the girl was taken away along with the grandmother. A wild fear took possession of the child; she screamed the entire time in the sleigh, and her small heart was not able to endure the strain. The grandmother carried a dead child to the fateful pit. When the mother found out about this, she went mad and was shot. The father was killed soon thereafter, and the entire family thus perished.

When we returned to camp in the evening, everything was as quiet and empty as at a cemetery. Soon the chief of police arrived and summoned me. He asked where I had been and where my child was. I answered that I had been at work and that he knew better than I where my child was. He left without responding.

That night my husband returned. He had left our boy with Anna Rud, a Ukrainian woman who promised to find him a refuge. We managed to throw her all our things across the fence, and the child was taken care of in a material sense — albeit only for the time being. The next day "Peewee" came to search the cellar and the attic for my boy. "Your blond boy was not on the truck," he said to me. "I remember him well." He had noticed him during the head count. . . .

Anna Rud gave my son to Polya Medvetsky, to whom I will be forever indebted. She guarded him for six months as if he were the apple of her eye. . . . He called her "Mama" and loved her very much.

On September 21 we were transferred to the village of Bugakov. There was a different German commandant there, and he was not subordinate to the authorities in Nemirov — Henig, "Peewee," and "Willy." I was appointed as a medical aide to all three Jewish camps: Bugakov, Zarudentsy, and Berezovka. It is difficult to describe the things that people experienced in those camps. The Germans told me to "cure them with the whip." A few of the old people who had escaped the execution could not take the strain and had collapsed. They were driven to work with clubs. The elderly Axelrod from Bukovina was driven to work with sticks on Saturday, and he died on Sunday. The elderly Mrs. Brunwasser had clots in the veins of both legs. She was dragged by the hair and thrown down the stairs. Two days later she died. Soon all the others died too. With the onset of winter the young people fell ill. We had to sleep on the cold ground and received a starvation diet. Epidemics began. There was no warm clothing, and it was bitterly cold. They beat us. The overseer Maindl harassed us more than all the others did. He particularly tormented my husband, whom he called the "damned engineer."

I did not see my child the entire time, and I was going mad from the thought that the Germans might have found him. In the beginning of April, I succeeded in visiting him. When I walked up to the gate, my heart was beating as if it was ready to burst. I looked around to make sure no one had noticed me. Polya Medvetsky opened the door and shouted: "Shura, come see who's here!" But Shura did not recognize me; he was quiet and sad and hid behind Polya. When I picked him up and took off my scarves, he began to remember everything. Polya told me that he never left the room nor even saw the yard. He had been taught that he was a nephew from Kiev and that his name was Alexander Bakalenko. When strange people came to the house, he hid. When I was leaving, Shura gave me an apple and said: "For Papa." He asked me if it was true that all the children had been killed and named all his friends. I thanked Polya from the bottom of my heart and left.

On February 2 a policeman called me aside and said: "Doctor, make sure that anyone who can stand goes to work tomorrow." I realized that the matter was serious and warned the patients, but they would not believe me. My husband was ill, and he stayed behind, as did almost all the sick. At 12:00 a number of sleighs drove up to the door. There were many policemen headed by Maindl. "Willy" had also arrived from Nemirov. I heard Maindl say: "Take the sick and the barefooted. . . ."

I hid in the rear so that they could not force me to point out the sick. It was a terrible scene: half naked people were dragged out by the hair into the snow. They took everyone who was older than 40-45 years old and also anyone who had no clothes or shoes. In the yard people were divided into two groups: those who could work and those who were to die. Mrs. Grinberg, a friend of mine from Bucharest, was a beautiful well dressed woman, but her shoes were ragged. She was noticed and dragged to the group of those who were to be killed. Then they grabbed me, because I too was wearing old flannel slippers. She kept saying: "I'm healthy." They answered: "You don't have shoes."

I thought of Shura, and that lent me strength. My husband was standing in the group of those capable of working. At the last minute, as we were being led to the sleighs, I managed to run across to the other group and hide. My friend tried to do the same, but she was noticed and severely beaten. An eighteen-year-old girl begged to be allowed to die with her mother, and permission was granted. She was already sitting in the sleigh when she became frightened and wanted to return, but they would not let her. One woman took poison and tried to give some to her daughter, but the daughter refused. A teenager attempted to escape and was shot. In an hour all those marked down for death were taken away, and the rest remained in camp. When the healthy returned from work at 10:00 P.M., they did not find their mothers, sisters, fathers. . . .

On February 4, 1943 we were transferred to Zarudentsy. Two thirds of the camp there had been shot, and space had been made available.

I arrived there on February 1 to check the sick, and I witnessed a terrible scene. The people were barefoot and draped in rags, and their bodies were covered with all manner of ulcers which one would not normally encounter. They were sitting on some rags on the floor and killing lice in a very serious, concentrated manner. So preoccupied were they with this activity that they did not even notice my arrival. Suddenly there was movement and shouting; people were jumping up; their eyes were gleaming; some were crying. What had happened? Bread had been delivered — an entire loaf for each person. What a joy! This was something new and unheard-of. The unfortunate people began to suspect that salvation was near. It turned out that the Germans in their precision had decided to give out an advance of an entire loaf before the "aktion" which was to take place on the fifth, since no one knew how many people would be left and it was impossible to calculate how much bread would be necessary. We learned of this calculation only after we found ourselves in the Zarudentsy death camp.

Along the way, all those who could not walk well were separated from the group and put on sleighs. Murder victims were collected in Chukov from Nemirov, Zarudentsy, Berezovka, and Bugakov. People were kept there naked for two days without food and water and then killed.

At work Master Dehr told us that he had been present at the execution (which he called "die Aktion"). He said it was not nearly as terrible as we imagined. Later we learned that Master Dehr and Maindl were SS men even though they were classified as employees of the firm in which we were working.

We were driven to work in the dark with whips, even before the severe winter dawn began to break. The unfortunate people hurriedly tied sacks stuffed with straw over their torn shoes so as to keep their feet from being frostbitten. People put blankets on their heads and tied ropes around their waists before getting into line. We were carefully counted and recounted and then herded off to work. It was difficult to lift tormented and wounded feet wrapped with rags and straw. The snow was deep and it kept falling. When we reached the work site, we breathed a sigh of relief, took up shovels, and began to clear away the snow. Suddenly there was a commotion: "black" Maindl was coming. All eyes reflected a wild fear, shovels began to swing furiously, and each person tried to become smaller and grow less noticeable. "Stop work," he shouted. "You have to take your shovels and clean the snow eight kilometers from here."

106

In the endless white steppe the snow was deep, and the storm swirled the flakes so strongly that it was impossible to see anything. A tall German dressed in black and with a long whip in his hands was driving on 200 wretched human shadows. My feet became heavier, and my heart seemed ready to jump from my chest. It did not seem possible that we would complete this wild march, but the survival instinct is strong, and we reached the spot. The sleigh stopped, and a vicious, arrogant and pleased gaze rested on the exhausted people.

Even though I was a "medical aide," I still had to go to work with other people. All this was called "clearing snow."

On February 8 a strange woman came to me and said: "I am Polya Medvetsky's sister. Take Shura. Polya has been denounced, and she hid him with a distant relative."

What could I do? While I was still working as a doctor, I sometimes treated the peasants. This was very dangerous, since Maindl had said: "If I learn that you were in a Ukrainian home, I'll shoot you on the spot."

There was no doctor in those villages, and I could not refuse if asked to visit a sick person. The family of Kirill Baranchuk lived next to our camp. I often dropped by, since his father was ill. Baranchuk once told me that he would like to press people such as us to his chest and carry them across the Bug River. I thought of him and asked Polya Medvetsky's sister to go to him and say that I begged him on both knees to go to Nemirov and take the boy for a few days. Later we would think of something.

Dear Uncle Kirill saved Shura, brought him from Nemirov wrapped in his fur coat. There his wife and children, Nastya and Nina, surrounded the boy with love. They came to the highway and said that Shura was alive and praying for us.

We decided to escape; we had to save Shura.

At 2:00 A.M. on February 26 my husband said: "Get up." We waited while a policeman came in to warm himself, and then we climbed over the wire. We went to Kirill Baranchuk, who took us in even though it could have cost him his life. We spent four days there, got our bearings, and on March 2 Kirill Baranchuk and his uncle Onisy Zmerzly took us to Perepelitsy, on the Bug River. The village was filled with German border guards, and no one wanted to let us in. We knew we had nothing to lose, and at 3:00 A.M. we crossed the Bug. My husband walked ahead carrying our child in his arms. It was a dark night. The ice had begun to thaw, and my leg went through the ice up to the knee. I sprained my ankle, but I said nothing. Shura noticed this, but he kept silent. Finally, we reached the other shore.

Some peasants took us into their hut, and we warmed ourselves and rested. They gave us some peasant clothing, and we went on foot to Mogilev-Podolsky, passing ourselves off as refugees from Kiev. On March 10 we arrived in Mogilev and ended up in the ghetto. We continued to be harassed and tormented, but we saw the day when the Red Army arrived. We could live freely. . . .

I know that my terrible wounds will never heal: my dear parents, my two young brothers, one of them was a gifted musician, all died. My other brother's wife and two children and also my mother-in-law and sister-in-law died. My heart is like a rock; I think that if it were to be cut the blood would not flow.

Prepared for publication by **Ilya Ehrenburg** and **R. Kovnator**.

The Murder of Jews in Lvov

The Germans entered Lvov on July 1, 1941. They marched, sang, and spread horror; no one left his house.

There was a German patrol on each corner. A Hitlerite demonstrated to a crowd of city thugs how the hangings would proceed. He shouted over and over: "Juden kaput!"

A dragnet was cast out for Jews. The local Fascists, accompanied by SS men, dragged Jews from their apartments and took them away to the prisons and barracks of Lvov.

At the entrance to the assembly point clothes were ripped off, and valuables and money were confiscated. The Fascists tormented and beat people until blood flowed and forced them to lick the floor with their tongues and clean windows with a chicken feather.

The Jews were lined up in a row and forced to beat each other. When the SS men decided that the blows were too weak, they dragged the intended victim from the row and demonstrated how to hit people in the face. The rest of the prisoners were forced to strike each other on the cheeks to the accompaniment of laughter on the part of the executioners. Then these people were shot.

During the first action, which was called "Bloody Tuesday," 5,000 Jews were murdered.

The remaining unfortunate people had not even had time to regain their wits when on Thursday, July 5, the Germans began to pick up men and women, supposedly for work.

The victims were assembled on the square next to Pelchinskaya Street and after two weeks of torture were taken from there to be shot. A few of the men succeeded in escaping. SS men took everything that caught their eye from the apartments and loaded the booty on trucks. The first pogroms and robberies were committed by regular troops. They were followed by the Gestapo and the German administration apparatus.

Lieutenant General Fritz Katzmann, the chief executioner of Jews in the Western Ukraine, issued an order on July 15, 1941, which contained the following:

1. All Jews twelve years of age and older were obliged to wear an armband embroidered with a six-pointed star. Appearance on the street without the armband was punishable by death.

2. Under pain of death Jews were not to change their domicile without permission from the German office of Jewish affairs.

Fritz Katzmann was the chief of the office of Jewish affairs in the entire Western Ukraine, and he appointed his own deputies: Lex in Tarnopol and Krüger in Stanislav. In each small town he had his own subordinates who organized concentration camps and systematically destroyed the Jews.

The Gestapo office headed by Major Engels was located on Pelchinskaya Street in Lvov.

The executioners attempted to divide the Jewish masses into groups so as to kill even the thought of any possible armed resistance. They created the appearance of safety for those whom they wanted to use and whose attention they wanted to distract from the true state of affairs.

Among the Jews there were many repairmen, mechanics, and skilled artisans who were needed by German industry. The Germans used their labor in military installations and factories. Naturally, there were many healthy and husky people, and they were forced to do the dirty work in the concentration camps.

Old men, women, children, the ill, and those who were incapable of work were killed first of all. They were destroyed during the pogroms, cast into prisons, shipped off to "forests of death."

A Jewish laborer was very profitable: in most instances he not only received no wage for his labor, but he even paid to get his *Arbeitskarte* (work card) so as to at least slightly delay his death or to avoid the camp, where death was also lurking.

If during the dragnet a Jew was unable to show the SS soldiers an employment certificate, he was killed.

Beginning in December of 1941, each working Jew was required to wear an armband with the letter "A" (*Arbeitsjude*) and his employment certificate number. Anyone who did not have an armband issued by the *Arbeitsamt* was killed during the extermination dragnets.

The unemployed forged employment certificates and embroidered armbands similar to those issued by the *Arbeitsamt*. When that happened, the former employment certificates were annulled and replaced with *Meldekarten*. In this fashion the German managed to control all the *Arbeitsjuden* and the *Nichtarbeitsjuden*.

A Jewish laborer received no wage for his labor. The 100 gram (3½ ounces) of bread which he was supposed to receive was actually sold by his superior for a high price.

* * *

Beginning in November of 1942, Jews working in German firms were required to wear, aside from the armband, a white patch embroidered either with the letter "W" (Wehrmacht) or "R" (Rüstung). This patch signified that the Jew in question worked directly for the arms industry.

The Germans surrounded the territory of the ghetto with a high fence.

On November 12 a large number of armed Gestapo soldiers appeared at the gates. They detained everyone who left for work. Anyone who did not have a patch either with the letter "R" or "W" was sent to be executed. As a result of this two-day check at the gates in November, 12,000 people perished.

In December the ghetto was closed. Two guard booths were placed at the gates. They were manned by Gestapo soldiers. It was possible to leave the ghetto only in the mornings in groups. As early as the end of December, 1941, the Germans began to transfer workers to barracks. Barracks were established for each factory. In this fashion those who worked were separated from those who did not work. The former were housed on Zamarstynovska Street, Lokietek Street, Kushevich Street, and Kresova Street. The latter were housed in the Kleparov suburb.

All those who did not succeed in getting work realized that Kleparov would soon be liquidated.

True, the Germans used their network of agents to spread provocatory rumors to the effect that a ghetto was being organized for *Nichtarbeitsjuden* (the unemployed). This calmed down the tormented unfortunate people and inspired a glimmer of hope in their hearts. All hopes were dissipated, however, after the tragic events that took place in Kleparov.

On the night of January 4 [1942] shooting began on the streets of the ghetto. This was the signal to begin a new "Aktion." Jews began to hide and to flee to their relatives in the barracks.

In the morning of January 5 the "January Massacre" began. Those who were employed were taken to work, and then a hunt began for the others.

During the November "liquidation campaign," Jews were taken to Belzec* and killed there. Many Jews, however, ripped up the boards in the train cars and escaped; the Germans never caught them. To prevent a repetition of this experience, the Germans

*Belżec — pron. Bél'zhets.

decided to conduct the "January Campaign" in a somewhat different fashion. They killed, burned, and deported Jews to Piaskowa Gora. Houses in which no Jews were found after a careful search were burned by the Germans. People hiding in secret passages, cellars, attics, and ovens perished in the flame.

The unrestrained representatives of the "superior race" did not miss a single woman during this campaign. They raped them or killed them, or threw them into the burning houses.

All of Kleparov was ravaged. Only the streets where the barracks were located remained.

After that about 20,000 Jews were left alive on a few small streets. Before dying they experienced the most varied of torments.

Those in charge of the ghetto stood next to the guard booths, checking to see if the "R" and "W" patches were authentic. This was not difficult to determine.

Many had themselves embroidered these letters to have the opportunity to leave the ghetto on a daily basis for the "Aryan side" together with those who were employed. By remaining in the ghetto, they subjected themselves to mortal danger, since the Germans searched the barracks daily and sent off all who were caught to prison. The letters issued by German concerns had been sewn by machine with a special stitch, and no one could perfectly duplicate it. Scharführer Siller was a specialist in catching people with falsified letters. For his success in catching Jews he was transferred to the Janowski camp.

The cells in the Jewish prison were low and dark and had no bunks or benches; they were also damp and smelled of decay. The windows were small and so heavily barred that no light could penetrate them.

The prison was located on Lontsky Street. It was surrounded on all sides by SS men and a mob of German soldiers who stripped anyone arriving of his clothes and shoes. The guards beat people whenever the mood was upon them.

People were forbidden to talk to each other in the cells. Prisoners were not fed. What for? The Germans were calculating and tight-fisted. The sick in prison were killed and hauled away at night to the cemetery.

Engels himself often visited the prison. Jews were led out in the yard to amuse this bandit. He tormented them and beat them till the blood flowed. He liked to play with his victim — promise him life and freedom and when he noticed a spark of hope on the face of the prisoner to laugh and kill him with a bullet from a revolver.

When the prison was too packed, the Germans would arrange "purges" or "shipments." Prisoners were loaded onto trucks and taken in groups to Piaskowa Gora, where they were shot.

On the other hand, the prison was always full. If a person came out onto the street without an armband, he was sent to prison. Another person might have too narrow an armband or he might not have bowed to a German, and he would also be sent to prison. People were hauled off to prison without any reason whatsoever. SS men would burst into an apartment and arrest a member of the family. "But why?" the victim would ask. "You don't know? Because you're a Jew. It doesn't make any difference — sooner or later you have to die."

Engels never made use of mass pogroms. Instead he arranged "purges" in the prisons. In this fashion he killed many thousands of the elderly, children, men, women.

In the fall of 1941 Govenor Frank issued an order about forced labor by Jews in concentration camps on the territory of the Western Ukraine. As early as the beginning of 1942 the Lvov, Tarnopol, and Stanislav regions were linked by a network of concentration camps.

The most terrible camp was the one on Janowska Street in Lvov. It was referred to by the name of the street. Several thousand Jews were taken there from all over the Western Ukraine. They were brought there to level a hilly area and prepare it for a new camp. Hungry and beaten, people worked there until they were exhausted. They slept under an open sky until the ground was leveled and barracks were constructed.

The work continued all fall and all winter. People died from cold and hunger and were replaced by new throngs of Jewish workers.

A roll call or so-called *Appell* was made every morning before work. All working groups were gathered together with their leaders — the *Oberjuden*. The *Oberjude* reported the number of persons in his group to the SS man on duty. After the report, morning exercises were conducted by the SS men. After an endless number of various sorts of jumping exercises to the commands of "Auf" and "Nieder," the sick and the weak were detected, led aside, and later taken to the other side of the barbed wire and shot with submachine guns. The dead were laid out in rows, and the living marched off to work. Along the way all those who limped were also

113

shot. Only the strong and the healthy were permitted to work.

After the camp territory had been prepared, it was paved with gravestones taken from the Jewish cemetery.

The Germans did not leave even dead Jews in peace. In many cities and small towns of the Western Ukraine grave markers were used to pave roads.

When the territory was leveled, the camp was surrounded by barbed wire and guarded by Fascist police. From the main entrance, one path led to the camp barracks and kitchen, and the other led toward the hills where the executions took place. One and two-story watchtowers were built all around the camp. The guards could thus watch the camp from a high point, and escape was made nearly impossible.

The appearance of the camp was a gloomy one: sentry booths, dismal barracks, people wandering in silence, and the unbearably sweet smell of corpses.

Approximately twenty camp barracks were situated around the vast empty yard which served as an assembly point for morning headcounts. All of the barracks had five-tiered bunks covered with a thin layer of dirty straw. Behind the barracks was a kitchen, where a watery swill was cooked twice daily, and two pieces of stale bread substitute were distributed.

Newcomers slept on the bare earth.

The cream of the SS bandits, distinguished pupils of the masters of Dachau and Mauthausen, worked in camp. The Janowski camp was a German Oxford, and its professors were the aristocrats of Hitler's Germany.

Having quickly graduated from their "university," Gebauer's erstwhile pupils went to various areas of the Western Ukraine to work "independently."

Inexperienced SS soldiers were also brought to Lvov, where they were taught the art of killing and torturing their victims, as well as various other brutal skills. When their superiors came to the conclusion that the young SS men were sufficiently prepared, they were sent to do their bloody work in various provincial camps.

On the other hand, whenever someone in the provinces became well known as a refined executioner and a master of his "trade," he was transferred to the Janowski concentration camp. There his less talented colleagues greeted him with respect. It was the custom for the executioners to compete with each other in perfecting the means of torture.

114

Under the direct supervision of Katzmann, Himmler's pupils practiced particular refinements of torture in addition to the normal program. Among these unusual measures were "races" and "boards," which were normally conducted on Sundays.

"Races" consisted of making victims run 300–400 meters nonstop while SS men on both sides attempted to trip the runner by sticking out their feet. If the runner tripped, he was taken "beyond the wire" and shot. There were many of these victims, since the camp prisoners were barely able to drag their swollen tortured feet.

The torture called "boards" consisted of the following: on Sundays exhausted from heavy daily work, the Jews were made to carry logs intended for barracks construction from one site to another. Each person was required to carry 150 kilograms (330 pounds) on his shoulders. Anyone who could not hold up under that weight was killed by an SS bullet.

The Germans' drunken orgies were terrible. They would burst into the nearest barracks, drag its occupants out into the snow, and torture them. On the days of the orgies the SS soldiers did not shoot anyone, but would pierce the prisoners' skulls with sharp poles or crush them with sledgehammers and strangle or crucify them, driving nails into their still living bodies.

Each SS man had his own particular passion. Gebauer strangled his victims in a barrel or between two boards. Another hanged the unfortunate people by the feet, and a third shot them in the back of the head. Twenty-three-year-old Schönbach invented new methods of murder by torture. One Sunday he tied his victim to a post and beat him with a rubber truncheon. When the man lost consciousness from the blows and dropped his head, Schönbach revived him, gave him food and water, and a minute later beat him again. All the prisoners were brought together in a circle around the victim to witness the torture. The unfortunate man's guilt consisted of having urinated behind the barracks. He had violated the rules of the camp and had been observed by a guard. He was tried on Sunday and tied to the pole, where he suffered all day. Blood gushed from his mouth and nose. By evening Schönbach grew weary. He ordered everyone to disperse and placed a guard next to the dying man. In the morning the people witnessed a terrible scene: a bloody pillar with shreds of a human body.

When management of the camp was transferred to Scharführer Willhaus, people were murdered on a mass scale.

From time to time the prisoners were checked. The ill and the emaciated were executed with submachine guns.

In camp the prisoners did not wear a white armband. Instead, a number was issued to them which was worn on the back, and a yellow patch was worn on the chest. Their bodies were covered with rags.

The Jews in the ghetto tried to save themselves in various ways. They hid with Ukrainian and Polish friends, fled under false names, joined the partisans.

The prisoner in camp lived behind a barbed-wire fence. He could not escape, and he was so depressed that it was difficult for him to even think of resistance.

In spite of all this, however, partisan groups were formed on camp territory thanks to the heroic efforts of the Jewish poets Sanya Friedman and A. Laun. They succeeded in obtaining weapons, but, unfortunately, the Germans learned of their organization and shot all the prisoners in their barracks. From that time on the Germans appeared more infrequently in camp, and they were always armed.

When the lawyer Mandel was being led to his death, at the last minute he shouted: "Long live the Soviet Union! Long live freedom!" This cry was widely discussed throughout the camp and had a great impact. It was as if people had awakened from a lethargic dream, and even those whom the Germans considered their obedient victims realized that passivity would help only the Germans.

A movement was begun among the camp prisoners to recruit young people to fight the Germans. One young butcher from Lvov attacked a Gestapo man and strangled him. In the Chvartakov camp a young Pole shot the head of the camp. Such incidents began to occur more and more frequently.

Jews intended for "liquidation" were brought to the gathering point of the Janowski camp. At the entrance a German pedantically wrote down in pencil his victims' names. Young men were left in camp, but all the other people were taken to the railroad station where they were put in local train cars. Everyone realized what this meant, and tragic scenes took place in camp. Some people cried, others went mad and laughed hysterically. Hungry children cried constantly. One of the chief executioners of the Janowski camp, the "musician Rokita," once came out onto the balcony of his apartment which overlooked the camp. He had been awakened from his afternoon nap, and he fired into the crowd with his submachine gun for a long time.

The August sun burned down mercilessly. People fainted with thirst and begged for water, but the henchmen guarding them remained cruel and implacable. The trains left at night. All clothing was taken from the people. Many ripped up the boards in the cars, jumped from the train and ran naked through the fields. The German guards in the last car shot at them in bursts of submachine-gun fire.

The railroad tracks from Lvov through Brzukhovitsy — Zhulkev to Rava Russkaya were littered with the bodies of Jews.

New trains with Jews from Brussels, Paris, and Amsterdam passed through Rava Russkaya. They were joined by transport from Tarnopol, Kolomya, Sambor, Brzeżany, and other towns in the Western Ukraine.

Fifteen kilometers from Rava Russkaya and Belzec, Jews who were supposedly being moved for "resettlement" were taken from the cars. Belzec was a terrible execution spot for Jews, and the Germans kept it top secret.

The railroad personnel who worked on the trains carrying the doomed victims, however, told their friends and relatives of how the Jews were being massacred in Belzec.

Jews were led into an enormous hall which held up to one thousand persons. The floors and walls of the hall were electrically wired and without insulation. As soon as the hall was filled with naked people, the Germans switched on a strong electrical current.

This was an enormous electric chair — something that no criminal imagination could ever have invented.

In a different area of the Belzec camp was a soap works. The Germans selected the plumpest individuals, killed them, and boiled them down for soap.

"Jewish soap" was printed on the labels. Izraelevich Rozenstrauch, a bank clerk from Lvov, actually held a bar in his hands, and he was one of the witnesses who provided us with this testimony.

The Gestapo thugs never denied the existence of this "production process." Whenever they wanted to frighten a Jew, they would say to him: "We'll make soap out of you."

In the beginning of February, 1943, management of the camp was transferred to SS Hauptsturmführer Josef Grzymek, who was an ethnic German from Poznan. Tall, heavy-set, and always carrying a submachine gun, he was terrifying.

Grzymek loved cleanliness and ordered that signs be placed on the ghetto fence: "Work! Neatness! Discipline! Everything in its place!"

Surrounded by his followers, he rode around the ghetto on a horse. During roll calls he broke windows and shot at people. When he was in charge of the ghetto, going to work became a true torment.

Sometimes he would force people to walk through the gates carrying their "W" and "R" patches in their hands so he could check their authenticity. On a different occasion people had to hold their work permits over their heads. Everyone was required to remove his hat in the presence of the master.

Grzymek ordered that all heads be shaved. A barber stood at the gates and shaved the middle of the skull of everyone who walked past.

An orchestra played military marches while people were leaving for work, and everyone had to march in neat columns to the accompaniment of this music. Anyone who did not manage to do so became the victim of Grzymek's rubber truncheon.

Every wing of the ghetto had a watchman and a cleaning woman. The streets were cleanly swept, and the houses were whitewashed. Grzymek himself saw to that. In these whitewashed houses, however, were crowded doomed, half-dead people who were swollen with hunger.

There was an outbreak of typhus at the ghetto, and almost the entire population fell ill with this disease. There was a hospital in the ghetto, but everyone knew that it was a place of death. Many died, and those who survived became cripples. The sick were not treated but were taken in groups from time to time to be shot on Piaskowa Gora.

Friends and relatives would conceal a sick person in a hiding place, where he suffered from cold and was frequently without food.

The employer crossed the sick person's name off the list of the working and gave it to the Gestapo. There was a special SS commission that searched apartments for the sick. Heinisch, an SS soldier as heavy as a bear, became notorious by making a profession of searching for the sick. He shot the unconscious on the spot and sent those recuperating to prison.

* * *

Honest Poles and Ukrainians were outraged by this unheard-of crime — the total massacre of innocent people, and it became necessary to somehow calm the local population. This was the task of the press: the *Lemberger Deutsche Zeitung*, *Gazeta Lwowska*, and *Lvivskiye visti*.

These rags printed daily articles on how "the genius of the German nation had demonstrated its implacability toward the lower race" (Jews) and how "historical justice was punishing the damned kikes with the German hand."

Such abuse pursued the goal of arousing hatred among the Poles and Ukrainians toward the Jewish population. Katzmann published a notice stating that the concealment of Jews was punishable by death.

The German newspapers conducted an "explanatory campaign." They wrote that the liquidation of the Jews was being conducted in the interests of the Aryan peoples. "The Jews have long planned to rule the world." To provide substance for this foolish thought, quotations were juggled from the Talmud and the Bible. The Germans wrote that they were "liquidating" the Jews in response to the attacks on the German population of Bromberg (Bydgoszcz), Poznan, and other cities. No one responded to this foolish provocation, however.

* * *

Under conditions of the cruelest terror and the most monstrous of violence, the Jewish population used all means at its disposal to save itself from doom. Many left Lvov and lived in Warsaw under false names. Others passed themselves off as Aryans and moved to Lvov's "Aryan section," where they lived and worked disguising themselves as Ukrainians and Poles. The Gestapo soon learned of this and resolved to put an end to these "false Aryans." With this goal in mind, they flooded Lvov with secret agents who eagerly carried out the mission entrusted to them. They were all over the streets, in the post office, at the railway stations. They peered greedily into the face of every person suspected of Jewish origin. They took their victims to "Kripo" (*Kriminalpolizei*), where officials quickly determined if the suspected individuals were Jewish or not. Women were tortured until they admitted to being Jewish. The Germans generously rewarded agents who caught "false Aryans," but it also happened that Jews rewarded them with bullets. A young Jew with false "Aryan" documents was approached on

Streletsky Square by a secret agent who demanded that he show his documents. Evidently, he had recognized him as a Jew. The young man immediately pulled a revolver instead of the documents from his pocket and killed the agent.

The story of Lina Haus, a student in the Jewish high school, attracted considerable attention in Lvov. Lina lived on Yakhovich Street as a Pole. She had changed her name and was employed in a German firm. A secret agent suspected her and went to her house to check her documents. He was found dead — strangled with a towel. The Germans pasted up "Wanted" posters with her picture and promised a large reward; it was all in vain, and Lina Haus disappeared.

Sometimes Jews who spoke good French dressed in the uniform of French prisoners of war and lived together with them in the concentration camps.

A large number of Jews hid among the Poles and Ukrainians. No matter how the Germans endeavored to corrupt the hearts of the people with the fear of death, executions, treachery, and greed, there were, nevertheless, courageous and honest people capable of heroism. Educated Polish people saved many Jewish children from death, although for the most part they could take in only girls (for obvious reasons).

Many Polish priests took in Jewish girls, hid them in the churches, and saved them from death. More than one of these noble people paid with their own lives for saving Jewish children. . . .

In January, 1943, after the Germans were defeated at Stalingrad, a committee was organized in the Lvov ghetto for armed struggle with the Germans. Among the members of the committee were the Jewish poet Shudrikh, who represented the ghetto, and the poet Sanya Friedman, who represented the camp.

The organization was in contact with the Polish committee and began to publish an underground newspaper which was circulated by hand. The money collected by the committee was used to buy revolvers, and some of the people who worked in German military organizations succeeded in stealing weapons. Soon secret military training was begun. Committee delegates managed to break through to Brody and establish contact with the Volhynia partisans. Among them was a woman, Dr. Lina Goldberg, who enthusiastically set about organizing the partisan movement in Lvov. The flow of weapons to the ghetto continued uninterrupted. Once, during a search, SS men found a weapon on the person of a teenager, and he was shot on the spot. From that day on, frequent searches were instituted in the barracks. A weapons cache was found on Lokietek Street, and the Germans unsuccessfully tried to find its organizers.

People began to flee the ghetto individually and in groups. The committee tried to find ways to send people to Brody so as to make it a center of armed resistance.

Three trucks were rented for a large sum of money, and the operation was carried out under conditions of absolute secrecy. The first three groups were successfully dispatched, and they joined the partisan movement. There were many young people in the group, and they knew all the places, roads, and paths in the area.

The partisans successfully attacked German estates and obtained provisions. They set up ambushes and took weapons from German soldiers.

They were not alone in their struggle. Volhynia's partisans sent them emissaries and provided them with explosives (tolite and dynamite) so that they could carry out sabotage.

Brody's partisans killed Germans left and right. On one occasion they attacked a German post near Brody — at the very border between the general governorship and the *Ostgebiet*. The sentry was killed, and submachine guns and grenades were seized. The partisans began to pose a threat to Germans throughout the region.

[German gendarmes did everything in their power to learn the location of the unit, but they were unable to capture partisan headquarters, since it was constantly moved from place to place.

When the committee received information that the ghetto was to be destroyed, the Jews decided to hide in the forests and continue the struggle. Shudrikh was supposed to go into the forest with a group of seventeen persons. Their departure was scheduled for 8:00 A.M., May 8, 1943. The next day, however, the truck that was taking the partisans to Zyblikevich Street was surrounded by an SS unit. The partisans realized that they had fallen into a trap, and they decided to sell their lives dearly. Shooting began, and several Germans were wounded. An SS unit arrived and disarmed the partisans. They all perished. On the morning of May 9 the forest near Brody was combed by a battalion of German infantry.

The partisans' struggle with the German force three times their strength continued for three days. Only a few of the partisans succeeded in breaking clear of the encirclement and making their way to the forests of the Lublin area where they continued their fight. The others died bravely with their weapons in their hands. Not a single one surrendered alive to the Germans.

* * *

Sensing that the end was approaching, the Germans began to speed up the destruction of the Jews. One after the other, the following ghettos disappeared: Przemyśl]*, Sambor, Rudki, Brzeżany, Tarnopol, Jaworów, Żółkiew, Przemyślany, Jaryczów.

In Lvov a certain calm ensued just before the liquidation of the ghetto. There were no guards at the gates, and the Germans arranged concerts and soccer matches within the ghetto. Grzymek rarely showed himself on the streets and no longer beat and shot people. The SS men stopped attacking Jewish dwellings. Nevertheless, everyone knew that this was the calm before the storm. On April 25 the Germans took 4,000 prisoners from the Janowski camp to Piaskowa Gora to be executed.

At 3:00 A.M. of July 1 [1943] the Germans entered the ghetto to finish the bloody work that they had begun in 1941. This was the final liquidation, and they took everybody — even those who worked in German concerns. Certificates with the seal of the SS and patches with "R" and "W" were annulled.

The liquidation campaign was led by Katzmann, Engels, Lenard, Willhaus, Inguart, and Schönbach. SS units and Fascist police searched houses all day, throwing grenades into cellars where people were hiding. On the third day fire trucks drove into the ghetto. The Jews were being burned alive. Lokietek Street, Kresowa Street, and Sharanovich Street were put to the torch. People hiding there chocked from the smoke and came out only at the last minute. The Gestapo soldiers did not shoot but tried to catch their victims alive and throw them into the flame.

During the first days a few people attempted to resist. Those who had weapons began shooting in a disorganized fashion. Two policemen were killed, and a few SS men were wounded. This enraged the executioners still more. They killed women and children by throwing them from balconies; they chopped off the men's heads with axes. The ghetto streets were filled with corpses.

The sky above the ghetto was black with the smoke of the fires as it silently hearkened to the terrible cries of murdered children.

* * *

*This part of the text was restored by a reverse translation from the Rumanian (See *Cartea Neagra, p. 138*).

122

We have told the truth. This Fascist crime cannot be concealed from humanity even though the murderers have done everything in their power not to leave any witnesses.

Witnesses remained: Naftali Nacht, a teenager from Lvov who escaped to Soviet Ukrainian partisans; Leopold Schor, also a refugee from Lvov; Jurek Lichter, who escaped his executioners by joining the partisans in the Zlochov forests; Artur Strauch, a bank clerk from Lvov; Lily Herts, who spent thirteen days in a sealed hiding place in the ghetto.

This crime cannot be forgotten or forgiven by humanity.

Information supplied by **L. Herts** and **Naftali Nacht**.

Prepared for publication by **R. Frayerman** and **R. Kovnator**

Transliteration verified by **Dr. Ada Friedman**.

Thirteen Days in Hiding

(The Story of Lily Herts)

We are sitting in our hiding place. On the streets of the ghetto, we can hear the Germans shooting and the screams of people being murdered.

Our hiding place is in the attic, which consists of two parts separated by a brick wall. The entrance has been well masked.

There are forty of us. It is stuffy, and we are thirsty.

The Germans rest at night, and so it is quiet till morning.

At about five o'clock sounds reach us which are like someone ringing a bell. At first these are quiet, shy, lonely sounds. Later they shift into a terrible scream rushing upward and drowning out even the shooting. The people being killed are screaming.

No one in the hiding place moves. The Rosenbergs' tiny baby groans quietly. Finally he begins to cry, and we are all in the power of his small lungs. He can reveal us. We give the mother some sugar, and someone has a bottle of milk. Anything to quiet the child.

* * *

Toward morning, when everything falls silent, we come out of hiding. The doors of the apartments are open. We lie down on the scattered bed linen to get a few hours of sleep after a torturous night.

Soon, however, we again hear shooting and go back into our crowded hiding place.

The footsteps of policemen come closer and closer. They are searching for us — unsuccessfully so far. Enraged by their failure but certain that there is someone in the house, they shout: "Come on out! Fools! We'll shoot!"

The baby begins to cry. . . . We are petrified with horror. This is the end. They'll find us. What can we do?

"We won't come out. Let them go ahead and shoot."

"Open up! Quick! Damned kikes!"

Someone pushes the door open, but the Germans won't come in. They are afraid. The baby screams at the top of its lungs. I say goodbye to my husband.

The Germans come up on the roof and begin taking it apart so as to shoot from there. The rafters are already cracking over our heads. In a panic, everyone rushes to the exit.

124

I try to hide. There is no one in the attic. I crawl under a mattress in the corner. Maybe they will go away. But a hand drags me out by my coat.

*   *   *

We are driven out into a tiny corridor. My dear husband Levka is leaning against a wall. He is pale and silent. I come up to him, and we again say goodbye.

They count us — one, two . . . thirty-five.

There is a sudden confusion. Someone is running up the stairs. Iska covers me with his own body and shoves me into the open door of an apartment.

"Save yourself, if you can!" he says quietly and disappears.

I run through the kitchen into a room. Everything is scattered around. I crawl under a heap of pillows and feather quilts and lie there motionless. I neither feel nor hear anything. My body has turned to wood, and only my heart beats. It is hard to breathe, and my throat is dry. I wait. I know they will notice that one person has disappeared and come to search for me.

My God, what is that? The shot was so close! It must have been in the kitchen.

"There's not even anything to get drunk on" someone says in German. He opens the cupboard and searches for vodka. Then he comes into the room. He looks around. I hold my breath. Let it happen as quickly as possible; let him shoot, but let it be quick. I gulp. He looks around, holding some papers in his hand. It is money. My leg is sticking out from under the feather quilt; I did not manage to hide it. He will stumble on it, and I will be doomed.

No! He goes away. He really goes away. Another minute of intense waiting passes, and I can hear steps moving quickly away from me along the stairway. I crawl out; this is no time to rest. I get up. There is someone else in the room — Bronya, Iska's sister.

"What miracle brought you here?"

"Iska pushed me in here at the last moment."

We have no time for talk and run back up to the attic. Behind the brick wall are other people who were not found. They are the owners of the home. . . . We knock.

"Let us in! Quick, the Germans might come back!"

There are sixteen people left in the hiding place — women, girls, men, and a three-year-old boy named Dziunya. We do not talk. The July sun beats mercilessly through the roof.

125

* * *

Night finally comes, and we crawl out of our hiding place and collect some water in a bottle so as to have a supply for the next day.

In the attic we all fall into a dead sleep. When the sun's rays break through the cracks we are still asleep.

Lusya wakes us anxiously.

"Get up! Get into the hiding place quickly! Some sort of fire trucks have arrived."

We again crawl into our lair. Explosions can be heard; it is the Germans driving people from their hiding places. Between the explosions we can hear groans, screams, and the shouts of Germans: "Leonard, did you see me take her with one shot? She was really far away!"

"Aha!" another German shouts. "Flutter out, little birds! That's it. And now we'll roast you goddamn kikes over the fire!"

"Just don't throw me in the fire! Shoot! Oh, my God!" a woman screams in a shrill voice.

A thin wisp of smoke comes through the cracks of the roof. It burns my throat, which is already dry from heat and fear.

Little Dziunya covers his mouth with both hands. He knows he must not talk. Large drops of sweat fall from his face.

"Maybe it's better to come out. It's better to die from a bullet than to burn alive," I say.

"We won't go," Bronya says. "Our house won't be burned, since it's next to the German hospital."

"They'll burn us alive. Open up!" Lida begs.

"Burn it down!" we hear the Germans on the roof shout.

"Give it more gasoline!" a fireman shouts.

There is a sinister sound, and the liquid from the hose strikes the roof. It soaks through the cracks and drips onto our steaming heads but — strangely — refreshes us.

"It is not gasoline, but water," we explain to each other with gestures. They wanted to frighten us and make us run out of the building.

If only the men standing on the roof don't find us! But they continue pouring on the water, and the sound of it flowing drowns out our breathing.

"Stop the water!" a fireman shouts.

Evidently they are protecting our house from the fire to keep the blaze from reaching the hospital.

The voices leave.

126

All we can hear is the rumble of the red-hot tin, the roar of the fire, and the screams of the dying people.

At night we come out of our hiding place to look through the cracks in the roof at blazing Lokietek Street.

The voice of a dying boy can be heard at the far end of the street: "Ple-e-e-ease, one more bullet, ple-e-e-ease!"

* * *

By morning the screams of people being burned alive have quieted down. Our hiding place has become a true hell. We are miserable from hunger and thirst, and the lice are relentless. We are sweating and gasping from the heat.

Dziunya keeps asking for sugar and water. He pounds at his mother and pulls me by the hair. We talk in a whisper. One person keeps up a constant wail at half-voice. Those who mourn their children groan and lament.

"If I could only strangle one of those thugs with my own hands, death would be a luxury. But I sit here helplessly and wait . . ." Lida says.

Evening comes, and I go downstairs for the first time. My head is spinning. We have not eaten for several days. I have to find underwear, because the lice won't let us rest. I steal into my apartment silently to keep the German patrol from hearing me.

In the darkness I find a jar of sugar and take it for Dziunya. Something white is hanging from a clothesline. Underwear! I grab it greedily and go back to the attic.

The underwear is torn from my hands, and we immediately change clothing.

"God! Is it possible for a person to feel such bliss?" one woman exclaims. "What a joy it would have been if you had found food as well. Don't be afraid. Go on back."

I again go downstairs and enter another apartment, where I stumble over the corpse of a dead woman. There is something cold and soft under my hand. I go back — without any bread. I do not want to eat any more.

I stand in the corridor leading to the balcony. I can hear Hitler's guards shooting at those who are attempting to escape. . . .

* * *

Someone must have spotted us during the night, because on the seventh day we hear German being spoken virtually next to us.

"There must be Jews here. We have to check carefully."

"Why fool around with them? Use the grenades," a German orders.

There is an explosion — then another. One grenade explodes on the roof. The dust from the explosion falls on our faces.

We remain calm. There is no frightening us with grenades. Nothing can frighten us. Dziunya, our little hero, helps us. He calms the others.

"Mama, if I sit quietly, will you give me some sugar?"

"I'll give you everything."

"Mama, we'll kill all the Gestapo soldiers when we leave here."

"Right, but just sit quietly."

And all the time the ghetto has been burning. We hear the voice of a man being killed on the street by the Germans. Before dying he begs his murderers for some water. What a strange person!

Something incredible is happening to our little Dziunya. He is talking a lot and crying. Again and again our house is searched; the Germans rap on the ceiling, floors, and walls.

"Tell me a fairy tale! I want a fairy tale. Or else I'll shout," little Dziunya says.

"Sweetie, I'll tell you a wonderful fairy tale as soon as things quiet down."

"But I want one now! Do you hear me? Or else I'll shout."

Suddenly there is a knock above us. Everyone falls silent with horror.

I begin to tell a fairy tale in a whisper, dragging out each syllable so as to hold the boy's attention as long as possible.

"You know, Dziunya," I say, "when we leave this hiding place, Papa will come and buy you a horsie."

Also dragging out each syllable, Dziunya answers:

"You're lying. Papa won't come. The Gestapo soldiers killed him."

"You know what, Dziunya? Pull me by the hair." I say.

He pulls my hair, but that does not distract him for long.

His face is burning, even though he is constantly drinking water. We even wipe him with a damp towel, but nothing helps. He hops around and screams at every sound from outside.

We are totally exhausted from fear, hunger, and thirst.

Toward evening some Germans enter the house. As usual, they speak in loud voices.

Suddenly Dziunya gets up and looks around with insane eyes:

128

"Now," he says, "I am going to shout loud so that they come."

We put a hand over his mouth. His mother pleads with him, kisses him, and cries. Nothing helps. He bites her hands and kicks at her stomach.

How great must be our sufferings if even a little boy goes mad!

He dies, and his mother takes his tiny body down to the cellar during the night and buries him there.

On the thirteenth day, a Sunday, silence comes to the ghetto. German guards bustle up and down the street, and shots are heard infrequently.

The night favors us. It is without stars, moon, or fires. We listen to be certain that there are no guards near. The silence surrounding us is broken only by individual shots.

"We are sure to die," Lida says.

"It is better to die from a bullet than die here from dirt, fear, and hunger," Bronya says. It is she who has kept up our courage for these twelve days.

We break up into two groups. One goes to the right, and we go to the left. It seems to me that I have been buried alive all these days, and that I have only now come out to freedom. Opposite us is Lokietek Street. To reach it we have to make only a few steps, but we are in no condition to move. Bronya forces us forward. We walk single-file, holding onto the walls of the houses. In certain spots bonfires are still burning to light up the ghetto and frighten off any refugees.

Lvov is asleep. The windows of the apartments are curtained. Some drunken men come out of a building, singing loudly. We squeeze through the gates so as not to be noticed. They pass by us without incident. The home of a Polish woman whom I know is not far away. Surely she will help us. I knock at the window.

"Leilya, it's me. Open up, I beg you." I say quietly.

She takes us in, brews coffee and cooks eggs, and serves them to us at the table.

"I'll hide you in the hay shed, since there is an order not to let any Jews into apartments under pain of death," she says.

"We'll be fine in the shed. If only they don't find us."

We sit, hidden in the hay, whispering.

About 10:00 P.M. I go to the house. I want to know if there is any information about Iska. I steal up to the window and quietly tap at the window pane. No one can see me from here, and I can talk to Leilya without being seen.

Suddenly Germans come riding into the yard on motorcycles. My first thought is that someone must have reported us.

I am not mistaken. One of them walks directly up to the shed and drags Bronya out.

"I beg you, let me go. I'm only nineteen years old. Why do you need my life?"

"Shut up, you bitch!"

I see all this from my hidden corner. Bronya stands upright and pale.

"Where's the other one?"

"She left this morning. I don't know where she is."

"We'll find her!"

Bronya is shoved with a rifle butt, and she stumbles as she is led away.

I have been saved once again.

Information supplied by **Lily Herts**
Prepared for publication by **R. Frayerman** and **R. Kovnator**

My Comrade — The Partisan, Yakov Barer*

(Letter of Boris Khandros, Lvov)

I was born in 1924. When I was fourteen, I became a member of the Komsomol (Communist Youth League). In 1941 I graduated from high school and went as a volunteer to the front. During the defense of Kiev I was wounded in the leg. An old woman hid me and brought me back to health. The front was far away, and I returned to Pridnestrovye. Together with Tamara Buryk, a village school teacher, I organized an underground group. We survived the terrible summer of 1943, and I again fought against the Germans, although I was thousands of kilometers from the front.

I met Yakov Barer in the beginning of 1944. He was a strong youth with an excellent command of German. He entered our unit and fought bravely. On March 17, 1944, I was seriously wounded in the chest; a bullet had pierced my lung. Yakov carried me away under fire.

*Yakov Barer now lives in Israel and is a lieutenant colonel in the Israel Defense Forces.

130

Before 1943 Yakov had lived in Lvov, where he was a furrier. He began his studies in 1939 and prepared to enroll in the university. But then the Germans arrived, and Yakov, like all the Jews of Lvov, was doomed.

The Germans took him to work one morning, and when he returned home in the evening, both his grandmother and his thirteen-year-old brother were gone; they had been taken to the "death factory" in Belzec. Soon Yakov was also sent there, but he jumped from the train.

In the fall of 1942 Yakov found himself in a concentration camp near Lvov. The commandant of this camp never sent any Jews to be shot. He would approach the doomed person, speak of planned improvements and the humanity of the *Führer* and, when the person began to believe that he would be saved, the commandant would strangle him. He was nicknamed "the strangler." He had a special glass booth built on a tower so that Jews could die in it before everyone's eyes. The "strangler" forced people to dig pits and then fill them in again with earth. On one occasion Jews were digging up the ground near the camp border. Yakov hid, and the column returned to the barracks. When a German sentry shouted at him, Yakov jumped up and killed the man with his shovel.* He removed the guard's uniform and checked his pass, which was issued in the name of Max Waller. After that, Yakov went to the barracks where his younger brother and eight friends from Lvov were being kept. He spoke in so alien a voice that even his own brother did not recognize him: "Get your things!" he barked. Silently all set out on their last journey. The sentry at the gates was not surprised, since Jews were led out to be shot every night. "Cleaning the air, friend?" the sentry joked.

This was Yakov Barer's first success.

Yakov decided to make his way to the east. They reached a railway freight station, and Yakov noticed crates of books in one of the cars headed for Dnepropetrovsk. The nine Jews hid behind the crates, and Yakov stood guard in the uniform of an SS soldier.

Yakov and his brother left the group in Dnepropetrovsk. They wandered for a long time. Yakov was forced to discard his uniform, since the gendarmes were on the lookout for deserters. In September of 1943 they reached Pervomaysk. There Yakov was befriended by his former teacher, Mikolaychik. Yakov obtained a

---

*Ya. Barer has testified that he killed two Germans.

radio, and they listened to Soviet bulletins and told others of the news. The *Sicherheitsdienst* became interested in Yakov, and he fled, but the Germans killed his younger brother.

I saw the photographs and documents of the Germans Yakov killed. He did not like to tell of his exploits; it was hard for him to remember the death of his friends and relatives.

He and I split up in the hospital. He was headed west with the Red Army and lived for one thing only: to see Soviet Lvov. A Siberian surgeon of the Kiev Division saved my life, and I will soon go back to fight, but I do not know what happened to Yakov Barer. Is he alive? Did he ever see his native Lvov?

June 22, 1944

Prepared for publication by **Ilya Ehrenburg**.

In the Penyatsky Forests

(The Lvov *oblast*)

There were two villages located in the Penyatsky forests. One was four kilometers from the other. In the village of Guta, which was in the Penyatsky region, there were 120 farms; now not a single one remains. Three hundred eighty Poles and Jews lived in the village; now they are dead. On February 22–23 the village was surrounded by Germans who poured gasoline on the houses and sheds and burned the village together with its residents. In the village of Guta Verkhobuzheskaya only two farms were left out of 120. None of the inhabitants survived. I, Matvey Grigorievich Perlin, am a scout in the Red Army, and I accidentally came upon two earthen shelters with eighty Jews not far from these villages. There were 75-year-old women, teenage boys, girls, and children, the youngest of whom was three years old.

I was the first representative of the Red Army whom they had seen after almost three years of daily fear for their lives, and they all tried to come as close to me as possible, shake my hand, and say a word of greeting. These people had lived sixteen months in these holes in the forests, hiding from persecution. There had been more of them, but only eighty remained. In their words, not more than

200 people remained alive of the forty thousand Jews of the Brody and Zolochev regions. How had they survived? They were supported by the inhabitants of the surrounding villages, but no one knew where they were hiding. When leaving "their" forest, they covered their tracks with snow sprinkled through a specially made sieve. They had a few rifles and pistols, and they never missed an opportunity to lessen the number of Fascist beasts.

They had spoken only in a whisper for the entire three years. It was not permitted to speak aloud even in the earthen shelters. Only when I arrived did they begin to sing, laugh, and speak aloud.

I was particularly touched during this meeting by the passionate impatience and firm faith with which these people had awaited us — the Red Army. Their songs and poems, their conversations and even dreams were overflowing with this faith and longing. Zoya, who was three years old, did not know what a house was, and she saw her first horse when I arrived. But when she was asked who was supposed to come, she answered: "*Batko** Stalin is supposed to come, and then we'll all go home."

A letter of **M. Perlin**.

Prepared for publication by **Ilya Ehrenburg**.

*Ukrainian for "father" or "leader" (J.G.)

The Letter of Siunya Deresh

(Izyaslavl)

April 14, 1944

Dear Uncle Misha,

I am writing from my home town of Izyaslavl, which you wouldn't recognize. Only the worst half is left of our small town, and there was no reason for it to have survived. It would be better if it had never existed, if nothing existed; it would have been better if I had never been born. I am no longer the same Siunya that you knew. I myself do not know who I am. Everything seems like a dream, a nightmare. Of the 8,000 residents of Izyaslavl only I and Kiva Feldman, our neighbor, are left. They are all gone — my dear mother, father, my precious brother Zyama, Iza, Sara, Borukh. . . . You dear people, how hard it was for you! . . . I can never recover,

I cannot write. If I began to describe the things I experienced, I don't know if you would understand. I escaped from concentration camps three times, and I looked death in the face more than once while fighting in the ranks of the partisans. It would have been better if the bullet of some Fritz had killed me. But I am healthy again. My leg has healed, and I am going to search out the enemy to take vengeance for everything. I would like to see you — if only for five minutes. I don't know if I will be able to. . . . For the time being I am at home, although all that is left of what was once called "home" is a ruin. I got a letter from Tanya. She was very happy to learn that someone is left. . . .

I am waiting for an answer to my letter. My dear people, if only we could see each other as soon as possible! Uncle Misha, remember that our most vicious enemy is the Fascist cannibal. What a terrible death all our family died! Kill the Fascist, cut him up in pieces! Never fall into his hands! This letter is disorganized — just as my life is disorganized and worthless.

Nevertheless, I am alive. . . . To take vengeance on the enemy. Goodbye, Uncle Misha. I hope we meet soon! Greetings to everyone! I feel as if I had returned from the afterworld.

I am beginning a new life now — the life of an orphan.

How? I don't know.

Write as often as possible. I am waiting for an answer. Why don't Uncle Shlyoma, Joseph, and Gita and the others write?

Warmest greetings,

Your nephew, Sinuya Deresh

P.S. My address is the same. No matter where you write, I'll get it, because there is no one left here but me.

Prepared for publication by **Ilya Ehrenburg**.

Letters of Orphans

(Botoşani)*

[Dear Comrade Ehrenburg,

I, Dina Leibl, was born in the village of Bregomet, which is on the Seret River in the Chernovitsy region. I am sixteen years old.

In 1941, when the Germans occupied North Bukovina, we were taken to the Krasnoye camp in the Vinnitsa region of the Ukraine. In 1942 the Germans killed my parents. I am the only one left of our large family.

I escaped to Rumania. I live in the house of a man who feeds me. I beg you: take me back to Russia. I want to study and become a real person. My youth is being wasted, and in Soviet Russia I can work.

Dina Leibl]

In 1941, when the Germans occupied the small town of Kalinovka in the Vinnitsa *oblast*, they took all the Jews off to work. They tortured us and beat us with whips. They gave us leaves and grass to eat. Three Jews were harnessed to a cart, and they were supposed to haul the Germans. They did not have the strength, and they were killed. In 1942 we were forced into the ghetto, and we could not leave it. Many people died there from hunger. Then they took us to the stadium. There they encircled us, shouted "Juden!", and began to kill everyone. The children were thrown into a pit. I ran away. A German chased after me, but I climbed a tree, and he could not find me. I saw them kill all the Jews, and the blood trickled through the grass for three days. I was ten years old then, and now I am twelve.

Nyunya Doktorovich

In 1941, when the war began, they came to Mogilev-Podolsky and took all the Jews to the Pechera camp in the Tulchin region. They made fun of us and shot my parents. We were taken to work, and the little girls had to dig peat with their hands. We worked

---

*The name of the city is crossed out in the text. In the collection, *Murderers of Peoples* (vol. II, p. 88), this material is titled "Letters of Orphans Living in the City of Botoşani (Rumania). The letters of Dina Leibl, Rokhl Rosenberg, and Khaya Hantwerker are absent from the manuscript of *The Black Book* which was received in Israel and are reproduced from the above-mentioned edition.

from 4:00 A.M. until late at night. Once we overheard them say that the *Yids* would be killed when the summer ended. We ran away in all directions. They chased after us and killed a lot of people. I was saved by a Ukrainian who took me to his home and hid me. His neighbor told the Germans that there was a "kike" in his house. The German came to shoot me, but the Ukrainian began to fight with him, and I ran away and ended up on Rumanian territory.

Rosa Lindvor, 15 years old

[On July 9, 1941, the Germans came to our village of Brichany. They sent us all to the Yampol camp in the Ukraine. The Germans would not let anyone go to the creek to drink, and everyone was suffering from thirst. Then they took us back to the Sukharki camp in Bessarabia. From there we were sent to the Kolaigorod camp in the Ukraine. My sister and I were orphaned. I was only twelve years old, but I lived through more than I can describe. I thank the Red Army for saving the people.

Rakhil Rosenberg]

I was born in the small town of Bagila on the Seret River. I am now fifteen years old, and I have yet to see anything good. We were all arrested and taken to the Yedintsy camp. I suffered there and saw death before my very eyes. Then we were taken to the beautiful Ukraine, but it was dark for us. There my beloved parents both died on the same day. The five of us were orphaned. I myself was not far from death. Now my sisters and I are in the town of Botoşani. That which we have lost will never return.

Enya Waltser

[I am from the city of Lipkany in Bessarabia. After the Red Army arrived in 1940 we again began to live well.

I studied in school and was an excellent student. Our entire life was destroyed because of the war. The Germans deported us to the Ukraine. There we were driven from place to place and beaten. There was no food, and the people died like flies. In 1942 father died. Two days later mother died too. My brother and I are left now. I am thirteen years old.

Khaya Hantwerker]

BYELORUSSIA

The History of the Minsk Ghetto

On June 28, 1941, German tanks rumbled down the streets of Minsk. Approximately 75,000 Jews (together with their children) had not managed to leave the city.

The first order required all men from 15 to 45 years of age to appear at the registration point. Failure to do so was punishable by death. On July 7, 1941, Germans burst into apartments, seized the first Jewish men that they came upon, loaded them onto trucks and took them away. The next day an announcement was posted of the execution by shooting of 100 Jewish communists for Bolshevik connections.

When the Germans appeared in town, people were robbed, raped, and shot for no reason. Jews were subjected to particular harassment.

No. 21 Myasnikov Street was heavily occupied; more than 300 people resided there. On July 2, 1941, the building was surrounded. The residents (the adults, the elderly, and even the children) were taken out into the yard and ordered to stand with their faces to the wall. No explanation was given. Forty guards held the people at rifle point for six hours. Meanwhile clothing, linen, blankets, footwear, dishes, and all foodstuffs were confiscated. (The pretext given was the confiscation of weapons.) The stolen goods were loaded onto two large trucks and hauled away. Only when all this had been accomplished were the people released. They were totally dumbfounded at the sight of their ransacked apartments.

That night groups of from four to five men returned to the apartments of the Graivers, the Rapoports, the Keonskys and ordered them to hand over their remaining belongings. "There were silver spoons here. . . . Where is the suit? What happened to the silk?" the bandits shouted.

The Stalin School was a large building also located on Myasnikov Street; its windows looked out on the courtyard of an apartment house, and through them the interiors of the apartments could be seen. The Germans settled in the school and selected the residents of the building as the objects of their amusement. For an entire day they shot from the windows, aiming at mirrors, furniture, and people.

Hundreds and thousands of men obeyed the order to go to the

registration point. All were sent to the Drozdy camp. There Russians, Byelorussians, and Jews were all subjected to the same harassment and violence.

After a time, the Russian men were released, but the Jews were kept in the camp. Those who remained were divided into two groups: white-collar workers and blue-collar workers. The former were loaded onto trucks, taken outside the city limits, and shot with submachine guns. Altogether, 3,000 people were murdered. Outstanding people perished: engineers, professors of the Polytechnical Institute, Mr. Eisenberg and Mr. Pritykin, who held Candidate's degrees in the technical sciences, Dr. Priklad, who was a Doctor of Mathematics, and others.

The second group, which consisted mainly of skilled laborers, was taken from the camp under heavy guard and imprisoned in the city. As they were being led along the streets, women and children ran out of the houses, attempting to pick out the faces of friends and relatives. The convoy met them with bullets. The columns of people were led along Communal Street. Mr. Zyskin's fourteen-year-old daughter ran out of the house to the gates in the hope of seeing her father. A shot rang out, and the girl fell dead.

The following is Comrade Partisan Grechanik's testimony about the days spent by the male population of Minsk in the Drozdy camp:

"When our column was about a kilometer from town, they stopped us and said: 'knives, watches, and razors are to be put in a hat and handed in.' The people obeyed. Of course, those who had their wits about them hid their watches and razors. Very many people buried their things in the ground rather than give them to the Germans. The Germans turned everyone's pockets inside out, took the belongings from the hats, and checked wallets. We were standing in a field and were surrounded by guards. People kept arriving at the field — group after group. That night it grew cold in the bare field, and people lay next to each other to keep warm. We spent the entire night in the field. There were very many people, but they would not give us anything to eat. People asked for water, but they would not give even that. Whenever anyone asked for anything, the Germans would shoot straight into the crowd. Thus, the second day passed. The people lay on the ground, cold and hungry. Some were dressed warmly, but others wore only summer shirts. Day broke, and people kept arriving. A German appeared with a bucket and began to distribute water. The people surrounded him and almost knocked him off his feet. Again those animals shot at the people.

"It was 12:00 on the third day, and the people were hungry. The weather was warm and pleasant. Suddenly an officer appeared with an interpreter and announced that from 10:00 to 4:00 relatives would be admitted to the camp with food packages. In the distance we could see women with baskets and children carrying bottles of water, but they were not permitted to approach immediately. They were all detained, and the contents of the packages were checked. It got noisy. Everyone tried to reach the women and children. The general mood improved; those who received food ate with gusto and shared with those who did not. It became even noisier in the field, and the children were asked to bring more water. They did so, and the men drank with pleasure. But then some twenty of the women began to cry. When asked why they were crying, they answered that their husbands and children had been killed.

"The day came to an end, and the women and children were forced to leave. The men lay in the field. Suddenly we heard steps, some shouts in German, and rifle shots; Red-Army soldiers were led up, but they were not permitted to mix with the civilian population. The morning of the fourth day came. The soldiers attempted to approach the civilians, but they were immediately fired on. That day more than ten people were killed. Again the women came and brought food and drink. On the fifth night the soldiers began one by one to run over to the civilians.

"The Germans fired at them, but the Red-Army soldiers paid no attention to the danger. They would run over and immediately lie down. The civilians gave them bread, water, and salt. Thus the civilians and the soldiers spent the entire night together — until just before morning. Then the soldiers ran back to their group and were again shot at. On the fifth day the weather was not particularly clear. More and more people were brought in — military and civilian. Suddenly a large column was led up; the people were dressed differently than we were and were carrying sacks and bags. They said that they had come from the west in an attempt to escape from the advancing Germans. They said that many had perished along the way.

"Again the women came and brought food. Some brought raincoats. There was a sudden rain, and it became cold and damp. The people lay on the ground, and the day passed. The sixth night began. It was dark, and the soldiers ran over to the civilians. The Germans shot at the people. Again shouts were heard; it turned out that someone's sack had been cut open. The sacks contained dried bread, and people surged toward the food. There were shots and a lot of noise, and about fifty people crawled away from the crowd. When they reached the German guards, the fugitives took off running. The Germans noticed them and began to shoot, but it was dark, and only three people were killed. The rest got away, and the sixth night passed.

"On the morning of the seventh day it rained. We could see the women and children in the distance. They came closer, and the crowd began to wait impatiently. It was already 10:00, but no one was admitted to the camp. A column of people dressed in shabby civilian clothes was brought up. Some were barefoot. When they passed the women who had brought food to their relatives, shouts were heard. The new arrivals attacked the women and children and took their baskets from them. The Germans chased the women away, and the column of people was admitted to the civilian area of the camp. Only then did we realize that these were people whom the Soviet government had sent to forced labor camps.

"Then in the distance could be seen a Gestapo unit on motorcycles, on bicycles, in cars, and on foot. They approached the crowd, and shouts could be heard: 'Line up four-deep!' Rubber truncheons were used to get the soldiers in formation and then the others. The people were taken two kilometers away. Along the road lay soldiers with leg wounds. They shouted and groaned, but the Germans would not permit anyone to leave the column to help them. In this fashion everyone was bivouacked next to the Svisloch River. Military personnel were in one area, and civilians were in another. Thus the day passed.

"The eighth day dawned. The people lay on the ground, since they had been warned that anyone who stood up would be shot. The machine guns were used frequently, and we heard people scream: 'They killed him!' Anyone who got up to discharge his bowels was shot. One man lay on the ground. A bullet had entered the small of his back and passed out through his stomach, ripping out the intestines. He was still alive and asked people to take down his address and write to his wife and children to tell them how he had died. A German walked up and asked: 'Whose knife ripped open his stomach?' Thus the eighth day passed.

"The ninth day arrived. The people did not ask for water, since there was enough in the stream. A German stood next to the stream and permitted people to get water one after the other. A truck drove up, and an interpreter shouted some names through a megaphone: doctors, cooks, bakers, electricians, and plumbers. They were told to go to the truck; they would be permitted to return home on condition that they appear for work.

"Another truck appeared with Germans and a movie camera. They began to throw dried bread to the military prisoners, who scrambled for it frantically as they were filmed by the movie camera. An officer on the truck shot at the hands of the Red-Army soldiers who grabbed for the dried bread. He got down from the truck and examined the hands of those who had been shot. If the bullet had struck a bone, the man was put in one group. If it had penetrated only the flesh of the hand, the man went to a different group. The first group was shot in full view of everyone. The officer gave the Red-Army soldiers shovels and ordered them to bury the dead.

"The tenth day arrived. It was very dark, and the military prisoners again ran over to the civilians. Amid the noise and shooting many of the military prisoners — about three hundred — crossed the stream to the other shore, where there was a small forest. Suddenly a shot rang out from the woods. The people were lit up with headlights from three sides, and machine guns began to fire. Bullets flew overhead, and the people pressed their bodies to the ground. Those who were lying on higher ground crawled lower. By that time all the escapees had reached the woods. Only two were killed crossing the stream. The shooting stopped, the headlights went out, and the prisoners of war ran back to their places. The night came to an end.

"The eleventh day began. The weather was bad. Some officers came to make a speech, and the sentries began to put things in order. On the other side of the stream a German sentry was washing his feet. Suddenly we heard the roar of planes and several explosions. The sentry grabbed his boots and ran for the woods. The officers jumped into their car and left without saying anything. The people saw the sentry grab his boots and run, and they burst out laughing. Then the women came again and brought food, underwear, and some warm clothing. The day ended.

"On the twelfth night the prisoners of war ran over to the civilians, who gave them something to eat. Many of the soldiers changed into civilian clothing and remained with us. The night passed in this fashion.

"It was already 10:00 on the thirteenth day, but the women were still not permitted to enter the camp. Suddenly a car drove up, and it was announced that Poles were to gather on the left, Russians on the right, and the Jews next to the stream. The area was surrounded by wires, and the crowd began to split up.

"Germans with rubber truncheons were everywhere. They beat the Jews and drove them toward the wire. Anyone who resisted was beaten to death or shot. Suddenly it was announced that they would let us go home. Poles and Russians were to be released first. No mention was made of the Jews. They began to release the Poles, and the day came to an end.

"On the fourteenth night it was dark and cold. Again the prisoners of war ran over to the civilians, and the Germans shot at them. Suddenly an uninterrupted round of shooting began on the other side of the stream. We asked the prisoners of war what was going on, and they replied that the Germans were shooting the officers and political instructors. The shooting continued almost all night.

"It rained on the morning of the fifteenth day. The women again gathered to have their packages checked. They had brought food, and part of it was confiscated before they were admitted to the camp and shown where to go. Some of the women who were looking for their men could not find them. . . . They had been killed on the previous day. The women left sobbing.

"It grew warm, and a German was posted beside the stream, but he would not permit anyone to go for water. He pushed each man who approached into the river and told him to dive three times in his clothing before taking water. There were fewer and fewer Poles in camp. In this fashion the day came to an end.

"The sixteenth night was dark and rainy. The prisoners of war again ran over to the civilians, who fed them. Many changed into civilian clothing. It rained all night.

"At 10:00 on the seventeenth day a car arrived with an interpreter who explained that all Jewish engineers, doctors, technicians, bookkeepers, and educated persons must be registered. They would be released from camp and sent to work. There were 3,000 such persons, and they began to register. Later the people learned that all these educated persons were shot. The women came and brought food. There was a heavy rain, and everyone was soaked; some of the men shaved. A group of women gathered around while three freshly shaven men put on women's clothing and covered their heads with large kerchiefs. The old women took them by the hand, and they picked up baskets with pots and set off for the exit. The sentry paid them no heed, and the people watched intently. They got through, and everyone breathed freely. That day twenty men escaped from the camp. Almost all the educated people were registered and marched off — away from the workers. Then the workers were registered as well. When it became dark, there was no one left in the field except for Jews and prisoners of war. Suddenly a shot rang out. A sentry had recognized a man dressed as a woman and had shot him. Then it all began. Brandishing sticks, the Germans ran toward the Jews. They searched for razors, cups, raincoats, and good boots. The crowd pushed back and forth and in the confusion threw all razors and valuables into the stream. Thus the day ended.

"The eighteenth day was dark and rainy. The prisoners of war ran over to the civilians but no longer changed into their clothes, for only they and the Jews remained in the middle of the field to face their bitter fate. The Jews gave them something to eat, and they lay down and warmed themselves together with us. It was dark, but the roar of trucks could be heard. The prisoners of war ran back to their places. The trucks pulled up to the group of educated people and took them away — supposedly to work. We now know what sort of 'work' this was.

"About twenty minutes after the trucks left we heard bursts of machine-gun fire, and in another fifteen minutes the same trucks returned for more people. In this fashion they took away all the educated people. At dawn an officer arrived and selected 200 workers. He sent them off on foot to 'work' and announced: 'All Jews will be taken from here to a different place. It will be warm there, and there won't be any rain. You will be taken through the town. Be sure to tell your wives, relatives, and friends that you will be taken through the town tomorrow. If even one of them approaches you, both you and they will be shot.'

"They began to lead out the prisoners of war. The women came and brought food. Many wept, for their husbands, relatives, and children were no longer among the living. They were told that we would be taken through the town on the next day, but that no one should approach us or else they would be shot. They left crying. The last day in the Drozdy camp came to an end.

"On the nineteenth night the prisoners of war were taken from camp. Red-Army soldiers were hauled away all night under the glare of headlights. There was no longer anyone left in the field except the Jews. In the morning a Gestapo unit arrived; they were all wearing red silk neckties. The simple Jewish people were assembled in formation and led away. Sentries stood all along the road leading to the prison. When the people approached the prison, the Gestapo men opened the gates and let them in. And the gates closed."

The workers spent a few days in the prison, after which some of them were released and sent to work, while others were loaded onto trucks, taken outside of town, and shot.

The German authorities ordered that the entire Jewish population be registered by the *Judenrat*, a Jewish committee which had been specially created for this purpose. The order warned that any unregistered Jews would be denied apartments during resettlement. During the registration, the first name, surname, age, and address were taken down.

The Jewish committee was created in the following fashion: members of the Gestapo seized ten men on the streets, took them to government headquarters, and ordered them to carry out all instructions of the German authorities. The slightest violation was punishable by shooting. Ilya Mushkin, the former vice-director of the Ministry of Commercial Trade, was appointed chairman of the committee.

By July 15, 1941, the registration of the Jews was completed. From that date on Jews were ordered to wear yellow tags on their chests and backs beginning on that date. The tags had to be ten centimeters wide. Instructions were issued forbidding Jews to walk down the main streets. Jews were also forbidden to greet non-Jewish friends. After that the German authorities announced that a ghetto would be formed.

On top of all this, the Jews were required to pay an indemnity in gold, silver, Soviet currency, and certain bonds.

Crowds of Jews left the places where they had lived for so long, leaving behind their apartments, furniture and possessions, and taking with them only the most essential items. There was no form of transportation, and they had to carry everything on their shoulders. 1½ square meters (about 12 square feet) were allotted per person, not including children.

The resettlement did not take place without harassment: a strictly defined area was set aside for the ghetto, but as soon as people moved into an apartment, a new order would be issued including certain streets and excluding others.

During the two weeks extending from July 15 till July 31, 1941, Jews were tormented and shifted from place to place. By August 1,

1941, the resettlement of the Jews had been completed. In instances of mixed marriages the children remained with the father. If the father was a Jew, the children left with him for the ghetto, and the mother remained in town. If the father was not a Jew, the children lived with him in town, and the mother had to leave for the ghetto. It is known that Professor Afonsky, a Russian married to a Jew, bought his wife's release from the ghetto from the German commandant's office. She was permitted to live with her husband and daughter in town (outside the ghetto) on condition that she be sterilized. The operation was conducted by Professor Klumbov under German observation. This case was unique. Professor Afonsky had a large supply of gold coins plus the money he had received from selling his property, and he gave it all to the Germans as ransom.

The following streets were included in the ghetto: Khlebnaya, Nemigsky Lane, part of the Respublikanskaya Street, part of Ostrovskaya Street, Yubileyny Square, part of Obuvnaya Street, Shornaya Street, Kollektivnaya Street, the Second Apansky Lane, Fruktovaya Street, Tekhnicheskaya Street, Tankovaya Street, Krymskaya Street, and others. These streets were isolated from the center of town and from commercial and industrial concerns. On the other hand, the cemetery was included in the territory of the ghetto.

The ghetto was surrounded by five strands of barbed wire, and anyone who went beyond the wire was shot. Jews were forbidden under penalty of death to engage in trade or buy food. The Jews received a new companion in their lives: the firing squad.

The family of the laborer Cherno consisted of six persons — two adults and four small children. Cherno's wife Anna could not endure the suffering of her hungry children and she went to the Russian area to ask her friends for help. On the way back, she was stopped by the police who confiscated everything she was carrying, took her to prison, and shot her. The same fate befell Rozalia Taubkin, who had crossed the wire to meet her Russian relatives.

As soon as the ghetto was surrounded with barbed wire, robberies and violence began to occur. At all hours of the day and night Germans drove or walked up to the ghetto and entered Jewish apartments, where they felt themselves to be unlimited masters; they robbed and took everything from the apartments that caught their eye. The robberies were accompanied by beatings, harassments, and — not infrequently — murder.

The Germans attacked Jewish houses at night and killed their inhabitants. The murders were committed in cruel fashion — by poking out eyes, cutting out tongues, severing ears, crushing skulls, and so forth.

The area of Shevchenko Street, Zelenaya Street, Zaslavskaya Street, Sanitarnaya Street, Shornaya Street, and Kollektornaya Street was particularly afflicted. The Jews defended their apartments by making double doors and iron latches. When the bandits knocked at their houses, they refused to open the door. They arranged watches and self-defense groups, but even so they had to surrender to the strength of arms. Doors and windows were smashed, and the bandits burst into the apartments. The Germans broke into the apartment of Dr. Esfir Margolin, beat everyone, and killed two persons. Dr. Margolin was shot four times, and her wounds were quite serious. The Kaplan family, who lived on Zaslavsky Lane, was tortured for a long time: the Germans poked out the eyes of the father, cut off the ears of the daughter, crushed the skulls of the other members of the family, and finally shot everyone. . . .

A camp was set up on Shirokaya Street. Russian prisoners of war and Jews were forced to do heavy, exhausting work there. The Jews were made to carry gravel and sand from one area to another and then back to the original site. Digging was done without shovels. Workers were given 300 grams (⅔ of a pound) of bread once a day and a murky water called soup.

Gorodetsky, a former member of the White Army, a thief, rapist, and murderer, was simultaneously appointed commandant and master of the camp.

Professor Siterman, a doctor of medicine, was one of the most respected scientists of the Byelorussian Soviet Socialist Republic. He had not managed to evacuate from Minsk, and Gorodetsky and the Gestapo began to torment him as soon as they learned of his whereabouts. Gorodetsky burst into his apartment, took everything that caught his eye, and beat the old man. Gestapo men came to his apartment, took him away, and forced him to perform heavy filthy work — cleaning cesspools and toilets. In October of 1941 Professor Siterman was placed in a toilet and photographed with a shovel in his hands. Once he was forced to crawl on all fours in the middle of the ghetto square; he was photographed with a soccer ball on his back. A few days later a car came for him and took him away. His relatives were told it was for a "consultation." He was not seen again.

148

All men in the ghetto were registered in the labor office. Subsequently this office was given the title of "labor exchange." From there people were sent to do heavy work in the military units and in the camp on Shirokaya Street.

On August 14 a rumor spread through the ghetto: "They're picking up the men." The ghetto had been surrounded, and many men were loaded on trucks and taken away. The Gestapo explained that these people were being taken to work at military sites. That which the Gestapo called "work" is called death in all other languages.

At 5:00 A.M. on August 26, 1941, a number of cars sped up to the ghetto; in five minutes they had surrounded it. They had brought Gestapo agents who burst into Jewish apartments shouting: "Männer!" (Men!). All the men were driven out onto Yubileiny Square, beaten, tormented, and then taken away.

On August 31, 1941, this dragnet was again cast out. Again the ghetto was surrounded, but on this occasion some women were arrested in addition to the men. At the same time the Jewish apartments were looted.

The people arrested on August 14, 26, and 31 were taken to prisons and shot (all in all, about 5,000).

The Germans tried to sow panic among the Jews, to shackle their thoughts and actions, to inspire in them the belief that all was lost and that there was no escape.

In August 1941, however, organized resistance forces began to emerge within the ghetto. The communists who had remained in Minsk agreed to call a party meeting for the end of August. The house at 54 Ostrovsky Street served as the meeting place. Among the communists were Weingaus, a member of the Soviet of People's Commissars of the Byelorussian Republic, Shnitman, Khaimovich, and Feldman — all employees of the Bialystok Textile Factory — and Smolyar* — an employee of the Union of Soviet Writers.

At the meeting it was decided to create an underground party organization which would pursue the following goals:

1. Put an end to the panic among the Jews.
2. Organize the systematic publication of leaflets.
3. Establish contact with communists in the Russian sector.

*H. Smolyar worked in the Bialystok Division of the Byelorussian Writers' Union until June, 1941. He now lives in Israel, where he is a researcher and writer. See note on page X.

4. Establish contact with the partisans.

5. Set up a radio receiver.

The first steps of the party organization were successful. The Germans had ordered that all valuables, gold, and silver be turned in, but the underground party organization resolved that these valuables should be sent to the partisan units. Some of the valuables were, in fact, smuggled out to the partisans.

The underground party group set about systematically producing leaflets. The leaflets were read with extreme attention and handed on. In meeting, people no longer greeted each other, but asked: "Any news today?" It seemed that the only word on everyone's lips was *Nayes* ("News"). The Jewish underground put out leaflets summarizing the latest Moscow radio broadcasts which had been received on the secret receiver. Weingaus was appointed editor, and the leaflets were copied and passed from house to house.

In September, 1941, one of the leaders of the party group in the ghetto, Kirkoeshto, was killed. His place was taken by Misha Gebelev, an instructor from the Kaganovich Regional Committee in Minsk. It was Gebelev's task to establish contact with the communists of the Russian sector. The question was raised as to calling a joint party conference.

The Hitlerites attempted to sow national enmity, and Gebelev, a Jew, went to the Russian sector at the risk of his own life to save Russian communists and hide his comrades in the apartments he located. Some of them he hid in secret apartments in the ghetto. Reserve apartments were established within the Russian sector near the ghetto; these were used both by communists from the Russian sector and from the ghetto.

In September 1941, contact was established with the partisan unit of Captain Bystrov. (This unit operated in the east.) Guides arrived, and the first group of people from the ghetto — 30 persons — was sent to join the partisans. These were, for the most part, communists and people with a military background: Shnitman, Khaimovich, Gordon, Lenya Okun, and others.

The underground party organization resolved to organize systematic assistance in the form of warm clothing, soap, salt, etc. for the partisan units.

The underground group viewed the Jewish Committee (the *Judenrat*) as part and parcel of the policies of the invaders. Nevertheless, contact was established with those elements within the *Judenrat* which were prepared to render assistance to the partisan movement and in the evacuation of Jewish units to the partisans. First of all, contact was established with Mushkin, chairman of the *Judenrat*. Later Serebryansky and Rudintser, chairman of the production sector, were asked to help in rendering aid to the partisan movement. Both these men turned over to the leaders of the party group items intended for the partisan group: footwear, leather, underwear, warm clothing, typewriters, office supplies, soap, medicine, and sometimes even food and salt.

The Fascist thugs roamed around the ghetto harassing every Jewish apartment. In spite of this, however, Jewish women — even the older ones — helped the partisans by sewing underwear and camouflage suits, and by knitting socks. The workshops of the ghetto were run by Goldin and functioned primarily to support the partisans.

At that time the communists of the ghetto and the communists of the Russian sector decided to call a joint meeting to create a united party organization in Minsk.

In September 1941, a preliminary meeting took place, but the general conference could not be called at that time.

The twenty-fourth anniversary of the October Revolution was approaching. Beginning in November, the rumor spread through the ghetto that there would be a pogrom in the Minsk ghetto on the anniversary of the October Revolution. Gorodetsky came to the ghetto and selected the skilled workers to be sent together with their families to the camp on Shirokaya Street during the pogrom. Certain employees of the *Judenrat* were also sent there. The following is a brief description of this camp; it was provided by Comrade Grechanik:

"No one was allowed to leave the camp on Shirokaya Street to go home. The camp contained prisoners of war. The Germans sent mainly Russians, Byelorussians, and Poles there who had violated some rule of the German authorities. Everyone was ordered to sew red patches onto their clothes. In the same camp the Germans appointed a Western Ukrainian as head of the camp. He beat everyone indiscriminately — Jews and Russians. . . . Many were ill, and new persons were constantly being brought in. In the camp on Shirokaya Street people were used up quickly."

On that anxious night the Jews did not sleep, they were waiting for morning. As soon as it began to get light, large covered trucks drove into the ghetto. The Gestapo agents were armed with whips, revolvers, and light machine guns. On November 7, 1941, the Germans carried out a massacre — and not just of Jews. Gallows were thrown up all over Minsk — on the streets, in the parks, in the bazaars, and on the outskirts of town. On that day approximately 100 persons were hanged in various part of town. From their necks dangled plywood signs with the words "Partisan," "For collaborating with the partisans," "Communist," etc. Naturally the most terrible blow was aimed at the ghetto. The people were ordered to put on their best clothing and to dress their children as if for a holiday. Even small babies had to be taken. All the people were lined up in columns of four and taken under guard to Novokrasnaya Street. A truck was drawn up next to the park and used as a platform from which to photograph one of the columns. The machine gun began to bark, and the column was massacred. Trucks drove up to Novomyasnitskaya Street and picked up people. The workers taken from the ghetto had learned that morning that a pogrom had begun. At noon the workers entreated for and received passes for their families and ran to the ghetto. Very many of them found no one at home. It was apparent that they had been taken straight from their beds. The workers rushed to the trucks onto which people were being loaded. Some of them did not find their families and asked if they could go with these trucks in the hope that they would find them.

An officer replied that those who had been taken were no longer alive. He said: "You can go if you like, but I don't know if you will return." Many workers saved women, girls, children, acquaintances, and strangers by passing them off as members of their own families.

The trucks went back and forth all day. About twelve or thirteen thousands Jews were taken to Tuchinki that day and kept there two days. The groans and crying of thirsty children crowded upon each other carried for long distances. On the third day the machine guns were used. Thousands of bodies were laid out in trenches which had been prepared in advance. Of thousands who were taken to the execution site two or three returned.

A ten-year-old boy returned to the ghetto. He said: "At 7:00 P.M. very many women and children were brought in trucks to the barracks. They were kept there for three days. They were not given anything to eat or drink. Some of them, the small babies and the old folks, died in those three days. When they took us from there, I was with my mother's sister. There were no other trucks behind us, and my aunt picked up the tarpaulin and said: 'Jump, sweetie, maybe you'll survive.' I jumped as the truck drove down the road. I lay on the ground for a while, and then I came here."

The next story is that of a woman who had been led out into a field to be shot. She came to the ghetto, her body swollen and bloody. She was naked and wounded in the arm. She had seen long wide trenches, alongside which Germans and policemen were forcing people to undress. As soon as the small children got down from the trucks, the policemen took them from their parents and broke their spinal columns against their knees. Small babies were thrown in the air and shot at or caught on bayonets and then flung in the trenches. Naked people were lined up next to the pit and shot with machine guns. Those who refused to undress were murdered in their clothing. If their clothing was of good quality, they were undressed after being killed. One woman was forced to undress and stand beside a pit. They wounded her in the arm; she fell and was covered up by bodies. That night, when things quieted down, she crawled from the pit and came to the ghetto.

The following streets were encompassed by the pogrom: Ostrovsky Street, Respublikanskaya Street, Shevchenko Street, Nemig Street, Khlebnnaya Street, and others.

By the evening of November 7, the pogrom began to die down.

After this pogrom the Germans began to create "specialists' sectors"; they called all the skilled craftsmen "specialists."

The labor exchange asked the German managers for lists of their Jewish workers. The managers submitted the lists, and the exchange began to issue special cards to the "specialists."

Unskilled laborers were not issued cards. All non-specialists were ordered to move immediately to a different sector. A new resettlement began, and everyone knew what that meant. The women began to look for specialists, and the young girls began to marry old men. Many of those who were denied "specialists' cards" and were thus condemned to die lost their minds.

When the first resettlement of non-specialists was concluded, the Germans began to issue address tablets to be affixed to the doors. These tablets were attached to the outside door and indicated who lived in the apartment, who worked, and who was whose dependent. When all this was accomplished, the Germans ordered that each resident "specialist" go to the *Judenrat* for the number of his house and sew it on his chest, under a yellow badge, and also on his back. This number was written on white canvas and stamped.

153

The Germans warned that if any of the residents of a house failed to wear the number, all residents of that house would be shot.

The "specialists" from the camp on Shirokaya Street and the employees of the *Judenrat* returned on November 8, 1941.

Part of Nemig Street, Ostrovsky Street and certain other streets were declared by the Gestapo to be part of the Russian sector. The territory of the ghetto was diminished. Within the ghetto, life proceeded — hungry and difficult — but even this life was snuffed out for many.

German Jews began to arrive by the thousands. They were dressed in strange fashion — in feather capes with hoods. Some wore pink clothing, others wore navy-blue, and still others wore light blue. All this was made from artificial leather, and each person wore a six-pointed star sewn to the right side of his chest. They spoke only German. Gestapo agents arrived and forced everyone to leave Respublikanskaya Street, Obuvnaya Street, Sukhaya Street, and Opanasskaya Street to make room for the newcomers. The entire area was surrounded by barbed-wire fences, and a warning was issued that anyone who approached the wire would be shot. During the first days sentries were placed to guard the fence.

When the people approached the barbed wire surrounding the German Jews, the newcomers proved eager to talk. It was learned that they were Jews from Hamburg, Berlin and Frankfurt. Approximately 19,000 people arrived during the period of the Minsk ghetto's existence. All their property had been confiscated, and they had been told that they would be sent to America. Their destination, however, turned out to be a ghetto in Minsk surrounded by barbed wire. They thought that Russian Jews could walk about freely and buy food, and they asked for bread. The Gestapo found "work" for the German Jews. Every night they would come to the ghetto and kill seventy of eighty of them. The Germans forced them to haul the bodies to the cemetery in baby carriages. There pits had already been dug, each of which could accommodate about three hundred bodies. When a pit was filled, it was covered with earth.

On November 20, 1941, morning had not yet arrived but the Germans and police were already walking down the streets of the ghetto: Zamkovaya Street, Podzamkovaya Street, Zelenaya Street, Sanitarnaya Street, and others. Again the people were driven from their apartments, marched in columns to the graves in Tuchinki.

Lime had already been prepared at the graves, and the people were thrown alive into the pits. There they were shot and burned.

Among the people who were seized on November 20 were good "specialists" needed by the Germans. An officer arrived at the gathering place, but the people taken from the ghetto were no longer there. The officer learned where they had been taken and went to the field outside of town where they were being murdered. It turned out that almost all his workers had been killed, but he recognized a few who were still alive and arranged to have them spared. One of them was a skilled furrier by the name of Alperovich; another was the barber Levin, who shaved all the officers. The destruction "boss" released only the barber and Alperovich. In a cruel mockery, he permitted the barber to take either his wife or his daughter. Levin selected his daughter. The officer told them not to tell anyone of what they had seen. When they were brought to the factory, their faces were whiter than snow and they could not speak. Alperovich was sick for a long time after this.

Seven thousand Jews perished on November 20. The people began to hide themselves in specially prepared cellars, pits, concealed rooms, but the raids of the Hitlerites were too sudden for this to save them. The Germans explained away the pogrom of November 20 by saying that the "plan had not been fulfilled" on November 7 — that is, that a smaller number of Jews had been destroyed than was demanded by the authorities.

Pogroms and the deaths of certain underground leaders did not weaken the resistance movement. During the pogrom of November 20, 1941, Weingaus perished. He was replaced in the party group by Pruslin (Bruskind), propaganda secretary of the Voroshilov Regional Committee in Minsk. At the end of November the communists called a general party conference, which was chaired by "Slavek." Gebelev was selected as representative of the ghetto party group. This meeting marked the beginning of the smuggling of people to the partisan units. The general party conference resolved to organize the party organization in cells of ten. Each cell was to be headed by a secretary. Cells were formed only on the basis of acquaintanceships and personal recommendations. All secretaries were in contact with the central leader of the zone. Altogether there were four zones, of which the ghetto formed one. At the party conference an underground party committee was created. "Slavek" was elected secretary.

The ghetto representative of the Party Central Committee was Smolyar, who lived in the ghetto under the name of Smolyarevich; his code name was Skromny. The boiler room of the Jewish hospital where Smolyar worked was headquarters. Communists went there to discuss and decide the most important questions.

The cells were headed by Naum Feldman, Zyama Okun, Nadya Schusser, Maizels, Rubenik, and others. Emma Rodov was selected to maintain contact with the communists of the Russian sector.

The cells were assigned the following tasks:

1. The selection of candidates from among the communists and persons with military training to be sent to join the partisan units.

2. Collecting weapons.

3. Material assistance in the form of warm clothing to be sent to the partisan units.

4. The collection and shipment of medicine.

5. The creation of a fund to aid needy communists.

The winter was a difficult period for residents of the ghetto, since they all suffered from hunger and cold. Jews working in the Russian sector were in contact with the Russian population and thus were not in such dire need as those Jews who worked behind the barbed wire and who were hungry and needy.

Thanks to the connections of many members of the *Judenrat*, it was possible to place people in the city in such a fashion as to use their work in the German concerns to aid in the struggle with the invaders.

Groups of young people went to the factories involved in the production of weapons so as to have the opportunity to smuggle out arms. Women worked in places where it was possible to obtain underwear and warm clothing to send to the partisan units. Shipments of military supplies and clothing were usually sent from the Openheim apartment at 16 Respublikanskaya Street. Gathering took place at the bazaars. Since the units moved from place to place, contact was lost with some of the partisan units in February of 1942. Information was received that the unit of Nichiporovich was active in the direction of Dukor. A group of people, among them Dr. Margolin and Skoblo (one of the first Stakhanovites of the Byelorussian Republic), set out to find this unit. The group was armed with four rifles and four grenades.

The operation was not successful. The people were surrounded by the Gestapo and some of them — including Skoblo — perished. The rest returned to the ghetto with frostbitten hands and feet and spent a long time in the hospital as well as attempting to reestablish contact.

The underground group searched for and purchased weapons. Naum Feldman was in charge of this operation. The party committee made plans to smuggle people out of the ghetto who were unable to join the partisan units. At first it was believed in the ghetto that it was sufficient to take people beyond the barbed wire, settle them in the Russian areas, and ensure their security.

The underground party committee searched for places to send old men, women, and children. Nina Liss was selected to perform this task, and she set out for Western Byelorussia to find villages and farms near the railroads and highways.

In February 1942, the Germans arrested Mushkin, the chairman of the *Judenrat*. His role had been a difficult one: on the one hand, he had participated in the struggle with the invaders and materially aided the partisan units; at the same time he had had to preserve an appearance of normal relations with the German authorities and pretend to carry out all their directives and orders. He was forced to conceal his activities even from certain members of the *Judenrat* such as Rosenblat and Epstein.

A provocateur betrayed Mushkin. Mushkin was tortured for a long time in prison, but he did not name his friends and silently endured his suffering. Only after a month of torture following his arrest was he taken from the prison and shot.

It was winter of 1942. . . . It brought hunger, cold, and disease with it. The pitiful existence of the people could hardly be called living. The crying of children and the groans of the ill filled the homes. People ate the refuse from German kitchens. A command dish of the Jewish population was potato skins cooked as pancakes and baked in a pudding.

Diseases appeared: furunculosis, dystrophy, scurvy, typhoid, and typhus. Illnesses had to be concealed from the authorities since the Germans demanded a daily list of new patients in the hospital. The Germans were wary of infectious diseases, and the Jews knew that as soon as the German authorities learned of typhoid, a pogrom would be inevitable. The Germans never found out about such diseases in the ghetto. Nevertheless, a pogrom of a new, horrifying magnitude was unleashed on the Jews.

On March 2, 1942, cars with Gestapo agents drove up to the ghetto; in one of them was *Obersturmführer* Schmidt, who was totally drunk. This was a bad sign, and the Jews were worried. Columns of workers, however, set out as usual for work. The Gestapo agents went to the office of the labor exchange and began to drink. There was no shortage of vodka and expensive wines; everything had been brought to the ghetto in a truck. Not all of those who had arrived were able to squeeze into the apartment, and some of them remained in the street and on the square. They called for the policeman of the fifth sector, Richter, who was in charge of the ghetto. The Gestapo agents began to drink and stuff themselves on the street, after which they set about "work." They burst into apartments with whips and revolvers and drove the people into the yard of the wallpaper factory on Shpalernaya Street. Crowds of people — women, children, the elderly — stood and waited for their turn to die. In two houses along Tekhnicheskaya Street the executioners did not find the residents, since they had hidden in concealed apartments. The Germans put these houses to the torch and burned the people alive. When columns of workers began to return they were met by a member of the Gestapo. These workers, along with the crowd awaiting death in the yard of the wallpaper factory, were led to the railroad, loaded on cars, and sent to Dzerzhinsk.

There everyone was shot. Many attempted to escape, but the murderers' bullets caught up with them. 5,000 people were killed there.

Gestapo agents surrounded the column of workers from the prison. The column was headed by Levin, a former artist and children's writer who wrote under the penname "Bersarin."

Levin demanded that the column be released, arguing that it consisted only of specialists. He himself was released, but he insisted on the release of everyone. He was beaten with rifle butts and driven off. Levin had the lid of a tin can in his hands, and he used it to attack the Germans. He was shot on the spot.

In the evening, when the bloody work was coming to an end, *Obersturmführer* Schmidt shouted in unaccented Russian: "Today was more successful and perfect, more successful and perfect than ever." Whip in hand and surrounded by Germans and policemen, he was completely drunk. For having organized the pogrom so well he received an award and a promotion.

As in the first pogroms, the orphanage and the nursing home were destroyed. Some of the employees of the *Judenrat* were killed.

The column of children of all ages from the smallest to 13-14 years of age presented a terrible sight. It was led by the director of the orphanage. The children shouted: "Why? Our people will come and take vengeance for our blood and the blood of our fathers and mothers!" They were whipped on the heads and went on, covered with bruises, their faces swollen from beatings, their clothes in rags. If a child fell behind, he was shot. The entire street was littered with the bodies of children.

A female employee of the Orphanage Amsterdam, committed suicide by opening a vein.

The population of the ghetto began to shrink. The Germans carried out a new resettlement and shifted Jews from one apartment to another, from one sector to another. The territory of the ghetto grew smaller, and the ring around it tightened.

The pogroms carried out by the Gestapo did not stop the work of the communists. Within the ghetto, Jews continued to leave to join the partisan units; every day more and more people left. The Gestapo learned of this and responded to each departure with acts of bloody terror.

In those instances when the Gestapo tracked down a person connected with an underground organization, not only he was held responsible, but so also was the entire column in which he worked or all the residents of the building in which he lived. The house would be surrounded at night, and the people led out to be shot.

At the end of March 1942, a new wave of night pogroms began. The residents of the ghetto listened in horror to the bursts of machine-gun fire and the screams and groans of those being shot. At night the sounds of people attempting to escape the bullets could be heard.

Pogroms occurred on the night of March 31, April 3, April 15, and April 23. During the pogrom of March 31, 1942, Nina Liss died. She had just returned to Minsk the previous day, having carried out her assignment in Western Byelorussia.

A traitor handed over to the Gestapo the lists of those working in the underground party committee. The list contained addresses. Nina lived at 18 Kollektornaya Street. When the bandits surrounded the house in the night, they knocked and shouted: "Nina, open up!"

The Gestapo demanded that Gebelev, Smolyar, Feldman, and Okun be handed over. Otherwise they threatened to shoot all employees of the *Judenrat*. Ioffe, who had just been reappointed chairman of the *Judenrat* [after Mushkin's death], knew that the

Germans would carry out this threat. Nevertheless, Ioffe refused to submit to this demand.

Gebelev conspired to bear three different names and thus confuse the Gestapo. There were many Feldmans in the ghetto, and three of them were sent to prison — never to return. Okun was arrested after a period of time.

Smolyar (Smolyarevich), who headed the underground party organization, could not be caught. The Gestapo demanded that he be handed over, and Ioffe tried a trick: he filled out a blank passport in the name of Yefim Smolyarevich, smeared it with blood, and went to the Gestapo, where he reported that the passport had been taken from the clothing of a dead man found in a house where a pogrom had taken place the previous night. The Gestapo accepted this version and was satisfied.

Smolyarevich, Gebelev, and Feldman lived on and continued to fight the enemy.

Feldman's task was to supply weapons. Groups of people sent to the partisan units were armed with rifles, pistols, and grenades. Aside from obtaining weapons, the efforts of the underground were directed toward obtaining a printing press and sending it to the partisan units. Two printing presses were sent to the partisan units, and a third was handed over to the party committee in the city.

A major role in shipping the printing presses to the partisan units was played by Vilik Rubezhin. This boy had lost his parents, and the war found him in a Pioneer camp near Minsk. In the face of enormous risk he pulled a sled with the type covered with a rag through the entire city.

It was Vilik who led a group of thirty Jews to the partisans. Later he himself joined the partisans in the forest and participated in many acts of sabotage and also in ambushes. He was awarded the medal of the Red Star.

The Gestapo explained the night pogroms as part of the struggle with the partisan movement. Such "aktions" also occurred in the Russian sector. An enemy had penetrated the party organization and betrayed several members of the underground party committee.

Gebelev brought ten communists from the Russian sector, gave them Jewish passports, and hid them in conspiratorial apartments.

The sudden and brief pogrom of April 23, 1942, was particularly cruel. The murderers surrounded the houses on Obuvnaya Street,

Sukhaya Street., Shornaya Street and Kollektornaya Street. The pogrom began at 17:00 and ended at 23:00. 500 people perished.

Another night pogrom which was horrifying in its cruelty was that conducted by the Germans and the police in May, 1942. They surrounded two four-story, heavily settled buildings on Zavalnaya Street, set them on fire on all sides, and burned the people alive. Several hundred people perished in the flame.

The German thugs were rotated; some arrived, and others left, but each of them occupied himself with the destruction of Jews under the pretext of restoring order.

Shortly before his departure from the ghetto, Richter decided to check that the Jews were going to work as ordered. He stopped the first three persons he met on the street, took them to the labor exchange, ordered that the police strip the unfortunate people, beat them half to death, and took one of them out into the square, where he tied him to a post and shot him. A piece of cardboard hung from the chest of the murdered man; it read: "Anyone who dares not to report for work will receive this very same treatment."

Richter's replacement was Hettenbach, who issued an order transforming the ghetto into a camp. All buildings in the ghetto were renumbered, and the residents had to wear their house numbers in addition to the yellow patches. Hettenbach personally shot hundreds of Jews for violating this order.

People were shot in the ghetto for no reason at all. In May three workers were brought from the Trostinets camp. They did not feel well and asked to be examined by a doctor. Hettenbach took them to the cemetery and shot them. There were many analogous cases.

Work at the October Factory was considered the most advantageous. Aside from 200 grams of bread, the workers received a mug of hot water and some thin soup for dinner.

In May 1942, thirteen women were fired from the factory. They decided to march in a column to the factory to find out why they had been let go. They were not permitted to speak to the head of the factory but were taken to the prison. They were tortured and kept in the prison for two weeks; then they were taken under heavy guard to the ghetto square opposite the *Judenrat*. The residents were forced to come out of their houses, and then these unfortunate thirteen women were shot with hollow-point bullets. The Germans would not permit the bodies to be removed, and they lay on the square for two days.

In April 1942, the Gestapo ordered all Jews to appear at the square in front of the *Judenrat* precisely at 10:00 every Sunday.

These appearances at the square were always accompanied by whips and beatings. People were tense and did not know what awaited them on the 'square. Each Sunday Richter, Hettenbach, Fichtel, Menschel and others called meetings at which they made speeches, attempting to persuade the Jews not to leave the ghettos to join the partisan units and claiming there would be no more pogroms. Every Sunday they repeated the same speeches, and the Jews were forced to perform as on stage — by singing and playing instruments. Some were photographed.

On one of the Sundays the police went from house to house to check that all the Jews had gone to the *Appell* (roll call). They found fourteen men in the apartments. They were brough to the square and shown to everyone. It was announced that they would be taken to prison and would never return. These roll calls continued until June 28, 1942. After one which took place on a Sunday in June, a group of Jews were standing next to a public water faucet on Tankovaya Street. A policeman came down the Second Alpansky Lane with a woman. When they approached the barbed wire and saw the crowd standing in line for water, the policeman said to his companion: "See what a good shot I am." He shot into the crowd with his rifle, and a sixteen-year-old girl, Esther, fell to the ground. She died an hour later. Such instances were not unique.

After the Minsk party group was arrested, guides stopped appearing from the partisan units, and the connection with them was temporarily lost. The ghetto party committee discussed the matter and decided to create its own base for sending people to the partisan units. To achieve this aim, a group of twenty persons headed by Comrade Lapidus was selected. The people were to be sent by truck, but since the whole contingent could not fit in the truck at one time, it was decided to send the first group of twenty people forty-five kilometers from town and to return the truck to the fifteenth kilometer for the second group. In the second group were Feldman, Tumin, Lifschits, and others. They did not meet the truck in the agreed-upon place. The first group arrived successfully, but the second was attacked by Gestapo agents and traitors. Some of the people, among them Feldman and Tumin, returned to the ghetto, and the rest died.

At the end of 1942 the communists remaining in the ghetto resolved to reestablish the city party committee. A party meeting was called in one of the houses on Torgovaya Street. It was attended by communists from the Russian sector. After the meeting the party organization was reestablished, not on the basis of cells of ten, but on the basis of territory and work location. The party organization was formed into an independent group which was part of the Kaganovich Regional Party Committee. At that time the order was received from the Central Committee to begin smuggling people out of the partisan units on a mass basis.

With the help of the underground party committee of the ghetto a unit was formed (in the direction of Slutsk) under the command of Captain Nikitin. Ghetto Jews were sent to this unit. Prisoners of war working in the camp on Shirokaya Street, at the felt factory, and in other concerns were systematically sent to the partisan units.

While sending prisoners of war to the partisan units, Misha Gebelev was arrested at the wire. He had dedicated himself to serving the people and had known neither fear nor exhaustion in his struggle.

At the same time that prisoners of war were being smuggled out to the partisan units, sabotage was taking place at the meat-packing factory, the felt factory, and the distillery. A Jewish blacksmith who worked at the distillery regularly poisoned the alcohol destined to be sent to German soldiers at the front.

The ghetto party committee was directed by Naum Feldman, one of the earliest participants in the underground party organization, to set up partisan bases to the west of town. Feldman's path was a difficult one; he waited for two days at the ninth kilometer for a guide to lead him and his group to the intended spot.

Finally Feldman found Skachkov's unit, which was just being formed. Skachkov refused to accept Feldman's group, and Feldman decided to organize a unit himself. He sent messengers to the underground party committee, and the ghetto sent him new comrades. The group was already armed with light machine guns, rifles, pistols, and revolvers. At the end of May, Nikitin's unit took those of the unit who had weapons. The rest occupied themselves with searching for weapons. Again the ghetto party committee came to their aid. The liaison between the two groups was uninterrupted. In June 1942, an escape was organized for Semyon Grigorievich Ganzenko, a prisoner of war in the Shirokaya Street camp, and he was sent to be commander of a unit, named in honor of Comrade Budenny. Feldman was party organizer of the unit, which then joined the Stalin Brigade and became one of its military subunits. Later Ganzenko was appointed brigade commander, and Feldman became commissar of one of the brigade units.

All these escapes involved colossal difficulties. The ghetto was guarded night and day, and ambushes were arranged everywhere.

On June 27, 1942, the Gestapo issued another order: as well as the yellow badges and their house numbers, all Jews were to wear additional signs. Workers were to wear red badges and the dependents of workers and the unemployed were to wear green badges. Workers were to receive their badges at the place of employment, and dependents and the unemployed were to receive theirs in the square in front of the *Judenrat*. No one supposed that this seemingly innocent order was part of the preparations for a terrible bloodbath.

July 28, 1942, was the ghetto's blackest day.

In the morning, after the columns of workers had left the ghetto, the Gestapo and police arrived. The whole area was surrounded by an unbroken ring of patrols. Residents were driven from their apartments to the square, and large black covered trucks with gassing equipment began to pull up. During this pogrom the orphanage, the home for the disabled, and the hospital (which had been spared in the former pogroms) were destroyed by the Gestapo. The sick were shot in their beds. Among them was Kroshner, the composer and laureate. Doctors and medical personnel were formed into a separate column and led in their white gowns to the square. There they were loaded into the trucks and gassed.

Forty-eight doctors, the leading specialists of the Byelorussian Republic, perished. Among them were Professor Dvorzhets, holder of a "candidate's" degree in medicine; Associate Professor Mayzel, a "candidate" in medicine; Turvel, Kantorovich, Gurvich, Sirotkin, and others — all experienced senior doctors.

The Germans found two Jews in a hideout. One was thrown to the ground and covered with pieces of broken glass; the other was forced to stamp on the glass. Seeing that the Jew was coping badly with the task that had been forced upon him, the villains themselves crushed the glass and shot both men.

This terrible, unthinkable pogrom lasted July 28, 29, 30, and 31. The executioners drank and made merry during the short pauses.

At 13:00 on July 31, 1942, the order was issued to halt the pogrom, but the Fascist violence would not stop. The thugs continued to run from apartment to apartment, searching for conspiratorial apartments, dragging people from them, and shooting them. Approximately 25,000 people perished in this last monstrous bloodbath.

The following is a description of this pogrom by Lilya

Samoilovna Gleizer, who personally lived through every hour of it:

"It rained all night, and on the morning of July 28 it began to rain even harder. Nature seemed to be lamenting in advance for the innocent blood that was to be spilled on that day. That morning those who were able to leave marched off to work. Once they were outside the ghetto some of them hid with their Russian acquaintances or in hideouts.

"Those in the workers' columns thought that their children, who had remained in the ghetto, would not be harmed, since they had received formal guarantees to this effect. In the morning I descended into a special hideout which was separated from the other hiding spaces in our building. It was just under the stove, and the entrance was so well concealed that even the most experienced detective could not have found it.

"Through the underground walls I could hear the crying of babies and the muffled speech of adults. Past experience made it clear that such hiding places would be found if the Fascists decided to search for them.

"During pogroms persons in hiding suffer most of all because of the children. Children cannot for days on end silently endure hunger or the unbearable stuffiness and crowding. They become capricious and begin to cry and thus give away the location.

"Through the wall I could hear people preparing frantically for something unusual. Everywhere were the sounds of people hurrying, doors squeaking, babies crying, excited conversation. Soon the noise increased, and I could hear the police drive the people out of the building into the street. There were wails; people begged that the very old and the little children be allowed to stay. All these pleas and cries, however, were drowned out by the violent swearing of the police. In an hour everything fell silent. Curiosity induced me to crawl out of my hiding place into the room. Our building, in which 900 people had lived, was as silent as if everything in it had died. The street was also quiet and empty. I stood there a minute straining to hear. The hysterical cries of a woman begging for mercy reached me and then were followed by a long-drawn-out noise and several rifle shots. I scampered back to my hideout as quickly as a mouse. From there the noise and the shooting seemed to be getting louder. I realized that the police were making a second, more careful inspection, and that those who were caught were being killed on the spot.

"In a few minutes steps reverberated on the stairs of our building. Dishes crashed, rifle shots rang out, and I could hear the brief sharp crunch of doors being broken and the guffaws of policemen. Several minutes passed, and the noise began to die down. The "bobbies," as the police were usually called, had left. Several more rifle shots rang out in the building, and then everything fell silent as the grave.

"Silence ensued, and I could hear only infrequent cries from nearby hiding spots. My curiosity overcame my fear, and I again crawled out of my hideout. Suddenly I heard a noise in the neighboring apartment. After standing a minute and listening to it, I realized that its source was a woman who had lost her mind when her husband was shot before her very eyes. This was during the first days of the ghetto. Listening for the slightest noise, I tiptoed like a cat to the doors of her apartment, opened the door slightly, and saw her; she was carrying her baby about the room in her arms. By sheer chance the police had not noticed her. "She must be fated to live," I thought. She did not notice me, but kept asking for something to eat, addressing empty space. When I saw this mad woman with her baby in her arms, I burst into sobs, and I felt an immeasurable pity for her. I recalled that in the cupboard I had a crust of half-wooden bread that the Germans gave to Jews and prisoners of war. I immediately rushed to the cupboard, brought the bread, and used it to lure the mad woman into my hiding place so as to save her. We had barely crawled in when a knocking was heard at the outside door and we heard the voice of the Hitlerites: "Aufmachen!" (Open up!) Even though the door was not locked, they shouted furiously for it to be opened. In a few minutes we heard the blows of rifle butts. I crawled farther into the hole and leaned against the earthen wall, trembling with fear. We heard the Germans burst into the apartment and shoot at the walls, ceiling, and floor. These were Germans selected to find hiding places, and they were particularly brutal. The Hitlerites shouted and swore furiously, but I could tell from their garbled speech and swearing that they were drunk.

"The mad woman's baby was frightened by the shooting and began to cry loudly.

"The mother clapped her hand over its mouth, but the cry had been heard by the Hitlerites. They stood silently for a moment and then began to rip up the floor above our hiding place, swearing violently.

"'We're doomed,' I thought. When they had ripped up the

boards next to the stove, the Hitlerites threw several hand grenades into the area. The explosion revealed neighboring hiding places, since the entire earthen layer which served as our ceiling collapsed. They began to shoot mercilessly into the hiding places. The wails of women and children begging for mercy did not affect the Hitlerites. They threw several more hand grenades into the openings of the cellars, from which could be heard the groans of the wounded and pleas for mercy. These explosions again shook everything around and revealed my hiding place. For a moment the groans and wails stopped. I had been deafened by the explosions, but I soon again began to hear the growls and shouts of the Fascists: "Herausgehen!" (Come on out!) The only response, however, were the heartrending screams of the wounded. Having fruitlessly repeated their order, the Germans descended into our cellar and illuminated with flashlights the semidarkness from which issued the wails and groans of the dying. I pressed myself against the earthen wall of the cellar and held my breath when I saw the rays of light from the flashlights. The Germans did not discover me, since I was behind a bend. They shouted "Herausgehen!" several more times, finished off the dying with daggers, and crawled back upstairs. Drunk with the madness of destruction, the Hitlerites began to break the dishes, furniture, and windows. Then they burst into other hiding places in our building, and the same horror repeated itself. In a few hours everything fell silent. The silence was broken from time to time by groans from nearby hiding spots. In the darkness, alone among the dead, I was overcome by horror and hurriedly crawled toward the door which had been ripped open by the grenade explosions. A faint light was coming from there and lighting the cellar. At the very exit of the hiding place I came upon the prone body of the mad woman whom I had attempted to save. Her body was cut all over by grenade fragments, and she had evidently died instantly. Next to her lay the tiny body of her dead baby; its mouth and eyes were open.

"I crawled out into my room, which was littered with smashed dishes and broken furniture. The floor and remaining things were covered with a thick layer of lime and also by feathers and down from feather blankets and pillows. The windows had been knocked out, frames and all, and there were holes made by grenade fragments in the ceiling and walls. My head began to spin. I covered my face with my hands and almost fell on the remnants of the shattered door, but a thirst for life returned me to consciousness. When

I regained my senses, I rushed up to the attic. From there I could see the pogrom continue in other houses on our street. I could hear the constant random roar of grenades exploding and burst of machine-gun fire. The bloody corpses of women and children littered the street. The Hitlerites were dragging all sorts of bundles and other objects from the buildings, loading them on carts, and hauling them away. This, however, was not the pogrom itself, but only the beginning of the pogrom."

At noon everyone left within the bounds of the ghetto was herded into Yubileiny Square. In the square enormous tables were decorated as if for a holiday. They were heaped with all sorts of delicacies and wines. At the tables sat the directors of the most fantastic slaughter in world history.

In the center sat Richter, the head of the ghetto, who had been rewarded by Hitler with the Iron Cross. Next to him were members of the SS and one of the chiefs of the ghetto, Rade, an officer with wide cheek bones. There too was the chief of police in Minsk, Wentske. Not far from this devilish throne stood a specially constructed speaker's platform. The Fascists forced Ioffe, the composer who had been a member of the Jewish ghetto committee, to speak from this platform. Deceived by Richter, Ioffe began to calm the frantic crowd, saying that today the Germans would only conduct a registration and exchange identity badges. He had hardly finished talking when covered trucks with gassing equipment drove into the square from all directions. Ioffe immediately realized what this meant and shouted "gassing trucks"; the terrible phrase passed like lightning through the frantic crowd:

"Comrades! I was deceived. They're going to kill you. This is a pogrom!"

The insane crowd scattered, seeking salvation from the terrible death. Confusion reigned, people rushed back and forth, and an infinity of six-pointed stars flashed by. The Fascists, who had already surrounded the square, opened a steady stream of fire on the defenseless people. Nevertheless, the people continued to push forward. Finally the unarmed Jews met in hand-to-hand battle with the Fascists, who were armed to the teeth. Many of the Fascists paid a high price to control the crowd. The entire square was littered with bodies and reddened with blood. The Germans lined up endless numbers of women and elderly before the gassing trucks; the shooting had suppressed the rebellion. The children were separated from the adults and made to kneel with their hands raised. Small children, exhausted and weak, began to cry, and their small arms immediately grew tired and fell. For this they were slaughtered with knives or their spines were broken. Sometimes a Fascist would lift a child above his head and throw him with all his might against the cobblestones of the pavement. The brains of the child's crushed skull sprayed in all directions from such a blow. The mothers who stood in line next to the gassing trucks either went mad when they saw this or attacked the Germans like enraged tigresses. They were killed with machine-gun bursts. A terrible fate awaited those who refused to crawl into the gassing trucks. They were dragged to the pillars where drunken toasts were accompanied by accordion music. The drunken Hettenbach, Richter, Raede, and others announced the sentence: "Cut off the nose and ears"; "Kill with fists and whips"; and so forth. These sentences were carried out right at the table either by the judges themselves, the police, the Gestapo men, or the garrison soldiers.

The actor Zorov, who had received the title "People's Artist of the Republic," rushed cursing at the Fascists when he saw the bloody spectacle. He bit, hit, and kicked until he was knocked unconscious and thrown into a gassing truck.

This continued until late evening. The square emptied, and the organizers of the massacre fell asleep at the festive tables. Only the soldiers of the Minsk garrison, the inevitable participants in violent acts in the ghetto, rushed about searching for valuables. All the children who had been forced to hold up their hands were killed in the square. The gassing trucks did not return.

That night the members of the Jewish militia who were still alive were ordered to remove the corpses and the blood from the square. By morning the order was carried out.

The morning of July 29 arrived. The day was overcast — as if in premonition of a continuation of the slaughter. From time to time the sun emerged from behind the black storm clouds and then immediately disappeared again. The ghetto was deserted.

At 10:00 A.M. German trucks appeared on Yubileiny Square, their horns honking. A group of soldiers from the Minsk garrison under the command of the chief of police, Major Wentske, set out to loot and discover new hiding places. Wentske was a German officer and executioner. Since it was about to rain, the festive tables were removed from the square and carried into the committee building. The elderly, the women, and the children discovered in hiding places were also brought there to be killed. Many hiding places were discovered on that day, and many homes were looted. Furniture and dishes were smashed in the apartments.

The Germans and police burst into the ghetto hospital, which had not been touched on the first day of the pogrom, and killed all the patients and personnel with daggers.

On August 1, after four days of slaughter, the Germans again dragged a table out onto Yubileiny Square. It was heaped with food and wines, and the same leaders sat at it.

The Gestapo agents and police were ordered to deliver up the last inhabitants of the ghetto who were still in hiding.

On this last day of the pogrom the Fascists exceeded all boundaries of human imagination. Before the eyes of the mothers, who were either fainting or losing their wits, the drunken Germans and policemen shamelessly raped the girls before each other or others. They cut out the sexual organs with daggers, forced living and dead bodies to assume the most disgusting poses, cut off noses, breasts, and ears.

Mothers rushed at the Fascists in a rage and fell dead with crushed skulls.

Feeble old people were killed by blows on the head with rubber truncheons or were beaten to death with leather whips. The hysterical cries, wails, and curses did not cease all day; the dozens of accordions could not drown them out.

At 3:00 P.M. everything was over. In an hour Richter's assistants had left the ghetto.

After the massacre was over, the Gestapo sent out an order to the factories where the Jewish workers had been kept during the four-day pogrom directing that they return to their homes in the ghetto.

In the evening columns of workers set out for the ghetto. All walked slowly and in total silence, their eyes directed at the ground. In this fashion they reached the check point at the ghetto gates. Who would meet them at the gate?

Normally the entire population incapable of working came out to meet the workers' columns returning from hard labor. Mothers, wives, elderly fathers, children, sisters, and brothers rejoiced to see each other alive after a fourteen-hour separation. This time, however, no one stood at the gates.

Only at the check point did a German sentry run out of his booth and loudly and firmly click his metal-tipped boots as he saluted the officer who walked at the head of the guards. The officer touched his cap and ordered the soldier to open the gates. The column entered the silent ghetto. Pieces of broken furniture, shreds of paper and books, fragments of dishes lay all over the streets. Feathers from feather quilts and pillows covered the pavement and sidewalks as well as the smashed household utensils.

Cupboards, buffets, and tables protruded from broken windows, so far it was a miracle that they had not fallen out. Everywhere, all around, lay the bodies of those whom the returning workers had hoped to see. They lay in enormous pools of blood. The German officer who was leading the column and who evidently had never seen such a sight suddenly screamed and went into a hysterical fit on the blood-soaked pavement. The column came to a shuddering halt. The women sobbed in grief; the men groaned, wrung their hands, and tore their hair. Had the world seen anything more terrible than this since its creation?

The people rushed insanely to their apartments, hoping to find their relatives safe in their hiding places. But the hiding places in the stoves, under the floor, between the walls had been ripped open by grenades. There the workers found the remains of their families who had been ripped to pieces by the grenades. The majority, however, did not find even remains. Suffocated in these machines of death, robbed, and stripped, the people had been taken in the gassing vans to Trostinets and Tuchinki and dumped into pits which had been prepared in advance. Even the horrible pogrom of March 2 pales before the July massacre. Of 75,000 Jews only 8,794 people were left by August 1, 1942.

The German Jews also suffered in this pogrom; 3,000 of them were asphyxiated in the gassing trucks. They had been told to gather their things — supposedly to go to work. Hettenbach and the *Obersturmführer* made a speech to them.

The German henchmen changed; Richter left and was replaced by Hettenbach, then by Fichtel and Menschel. Each such arrival and departure cost new victims.

In January 1943, the police discovered the bodies of two Germans in the Russian sector. The Gestapo responded with terrible reprisals. At 3:00 P.M. on February 1, 1943, gassing trucks entered the ghetto. They brought Gestapo agents headed by the bloody *Obersturmführer* Miller.

People were driven from their homes, seized on the street, and stuffed into gassing trucks. 401 people were missing in the ghetto on the next day.

Soon fifty-three Jewish "specialists" from Slutsk were brought to the ghetto. They told of the horrors of the gradual liquidation of the Slutsk ghetto. In their stories they frequently mentioned the name Ribbe — an incredibly cruel member of the Gestapo.

In the first half of February, 1943, two previously unknown Germans appeared on the streets of the ghetto. On their clothing they wore insignias distinguishing them as members of the Gestapo. They stopped a woman, searched her, took the eight marks they found on her person, and went on. They then came upon another woman with a four-year-old son. They asked her why she was not working. (One of them spoke Russian; it turned out that he was the translator, Michelson.) The woman presented a certificate of illness, but they both fell upon her, beat her, and dragged both her and her son to the graveyard, where they shot them. Returning from the graveyard, they met a boy of about fifteen years who was carrying two logs in his arms. "Where did the wood come from?" they asked. "My boss gave it to me at work," the boy replied. They led him to the cemetery and shot him there. In the evening, when the people returned from work, the Jews from Slutsk recognized their executioner. "They are Ribbe and his translator Michelson," they said. "If he is here, that means that the ghetto is to be totally liquidated."

It was indeed *Hauptscharführer* Ribbe and his assistant and translator Michelson. Ribbe had carried off many pogroms and had received many awards.

After Ribbe's arrival the Jews did not know a single moment of rest. His assistants in the bloody acts of violence were Michelson, the new police chief Bunge, and his deputy, Corporal Scherner.

Shots rang out in the ghetto from early morning till late at night. People were dying everywhere. If Ribbe happened not to like a person's face, he would shoot hm. If his clothing was not the sort that Ribbe approved of, he was shot. If his identification badge was not sewn on properly, he was shot.

The streets emptied, people were afraid to leave their apartments, but it made no difference. Ribbe and his band burst into the apartments. If they found a German-baked roll, a piece of butter for a sick child, a geographic map, or a book, the people were shot.

Jewish children were driven by hunger to go begging for a crust of bread in the Russian sector. Usually they would gather in the evenings at the railroad bridge and wait for the workers' columns so as to return to the ghetto with them. In February Ribbe set up a dragnet for the children. If they were caught in the Russian sector, they were put in a truck, taken to the Jewish cemetery, and shot there. When the children were loaded on the truck, they screamed.

On February 19 Ribbe made the rounds of the factories where the German Jews were working and noticed several beautiful young women and girls.

He selected the most beautiful women — twelve German Jewish women and one Russian — Lina Noy. Ribbe ordered them to report to the labor exchange at 6:00 P.M.

Ribbe came to the labor exchange together with Michelson. The victims, ignorant of their fate, were already there. The street was noisy. The columns of workers were returning home, and many stopped and waited. Everyone wanted to know why Ribbe had selected the most beautiful girls and women. Ribbe gave the order to take the women by the arm and lead them down Sukhaya Street at a slow pace. A groan went through the ghetto: Sukhaya Street led to the cemetery.

It was a terrible procession: thirteen young, beautiful women walking slowly toward the cemetery gates. One German Jewish woman asked to be allowed to say goodbye to her husband. Ribbe granted permission, and the husband was brought to the cemetery and shot before his wife's eyes. The animals stripped the women naked and mocked them. Then Ribbe and Michelson personally shot them. Ribbe took Lina Noy's bra and put it in his pocket: "To remember a beautiful Jewess," he said.

At 11:00 P.M. on February 19, 1943, a truck of Gestapo agents drove into the ghetto. After they had picked up Epstein, a traitor who always helped them, they set out for No. 48 Obuvnaya Street. They surrounded the building on all sides, led the people out onto the street, and formed them into a column of four. The children's screams were so piercingly loud that they drowned out the bursts of machine-gun fire. All 140 residents of the building were killed. Only two people, a man and a small boy, survived that night. The Germans sealed the house, and on February 20, 1943, Ribbe pasted a declaration on the building stating that weapons had been kept in building No. 48 and that all its residents had been shot. The order demanded that everyone hand in his weapons. Anyone who was afraid to come personally could throw them near the police head-quarters without being noticed.

The order warned that failure to turn in firearms would lead to mass executions. The Jews read this order with horror and disgust, but not a single person handed in any firearms, even though they were being received daily in the ghetto and were being smuggled out to the partisan units.

Ribbe liquidated the ghetto in a leisurely fashion. He took control of the workers' columns; he and Michelson met them every evening and searched them. If Ribbe found a few potatoes or a bottle of milk or fat, the "criminal" was taken to the cemetery and shot. The food went to the apartments of Ribbe and Michelson.

Ribbe claimed that he was persecuting only those who were involved in political activity or who were part of the partisan movement. In those instances when Ribbe established that a person had escaped from a workers' column, the entire column was shot. This was how the workers of the distillery, the prison, and other institutions were murdered. Jews working in the prison were warned that they did not have the right to reveal what they had seen inside the prison. In order to isolate them and prevent them from having any contact with the ghetto Jews, they were forced to live in barracks within the prison.

In May 1943, the prison warden Ginter ordered that all working Jews be lined up, stripped naked, loaded into trucks, and taken out of town to be shot.

"They knew too much," Ginter said.

After that he came to Epstein in the *Judenrat* to get new workers. A fresh group was sent to the prison. In three weeks they too were shot.

Soon Ribbe issued an order demanding that all parentless children be sent to the labor exchange. The ragged, hungry children arrived, and among them were children whose parents were still alive. The children were taken to prison in a truck and from there to be executed.

After this incident the mothers feared to leave their children at home and took them along to work, frequently carrying them in sacks. Once Scherner, a German, walked up to a truck, dragged a six-year-old boy from it, threw him on the pavement, and stepped on his neck with his boot. He trampled the boy with his boots and threw the dead mangled body to the side.

The next day Bunge met a column of workers and seized an eleven-year-old boy, took him to the cemetery, and shot him. When he returned to the columns, Bunge grabbed a second boy by the arm, pulled him out of the column, and shot him right there on

Sukhaya Street. The elderly and the unemployed, in the opinion of Ribbe, also were a burden on the ghetto. Even people who had a good reason for not going to work and had official permission to stay home for two or three days were considered unemployed. One hundred fifty "unemployed" and elderly were taken from the prison and shot. The ghetto shrank as each day the number of those left alive lessened. The prophecy of the Slutsk Jews came to pass: Ribbe had been sent to Minsk to liquidate the ghetto.

In carrying out his policies, Ribbe tried to prevent news of his evil deeds from going any farther than the bounds of the ghetto. He was not able to accomplish this, however. Inspector Schultz, a German Luftwaffe officer, agreed to get the Jews who worked with him out of the ghetto. He put thirty-seven Jews in a truck, armed them with machine guns, revolvers, and rifles. He himself seized a radio receiver and left with the Jews to join a partisan unit. This incident was quite exceptional, and we consider it essential to mention it.

After the children, the "unemployed," and the elderly, the turn came for the doctors to die.

At the end of April, 1943, Ribbe requested lists of the doctors. A few days later a new order was issued: all the doctors were to appear at the *Judenrat*. From there they were taken to Gestapo headquarters.

Ribbe pointed out to Epstein that there were elderly persons among the doctors, such as Dr. Gekhman and Doctor Kantsevy (she was an invalid and limped). He asked Epstein to take special care of them and lead them through the town to make sure that they did not overtire themselves and fall behind.

Everyone was amazed by such concern on the part of this monster — amazed and frightened. Ribbe ordered the doctors to appear at the Jewish labor exchange at 4:00 P.M. The doctors arrived to find Ribbe and Michelson already waiting for them. The doctors were quickly divided into groups — the elderly (Gekhman and the two women doctors, Shmotkin and Kantsevy); pediatricians (Savchik and Lev); doctors from the orphanage; doctors from the home for the disabled. A large number of specialists in internal diseases, dentists, and ear specialists were led to the side.

The selected doctors were taken to the bunker which housed the labor exchange. As soon as it became dark, their families were sent for. Among those brought in were Lev-Mlynsky (a historian and scholar) and his two children, Dr. Shmotkin's son, Dr. Savchik's

175

three children — in all, approximately 100 people. Bunge and Scherner arrived about 5:00 A.M., before the workers' columns left. They brought with them a group of policemen and took the column to prison. There they stripped them of their clothes, beat, and killed them.

When the doomed doctors and their families were being led to the prison, Dr. Savchik's twelve-year-old daughter shouted: "It's all right, Momma, walk bravely. Our blood will be avenged."

Next came the turn of the orphanage and the home for the disabled. One clear, moonlit night at the end of April, 1943, a car and a truck drove up to the large two-story building in which children, invalids, and service personnel lived. Ribbe and Michelson emerged from the car, walked up to the building, pointed it out to the men sitting in the truck, and left. The building was located on Zaslavsky Street, next to the very edge of the Russian sector. The police cut the barbed wire and surrounded the building. The children and personnel were seized naked and thrown into the back of the truck. The sick, invalids, and small children were shot on the spot. Everything was over in an hour.

Loaded with people, the truck left for the prison. No one ever saw those children again.

Bunge and Scherner arrived in the morning to check the work done during the night. Among the bodies, which were literally floating in enormous pools of blood, they found several seriously wounded women, whom they finished off on the spot.

Next to this large stone building stood a small hut. This was the isolation ward of the orphanage. It contained thirty sick children. They began to shoot the children and, when they ran out of bullets, Bunge and Scherner killed them with daggers.

The hospitals remained. In May Ribbe came to the hospital, inquired as to the condition of the sick, and asked to be shown the wards. Two days later, precisely at 12:00 and during a period of clear, warm weather, residents of the ghetto heard shooting coming from the hospital for German Jews. Everyone rushed there. A large black gassing truck stood in the hospital yard. The German Jews said that Miller, Ribbe, Mikhelson, and four other persons dressed in civilian clothing and concealing submachine guns under their raincoats entered the hospital and the orphanage and shot the sick and the children point-blank. Having completed their murders in this hospital, the bandits immediately went to the hospital for Russian Jews. The sick jumped from second-floor windows, and several people escaped. All the others were shot in their beds.

The hospital personnel was ordered to remove the bodies, wash away the blood, and put everything in order so that the hospital would be ready to receive new patients by 4:00 P.M.

Ribbe said: "The German authorities do not carry out pogroms, but we do need healthy people — not sick ones."

After these liquidations Ribbe began to occupy himself with the German Jews. He used to say to them: "What kind of work do you do? If it's too hard, we'll send you to a camp to peel potatoes."

There were naive people who believed that Ribbe really would give them an easy job. They asked for permission to take members of their families with them to the camp. Ribbe granted permission: "I don't believe in separating people who are close to each other."

At 2:00 P.M. he came to Epstein's, had dinner, drank vodka and wine, and then went out into the yard to order his underlings to get ready for the operation. For the meantime, however, he decided to amuse himself. The whim came to him to hear a concert, and precisely at that moment the violinist Varshavsky was walking past. Then came Barats, a violinist in the Minsk Philharmonic. He had been walking past the ghetto for German Jews and realized that a pogrom was being prepared when he saw how the people were preparing themselves.

He was stopped. He vainly attempted to convince them that, after a two-year break, he was in no condition to play, but they forced him. Pale, with tears in his eyes, Barats played before the executioner. When the concert was over, Ribbe let Barats go and went with his unit to the ghetto for German Jews. Ten minutes later a crowd of people with children, bundles, and packages were locked in the bunker. A few minutes after that a large closed truck drove up, and they began to put people in it and haul them off to prison. There was a deadly silence. In the prison Richter and Menschel received the German Jews. They stripped the doomed people, hosed them down with water, mocked them, and then shot them. 175 people were murdered on this occasion.

In spite of the terror and the daily murders, people still attempted to fight and to escape from the ghetto.

The departure of Jews from the ghetto increased considerably in April and May 1943, when Parkhomenko's unit and Zorin's unit were organized in Pushcha. Zorin knew of the sufferings of the ghetto Jews, since he himself had endured them. Zorin organized Jewish family unit and systematically sent guides to bring everyone to his unit — old men, women, and children. This unit had about 500 people. Many Jews became excellent partisans; they undermined railroad tracks and derailed trains containing military supplies, troops, and machinery.

Many perished in attempts to escape the ghetto. Fourteen Jews worked at the *Verpflegungsamt* (supply office) as cobblers, tailors, blacksmiths, and house painters. The communist, Uri Retsky, and his friend, Ilya Dukorsky, worked among them. Retsky often told his comrades at work that he would sell his life dearly and the Hitlerite would die who raised his hand at him. . . . He made a Finnish knife and carried it with him.

The people worked on Dolgobrodskaya Street and walked several blocks away to the Bakery to eat (that is, to drink thin soup). Once, during the lunch break, Retsky met Savich, an old acquaintance who had formerly managed the cafeteria of *Belgosstroy*. Savich claimed he was a Soviet patriot and that he had connections with the partisan units and guides. For money he offered to obtain a large quantity of weapons. Two days later Retsky arranged to meet Savich and get a final response to his request for firearms and a guide. When he had thought through Savich's offer, Retsky decided to check up on him, since Savich had made a bad impression. The traitor Savich beat Retsky to the punch and went to the *Verpflegungsamt* two days later with his boss Kovalev (a local German) and a whole band of Gestapo agents. Kovalev quickly entered the shop, and Savich stood and observed him. The rest of the bandits surrounded the building. Retsky grasped what had happened and exchanged glances with Dukorsky. Dukorsky slammed the door, and Retsky whipped out his knife and began to stab Kovalev. The others came running. Retsky and Dukorsky were shot on the spot, and they tried to arrest the others.

Two workers, Bykhovsky and Silberstein, shouted to their comrades: "Don't give up alive, run but don't ask for mercy and don't cry!" The police did not take anyone alive. Everyone tried to escape; people were jumping over the fences. A bullet caught up with Misha Belostoksky at the third fence. Among the workers was a twelve-year-old boy by the name of Bliakher. He tried to escape, but was also brought down by a bullet.

For his struggle with the partisans Kovalev was awarded the Iron Cross.

Another act of treason took place on May 8, 1943. Solomon Blyumin, who managed the housing bureau in the *Judenrat*, had been rendering all possible assistance to the partisan movement.

When the party organization was destroyed and the guides moved from the units to the ghetto and perished, the link with the partisans was severely hindered.

With the aid of a female acquaintance, a certain Sonka, Blyumin got in touch with Ivanov and Kuzminov. They both worked as truck drivers in the housing bureau in Minsk. They met with Blyumin many times and worked out a plan for escape from the ghetto and the forgery of documents. Blyumin wanted to take firearms from the ghetto and take with him the rest of the communists. Not wanting to acquaint any superfluous persons with the truck drivers, he met with them alone.

It was difficult for Blyumin to leave the ghetto, since everyone there knew and loved him. Tall and handsome, he cut a striking figure. The departure day was set for May 8. Trucks arrived in the ghetto, but they were not the ones on which Blyumin and his people were supposed to leave. They were gassing trucks; Ivanov had betrayed them. At 6:00 A.M. the Gestapo surrounded the block where Blyumin lived.

Blyumin appeared in the doorway, and they began to beat him with rifle butts. Stunned and bloodied, he fell to the ground. He was bound and thrown into a truck; his family and the residents of the building were also forced into the truck. Blyumin spent three weeks in the Gestapo, and for three weeks — day and night — they tortured him, demanding that he reveal his accomplices, connections, weapons' locations. Blyumin suffered in silence, and not a word, not a sound, passed his lips. When the Gestapo realized that it was impossible to get anything out of him, they paraded him down the streets of the ghetto and then took him to the cemetery, where they shot him and threw his body into a pit. The people had difficulty identifying their Blyumin. He had been tall and broad-shouldered, but he was thin and toothless when they took him to the cemetery. The people stole his body from the common grave and buried him with honor.

In June of 1943 guides from a partisan unit arrived demanding medicine and a doctor. Anna Isaakovna Turetsky was selected. At one time she had managed an orphanage. The children and the employees spoke of her with pride as "our Niuta," "our Momma." A beautiful, intelligent woman, she was able to get along with everyone. In difficult times she knew how to encourage, to be discreet, and to inspire hope and cheerfulness in those who had despaired.

She was happy to serve her people in those difficult days. Niuta attempted to escape the barbed wire four times, and each time she was unsuccessful.

Finally, at 11:00 P.M. on June 16, 1943, a group got out. Two kilometers from the ghetto they came on Scherner and a group of policemen who were checking sentries. The guide was killed, and Turetsky was wounded in the leg. The others scattered. Turetsky crawled into a hole, and the bandits searched for her for three hours. She was found and taken to the Fifth Police Station, beaten, and thrown on a stone floor, where she lay bleeding and crushed. Scherner tortured her for a day, asking in German and Russian: "Where were you going? With whom? Whose assignment were you carrying out?" Every word was accompanied by a blow. He kicked her wounded leg with his boots. Struggling to keep her wits about her, Anna Isaakovna answered that her condition did not permit her to answer questions. Scherner realized that he would not get anything out of her. In the morning he dragged her to the truck and took her to the Jewish cemetery. She was carried to the common pit on stretchers. It was there that Niuta began to speak. To Scherner's question of where she had been, she responded: "All my people were with me. I don't know their names. You can kill me, but no one will suffer from that. On the contrary, after my death, you will be hated all the more. Look at your hands; they are covered with blood. How many children have you strangled? I am not afraid of you. The entire Soviet people will avenge us. Kill me!" Gathering her last strength, Niuta Turetsky raised her body and calmly waited for the bullet.

She was killed by a bullet from Scherner's pistol, and her body was also stolen from the common pit and buried in a separate grave with grass and wild flowers.

The surviving Jews of Minsk will never forget their Niuta.

In June of 1943, the Germans began to eliminate the workers' columns. In June the Germans gathered seventy women under the pretext of sending them to the radio factory; twenty were sent to the factory and fifty to the Gestapo. Flanked by Gestapo officers, Ribbe told the women that they would be put on trucks and taken outside of town, where they would work and be fed well. The trucks arrived, and the women recognized the familiar gassing equipment. They realized that they were not being taken to work, but to die.

Many were shot on the spot, and the rest were forced into the truck and gassed. Only one of the fifty women, Lilya Kapilovich, managed to escape. She hid between the trucks standing in the yard.

It was from this time that the destruction of the workers' columns dates. Ribbe made the rounds of the firms which employed Jews and wrote down the names of the workers. After Ribbe's visit, one after the other, the columns disappeared.

Early in September, 1943, Ribbe appeared in the ghetto for German Jews and selected the three hundred healthiest and youngest men. They were loaded onto trucks and taken away. In a few days the same thing happened in the ghetto for Russian Jews: two trucks arrived, were loaded with men, and were sent to the camp on Shirokaya Street. A few days later the men were taken from there as well.

On September 12 it was announced to the German Jews that they should prepare themselves to return to Germany. They began hurriedly to collect their possessions and make preparations. In September they were loaded into gassing trucks and taken away.

By October 1, 1943, a total of 2,000 Jews remained in the ghetto.

On October 21, 1943, the ghetto was again surrounded, for the last time, by the Gestapo. Everyone was loaded into trucks and taken away to die. In those instances when no one was found in an apartment, the building was blown up with grenades to ensure that anyone concealed in a hiding place would also die.

October 21 is the last day of this great tragedy. The Minsk ghetto ceased to be, and its last inhabitants disappeared. Not a single living being was left. Only the ruins stood in testimony to the suffering and terrible torments which had rained down on the heads of tens of thousands of Minsk Jews for two and one half years.

Based on information provided by: **A. Machiz,**
Grechanik, L. Gleyzer, P. M. Shapiro.
Prepared for publication by **Vasily Grossman.**

The Story of an Old Man,
Shmuel Dovid Kugel

(Pleshchenitsy)

I am almost seventy years old now. Germans arrived in our small town of Pleshchenitsy (Minsk *oblast*) on July 27 [1941]. At the first sound of shooting, we very old Jews went to a grove five kilometers from town and returned only when the battle was over.

Half the town was burned to the ground, but my small home was left standing. My wife and I came home, locked the outside door, and drew the curtains. We could hear shooting in the distance. When it stopped, we were gripped with horror, since we found ourselves on the other side of the front.

The temporary German commandant in Pleshchenitsy issued an order stating that special laws were to be applied to Jews: they would have to live apart, in a ghetto, and wear yellow identification badges on the chest and back. This was required even of children. Jews were forbidden to use the sidewalks. Christians were forbidden not only to deal with Jews, but even to talk to them or respond to their greetings. All heavy labor had to be done by the Jews without any compensation, and so on.

In the very first days several Jews and Christians who had occupied positions of responsibility under Soviet rule were killed.

A few days later we learned that about two kilometers from us, in the small town of Zembin, the Jews had been forced to dig a large pit. When it was ready, all the Jews of Zembin were herded to the bazaar, supposedly for registration, and then to the pit, where they were shot. Some of those thrown into the pit were still breathing. When the pit had been covered over with earth, the ground was still heaving from the movements of people buried alive. We learned of this from those who had been forced to fill in the pit.

Only ten Jews succeeded in escaping. One of them came to us two weeks later.

This vicious act seemed unthinkable to us. We wanted to believe that it was an unfortunate accident. Perhaps the Germans had discovered murdered Germans in Zembin and that was why they had committed this act of violence on the Jews. It was known that the Germans slaughtered entire small towns and villages as retribution for one dead German.

We assured ourselves, however, in vain. The violence was repeated in the small town of Logoysk, 26 kilometers from us, and

182

later in several other places. A particularly large number of Jews were killed in the city of Borisov, in the small towns of Smilevichi and Gorodok, and in other places. Everywhere the same "Jewish wedding" was being celebrated.

It was then that we realized that the events in Zembin were no coincidence, but that they were being carried out on the basis of Hitler's criminal order. By that time, we had already been resettled to the ghetto. Fifty houses were set aside for the ghetto, and approximately one thousand people were settled in them.

For two weeks we lived in great terror in the ghetto, since we realized that the matter would not be limited to this move and that we would have to drink this bitter cup to the bottom.

Once we saw dozens of policemen coming toward the ghetto, bringing with them a large number of empty carts. Several families managed to escape to the small town of Dolginovo, about 40 kilometers away, in the Vilnius *oblast* (formerly part of Poland). At that point there had still not been any total slaughter of Jews. But by evening the ghetto was surrounded, and it became impossible to escape.

On the next day the policemen went to all the Jewish houses and chased everyone out into a field. Those who walked slowly were urged on by whips. In the field, some of the craftsmen — cobblers, tailors, blacksmiths, and also the elderly — were separated from the group and allowed to return to the town. My wife and I ended up in that group, but our entire family of eight — including our daughters and granddaughters — were put on the carts and taken away. We were not even able to say goodbye and embrace them for a last time. Those driving the carts told us that they took the unfortunate people to a forest near Borisov, about fifty kilometers from us, where the German executioners were waiting for them. The drivers and their horses were sent back, and we never heard anything of the victims again.

How can I describe our state of mind when we returned home? The town was as silent as death itself. my wife rushed from room to room as if hoping to find some of her children. The books, maps, and musical instruments were all in their places, but the children were gone. She began to tear her hair and fell unconscious.

About three weeks passed. The holiday "Sukkoth" (Feast of Booths) passed. I was returning from work with four Jews. Near the town we were warned: "Run to the forest right away. The Gestapo is picking up all the remaining Jews."

I wanted to run home to save my wife or die together with her, but my companions would not let me go and took me with them to the forest. The Germans shot at us but missed. I could not keep up with the young people, and I sat down in a clearing and remained there in a cold rain until darkness. That night I went home. I hoped that my wife had hidden herself somewhere close to the house and was waiting for me. I did not find anyone, and our hut had someone else's lock on it. There was nothing left to hope for. I crawled under a haystack to get warm and decided what to do next. I had no desire to remain there until morning and end up in the clutches of the Germans. I wanted to live to see, with my own eyes, innocent blood avenged. I decided to go to Dolginovo in Poland. It was raining, and I did not have anything warm. I found only a large sack, put it over my head, took a staff in my hand, and left my home and native land. The last of the *shtetl* Jews set out into the dark night.

It took me four days to reach Dolginovo. I walked through forests and fields, spending the night in haystacks belonging to peasants who fed me and mourned my fate and their own.

In Dolginovo I met a relative, and we both burst into tears. He had experienced his own tragedy. About five days before my arrival a punitive unit had come to their village. After it left, a few of the bandits returned and claimed that they had lost a whip. They announced that if it was not found in ten minutes, they would kill several Jews. The whip was not found, and the murderers shot five young workers who were returning home. One of them was the son-in-law of my relative. His young daughter was left alone with a two-month-old baby to grieve for her husband.

I spent the winter in Dolginovo. There had been no total slaughter of Jews there, and they suffered only from individual acts of violence, taxes, and forced indemnities.

After the holiday of Purim the rumor spread that mass murders had begun in Poland. We began to prepare hiding places for ourselves so as not to fall into the murderers' clutches. Shortly before Passover, Gestapo men drove up to the town. They immediately began to shoot Jews — regardless of age. We hid in the attic and could see the slaughter through the cracks in the roof.

The Gestapo men, however, were not satisfied with this. The next day they mobilized all the policemen from the nearby villages and searched the houses, barns, and attics. They threw grenades into hiding places. Everyone who ended up in their hands was stripped naked, beaten, and led off to slaughter outside town.

Those who could not walk quickly were shot on the spot. The blood of martyrs bespattered the walls of the houses. Outside the town, people were shot in groups, and the bodies were left unburied. Several hundred people were driven into a barn; kerosene was then poured on the barn, and the people were burned alive. In those two black days 1,800 people were destroyed. We were among the 1,200 who survived.

On the third day the murderers left. They said that the majority of Jews had been killed and that the rest would not be hurt if they registered with the police. Those who did not register would be shot.

Almost everyone came to register, and in a few days they were resettled to forty small houses of the ghetto. The ghetto was surrounded with barbed wire and a board fence. The Jews had to do all this themselves. Within the ghetto, however, we immediately began to create hiding places. Everyone realized that it was not possible to believe these cannibals.

Once we were ordered to join a military wagon train as drivers. None of us had any desire to end up in the maw of the beast, and people began to hide themselves. As my relative was crawling into the attic, he was noticed and shot in the leg. The next day the murderers began again. In two days eight hundred more people were killed, but the Germans never found four hundred of us. In the house where I lived many were so tired that they made no effort to hide; they felt it was only a useless torment. Ten persons, however (including me), hid in the attic. The bandits ripped open the roof. They were in the attic several times, but we were not found. In this fashion I again remained alive.

When leaving, the Germans once more made arrangements for a registration and promised life to everyone who came. But no one was in a hurry. How could we believe the word of a cur? We began to prepare to escape, and one night approximately two hundred people broke through the fence and left for the forests of Byelorussia. There we met our friends and brothers — the partisans. They received us warmly. The young were taken into their units, and the children and old people were given shelter and food. Comrade Kiselev, a good, educated man, was appointed to be in charge of us as political instructor.

We spent the summer and fall with the partisans in the forests. When cold weather set in, the commander ordered that the weakest be led through the front line to our dear native land. A special unit was formed for this task under the leadership of that same Kiselev.

The march lasted about two months. We walked at night and rested during the day. Every day we came to a new forest. We covered up to twenty kilometers a night. If the area was particularly dangerous, we covered as much as thirty kilometers. When we reached areas occupied by the partisans, we moved during the day and rested at night, two or three persons to a peasant hut. The peasants fed us. Altogether, we walked about one thousand kilometers (600 miles) on foot.

This was how we survived. I, seventy-year-old Shmuel Dovid Kugel, bear true testimony to the world.

Shmuel Dovid Kugel

Prepared for publication by **Vasily Grossman**.

The Massacre of Jews in Glubokoye and Other Small Towns

The Germans entered the small town of Glubokoye on July 2, 1941. Fear and horror seized the population. Byelorussians, Jews, and Poles had lived there friendly for decades and decades.

The German authorities first demanded that all excess grain be handed in. Each family, regardless of size, was permitted to retain only twenty kilograms (forty-four pounds) of flour and grain.

The rest of the grain had to be taken to the magistracy within a few hours. The enormous line of people bringing their "excess" of 3-5 kilograms was a sad sight. Osher Gofman was found to have more flour than the amount permitted by the Germans. For this crime he, his wife, his children, and his elderly parents were arrested. They were taken out of town, ordered to dig a grave, and were all shot.

This villainous destruction of an entire family caused the entire population of Glubokoye to react in horror.

The same punishment threatened certain other families as well: the Olmers, the Druts, the Kantoroviches, the Pliskins, the Ponyatovskys, and others. At the house of Druts, for example, the police found bran which he had not handed in, since he did not consider it part of the grain quota.

All these people were arrested as criminals, and they succeeded in escaping death this time only by paying a large bribe.

From the very first days of the occupation, the Germans began to take the entire Jewish population (including children) to forced labor.

Jews were made to perform over-taxing work and were at the same time mocked and tormented. There were instances when people were beaten unconscious and had to be carried home from "work." Natanzon, Pintov, Ozhinsky, and the lawyer Slonimsky, were among these unfortunate victims. The German overseers conducted themselves as if they were masters dealing with slaves. The Jews were forced to carry out their basest whims — sing songs, crawl on all fours, imitate animals, dance, kiss the Germans' shoes, etc.

The Germans began to refine an entire gamut of mockery. For example, people working at the train station in Krulevshchina were made to stand under the water tower and were soaked with cold water. Very frequently, after an exhausting day of work, the people were forced to enter the water clothed to "bathe" and then lie down in the sand, and so forth.

All these things, however, were only innocent amusements for the "Aryans."

On October 22, 1941, the *Gebietskommissar* announced that the Jews had to move to the ghetto in a half hour. They were forbidden to take anything other than a small amount of old furniture, and even that required the permission of a specially appointed commission from the magistracy.

M. Rayak has provided an eloquent description of this "resettlement":

"The whole town looked like a bazaar. All the streets were piled high with old furniture. The Jews were taking their pitiful belongings to the camp established for them — the ghetto. There was an unheard-of noise, shouting, and pushing on the streets. For its part, the police was 'establishing order' and beating the people on the heads, arms, etc. with rifle butts, sticks, and anything that came to hand."

This was the way the resettlement to the ghetto was accomplished.

Conditions in the ghetto were terribly crowded; several families were packed into one room. Families slept on the floor.

At first the Jews were permitted to make purchases at the bazaar during a two hour period, but later it was categorically forbidden to go to the bazaar. The Jews were not permitted to buy butter, meat, eggs, or milk.

Contact with the peasantry was forbidden under pain of death. Nevertheless, in spite of all the cruel limitations which doomed the Jewish population to hunger, these cannibalistic regulations were circumvented in all sorts of ways.

Many of the peasants ignored the danger threatening them and gave food to the ghetto, sometimes even bringing it themselves. There were instances when peasant women put "Jewish badges" on their sleeves and brought food to their acquaintances in the ghetto.

The Rayak brothers told of how Shchebeko, a peasant, secretly brought milk to their sick mother every day.

The peasant Grishkevich secretly brought cabbage, potatoes, and other vegetables for several families — Dr. Rayak, the tailor, Shames, Gitelson, and others.

If such "crimes" were discovered, the guilty paid with their lives.

People were beaten to death if they were found to have a piece of meat or a pinch of salt. This was the policy of the Germans during their rule.

Zalman-Vulf Ruderman's wife was detained and beaten terribly for having attempted to bring two eggs to the ghetto when returning from work. In the beginning of May, 1943, the butcher Sholom Tsentsiper was arrested and shot. At the check point the "criminal" was discovered to have a rooster in his sack which he was attempting to carry into the ghetto.

Jews were categorically forbidden to eat berries. . . .

It is difficult to believe that people were persecuted for having eaten a few berries as if they had committed a terrible crime against the state.

The Glozman family had been tailors for generations. Honest, hard-working persons, skilled masters of their trade, they were respected and loved by all.

Zelik Glozman had a ten-year-old son Aron. The father viewed the successes of his first-born with hope. The boy brought only A's and B's home from school. He was always first in games and amateu-u-r activity, as the father explained in a slight drawl. The tailor's heart seemed to stop beating when he thought of his son's future: "Who knows, anything can happen in the Soviet state. Archik has a good head on his shoulders. He might become a doctor or an engineer."

The Germans arrived, and in a few days Archik Glozman was being searched for all over town. The Gestapo agent Hainleit made everyone search for the boy, whose "crime" consisted of having brought a few berries in the handkerchief. The boy managed to escape from the guards, and one can imagine what it cost the poor parents (with the aid of good-hearted acquaintances) to hide him!

Later, however, both the Glozmans and their son were destroyed. . . .

David Pliskin, a teacher, worked as an interpreter for the commandant Rosentreter. Once, in late June, 1943, Pliskin walked up to a raspberry bush and picked a few berries. He was seen by a German engineer who was looking out the window of a nearby house. Foaming at the mouth, the German ran up to Pliskin, began to berate him and shout that Jews were forbidden to eat berries. Pliskin promised to observe this regulation strictly in the future.

He was threatened with death, and only his "sincere repentance" and the fact that his superior put in a good word for him saved him

189

from being shot. The execution was replaced with a fine. . . . 2,000 rubles were demanded of him, but after long arguments this was reduced to 500 rubles. The fine was paid immediately. When paying the fine at the Gestapo office, Pliskin was warned that he would not escape punishment if such a crime were repeated. The new law decreed that Jews who ate berries, fruits, or fats would be executed.

N. Kraut was wounded and then killed for having attempted to carry a little salt into the ghetto in a sack.

In March 1943, the gendarmerie and police were searching for Zalman Fleischer, who was accused of having bought a lump of butter from a peasant.

Fleischer was warned in time that he was being searched for, and he managed to escape. . . .

But the crime had to be punished as an example, and the chief of the gendarmerie Kern ordered that the first Jews to be found on the street were to be arrested and punished. Leyvik Drisvyatsky, his eighteen-year-old son, Khlavne, and Lipa Landau were made "to answer for the sins" of Fleischer.

In April 1942, Drisvyatsky had lost his eldest son during an "aktion." The loss of this boy, a capable and educated youth, had deeply shaken the father. Life had lost meaning for him, and he could not recover. Drisvyatsky himself was a man of broad education: a talmudist, mathematician, and linguist. In Glubokoye he was respected and loved by all.

Lipa Landau also had a higher education, was a witty conversationalist, and liked to play jokes. The German henchmen had killed his wife and children during an "aktion" in June of 1942. He himself had survived by a miracle: he had crawled out of a pit of death from under a heap of corpses and had wandered through the forests and fields for a long time before stumbling into Glubokoye, where he remained.

In Glubokoye he became friendly with Drisvyatsky, and they often spent their hours of relaxation together.

Then they were seized, taken to the Gestapo, tortured all night, and taken in the morning to bloody Borki — a place of execution. This was the fashion in which German "law" took vengeance for a lump of butter "illegally" smuggled into the ghetto by Zalman Fleischer.

In December of 1941, the Jewish population began to be systematically destroyed in what were described by the Germans with the short and terrible word, "aktions."

Early one December morning the Gestapo men burst into the homes and, without any explanation, dragged several dozen people from their beds. These people, who were described as an "unnecessary element," were forced to walk naked in the freezing cold.

"One woman," M. Rayak writes, "lay down in the street together with her children and cried and screamed that she would not move from the spot. She was beaten unconscious, and everyone was herded off to Borki, where they were shot. The poor children were thrown into the pit and buried alive."

Borki was a rural area 1½ kilometers from Glubokoye. In peaceful times it was a place of recreation and relaxation.

"In Borki," the Rayak brothers write, "the Germans forced the young to dance at the edge of an open grave and the old to sing songs. . . . After this sadistic mockery they forced the young and healthy to carry the feeble old people and cripples into the pit and lay them down. Only after this were they to lie down themselves, and then the Germans methodically and calmly shot everyone."

What sort of demonic fantasy could have invented such an "organized" division of "labor"? This was how the seventy-year-old mother of the Rayak brothers died, and this was how all the residents of Glubokoye were gradually destroyed.

The murders were preceded by unimaginable torture: people were cut in half, teeth were pulled, nails were driven into the victims' heads, people were kept naked in the freezing cold and soaked with cold water, beaten with sticks and rifle butts until they lost consciousness. . . .

The Fascists tortured women and children with a special passion.

In Glubokoye, as in many other places, the Germans used their favorite provocationary method — splitting the people up into two ghettos.

The second ghetto, according to the Germans, was for Jews "of little use." In point of fact, many skilled laborers ended up in the second ghetto: cobblers, joiners, tailors. The Germans decided to use the second ghetto for a financial "aktion"; people could pay money to avoid being sent to it.

In this fashion, Jews who had paid a ransom were permitted to remain in the first ghetto. People who were not able to pay the set sum in money or valuables had to remain in the second ghetto, even if they were skilled laborers.

Resettlement to the second ghetto lasted about two weeks — from May 20 to early June, 1942. For two weeks old men and women were hauled on carts to the second ghetto.

Rayak writes: "This terrible scene can scarcely be described. The poor old men and women cried and sobbed, asking pitifully: 'Where and why are they taking us? What sins have we committed to be separated from our children?' Krasnoarmeyskaya Street was filled with groaning, crying old people and cripples. . . .

After the second ghetto was formed, the Fascists announced that all the residents of the first ghetto would receive workers' identification cards and that this would guarantee their safety.

Kopenwald, the executioner of Glubokoye's Jews, gave the representatives of the *Judenrat* his official "word of honor" that there would be no massacre of the Jews.

In July 1942, the *Gebietskommissar* ordered that all Jews left alive gather in the Glubokoye ghetto. In the order the *Gebietskommissar* gave assurances that no more Jews would be killed. He issued passes to members of the *Judenrat* to make trips to the forests and villages to find Jews in hiding and bring them to the camp.

By this time the camp — the ghetto in Glubokoye — had become a peculiar "Jewish" center. All the surviving Jews of forty-two cities and towns had been assembled there. There were husbands who had lost their wives, wives without husbands, husbands and wives who had been separated during the slaughter and had lost track of each other, but had now met again in the ghetto and asked each other what had happened to their children. There were boys and girls with no family and small babies who had been found under bushes in the forest and brought to the camp. There were Jews from Miory, Druya, Prozorki, Golubichi, Zyabki, Diona, Sharkovshchina, Plissa, etc. Exhausted, tormented, and crushed people had come together from all these places. The survivors of the slaughter in Dolginovo, Druysk, Braslavl, Germanovichi, Luzhki, Gaiduchishki, Voropayevo, Parafinovo, Zachatye, Bildichi, Shipy, Skunchiki, Porplishche, Sventsyany, Podbrodzie, and others.

The trick succeeded: all the Jews were collected in one place.

It is interesting to note that in Glubokoye the economic effectiveness and benefit derived by the Germans from the "aktion" perpetrated on the Jewish population were quite noticeable. Aside from furniture, the Germans hauled away clothing, footwear, linen, dishes, sewing machines, household items, machines for making stockings and hats, and milling machines. All these things were sorted out and stored in barns with typical German precision. After a time there appeared in Glubokoye (along Karl Marx Street) stores selling "ready-made clothing, footwear, and personal items," etc.

A short time later a china and glass store was opened, and also a furniture store.

The laundry which washed the murdered people's clothing worked night and day. Naturally, the people working in the laundry (and other "restoration" shops as well) were Jews.

When clothes were sorted and washed, strange scenes were played out. People recognized the underwear and belongings of their murdered relatives. Raphael Gitlits recognized his murdered mother's underwear and dress. Manya Freidkin had to wash her husband Shimon's blood-stained shirt. The wife of the teacher, Milikhman, had to put the suit of her murdered husband into "decent order" with her own hands.

Commercial activity was not at all exhausted by the German department stores — *Warenhäuser*. At 19 K. Marx Street there existed the special "Bureau of the *Gebietskommissar* in Glubokoye." The task of this bureau was to check that order was maintained in the factories and shops, to do bookkeeping, and to supervise the workers.

The bureau's basic task was the preparation of packages according to the orders of German concerns and private parties and the shipment of those packages to Germany.

The main clients of this bureau were: Gachman (*Gebietskommissar*), Heberling and Hebel (consultants), Kern (chief of the gendarmerie), the officers Hainleit, Wildt, Speer, Zanner, Bekkar, Kopenwald, Seif, Schultz, and many, many others. Every day packages of food and bed linen were prepared and sent in massive quantities to Germany.

To support this enormous flow of packages, a special operation was set up for the production of cartons. Jewish children from eight to twelve years of age worked in this shop, and they paid heavily if even the tiniest defect was discovered! They were punished as cruelly and implacably as adults!

Dozens of train cars left Glubokoye, Krulevshchina, and Voropayevo loaded with cloth, leather, wool, footwear, knitted items, and large quantities of foodstuffs.

The Jewish population was impoverished, and the Germans were sucking the life blood of the village. The economy was exhausted, but German pockets continued to swell. Aside from the mass acquisition of edibles and consumer goods, metals were the object of intensive looting. The Germans organized a special storehouse for metal items: samovars, pots, candle sticks, mortars, copper pots, door handles, etc. In Glubokoye the police walked from house to house checking to see if the populace had any other metal items. All the stolen metal was shipped by the train car to Germany. The German authorities used everything; in the summer and fall of 1942, Glubokoye was the source of dozens of tons of "light" materials: the down and feathers of quilts and pillows that had been ripped open. . . .

The grief and suffering which befell the people of Glubokoye were immeasurable.

Aside from physical torments, the Germans also subjected the Jewish population to moral torture and mockery.

The terrible cruelty of the Germans was aimed, not only at the living, but also at the dead.

The Germans forced the Jews themselves to break up the stone fence around the cemetery, cut down all the trees, and destroy the markers.

On the night of June 18, 1942, a bloody "aktion" took place. There was a heavy rain, and the earth shuddered from the screams of women and the cries and groans of their children. Suddenly, in the frightening nocturnal darkness, the old men began to recite the sad sounds of *El Male Rahamim*, the prayer said after a death. As soon as it became light, the people were herded to the place of execution in Borki. A young girl, Zelda Gordon, gave a shout and set off running in the direction of the lake, and others followed her.

Bullets cut down the runners, and for a half hour the entire field — all the way to Borki — was littered with bodies. Bloody torture awaited anyone who refused to go meekly to his death. Samuil Gordon tried to hide in the first ghetto (the "aktion" was directed mainly toward the second ghetto), but he was caught. He was beaten terribly, and then dragged by the neck with a poker through the streets until he died.

Those left in the field after this "aktion" knew that their days were numbered.

Even though they were deprived of all human rights and had to endure the terrible conditions of the ghetto, Jews ignored the danger and helped the Soviet prisoners of war. One and a half kilometers from Glubokoye, in the village of Bervechu, there was a prisoner-of-war camp. The Kozliner family brought the prisoners bread. Kozliner was observed doing this by the Germans, and his entire family of eight was shot.

It was difficult to leave the ghetto. There were sentries everywhere, and the Germans kept the people terrified and passive by holding them responsible for each other. The thought of struggle and vengeance, however, lived on in the people's hearts.

In spring of 1942, Jewish youths displayed great resource and inventiveness in obtaining weapons. We are obliged in this regard to remember the first heroes to sacrifice themselves. Ruvim Iokhelman, from Gayduchishki, got a job at the warehouse of the gendarmerie to be able to smuggle out weapons and medicine. In spite of the enormous risk, he did this for a rather long time before he was caught by the Germans and subjected to a horrendous death. . . .

Yakov Friedman became a "specialist" in obtaining weapons in the villages. In the fall of 1942 he joined the partisan unit "Mstitel" (The Avenger) and fought in its ranks without regard to his own safety until the Red Army arrived.

Moisey Berkon's son-in-law brought rifles, grenades, and revolvers and shipped them in significant quantities to the partisan units. He was turned in, and when the Germans came for him, he resisted desperately.

Klainer from Luchai (near Dunilovich) also sent weapons to the partisans, and also to the camp-ghetto in the fall of 1942. He struck a German who was standing guard, grabbed his submachine gun, and disappeared into the forest.

In the summer of 1942, a group of young people went into the forest with weapons in their hands and joined the partisans.

The most famous of the original partisans from Glubokoye was Avner Feigelman. This youth was intelligent, level-headed, and decisive in his actions. He fought in the Voroshilov Brigade. Others who fought manfully and without regard to their own safety were Isaak Blat (in the Chapayev Unit of the Voroshilov Brigade), Borya Shapiro, and Khasya, a girl from Disna.

Bomka Genikhovich from Plissa was an avenger of the people. The German, Koppenberg had killed his father, and the youth tracked Koppenberg down and killed him. The German bitch Ida Oditsky was notorious for her cruelty and had taken part in mass murders and in persecuting the partisans. Genikhovich and several of his comrades succeeded in luring her into the forest. There they conducted a speedy, but just trial and hanged her.

In September, 1942, another armed group of seventeen persons left to join the partisans. These were the Katsovich brothers, Zalman Milkhman, Mikhail Feigel, Yakov Ruderman, Rakhmiel Milkin, David Glezer.

This group had been in contact with the partisan unit "Mstitel" (Avenger) while still in the ghetto and had sent weapons to the unit. Now they joined the unit, which was located near the village of Univer in the Myadelsky region.

A few months later another eighteen people left the ghetto to join the partisans. Among them were Israel Shparber, Moisey and Sonya Feigel, Girsh Gordon, Simon Soloveychik, Girsh Izraelev.

Two days after this group left, the Gestapo surrounded the homes in which the families of the partisans Feigel and Milkin lived and killed fourteen people after torturing them terribly.

Iosel Feygelson's sons Zalman and Don joined the partisans, and rumors of their courage spread throughout the region. In July 1943, the Gestapo viciously murdered their father, their aunt Sarra Romm, and her daughter Nekhama Romm.

On August 17, 1943, in Krulevshchina — 19 kilometers from Glubokoye — a heavy battle took place between the Germans (supported by the local gendarmes) and the partisans. In this fight Kern, the chief of the gendarmerie in Glubokoye, was killed. Along with this rabid Hitlerian dog, several dozen Germans were also killed. The dead were taken to Glubokoye.

Naturally the Jews were forced to dig the graves, and it must be said that this was the only work that they performed with pleasure.

The fateful day was approaching; the Germans were preparing the final liquidation of the ghetto.

All those who seemed even a little suspicious were "fished out." A radio receiver was found in the attic of Zayats. He was tortured for several days, but revealed nothing.

Shloma Kraines, a blacksmith, started to shoe a horse at the request of a peasant who was an old acquaintance. This was noticed by the guard, and Shloma was shot.

The entire town knew and respected sixty-year-old Mordukh Gurevich. He was a quiet, calm person who never bore a grudge. He had lived in Glubokoye all his life, and the peasants in the area loved and respected him. Once, when sweeping the street, he greeted a peasant who was an old acquaintance. Mordukh's bow was noticed, and he was arrested, taken to Borki, and shot.

The cheerful and pleasant Salya Braun was shot for her friendship with a peasant lad, Vitya Sharobaiko.

In August 1943, the ghetto in Glubokoye was liquidated. The

German newspapers announced that they had destroyed a major partisan nest with 3,000 members and headed by a seventy-year-old rabbi. . . .

* * *

The German-Fascist troops brought destruction and death everywhere they went. On July 2, 1941, the Germans appeared in the town of Krivichi.

Several days before this seventy-year-old Zilberglayt gathered his last strength and reached Budslave, where the Red Army was positioned, and reported that German scouts had appeared in Krivichi. This information proved to be very valuable, and the Germans in Krivichi were destroyed. Old Zilberglayt paid with his life for this patriotic act. . . . He was denounced and killed on the very first day of the German occupation of Krivichi.

As everywhere, the Germans tried to isolate the Jews from the rest of the population.

In Krivichi the residents were obliged to daily hang out flags on their houses — at first, white, and then black-and-white, and then other colors as well. A distinction was made for Jews; their flags had to be of a different color so as to distinguish their houses from those of the peasants. The Rayak brothers write: "Many of the peasants found this very difficult to do, and they wanted to refuse those services. They could not reconcile themselves to the fact that their neighbors, with whom they had always lived in friendship, were enslaved and forced to work for them."

There were five Soviet prisoners of war in Krivichi, and the Jews helped them in every way possible.

The local police daily summoned the Jews to the police station, and people who were known and respected in town were whipped with birch rods for no reason whatsoever.

As soon as morning broke, the Jews would be herded off to work. The mockery they had to endure, however, was an even greater torment than the work itself. The Jews were forced to dance, to run, to sing "The International" and "Katiusha." As they worked, they were beaten with sticks and whips for the slightest error. Almost daily, people were brought home maimed and frequently unconscious. Jewish women were sent to do field work. Once, in the middle of August of 1941, the Germans gathered the Jewish girls who were working in the garden of the local priest Kropovitsky. After work, they were locked in the barn, and the

Germans attempted to rape them; the girls broke the windows and escaped. Bullets followed them, but many managed to escape.

Jewish property was stolen in pirate-like fashion, the synagogue was damaged, and extremely valuable books kept there were ripped up and burned.

Rabbi M. Perets and Movsha Dreizin became the next victims. The Gestapo men came to Dreizin's apartment together with the police. Everyone in the apartment was made to face the wall, and the book shelf was overturned. When absolutely everything had been taken from the apartment, they left.

In March 1942, government officials arrived in Krivichi from Smorgon with twenty carts of stolen articles and valuables. The Jews were called in to unload these goods.

It was a cold March day, and the Jews were kept outside in a piercing wind for several hours. During the work they were forced to run barefoot through the puddles, lie down in them, and get up.

In April 1942, the first "aktions" began: the Germans killed the Gypsies and the prisoners of war. The Jewish population was next in line. The residents of the town of Dolginovo died terribly; most of them were burned alive.

Dolginovo is fifteen kilometers from Krivichi, and the residents of the two towns were close to each other.

The few Dolginovo Jews who survived presented a terrible sight. Less than 100 of them were brought to Krivichi. Barefoot and virtually naked, they were forced to crawl on all fours, sing Soviet songs, dance.

It is difficult to imagine the general harassment to which the Jews were subjected. They had to clean latrines with their bare hands and carry excrement on their shoulders in sacks. The overseers took pleasure in their victims' suffering.

On April 25, 1942, about 1½ kilometers from Krivichi, the partisans derailed a train carrying gasoline, and it burst into flame. This incident was used by the Germans as a pretext to begin a general "aktion" against the Jews.

On April 28, 1942, twelve Jews who happened to be walking by were seized and sent to Smolovichi, where they were tortured terribly and, finally, shot.

On the same day a group of SS soldiers and gendarmes arrived in Krivichi, surrounded the town in an unbroken ring, and chased the Jewish population out into the square where they were kept all day.

In the square the doomed people were forced to strip naked and were then driven out into a field. There was a large barn there which the Germans set on fire. The people were driven into the flames.

The sight of children burning alive was terrible!

Twelve-year-old Sarra Katsovich struggled with all her might for her life; the girl had a great thirst for life. The dying child ran out of the burning barn, and the policemen pushed her back into the flame and shouted to her: "Well, my beauty, you got your savior, Stalin!"

Blyuma Kaplan also died in the flame; but the victims can never all be named.

Girsh Tsepelevich had led an active life under Soviet rule. A cripple, he could not go far with the retreating Red Army and was forced to return to Krivichi. For long months he hid in a small, dark, damp cellar.

He had forgotten what daylight, a bed, and clean linen were like. His sister M. Botvinnik secretly brought him a meager diet at night. When the "aktion" of April 28, 1942, broke out, Girsh Tsepelevich realized that there was no longer any sense in fighting for his life. Knowing that the hours of his life were numbered and not wanting to surrender alive to the enemy, Girsh Tsepelevich took poison which he kept on his person at all times.

Movsha-Leyb Shud had been hiding for a long time in an attic. During a search his hiding place was discovered. Shud, however, managed to knock down the policeman who came for him and run to the forest. He was caught and suffered a terrible death: he was thrown alive into a fire.

160 Jews died on April 28, and the same fate awaited the rest. Of the 420 Jewish residents of Krivichi, 336 perished.

The only survivors were those who had managed to join the partisans. In April 1942, ninety young people joined the partisan brigade "The People's Avenger." They fought manfully and without regard to their own safety, avenging the blood of their relatives and the insult to their people.

Eleven Jewish women worked in Slobodka, which was two kilometers from Krivichi. They managed to deceive the German guards, escape to the forest and join the partisans.

Five children worked in the small town of Pokut (four kilometers from Krivichi). When the ghetto was liquidated, the Germans killed the children as well. Only one boy, Gevish Gitlits, managed to run away to the partisans.

The Fascists wiped entire Jewish *shtetls* from the face of the earth. For example, 500 people were killed in Braslavl and 2,000 in Miory. The camp-ghettos in Plissa, Luzhki, and Novy Pogost were totally liquidated.

The slaughter of Jews in the *shtetls* was particularly cruel; people were thrown into fires. In the town of Sharkovshchina the Germans poked out eyes, cut out tongues, and tore out hair before killing the people.

The Germans also forced the Jews to do overtaxing jobs which were frequently unnecessary and senseless. At night people carried water in leaking buckets. In Dolginovo people were harnessed to plows and harrows.

Weak women were forced to carry heavy rocks and large boxes of sand, a job which turned out to be totally unnecessary. There was one goal: to torment the people. The fate prepared by the Germans for the people was terrible, and anyone who attempted to render aid to a Jew was also executed. We want to remember with gratitude the honest and self-sacrificing people who displayed strength and pureness of soul in saving Jews.

In the *shtetl* Borouchina Adolf and Maria Statsevich hid many Jews from nearby towns.

People came to the Statsevichs from all directions, and he helped them however he could. Statsevich died a martyr's death — he was hanged by the Germans.

The Jews in the towns established contact with the partisans and joined the partisan units so as to fight and avenge themselves. Forty people left the little town of Orany to join the partisans. The partisan Ayzik Lev derailed fourteen enemy trains. He fell bravely, and his memory will live on in the hearts of the people. Other partisans from Orany also fought boldly and courageously.

Particularly energetic activity was displayed by the Jewish partisans in Dolginovo, where the commander of the unit "The People's Avenger," Ivan Matveevich Timchuk, rendered them considerable assistance.

Dolginovo's Jewish partisans participated in many important operations. In May, 1942, they destroyed a sawmill, killed fifteen Germans, and seized a quantity of ammunition. In November, 1942, they took an active part in the destruction of a German garrison in Myadel; they freed the Jews from the ghetto and helped them cross the line of the front. In spite of the heavily armed German garrison in Glubokoye, the partisans smuggled out the type for a printing press.

Under the leadership of Yakov Sagalchik, the Dolginovo partisans destroyed more than thirty Germans in the village of Litvichi.

Thus did Jewish sons and daughters fight and avenge their people.

Based on materials of **M. Rayak** and **G. Rayak**.
Literary preparation by **R. Kovnator**.

The Story of Mrs. Pikman, an Engineer from Mozyr

I was born in Mozyr in 1916. From 1933 I worked in Minsk as an engineer-dispatcher. On July 25, 1941, I left the burning city of Minsk and came out onto the Moscow Highway, rested during streaming with refugees. I walked about thirty kilometers, spent the night, and set off again on my way. Fascist planes apeared and bombed and strafed us. There were many victims — old men, women, and children. I hid in the bushes. At night the bombing stopped.

I wandered in the forest without bread or water. On the fifth day I came to the village of Skuraty. There were many refugees there. The Germans came and herded everyone off to Minsk. At a check point near the city they detained all the men.

Minsk was unrecognizable; everywhere were ruins and charred bodies. Orders were pasted on the walls: all men from sixteen to sixty-five were to appear at the commandant's office; anyone who did not appear would be shot.

The men were herded off to a camp which was located at first in the Starorzhevskoye Cemetery. There people were detained for twelve days without food or water. When a barrel of water was brought, the people rushed toward it, and the Germans shot at them. Then the camp was moved to the Svisloch River, but it was forbidden to take water from the river. Jews were separated from the rest and severely beaten. Some were used for target practice. I saw my co-worker, the technician and storehouse keeper Berstein, tied to a post and shot at.

A few days later an order was posted demanding that all Jews be registered and that they make a "contribution." On July 15 all Jews were moved to the ghetto. It was announced that the Jews must build a stone wall, but then the order came to surround the ghetto with barbed wire. It was announced that any Jew — adult or child, man or woman — would be shot if found outside the ghetto. Moreover, Jews had to wear yellow circles on the back and chest.

Seventy-five thousand Jews were registered in Minsk. They were settled on several streets. Five families were crammed into every room, and people slept, standing up. The people were herded off to work without being fed and were beaten at night.

I spent three weeks in the ghetto. On August 6 I crawled through the barbed wire and began to make my way to Mozyr through country roads. I walked for a long time and became very weak.

Finally, on August 30, I came to my home town.

My father, grandfather, and great-grandfather were born in Mozyr. I had an uncle, an artist and engraver by the name of Razumovsky, who lived in Paris. In his old age he wrote a book about his life and described Mozyr lovingly. We were very much attached to our town.

Mozyr seemed totally deserted. There were no Germans in the town; they had moved on east. I met some old women and told them who I was. They said that my relatives had managed to evacuate. I went to our house and found it had been looted. Looters were rummaging through the houses. Of the Jewish population only the ill, the old, and women with children remained in town.

I was taken in by Aunty Glasha, a Byelorussian woman who was our neighbor. On September 6, while wandering down the empty streets, I suddenly saw German soldiers in camouflage uniforms. They were shooting at the windows of the houses as they walked along. It turned out that this was the first punitive unit. On that day the following people were killed: the old cobbler, Malyavsky, a Polish actress, a Byelorussian family that lived on Pushkin Street and had come from Pinsk, another Byelorussian family that lived on Pyatnitskaya Street, the elderly Lakhman and his wife, and many others. The dogs dragged Lakhman's body down Novostroeniya Street.

Aunty Glasha said to me: "Go away. There is a viper living in this building, and she said to me: 'When the Germans come, I'll tell them that you are keeping a Jewess.'" I left and moved in with my grandmother Golda Bobrovsky. She was seventy-three years old. She lived at the very outskirts of town.

On September 9 I went to Saet Street, where many Jews used to live. There were corpses in every apartment: old women, children, women with their bellies slashed open. I saw the old man, Malkin. He had not been able to leave Mozyr, since his legs were paralyzed. He lay on the floor, his skull crushed.

A young German was walking down Romashev-Rov Lane. He was carrying a year-old baby pinioned on his bayonet. The baby was still crying weakly. And the German was singing. He was so engrossed in what he was doing that he did not notice me.

I went into several apartments: everywhere were bodies and blood. In one cellar I found living people — women with children. They told me that the old men had left for the ravines near Pushkin Street.

On September 10 I heard shots: people were being executed. On Lenin Street I saw a sick old man, the hatter Simonovich. The Germans were beating him with rifle butts and pushing him along, but he could not walk.

I returned to grandmother Golda. I sat on the porch and considered how to reach the front. It was six or seven P.M. Suddenly I saw Jews being led down Novostroeniya Street. Some had shovels, and at first I thought they were being taken to work. There were about two hundred of them. Bearded, bent-over old men were walking in front, followed by boys of 12–15 years; then several men who were dragging cripples and the ill. One tall, thin man was leading two feeble old men by the hand. His head was bare, and he was looking upward. The Germans beat him with rifle butts, but he never once screamed. I will never forget his face.

They were led to the steep face of the mountain and were forced to crawl up it. The old men lost their grip and fell down. They were urged on with bayonets. Later I heard bursts of machine-gun fire.

A half hour later the Germans left the mountain; they were singing.

The people who were on the mountain said that the Germans threw the old men into the pit alive. Some tried to crawl out, and their hands were chopped off at the wrist.

As the Fascists were leaving the execution site, I saw two soldiers drag two Jews up the mountain. As soon as they reached the top, shots rang out. These people were not buried. The two soldiers ran to catch up with the others; they were also singing.

The house in which I spent the night was one hundred meters from the pit. All night I heard groans. Two years have passed since then, but every night I hear someone groaning.

The next morning Aunty Glasha met me with the words: "We are all doomed." She said the Germans were driving all the women and children to the Pripyat River and throwing them in. The children were lifted on bayonets. Aunty Glasha shouted: "Why the children? The animals! They'll kill everyone. . . ."

I went back upstairs. Golda Bobrovsky was praying. Toward evening the Germans and policemen came. They asked me: "Where are the Jews here?" I answered that I did not know, because I was not from this area. Just then they spotted old Golda. They attacked and beat her with rifle butts. I ran out and hid in the corn. The landlady came and said: "Stay here. They're looking for you." It was a very brilliant sunset. I waited for them to come. . . .

But they left. I changed clothes and stole out of town. I decided to make my way through the front. In the village of Kozenki I met a plumber who had come from Mozyr. I had seen him in the Bobrovsky apartment. He said that old Golda had been bayonetted and that her body had been discarded near the cemetery. There were many bodies of old men, old women, and children there. Pieces of heads, trunks, arms, and legs were scattered on the ground.

The Jews in town had all been killed. By that time the punitive unit had split up to cover the villages. The plumber said: "You're still young; I don't know who you are, but I feel sorry for you. Get away." In this village lived a Jewish woman who taught in the school. Her husband was a Byelorussian. I went to see her. She was young and very beautiful. She had three children, of whom the oldest was six and the youngest could not yet walk. I suggested to her that we leave together. She answered: "Where can I go with these three small children?" While spending the night in the next village, I learned that members of the punitive unit had come to Kozenki and killed the teacher and her children.

I witnessed many things. I saw the ghetto in Orsha. It was even more terrible than that of Minsk. Freezing old women rummaged among the corpses. Girls, bruised and swollen from hunger, asked: "When will they come for us?" Death seemed a relief to them. Twenty old Jewish carpenters who did not wish to surrender themselves into the hands of the executioners gathered at the home of Eli Gofstein on Pushkin Street, poured kerosene on the house, and burned themselves alive. Their charred bodies lay there unburied. . . .

I saw a prisoner-of-war camp in Orsha. The Fascists kicked the prisoners with their boots and beat them with rifle butts and whips. I saw a camp in Smolensk. Human shades had to bury the dead — 300–400 a day. In the city of Pochinka I was arrested and tortured; they wanted to find out if I was Jewish. I remained silent, and I was beaten with a whip, and my teeth were knocked out. In Pochinka I saw Russians hanged. I saw Germans rob, kill, and laugh at misery. Hungry and barefoot, I walked east. I gathered ears of grain in the fields and lived the life of a beggar. I was run over by a German automobile, and my leg was broken. I fell ill with typhus and asked the doctor not to treat me. I reached Orel and saw the partisans. I saw Soviet people fight the invaders. And finally I saw a miracle; on August 5, 1943, I saw a red star on the cap of a Red-Army soldier.

Basya Pikman

Prepared for publication by **Ilya Ehrenburg**.

The Story of Doctor Olga Goldfayn

The war caught me in the border town of Pruzhany, where I was a doctor in the hospital. I was on duty in the early hours of June 22, 1941. The Gemans began to bomb the town at 3:30 A.M.

The Germans entered the town on the twenty-third and immediately jumped out of their cars to rob and beat the Jews. They brought with them many White-Army soldiers who began to urge the people to carry out a pogrom. We all locked ourselves in our houses.

On the third day the Germans demanded that we surrender all eating utensils: knives, spoons, pots, dishes. Two days later they demanded our beds, bed linens, etc.

On July 10, after the army had passed through, the Gestapo troops arrived, and what began then is indescribable. First of all, they seized eighteen Jews and shot them two kilometers from town. We learned of the fate of these unfortunate people only ten days later, when a dog dragged in the arm of a doctor with a red cross on the sleeve.

On July 15, the Germans posted an announcement requiring the Jews to select a Jewish council — a *Judenrat* — within the next three days. If the *Judenrat* was not formed, 100 people would be shot. None of the Jews wanted to join the *Judenrat*. One Jew consulted with the Poles and decided it was necessary to present a list of Jews without their knowledge so that when they were summoned it would be a *fait accompli*. The list contained people with a higher education — lawyers, doctors. But the Germans took one look at the list and said that they needed skilled laborers and not scholars. A week later they themselves selected a *Judenrat*.

On July 20 Gestapo men appeared at the *Judenrat* and announced that a large indemnity would have to be paid to them. Three days later the Germans picked up the indemnity but did not leave any receipt with the *Judenrat*. Jews from surrounding towns asked us to help them pay the indemnity. We had no valuables or money. We collected all the valuables that we had left — brooches, rings, menorahs from the synagogue — and thus covered the indemnity for the towns of Shirokov, Malich, and Linovo.

From the very beginning of forced labor, people often returned from work crippled and beaten.

On August 10, the German High Command posted an announcement requiring all Jews in the occupied territories to move to the ghettos.

For two months we slept in our clothes, keeping a small bundle under our heads and ready at any minute to leave.

On October 10, it became known that a *Judenstadt* was being organized in Pruzhany. We would stay where we were, and residents of Bialystok would come to our *Judenstadt*. On October 25 we were moved to the ghetto. Part of the ghetto was surrounded by barbed wire, and part had a solid wall.

Jews from Bialystok kept arriving for six weeks — three thousand widows and two thousand orphans. Outside of town the Germans set up a "control chamber" where they mercilessly beat and robbed the new arrivals.

At the same time Jews from other towns and *shtetls* began to arrive — Belovasha, Bluden, Malich, Shereshovo, Bereza, Slonim, and others.

On January 3, 1942, the Germans demanded a second indemnity. They took our fur coats and all woolen and fur items. A Jewish woman did not have the right to wear so much as a fur button. All cameras, rugs, gramophones, and records were confiscated. We were presented with a bill for equipping the ghetto which we ourselves had been forced to build: 750,000 marks and then 500,000 marks in a second indemnity.

On January 9, the mayor, a German woman named Horn, announced that all Jews must leave the ghetto at once. Thanks to the large bribe which we paid Madame Gorn and the gendarmes, these Jews were left in the ghetto until spring.

In February a new mayor, Koschman, arrived in town and demanded a third contribution in money and clothing. In addition, a tax was established — ten marks per person. The *Judenrat* had to pay for those who had no money.

In March 1942, Jews began to arrive from Ivantsevichi, Stolbtsy, and other places. They were in terrible shape; they were half-naked, and their hands were frostbitten. In April more people than ever were packed into the ghetto. In May people began to be recruited for the camps, from which no one ever returned. In winter we cleared the snow from the rails from Dinovo to Baranovichi, but some young people were taken to the camps anyway. In the spring and summer we dug peat, removed stumps, cut trees in a one-hundred-meters-wide strip along the railroad, loaded ammunition, filled in pits with sand, etc.

The Germans set up shoe-repair, tailoring, and furniture artels.
The Germans transported all metal to Germany; they dismantled the narrow-gauge railroad in Pruzhany.

At 5:00 A.M. on November 2, Gestapo men encircled the ghetto and announced that we would be evacuated. They warned that each person could take no more than fifty kilograms of baggage. Our ghetto was like an oasis in the desert; the Jews in all the other towns had already been killed, and we understood what our fate was to be. Many decided to die and rushed to their medicine cabinets for poison. Forty-seven people took poison and died. I also decided to die. We had a supply of morphine, and we divided it among ourselves — one gram per person. I swallowed one gram and injected one gram into a vein. After that we locked ourselves in our apartments and tried to induce carbon-monoxide poisoning. The *Judenrat* learned of this and opened the apartments. Everyone was unconscious, and one fortunate person had already died. The medical personnel treated us for three days, and we returned to life.

On November 7, I received a note from a nun whom I knew — Sister Chubak. She asked me to meet her. I went to the barbed-wire barrier and saw her. She gave a liter of vodka to the sentry, and he permitted us to talk. She gave me 300 marks to bribe the guards. I told her that I was exhausted and in no condition to struggle any further; I said it would be better if I left this life. When we separated, I decided to be rude to the guard so that he would shoot me. At first the guard was amazed that I had the courage to address him. I asked him if he believed Hitler — that we were biologically not people. Could it be that the Germans, who considered themselves to be cultured people, were not ashamed to torment all these helpless widows, old people, and children? Could it be, I asked, that he did not know the situation of the German army? After all, they had not been able to take Stalingrad, they were surrounded in the Caucasus, and they were on the run in Egypt. They could not win the war, and without a "Blitz" they would lose. I told him that the *Führer* had inoculated the German people with rabies, and they had, in fact, gone mad — like dogs. "I want you to understand, sergeant," I said, "that I want you to survive, go home, and remember the words of this little Jewess who told you the truth."

But the sergeant did not shoot me.

Then I went to Berestitsky, a barber friend of mine. I knew him to be a resolute person. I called him out into the alley and said: "I wanted to take poison, but poison didn't work; I wanted to be shot, but German bullets won't kill me. There is only one way out left — escape from the ghetto." I asked him to help me. Berestitsky carefully raised the barbed wire; I crawled under it, crossed the street, the gardens, and the yards, and rushed to the convent. Soon I was with my acquaintance, the nun. She immediately gave me different clothes and hid me. I had three places to take refuge — in the cow shed, under the stairway, and between two cupboards. I sat locked up and constantly looked out of the window to see who was coming. All this time I had terrible toothaches, and I could not sleep at night, but I could not go to a dentist. The week passed in constant terror. In the daytime I hid in the room, and at night I would come out in the yard and listen to what was happening in the ghetto. It was dark and terrifying. Fires blazed around the ghetto, and machine guns and light tanks were stationed all around. Planes flew over the ghetto.

At the end of the fifth week of my stay in the convent a representative of the *Judenrat* came to me with letters from the chairman of the *Judenrat* and my husband. They wrote that the Germans were interested in my health. (The Germans believed that I was still sick after the poisoning.) If I did not return, the ghetto would suffer because of me.

I did not take long to think the matter over: if the ghetto was in danger because of me, I would return. But I did not know how to enter the ghetto. The messenger said that he would disguise me as an employee of the commissar who was going to the ghetto to find good wool to knit him a sweater.

A few hours later I was in the ghetto. I did not find my home. It had been walled off from the ghetto, and my husband and I moved in with my friend, Nitsberg-Mashenmesser, a dentist.

Upon returning to the ghetto, I learned that Africa was almost entirely liberated and that the Germans were surrounded in Tunis. Everyone was in better spirits.

On January 27, 1943, while returning from visiting a female patient, I heard shooting in the *Judenrat*. Ten minutes later I was summoned there. I found two wounded persons and one dead. It turned out that the shooting had been done by Wilhelm, the head of the Gestapo. He had burst into the building of the *Judenrat* at 7:00 P.M. and had accused the *Judenrat* of involvement with partisans. He killed the guard on the spot and wounded two members of the *Judenrat*.

At 5:00 A.M. of January 28, troops approached the ghetto, and at 7:00 an evacuation was declared. At 8:00 many carts were brought in to remove us from the ghetto. The head of the Gestapo, Wilhelm, ordered that only some of the carts remain and that the others be sent on the twenty-ninth, the thirtieth, and the thirty-first. The first group of carts set off at 9:00 A.M., and I was one of the passengers.

It took us five hours to reach the Linovo station, where the Germans told us to get out of the carts. Everyone was beaten on the head with whips until he or she lost consciousness. I received two such blows, and my head buzzed like a telegraph pole. Seeing death very near, I left my things on the cart. I lost sight of my husband at once. We were kept at the train station for three hours, and our train (unheated boxcars) arrived at 6:00. At 7:00 boarding commenced. On the platform we had to walk over corpses. We were thrown into the cars like sacks of potatoes. The Germans tore children from their mothers and killed them on the spot.

At the last minute, just before the car was to be sealed, I jumped out onto the tracks. My "badge" was covered with a large kerchief. I walked quickly down a street, came to a garden, and walked along a fence into a field. After that I walked only through fields, since there were Gestapo men on the road.

When I reached the military settlement, I was stopped by the shout of a sentry: "Halt!" I pretended to be a Byelorussian and said that I was going from my village to the neighboring one, where my daughter was giving birth. The sentry permitted me to go.

In this fashion I walked until 2:00 A.M. Finally I reached the town. I wandered around the outskirts of town for two hours, afraid to meet anyone. I approached the convent with extreme caution and quietly knocked at the window. The mother-superior opened the door and immediately began to rub my hands. My friend, Sister Chubak, put me in her bed, and I fell asleep.

In the morning (January 29) I was awakened by crying. It was one of the nuns; it turned out that she was afraid that my return to the convent would doom the nuns. Sister Chubak tried to convince her that we would leave the following day, but the other nun kept repeating: "Doctor Goldfayn has to die anyway, and we will die because of her." At that point I broke into the conversation and said that if I had managed to jump from a death train, I would manage to leave this house without causing any unpleasantness.

Announcements appeared in town declaring that all barns, attics, cellars, and outhouses should be locked to keep the Jews out. Dogs were to be unleashed. If a Jew was found in any house, the entire population would be killed.

The sixteen-year-old serving girl of the convent, Ranya Kevyursky, walked twelve kilometers to the village to find a cart for me. She returned late that night and said that a cart would come in the morning.

The cart arrived at 10:00 A.M. I donned the habit of a nun and put on dark glasses. Sitting on the cart, I stared stubbornly at the bundle in my hands. Sister Chubak went ahead on foot. I left the town under the eyes of the Gestapo men. Precisely at that time a third train of carts full of Jews was passing. Kalinovsky, a Polish woman whom I knew, came toward us and made a sign to Sister Chubak indicating that I was well disguised. This frightened me, because I was afraid that she would turn me in. My companion assured me that Kalinovsky sympathized deeply with the Jews in their misfortune. She had come out onto the road, because she had learned that there were plans to save me, and she wanted to be sure that everything went well.

We were on the road until 5:00. The horse was exhausted, and we decided to spend the night in the nearest village. My companion asked the village elder for permission to spend the night, but he declared that there was no room; twenty German gendarmes were spending the night in the village. We decided it would be better for us to leave, got back on the cart, and moved on. The exhausted horse could hardly walk. We entered an enormous forest — the Bialowieza Forest. Along the road we saw a small house. My companion went in and met a former pupil there. We were well received and spent the night in a warm place. We continued our journey at dawn. Finally we arrived at Bialowieza and headed for the Catholic Church. Then we went to Chainovka, from there to Belsk, and from Belsk to Bialystok by train. On the train we learned that the Germans had surrounded the ghetto on February 2 and that a slaughter was taking place there.

In Bialystok we went to the main convent. I asked the mother-superior to hide me, but she was frightened and ordered us to leave immediately. In leaving the convent I said to my companion that we should not reveal our secret to any other person.

That night we found ourselves on the street and did not know where to go. Then my companion remembered that she knew the address of the brother of one of the nuns. He was not home, but his wife received us gladly. At that moment the Jews of Bialystok were being slaughtered. The town was full of Gestapo men, and all the residents were afraid that they might be suspected of being Jews. There were no tickets being sold at the train stations. We asked the head of the station to give us poor nuns, who were forced to beg for charity, a ticket without a pass. At first he refused, but then he gave in. I was afraid to put the precious tickets in my pocket and held them in my hand the entire time.

In this fashion we left Bialystok on February 13 by train and went to the Lapy Station. From there we went by cart to various Catholic churches — Dombrovo, Sokoly, Mokiny. From there we travelled to Warsaw by train. In the Government-General we were no longer afraid to being detained, since no one asked for passports. From Warsaw we went to Lowicz, where my companion's family lived. We spent sixteen months there; no one knew that I was a Jew. I worked as a nurse and had a large practice.

In May, 1944, we decided to move to Naleczów, near the Bug River. This was about twenty-two kilometers from Lublin.

On July 26, 1944, Naleczów was liberated by the Red Army, and on July 29 I set out east — partly on foot, and partly by automobile. I eventually made my way to my home town of Pruzhany.

Pruzhany had been liberated on July 16. Of the 2,700 Jews who had taken refuge in the forest only about twenty young people returned to the town; all the rest perished. The local people were very happy at my return and my friends, acquaintances, and patients literally made pilgrimages to me. At the same time it must be said that there were people who were frightened when they saw me — a person who had come back from the other world, a witness to who knows what sinister deeds.

A stenogram. Prepared for publication by **Vasily Grossman**.

Brest

One of the first victims, Brest was occupied by the Germans at the very beginning of the war.

Before the war about twenty-six thousand Jews lived in Brest; among them were engineers, physicians, technicians, lawyers, highly skilled carpenters. Of all those people, no more than fifteen miraculously survived the violence.

This is what those few survivors tell about the first days of the German occupation of Brest.

Vera Samuilovna Baklyash:

"The day the Germans arrived, the Jewish population immediately felt the weight of the German paw. Searches were carried out, and people were herded off to forced labor. After work, the people were forced to dance and to crawl on their bellies, those who refused to obey were beaten."

Tanya Samuilovna Gutman:

"The life of the Jews became terrible from the very first day. The Germans took everyone off to work, tormented them pitilessly, then robbed them and demanded gold. Those who did not give gold were beaten and shot. Cruel as tigers, they (the Germans) ran from one house to another."

Osher Moiseevich Zisman:

"In the beginning of July, 1941, the Germans began to take the Jews to 'work.' In point of fact they took all captured Jews to the Brest Fort and kept them there in terrible conditions. In the July heat the people were not given water or bread for five days; then they were all shot. One Jew survived and he said that, when he crawled out of the grave, there were many living and half-living people left, since only the first rows had been struck by the bullets. When the Germans began to fill in the graves with earth and hot lime, many were still alive."

"In the city of Kobrin of the Brest *oblast*," Zisman writes, "the Germans burned down the Jewish hospital and the apartment of the rabbi. The local firemen were ordered not to extinguish the flame, and the fires spread to the rest of the town. The Germans threw living Jews into the flames."

On July 12, 1941, a search was carried out for Jewish men. The Katsaf sisters, Maria and Sulamith, write:

"They were taken at night from their beds. Those who hid

213

survived for another year. Five thousand men were arrested; among them were thirteen-year-old boys and seventy-year-old men. A large number of educated people were taken away — doctors, engineers, lawyers. Among them were our good friends: Doctor Gotbetter, a pediatrician; Doctor Frukhtgarten and Doctor Tanenbaum, specialists in internal diseases; the well-known lawyers, Berlyand, Adunsky, Belov; the engineer, Mostovlyansky; and others."

Tanya Samuilovna Gutman writes:

"They rounded up five thousand men in the search, took them outside of town, and shot them. Among them were doctors, engineers, lawyers."

Osher Moiseevich Zisman writes:

"Before shooting my elderly father, the German beasts pulled out his gray beard. My brother was a dentist. The mad German dogs knocked out all his teeth before the execution. When he fell unconscious at the edge of the grave, they laughed and ordered him to make himself false teeth."

Conditions of inconceivable horror were created for those Jews who survived the first days of the occupation. All Jews were ordered to wear yellow armbands with the "Mogendovid" sign; after a while these armbands were replaced with yellow circles ten centimeters (four inches) in diameter which had to be worn on the chest and the left shoulder; as a result Jews could be recognized a kilometer away. The Jews were forbidden to walk down the sidewalk. "They were permitted to walk only down the center of the street," T. S. Gutman writes. The Katsaf sisters write: "This created an emormous impression and was considered a terrible indignity; we did not know what horrors awaited us."

Jews were not yet deprived of life, but life had already been transformed into a hell. This is what the Katsaf sisters tell:

"From the very first days of the occupation the Jews were forbidden to go to the bazaar, and all those who succeeded in doing so were driven away with whips and submachine guns."

V. S. Baklyash adds:

". . . it was forbidden to go to the bazaar, and in the neighboring villages it was not permitted to sell anything to Jews. If anyone did succeed in buying anything, it was confiscated."

The Katsaf sisters write: "Robberies began at the very outset of the occupation; everything was confiscated: beds, linen, dishes, furniture. Nothing was taken into consideration; our daughter-in-law, a helpless, pregnant woman, lost her only bed and blanket. For some their own personal items were their only source of support, but it was almost impossible to sell anything, since it was forbidden to buy from Jews."

Nevertheless, this was something similar to freedom by comparison with the life that awaited the Jews.

At the end of November 1941, the Fascist authorities selected several streets in Brest, where they settled all the remaining Jews, and surrounded the area with barbed wire. This was how the ghetto came to be in Brest.

Vera Baklyash writes: "The police stood at the gates and would not permit anyone to leave the ghetto; non-Jews were not permitted to enter. People were herded off to work under police guard; Jews were forbidden to walk alone down the street. If anyone succeeded in buying anything along the way home, it was confiscated by the police, who searched all those returning from work. Ration cards were issued which provided people with 150 grams (1/3 pound) of bread a day."

"Living conditions were a nightmare," writes Sikorsky. "People in the ghetto were denied the opportunity to acquire any foodstuffs whatsoever. If anyone had any reserves, they were quickly confiscated by the German police, and the people were literally hungry."

Tanya Gutman writes: "We were taken from the ghetto to forced labor. Even teenagers were forced to perform the heaviest of tasks. I had to load heavy items, and I was sometimes beaten for not being able to carry out an order."

"Jews in the ghetto were forbidden under pain of death by shooting to get married or have children," writes Osher Moiseevich Zisman.

Such was the existence in the ghetto, and while people died by the hundreds from hunger, unbearable work, and devilishly contrived living conditions, the Aryan rulers calmly laid their plans without excessive nervousness or bustling and prepared the scene for the last bloody act of the tragedy — the destruction of the Jews.

An official document, written by a commission consisting of representatives of the Soviet government, partisans, and citizens of the Brest *oblast*, tells us how this act was conceived and prepared:

"*A Report on the Atrocities, Robberies, Harassments, and Destruction Caused by the German-Fascist Invaders in the Region of Bronnaya Gora, the Brest oblast.*

"The commission consisted of the chairman Arkady Ivanovich

Tarasevich and the following members: Vasily Nikolaevich Bury, Chairman of the District Executive Committee; Ivan Pavlovich Kashtelyan, representing the partisans; and Comrade Novik, representing the citizens of the Berezov Region.

"An examination of the scenes of mass torture and execution of Soviet citizens by German-Fascist invaders and the questioning of a number of citizens in this regard have revealed *the mass destruction of Soviet citizens.*

"Using plans drawn up in advance by the German-Fascist invaders, graves were dug in May and June of 1942 in an area occupying 16,800 square meters in the area of Bronnaya Gora, 400 meters from the Bronnaya Gora Railroad Station.

"From 600 to 800 persons from the nearby villages of the Berezov Region were mobilized daily to dig the graves. In order to complete the work as soon as possible, the Germans used missiles and explosives such as tolite.

"When the graves had been completed, the Germans began in June, 1942, to bring trainloads of Soviet citizens of various nationalities to the Bronnaya Gora Station. These were Russians, Byelorussians, Jews, and Poles; they included men and women, small babies and very old people.

"The arriving cars were accompanied by special German guards in the uniforms of the S.D. and the SS. The cars arrived from various parts of Byelorussia, the railroad stations Bereza, Brest, Dragichino, Yanovo, Goroda, and others. Soviet citizens were also brought to the Bronnaya Gora region on foot.

"The train cars were extremely overcrowded, and among the exhausted citizens there were many dead. As the cars arrived, they were shunted onto a side track which led to the military supply depots 250 meters from the Bronnaya Gora Station in the central rail system. The trains were stopped beside graves which had been dug in advance, and disembarkation took place in a specially prepared area surrounded with barbed wire.

"During disembarkation the people were forced to strip naked and throw their clothing into a pile. Then they were led along a narrow barbed-wire corridor to the pits. The first comers were forced to lie face down on the ground in compact rows. After the first rows were filled in, Germans in SS and S.D. uniforms shot the people with submachine guns. The same was done with the second and third rows — until the graves were filled.

"All these atrocities were accompanied by the harrowing screams of men, women and children. When the train had been completely unloaded and the citizens had been shot, the clothing and belongings of the victims were loaded into the cars and sent off in an unknown direction. The arrival of trains at the execution area and their return was strictly controlled by the Bronnaya Gora station master Heil, and also by Pike and Schmidt, the duty officers. All three were of German nationality.

"In order to conceal all traces of the crimes committed in the Bronnaya Gora region, the Germans shot the entire civilian population inhabiting the territory of the military supply depots (more than 1,000 persons). There were eight graves in the area where the mass executions occurred: the first was 63 meters by 6.5; the second was 36 meters by 6.5; the third was 36 by 6; the fourth was 37 by 6; the fifth was 52 by 6; the sixth was 24 by 6; the seventh was 12 by 6; and the eighth was 16 by 4.5. All graves were 3.5 to 4 meters deep.

"More than 30,000 peaceful Soviet citizens were shot by the Germans in the area of Bronnaya Gora."

On October 16 came the turn of the Brest ghetto residents to say goodbye to life. Here is what the survivors related about this day:

"On October 14, 1942, the (people of the) ghetto became very upset. Something was happening beyond the barbed wire encircling the ghetto. It was noisy, and there were very many police units about. What could this mean? By evening the police had left, and the people calmed down somewhat. At 6:00 A.M. on October 15 we were awakened by our neighbor who said the ghetto was surrounded. It had begun! It is difficult to describe what happened. Some people had hiding places, but those who did not rushed about the streets as if they were insane" (testimony of the Katsaf sisters).

Comrade Sikorsky has testified that ". . . on October 15, 1942, the entire ghetto was surrounded by SS and S.D. troops, and a bloody massacre ensued at 6:00 A.M. Hitler's pirates burst into houses and basements and dragged all women, old people, and babies out onto the street. They were lined up and led away to be shot."

Although they were refined in torture and execution and had no conception of pity whatsoever, these henchmen, nevertheless, knew the feeling of fear. An official commission document speaks eloquently of this:

"In order to conceal the traces of their beastly actions, the Germans brought 100 citizens by force from various parts of the Brest *oblast* to the Bronnaya Gora Railroad Station in March 1944. These people were assigned to digging graves and burning corpses. The corpses were burned in an area where the graves with the executed citizens were located. The corpses were burned day and night for fifteen days. The Germans disassembled 48 military warehouses and barracks located in the area to provide fuel for the fires. They also used an inflammable liquid which burned with a blue flame. Once the corpses were burned, the Germans shot and burned all the 100 workers who had done the digging and the burning.

"The Germans planted young trees over the graves and the areas where the burning had taken place. In the cremation areas were found fragments of charred bones, barrettes for women's hair, children's shoes, Soviet money, a shoulder bone, and the eighteen-centimeter-long arm of a baby."

Moreover, people came and told of what they had seen with their own eyes — Roman Stanislavovich Novis, Ivan Vasilyevich Govin, Borislav Mikhailovich Shchetinsky, Grigory Grigoryevich Yatskevich, and others. They were the ones who led the Soviet investigatory commission to another terrible place located near the village of Smolyarka in the Berezov region — six kilometers from the Bronnaya Gora Station, fifty meters from Smolyarka, and seventy meters from the Moscow-Warsaw Highway. This is what the commission established:

"The Germans used train cars to bring Soviet citizens from the town of Bereza and from villages in the Bereza region to the graves in the indicated area. Torture, harassment, and executions took place by the same methods as in the mass shootings at Bronnaya Gora.

Altogether, five graves were found containing the bodies of Soviet citizens. All the graves were of identical dimensions: 10 meters long, 4 meters wide, and 2.5 meters deep.

The mass execution of citizens in September 1942, on the Smolyarka territory, where witnesses testify that more than one thousand persons were shot, was confirmed by Ivan Ivanovich Gents, Ivan Stepanovich Gents, Andrey Ivanovich Levkovets, Iosif Yakovlevich Kutnik, and others.

Kokhanovsky, an engineer and resident of Brest who witnessed the Brest events, has testified:

"The entire population of approximately 20,000 Jews including the most prominent representatives of the educated class were shot: 1) Doctor Kalvarisky, an important specialist in neuropathology, 2) Doctor Ioffe, a therapist, 3) Doctor Manzon, 4) Doctor Kagan, 5) Doctor Keblitsky, 6) Doctor Mechik, 7) Mechik, a lawyer, 8) Doctor Rakif, 9) Doctor Kislyar, 10) Doctor Ivanov, 11) Zeleny, a famous woman engineer, 12) Bereshchovsky, an electrical engineer, 13) Zilberfarb, an economist, 14) Filipchuk, an engineer, 15) Golub, a technician, 16) Taran, a technician, 17) the engineer Kaminsky, and others.

"The Germans did not like the educated working class. Engineers were forced to clean livestock yards while people were called to watch them being taunted as they worked: "Engineer, Engineer." They were shot singly and together with their families. A Catholic priest was shot. The Germans destroyed all culture, the educated people, religion. The physically healthy population was taken away to Germany to forced labor, and those who remained in town were used to dig trenches."

In Brest the Red Army found people swollen from hunger, people who were half-dead, but who were miraculously saved from the German death: Tanya Gutman, Vera Bakalyash, the Katsaf sisters, and Osher Zisman. How did these people survive?

Tanya Gutman described the simple miracle of her survival as follows:

"My sister and I hid, together with my children, under a house from which we could see the Jews being led away to be shot. At first they shot people in the ghetto after they had forced them to strip so that their clothes remained behind. In my hiding place I ate raw buckwheat, flour, beets, pickles. The children became dehydrated from hunger. After two weeks I left the ghetto to see what was happening in the world. I got some bread, brought it to the children, and again left the ghetto. Even though there were already frosts, I had to sleep under an open sky. I made out this way for five weeks, but one day I came back to the ghetto and failed to find my children. Then I set out aimlessly, not knowing where I was going. Late that evening I decided to go to a Russian family that had had pity on me and had hidden me in a shed. I spent the entire winter with them, and then they hid me under the floor in a pit where I stayed until the Red Army arrived. On that day I came out to freedom, and the soldiers who had stopped in the yard gave me dinner, and I became a person again."

Osher Zisman tells the following:

"My wife, twelve other women and I hid in a pit under a shed. A few of the women who were with us went mad. Since my wife and I fell ill, we gathered our last strength and went to a different place — an attic. We lived in this miserable way for seventeen months — in attics, in cellars, in outhouses. When our town was liberated from the German bandits on the happy day of July 28, 1944, I was unable to move. Swollen from hunger and ill, I was not even capable of talking. Red-Army soldiers fed me, summoned a Soviet doctor, and thus saved my life."

Another witness tells the following:

"I did not have a husband. My sister and I took our children to a cellar which had a secret passage leading to our room. Our elderly mother pushed a cupboard in front of the entrance, and the Germans did not see it when they came. They took the old woman with them. In this fashion we remained there until November 1, eating raw beets, cabbage, raw buckwheat, and even flour mixed with salt. I decided to send my nine-year-old son to the village to our acquaintances. Two days later he returned home empty-handed and began to ask me to go for bread, saying that he would lead out the younger children after me. He cried and begged so much that I gave in. He and I left, and I managed to hide in a certain village, and the boy went for the younger children. But when he returned a few days later, he brought a thunderbolt instead of my children: they had been detained by the police. I lay unconscious for three days, but I could not stay there for long. I had to get up and set out. I spent several days outside of town in water where abandoned tanks were standing. In one village I hid under the floor of a good person until February 20. One night, however, I had to flee, since I had been reported, and a search was being conducted. I hid under a church not far from the village. I spent almost a month there with a two-kilo loaf of bread as my food supply. Hunger drove me out, and I fell exhausted in the forest. A good woman picked me up, fed me, gave me some bread, but asked me to go away, since she was afraid of the Germans. She led me to the forest, where I met partisans. I lived with their unit until the Red Army arrived."

The following is the "miracle" of Vera Bakalyash:

"At 6:00 A.M. on October 15, 1942, we took our mother and my sister's baby to a hiding place at our daughter-in-law's. Since there was no more room in the hiding place, we left them food and went out in the street, not knowing what to do with ourselves. At the last minute the idea came to me to go to the attic of our house, and sixteen of us spent five weeks in a boarded-off corner. It is difficult to imagine the conditions — hunger, cold, filth. But I consider all this unimportant. The main thing is that we were witnesses to the horrors. That is, we did not see anything, but every day we could hear 70–100 people being brought to the neighboring yard, ordered to strip. They were shot, and buried on the spot. Earlier in the morning the workers would come to dig the graves. Once we heard a child shout: 'Mama, I hope the bullet comes soon; I'm so cold.' This was in November, and the people had to strip naked. Mothers undressed their children and then undressed themselves. There are approximately 5,000 people buried across the fence from our house on 126 Kuibyshev Street. During the first three days the Jews were taken from Brest to Bronnaya Gora, where there was a lot of automobile traffic. The entire 'action' was carried out with the pomp of a major victory, such as the capture of a city or something like that. After the 'action' was carried out, singing and music were heard all night. Thus another 17,000 of Brest's Jews died, among them 25 members of our family. On November 20, 1942, the Ukrainian police found us, but they only robbed us and did not kill us. We had to leave with no idea of where we were going. We were almost naked, and we spent two miserable years like this, hiding in cellars, attics, and sheds, staying outside in the fiercest cold. The fact that we did not freeze to death was a miracle. We did not undress for a half year at a time. If that life had continued for two weeks more, we could not have endured it, but the Red Army liberated us, and our brother, a Red Army soldier, is taking vengeance for our family and the entire Soviet Union."

The entire time, in all these hiding places and cellars, from every pit and through every crack came scenes, each more terrible than the other. A bloody panorama of life was unfolding — a monstrous and daily spectacle of death.

"From the ventilation opening I saw the German henchmen mock their victims before shooting them. Under threats of being buried alive, the people were forced to strip naked. The Germans were short of bullets, and they heaped earth and hot lime on living people. I fell ill with dysentery in the cellar and I could not stand up, but through the ventilation opening I saw the Germans herd the young girls into a shed next to the graves and rape them before the execution. I heard one girl call for help; she hit the German in the snout, and for that the Germans buried her alive." This is the testimony of Osher Zisman.

Vera Bakalyash writes: "Screams and the cries of children were heard from all directions. People were put in trucks and taken away to Kartus-Bereza. There enormous pits had been dug in the clay. The children were thrown in alive and killed with grenades; the adults were buried alive."

When Vera Bakalyash learned that her children had been detained by the police, that is, learned of their death, she lay unconscious for three days. Then she got up and went through terrible trials until, at last, she reached the partisans. . . .

Of the 26,000 Brest Jews, 12 to 15 survived. It is a miracle that these people had the passionate will to live to continue their struggle for revenge in spite of the danger they experienced every day, every minute, in spite of the deaths of those near and dear to them, in spite of the most cruel and incredible denials of their bodies.

Here are the last words given to us in the commission's document:

"In the Bronnaya Gora region the Germans destroyed the railroad tracks and all buildings at or near the stations. During the retreat, the buildings were blown up and burned, and the railroad bed was destroyed by a special machine which tore up the ties and the rails. There were special railroad destruction teams; they were called *Pimaschzug* (Pioneer machine train). The commander of the team was Captain Sporberg, a German by nationality. The damage caused to the Bronnaya Gora station amounts to 1,152,000 rubles. By interrogating the population and gathering data in the Brest *oblast*, the commission established that the mass execution by shooting of Soviet citizens in the area of Bronnaya Gora and the Smolyarka lands of the Berezov region was conducted by special teams of the S.D. and the SS under the direction of the following persons:

1) The chief of the regional police bureau, Major Rode (up till the beginning of 1944).

2) The chief of the regional police bureau, Biner (from the beginning of 1944 till the Germans were driven out of Brest).

3) The chief of the First Police Sector of the town of Brest, Lieutenant Hofman.

4) The chiefs of the First Police Sector of the town of Brest, *Meister* Golter, *Meister* Grieber, and *Meister* Boss.

5) The chief of the Second Police Sector of the town of Brest, Lieutenant Prisinger (until the beginning of 1944).

6) The head of the criminal police, S.D. *Oberscharführer* Sanadsky (a German).

222

7) The commandant of the criminal police, Ivanovsky (a Pole).

8) First Deputy of the chief of the S.D., *Obersturmführer* Zibel.

9) Chief of police in the *Gebietskommissariat*, Captain Dauerlein.

10) Gerik, a member of the S.D.; in charge of the executions.

11) The chief of police in the city of Kartus-Bereza, First Lieutenant Gardes.

12) Officers of the S.D., Grieber and Wanzman, who participated directly in the executions."

Signatures of commission members
These names were preserved in the shocked memory of the witnesses and have become known to us. Let them join the ranks of henchmen who will receive a just and deserved punishment.

Oral and written testimony of the residents of Brest.

Prepared for publication by **Margarita Aliger.**

Our Struggle in Bialystok*

My name is Riva Yefimovna Shinder-Voyskovsky. I was born in Western Byelorussia, in the small town of Krynki. My parents were not wealthy, but they tried to give their children a good education. Like all inhabitants of our town, they wanted their children to "become somebody" and be spared the joyless, precarious, and beggarly existence which was the lot of so many "luftmenschen." For that reason I was given the opportunity to study. I finished high school in Grodno, and in 1923 I graduated from the Pedagogical Institute in Warsaw. For many years I worked as a history teacher in the Jewish schools of Brest-Litovsk and Lodz. I loved my work, and I can say that my pupils had a good attitude toward their studies. My classroom was quiet, and many students read the books recommended by the school program. It was a true joy to see a lively, inquisitive child's mind work and develop. My teaching was interrupted quite unexpectedly. In 1932 I was arrested for communist activities, and I was denied the right to teach school after release from prison. I was unemployed for a long time and then got a job operating a grooving machine at a textile factory. When the Second World War began, I was living in Lodz. On September 1, 1939, my husband and I left Lodz and set out in the direction of Bialystok. We reached my home town of Krynki (about 40 kilometers from Bialystok), where I became the director of a school. Soon we moved to Bialystok.

The Red Army liberated Western Byelorussia, and there was a flowering of cultural and economic activity in the towns and *shtetls*. It was a joy to live and work!

Hitler's treacherous attack took place on June 22, 1941; like a sharp knife, it cut through our life.

The Germans entered Bialystok on June 27, and almost no one managed to evacuate. In 1941 there were about 100,000 people living in Bialystok, of whom roughly 50% were Jews. The Germans immediately began to commit outrages. It was clear that the sword of death had been raised above our people. When the Germans entered the city, the first thing they did was to put to the torch several streets in one of the Jewish areas. Out of "sheer mischief" they burned down several houses together with the inhabitants. On

*The Bialystok voyvodshaft (*oblast*) was annexed by the USSR in September, 1939, and returned to Poland after the war.

the first Saturday of their rule the Germans set fire to the synagogue with 300 men in it.

The Hitlerites wanted first of all to destroy the male Jewish population. They hunted for men in the streets and entered houses, spiriting people off without regard for age, position, or health. Men went out into the street and . . . disappeared. At first men were picked up on the pretext of sending them to work. But these thousands of men were "transported" in "an unknown direction," and all trace of them was lost.

The Germans destroyed educated Jews with particular zeal and consistency.

The Hitlerites wanted not only to destroy a person physically, they wanted to destroy his dignity, his fighting spirit. In their efforts to degrade people, the Fascist monsters invented all sorts of moral torture. The strict order concerning the wearing of badges with a yellow star on the chest and back was no doubt intended primarily as a moral indignity. Many were inclined to think that there was no particular motive behind this. They said: "So what if we wear yellow stars; we are not killed or tortured." This was not the truth. We experienced a feeling of painful shame. Many would not go out into the street for weeks. The following incident happened to me. The first time that I went out into the street with my "decoration," a group of Germans was crossing the street. Together with some passers-by, they rushed at me and began to shout out terrible curses. I leaned against the wall. Tears of anger and grief welled up in my eyes, and I was not able to say a single word. Suddenly I felt someone put his hand on my shoulder; it was an elderly Pole. He said, "My child, don't be upset and don't be offended. Let those who did this be ashamed." He took me by the arm and led me away.

This meeting made a strong impression on me. I realized that not everything was over and that there were still honest and firm people. The Germans would not succeed in seducing and confusing everyone by their misanthropic policies.

Thoughts of struggle were with me constantly from that moment on. I understood that each of us could help our native Red Army and that only by a struggle could we save our own dignity and the honor of citizens and Jews. On July 12, 1941, my husband was arrested together with several thousand other men. My grief was great. But I saw that it was a small part of the grief of all the people.

My only desire was to fight and take vengeance on the Germans;

it was a desire that permeated my entire existence and burned in my blood.

The Germans demanded a colossal indemnity: one million rubles, several kilograms of gold and silver, etc. All this had to be delivered within 48 hours, or else they threatened to burn down the Jewish quarter and destroy the entire Jewish population.

One can imagine how difficult it was to carry out this brigandish order. There were instances when Poles came to the Jewish community with gold objects and said: "Take this from us, save the Jewish population — your brothers and ours." In general it must be said that in those difficult days the friendship of the Polish and Jewish peoples burned particularly brightly. Of course, the Germans succeeded in organizing certain Polish riffraff and setting them on defenseless and persecuted Jews. But the best of the educated Poles, honest representatives of their people, helped us as best they could.

When the indemnity had been collected, a new order was issued: all Jews had to move to the ghetto. According to the order, there were three meters of space for every person, but in point of fact this "residential" quota was even lower; two and three families were squeezed into a single tiny room. People had to carry their things to the ghetto on their backs; the Germans forbade the Poles to render any aid whatsoever. Of course, many disregarded this order and gave the Jews carts. I too was given a cart by a Pole, and in addition I carried a large bundle in my arms.

A Polish woman whom I had never seen walked up to me and offered to carry my bundle; in those days there were many instances when German soldiers and local hooligans tore things from the hands of the Jews.

On August 1, the Jews of Bialystok were locked up in the ghetto.

The ghetto was a prison; no, it was not a prison, since that is too weak a definition. The ghetto was hunger, degrading oppression, executions by shooting, gallows, mass murders.

The people were subject to total arbitrariness. The Gestapo agents walked into houses whenever they felt like it and took everything that caught their eye.

An announcement hanging from the ghetto gates declared that it was forbidden to bring in food. If even the smallest amount of food was discovered, the punishment was execution by shooting.

They began to select people for work. Those selected were issued passes indicating which streets they were permitted to use. Anyone

226

found on streets not indicated in the documents was arrested and shot.

Jews were permitted to walk only on the pavement. I myself know instances when people were cruelly beaten for merely putting a foot on the sidewalk while attempting to avoid automobiles.

All the vicious acts of the Germans, however, could not break the fighting spirit of man, or kill his love of freedom.

In spite of the terror, an anti-Fascist organization was organized in December, 1941. The Polish comrades, Tadeusz Jakubowski, Niura Czerniakowski, and others, played an important role. I was secretary of the Committee.

I had to be able to leave the ghetto regularly so as to maintain contact with our Polish and Byelorussian comrades. A friend helped me get the job of janitress at a factory.

The Committee accomplished an immense amount of work in conditions of inhuman terror and amid the cruelest of persecutions. The ghetto believed unswervingly in the victory of the Red Army. We should bow to those people's grandeur of spirit!

Radio connection was established in the ghetto. Bulletins of the Soviet Information Bureau and English bulletins were received almost daily.

The grandson of an old woman by the name of Bramzon worked as a radio repairman in the German "castle."

He received bulletins in German and also succeeded in listening to English broadcasts. As soon as the youth came home in the evening, he was visited by both young people and ordinary elderly Jews. With what strained attention people followed the map which had survived (God only knows how in this hell!) and with what joy and delight they noted the cities liberated from the German monsters! Bramzon's grandson was not by any means our only or even our main source of radio information.

We had our own radio man, Comrade Salman, who had rendered many services to the anti-Fascist organization. His wife and son had perished in the ghetto, and he had dedicated his life to the struggle with the German cannibals.

Comrade Salman knew several languages and shorthand. This helped him a great deal. He worked in unusually difficult circumstances. Only boundless dedication and the iron will of a fighter helped him to overcome everything.

The radio was located in a pit, where there was barely enough room for one person. He had to kneel while writing. In the winter, when it was bitterly cold, this was devilishly difficult, but Comrade Salman did not abandon his post for a single day.

We must also remember the Kozhets Brothers (who later became partisans in the "October 26" unit). Our radio receiver was kept in their apartment for a long time.

Thanks to our dedicated radio people, we carried on intensive propaganda and put out bulletins from the Soviet Information Bureau and the English broadcasts on an almost daily basis.

We published Comrade Stalin's speeches and gave wide distribution to material about Treblinka and Oswiecim. Through reliable people we received and circulated a broad spectrum of material about Warsaw.

Our "technical resources" consisted of typewriters and duplicating machines, and we were not in bad shape in this regard.

We had a chemical engineer in our group whose name was Musya Davidzon. She worked in the same chemical factory where I was a janitress. She helped us in our cause. Aside from her, I also became acquainted with a certain Jewish repairman, and he helped me to steal a duplicating machine from the factory. I put it in a bag and covered it with a thick layer of wood scraps. We were permitted to take such "fuel" into the ghetto.

Aside from this, our comrades who worked in the German factories typed many materials.

Other of our "technicians" were Frida Fel, Sonya Ruzhevsky, Kveta Liaks. Later they all died at German hands. . . .

My entire family perished in November 1942. First my sisters and their husbands were taken away, then my other relatives. My brother was left behind when his wife and child were first taken, but three weeks later they took him away too. I remained totally alone.

Residents of the city of Bialystok knew what awaited them. None of them harbored any more illusions. The mass destruction of Jews was an incontrovertible fact, but no one wanted to perish without a struggle.

Each of us knew that the enemy's strength was incomparably greater than ours, that the enemy was armed to the teeth, that it was a fight to the death, but we firmly resolved not to retreat without a struggle.

In the apartments of Velvl Messer, Berko Savitsky and others we held numerous anti-Fascist meetings at which we heatedly discussed our current affairs and tasks.

With the knowledge and consent of the organization, our people carried out many acts of sabotage at the textile factories, the power stations, the tracks and railroad stations of Lapy, Staroseltsy, and others.

The inventiveness of our comrades in the struggle with the Germans was truly inexhaustible. For example, Anya Liskovsky sneaked into the kitchen of the SS and threw poison into the kettle. Fifty Germans were poisoned, and our organization justifiably assumed responsibility for this!

We established contact with the partisan movement. The contact was through a group of Soviet prisoners of war who had escaped to the forest and organized the partisan group of Mishka Sibiryak. Sibiryak himself tragically perished in the process. He had gone to a meeting in town, and the Germans surrounded the house when they learned of this. Mishka jumped out of a window, but was seriously wounded. A Pole hid him in his house, but Mishka nevertheless ended up later in the paws of the Gestapo and died.

The intelligence work of our anti-Fascist organization helped the partisan movement. Later we passed valuable materials to the headquarters of the Red Army through the Kalinovsky brothers. Aksenovich, Lyarek, Leitish, and others were excellent scouts. Miracles of courage were displayed by the Jewish girls, Marilya Ruzhitsky, Anya Rud, Liza Chapnik, Khayka Grossman*, Khasya Belitsky**, Bronya Vinnitsky***.

Through a Polish friend who worked in the German passport office they obtained Polish passports. For that reason they were able to live outside the ghetto. Naturally, they used all the advantages of their situation to aid our cause.

We helped the partisans a great deal — gave them radio receivers, medicine, clothing.

The aid rendered to Soviet prisoners of war was a wonderful page in the history of our anti-Fascist organization. A committee of three persons was in charge of this aid: Leybush Mandelblat (a shoe repairman from Warsaw and a member of the Polish communist party), Yudita Novogrudsky, and Velya Kaufman.

*Khayka Grossman lives in Israel, is a deputy in the Israeli parliament (the Knesset), and is a leader in the "Mapam" party. She is also a member of the *kibbutz* "Evron."
**Khasya Belitsky-Bronstein lives in Israel and is a member of the "Lakhavot Khabasha" kibbutz.
***Bronya Vinnitsky-Klibansky lives in Israel and directs a branch of the Yad Vashem Martyrs' and Heroes' Remembrance Authority in Jerusalem.

The prisoners-of-war camp was located in Bialystok. The officers were kept in the camp itself, and privates were taken to work in various points. It was necessary to establish contact with the officers. Since the camp was surrounded with strong walls and barbed wire, this was very difficult. The prisoners of war were starving.

A sewer repairman, whose name I do not remember, was permitted to enter the camp, and he contacted an officer. The repairman was a member of our anti-Fascist organization; we gave him the food and medicine we had collected.

No matter how great the hunger was in the ghetto, there were nevertheless self-sacrificing people who, in a spirit of brotherly love, gave their last morsel for the Soviet prisoners of war.

At the factory where I worked was a young man who was a workgang leader among the prisoners of war. Denying ourselves our last morsels, we took to him our rations, and he passed them on. Once he told us that a leader had been elected who divided everything up between the prisoners of war and that they very much wanted to know who was bringing them all these things. We hid behind some trees, but the prisoners saw us. It was a touching scene; they began to wave and smile.

Polish and Jewish women who worked at the factory rendered this aid. The guards killed one girl who had taken part in the committee to aid the prisoners of war, but this act of violence did not frighten the people. We managed to help one group escape from the camp. These were privates who lived in the barracks.

In 1942 the Red Army bombed Bialystok. Many took advantage of the moment to escape from camp. I did not see these people again.

The anti-Fascist organization founded a fighting unit in the ghetto entitled "Self-Defence." This unit had to be armed. Jews worked in various arsenals and in the barracks. Disregarding the danger, they smuggled arms from the tenth and forty-second regiments and from the Gestapo arsenal. In the streets the Gestapo very frequently checked passers-by, especially Jews. One can imagine what it meant for a Jew to carry a weapon through the entire town. But the most difficult thing was to get the weapons into the ghetto. On the gates of the ghetto hung a sign: "It is forbidden to carry food into the ghetto; the punishment is death by shooting." Even to bring a few kilos of potatoes into the ghetto was fraught with risk. One can imagine the fear that had to be overcome, the courage that had to be displayed, to bring weapons into the ghetto. Nevertheless, weapons were brought in through the gates during the day and thrown over the fence at night. Marek Bukh and Berknvald frequently removed their badges and carried weapons through the town.

Berestovitsky brought eight pistols into the ghetto as well as a good deal of ammunition. Natek Goldstein and Ruvim Levin, both of whom later died with the partisans, smuggled 24 ten-shot guns and 20 rifles from the Gestapo arsenal and brought them to the ghetto. Jerzy Sochaczewski (later commander of the Jewish partisan group, "Vpered" [Forward]) carried a pistol out of the Gestapo trophy museum. Motl Cheremoshny smuggled our rifles from the same place. Many weapons were carried into the ghetto by Mulya Nagt, who was known by his partisan *nom-de-guerre* "Volodya."

It is difficult to enumerate all the facts and all the participants in this work. Eternal glory to their names!

Weapons were also brought from Polish villages. Bronya Vinnitsky transported weapons from Grodno in a suitcase.

Farber, an engineer, directed the preparation of grenades and explosives in the ghetto.

It was impossible to provide the entire population of the ghetto with weapons, but many houses were provided with various toxic substances.

Jews working at the Miller factory brought several hundred liters of sulphuric acid to the ghetto.

Etl Bytensky organized self-defense in several buildings on Kupecheskaya Street and provided the residents of these buildings with sulphuric acid and axes.

The most terrible days were approaching. We knew that Hitler's monsters were liquidating the ghettos in various towns. They began to liquidate the Bialystok ghetto in February, 1943, and completed their bloody business in August, 1943.

February 1943 was the period of great victories near Stalingrad! The Germans decided to take revenge on the Jews for their defeat. At 6:00 P.M. on February 4, 1943, the residents of the Bialystok ghetto already knew that the "action" would begin at 4:00 A.M. on February 5. At 10:00 P.M. the people were reading bulletins of the Soviet Information Bureau and knew that death was inescapable. But this did not frighten them. This did not frighten the hero Malmed! When the Germans appeared in the ghetto, he was the first to kill a Hitlerite bandit. His wife and small daughters were shot before his very eyes, hundreds of tenants of his building were shot, and then Malmed was himself hanged. For seven days (the length of the Bialystok "Aktion") his body hung on Belaya Street, and the Germans would not permit it to be removed. Hundreds of Poles approached the ghetto fence to bow to the body of this fearless fighter!

Malmed was not the only one. The Fascist murderers had to take each building as if storming a fortress. Many buildings were blown up with grenades or put to the torch.

Not surprisingly it was learned later that the Gestapo assessed the action in the Bialystok ghetto as a failure.

The second "action" began on August 15, 1943. It began suddenly, but this did not help the Hitlerites. No one panicked. The Germans attacked the ghetto with tanks and planes, and the fighting lasted for a whole month.

The bright names of the participants and leaders of the uprising in the Bialystok ghetto will live eternally in the grateful memory of the people. The leader of the uprising, Daniel Moszkowicz, and his deputy, Mordekhay*, were posthumously given the highest award by the Polish government.

Hela Shurek and her ten-year-old daughter, Bira, died a heroic death together with seventy youths; they did not drop their weapons until their last gasp. Velvl Volkovysky saved dozens of people and sent them to the partisan unit "Vpered." He fearlessly risked his own life, just as did Kalmen Berestovitsky and also Khaim Lapchinsky, who fought with an ax in his hands. Leybush Mandelblat fought even though he was seriously ill and had a temperature of 40° Centigrade (104° Fahrenheit). Miller, an artist, also refused to leave the field of battle, as did hundreds of others.

Anyone who saw and knew the terrible conditions in which the Jewish population lived under the German yoke and how heroically it fought with the German murderers will understand how great was the contribution of the Jews in the defeat of Fascism. All these honest people revered the heroic feats of the fighting Bialystok Jews. Many Poles gave us weapons. Wrublewski and Wladek Mstyszewski actively helped the Jews arm themselves. Several Polish shoe repairmen hid Jews in their apartments who were active participants in the anti-Fascist struggle. The Pole, Michail Gruszewski, and his wife from the village of Konnykh hid a group

*Mordekhay Tennenbaum.

232

of Jews in the forest. They took care of these people, until they were able to contact the partisans.

Doctor Dokha from the village of Zukewicz and the paramedic Ryszad Pilicki rendered aid to wounded Jewish partisans.

The Gestapo subjected the residents of the village of Kremenoe to cruel punishment, but in spite of this they did not cease to help the Jewish partisans in any way they could.

Many Jewish families from Grodno were saved by peasants of the villages in the Grodno region.

Those who succeeded in escaping from the Bialystok ghetto went into the forest. The Germans began to carry out searches. They caught one girl and shot her. The forester, Markewicz, came out onto the highway and warned: "Don't go past Lesniczewka." He hid Jews, brought them food, and protected them until the partisans came. The forester from the preserve "The Three Pillars," his wife, and three daughters were stripped naked in the forest and tortured, but they did not reveal the location of the Jewish partisans, even though they knew it perfectly.

I have given only some of the facts from the history of the struggle of the anti-Fascists of Bialystok and the Bialystok region during the three nightmarish years of German occupation. I have told only a little of that which I saw with my own eyes as an active participant in that life and death struggle.

Stenogram and letter of **Riva Yefimovna Shinder-Voyskovsky.**
Literary preparation by **R. Kovnator.**

The Tragedy of My Life

Diary of the Red-Army Soldier, Kiselev

I am Salman Ioselevich Kiselev, a soldier of the Red Army and a resident of the small town of Liozno in the Vitebsk *oblast*. I am in my forties, and my life is twisted; the bloody German boot has trampled my days. I studied for a long time in the *Talmud-Torah*, a school for the children of poor people. My poor parents took me there. In 1929-30 I attended the regional collective-farm school. I read books — Victor Hugo, Shakespeare, Jules Verne. My reading took place in conditions of work and material deprivation. I will now describe my life's tragedy; I am the protagonist of the story and the author is the Patriotic War. I was born in 1900 in the family of a drayman, happiness was a game, and a horse died every year. As I have already mentioned, I studied in the *Talmud-Torah*, and a former student gave me free lessons. In 1920 I went with my mother on a visit to the small town of Babinovichi. There I took a liking to a girl — my third cousin. She was tall, chubby, and had a rather pretty face. Her personality was not bad, and I liked the fact that she was not from a rich family, since she would not despise me, knowing my poor situation. She must have liked me too. I got a cow as her dowry, and we celebrated our wedding. I had only forty rubles when the wedding took place, but that did not bother us, because our love was more precious than anything. I was a cattle driver for some merchants at the time, and I had discovered life. Since I had someone to love, nothing bothered me; I worked day and night, and I was happy. By 1928 I had two pretty little girls, and my wife was getting prettier. I thought I was the happiest person in the world. I went to work for Belmyastorg (a meat market), studied at night school, and read books. 1934 was a difficult year. I had to give up my studies and switch to a job stocking groceries. I was given bread to keep me going — but not enough. My wife bore all this together with me and never urged me to take up crime. In general I considered myself happy and lived peacefully, though poorly. I was innocent of any wrongdoing, and I was respected by my neighbors. By 1941 I had a cow, a couple of pigs, two beehives, and a garden. My wife worked, and I worked. We had six children — five girls and one boy. As everybody knows, the war began, and the enemy attacked our country. On July 5, 1941, I was sent to the army, and my wife remained in Liozno with the children and my mother, who was 75 years old. On July 12 the

Germans seized Liozno. I lost touch with my family. In May, 1942, I received a letter from my wife who was in the Chkalov *oblast* (the city of Saraktash). She sent greetings from our children. I was happy, and our correspondence lasted for over a year. I saw that my wife's letters were full of grief, and in June, 1943, I got a letter which said: "Your wife, Fanyusya Moiseevna, is sick. Come." We were stationed in the Kursk Bulge, and the situation was an intense one. I did not go, and two weeks later I got a letter that said: "Your family has left Saraktash." I immediately realized what the word "left" meant; that was what we called "leaving ranks." I wrote and asked the landlord of the apartment where my wife had lived how many of the children were with her. The landlord answered that Fanya was alone, that she had lost the children while crossing the front line. It happened this way. In early March, 1942, after the mass murders of my relatives, my family and several other families left with the partisans. They reached the front positions. My wife left the children with my mother and went to a nearby village for bread. She spent the night there, and our units came up during the night, so that she was not able to go back. And that is how my Fanya lived without her beloved children. She did not want to cause me pain and so did not write to me about this. To spare me she took her grief with her to the grave. She was a true friend and partner in life. I ask you to write the story of her fate in your words.

Prepared for publication by **Ilya Ehrenburg**.

Letter of the Red-Army Soldier, Gofman

(Krasnopolye, Mogilev *oblast*)

I am going to tell of another tragedy — that of Krasnopolye. 1,800 Jews perished there. My family was among them — my beautiful daughter, my sick son, and my wife. Of all the Jews of Krasnopolye, only one survived — Lida Vysotskaya. It was she who wrote to me about everything. I learned that, a day before the execution — when it was no longer permitted to leave the ghetto — my wife managed to go to town to get dried apples for our sick son. She wore a shameful tag on her chest. She wanted to prolong her son's life — if only for a day. The heart of the unhappy woman beat with love for her son. On October 20, 1941, the Germans herded everyone together and shot them. The children were tormented for two months and then shot. My son had been ill for a long time, but the doctors were keeping him alive. Soviet science saved him, and those beasts killed him with a submachine gun.

I am a husband without a wife and a father without children. I am no longer young, but this is my third year in the fight. I have taken revenge and will take revenge. I am a son of a great fatherland, and I am a soldier of the Red Army. I raised my younger brother, and he is fighting now as a lieutenant colonel on the first Ukrainian front. He too is taking revenge. I have seen fields sown with German bodies, but that is not enough. How many of them should die for every murdered child! Whether I am in the forest or in a bunker, the Krasnopolye tragedy is before my eyes. Children died there. In other towns and villages children of all nationalities died. And I swear that I will take revenge as long as my hand can hold a weapon.

March 10, 1944

Prepared for publication by **Ilya Ehrenburg**.

Orphans

1. In the Pit

Little Khinka Wrublewicz told her savior, V. Krapivin, a brief but terrible tale. Krapivin was a captain in the Soviet army, and when this strange creature with long tangled hair, bare feet, dressed in dirty rags and suffering from cracked skin on her wrists was brought to him, he did not realize at first that it was a child, a girl.

This wild creature, which had lost all semblance of humanity, began to speak. The little girl's story recreated, step by step, her path of suffering and loneliness.

Khinka Wrublewicz was born in the small town of Vysoky Mazovetsk. Her father, a shoemaker, had lived there until 1941. When the Germans arrived, their entire way of life changed. All the misfortunes of the Wrublewicz family stemmed from the fact that they were Jews. The Germans' first concern was to create a ghetto in the town. The Wrublewicz family consisted of the father (37 years old), the mother (40), three brothers (17, 10, 7) and Khinka; they lived a year in the ghetto — if half-starved existence passed in constant fear of death can be called living. But even this existence came to an end when all Jews from the nearby areas began to be brought to the Zambrov barracks, an area which had become notorious during the occupation. Thousands and thousands of people were collected there, taken away somewhere, and never seen again. The fear of Zambrov was so great that the entire family fled to the forest. After two weeks of wandering about the forests, they met two Poles who were German collaborators from Vysoky Mazovetsk — Leonard Szikorski and Wysocki. Yes, Khinka knew them well. They had managed to take away her mother and two younger brothers to town. Khinka knew only that her family had been sent to Zambrov; she did not know their subsequent fate. She was convinced that the Germans had killed them.

The father, the surviving older brother, and Khinka went deep into the forest, dug themselves a pit, and for a year lived off berries and charity received during the night from nearby villages. Soon the father was tracked down and killed before the eyes of little Khinka and her brother. The children were left alone in the pit. . . . All around was the lonely swamp and forest wilderness. . . . Some time later another Jew joined the children. He had also been hiding

237

in the forest, and he brought misfortune with him. Evidently he had been followed, and two strangers again appeared and took the last things from the newcomer. They were the same ones who told the Germans about the location of the pit. The most terrible day in Khinka's life arrived. When they heard the Germans approaching, all three jumped out of the pit and fled. A dozen submachine guns barked after them. Khinka's brother, who was running beside her, was killed on the spot. She never saw the third inhabitant of the pit again either. Later she crawled back to her empty den. . . . She was left alone in the forest — without mother, father, brothers, or relatives. Alone. But if it was terrifying in the pit, it was even more terrible to learn that German murderers and henchmen were all around.

Nevertheless, Khinka drew support from the hope that the Germans would be driven away. This lent her strength, and she continued to go to the villages at night where good-hearted women would furtively give her a piece of bread.

"Just imagine — a winter night, a howling snowstorm, and hundred-year-old fir trees bending under the raging wind! And that little half-dressed figure with a bread crust in her frozen fist slipping alone to her cold, narrow den — hurrying to beat the dawn so as to sit there, trembling from the cold and tears, until the next night.

"Our submachine gunners found her in the pit, in the forest near the village of Golashi, which is ten kilometers east of Zambrov. . . .

"I don't know if I have been able to tell of this tragedy the way I myself perceived it. When she finished her story, we front-line soldiers, who had seen many things, were afraid to look each other in the eye. Before this child we were full of shame that two-legged insects with a swastika still walked the earth, that the author of *Mein Kampf* was not yet swinging at the end of a rope, that Alfred Rosenberg, that preacher of racial hatred, was still alive."

Thus did Red-Army commander V. Krapivin finish the tale that he had written down from Khinka Wrublewicz after he had saved her from a terrible death.

We wish to add here that the little orphan Khinka found a home and love in the family of Red-Army lieutenant R. Shulman.

2. The Story of a Small Girl from Bialystok

The memoirs of ten-year-old Dora Shifrin were written down in careful handwriting in a lined notebook. She writes: "In the house where we lived about twenty men were killed. When I saw that, I grabbed my little sister and brother and ran to our uncle, who lived not far from us. I was terrified. The screams and wails of mothers and the cries of children were frightful. I was simply overcome by pity when I saw this scene. Our whole house and all we possessed was burned. We moved in with our uncle temporarily. The Germans were carrying on in the most savage fashion. They killed many Jews; in our yard and the next one alone they killed 75 people. They took away 16,000 people — supposedly to work. They said they would let them go when the indemnity was paid, but they never let anyone go. They killed everyone and burned them. . . .

"When everything, including the synagogue, was burning, the barbaric Germans began to seize Jewish men, women, children, and the elderly and thrown them alive into the synagogue."

Dora Shifrin's parents did not manage to escape. They were murdered before her very eyes.

This ten-year-old girl remembers this. She will never forget it.

Prepared for publication by **Valeria Gerasimov**.

Liozno

I was born in 1928 in the small town of Liozno in the Vitebsk *oblast* and lived with my grandparents before the war.

The Germans arrived on July 16, 1941. On the very first day they confiscated everything. The house burned down. Along with three other families, we moved in with my third cousin.

The first announcement that I read required under fear of death that all Jews wear a band with a six-pointed star on the left arm. One street was marked off for us; approximately 600 people lived there in 30 or 40 houses.

In the fall of 1941 a young German wearing glasses came to this street. He had a skull on his sleeve and on the lapels of his coat. After searching around for a long time, he led away six old people. Among them were the wood carver Simon (one of the most respected Jews in town), two invalids, and Velvele, who was mentally ill. They were locked in a barn. In the evening they were taken to the river and forced to crawl on all fours on the river bottom in icy water. They were tortured that way for three days and shot on the fourth.

Near Koyanki Station the partisans derailed an ammunition train. The Germans hanged six of the station's residents and began to fire at the suspended bodies with explosive bullets. I will never forget how one of the German officers climbed the gallows to photograph the profile of one of the murdered people.

I saw two pregnant women whose bellies were sliced open and breasts cut off. Beside them lay the bodies of their babies. I saw the bodies of twenty-five Jews from the Babinovichi *Shtetl*. The Germans had scattered their bodies along the road from Babinovichi and Liozno. I saw a truck loaded with Byelorussians being taken to be shot. For a fifteen-year-old, I saw very many things.

The police burst into ghetto houses in the winter at any time of the day or night. They broke the windows, beat the Jews with sticks and whips, and chased them out into the freezing cold.

Not a single pane remained in one of the houses where there had formerly been a cobbler's shop, even though forty people lived in that house in −40° Centigrade weather. Infested with lice, the people slept on rotten, wormy straw. A typhoid epidemic began. Several people died every day, and new Jewish families who had escaped from Vitebsk, Minsk, Bobruisk, and Orsha were immediately herded in to take their place.

"At 2:00 P.M. on February 28, 1942, the Germans and police began to truck all the Jews to one place. I was not at home. When I returned, my relatives had already been put in a truck. Russian comrades hid me in a toilet and nailed the door shut from the outside. Two hours later, when the policemen were gone, I crawled out of my lair. I saw them shoot the Jews, and I saw many go mad. My grandfather and grandmother kissed before death. They loved each other and did not betray their love even in their last minutes of life.

"After that I lay unconscious in the snow for a long time. I do not have the strength to describe how I felt. I could not even cry.

"When it got dark, I went to a Russian woman whom I knew, but I understood that I could not stay with her for long. That was why I went away to Liozno and crossed the front line.

"I don't have anyone now. But I live in the Soviet Union, and that says everything."

A letter of **V. Chernyakov**.
Prepared for publication by **Vsevolod Ivanov**.

Letters of Byelorussian Children

(The Village of Starye Zhuravli, Gomel *oblast*)

1

The Germans herded all the Jews to one place and forced them to work for them. They lived there for two months. Then the Germans came and began to chase out the Jews. One German walked up to a shoe repairman; the shoe repairman hit him on the head with a hammer, and the German fell down. The shoe repairman was shot. All the other Jews were put on trucks and taken away to be killed. Along the way, one woman jumped out and ran away. The Jews were taken to the hospital and killed there.

V. Vorobyev, 4th grade

2

The monsters mocked the Jews and beat them with a whip. When they were taken to be shot, one Jewish woman threw her baby from the truck. The people wanted to take it, but the Germans would not let them. They took it to the pit and killed it. But the mother ran into the forest. She was in the forest till night, then she came to look for her baby, and the Germans shot her.

Lyuba Mayorov, 3rd grade

Prepared for publication by **Ilya Ehrenburg**.

The "Brenners"* from Bialystok

(The Story of the Workers of Bialystok, Zalman Edelman and Shimon Amiel)

We will never forget the dark days of the ghetto. We will never forget the barbed wire which surrounded the streets of Bialystok — Kupecheskaya Street, Yurovetskaya Street, Czenstochovskaya Street, Fabrichnaya Street, and many others over which death hung for three years. By the end of 1943 the streets of the ghetto were empty; more than 50,000 of its inhabitants had perished in the ovens and gas chambers of Maidanek and Treblinka, in the "extermination camps" near Bialystok.

The Germans selected 43 people from among the last inhabitants of the ghetto on August 16, 1943. We two workers from Bialystok were among them.

All those who were selected were thrown into prison. On the next day we were ordered to forge two-meter-long, twelve-kilogram chains for ourselves. We were kept there until May 15, 1944.

Three months before this unhappy day we were transferred to a special regimen. Every day we were led away somewhere, and this procedure was given all the trappings of an execution. The fear of death, however, gradually faded away. We lost all hope of salvation. We were constantly beaten and mocked; Shlema Gelbort and Abram Klyachko fell ill with a nervous disorder. They refused food (1.5 liters of thin soup), suffered from hallucinations, and finally died after about ten days. In spite of the fact that these people had lost their senses days earlier, the Germans beat and tortured them, accusing them of simulation. A state of animal-like torpor predominated among the prisoners. Everyone expected the same end.

After three months the doomed people lost all human appearance.

Early one morning the prison was visited by Makhol, the deputy Gestapo chief. He ordered us to put on different clothing. Our new suits had bright white patches on the knees and a big white patch on the back. These patches could be seen from a distance of 500 meters. The clank of the two-meter-long chains on our hands and feet reminded us that any attempt to escape was futile. We were put into a "death machine" (something like a gassing truck) and were taken in the direction of Augustow. The truck stopped. Upon

*Brenner — cremator.

getting out, we were ordered to get in formation, and we found ourselves surrounded by 50 gendarmes armed with submachine guns, pistols, and grenades.

Makhol delivered a speech for our benefit; he said we would do construction work which would last for three years. Not a single one of us would be shot if the work was done conscientiously. There was no sense in trying to escape, since the chains would not permit that. If anyone did succeed in escaping, the rest would be shot on the spot. Then we were taken under armed guard deeper into the forest to a hill which we were supposed to dig up.

We were issued picks, shovels, and other tools. When we began to dig the earth, we came upon the corpses at a depth of 15 centimeters. We were ordered to drag these bodies out with hooks and stack them on two-meter-high heaps of wood. The stacking took place in the following fashion: each row of corpses was alternated with a row of wood. (We cut the wood in the forest.) When the height of the bonfire preparation reached three meters, kerosene or gasoline was poured over the wood, inflammatory cartridges were inserted in a few places, and the entire structure was set afire. An hour later it was impossible even to approach the fire, since clothing caught fire at a distance of one meter. The burning of a group of corpses took 12–18 hours. After that the bones were removed from the ashes and were ground to dust in large mortars. Then the ashes were sifted through sieves to discover melted crowns of teeth or other gold or silver objects that the murdered people may have had on their persons.

Then the ashes were buried in the same pits from which the bodies had been taken for burning.

The Gestapo men ordered that the hills above the pits be levelled and the surface planted with trees and flowers.

The regimen was a strict one. The Germans were afraid that one of the "Brenners" might escape, so they watched us carefully. In the course of the day, the Gestapo men would check several times to make certain that all the "Brenners" were in their places. (Those who burned the corpses were called "Brenners.") We were forbidden to talk. At 6:00 A.M. we were awakened and led to the site scheduled for digging up and cremating bodies.

The first three pits in the forest near Augustow contained 2,100 bodies. These people had been killed, for the most part, by rifle and submachine-gun bullets. The corpses were in clothing which had rotted or decayed. The corpses themselves, particularly the upper layers, were in a state of decay. The skin and fatty tissue were soft and had the appearance of raw white soap.

The bodies were dragged out with the aid of hooks attached to ropes. One or two hooks were thrown into the pit and would snag a corpse.

The Germans watched carefully to ensure that the entire contents of the pit were destroyed.

From the very first days we decided to do what we could to make what we were doing known to the world. Once a German walked up to me and said: "You won't live anyway, and even if you do stay alive and tell anyone about this, no one will believe you." This sentence influenced me strongly, and I resolved to do everything in my power to preserve traces of our work. I watched the gendarmes who surrounded us and waited for moments when their attention was distracted; then I would throw a hand, a rib, a skull into a hole and cover it up with sand. My other comrades did the same. We all had great faith that one of us would remain alive to tell the court of the horrible things which we had been forced to witness.

From Augustow we were taken to villages inhabited mainly by Byelorussians. Near every village was a distinctive hill under which were buried murdered Jews. It was impossible to count those graves. We could bury 200-300 bodies and bury the ashes in the pits by working from morning till late at night. In the vicinity of Grodno, near Staraya Krepost, we burned several thousand corpses. We burned a particularly large quantity of corpses fourteen kilometers from Bialystok, in the small towns of Novoshilovki and Kidl.

Near Bialystok we dug up a pit with 700 women. One can imagine what these unhappy people experienced before being killed. The bodies were absolutely naked. The breasts of many of the victims had been cut off and were lying beside them in the pit. This sadistic act must have occurred toward the end of 1943.

I met one of the survivors, Mikhel Perelstein, a resident of the *Shtetl* Yedvabny, who told me that he was in the ghetto on the day when 700 young women capable of working were selected. They were supposedly sent to a knitting factory. On the way to the factory they were evidently forced to turn off the road into a forest grove, dig pits, strip naked and, after terrible torture, were shot.

Near Lomża, in the village of Golnino, we dug up four pits, each of which was five meters wide and four meters deep. There I succeeded in hiding several legs, one skull, and several ribs. The

Germans were nervous, and it was evident from their conversations that the Red Army was near. The haste which the Germans displayed told us that our days — and perhaps even our hours — were numbered. They guarded us less closely, but even so it was impossible to dream of escape, since sixty gendarmes, armed to the teeth, surrounded us.

I will always remember that early summer morning. At dawn we dug up one large pit. We had not finished digging it up when Makhol appeared. He summoned *Obersturmführer* Schultz and Tifenson, whom we called "chief bandit," for a discussion. We immediately realized that something serious had happened. Makhol's nervous tone and several words which we overheard told us that our end was near. Gudaiski and Paul used clubs to drive us off to the side, and we were ordered to immediately dig a pit four meters wide and two meters deep. We realized right away that this pit was intended for us. Each of us began to think of how he could tear himself free from the claws of death. We could not talk the matter over with each other. The smallest word pronounced in a whisper was punished with a "Gummi" — a blow with a rubber truncheon. When the pit was ready, we were all checked and stood in formation facing the pit. Makhol waved his glove, and *Zugwachmeister* Wacht gave the orders: "Into the pit!" I shouted: "Save yourselves, run in different directions!" From the terrible nervous tension everyone screamed and set off running. Submachine-gun bursts resounded and many of us were killed, but even the wounded tried to run into the depths of the forest which was 200 meters from the pit. That evening I came across Edelman. For three days the two of us wandered through the forest, eating roots and leaves. We drank water from puddles and were afraid to come out of the woods. On the fourth day we came to Grabovka, which was not far from Bialystok. We learned that the Red Army had occupied the town that morning. Our hearts beat with a great joy, and we realized that we were saved. Of all our group nine people survived: myself, Edelman, Rabinovich, Gershuni, Felder, Vrubel, Abram Lef, Shif, and Lipets. Eleven days later we were all in Bialystok. It is difficult to tell what we felt when we stepped on land occupied by the Red Army. Even today, the death order rings in our ears and will probably always be with us: "In das Grab, Marsch!" — "Into the grave — March!"

Material provided by **Nukhim Polinovsky**, major in the medical service.
Prepared for publication by **Vasily Grossman**.

A Letter Written by Zlata Vishnyatsky Before Her Death

(The Small Town of Byten)

I found this letter in the small town of Byten in the Baranovichi *oblast*. It was written by Zlata Vishnyatsky and her twelve-year-old daughter Junita to their husband-father. Approximately 1,800 Jews from Byten were killed by the Germans.

Major Vladimir Demidov

July 31, 1942

To Mister Vishner, Orange, New Jersey, U.S.A.

Dear Moshkele and all my dear people,

On July 25 a terrible massacre took place here — as happened in all the other towns. It was a mass murder. Only 350 people are left. 850 died a black death at the hands of the murderers. They were thrown like puppies into latrines. Living children were thrown into pits. I will not write much. I think that someone will survive and that that person will tell of our torments and of our bloody end. We have survived for the time being. . . . But for how long? Every day we wait for death and mourn our near ones. Your family, Moshkele, is already gone. But I envy them. I cannot write any more; it is impossible to tell of our torments. Be healthy — all of you. The only thing that you can do for us is to take revenge on our murderers. We shout to you: Avenge! I kiss you fervently and bid you farewell before we die.

(Added on:)

Dear Father! I say good-bye to you before dying. We very much want to live, but all is lost — they won't let us! I am so afraid of this death, because the small children are thrown alive into the graves. Good-bye forever. I kiss you over and over. A kiss from G.

Your I[ta]

The Temchin Family from Slutsk

(Excerpts from Letters Received by Yefim Temchin, a Flyer)

1

September 27, 1944

Dear Yefim, I dropped into the town council and found the letter you sent there asking about your family. I must tell you as a warrior with a strong heart that many of those who remained here are no longer alive. The same is true of my family. I heard that you accomplished great things in battle. I always knew that you would be that kind of person. Your childhood friend, Anatoly Potekhin.

2

October 2, 1944

My dear and only brother, Yefim! Finally, of all our family, I found one person who is close and dear to me. But the wound in my soul will never heal. You and no one else knows how I loved and respected our family and how mother frequently cried over us. Now there is no one left alive. Yefim, you can imagine how I mourn for mother, father, Pinkhos, Freida, Nekham, Roza. I still have not been able to learn Manya's fate.

I saw our family for the last time at 10:00 A.M. on June 22, 1941. You didn't see them for an even longer time, since you went away to study. I said good-bye to them and went to the front. We went into battle on June 24. On August 26 I was seriously wounded near Chernigov. I spent eight months in hospitals. Then I went to the front again and again was seriously wounded. I am now in Lithuania in a non-fighting unit. I kept trying to find out something about our family — but without any results. I always had the family on my mind, remembered them when I got up, sat down to eat, went to bed. But I was prepared for the blow I received when the letter arrived about their fate, since I had seen what the Germans did to the Jews. In Kaunas they shot and burned 65,000 Jews. After the town was liberated, I saw the charred corpses being dragged out. Yefim, you have to keep control of yourself and be a man. I ask you to be a man. You yourself know how I loved the family. When we were at home, I, as the oldest brother, worked more than anyone and helped the family, because I loved the family — especially mother. Mother is the closest and most precious thing in life. I worked, because I felt sorry for mother. Oh, Yefim, what a pity it is that we do not have even one photo of our family.

There is nothing to look at to remember them. Yefim, I ask you once more to keep control of yourself and be a man. Do not be offended at me for writing to you in this fashion; I have no one left aside from you. You are my greatest happiness.

Your brother, **Leyzer**

3

(A letter attached to the previous letter)

August 29, 1944

Dear Leyzer, I am answering your letter about what happened in Slutsk. Your father was a skilled worker at the dyeing plant. Then the Germans arrested him and took him home for a search. He was still alive. In the house they took everything that caught their eye. Four days later I heard that he was killed. Your mother was not told, and she kept coming out onto the street and walking around town in the hope of somehow seeing him. All the Jews lost their cows, and it became very difficult to feed small children. In the beginning of October a ghetto was formed, and all the Jews were brought to it. At first there was only one ghetto, and then a second one was formed. One was called the "field" ghetto, and the other was the "city" ghetto for working Jews. It was easier to live in the city ghetto; people went to work and were able, little by little, to obtain food and sell their things. The "field" ghetto was stricter; people were not permitted out to go to town. Your people went to the field ghetto, since only Pinkhos could work — even though he was very young. Even so, he did not have any work at the time. They soon began to shoot the people in the field ghetto — usually on Mondays and Saturdays. Two, three, or four trucks would take the people away to the vicinity of Bezverkhovichi, in the forest. Pinkhos managed to become a worker, and he avoided the first group of those sentenced to be shot. He was transferred with the entire family to the city ghetto, where he remained until the last moment, that is, until February 8, 1943, when the city ghetto was totally destroyed. The field ghetto had been destroyed in March 1942. During the move from the field ghetto to the city ghetto, the Germans confiscated many of the Jews' belongings. I helped your family move, and they would drop in on me once or twice a week. But what could I do as a teacher with a salary of 350 rubles a month when a kilo of lard cost 500-600 rubles (and was as high as 1,000-1,100). They sold the sewing machine, the bicycle, and the clock. Manya is gone now. She escaped from the truck that was taking her to the execution and came to my place in tears. I gave her a few things, and she went into the forest.

Your neighbor, **Sulkowski**

4

October 20, 1944

My dear friend Yefim! I hid in the city, but several Jewish pogroms occurred before my very eyes. The Germans shot your father before the pogroms. During the pogroms we hid with Pinkhos several times. Your mother and Manya together with all the little ones also hid with us. It is very difficult to tell about this tragedy. It was easier for me, since I was alone. In the beginning of 1942, I joined the partisans. Pinkhos decided to stay because of the family; without him to work, the Germans would have shot everyone. I was with the partisans until July 1944 and was deputy commander of the unit.

Your Senya

5

Hello, Yefim! I have just arrived from Slutsk, where I was on leave. Slutsk has been almost entirely burned down, and only a few houses are left on the island, on Reiczani, and on Volodarskaya Street. Father was shot in August, 1941, in the Monakhov Orchard. Before being shot, he was tortured. His arms and legs were broken, and he was taken in that state to the search. Mother, Pinkhos, Freida, Roza, and Nekhama were shot in February, 1943, in Mekhorty. When Roza was put on the truck, she tried to escape, but she was wounded in the legs. She fell and was thrown bleeding into the truck; mother held her in her arms. I was told all this by witnesses. In Slutsk more than 20,000 peaceful inhabitants were shot. Yefim, it is terrible to see what the Germans have done to Slutsk and to hear what they did to the people. It is nothing but a horror. But Manya is alive! She is in Pinsk. She jumped off the truck, ran away, and became a partisan. I wrote to her and am sending you her address.

Your brother, **Leyzer**

6

October 28, 1944

Hello, my dear and very beloved brother, Fima! Today is the biggest holiday I have ever had in my short life. I received a letter from Leyzer and learned that you are both alive!

When the cursed Germans came, we all lived together and even helped Aunt Sonya. Papa was with us. Papa did not want to work for the Germans, but they forced him to, because he was the only

249

one skilled in pickling vegetables. It was learned that he had worked under Soviet rule, and he was arrested. On July 26, a Saturday, he was brought home. He had been beaten. His arms and legs had all been broken. I saw him. Mama asked and begged, but nothing helped. We were robbed, everything was taken, and father was taken away. Mother said good-bye to him; they kissed. His last words were: "Raise the children; they'll kill me."

He was shot in the Monakhov forest, which is a real cemetery with thousands of corpses. Then our life became even worse than that of beggars. Devils invented the ghetto. Cold and hungry people were kept in a single building — the barracks. No one was allowed to leave. Then they began to take people away to shoot them. We were on the brink of doom seven times, but somehow we survived and were not put on the trucks. Simon Strugach was paralyzed in the ghetto, and he was carried into the truck. Many people whom we knew died then.

Leyzer writes that no one survived except the partisans. On Easter 1942, the ghetto was destroyed, and only the workers were left. Thanks to Pinkhos we were transferred there. But there was no room. Mama and the children spent the nights in a barn during bitter cold periods — sometimes even on the streets. We ate potato peels and bran. It was frightening to look at Mama; she was a living corpse. But the children did not understand anything and kept asking for food. On Monday, February 6, 1943, the entire area was surrounded, and they began to load people on the trucks. Pinkhos was taken first. Then they took mama and the children. That was at 9:00 A.M. They took me at 1:00 in the afternoon. I can still hear the screams of our little sisters as they were taken to be shot. Roza was shot. Children and men who had been wounded resisting were with me in the truck. We were taken down the Bobruisk Highway. The truck bed was covered with a tarpaulin. Two Germans sat with us. I decided to jump off. It was better to die on the road. The truck was moving very rapidly. I had a razor blade. I cut the canvas from the window down and jumped out. When I recovered my senses, the truck was gone. I went to Valya Zhuk and said to her: "Save me!" She and her mother hid me for six days in a shed. Then I went to Slutovsky's, and then into the forest, where I came upon a partisan unit. I was in the unit until the Red Army arrived. Now I work in Pinsk as a bookkeeper for the Red Cross. My dear brother, I beg you: Avenge, avenge, avenge!

Your sister, Manya

Prepared for publication by **O. Savich.**

THE RUSSIAN SOVIET
FEDERATED SOCIALIST
REPUBLIC

Smolensk Area

1. Shamovo

This happened in the small town of Shamovo of the Roslavl region of the Smolensk *oblast*. On February 2, 1942, the commandant of Mstislavl, Lieutenant Krause, announced to the policemen that all Jews residing in Shamovo had to be destroyed. The doomed people were herded together on the square in front of the church. There were 500 old people, women, and children. Several girls attempted to escape, but the police shot them.

People were led to the cemetery in groups of ten to be shot. Among the doomed people were the two Simkin sisters. The younger, Raisa, was a student at the Leningrad Pedagogical Institute; she was one of the first to be killed. Her older sister, Fanya, was a teacher; she survived and told the following:

"It was toward evening of February 1. My sister and I kissed each other and said good-bye — we knew that we were going to our deaths. I had one son, Valery, who was nine months old. I wanted to leave him home in the hope that someone would take him in and raise him, but my sister said: 'Don't do it. He'll die all the same. At least he can die with you.' I wrapped him in a blanket, and he was warm. My sister was the first to be taken away. We heard screams and shooting. Then everything grew silent. We were in the second group led to the cemetery. The children were lifted by their hair or by the collar — like kittens — and were shot in the head. The entire cemetery was screaming. My boy was torn from my arms. He fell into the snow. It was painful and he was cold; he cried. Then I fell from a blow. There was shooting. I heard groans, curses, shots, and I understood that they were striking every body to check that the person was dead. I received two strong blows, but I remained silent. They began to take the things from the murdered people. I was wearing a shabby skirt; they tore it off. Krause called for a policeman and said something to him. They went away. I reached for Valery. He was completely cold. I kissed him and said good-bye. Some people were still groaning and wheezing, but what could I do? I left. I thought they would kill me. Why should I live? I was alone. True, I did have a husband at the front. But who could know if he was alive or not? I walked all night. My hands were frostbitten. I don't have any fingers, but I reached the partisans."

In the morning Lieutenant Krause sent policemen to the cemetery to finish off the wounded.

Two days later four old Jews came to the police station. They had tried to escape death but had not found refuge. Shmuilo, who was seventy years old, said: "You can kill us." The old men were led to a barn and beaten with an iron rod. When they lost consciousness, they were rubbed with snow to revive them. Then a rope was attached to the right foot of each of them, and the end was thrown across a rafter. Upon command, the policemen lifted the old men two meters above the ground and dropped them. Finally, they were shot.

2. Krasny

Before the war I lived in Minsk. On June 24, 1941, my husband left for the front. With my eight-year-old son, I left town and headed east. I decided to reach my home town of Krasny and take my father and brothers. The Germans overtook me in Krasny; they arrived on July 13.

On July 26 announcements were posted. The town residents were called to a meeting, where the Germans said that anyone could move into the house of a Jew. Moreover, the Germans announced that all Jews were to obey totally all orders of the German soldiers.

They began to make the rounds of the apartments, strip people, take their shoes, and beat them with whips.

On August 8, Germans burst into the house where I lived. They had tin cans with the picture of a skull. They seized my brother, Boris Semenovich Glushkin. He was 38 years old. First they began to beat him, and then they threw him out into the street, mocked him, and hung a board on his chest. Finally they threw him in a basement. On the next morning announcements were posted: "All town residents are invited to the public execution of a kike." My brother was led out, and it was written on his chest that he would be executed that very day. He was stripped, tied to the tail of a horse, and dragged. He was half-dead when they killed him.

At 2:00 of the next night there was a knock at the door. The commandant had come. He demanded the wife of the executed Jew. Shaken by the death of her husband, she was crying, and her three children were also crying. We thought she would be killed, but the Germans were even more base — they raped her right there in the yard.

On August 27 a special unit arrived. The Jews were herded together and it was announced that they must immediately bring their possessions, hand them over to the Germans, and then go to the ghetto. The Germans fenced off a piece of ground with barbed wire and hung a sign: "Ghetto. No entrance." All Jews, even children, had to wear on their backs six-pointed stars cut from bright-yellow material. Anyone had the right to insult and beat a person with such a star.

At night, "checks" were carried out in the ghetto. People were herded out into the cemetery, girls were raped, people were beaten unconscious. They shouted: "Let everyone raise his hand who thinks the Bolsheviks will return." They roared with laughter and then beat the people again. This went on every night.

The following happened in February: SS men burst in and began to wave flashlights. They picked Etya Kuznetsov, an eighteen-year-old girl. She was ordered to take off her shirt. She refused. She was beaten with a whip for a long time. Her mother, fearing that they would kill her, whispered: "Don't resist." She undressed, and they stood her on a chair, turned their flashlights on her, and began to mock her. It is hard to tell about this.

The fortunate ones were those who escaped to the forest. But what could the old people, women with children, and the ill do? I had comrades in Krasny on whose side I wanted to fight as a partisan. We waited for the weather to turn warm. But on April 8, 1942, my comrades informed me that a punitive unit had arrived. We decided to try our luck.

I left town a half hour before it was encircled. But where could I go?

The police were everywhere. We were being hunted like rabbits. I reached the prisoner-of-war camp; I had connections with them.

The town was surrounded. All Jews were herded out into a yard and forced to strip. My father was the first to go. He was seventy-four years old. He carried his two-year-old grandson in his arms.

Evgenia Glushkin, the wife of my eldest brother (whom the Germans had killed in August), took her two children with her; one was twelve, and the other was seven years old.

She left her third child, a year-old-baby, in the crib in the hope that the beasts would spare him. The Germans, however, when they had completed the execution, returned to the ghetto for rags. They saw Alik in the cradle. A German dragged the baby out into the street and struck his head against the ice. The head of the unit ordered that the body of the baby be chopped to pieces and fed to his dogs.

I joined the partisans. It was difficult for me with a child. But in these extremely difficult conditions comradeship, togetherness, and human kindness made themselves felt. There were long marches and many guard posts. I was a messenger. Twice I met punitive units, but I escaped. My child was prepared for everything. I said to him: "If they catch me or if they beat me or poke me with needles, if I cry or scream, stay quiet." The eight-year-old boy never complained. He knew how to conduct himself with the Germans. He was a true partisan child.

We fought for two years, and the day arrived when I saw the Red Army.

Sophia Glushkin, agronomist
November 9, 1943

3. The Fate of Isaak Rosenberg

Many Jews lived in the small town of Monastyrshchina in the Smolensk *oblast*. There was a large Jewish collective farm there. On November 8, 1941, the Germans slaughtered all the Jews — 1,008 people. Adults were shot with submachine guns, and children were buried alive. When the policeman, Dudin, was caught and asked if he had really thrown living children into a grave, he answered: "I didn't throw them; I put them there."

Children of mixed marriages were also killed. Lyubov Aleksandrovna Dubovitsky, a pedagogue of Russian nationality, was married to a Jew. She was arrested and tortured. Her children (seven, four, and one-year-old) were killed. Dubovitsky is twenty-seven years old; after all that she has lived through, she looks like an old woman.

Monastyrshchina was burned, and only the stoves were left of the houses. Of the house of Isaak Rosenberg, an employee of the regional civil registry office, only the stove is left. He was married to a Russian woman who was born in the Zhiryatino region of the Orlov *oblast*. Natalya Emelyanovna Rosenberg had two small children. They survived; the mother succeeded in convincing the executioners that they were from her first marriage.

Natalya Emelyanovna hid her husband in a hole under the stove. He spent more than two years there. He had to sit bent over, since there was not room to lie down or stand up. When he sometimes came up at night, he was not able to straighten out. It was concealed from the children that their father was hiding in the cellar. Once the four-year-old daughter looked in a crack and saw large black

256

eyes. She was frightened and shouted: "Mama, who is there?" Natalya Emelyanovna calmly answered: "It's a very large rat; I noticed it a long time ago."

Isaak Rosenberg used a manganese solution to keep a diary on scraps of German newspaper. He also wrote down the stories of his wife about the "new order" in Monastyrshchina. Frequently the hole was filled with water. Sometimes Rosenberg wanted desperately to cough, but he did not dare. He wrote about this as well.

The house was a good one, and the Germans took a liking to it. Then Natalya Emelyanovna took apart the roof. The house was flooded with water, and it was cold in winter, but the Germans did not occupy the house.

Natalya Emelyanovna fell ill with typhus. She was taken away to the hospital, and a neighbor took in her children. At night Isaak Rosenberg crawled out and ate the glue from the wallpaper for two weeks. In the hospital Natalya Emelyanovna worried that she might give away her husband in a delirium.

In September, 1943, units of the Red Army came almost right up to the small town. Monastyrshchina is a crossroads, and the Germans resisted strongly at that point. The battles went on, and armed Germans were next to the Rosenberg house. Like the other residents of Monastyrshchina, Natalya Emelyanovna took the children and fled into the forest. She returned when Red-Army soldiers entered the town. She found still-smoking ashes and the stove; the house had burned down. Isaak Rosenberg had died from asphyxiation. He had sat out twenty-six months in the cellar and died two days before Monastyrshchina was liberated by Soviet units.

Prepared for publication by **Ilya Ehrenburg**.

Rostov-on-the-Don

On August 4, 1942, an announcement requiring the registration of Jews was posted on the walls of Rostov: it was signed by the "Jewish elder, Lourié." According to the announcement, Jews could live calmly in the town, since "the German command would guard their safety." Five days later there appeared a new announcement signed by the same Lourié: "In order to protect the lives of the Jews from irresponsible acts of enraged elements, the German command has to resettle the Jews outside of town and thus make easier their protection." The Jews were directed to gather in the indicated points on August 11, 1942, taking with them only valuables, clothing, and the keys to their apartments, in which their belongings were to remain untouched.

There remained in Rostov many Jews who were not able to leave — the elderly, the sick, their relatives, mothers with children. Some realized immediately what the German order meant. Fedor Cheskis, a research worker at the agricultural institute, opened his veins and lost a great deal of blood but did not die. His wife hauled him from hospital to hospital in a wheelbarrow — but it was all in vain. They were stopped by a German patrol. Cheskis was executed, and his wife (who was Russian by nationality) was put in prison. One woman threw her three children in the Don River and then jumped in herself. She and one boy were saved; the other two children drowned.

Two elderly people, a man and wife, barricaded themselves up in their apartment. The Germans broke down the door, threw aside the furniture that had been heaped up in front of it, and took the old people away. A woman dentist lived with her daughter and eleven-month-old grandson on the corner of Budenny Avenue and Sennaya Street. When she learned about the German order, she decided to drown herself together with her daughter and grandchild. The daughter and grandson drowned, but the grandmother was saved by good people. Crazed from despair and anxiety, she ran to Doctor Orlov at the hospital and begged her to inject her with morphine, since she was being hunted. In point of fact, the same "good people" called the Germans when they learned whom they had saved. The Gestapo took her from the doctor's office to her execution.

Yekaterina Leontyevna Itin was eighty-two-years old. She lived with two former nuns, who loved her and took care of her. She said: "I will not go anywhere. Let them come and kill me." The Germans announced that if she did not come they would kill the nuns as well. Then the old woman went to the point.

The two eldest doctors of Rostov went to their deaths: Doctor Ingal and Doctor Tiktin. Doctor Garkavi, a woman, was considered the best specialist on tuberculosis. Her husband, who was Russian by nationality, decided not to abandon his wife, and they went to be executed together.

Mr. Okun, a paralyzed old man, lived with his wife and daughter on Maly Prospekt. The girl did not want to leave and thus cause pain to the old people. When the elderly Mrs. Okun read the order, she began to give her belongings to her neighbors. On August 11 she went with her granddaughter to the gathering point. The paralyzed old man remained alone. He kept asking the neighbors if his wife would return soon. The next day a car came for him.

Residents of Rostov who frequently walked down Maly Prospekt knew the old woman, Maria Abramovna Grinberg. She always sat at the window, greeted her acquaintances, and treated the children with sweets. Everyone loved her. Maria Abramovna's children managed to leave — with the exception of one daughter, Doctor Grinberg, who decided not to abandon her elderly mother. The daughter went to the gathering point. The old woman could not leave and remained at home. She did not understand why her daughter had left for the entire day. The old woman asked the neighbors: "Let me sit with you a while until the car comes for me. . . ." When she said this, she did not realize why the car would come. She did not understand why her neighbors asked her to leave. She said: "I don't recognize you; you are such good people, and you don't want to take me in for one evening. . . ." She was taken away that evening.

The following is the testimony of Ludmila Nazarevsky:

"On the morning of September 11 I was walking down Pushkin Street past the gathering place. Trucks were standing in front of the building, and people were crowding around in the yard. Rozalia Oguz, an old woman who taught music, caught sight of me. A half century earlier she had given lessons to my older sister. She was very happy to see me and said: 'Ludmila, you must have come to see us off. Please go to my apartment. I live with Goncharov, tell her that we are being taken to the military offices. Have her bring me and my sister some food.' I promised her I would do everything and said good-bye.

"I walked on for a few steps and saw a mother and daughter. The mother was blind, and the daughter was deaf. They stopped me and asked where the point was located. A tall girl who was walking behind me threw her hands up and shouted: 'My God, you poor people, where do you have to go!' She burst into tears and she took the unfortunate people to the point.

"I set off for the military offices. Traffic was moving incessantly along Budenny Avenue and farther across the Don to Bataysk. Two workers waled past me, and one of them said gloomily: 'It's hard to overpower them. . . .' I walked around the military offices. This was about fifteen kilometers from town. I did not see anyone. Returning through the workers' residential area, I sat to rest on a bench at the market and suddenly saw a group of modestly dressed women and several old men — among them Doctor Tiktin. I followed them.

"German soldiers were walking in front and behind them. At the very front was a man in a white shirt. He was evidently enjoying his role and turned around from time to time and waved his arms as if he were directing.

"Outside of town the road ran parallel to the railroad. It was there that the bandit in the white shirt stopped me. He called the Germans, and they told me that I could not go any farther.

"While returning to town, I met several vehicles in which Jews were being transported. In one was a youth who tore the cap from his head and waved it at the bandit in the white shirt. Perhaps he wanted to say good-bye to a living soul? The bandit burst out laughing in response. I remember the face of a woman in a different truck; she was holding a small baby in her arms, and her face was strained and had an insane look about it. The truck rushed on, jolting the woman and child. I also saw our old woman, the midwife, Rozalia Solomonovna Fishkind. She was wearing her everyday coat and a white cap. Her face was sad and thoughtful, and she did not see me. . . ."

What happened in the place to which Doctor Nazarevsky was not admitted? It was a largely unsettled area — just five small houses for railroad workers and a few houses to the east of the Olimpiade farm. The residents of these houses had been forced to leave two days earlier. Under threat of being shot, they had been ordered to lock up their homes and leave. Some of them, however, fearing for their property, hid in sheds, gardens, and ravines. They saw everything.

On the eve of the August 10 execution of the Jews, the Germans killed 300 Red-Army soldiers on the same spot. The Red-Army soldiers were brought in trucks to the transfer point. There they were put in a special gassing truck, from which their dead bodies were later dragged. Those who showed signs of life were shot.

The Jews were ordered to strip. Their belongings were set off to the side. They were shot in the Zmiev Ravine and immediately covered with clay. Small children were thrown live into the pits. Some of the Jews were killed in the gassing truck. One group was led naked from the zoological garden to the ravine. A beautiful woman, also naked, was with them. She led by the hand two small girls with ribbons in their hair. Several girls walked arm in arm and sang something. An old man walked up to a German and hit him in the face. The German shouted, then knocked the old man down, and kicked him to death.

The local residents saw a naked woman crawl out of the pit on the night of the eleventh, take a few steps, and fall dead.

On the next day the newspaper, *The Voice of Rostov*, which was published by the Germans, announced: "The air has been cleaned. . . ."

Prepared for publication by **Ilya Ehrenburg**.

Doctor Kremenchuzhsky

Doctor Ilya Kremenchuzhsky lived in the town of Morozovsk together with his wife and two daughters. The husband of one of the daughters was at the front. She was nursing a baby. Kremenchuzhsky's wife was Russian. She had survived by a miracle. She told the following:

"The Germans killed 248 Jews. But on that night they killed 73. They came to our house in the evening, shouting: 'Is Doctor Kremenchuzhsky here? You and your family — get your things.' My husband understood everything immediately. In the truck he gave a powder with poison to me and our daughters. He said: 'When I give a sign with my hand, swallow this.' He left one dose of poison for himself.

"We were brought to a cell. It was very crowded there. We all stood. Under the windows the SS men were shouting: 'We'll put an end to you now. Just wait. . . .' My youngest daughter wanted to take the poison, but my husband grabbed the poison from her hand and said: 'No, we can't. What will happen to the others if we take poison? We have to support them and share the common fate.' My husband did not speak Yiddish. He had lived his entire life on the Don, but in that place he remembered two words — 'Brider, Yiddn' — 'brothers, Jews.' Everyone began to listen intently, and my husband said: 'We must die with dignity — without tears, without screams. We must not give any pleasure to our executioners. I beg you, brothers and sisters, be silent.' A terrible silence ensued. Even the children were quiet.

"An engineer whom we knew had arrived with us. He suddenly began to bang on the door and shout: 'This is a mistake! There are Russian women here. . . .' A German asked: 'Where?' They pointed to me and my daughters. The German led us out into the corridor: 'We'll clear this up tomorrow.' Then they began the slaughter. They did the killings in the yard. No one screamed. I thought: why should I live? But my grandson . . . I wanted to save my grandson, and we ran away. The teacher hid us. . . "

Prepared for publication by **Ilya Ehrenburg.**

262

"Where Are They Taking Us?"

There were children in a village near Morozovsk doing field work. Rumors about the murders of the Jews reached the village. Six Jewish children, ages nine to twelve, set out for Morozovsk. When they learned that the Germans had taken away their parents, the children went to the commandant's office. From there they were taken to the Gestapo.

There were two Russian women in the cell — Elena Belenov (47) and Matrena Izmailov. Izmailov tells the following:

"The children were crying. Then Belenov began to calm them and said that their fathers and mothers were alive and that nothing terrible had happened. She caressed them and lulled them to sleep. At 3:00 A.M. the Gestapo men came for them. The children began to scream: 'Lady, where are they taking us?' Belenov calmly declared: 'To the village. You will work there. . . .'

"In a pit near Morozovsk were found the bodies of Elena Belenov and the six Jewish children."

Prepared for publication by **Ilya Ehrenburg**.

In Stavropol

On May 5, 1943, I returned to my home town of Stavropol, which had been liberated by the Red Army. The Germans killed my entire family: my elderly father, mother, my brother together with his wife and children, and my four sisters together with their children, among whom were nursing babies.

When the Germans occupied Stavropol, they established "The Jewish Committee to Protect the Interests of the Jewish Population." The Jews were registered. A week later the Germans directed The Jews to come to the square at the train station, taking with them luggage weighing up to thirty kilograms. They were to be "resettled to areas with a lower population density." All those who came were put in vans of a special construction and gassed. Their belongings were taken to the Gestapo.

Two days later, on August 14, 1942, the Germans directed that all local Jews come to receive armbands. Everyone — including my family — went. They were kept at the Gestapo offices until evening and then told that they would be allowed to return home in the morning. In the morning they were stripped naked, put in gassing vans, and taken outside of town.

Officers and Gestapo men sifted through the Jewish apartments in search of booty.

I want to tell about my mother. She had great-grandchildren. She raised seven children. She had been sick for the previous two years, cooked dinner at home, and almost never left the house. Her grandchildren used to come to her and bring her flowers. She sat among them, weak and happy. She was seen going to the Gestapo. She walked bent over, in a worn housecoat, covering her gray hair with a black shawl. How empty and terrible must have been the heart of the person who pushed her into the grave!

My relatives lived a peaceful life, fixed watches, repaired dresses, made boot tops. The children went to school and did field work. Lina, my sister's oldest daughter, was a strong, beautiful girl and an athlete. During the first days of the occupation, German officers would not let her alone. A proud Soviet girl, she cried when she came home. Then they killed her.

They also killed my brother's little son. He was ten months old. First the Germans announced that all children older than eight years of age had to appear. Later they ordered the women who had gathered to bring all their children "for registration." And they killed them.

My mother did not take one of my nieces with her. The girl hid with the neighbors. The Gestapo learned about this. Soldiers with automatic rifles spent an entire evening searching for this twelve-year-old girl. They did not find her. On the next day, even though the neighbor women tried to dissuade her, she herself went to the Gestapo and said: "I want to go to mama." They killed her as well.

Information supplied by **A. Nankin**.
Prepared for publication by **Ilya Ehrenburg**.

Evenson's Story

(Kislovodsk)

Moisey Samoylovich Evenson, who wrote down his memoirs about the Germans in Kislovodsk, is now seventy-nine-years old. He was born in Kaunas. While still almost a boy, he was forced to emigrate. He worked for a long time as a reporter in Vienna. Evenson returned to his native land without graduating from the philosophy department, where he had studied intensively. He was twenty-one-years old then.

He worked for the famous Russian bibliographer and historian of Russian literature, S. A. Vengerov, and participated in the creation of the Brokhaus and Efron eighty-four volume encyclopedia. in 1892 he began work as a journalist and authored a number of small articles on philosophical questions and the history of the Jews. As a Jew, he was forced to leave Petersburg for Kiev. In Kiev Evenson worked in the newspaper, *Life and Art*.

Nor did he have the right to live in Kiev, and this talented writer, the father of a family, was often forced to spend days and nights at the chess club. The police never went there to check documents.

From Kiev Moisey Samoylovich was forced to move to Zhitomir where he virtually single-handedly published the paper, *Volyn*. At one time the famous Ukrainian writer Kotsiubinsky wrote for this paper. *Volyn* was closed down, and Evenson moved to Kiev, where he took up the life of a wanderer.

Evenson's son died in 1915 near the town of Buchach in the war with the Germans.

The revolution of 1917 put an end to the state of affairs where the Jews in Russia had no rights.

The young republic conducted a fierce struggle with its enemies. The German imperialists invaded the Ukraine and attempted to deprive the Ukrainian people of their freedom. In 1919 Moisey Samoylovich's second son, a lawyer and chess expert, died at the hand of the enemy. Evenson left for Baku. He worked in the People's Commissariat of Foreign Trade until 1924, then retired, and lived near the small railroad station, Minutka, which is close to the resorts of Kislovodsk. There he married for a second time. His wife was Russian, and she saved him during the German occupation. Such was the life of the author of these notes.

The Germans in Kislovodsk

The Germans broke through to the Northern Caucasus suddenly; life in Kislovodsk was that of a town far from the front. There were many evacuated persons and refugees in the town.

On August 5, 1942, the population learned that the Germans were approaching Mineralnye Vody. Institutions and sanatoriums began to be evacuated. But there was no means of transportation. In order to leave, it was necessary to have a pass, and people were detained while their documents were being processed.

Many attempted to leave on foot for Nalchik, but on August 9, German cavalry units had already appeared on the roads.

On August 14 German motorcycle units appeared. After them came many German vehicles with machine gunners and sub-machine gunners. Then the infantry was brought in, and then light vehicles with the German authorities arrived.

Precisely-drawn cards appeared on many sanatoriums; they read: "Occupied by the German command. Entrance forbidden."

The center of town was occupied by the commandant's office and its numerous branches. In town printed announcements were posted for the population. They stated that the German army was fighting only with the G.P.U. (the Soviet secret police) and the Jews. The rest of the population was asked to maintain calm and order. Everyone was to go to work. The announcements stated that the collective farms were being disbanded, and that trade and the crafts were free. It was announced that acts hostile to the occupying forces would be punished by military law. First among such acts were aid and support of the partisans, refusal to report them to the authorities, the spreading of unfavorable rumors with regard to the actions of the German army and the occupational authorities, and also any refusal to carry out the orders of the commandant's office and those of the civilian authorities.

A few days later a newspaper began to be sold in Kislovodsk. It was called the *Pyatigorsk Echo* and was printed in Pyatigorsk. The paper was three-quarters filled with vicious anti-Semitic propaganda and foolish, false attacks on the Soviet government.

By the time Kislovodsk was occupied, a rather large number of Jews had evacuated to the town from Donbass, Rostov, and the Crimea.

One of the first orders of the German command was to appoint Kochkarev mayor. The mayor issued an order that weapons be surrendered, that the property of the sanatoriums be handed over, and that "Jews and persons of Jewish origin" be registered.

The elder of the Jewish committee formed by the Germans was Doctor Benenson, a dentist who was popular in town.

Two days later a new order appeared. The Jews were required to sew a six-cornered white star, six centimeters in diameter, on the chest.

Thus there appeared on the streets of Kislovodsk people already marked by the seal of death.

Orders were hung on the city walls as to the protection of crops and the reestablishment of medical institutions, which were to charge for their services.

There was no fuel or kerosene in town. The bathhouses were closed. Soap was sold for as much as 400 rubles for one piece. The schools were opened. The teachers were ordered to apply corporal punishment in the schools, but they refused to submit to this. There was no medicine in town. Unemployment reached cruel proportions.

The Germans announced a forced rate of exchange — ten rubles for one mark.

Deprived of all means of existence, the people sold their belongings. Second-hand stores appeared which at first charged twenty-five percent, then ten, and even five. Prices kept falling, and the Germans were buying things.

In the center of town there appeared officers and soldiers from various types of military units who were decorated with all sorts of badges and stripes. Women in thin stockings and dress shoes appeared. All men capable of working were required to work for the invaders two days a month, and an announcement soon appeared to the effect that the work had to be done several months in advance. Peddlers beat a path to the huts of the Karachaev mountaineers. Flour became expensive, and manufactured goods became cheap.

The Germans initially dealt with the Jews on a gradual basis. In the earlier days the Jewish committee was ordered to deliver five-hundred men's overcoats, fifty women's overcoats, the same amount of footwear, table linens, etc. for the needs of the German command. Later all watches and valuables were demanded. Then it was ordered that people be sent to clean the squares and participate in earth-moving projects. The work had to be done with bare hands.

On September 7 an order from the commandant's office was posted: "In order to populate certain areas in the Ukraine, all Jews and persons of Jewish origin (except for metis) are ordered to appear on September 9 at the rail-freight station. They should have with them the keys to their apartments attached to tags indicating their addresses and names. Persons being moved may have with them not more than twenty kilograms of baggage apiece."

Many realized that this was an order to go to their death. Doctor Vilensky together with his wife and Doctor Bugaevsky took poison. Doctor Feinberg together with his wife and daughters opened their veins.

On September 9 as many as 2,000 Jews came to the rail-freight station. The Jews passed by Gestapo men, who collected their apartment keys in a basket. Among those being moved was an old man, Professor Baumgolts, the author Bregman and his wife, Doctors Chatskin, Marenes, Schwarzman, the dentist Benenson and his family. His seriously ill son was carried on stretchers. People walked up to the train. The Hitlerites demanded that belongings and foodstuffs be handed over. Timid protests were heard: "But how about the children's underwear?" Embarkment proceeded. An automobile arrived with nine small girls from the orphanage. The frightened people became upset and started to grumble.

"Why are you sending these small girls?" shouts rang out.

A Gestapo man answered in Russian. "If they aren't killed, they'll grow up to be adults."

The train set out at 1:00 P.M. The guards were in the first-class car. The train passed the station of Mineralnye Vody and stopped in a field. The Germans began to look through their binoculars. They found the area to be a convenient one. The train backed up to Mineralnye Vody and was shunted to a sidetrack leading to the glass factory.

"Get out," the Germans said.

One woman, Deborah Reznik, was unnerved and weak from hunger; she fell out of the rear doors into the tall weeds.

The people got out, and the Germans said:

"Turn in your valuables."

The people removed their earrings, rings, and watches and threw everything into the caps of the guards. Ten minutes more passed. A car arrived from headquarters. The order was issued: strip to the underwear. The people began to scream and rush about. The guards herded the crowd to an anti-tank trench which was located about a kilometer from the glass factory. The children were dragged by the hand. Several automobiles sped back and forth across the field, shooting at those trying to escape.

268

The execution lasted until evening. That night trucks arrived from Essentuki.

1,800 people were brought from Kislovodsk; 507 adults and 1,500 children and old people were brought from Essentuki. By morning all were killed.

Debora Reznik left the grass. She had nearly lost her mind.

She wandered along the roads and remained alive by sheer accident — perhaps because she did not look like a Jew.

Fingerut, an old man, also remained alive.

In Kislovodsk the Germans left alive only a few cobblers and tailors. Before retreating, they summoned their families and shot everyone.

A few people were saved. Shevelev, a female employee of a Leningrad institute, saved three Jewish children by passing them off as her nephews. The employees of the medical institute helped her to hide the children. Doctor Gluzman with two daughters were saved. One Russian woman, Zhovty, hid a young Jewish woman and her small baby in her home.

A few Jews survived in the caves.

The weather was marvelous. Rumors spread that the Germans wanted to create a resort in Kislovodsk for Germans only. The Russian population was supposed to be evacuated.

Very many Russians died in Kislovodsk.

On November 6 a trainload of young people was sent to Germany.

Poverty increased in town, and the mood was an anxious one. Executions were discussed with the greatest caution, but even so anyone could hear the bursts of gunfire at night.

In December vague rumors were received about Stalingrad. Groups of wounded arrived in Kislovodsk. Soviet planes bombed Pyatigorsk. The invaders became quiet, and their faces grew ashen. Mayor Kochkarev was removed from office for embezzlement, and his position was taken by Topchikov. Many pine trees were cut for Christmas, but the Germans did not arrange any merrymaking during the Christmas season. The evacuation began.

On January 4-5 a search was carried out in the apartments for Jews and communists. An announcement was posted declaring that the rumors about the evacuation of Kislovodsk were false and that people would be shot for spreading them.

Explosions began in early January. The railroad bed and the rail-freight station were blown up. The searches were repeated. The Germans fled suddenly on January 10. This saved the lives of many people. At the stations the Germans abandoned barrels of sauerkraut, wine, bags of salt. It turned out that the wine had been poisoned. The salt had also been poisoned, but the cooks noticed that soup with German salt was covered with a green scum, and there were not very many cases of poisoning.

On January 10 the Germans were gone from Kislovodsk. Soviet troops entered town, and the bodies of the murdered and tortured began to be dug up.

The bodies of 6,300 viciously murdered Soviet citizens were found in the anti-tank trench. At Mashuk-Gora in Pyatigorsk 300 Russian bodies were found. 1,000 more bodies were found at Koltso-Gora in Kislovodsk.

That which the Germans did in Pyatigorsk and Essentuki was done calmly and methodically.

Prepared for publication by **Viktor Shklovsky**.

Essentuki

The Germans occupied Essentuki on August 11, 1942. On August 15 a Jewish Committee was appointed to register the Jews. 307 persons capable of work were registered; together with children and the elderly, they comprised approximately 2,000 people.

Jews had to appear at the Committee at dawn. They were sent to do heavy labor, and they were mocked and beaten by the Germans. Particularly zealous in this regard was the "Overseer of Jewish Affairs," Lieutenant Pfeifer. This fat, red-faced German came to the committee with a whip and directed the beatings.

On September 7, by order of the commandant von Beck, the Jews were directed to move to "lightly settled areas." All Jews had to appear at the school beyond the railroad bed, taking their belongings with them (not more than thirty kilograms), a dish, a spoon, and food for three days. Two days were allotted for preparation.

When Gertsberg, an associate professor at Leningrad University, learned of this "resettlement" and realized what this meant, he committed suicide. Efrusi, a professor of the Leningrad Pedagogical Institute, and assistant professor Michnik took poison but were saved by German doctors who believed that Jews should be killed in accordance with the established rules.

It was also ordered that all patients in the hospital be taken to that same school.

On the morning of September 9, Jews began to gather at the school. Many were accompanied by Russians, who cried when saying good-bye. The building was surrounded, and the doomed people spent the night in the school. The children were crying, and the sentries were singing songs. At 6:00 A.M. of September 10 the Jews were put on trucks but were not permitted to take their belongings with them. The trucks set out in the direction of Mineralnye Vody.

One kilometer from the glass factory was a large anti-tank trench. The trucks stopped next to the trench. The Jews were stripped and put into gassing vans. Those who attempted to escape were shot. The lips of the children were smeared with a poisonous liquid. The corpses were thrown into the trench in layers. When the trench was filled, it was covered with earth and stamped down with machines.

Aside from those named above, many scientists and doctors were

271

among the murdered: associate professor Tinner, Doctors Livshits, Zhivotinsky, Goldschmidt, Koznievich, Lysy, Balaban, the lawyer Shats, the pharmacist Sokolsky.

Doctor Eisenberg worked in Essentuki. He had been appointed head of the field hospital at the beginning of the war.

Doctor Eisenberg arrived in Essentuki after it has been liberated by the Red Army. He learned that the German cannibals had killed his wife and ten-year-old son Sasha. Together with representatives of the Red Cross and workers of the glass factory, Doctor Eisenberg placed a memorial plaque at the trench.

At this place were buried not only the Jews of Essentuki, but also of Pyatigorsk, Kislovodsk, and Zheleznovodsk. At this same place were also buried seventeen railroad workers and many Russian women and children.

Prepared for publication by **Ilya Ehrenburg**.

The Story of Joseph Weingartner, a Fisherman from Kerch

When the evacuation of women and children from Kerch began, my wife did not want to leave. Our fishermen and canning factory were filling orders from the front, and I could not leave my work. My wife would not agree to leave me alone in town.

"If you have to leave," she said, "we'll go together."

An order was posted in town: all Jews — from small children to old men — were required to appear for registration. Those capable of work would be given work, and children and old people would be provided with bread. Anyone who did not have a document stamped by the registrar would be shot.

I went and registered together with my family.

My heart was heavy, however; I did not like the fact that there were so few Kerch residents on the streets and almost no Jews.

"You know," my wife said, "let's talk to Vasily Karpovich about the child."

We dropped in on Vasily Klimenko, who lived in our courtyard. He and his wife, Elena Ivanovna, were old people who had asked us several times to drop in for a visit.

"When times are bad, it's better for people to stick together," they said.

We did not want to leave our home, however, and we took only our youngest son, Benchik, to them. Our oldest son, Yasha, was never home anyway. The schools were closed, and he passed the days running around with his friends.

One morning two policemen and a German came into my apartment. The German read aloud my name, my wife's, and those of both children from a piece of paper.

He said: "Take the things you need most, since you are being sent to work on a collective farm, and your apartment will be occupied by other people. Take your two children with you — fourteen-year-old Yakov and four-year-old Bentsion. Where are they?"

"That is a mistake," I answered. "We don't have any children."

The thought flashed through my head — what would I do if they were to walk into the room at that moment?

The German wrote something down and ordered us to follow

him. But I could sense our frightened neighbors secretly watching us from the windows of their apartments.

We were brought to the prison. It was filled to overflowing. There we found all our friends and acquaintances. Since no one knew why or for how long we had been arrested, the most terrible thoughts came into our heads. Everyone was excited because of the crowding and gloomy forebodings. Children were crying, and people were talking loudly; it was enough to make a person go mad.

Toward evening the head of the prison arrived.

"Citizens, there is no reason to be upset!" he said in a saccharine voice. "Get some sleep, rest up, and tomorrow we'll take you to your collective farms to work. You will receive two kilos of bread per day."

The people calmed down. Acquaintances began to agree to get on the trucks together and work in the same collective farm.

The next morning five trucks drove up to the prison. I, my wife, and our friends could not even get close to the trucks — so great was the shoving and pushing. The people wanted to get out of the prison as soon as possible and find freedom in the collective farms. The strongest ones pushed their way to the front. We all remained behind, even though the trucks kept coming back for new passengers all day.

That night someone remarked that it was strange that the truck took only twenty-five minutes for a round trip. Where could they take the people in such a short period? This was such a startling thought that we were all seized by horror. We spent a miserable night.

In the morning the trucks came again, and we, together with our friends, finally got places. I sensed that something was wrong as soon as we left town. Before I managed to think things over, I saw a mountain of clothing and the antitank trenches.

It was at precisely this point that the truck stopped, and we were ordered to get out. We found ourselves surrounded by soldiers pointing rifles at us. Legs, arms, and still-moving parts of bodies barely covered with earth protruded from a pit. For a second we were numb with horror. A fourteen or fifteen-year-old girl pressed up against me and cried: "I don't want to die!" We were all so shaken that it was as if we had awakened. I will never forget that girl! Her cry lives in my blood, my brain, my heart.

They began to tear off our outer clothes and herd us toward the pit — directly toward the bodies of the people who had been shot. We could hear terrible wails. The soldiers drove us toward the pit so as not to have to drag our bodies there later. The ring surrounding us became tighter and tighter. We were pressed up to the very edge of the pit and fell into it. At that moment shots rang out, and those who had fallen immediately began to be covered with earth. I said good-bye to my wife. As we stood, embracing each other, a bullet struck her in the head, and the blood spurted in my face. I picked her up and began to look for a place to lay her down. At that moment, however, I myself was knocked off my feet, and other people fell on top of me.

I lay unconscious for a long time. My first sensation was that the hot mass on which I lay was swaying. I did not understand where I was or what had happened. I was being crushed by the weight on top of me. I wanted to wipe off my face, but I did not know where my hand was. Suddenly I opened my eyes and saw the stars gleaming very high above me. I recalled everything, gathered up my strength, and pushed away the earth that was covering me. I even dug in the earth lying around me in an attempt to find my wife. But it was dark all around. Each time I would take someone's head in my hands and peer into the face to determine if it was a woman. I touched the faces with my fingers in the hope of recognizing her by touch. Finally I found her; she was dead.

I crawled out of the pit and set out in a random direction. I saw a light and went to the peasant hut from which it emanated. There were three men and two women there. Evidently they guessed immediately what had happened. The women removed my shirt, which had been smeared in blood, put iodine on my wounds, gave me a fresh shirt, fed me, and gave me a cap. And I left.

Along the road a woman asked me:

"Was Ilya Veniaminovich Valdman among you?"

"Yes," I said, and the woman began to wring her hands and fell to the ground.

I walked in the direction of the city. I do not know why, but I did not experience any fear. I wanted to learn about the children. It was night in the courtyard, and I did not want to waken my acquaintances. I saw the ruins of a building that had been destroyed by a bomb, and I went to the basement.

In the early morning, however, I tried to get up — and couldn't. My wounds were bleeding, I had a fever, and I could not leave the spot where I lay. From the fragments of conversations and the screams and desperate wails that reached me I realized that a large pogrom was taking place in the town. Later I learned that the pogrom exceeded my expectations by far. The Germans surrounded the workers' suburb and killed about 2,000 people.

I lay in the cellar, unable to move. Evidently someone guessed that there was a living creature in the cellar. From time to time this person would lower into the cellar a loaf of bread, a boiled potato, or an onion. Sometimes there would be a bottle of water. I lay there in that fashion for fifteen days. Suddenly I realized that I was rotting alive. At that point I gathered my strength and went to the medical clinic. When I entered the doctor's office, he asked: "What is the matter with you? What is that stench?" I showed my wounds.

"There is no place," he said. "Do you have money and papers?"

"No."

"In that case I have no right to treat you," the doctor said and immediately whispered to the sister to prepare a place for me in the ward right away.

He treated me without money or papers, kept me there for two weeks, and released me when I was again in good health.

I went to Russians whom I knew and received from them food, money, and a place to live.

I struggled with the sea and hurricanes for thirty-five years. My small boats were capsized more than once, but I was not defeated. How many times I was swallowed by the waves! And now a despicable dog wanted to put an end to me without further ado. . . . He would never live to see that day! My brothers and the brothers of my wife were fighting at the front, and they already know what the Germans did in Kerch.

I began to look for my children. No one knew what happened to Yasha. For several nights in a row I hunted through the pits. But how could I find anyone among all the corpses in the dark? Besides, dead people often are so changed that they cannot be recognized.

Nevertheless, I do not believe that my son is dead; he grew up at sea. As for Benchik, everything went as the Klimenkos promised me: "No matter what happens to us," they said when I gave them the child, "Benchik will be saved."

A few days after we were taken to be shot, the police and Germans came to our courtyard and demanded Bentsion Weingartner from the neighbors. A German pointed to a paper to show that he needed the four-year-old boy Bentsion of the Weingartner family.

He wanted to be told where the boy was being kept. The neighbors claimed that the child had been taken together with his parents, even though they all knew that he was at the Klimenkos.

The next day a German and a policeman came again. This time the policeman appeared unexpectedly, in the middle of the day, when there were a lot of children playing in the courtyard.

"Anyone who tries to run away will be shot," the German warned. He again pulled out his list and began to ask every child individually: name, patronymic, surname. Benchik was among the children. He looked older than his years. When the line reached him, he answered that his name was Nikolay Vasilyevich Klimenko. The adults and children standing there remained silent.

The German started to question them.

The matter did not end here, however. A few days later the Germans came directly to the Klimenkos to get the child.

Mrs. Klimenko hid the boy and claimed that he was their son. The Klimenkos didn't give up, they found papers, and brought living witnesses who testified that the child really was theirs.

There began a long struggle between the Germans and the Klimenkos over four-year-old Benchik.

In the meantime, the Klimenkos were not to be caught napping. They consulted with their neighbors and made a decision.

One night they left their home in the care of their neighbors and secretly left town together with Benchik. Along the way good people helped them, and thus they brought the child to an abandoned collective farm in the steppes near Dzhankoy. The Klimenkos had relatives there, and they were known.

That is how they saved my Benchik.

Prepared for publication by **Lev Kvitko**.

277

Yalta*

On November 7, 1941, the last Soviet ship left Yalta. Many did not manage to leave. A black fog stood over the town: the oil-reservoirs were burning. On November 8 the Germans occupied the city.

On December 5 the Jews were moved to the ghetto which had been set up on the outskirts of Yalta and surrounded by barbed wire. Jews were starved and mocked; no one knew what was in store for him.

On December 17 the Germans led the healthy men out of the ghetto and took them down the road leading to the Nikita Gardens. The truck stopped at the Red Shelter (the guard booth for the Massandra vineyards). The Jews were ordered to dig two deep trenches at the bottom of a ravine. When the work was completed, the Jews were shot.

On the morning of December 18 all Jews — women with children and old people — were loaded on trucks. They were forbidden to take any belongings with them. People stuffed a piece of bread or an apple in their pockets. The truck stopped next to the ravine. The doomed people were stripped and driven with bayonets to the edge of the trench. Children were taken from their mothers and flung into the trench. The adults were shot with machine guns.

It was a clear, sunny day. The sea splashed twenty meters away. The vineyard workers of Massandra and Magarach saw everything.

By evening it was all over, and the Germans covered 1,500 Jews with a thin layer of earth.

Then the executioners went to Magarach. At the apartment of Yelizaveta Poltavchenko they bragged that they had killed 1,500 people and that soon there would not be a single Jew left alive in the entire world.

Among the murdered were many doctors. In the "Tourist's Guide to the Crimea," published in 1898, "L. M. Druskin — pediatrician" and A. S. Guryan — woman doctor; midwifery and female illnesses" are listed among the practicing doctors. Anna Semenovna Guryan managed to leave Yalta, but she fell into German hands in

*Before the war Yalta, Yevpatoria, Dzhankoy, Feodosia, and Simferopol were part of the Crimean Autonomous Soviet Socialist Republic, which was part of the Russian Soviet Federated Socialist Republic. After the war the Crimean Autonomous Socialist Republic was liquidated; in 1954 it was incorporated into the Ukrainian Soviet Socialist Republic as an *oblast*.

Kislovodsk, where she was shot. Doctor Druskin was killed in Yalta on December 16. He had treated children for fifty years. His former patients had long since grown old. He was shot at Red Shelter, and the bodies of small children were thrown on the body of this specialist in children's diseases.

The winter of 1941-1942 was a severe and hungry one. Homeless dogs dug up the graves at Red Shelter and dragged out the corpses. In the spring water flowing from the ravine washed away the earth, and the half-decayed corpses were revealed. The Germans blew up a part of the ravine and covered up the bodies.

Once German police discovered flowers on a grave. An investigation was initiated, but the Germans never succeeded in finding the "culprits."

Prepared for publication by **Ilya Ehrenburg**.

Ms. Fishgoit's Letter

(Yevpatoria)

The Germans entered Yevpatoria on October 31, and the Gestapo arrived three days later. On November 5 ten Jews were detained on the street. Among them was my friend Berlinerblau; all were appointed members of the Jewish Committee. On the morning of the sixth an order was issued that all Jews be registered. The order was posted on the streets. Above it was drawn a six-cornered star. All Jews were ordered to wear a star on the back; all valuables and money were to be turned over to the Committee. People were permitted to keep only 200 rubles. The order ended with the words: "Disobedience will be punished by shooting."

On November 11 an order was posted that all Jews be evacuated from the Crimea. Jews were ordered to gather at Military House; they were permitted to take any amount of things with them, but the keys to their apartments had to be turned over to the Committee. The deadline for coming to the gathering place was set as November 20. On the morning of the twenty-third I came out into the street, and my eyes witnessed a terrible sight. Women were carrying children in their arms or leading them by the hand and crying. Men were carrying bundles, and the sick and paralyzed were being moved on carts. A young woman was leading two children; she had insane eyes and was shouting: "Look, my children have two arms and two legs just like yours, and they want to live, too!" After being mocked and harassed, all these people were soon killed. I survived, since my friends had brought me a passport on the evening of registration. The passport was given to me by a Karaite woman whom I knew — Dr. Neiman. It was the passport of her sister who had been killed by a bomb. With this passport I went by foot from Yevpatoria down the road to Simferopol. In the village of Vladimirovka a woman agreed to take me in, since it was dark and not possible to go any farther. We had just lain down, when a truck pulled up. The landlady got up to answer a knock at the door: "Do you have any *Juden?*" a German asked. She answered in the negative. All night vehicles roared past — they were looking for Jews. The weather changed radically overnight — a snowstorm had begun. I left early in the morning and reached the next village by evening. I managed to spend the night there. During the night the landlady's son returned from Saki and said that the Jews had been executed there at 5:00 P.M. I set out again in the morning. The snowstorm was so severe that it knocked me off my feet three times. It was terribly cold, and I was only lightly dressed. I walked that way for three days. I reached Simferopol by evening of the third day. In Simferopol the Jews were shot a month later than in Yevpatoria. Here Jews were robbed in an "organized" fashion, but in addition apartments were broken into by anyone who felt like it. People were beaten, robbed of anything that caught the assailant's eye, and driven out of grocery lines. On December 10, citizens who were late (movement about the town was permitted only until 4:00 P.M.) were gathered at the movie theater, where they spent the night lying on the floor. The Jews were tied to each other in such a fashion that they had to stand the entire night. After a time an order was issued that Jews be "evacuated." For three days I saw people go to their deaths. An old man from a neighboring court-yard came to us for advice as to whether he should go to the camp or not. He had heard that the order did not apply to persons older than eighty years of age. Our people advised him not to go. I wanted to embrace this helpless old man. Two days later he was taken away by the Gestapo.

On January 7 I left Simferopol and began to wander through the villages. In each of them I learned of horrors and tortures perpetrated on the Jews. I walked past wells and pits stuffed with Jews. In the Politotdel collective farm I learned of the noble act of village elder Kazis (later shot by the Germans as a partisan), collective farm worker Pavlishchenko (a partisan), the Yevpatoria nurse

Ruchenko, and the collective-farm worker Nina Lavrentyevna Ilyichenko: they alternately hid in their homes the Jew Birenbaum, a cobbler from Yevpatoria.

Ruchenko brought him to Ilyichenko's apartment. There a pit was dug in which he hid during the searches. Four families risked their lives to save one Jew. In July of 1943 caution even forced Ilyichenko to change her place of residence. She moved to Yevpatoria, rented a small house there, and lived there together with Birenbaum. They dug him a pit in the entrance way with an exit to the street. She hid the Jewish cobbler in this pit until the liberation of the Crimea. At the present time Birenbaum is in the ranks of the Red Army.

I had parted with my son while still in Yevpatoria; he was wandering somewhere with documents issued in the name of Savelyev. When I learned that he had set out in the direction of the Freidorf region, I also set out in the direction of Freidorf. I passed trenches where Jews and other peaceful residents were buried. Bloody clothing, footwear, galoshes were scattered around; the stench was terrible. There was a funeral going on in the first village to which I came. They were burying sailors from the Soviet navy who had come ashore secretly to fight and who had hidden in a haystack. There were eighteen of them, and the Germans burned them alive. The Jews had already been shot in all the collective farms, and only some mountain Jews were still left alive in the Shaumyan collective farm. They were shot later, in 1942. I spent entire days in the steppe, eating frozen corn. I went to the villages to spend the night. I told everyone that I was looking for my sister who had fled from Yevpatoria after the attack. I attempted to remain in some of the villages, but the elders refused to permit that, since my passport showed no mark of registration by the Germans. I went on and knew that ultimately I would be recognized and hanged or thrown in a well. I walked from village to village, asking about the prisoner of war Savelyev, but I could not find him anywhere. I was in such a state that I bellowed like a beast in the steppe and cried aloud for my son. Somehow this helped.

In the villages concealed Jews were being hunted down. Each time that I learned of the arrest of a Jew, I went to that village to learn if it was my son. I imagined my son's execution dozens of times. Each time I learned that the arrested person had managed to commit suicide (and there were many such incidents) I was happy in the hope that it was my son. I no longer dreamed of saving him, but only hoped that he would manage to commit suicide and not be tortured by the Germans. In Freidorf I learned from the cook of a punitive unit that the gendarmes had brought Jews there for twelve days, shot them, and thrown them in wells. The lips of children were smeared with poison. I was told by one witness that in the village of Imansha the children were thrown alive into the well, because there was nothing with which to smear their lips. Some adults went mad and themselves jumped into the well. Cries for aid resounded from the well for several days. The same collective-farm worker pointed out a dog to me that belonged to a Jew from Imansha and that it had lain next to the well for five days and howled. Jews were brought from the Tartar and Jewish areas of Munus to the Russian area of Munus, where there was a well. They were lined up three abreast; those standing in the rear had to throw in the bodies of those who had been standing in front and had been shot. This was told to me by a girl who had observed the scene from an attic. When they were being led to the well, one old man fell behind, and a Gestapo man killed him with a rifle butt.

Not far from Nikolayev I saw a frozen old Jew on a burial mound. I was told that he was lucky to have escaped the Fascist executioners. In Kori I learned of the tragedy of three small brothers — eight, ten, and eleven years old. They fled when their parents were being driven toward the well. This had happened in the fall, and they returned to the village of Kori in the depth of winter. They returned, because they had no place of refuge. They came back to their parents' home and found new people already living there. The children stood next to their hut for a long time, not asking for anything or even crying. Then they were taken to Freidorf and killed.

Once, while wandering through the steppe, I found a packet of flyers; among them was the New Year's speech of Comrade Kalinin. From it I learned of the successes of our Red Army. The address — "Dear brothers and sisters!" — seemed to appeal to me personally, and I again felt like a human being. At that moment it seemed to me that I could see our mighty Red Army with Comrade Stalin at its head coming toward us.

In better spirits, I hid two of the flyers and went on. A thick fog formed, and I lost my way. If I had remained in the steppe, I would either have frozen to death or fallen into the hands of a police patrol. I prepared a knife to slit my veins. Suddenly I heard the barking of a dog in the distance, and I set out in that direction. By the time I reached the village, the fog had partially broken up. It was the village of Krasny Pakhar. I went to a hut and asked for permission to spend the night. The owners agreed. We had a long talk that evening, and they said that they were willing to keep me and that I could take care of their baby, but that I had to give them some things in exchange. I offered them my watch, and they agreed to let me stay and even to feed me (if the village elder permitted that). On the next day I became acquainted with the elder; his name was Ivan Nazarovich Novogrebelsky. He agreed to let me stay even though I had not been registered by the Germans. As soon as he began to speak, I sensed that Novogrebelsky was one of us. I began to visit them. His wife, Vera Yegorovna, turned out to be a very pleasant person. From them I learned that the Germans were robbing the people, confiscating livestock and poultry, and demanding unbearable taxes of the people. The commandant beat people. Corporal punishment was a common phenomenon. I saw a woman who lay on her stomach an entire month after corporal punishment. The Germans began to send many young people to Germany.

On one occasion I secretly visited my friends in Yevpatoria who had given me my passport, and I received morphine from them. My situation in the village was becoming more and more dangerous. On my last visit to Yevpatoria I learned from the neighbors that my son had left the Crimea in February with the intention of crossing through the line of the front. It was as if a mountain rolled off my shoulders. When I returned to the village, I dropped in on Novogrebelsky, and he offered to let me stay the night. That night he revealed a secret to me — he had a radio. They had an organization which included (aside from the elder himself) his brother, the old partisan Suslov who was working as a bookkeeper, the elder's wife, his mother-in-law, his brother-in-law, the collective-farm worker Oksana Nikitich, and three people from a different village. Novogrebelsky began to receive bulletins and asked me to translate them into German. Suslov typed them, and other people distributed them in the villages. I was happy that I could carry out even this small task, and it served as a justification for my existence. I also translated into Russian our leaflets which were dropped from the air and were intended for the Germans. Suslov typed them. My happiness, however, did not last long. In the last part of September, during the registration of passports in the village, I was recognized by the registrars who had arrived from Yevpatoria. A few days later I fled. Novogrebelsky gave me a certificate stating that I worked in the labor exchange. I joined two women who had passports and who had been evacuated by the Germans to our village; they were leaving for the Ukraine. With great difficulty I managed to cross the Perekop. We reached the village of Rubanovka in the Zaporozhskaya *oblast*, where I met one of our prisoners of war who was making his way from a camp to the line of the front.

After liberation, fate sent me an enormous joy. From a female friend of our son I learned that he had reached our people, had studied in Nalchik, was a lieutenant, and had been seen on the south front in 1943. I do not know if he is alive; I do not have any information about him. The thought, however, that he broke free from shameful captivity and that he is defending the motherland is a source of enormous happiness for me.

Prepared for publication by **A. Derman**.

Murder in Dzhankoy

Before the war we used to sing a beautiful cheerful song about the Jewish peasantry of Dzhankoy. The song ended with a lively chorus: "Dzhankoy, Dzhankoy." But then the animal Hitler came and slit the throats of Dzhankoy's Jews.

Grigory Purevich, a mechanic at the tractor station that served the Jewish collective farms of the region lived in Dzhankoy during the mass murders.

He brought me to the Jewish camp and told me the following:

"Here in the attic of the creamery, in the very center of Dzhankoy, the Germans locked up many Jews who had been brought there from surrounding villages and from town. The conditions were so crowded as to be unbearable. The children were exhausted from hunger and thirst. Every morning we found several dead people. The following happened to me: several days before the Germans arrived, the director of the mill where Kolya worked asked me to come and work there. My wife remained in town with the children. She is Russian. I am sixty years old; how could I evacuate? Somehow we would survive this difficult time. . . . I went with Kolya to the director of the mill and spent several days there. But then all sorts of talk began, and I decided not to expose the people who had taken me in to danger, and I returned to Dzhankoy.

"I came home and found the Germans there.

"'Who are you?' they asked.

"'The owner,' I said.

"'Get out of here!'

"And they kicked me out. I didn't see my wife, my two daughters, or my son. They had hidden.

"I spent three days in a destroyed room near my home without water, bread, or any information about my family. Soon the Germans left, and I moved back into my apartment. The members of my family came out of hiding.

"Two days later the local police came.

"'Who are you?'

"I showed them an old paper from my savings account; it said that I was a Karaite. They looked at it and went away.

"All the Jews of Dzhankoy were already in the attic of the creamery. They were used for heavy work — dragging stones. The

285

overseer made sure that stones, even the heaviest ones, were carried by one person only. Anyone who fell under the burden was shot on the spot.

"They came to take me and my neighbor woman to the Gestapo.

"'I'm a Muslim,' the neighbor woman said.

"'And who are you?' they asked me.

"They let the neighbor woman go but sent me to the creamery.

"When I found myself in that damned attic and saw what was going on, what had happened to the healthiest and strongest workers from the collective farm, I nearly lost my wits. Several people were bustling about in the corner. It turned out that the cobbler Kon had hanged himself. . . . I had known this young, cheerful man. I was shaken by this, but the others regarded it as an ordinary event. In these crowded conditions I met all the Jews who had not evacuated from Dzhankoy; I also met Jewish collective-farm workers from nearby villages and also non-Jews. The non-Jewish peasants were being kept there for having given food to the unfortunate people or having helped them.

"In that mass of pale faces, the Russians and Ukrainians did not stand out at all. Their eyes, like the eyes of the others, expressed grief and anger. Misfortune, it is said, is the great equalizer.

"I managed to get released for work — to pave the road. It is better to die on the street than in an attic.

"The Germans picked groups of adults, children, and the elderly from the camp and herded them to the antitank trench outside of town. It was winter, and there was snow. The people were hungry and sick and could barely drag themselves along. They were driven on nevertheless. A three or four-year-old child fell behind, and a German beat him with a rubber truncheon. The child fell, got up, ran a few steps, and fell again. Again the rubber truncheon struck him on the back.

"The people were arranged in formation next to the trench and shot. The children scattered in all directions. In a rage, the Germans chased after the children. . . . They shot at them and grabbed them by the legs when they caught them and beat them against the ground.

"We were working on the road leading from Kerch to Armyansk. There were many captured Red Army soldiers lying on the road who had been killed or tormented to death.

"In the evenings we were led back to the attic. They brought a Russian there as well; his name was Varda, and he was a bookkeeper from the creamery. They came for his Jewish wife and child. He started to resist and grabbed a gendarme by the throat.

"'Take me too!' he shouted. And they took him.

"One night a young woman by the name of Katzman began to experience birth pains. The woman's quiet crying was heard by everyone. Her husband Yakov Katzman, who worked on a combine in the Jewish collective farm, was somewhere at the front, in the ranks of the Red Army. He was constantly being remembered. . . . He never thought that his young wife would give birth to his first child in this grave.

"At dawn the senior gendarme came with his assistants to take control of the camp. He walked up to the mother, turned the newly born baby to him, took a rifle from one of his assistants, and jammed the bayonet directly into the eye of the baby.

"In camp Redchenko was 'quartermaster.' He pretended to be mean, but he actually helped the children secretly whenever he could.

"Every day several dozens of people were selected from among us and herded to the burial trench. Every day we had to endure inhuman torments and degradation. We were forced to do things about which it is impossible to speak without disgust.

"I obtained a piece of electric wire and once at dawn attempted to hang myself. I was on the point of dying, but my wheezing was heard, and I was taken down. As a punishment I was beaten in the morning, and three of my ribs were broken. I did not have the right to make such decisions regarding my life; this right belonged only to the Germans.

"Once trucks arrived, and they began to stuff people into them from the attic. Everyone knew that they were being taken to their deaths. Major German units guarded the building and the road leading to the mass grave. In the beginning of the confusion some of the people attempted to escape. Some of them succeeded; I was among them. I went home, but I could not remain there. Precisely at that time a young acquaintance of mine came to Dzhankoy. His name was Onishchenko, and he was a collective farmer; he dropped in on me.

"He said: 'Come and live with us. I'll hide you.'

"I went with him and spent six months there. Then he brought my entire family to the village. A lot of Jews were hidden and given work in that collective farm. A reliable Soviet hand defended them there.

"An elderly Russian man Sergeyenko arrived there from Sim-feropol with his wife and three children. We learned that two of the children — boys six and seven years old — were not his; they were Jewish. When the Jews were being herded to a sure death in Simferopol, Sergeyenko's wife pulled the boys from the crowd and brought them home. Since it was impossible to remain in Sim-feropol with two Jewish children, the entire Sergeyenko family had moved here, to the village. They were given work in the collective farm.

"In this village it was possible to openly rejoice when Soviet planes appeared over us. We were in this village when liberation came. The joyous day when the Red Army showed up in our village will always remain in our hearts, and this joy will be passed on to our children and grandchildren together with their mothers' milk."

Prepared for publication by **Lev Kvitko**.

How Doctor Fidelev Was Killed

Fifty years ago a young doctor by the name of B. M. Fidelev arrived in the Crimean port of Feodosia. He had wanted to become a pediatrician, but fate willed otherwise. A ship from Yaffa brought plague to Feodosia, and it was lurking somewhere in the depths of the port. The port was surrounded and the sick and those who had been in contact with the sick were put in quarantine. There was a place on the beach surrounded by a high wall; from time immemorial it had been used to isolate persons ill with cholera and the plague. Doctor Fidelev voluntarily entered this gloomy place with its stone barracks and cemetery spread with quicklime. Its laboratory was the headquarters for those who struggled with the terrible disease. . . . Fidelev lived in quarantine for three months. Many people around him died. Many, however, owed their lives to the skilled and self-sacrificing care of this young doctor. Doctor Fidelev became an epidemiologist and, thanks to his efforts, the Feodosia quarantine area was rebuilt and transformed into one of the best naval medical-observatory stations on the Black Sea and the Mediterranean. . . .

Fidelev believed deeply in the curing powers of the Crimean sea air and sun rays, and he managed to get a new city hospital built just outside of town. The windows of the large light rooms faced the sea. Next to the building were lawns and flower gardens. With the years tall acacias, poplars, and cypresses grew up next to the hospital buildings.

When war with the Fascists broke out, Doctor Fidelev was chief physician of the Feodosia hospital. Soon its ward rooms were filled with people wounded during the bombings of neighboring settled points. Feodosia itself came to know the howl of the sirens, the road of ack-ack fire, and the explosions of bombs.

When the Germans reached Perekop, Doctor Fidelev was advised to leave.

"I never was a deserter," he said, "and I will not abandon hundreds of sick people to their fates. That would be the equivalent of desertion in a moment of danger."

On the third day after the Germans had broken through to Feodosia, they issued an order for all Jews to report to the city prison so they could be "sent north." Apartments were to be left untouched, and they could take with them only a change of underwear, a coat, and food for several days.

Doctor Fidelev and his wife also went to the prison. After his documents were checked, however, the doctor was told to return home.

That evening Chizhikov, a repairman from the quarantine area, secretly came to see Fidelev.

"The Germans want to set up paraformaline chambers in the quarantine area, but they're having trouble carrying out their plans. They don't have the blueprints, and part of the equipment has been dismantled. Someone told them about you. I want to warn you that they are evidently preparing the wards for purposes other than disinfection. . . . When they were trying them out, I saw them take Isaak Nudelman there. Afterwards they threw his dead body in the sea. . . ."

The Germans actually did demand of Fidelev that he help them set up paraformaline chambers. They explained to him that they were intended to "disinfect your countrymen before sending them to other places."

The doctor's reply was: "No."

He was arrested together with his wife and taken down the main street of town. Some Rumanian soldier pulled the fur hat off the doctor's head, and the fall wind tousled the old man's thick hair. There was not a person in Feodosia who did not know Fidelev, and everyone who saw them took off their hats, realizing where the old people were being taken. They passed the Fidelev ambulatory clinic, the tobacco factory clinic — also organized by him — and the nursery which he had run.

The prisoners were not brought to the prison, but were put in one of the cellars of the former clinic. The Germans probably applied various forms of "medical" torture, but Fidelev did not go to the quarantine area to help them. A few days later the doctor and his wife were tied up with telephone wires and thrown in the clinic well, which was used to dump seepage water from the cellars. This broad pit filled with water as high as a man is tall only after eight hours of use of the sump pump. Through a crack in the fence the cleaning woman in the clinic, who lived in the next courtyard, saw the Germans push the bound old people into the pit. She heard the electric pump work all night, sighing and splashing as it pumped the dirty water.

Doctor Fidelev drowned in the liquid mud which filled the pit. He gave his life to fight the people's enemies — diseases — and he did not retreat when he came face to face with a new "variety." It was not a lung or bubonic plague; it was the brown plague. The Germans in the Crimea were crushed and thrown into the sea, the city hospital named in honor of Doctor Fidelev is operating again. . . .

Information supplied by **A. Morozov.**
Prepared for publication by **A. Derman.**

The Painter Zhivotovsky

My childhood and youth passed in Dzhankoy. Dzhankoy was inhabited by hard-working craftsmen, and life there was rich and cheerful. The favorite of the entire town was Naum Zhivotovsky — "the cheerful painter."

Zhivotovsky was an amazing craftsman — inexhaustible in his love for work. He painted bright signs that made every passer-by stop in his tracks. He did attractive posters for the movie theater and fantastic decorations for club performances. The collective-farm carriages looked as if they had been prepared for wedding when he got done with them.

I never saw Zhivotovsky in a gloomy mood. Perhaps he had his bad days, but he used to say: "Let my grief stay with me, and the people can have my joy." He liked people, and people liked him. In the evenings Zhivotovsky liked to stroll down Krymskaya Street with his entire family. Beside him walked his wife, a cheerful, dark-skinned beauty wearing a colorful elaborate dress. Around them their children formed a noisy crowd — four mischievous, tanned boys and three girls — beautiful and flirtatious. They took after their mother, and they were dressed just as elaborately.

Zhivotovsky took pride in his family and his numerous relatives. He used to say: "Oh, there are a lot of Zhivotovskys; soon we'll fill up the entire Crimea."

In August of 1941 I was passing through Dzhankoy to the Perekop Isthmus. In the center of town a German bomb had destroyed the kindergarten. One wall had collapsed, the roof was gone, and everywhere were twisted children's beds, tiny tables, chairs, and playthings. On the inner walls, however, an artist had depicted everything that formed the wealth of the Crimea of the steppes. Enormous striped watermelons lay in a colorful heap next to a shed in a melon field; in the gardens tomatoes were ripening, pumpkins gleamed yellow, field pods were bursting with peas. On a side wall were drawn two seas. One of them was indicated as the Sea of Azov, and the other was the Black Sea. Flat-bottomed fishing boats with slanted sails moved across the mirror-like surface, military ships with cannons stood immobile, and an enormous steamship with the name "The Ukraine" was blowing smoke through its three stacks. Between the seas lay the Crimean steppe, and it also reminded the view of a sea. Combines that looked like schooners sailed through the steppe, and the golden wheat stretched its ripe ears to them.

"The children must have liked that very much," my companion said. "Who painted it?"

"Zhivotovsky," I answered confidently.

And I was not mistaken. A resident of Dzhankoy was passing and said:

"It was him."

Three years later I had heard nothing more of Zhivotovsky. But then a letter came:

"Dear countryman, someone told me that he saw with his own eyes that you were killed. But you are alive, and that is great; I can't tell you how happy I am. They tried to kill me many times, too, but the people of the steppe don't drown in water and don't burn in fire.

"Maybe you have forgotten me, but I don't think so. After all, you remember I always was with people, and the people remember me, because I was too noisy a person. But there is not much left now of the former Zhivotovsky. Terrible things have happened to me. I'm even surprised myself that I am still alive, that I breathe, eat, joke with my comrades.

"In April of this year I fought at the Perekop, forced the Sivash, and now I reached my native village — my beloved Dzhankoy.

"The town was destroyed. Everything was burning. I hurried to my house. It was in one piece, unharmed, and on the shutters were the flowers that I had painted, and the gate still had the mean dog that I had painted on it. I opened the gate and walked into the garden. A strange boy was standing there, smiling and looking at me. But I could not see anything; I was blinded from fear, and I could not ask anything.

"The Germans pulled Zhivotovsky's root out of the ground! My soul is as empty and cold as if I had been frozen, and even my tears have frozen.

"Dear countryman, I learned that the Germans had destroyed my wife, my children, my sick mother, my aging father, my sisters and their small children. Altogether I know of forty-two people. The fate of the rest is unknown to me.

"I decided then that life was not worth living, and I wanted to commit suicide with a war-trophy pistol.

"But then I decided that it was not proper for a soldier to die that way. And when I again found myself in combat and saw the

Germans, I no longer wanted to die. I attacked the Germans and shouted: 'Your trial has begun!' In that fashion I reached the very tip of the Crimea — the Cape of Kherson. Here, near Sevastopol, I killed a German on the shore and said: 'Sentence has been executed. Let the others tremble! Their trial has begun! I will reach your Berlin!'

"I was given a medal, and the regiment commander told me to rest up in Yalta and catch up with the regiment later. But I went with the regiment to a new area of the front. Now we are moving farther and farther west, and we conduct a just trial on the field of battle every day."

Your countryman, **Naum Zhivotovsky**,
the former "Cheerful Painter"

Information supplied by **L. Feygin**
Prepared for publication by **A. Derman**.

LATVIA

AIVTAJ

Riga

1. The Germans Enter the City

The Germans' approach to Riga was heralded by the incessant roar of bombs near the Western Dvina River crossings and the railroad station. From the very first hours of the war dozens of Junker and Heinkel fighter bombers roared over the streets and squares of Riga. They dropped bombs from great altitudes and at close range; then they swooped down and strafed the boulevards, killing many passers-by. The bombers were echoed by machine-gun and automatic-rifle fire from some attics and rooftops — German paratroopers and saboteurs who had infiltrated the city were already ensconced there. Hitler's secret agents, who had remained in the Baltic after the Soviet authorities had established themselves in Lithuania, Latvia, and Estonia, also made their presence known — the Fascists tried to blow up bridges, seize government buildings, and paralyze traffic on the most important military lines of communication.

A sinister threat hung over the Riga Jews. Tens of thousands of leaflets dropped from German airplanes painted a detailed picture of what would happen to the Jews. Russians and Letts were warned categorically that they would be severely punished if they helped the Jews to evacuate. Jews streamed to the railroad stations, over-filled the empty freightcars, sat for days on the railroad platforms, waiting for the trains to leave for the East. The railroadmen did everything in their power; under the whistling of bullets and the rumbling of bombs they carried out maneuvers on the station's tracks and got the trains moving. Many, who had no hope of leaving by train, put their bags in carts and started a long journey on foot. All the roads were covered with refugees. Women and children became the targets for German pilots.

With each hour the evacuation became more complicated. There were jams at the railroad stations between troop trains rushing to the front and the trains carrying evacuees; German airplanes became more and more fierce in their attacks on the roads; at times they pursued one person or one cart. It became increasingly difficult to get out of the city and past all the ambushes by German paratroopers. The brazen Hitlerites even made a sortie on the main highway of the city — Brivibas Street. Regiments of the Red Army held back the onslaught of the German troops by protecting the mobilization in the remote regions of the country. The Germans had superiority both in manpower and in tanks, but especially, in air power. Soviet regiments were ordered to fall back in delaying battles, to fight at each line, to gain time. Ultimately, about eleven thousand Jews were evacuated from Riga.

* * *

On the morning of July 1 the Germans were already in Riga. The first Jewish men they encountered were tied to their tanks, and their bloodied bodies were dragged for hours through the streets of the city. By noon they began to seize Jews on the streets and herd them into synagogues. Many of them did not reach the synagogues — they were shot on the way.

When the Germans decided that a sufficient number of Jews had been herded into the synagogues, they began to invite the people of Riga to assemble near the synagogues for an interesting sight. But here the Hitlerites encountered their first surprise — the Jewish houses of prayer became strongholds which crackled with the fierce fire of rifles and automatic weapons. It was obvious that the people who had settled inside there were doomed; by this time there was already a large concentration of German infantry and tank forces in Riga, but the besieged people decided to give up their lives and to die fighting. The Germans in several instances had to storm the synagogues with tanks. The uneven battle lasted several hours and by the end of the day all the synagogues in Riga were ablaze. In some instances the Germans burned down the synagogues, in others — the Jews themselves set fire to the buildings, preferring to die rather than surrender to the Hitlerites. Loud cries of women and children were heard from the burning buildings. Rabbi Kilov in the large choral synagogue read prayers aloud, while from underground gun-ports there were bursts of machine-gun fire. A saw-mill worker, Abel, shot with an old fowling piece two Germans who were trying to break into his house. A German officer summoned a whole platoon to be sure to take him alive. But Abel did not surrender; he died, fighting to the last minute. The synagogue on Gogol Street was stormed by two companies of German soldiers.

Centers of resistance sprang up outside the synagogues too. In some Jewish apartments the pogrom-makers encountered gun fire. A school director named Elkishek, a Doctor of Philosophy from the University of Vienna, died with a rifle in his hands.

Many recollections remain about the courage, dignity, and the special kind of pride with which the Jews met their executioners in Riga. Two SS men led a woman textile worker, Ganstein, to a synagogue; along the way they beat her with their rifle butts and jabbed her with bayonets. She walked silently for a long while, at times wiping the blood from her face so she could see where she was walking. At an intersection where a group of Letts stood, Ganstein suddenly broke away and shouted: "People, remember these beasts! The Soviet authorities will never forgive them for this. Our people will come, tell them how we were tortured here. . . ."

The Germans did not allow Ganstein to finish speaking and shot her point-blank; then they fired several shots from their automobiles into the air and ordered the crowd to disperse.

That same day a group of Jews made a desperate attempt to break through to join units of the Red Army. The leader of this group was Abram Epstein, a student of the University of Riga. The plan was as follows: since the Germans were busy plundering in the city and whole battalions had left their positions, they were to take advantage of these circumstances, go into the woods outside the city, and then, after discovering a poorly guarded area, they were to break through the front and join their own people. Three hundred women and children stretched into a long column. The people from Riga knew the area surrounding their native city very well, and this mass of people managed to safely pass the guards, go through the woods to the suburbs, and reach an area that was comparatively safe. Someone, however, informed on them to the Germans, and several tanks and an infantry battalion rushed in pursuit of the escapees. The Germans overtook the column fifteen kilometers outside the city. Abram Epstein ordered his unit (about sixty armed boys and girls) to protect the women and children. As a line of defense they chose a small river called the Maza-Yugla, which flowed to the east of Riga. A battle was waged there for several hours between the Riga students and the German attackers. This gave the women and children the opportunity to hide in the woods and, using inconspicuous paths, to reach the Madonsky highway where regiments of the Red Army were fighting. Abram Epstein's unit was almost completely wiped out along with its commander, but in that heavy battle on the Maza-Yugla River it killed more than one hundred Germans and it gave several hundreds of Jewish women and children the opportunity to reach Soviet troops.

There were attempts by Latvians and Russians to save Jews from inevitable violence. A student named Ilya Abel hid several Jewish comrades in his apartment for a number of days. During the first days of the pogroms Father Antony hid several dozens of Jews in his Polish Roman Catholic church. Another Catholic priest helped an engineer named Lichter to escape from the city. But all these measures did little to help these unfortunate people. Even if they were saved during the first days, later they inevitably fell into the hands of the Germans and suffered the fate of all Jews in Riga.

2. Night over Riga

The first night under German occupation fell. Hitler's agents crawled out of attics, roofs, and cellars. German "repatriates" appeared in the city — people who in 1940 had emigrated from Latvia. The Germans transported them in by train to be informers, undercover men, the future commandants of the prisons and camps, and plain executioners. The Baltic Germans justified the hopes of their hosts; among the Hitlerite scoundrels, they were the most vicious, among the executioners — the cruelest, among the interrogators and overseers — the meanest.

Each hour the Jewish pogrom took on more and more licentious forms and increasingly broader dimensions. The indiscriminate pillage of Jewish apartments began. Then came mass arrests. Everyone the Germans could lay hands on was seized, taken to prison, to the prefecture, or directly to Bikernieki Forest.* That night a total of six thousand Jews were arrested.

Bikernieki Forest has an unforgettable and sad page in the history of Latvia. In 1905 the Baltic barons who occupied all the command posts in this area drowned in blood the wave of the first Russian Revolution. Thousands of participants in the revolutionary movement were shot at that time in the Bikernieki Forest. During the Civil War years mass executions of fighters for Soviet Latvia were conducted there. In this forest, like geological stratification, lie the bones of fighters and martyrs of two generations. This was the place chosen by the Germans for the mass annihilation of hundreds of thousands of Jews from Riga and of Jews brought from Western Europe.

The Germans tried to outdo each other in their refined methods for exterminating defenseless people. *Sturmbannführer* (Major) Kraus from the *Sicherheitspolizei* (security police), for example, worked out his own favorite device. On the streets of the Moscow

*Most of the mass executions of Jews occurred in Rumbuli, a suburb of Riga.

Vorstadt (suburb) he lined up groups of Jews and covered their faces with portraits of Lenin and Stalin. He then armed Lettish boys with rifles and ordered them to "shoot the Bolsheviks!" Whenever the boys refused, he would catch one or two of them, cover their faces with the portraits too and push them into the crowd of Jews. And then the whole team of SS men would shoot the column of "portraits." *Untersturmführer* (Second Lieutenant) Bruns would force the Jews to dig graves for themselves in advance and lie down in them; then he would measure their height and spend a long time meticulously trying to make each grave have the correct geometric forms. Only when he had thoroughly enjoyed himself would he shoot his victims.

The Germans celebrated a bloody orgy in the building of the prefecture. Jews were continuously brought there to be "registered for work." The Germans filled out some sort of forms, measured the noses, foreheads, cheek-bones of some of the people and spent a long time writing something down. Then, laughing loudly, they burned the documents they had just filled out in the stove and made a "decision" — to Bikernieki Forest.

Once at midnight an SS man issued an order to get a barber. When the man came, he ordered him to shave half of the beards of all the elderly Jews. The Jews were to rip out one sleeve from their jackets, take off one shoe, and begin to dance. A half hour later the commander of an SS unit appeared, completely drunk, and announced that he would now make a political report. He spoke incoherently for a long time, but the one thing that could be understood was that he, the *Sturmbannführer*, would give no mercy to the Jews. Once they fell into his hands, they could consider themselves dead men and begin to prepare to meet their maker. And as proof that he meant what he said, the *Sturmbannführer* immediately shot several people with his pistol. That night about three thousand people underwent "re-registration" in the prefecture. More than a thousand were immediately sent to Bikernieki Forest and shot. The rest were locked up in the city's prison.

In the yard of the Central Committee of MOPR* the Germans found a number of placards, portraits, and several banners. The Hitlerites ordered some Jews to gather there and to take the banners and placards and have a mock "demonstration," sing the *Internationale* and other revolutionary songs. When the butchers

*The International Organization of Aid to Revolutionaries.

301

decided that the rehearsal was over, they led the "demonstration" into the street, trying to set the population on it. But the Hitlerites' provocation failed. The Letts and Russians were horrified by that awful sight. Then the Germans opened fire with automatic rifles and machine guns, and the whole "demonstration" was shot right there on the street.

That night in house N° 10 on Mariinskaya Street officers of the Württemberg-Baden Grenadier Regiment celebrated their successes. They herded several dozens of Jewish girls to their orgy, forced them to strip naked, dance, and sing songs. Many of these unfortunate girls were raped right there and then taken out in the yard to be shot. Captain Bach surpassed everyone with his invention. He broke off the seat cushions of two chairs and replaced them with sheets of tin. Two girls, students of Riga University, were tied to the chairs and seated opposite each other. Two lighted Primus stoves were brought and placed under the seats. The officers really liked this sport. They joined hands and danced in a ring around the two martyrs. The girls writhed in the torment, but their hands and feet were tightly bound to the chairs; and when they tried to shout, their mouths were gagged with dirty rags. The room filled with the nauseating smell of burning human flesh. The German officers just laughed, merrily doing their circle dance.

3. The First Days of the Occupation

Jewish affairs were turned over to the Baltic Germans who had returned to Riga. These scoundrels had long been possessed by a savage hatred for the Jewish population. The Baltic German was a special type of colonizer, mean and unrestrained, who had pillaged all the resources and wealth of the Baltic lands for centuries and who had never concealed his contemptuous attitude toward the local people nor his hatred of the Jews. Only after the unification of Latvia with the Soviet Union did Latvia and Estonia rid themselves of the age-long yoke of the Baltic Germans.

Now they returned in the capacity of storm troopers, invested with unlimited rights and power. In Riga police stations a certain Hans Mannskeit was known in his day as an incorrigible hooligan. People in Riga breathed a sigh of relief in 1940, when he was repatriated to Germany. He returned along with the German troops to occupy a position as Gestapo interrogator for Jewish affairs. A number of Baltic Germans began to play prominent roles under the Gestapo: accountant Lorenzen, Doctor Bernsdorf, accountants Schultz and Brasch. Other Baltic Germans who rushed back to Riga, while not occupying official positions in the Gestapo, nevertheless excelled in tormenting the defenseless Jewish population no less than the Gestapo men.

By special order, Jews were forbidden to buy food in the same stores patronized by Germans and Letts. They were also forbidden to perform "free" labor — all Jews had to do forced labor. Jews were required to wear a hexagonal star, the "Shield of David," on their chests and were forbidden to walk on the sidewalks; they were only allowed to use the roadways.

Arrests and mass executions continued without interruption. People were seized on the streets and in their apartments, and were dealt with on the spot. On Gertrude Street a group of storm troopers had climbed up on the roof of a six-story building and were throwing Jewish children to the ground. Some official was about to order them to stop these executions. They answered him from the roof:

"We're carrying on scientific work here. We're testing the validity of Newton's law of universal gravity."

"Donnerwetter! Well said! Continue gentlemen. Science requires sacrifices."

An old Jewish tailor was walking down Lacplesa Street, stooped over under the weight of a sewing machine. German officers tried to run him down with their automobile, but the old man managed to jump to the side and lean against a telephone pole. The Germans were indignant with this kind of "recalcitrance." They turned the automobile around and organized a regular hunt for the old man. They chased him for five minutes; finally, they pressed him against a newspaper stand, and he jumped out of the way onto the sidewalk.

"What? You would violate the laws of the German Empire?" the Hitlerites shouted.

They dragged the old man out into the road and began to beat him with iron rods. When, covered with blood, he fell down unconscious, the Germans walked to their automobile and, lighting cigarettes, began to talk merrily among themselves. A Latvian woman, Petrunya Salazas, who had witnessed this savage scene, brought a mug of water to the old man to wash off his face and give him something to drink. The Germans noticed this, and one of them knocked the mug from the woman's hands and threw it with all his might at her face; then he beat her with his rod and after making a threatening gesture with his pistol, he chased her away. The old man died two hours later right there on Lacplesa Street next to the newspaper stand.

Those days cruel violence was practiced not only against Jews, but also against anyone whom the Germans suspected of being in sympathy with the Soviet authorities. Jews were killed because they were Jews; Letts were accused mainly for sympathy to the Soviets. This put both nationalities on the same footing in the eyes of the executioners. On July 3 in the yard of the Riga prison fifty pairs of people were tied back to back and lined up; in each pair there was one Jew and one Lett. In the first pair stood the Lettish girl Elvira Damber and the Jew Yakov Abesgaus.

"You wanted equality," shouted the *Untersturmführer* who was in charge of the execution. "Now you'll get it."

And one hundred people, Jews and Letts tied together, were shot. Each bullet penetrated two bodies consecutively, and the blood of one hundred people flowed in a single stream in the prison yard. It is difficult to list all the refined tortures to which the Jews were subjected. Many people from Riga remember the martyr death of nineteen-year-old Lina Gottschalk. She was caught on the street and was taken to an apartment on Elizabeth Street where some drunk Germans were having a good time. The Hitlerites began to discuss how they were going to kill their victim. The girl knew German very well and silently listened to the discussion in which her fate was being decided. After a lengthy debate the Germans came to a decision — to convert the girl into a being without bones. She was tied up inside a sack and beaten methodically with ramrods. The beating lasted two hours. The girl was already dead, and all her bones were broken. The Germans would not leave their venture until they were convinced that every last bone was broken. So they rolled up the body of Lina Gottschalk into a bloody ball of flesh and ordered a soldier to throw it onto the boulevard near the opera theater.

A few days later the Germans began to carry out the order concerning the labor conscription of the Jews. The rulers of destinies in Riga — the Kommissar-general of Latvia, *Obergruppenführer* Drechsler and the *Gebietskommissar*, Witllock, ordered that all labor-intensive jobs be performed by Jews alone. With this, jobs were created for which there was absolutely no need and which amounted to an unnecessary waste of materials.

The Jewish labor exchange was headed by Lieutenant Kraus and

Sonderführer Drawe. They were especially sadistic in torturing their victims. In the beginning a large group of Jews, primarily youths, was charged with cleaning up buildings which were half demolished as a result of the war. The tasks were so enormous that many youths, particularly the girls, literally strained themselves. On stretchers which were carried by two people, the Germans ordered them to load eight to ten *poods* (400-500 pounds) of stone or brick. Those who fell from exhaustion were beaten with clubs, and often — to death.

The work day began, as a rule, with a beating and usually ended with murders. Floggings began in the morning as punishment for people who disobeyed the order to wear the hexagonal stars. In the beginning the star had to be worn on the left side of the chest; then an order was given to wear the star on the back. A little while later there was yet another order that the star was to be worn both on the back and chest. Then the rules underwent some additional changes — the Germans returned to the first variant, then to the second and so on without end.

Every morning people would ask themselves where they should attach the star, and every morning the Germans would find "violators," and a mass beating would begin.

Measures for ensuring even a relative degree of safety in cleaning up the buildings did not even enter the minds of the Germans. On the contrary, they forced people to remove the bricks near the foundation of demolished walls so that the unnecessary buildings could be brought down faster. Almost every day walls would collapse, burying dozens of people under the debris. And every day the Jews who returned from working found fewer of their friends and close ones.

Hundreds of Riga Jews died in a peatery near Olain.

The *Gebietskommissar* of the Yelgava (Mitava) district was a Baltic German, Baron Emden. He was nicknamed the "King of Zemgale," because his former property was there in the environs of Mitava and because in the district under his command he behaved like a cruel despot, unrestrained in his hunger for power. There is evidence that he organized several "hunts" and "roundups" against defenseless Jews. The list of his accomplices in one of these "hunts" is also known: Captain Cukurs, Major Arajs, the prefect of the city of Riga Stiglitz, *Untersturmführer* Jäger and the Baltic Germans — the Bruns brothers and *Gruppenführer* Kopitz.

Once this group went to see the director of the peatery and

demanded that they be given two hundred Jews. The director tried to object, saying that the removal of that number of people could interfere with the delivery of the peat at the scheduled time, but the all-powerful *Gebietskommissar* stood his ground. True, even he had to make a few "concessions" — he was given only women and children. Soon, the "hunt" began. These unfortunate people were driven out into a field in groups of ten to fifteen and warned that if they could run and hide in the woods nearby in eight minutes time, then they had a chance to save themselves. Otherwise, they would be shot as saboteurs and inferior subjects. At the sound of a whistle, the women and children ran as fast as they could toward the woods. They had to run a whole kilometer through canals, hummocks, and thickets. The Germans, watching a chronometer, held back the packs of hunting dogs. When eight minutes were up, the dogs, yelping and barking, tore after their victims. They overtook a lot of people who were still in the open field or in the short bushes. The specially-trained dogs ripped open their throats and took off for the others. Some of the dogs, after bringing their victims down to the ground, waited for their masters to arrive. The master would shoot the person lying on the ground, and the dog, after receiving a piece of candy as a reward, would run off in search of new game.

When the Germans had finished off the people they caught in the open field, the roundup in the woods began. It was conducted according to all the rules of the art of hunting: wide encirclement, the chase, pointers, ambush.

The murder of Jews continued daily. Hundreds of people were killed upon returning from work or just appearing on the street. Many preferred to stay put in cellars and go without food so as not to risk being seen by some Fascist. Particularly memorable days are July 16, when one thousand people were shot, and July 23 — the anniversary of the incorporation of Latvia into the Soviet Union, when more than two hundred people were killed and about eight hundred arrested. Jews were persecuted by the Germans even after they were dead — a special order was issued not to accept corpses of the Jews in the morgue. For seven days Jewish corpses lay scattered about on the streets of Riga.

Then the Germans began in earnest to plan for the complete annihilation of the Jews. For this it was necessary to gather the Jews in one place and isolate them from the rest of the population. The district chosen by the Germans for the resettlement of the Jews was the Moscow *Vorstadt* (suburb), where a Jewish ghetto had been located during the Middle Ages. It was not that the Germans were influenced by historical considerations. It was simply that the Moscow *Vorstadt* was the part of the city that was in the poorest condition and located very close to the Bikernieki Forest — the traditional place for mass executions.

Soon a governing board for the Riga Jewish community was formed which was responsible to the German authorities. Doctor Schlitter, a Viennese Jew and former state advisor of Austria, was appointed Chairman of the board. Members of the board included lawyers Michael Ilyashev and Mintz, Doctor Rudolf Blumenfeld, a former director of a textile factory, Kaufer, bookkeeper Blumenau, and others.

During the first days it became clear that the appointment of the board had not created any possibilities for improving the conditions of existence. The size of food rations were cut — Jews received half of what the rest of the population received, and that amounted to one-hundred grams of substitute bread per day. Jews were strictly forbidden to go to the villages to buy food. The Jewish population began to starve. Cut off from the whole world (correspondence through the mail was forbidden), the Jews of Riga anxiously waited for the events that lay ahead.

4. The Ghetto

The Germans did all sorts of things to speed up the resettlement of the Jews in the Moscow *Vorstadt*. Sometimes Jews were given only two or three hours to prepare to leave. Their furniture and property were confiscated by the Germans.

The area set aside for the ghetto was very small, but people kept arriving. On October 21 an order was issued by the commissar-general concerning the creation of the ghetto and the imposition of new, severe restrictions. Henceforth Riga Jews would be subject to the inhuman "Nuremberg Laws" and the "Goebbels Novella," promulgated as an elaboration of it. According to the creators of these "laws," Jews were no longer subjects in society, but had become objects of a racial policy.

The order of the commissar-general forbade Jews to leave the boundaries of the ghetto; they could go out beyond the barbed wire only under guarded escort. The enterprises at which the ghetto prisoners worked had to deliver their workers to the work place and back under guard. The city population was strictly forbidden to talk to the Jews or even come close to the ghetto fence.

A double fence of barbed wire closed off several blocks in the Moscow *Vorstadt*. On the evening of October 24 the German guard admitted the last Jews through the hastily raised gates. The Riga Jews had been herded into an enormous trap.

Days passed, full of anxiety. Each morning the gates of the ghetto were flung open, and thousands of people went to work under guard. The directors of the enterprises, contractors, and commandants of the German military units made extensive use of the free labor of the ghetto inhabitants. Lieutenant Kraus, who supervised the Jewish section of the labor exchange, refused no one's request for a work force. A poster hanging on the ghetto gates read: "Jews given out for a fee. This applies to military units too."

Every day the Jews who were returning from work were searched at the ghetto gates. The Germans examined everyone carefully. They looked for newspapers, books, food. Once they found a sandwich on a student named Kremer, and the boy was shot on the spot. Meanwhile, hunger in the ghetto was increasing and many were falling from malnutrition.

The community council took some local measures to improve the living conditions. Conditions were extraordinarily crowded and unsanitary (the Germans did not permit the removal of sewage from the ghetto). Nevertheless, doctors in the ghetto did what they could to guard against the outbreak of epidemics. Out-patient clinics, shelters for orphans, and an eatery for the elderly and the invalids operated in the ghetto.

On November 27 the community council was informed that, by order of the authorities, the male "Specialists" working as servants for the German military units would be separated from the rest of the ghetto inhabitants, including their families. On November 28 they began to build an inner fence in the ghetto. In this way the "Small Ghetto" was formed — the one where only able-bodied men lived, of which there were about nine thousand. Fenced off by barbed wire from the others, they were unable to communicate with the "Big Ghetto" to see their wives and children. The ghetto guards more and more often poked around the buildings with an ominous smirk on their faces. Everyone felt that catastrophe was near.

On November 29 *Sturmbannführer* Brasch summoned the entire community council to his office. He behaved more insolently than usual, as if he were flaunting his frankness. He declared that, by order of the authorities, part of the Jewish population of Riga would be destroyed, because the ghetto was too overcrowded. The council was to participate in this measure by helping the Germans select people for execution. For this purpose they had to immediately draw up a list of old men, the sickly, criminals, and other people whose presence in the ghetto was considered undesirable by the Council.

The members of the council silently heard out what the executioner had to say, looked at each other, and hung their heads. To argue with him, to try to persuade him of anything was useless. The members of the council knew each other well and therefore silently, after exchanging a glance, they made a decision. Doctor Blumenfeld gave Brasch an answer:

"The council will not give anyone up for execution. I am a doctor, and my whole adult life I have studied how to treat sick people — not to kill them. Our conceptions of human values are too different. Also different are our conceptions of who would be considered a criminal. In our opinion, the criminals should be sought outside the ghetto. . . ."

Brasch interrupted Blumenfeld and ordered the council to leave.

No matter how the members of the council tried to hide what Brasch had told them, the ghetto found out about the execution which the Germans were preparing. On November 29 the commander-in-chief of the police forces in Ostland, *Obergruppen-füehrer* Jeckeln informed all the enterprises and offices not to send the Jews to work until a special order was issued. On November 30 the ghetto gates were not opened; the guards who came to escort the Jews to work were sent back. From all the preparations it was obvious that something extraordinary was going to happen.

5. The First "Action"

The first "action" in the Riga ghetto took place on November 30 and December 1, 1941, five weeks after the creation of the ghetto. It began with the order for all the men to line up on Lodzinskaya Street. No one knew what was going to happen — the most discrepant rumors were circulating. Some of the men, fearing execution, hid with their families. And some of the women, having changed into men's clothes, tried to get into a column of men, hoping that they would save themselves there. Soon the men were led away — some to the "Small Ghetto," the rest to the Salaspils concentration camp. Toward six o'clock in the evening the women, children, and old men were forced from their apartments. Police swept through the apartments in Moscow *Vorstadt*. The sick were finished off on the spot; to mothers burdened with large families they left no more than two children, the rest were shot immediately. Three hundred old men from a poorhouse for the aged were killed to the last man. In the ghetto hospital all the patients were tortured to death. The ghetto streets were covered with blood and corpses. Death cries were heard everywhere. Groups of women and children who had been ejected from their apartments stood on street corners. Numb with cold and shivering, they watched the bloody orgy with horror. By morning the Germans had begun to form columns of two to three hundred people; escorted by an equal number of policemen, they were sent in an eastern direction.

Near the building where the community council was housed stood, surrounded by Hitlerites, the members of the council, and among them was the chief rabbi of Riga, Zak. Doctor Blumenfeld managed to whisper to Abram Rosenthal, who was passing by:

"Our minutes are numbered. Perhaps, you will live until brighter days; tell our families that we died with the firm belief that our people can not be destroyed. We will be executed — that is perfectly clear. Remember, in a house nearby, by the light of a wick lamp, Dubnov* is writing the last lines of his memoirs — like a chronicler of ancient times. He is sure that they will reach their reader."

One of the commandants of the ghetto was the German Johann Siebert, a butcher with a higher education, who once studied at the University of Heidelberg. Semen Markovich Dubnov periodically gave a series of lectures on the history of the ancient East and the general history of the Jews in Heidelberg. And here student and professor met in the Riga ghetto; one in the capacity of an all-powerful boss and cruel butcher, the other — a prisoner condemned to death. Siebert recognized his former professor and at every chance he could, he tried to insult and taunt the eighty-two-year-old man:

"Professor, I was once foolish enough to listen to your lectures at

*Semen (Shimon) Markovich Dubnov (1860-1941) was a Jewish historian, publicist, and public figure. The third volume of his *Book of Life* was published in Riga at the end of 1940. The entire edition was destroyed by the Nazis. Only one copy survived, and it was used to republish the edition — S. Dubnov, *Book of Life: Memoirs, Thoughts*, vol. 3, New York, 1957. In the Riga ghetto Dubnov began to write an article under the title "The Ghetto." He also kept a diary.

the university," Siebert once said to Dubnov. "You spent a long time talking to us about the ideas of humanism which would triumph throughout the world. I recall, you criticized the anti-Semites and made a prophesy about the twentieth century — a century that would see the complete emancipation of the Jews. You know, you almost foresaw everything. Yesterday I was in the Bikernieki Forest; four hundred and eighty Russian prisoners of war were executed there, and — imagine — just as many Jews. You can celebrate, Dubnov. You've already attained equality with the Russians."

"How many Jews were executed yesterday?"

"Four hundred and eighty."

"Thank you for the information. I am still working, and this is important for me to know."

Right up until the last day the author of "The General History of the Jews" kept a diary in which he gave an account of the Riga ghetto. Notebooks with his notes were secretly carried out of the ghetto to Latvian friends in the city. These notes have not yet been found — the people who were keeping Dubnov's diary were driven away by the Germans.

. . . Dubnov walked out of the building, urged on by two Germans. He had the look of a man who had, to the end, fulfilled his duty to his conscience and to his people. He turned around — it was snowing. But the customary whiteness was not there. Blood saturated the snow. Hundreds of women and children, urged on by SS men, were walking to their death. Dubnov looked at the Germans. Baring his teeth, Johann Siebert grinned. Dubnov wanted to say something to him. But automatic rifles began to crackle. . . . The tallith of Rabbi Zak turned red. . . . Dubnov fell too.

Witnesses of the mass murders in the Riga ghetto unanimously maintain that nothing that happened bore any traces of impulsive activity; on the contrary, everything was done according to a definite plan which was preconceived and worked out to the smallest detail. Inside the ghetto itself no one cleared away the corpses, but when the column went out beyond the barbed wire, wheelbarrows and carts were immediately brought forth to accompany it. People who lagged behind and crying children were shot by the guard without a moment's hesitation, and their bodies were thrown onto a cart or wheelbarrow.

Brasch stood with his pistol by the ghetto gates and shot into the moving columns of prisoners. He did this calmly, methodically taking aim. A member of the "order service," composed of Jews from the ghetto, Izidor Berel, walked up to Brasch and asked:

"What are you doing, Mr. Brasch? Is this what you call German culture — the willful shooting of defenseless people?"

Izidor Berel during the dictatorship of Ulmanis served in the Latvian police and rose to a high rank. Therefore, when he was assigned to the "order service" in the ghetto, he was ordered to wear a police uniform with the badge of rank he had earned. Brasch was below Berel in rank and like a proper German functionary, he felt it necessary to give him an explanation:

"We are acting in complete accordance with the instructions we received. We are supposed to adhere strictly to the time schedule for moving the column to its destination, and therefore we are eliminating from the ranks everyone who could slow down the pace of the column. Judge for yourself, do you think that old woman wearing the violet house-coat will be able to walk at the necessary speed?" After taking aim, he fired a shot at the old woman.

That is just how calmly and methodically all the executioners acted. If something did upset them, then it was only the danger of deviating from the column's precise time schedule and the completion of the "operation" in due time. Only once did Brasch lose his self-composure — engineer Volf quickly stepped out of the column and slapped the executioner in the face. Brasch discharged the whole cartridge clip of his pistol into the engineer. In other instances he saved his cartridges.

It was somewhat surprising for the leaders of the "action" to find so many orphans in the ghetto — many of them had become orphans only a few hours earlier. A special children's battalion made up of six hundred boys and girls was formed. It was escorted by two hundred policemen from the *Ordnungspolizei*. On the way they would throw children up into the air and shoot them.

When the column was walking past an Old-Believer church, several dozen Russian Old Believers led by a priest walked out with icons in their hands and, kneeling by the side of the road, they began to sing church songs. The police tried to break them up, but the priest said:

"Do not try to stop us from bringing prayers to God. It is not simple folk you are leading, but holy martyrs. They will soon appear before the Most High and tell him what is happening in our sinful land. Let our prayers go with them to God."

The mass murders roused deep indignation among the workers

in the "Quadrat" rubber factory. As a sign of protest they stopped working. The gendarmery intervened. The affair developed into armed skirmishes, and many workers died in the uneven battle.

In Bikernieki Forest eight enormous pits had already been dug. As soon as the columns arrived, everyone was ordered to undress. Boots had to be put in one pile, galoshes in another. The unclothed people were prodded by SS men with the butts of their rifles toward the precipice where the Baltic German, Baron Sievers, stood. He shot from his submachine gun in short bursts. Two aids changed the cartridge clips on the automatic rifles and took turns handing them to Sievers. He stood there, completely spattered with blood, but for a long time did not want to give his place to someone else. Later he boasted that on December 1 he executed three thousand Jews with his own hands.

Cameramen furiously turned the knobs on their cameras. Photographers bustled about, and many SS men also clicked their "Leicas," taking amateur snapshots.

The Germans thought up various methods of taunting their victims. They picked out old men with long beards and ordered them to play soccer right there in the snow. This idea pleased the Germans no end. The cameramen and photographers continuously photographed this unusual soccer match. But an officer rode up on horseback and gave Lange the order to speed things up.

The poor victims were overcome with numbness. Shivering from the cold, they hoped to the last minute to be saved. Many people thought that, once the butchers had seen enough blood, they would calm down and herd the survivors to a concentration camp. Suddenly, someone's nerves gave out, and a loud weeping was heard in the forest. He was joined by hundreds of voices, and people broke into hysterics. It seemed that nothing was capable of bringing calm to this half-senseless crowd of people. But Mrs. Malkin jumped up on a tree stump and shouted:

"Why are you crying, Jews? Do you really think these monsters will be moved by tears? Let's be calm! Let's be proud! We are Jews! . . . We are Soviet Jews!"

And everything grew quiet in the forest, only the frantic rattle of automatic rifles broke the silence. One of the SS men walked up to the column and asked with a jeer:

"Why have you quieted down? You have only a few minutes left to live, so make the most of them. Sing something."

313

In answer someone in an old man's voice began to sing the *Internationale*; he was joined first by isolated persons, and then everyone all at once began to sing the grand hymn. This episode was reported by the seamstress Frida Frid,* the only Jewish girl who survived that day in Bikernieki Forest. The story of her escape and the three-year-long wandering of this lonely, persecuted woman through the farms of Latvia could fill the pages of an entire book.

"Our column was divided up," relates Frida Frid, "and everyone was ordered to undress. I also undressed to my underwear, then I felt ashamed — there were men standing all around, and I was wearing only a slip. I took my cotton work smock and put it on. I was very cold. I stuck my hands in the pockets of my smock to warm up, and I felt a piece of paper there. I looked at it — it was my diploma indicating my graduation with honors from seamstress's school. I had kept it for about fifteen years. God, I thought, maybe this paper will save me. I ran out of the column and rushed up to a German — he seemed to me to be an officer.

"'Officer, sir,' I spoke to him in German, 'Why do you want to kill me? I want to work. You shouldn't kill me. Look, I'm not lying, I have a diploma. Here is the document.'

"He pushed me away, and I fell down. When I started to get up, he kicked me again and shouted:

"'Don't bother me and don't come up to me with all sorts of papers. Go to Stalin with your documents.'

"And once again I was back in the column. I looked at the people — they were obediently doing what they were told. I began to tear at my hair, grabbed a tuft of hair and pulled it out; it was in my hand, and I didn't even feel the pain. And the Germans kept prodding us with their rifle butts closer and closer to the pit. Once again I addressed the policemen, trying to prove to them that I was a dressmaker, that I wanted to work. I showed them the diploma, but no one would even listen to me. I had already approached the pit, tall trees grew on two sides of it, and behind it a narrow path. Jews were already walking there one at a time, and vanishing behind the precipice — one could only hear the rattle of the automatic rifles.

"'Is it really the end?' I thought. 'A few minutes will pass and I

*Frida Frid-Mikhelson now lives in Israel, where she has published the book *I Survived Rumbuli* (The Hakibbutz Hameukhad Press, 1973). According to her memoirs the execution which she survived took place in Rumbuli Forest.

will be dead, never to see the sun again or breathe the air.' How could this be? After all, my documents are in order, I worked honestly all my life, customers were never angry with me, and the Germans are not taking any of this into account. I do not want to die! I do not!

"I ran up to the officer who was in charge of the execution and shouted in a voice that seemed strange, even to me:

"'What are you doing to me? I am a specialist. Here are my documents. I am a specialist. . . .'

"He hit me in the head with his pistol, and I fell down. I was right next to the pit where the dead were being thrown. I pressed myself to the ground and tried not to move. A half an hour later I heard someone shout in German: 'Put the shoes here!' By this time I had already crawled back a little. Just then, something was being thrown at me. I opened up one eye slightly and saw a shoe lying next to my face. I was being covered up with shoes. Probably, my gray cotton smock blended with the color of the shoes and they didn't notice me. I began to feel a little warmer — there was already a whole mountain of shoes on top of me. Only my right side was completely frozen. The fluffy snow that had fallen in the morning had completely melted underneath me; first it was terribly wet; then the water began to freeze, and I was covered with a crust of ice. I could have put several shoes under me, but I was afraid that the pile would move, and I would be noticed. I lay like that until dark, with ice frozen to my right side.

"Shots resounded quite close to me, and I could distinctly hear the last cries of people, the moans of the wounded who were thrown alive into the common grave. Some died cursing at their executioners, others died remembering their children and parents, others read prayers aloud . . . others asked at the last minute if they could dress their children, or else they would catch a cold. And I had to lie still and listen to it all. Several times I thought I heard my brother's voice, then — my apartment mate's. At those moments I thought I was losing my mind.

"By evening the shooting had stopped. The Germans left a small guard near the clothing, and they went off to rest. Several Germans stood there steps from me. They lit up their cigarettes and talked among themselves. I listened to their cheerful, content voices: 'We did a great job today.' 'Yes, it was a busy day.' 'There are still a lot of them left there. We'll have to work a little more.' 'Well, see you tomorrow.' 'Pleasant dreams.' 'Oh, I always have good dreams.'

"I decided to crawl out from under the piles of shoes. The first thing to do was get dressed. I crawled over to another pile — it was men's clothing. There was no time to deliberate — I put on someone's pants and jacket and tied a big kerchief around my head. Just then I heard the faint crying of a child coming from the pit where all the dead lay: 'Mama, I'm cold. . . . Why are you just lying there, Mama?' Well, I thought, what will be, will be. I would try to save the child. But the Germans were a step ahead of me. They walked up to the pit, found the child with their bayonets, and stabbed him. One of the Germans said, laughing: 'No one gets away alive from us.'

"I saw that there was nothing more to do there. I had to get as far away as possible from that awful place while it was still night. But there were guards all around; they could see me in the white snow. Then I remembered the film "War in Finland," where soldiers dressed in white uniforms were very well camouflaged in the snow. Not far away I saw a pile of sheets in which some of the mothers had carried their infants. . . .

"I came across a blanket cover, wrapped myself in it and began to crawl. . . ."

Those who were left in the ghetto waited for the pogrom to continue, but to their surprise, it was quiet. Only now and then one could hear the moans of a wounded person; a policeman would quickly walk up to him. . . . A lone shot resounded between the buildings, and silence settled in again. No one cleared away the corpses, no new orders came, except one — to inform the police of any wounded. The Germans invariably finished off the wounded.

Only on the fifth day was there an order to bury the dead. In the old Jewish cemetery, which was located inside the ghetto zone, a single enormous grave was dug. A doctor carried his wife and two children to the grave; some people buried all their relatives, close and distant — from the oldest to the youngest generation.

6. "Deportation" from the Ghetto

A week after the first "action" it was announced that the "Big Ghetto" would be "deported" from Riga. What that word meant, no one knew exactly. The Germans explained that "deportation" was substantially different from "evacuation." If the notion "evacuation" entailed moving into a new place, then "deportation" entailed only eviction. . . . Whether those being "deported" would move in anywhere, was not known.

In the evening of December 9 in –20° Celcius the inhabitants of the ghetto were ordered to get ready for "deportation." From seven o'clock in the evening until early in the morning people clustered in the freezing cold. By that time the Germans had already plundered the ghetto and taken all the warm things. A lot of old men and women froze to death that night. At dawn they began to lead the columns out under escort. Not far from Shkirotava Station on a dead-end track stood several trains without engines. The "deportees" were put into freight cars. From these mobile prisons people were taken by the hundreds to the Bikernieki Forest, where the Germans massacred them with machine guns. In total, about 12,000 people were killed that day.

A few days later the Germans announced everywhere that they would soon celebrate the liquidation of the "Big" Riga ghetto. Everyone in Riga and the surrounding area who "enjoyed" such things took part in the holiday. German soldiers with all types of weapons thronged to the area of the Moscow *Vorstadt*: Germans dressed in civilian clothes, policemen, and gendarmes, the dregs of Riga's criminals, Fascist scoundrels from among the Latvian nationalists. The violence lasted for a long time — small children were tossed into the air; naked girls were forced to play volleyball, and the losing team was shot; then the game began again with new players. This entire holiday was directed by *Untersturmführer* Jäger who was widely known for the fact that he had long been a member of the Nazi Party — he had participated with Hitler in the preparation of the Munich putsch.

After the festival there were only 3,800 people left in the ghetto, including three hundred women and several dozen children. But in a day the Riga ghetto began to fill up again — the first trainload of people had arrived from Germany.

7. The Jews from Germany

It is difficult to explain why Riga was the place chosen for the murder of several hundred thousand German Jews. Once the commandant's adjutant, *Untersturmführer* Migge, having had too much to drink, bluntly explained in his own way why the Jews from Germany were brought to Latvia: the Germans were afraid to kill them at home, because it would not go unnoticed; every executioner would have become well known to a wide circle of people.

The German Jews were brought to Riga under the pretense of resettling them to a new place of residence. The Germans arranged

317

the export of the Jews to their annihilation in such a way that the poor victims did not know until the last minute what fate would befall them. It was explained to everyone that the move was being made for the purpose of German colonization in the East, that Germany, as before, still considered German Jews its citizens, but found it more expedient to settle them in *Ostland*. It was recommended that people take all the things that would be useful in their new place of residence. On the corpse of one of the people killed in the Riga ghetto the following directive was found regarding the evacuation from Berlin:

"Berlin No. 4, January 11, 1942.
To Mr. Albert Israel Unger and spouse.

"Your departure has been set by order of the authorities for January 19, 1942. This order concerns you, your wife, and all the unmarried members of your family who are included in your property declaration.

"At noon of January 17, 1942, your premises will be sealed up by an official. You must, therefore, prepare by the designated time your large baggage and hand baggage. You are to hand over the keys to your apartment and rooms to the official. You must go with the official to the police station in the district where your apartment is located, having taken with you both your large as well as your hand baggage. The large baggage you are to surrender at the police station. From there it will be delivered by our baggage compartment by truck to a collection point — Lowetzov Street, 7/8.

"Following the delivery of your large baggage to the police station you are to go with your hand baggage to the assembly point, to the synagogue on Lowetzov Street (the Jagow Street entrance). You may go there by the customary means of transportation.

"We will take charge of your belongings at the assembly point and during your train ride. It would be a good idea to take along in your hand baggage some food from your house, especially something for supper.

"Both at the assembly point as well as on the trip, medical and food services will be available."

Enclosed was a memorandum with essential instructions:

"It is necessary to follow these instructions to the letter and to prepare for the trip calmly and thoughtfully."

318

. . . The train pulled up to the platform of the Riga station. It was met by *Obersturmführer* Krause or by one of the high-ranking officials from the general-commissariat. The German smiled politely and, using the most refined expressions, he congratulated the eldest of the train with his safe arrival at his new place of residence. After a mutual exchange of compliments the German in an apologetic tone reported that due to unforeseen circumstances there had been a slight misunderstanding regarding transportation — there were not enough buses. Therefore, he asked the eldest of the group to separate the men and the healthiest women, who would have a three to four kilometer walk ahead of them; the old men, children and the rest of the women would make the trip in buses. The boarding of the buses was extremely well-organized. Policemen and gendarmes with courteous smiles and jokes helped the women and old men find seats in the buses, and the children were lifted up and handed to their mothers.

The men walked to the Moscow *Vorstadt* to occupy the apartments vacated by the Riga Jews; the women, children, and old men were taken to Bikernieki Forest. And there the manner of treatment changed with amazing speed. The doors of the buses were opened, the lines of policemen and gendarmes stood as they had at the station. But here they were not smiling and did not try to appear gallant. Everyone they got their hands on was rifle-butted, some were shot on the spot. Then came the order to undress, fold their clothes, and walk to the precipice where enormous pits had been dug in advance. . . .

Other trainloads of people were brought in their entirety in Bikernieki Forest; from others the most able-bodied were removed. Soon the greater ghetto was once again populated with Jews — from Berlin, Köln, Düsseldorf, Prague, Vienna, and other cities in Europe.

After the arrival of the German Jews, the ghetto in Riga existed for a whole year. It consisted of two parts — a big one and a small one. German Jews lived in the big part, Riga Jews in the small part. A barbed-wire fence was erected between the two parts. The boss of the whole ghetto was commandant *Obersturmführer* Krause, who had the right to personally judge and execute people, but the general management of the extermination of the Jews belonged to *Standartenführer* (Colonel) Lange, who commanded the Latvian

319

police and who in Germany had the official title "Doctor of anti-Semitism."

Among other restrictions and prohibitions which existed in the ghetto, it was forbidden to give birth to children. When Krause found out that Klara Kaufman, who had come from Germany, was soon to give birth, he ordered that she be transferred to the hospital. An hour after the birth several hundred people were herded to the hospital. Krause stood on the balcony in full dress and, with a signal, he gave the police the order to act. *Wachmeister* Kabnello carried the child out and, lifting him high over his head, he showed it to all the people who had gathered. Then, holding the child by its feet, he swung his arm and struck the child's head against the porch steps. Blood spurted out. Kabnello wiped off his face and hands with a clean kerchief and then brought out the mother and her husband. They were both shot on the spot, next to the corpse of their first-born.

Beyond the fence of the ghetto the Germans unleashed an active campaign to "preserve the purity of the race." No matter how the Hitlerites tried, they still had to make certain concessions in one area. In the hopes of winning over former officers of the Latvian Army and important officials of the bourgeois government of Ulmanis to their side, they permitted these people to take their wives of Jewish descent out of the ghetto. But soon they all received notice to report to the commissariat for registration. There they were received by Fritz Steiniger, the person who reviewed racial questions. He spent a long time questioning each woman, was interested in their genealogy, their state of health, etc. Each visitor was ordered to report to the clinic of Doctor Krastyn and to pay money for the two weeks that they would stay there. They were all sterilized. The sterilization was carried out under the observation of German doctors in full accordance with the "Nuremberg Law."

8. The Salaspils Camp

A year later the Germans decided that the ghetto was ruining the view of the capital of Ostland and moved all the Jews to the Salaspils camps. The center of the other camps was the camp at Kaiserwald, which served as a unique transit point. No one was able to avoid this horrible place. The Germans made *Sturmbannführer* Sauer, a well-known criminal in Germany, head of the camp. Sauer perfected searches. Everyone who came to Kaiserwald had to observe a two-day "diet" — they were fed only castor oil to see if the person had swallowed any diamonds or gold coins. "Third-degree criminals" who were brought from Germany were put in charge of the Jewish barracks. These were criminal prisoners who had served half their time in prison and had shown their devotion to National Socialism.

In liquidating the ghetto all the children were killed. An inexorable and consistent process of annihilation of adults went on at the Salaspils camp. Several "disinfections" were conducted in the barracks, after which hundreds of people who had been poisoned with gas were taken out to nearby ravines. Thousands of people were tormented at back-breaking work that was beyond their strength.

Many people were exterminated in the "experimental units" at German "Scientific" institutions which functioned in Riga — at the Hygienic Institute and the Institute of Medical Zoology. In these institutes licensed butchers cultivated and perfected the science of death. The Germans cut open the veins of several Jews, including those of an associate professor from the Sorbonne named Schneider, in order to study how the hormones and endocrine glands function during hemorrhaging. One of the scientific workers in these institutes was preparing a dissertation on the historical development of the method for hanging people. He thoroughly studied which sorts of rope gave the most effective results. This "dissertation" cost the lives of thirty-five Jews.

. . . The year 1944 came. The front line drew closer and closer to the Baltic. The Germans were in a hurry to do away with the Jews. One "action" followed another. Finally, all the inhabitants of the concentration camp were loaded onto a steamship and taken to Zemgale, where they were all executed.

The Germans celebrated — the Baltic was free of the Jews. But from time to time they had to admit that they had not managed to get rid of them all. Here is an excerpt from a German newspaper which was published in Riga and dated August 28, 1944:

"Jewish Gang Rendered Harmless"

"The security police and an S.D. unit in Latvia made the following report: on the basis of an investigation, on August 24 a Jewish gang consisting of six men and one woman was rendered harmless. They were all hiding in one of the apartments in house No. 15 on Plovuchaya Street. During the arrest, the male Jews, who had revolvers, shot at members of the security police. One of the policemen was fatally wounded. Two Jews who tried to offer resistance were killed by the police; the rest tried to escape to nearby buildings. A heavy guard consisting of police units and a unit of the field gendarmery, as well as SS patrols, was immediately set up around the buildings on the block. The whole gang of Jews, who had taken refuge in the house, was arrested.

"The police arrested the Latvian woman, Anna Polis, the owner of the apartment, who hid the Jews in her apartment and supplied them with food. She will receive the deserved punishment. In addition, all the residents of house No. 15 on Plovuchaya Street were arrested.

"The Jews who were arrested, as well as those who harbored them, will be brought to justice immediately after an investigation."

On that day on Plovuchaya Street the Germans killed Doctor Lipmanovich, Gruntman, Manke, Blyum, Berkovich and others. Anna Polis, who hid them, was executed two days later. But on the next street a teacher, Elvira Ronis and her mother, seventy-year-old Maria Veninzh, hid a group of Jews for half a year and were able to save their lives right up until the arrival of the Red Army. The Latvian Jan (Janis) Lipke hid more than thirty Jews on his farm for several months and later led the majority of them through the front line.

* * *

On the third day after the Germans were driven out of Riga a spontaneous demonstration of many people took place in the city: in the morning the people of Riga found out that at two o'clock that afternoon, units of the Latvian army corps, which were being shifted to another area of the front, would be marching in the streets of the city. Thousands of residents of Riga, with flowers in their hands, walked out into the main street of Riga — Brivibas.

The military orchestra played. Everyone waited impatiently for the troops to appear. Then the people who had gathered there saw a small column of demonstrators, about sixty to seventy people, who appeared from the direction of the Western Dvina. The standard-bearer, his assistants, and many in the column were dressed in striped prison clothes, and on the chest of each could be seen the yellow hexagonal star, and on the back — a number printed in big, black letters. They were pale as death, and it was obvious that these people had not seen daylight in a long time; the faces of some of them were bruised and scratched; some of them walked with a severe limp. At first it seemed that these were not people walking on the asphalt of Brivibas Street, but the shadows of those who had been tortured and shot and who had risen from their horrible graves to meet the soldiers of the Red Army.

And in fact, in this column there were people who had lain in mass graves, people who had crawled out from under the corpses of their fathers and children and then, for three years, persecuted and hunted, fought for their lives.

This column consisted of people from the former Riga ghetto. They were all that remained of the forty-five thousand Jews of Riga.

The people of Riga who saw the column of Jews lowered their heads. Generals and admirals who stood at the foot of the Obelisk of Freedom paid military honors to the demonstrators. And suddenly it became unusually quiet on the overcrowded square.

Battalions of the Latvian corps walked by in orderly ranks. People threw flowers at the soldiers and officers. Suddenly someone cried out in Yiddish from the crowd:

"Meyer, is that you?"

"Yes, it's me!"

A young, pale girl and an old man with a long gray beard ran out of the ranks and threw themselves at Sergeant Moreyn, hugging and kissing him. The sergeant with two medals on his chest, who had covered the long path of the war from Narofominsk to Riga and fought together with his comrades-in-arms, saved his father and sister. And they began to walk alongside him in the festive streets of Riga in the ranks of Red-Army soldiers.

An hour later in one of the empty apartments on Gertrud Street I met people in striped prison clothes. I heard from them the story about the murder of thousands of their brothers.

Riga Jews walked onto Gertrud Street with rifles and submachine guns strapped to them — fighters, sergeants, and officers of the Red Army. They came to inquire about their relatives and close ones. Most often they received sorrowful answers: "Shot during the first 'action,' 'committed suicide,' 'tortured to death by the Gestapo.'" The soldiers tightened the straps of their automatic rifles, saying: 'We will make them pay for everything in full.'"

By Captain **Yefim Gekhtman**

Transliteration verified by Dr. Gertrude Schneider, CUNY.

From the Diary of the Sculptor Rivosh

(Riga)

In the Moscow *Vorstadt* they are beginning to fence in several blocks — they are building a ghetto. The Middle Ages have come to life before our eyes. Jews are forbidden to shop in the stores, to read newspapers, and even . . . to smoke.

A so-called *Judenrat* has been formed — representatives of local Jews. The Jewish council is supposed to take care of medical assistance, to find living space for the Jews, etc. Its members include G. Minsker, Blumenau, Kaufer, and M. Mintz. On their sleeves there is a blue band with a star; on their chest and back there is, of course, also a star — in a word, they have been decorated all over. The *Judenrat* is housed on Lacplesa Street near Moscow Street, in a former school.

There have been many suicides in the city, mostly among the doctors.

My little son Dimochka has become fearful, nervous. As soon as he sees a German soldier on the street, he immediately runs into our building. The poor child is afraid, he does not even know what a Jew is. Our little daughter is all right, she is still quite unaware, she knows neither grief nor fear. . . .

Mama brought something edible from the Moscow *Vorstadt*. The Jewish portions are, of course, much smaller than the normal ones, and the food is of the poorest quality. Mama is depressed by what she sees and hears.

The fence around the ghetto is being built zealously; barbed wire is already being put up in places.

In the Moscow *Vorstadt* one is dazzled by the yellow stars. Men are almost nowhere to be seen — only old women and children. But one never sees even one child playing; all of them, like beasts at bay, cling timidly close to their mothers or sit in the gateways.

Jews come from all sides pulling carts containing various junk. A large former school yard is overcrowded with people. Even here there are very few men. The majority are women; they have sad faces and eyes red from weeping. Along the fence there are huge piles of furniture and junk which they were permitted to take with them after they were moved out. Some of the furniture has come unglued from being out in the rain.

We meet acquaintances — there is no one who has not lost close relatives. We met Noemi Vag. She has decided to give up on life

324

since her husband Monya was burned alive in a synagogue. She creates the impression of being somewhat unbalanced.

We met Fenya Falk; her husband and brother have been taken away. She has a sick mother on her hands, a small son Felix, and a sister-in-law with two tiny children. It was painful for me to see her sunken cheeks and how she had aged. Once I was riding a bicycle with her on the highway, and she frightened me. Fooling around, she rode full speed straight toward the oncoming automobiles. I got angry, yelled at her, but she assured me that nothing bad could ever happen to her, that she would die when she was a very, very old lady. . . . Who can know what his fate will be? Now death has raised its horrible, murderous, Hitlerite paw over her. . . .

Betty Markovna told me about an incident with her stepdaughter Heidi. Heidi — a model of the beautiful northern Aryan — is tall, well-proportioned, has light blond hair with cornflower blue eyes and a straight nose. She grew up in Vienna and, naturally, speaks excellent German. She was stopped on the street by a German officer who sharply charged her with provocation for having the Jewish star pinned to her. When she calmly told him that there was no reason at all to get excited, since she had a perfect right to wear those "medals," he flew into a complete rage.

It is a psychological riddle. The last months before the war I worked in a shop where there were four of us: Noe Karlis, foreman L., myself, and one other fellow named Anraus, whose profession was not known. I had been told all sorts of unflattering stories about him and, in general, people were hostile toward him in every way possible. I had no dealings with him — neither good nor bad. When I found myself beyond the protection of the law, all my Aryan former childhood friends, all my friends from work disappeared and here, like a miracle, Anraus appears. He came and said simply that he wanted to help me and my family, that he was prepared to do everything that he could. He said that he had decided to take a job repairing the facades of buildings that had been damaged by the war, and that he would give me a job with him. He began to bring Dima presents, played with him, in a word, he was showing a deep interest in our fate. This could only come from a person with considerable spiritual fortitude and nobleness. There is great human joy in finding friends when one is in trouble.

The Jews began to be moved into the ghetto by districts. The first to go were the residents of the central districts. Many who had moved to the Moscow *Vorstadt*, but who had settled on streets that were not part of the ghetto, had to move again.

Dima's nannie, Melanya, arrived from Limbazhi, crying and pleading that I give her the boy. I was ready to agree, but Alya said that if we are fated to perish, then she did not want to leave an orphan. The right to take charge of the children belongs to the mothers — Dimochka was not given to Melanya.

Evening. It's windy, there's a pouring autumn rain. In such weather one feels more calm; one knows that uninvited guests will not show up. I sit with Alya and Dimochka on the bed and, sinking into my thoughts, I hum a Soviet song. Dimochka climbs up on his mother's lap. Suddenly I hear her exclaim: "Dimochka, what's the matter, my love, why are you crying?" Dimochka does not answer, he is all red and rubs his face against her neck. Through the tears he says in a soft voice: "Papa is singing a Soviet song, I like that song so much, and I haven't heard it for so long. Mama, I just hope the Germans don't hear it." Tears flow down Alya's cheeks. I light up a cigarette. He is such a little person, but his heart is already broken. And I did not even know that my little son was suffering so deeply.

Our turn came to move into the ghetto.

I went with Alya to look for a place to live.

I try in every way I can to calm her, to distract her from dark thoughts; I paint her a picture of how we will live and assure her that I will even build a pigeon house in the attic. We kiss and joke because we want to deceive each other. It is growing dark. We take a trip to the other side of the Dvina; it may be the last time that we take this walk. We walk holding hands; in closeness we hope to find solace.

Tomorrow we have to vacate our favorite nest, our home of many years. I walk from room to room feeling indescribably sad: I am choking with anger and despair. Dimochka is also terribly upset, and he keeps reminding us not to forget to take his toys. He lists the things he wants: the plaster dogs and elephants, blocks, his train, and his trucks. He asks anxiously: "Mama, what if the Germans don't let me take my airplane, will you hide it?" Like an adult, he comforts his mother: "If they take my bed, Mama, don't worry, I can sleep with you."

Morning. An autumn wind.

Two policemen with briefcases, very businesslike and accompanied by a janitor, appear in our yard. They walk by with an air of importance, disdainfully examining our apartment.

I go to look for a cart.

Jews are not allowed to ride in an "Aryan" cart, with an "Aryan" horse and an "Aryan" driver — apparently, that is also considered a desecration of the race. But we decide to ignore this order.

We load up our cart. The cart grows bigger, the pile of junk in the yard grows smaller. We tighten the ropes. It's time to say farewell. . . .

The cart slowly, but surely, approaches its destination. The bridge is already behind us. We get closer and closer to the barbed wire. The cart turns from Moscow Street onto Lacplesa Street. There's a fence on the right, a few minutes later we drive through the gates of the ghetto. Sadovnikovskaya Street. The cobblestone is rough, and the cart rocks and shakes. There are also carts in front and behind us. The streets are full of people. We arrive at our "apartment": Maza Kalnu Street, house 11/9/7, apartment 5. Taking a running start, the horse wheezes and pulls the cart through the gates. Hurriedly we drag in our things, and for the time being we lock them up in the shed. I set out to see the Gutmans — to drag in the old people's things. On Ludzas Street, near a small house, someone calls to me. I see in the window my friend, the tinsmith Markushevich. He asks me if I would please drop in for a few minutes, he would like to have a cigarette and at the same time to chat awhile. Markushevich has a large family — several grown daughters, one with children. They all live in one room. His wife, although she is no older than forty, looks like an old woman. I ask him where he works and how he's getting along. He doesn't complain, he's been poor his whole life, and poverty is as familiar to him as his mother. He works for the Germans. I thought that as a master-tinsmith he would get better treatment and that his situation would be easier. When I told him this, he even recoiled: "What are you saying, do you think I would start working for them as a specialist and have them derive benefit from my work? They don't even know that I know how to cut tin. I work for them as an unskilled laborer. Even if I were dying of hunger, I still wouldn't tell them that I was a tinsmith." This encounter has remained a source of inspiration for me. A small, unremarkable, and unnoticed man, but how brave and spirited! After this encounter I never again saw him in the ghetto; he was probably shot.

The last cart arrived with the small belongings and firewood. The driver is in a hurry and so he just dumps the wood in the yard. It is raining, we can't leave it in the yard, so we amicably set to work. Although she's tired, Alya still carries the logs, keeping right up with me. Tsapkin runs out into the yard, Alya is worried that he might get lost. I'm glad that she still cares about the cat — it means she's still "alive." We are seriously concerned about our daughter. We left her with Mimi, and the ghetto could close at any moment. We, of course, are not given advance notice of any measures or orders but are presented with a *fait accompli*. In just a matter of minutes people are taken out, put to work, and shot without warning.

I personally think that, in general, it's better to leave the girl there. Mimi won't throw her out. She is a girl, not a boy, which means it is impossible to prove that she is not an "Aryan." It's true, Mimi is old, but even if she were to die, the neighbors would bring up the girl. If we are saved, we'll find her; if we die, she will grow up and will live without us. But I'm afraid to even talk with Alya about this.

Mama arrives. Her "friends," the Romms, offer her a chair as accommodations for the night — she spends the whole night in it. Poor Mama, she probably envies Papa that he died a long time ago. I look at her, and I feel awful. How quickly people who feel grief melt away.

Alya and Mama spend the whole evening measuring and arguing about what to put where. I'm not really interested, so I don't interfere with what they're doing. We are even beginning to get used to the new place; we are slowly being reborn and will soon become different people. Dima's favorite pictures are hanging above his bed. The rug on the floor is folded in four so our little girl doesn't catch a cold — after all, we are actually living in a shack.

Children play, run, and fight in the yard, but Dimochka is afraid to leave the house. When he goes out with me or with Alya, he doesn't leave our side.

Our building is set back from the street, so it is very, very quiet. But in the central part of the ghetto there is a hunt going on — people are being caught and put to work. Three people are involved in this: the German Lieutenant Stanke, Sergeant Major Tuchel, and a local German Dralle. Jews are afraid of these jobs, not because they involve work, but because people are beaten unmercifully when they leave and return from them. The Germans beat whomever and however they choose — with fists, sticks, or with their feet.

After lunch, Alya brings Lidochka. They are both tired and upset — it is difficult for them to say good-bye to Mimi. Mimi and our janitor promise to pass us food through the wire.

328

Finally, the ghetto is closed. It is officially announced that all contact with the outside world is forbidden. If there is any conversation or passing of items through the wire, the guards will shoot. The guards at the gate search all the people very carefully who leave and return from work, especially the young women. Amidst general laughter and comments, they feel underneath the women's clothes with their cold, dirty, and rough hands, fumble about their naked bodies. After a search many women have scratches and bruises on their breasts. The men are searched superficially, but to make up for it they are seriously beaten. The day after the ghetto is closed, they catch a Jewish fellow in the city who spent the night with his Christian girlfriend. He is brought into the ghetto and shot in the yard by the guards. His corpse is left there to serve as a warning. . . .

Everyone is depressed; it feels like we're in a mousetrap. The hunt for people has intensified, and now they're catching people at night in their apartments. Our situation reminds one of fishing in an aquarium or hunting in a zoo. In a forest an animal can run away, hide, resist, but what can a person do in the ghetto? There is wire on all sides, beyond it are the armed guards, and we are like livestock in a pen. . . .

I talk to engineer Antokol who worked for twenty years in the town council as a civil engineer. Antokol says that in the whole ghetto there is not a single stove maker, and if I could try to become one, it would be a blessing for the ghetto.

The news that the *Judenrat* has acquired a stove maker spreads throughout the ghetto. That same evening the first customer turns up at my apartment.

The next morning I do not even have a chance to eat breakfast when there is a knock at my door. Some man wants to see me. I ask him what he wishes with me? He says that he rented a former shop not far from me and that his mother and sister are living there. But the shop doesn't have a stove, and he wants me to build just a small stove. This customer has barely left when my cousin Roza Girshberg appears. In a word, it seems that I can't satisfy all the requests and that I will have to become "inaccessible."

There is a new unpleasant surprise — the distribution of milk has been cut off. Jewish children are not allowed such a luxury. The hospital is also refused milk.

Since it is noticed that there were instances when food was passed over the fence, a second row of wire is erected, but of course, not at the expense of the street, but rather of the sidewalk. In certain places — on Gersikas, Lazdenas, and other streets — the sidewalks are so narrow that one can only pass there sideways to avoid tearing one's clothes on the barbed wire. A fat person can not get by at all. To avoid trouble, the *Judenrat* has ordered that all yards on streets adjoining the periphery of the ghetto be connected and that people walk through the yards. Ours has also become a linking courtyard and people are always scurrying past our windows.

The following incident happened to a boy we know, B. Zaks, our former neighbor in Sassenhof. He was walking on Bolshaya Gornaya Street. A sentry yelled out "Jew, tell me, what time is it?" The boy turned back his glove and, having taken a look at his watch, he answered the question. The soldier pointed the muzzle of his rifle at him: "And now, quickly, while you're still in one piece, throw your watch into the snow!" That's the way sentries earn their watches.

In the evening we bathe our little daughter. She has no cares, sitting in her little bathtub, splashing like a duck, playing and having fun. In spite of the ghetto, she is healthy and round; it's sheer pleasure to hold her in my arms. Dimochka wipes off her little feet and kisses her rosy heels. She laughs merrily and pulls at his hair. Alya and Mama are beside themselves with delight over this idyll. It is said that only in grief do people express their true feelings for one another. Never before have Alya and I shown so much mutual tenderness.

After Lidochka, Alya "bathed" in the same water. She had become so thin that the child's bathtub was almost the right size for her. The soapy water was not poured out, but was used instead to wash her underwear. That's economizing!

Seven o'clock in the morning. Mama has already gotten up, lighted the stove, cooked potatoes, and made tea. During breakfast Friedman's son Izka came with his friend; they are my "apprentices." I have tools in my briefcase, the boys loaded the sleighs with a box for material, and the three of us set out for Gertsmark's place. On Ersikas Street we walked on such a narrow sidewalk that I had trouble getting by. Alongside of us there were Russian and Latvian workers going to work, the same kind of toilers as we, but between us is the wire and it creates a chasm. I try not to see or notice people on the other side of the fence. . . .

House No. 5. Old, heavy gates, a rickety wicket. To the right is a big building, to the left an old half-torn-down hut. A steep, narrow, wooden stairway, the steps are worn down. I lean against the door with a small window half-boarded up with plywood. I knock once, twice; no one answers. Finally my energy has an effect, the door opens. I walk in — a garret, average size room, the walls are slanting and black, just like the windows; several squares are covered with paper. It is as cold as outside. The floor is full of dents and holes, along the edges the rat cracks are stuffed with bottles. In the middle of the room is a table, a stool; near it is a big, old axe. Next to the wall is a shabby, iron bed buried in a pile of rags. The landlady of the "apartment," having let me in, went back and covered herself again with the rags. And only after this did she want to know who I was and why I had come. I thought that she would be glad, but I was deeply mistaken. I looked at her with curiosity. She was a 60 to 70-year-old woman. Her face expressed such indifference to everything that one felt uncomfortable. I began to take the stove apart and to "examine" the oven; it was all in terrible condition. Like a "specialist," I had to give careful thought to how I was going to repair everything. My day was as hard as a rock; I needed hot water, and I asked the old woman to help. With the same indifferent look she crawled out of her lair and went to her neighbors for some hot water. After returning, she said that the water would be ready soon.

I warmed up from working. I took off my coat, saw a nail in the wall. I asked: "Tell me, ma'am, are there any bedbugs or midges on the wall, is it all right to hang up my coat?" "Of course, dear, we have everything, bedbugs and lice, but you don't have to worry about hanging your coat; they don't come out of their holes in such cold," was her wordy reply.

I did not want to bother the old woman, and I went for the water myself so that I could take a look at her neighbors. Next to her door was another door, covered up with an old blanket. I was let in by a little girl. The room and the kitchen were in approximately the same condition as my old woman's, except that they were cluttered with all sorts of junk. A large family was living there — several small children, teenagers, adults, and an old woman. In the middle of the room a little girl sat on a pot, playing with a rag.

My hands became numb with cold from the cold clay, and from time to time I put them into the hot water. I was in a hurry because it was almost four o'clock and I had a "special" order, for which I expected a whole treasure — two eggs and a package of tobacco.

I was as dirty as a chimney sweep, but my spirits were high. It is very satisfying when a job benefits not only yourself, but also people whom you want to help. I was certain that in the winter a stove maker in the ghetto was no less important than a doctor during an epidemic.

Having washed and had supper, I went to see Friedman. I wanted to "repay" a good deed — he had once given me a matchbox filled with tobacco and now I was rich and could give him a treat. Friedman has a comparatively nice little apartment — a room and a small kitchen; it's impossible to sleep in it, but still, it is a room. His wife is a charming woman — one can tell that she is very kind and warm. As is the case in most families, they have their cross to bear. Aside from their two sons — my assistant Izka and a younger, sixteen-year-old son, they also have a girl. She is 12 years old, but she is Dima's size, a cripple with so-called withered feet. She sits for days on end, cutting things out of paper, threading beads, or sewing rags together. She is always sad and speaks intelligently like an adult. She loves it when children come to see her, but how she must suffer seeing them run! The little girl is adored by her parents and brothers. Her younger brother tries to cheer her up and make her laugh. I did not expect such tenderness from a boy his age. While Friedman and I were having a smoke and exchanging the news and hopes, the neighbor from the adjacent apartment came in. He said that he was working today at Bikernieki. They were digging pits in the forest, long and deep. "Without a doubt," he said, "these are future fortifications and if this is so, then they are expecting a Soviet offensive."

We, that is, those of us who are optimists, have developed an ability to perceive the good side in all events. I don't know whether this is smart or stupid, but in any case it is easier to live that way. I have made it my duty in the presence of others, friends or strangers, to joke and try to cheer them up in times of misfortune and failure. I was certain that these pits were not being dug for fortifications. But for what other purpose? Is it possible? . . . I drove away these dreadful thoughts.

With each day the number of beggars in the ghetto increases. They go from one apartment to another, trying to get something to eat. They are given a few potatoes, turnips, a bowl of soup. There is another kind of beggar who does not live by begging. In a yard on Sarkanu Street I saw a little old man searching in a garbage dump for potato peelings and occasional crusts of bread. The fact that he was being careful not to be noticed made it clear that he was not a professional. He saw me when I had already walked past him and he became so flustered that he tried to act as if he were doing something completely different.

An anthill in the forest will not make a special impression on a chance passer-by — piles of ants, and that's all. That's just like our ghetto — outwardly it is all gray, bustling, frightened, half-starving. But in fact inside the ghetto life is full of tensions and tragedies. . . .

In a shelter on Sadovnikov Street, in a closet, lives Professor Dubnov who is writing a sequel to his "Jewish History." In the hospital on Ludzats Street doctors are operating on patients.

Each day there are several funerals in the ghetto. Throughout the day simple sleighs with a black box, and 2-5 people behind them, move slowly along Ludzats Street toward the cemetery. Sometimes the sleighs with the box pass by quickly; this means there were no relatives. . . .

Recently another young man was shot near the wire.

Announcements have appeared on houses: all Jews are ordered to surrender all their gold, silver, valuables and rugs within a week. At the end of that period there will be searches, and those who have not surrendered their things will be severely punished. We know of only one form of punishment — execution.

Alya and I have only our thin wedding rings, and Alya has two or three other small rings, and that is all.

Friends come and ask if they can hide their valuables. I've gone to the homes of many friends to make "safes," for one in a door, for another in the cornice of a cupboard, for another under the floor, and still another in the heel of a shoe. I've advised people to throw their silver into the toilet or to bury it, just so long as they don't give it to the Germans.

The lack of food is having its effect on Alya. The other day she was standing in line for a long time and when she finally had her turn and was about to leave, she became dizzy and fainted — for the first time in her life.

I went to work. I opened the door. The first thing I saw was a bed and on it was an exhausted woman. Next to her under a blanket was a child with something wrapped around its neck. At the foot of the bed, pressed against each other like small wild animals, were three other children in coats. On the opposite wall was a door, placed on bricks, and on it was a blanket and several gray pillows. An earthenware pot, a pail, and a chair — these were the only furnishings. "Who are you, why have you come here?" I explained that I had been sent by the *Judenrat* to repair the stove and the heater. I asked if there wasn't anything I could do to help her. "How will you be able to help me, I have gallstones and, probably, cancer. We have no heating fuel and nothing to eat."

There was a dejected man standing in the kitchen, his name was Khaim. He was the owner of this wealth. I began to work. Khaim began fidgeting around, ran off to get some hot water; in a word, he came to life. It was obvious that it was awful for him to remain alone with his family; he was glad to see other people. It was rather dark in the kitchen; part of the window was covered with paper. On the floor were several pots, dirty dishes, a basket containing frozen potatoes, a box; that was all. It was awfully cold. And again from behind the door I heard a pitiful, tormented voice: "Poor man, my poor Khaim, who will take care of you when I'm gone, what will you do with the little ones without me?"

There was a knock at the door. Khaim let in a young man who spoke German with a foreign accent. He was a Czech emigrant who had not eaten anything for three days and was asking if something couldn't be found for him to eat. Without saying a word, Khaim pulled out an earthenware pot which contained boiled potatoes that were still warm. He got a small cup with salt from somewhere: "Eat right from the pot, then it won't get cold so quickly, eat as much as you like, we have enough potatoes, don't be bashful." Khaim expressed his regret that he didn't have anything else to offer. The young man was hungry, but he saw that he was being treated by a beggar, and, moreover, one who was prevailing upon another beggar not to be bashful! When saying good-bye, Khaim crammed several potatoes into the man's pocket.

The days are flying by, and I have more and more work to do. Rumors, one more incredible than the next, are spreading throughout the ghetto. I try not to pay attention or to think about them.

There has been a new announcement in the ghetto: all Jews must immediately tell the police about any non-Jews who are hiding inside the ghetto. If the order is not carried out, the whole ghetto will suffer.

They say that German deserters are hiding in the ghetto. I found out from a friend that there had been a search and that two people were caught; judging from their descriptions, one of them was the same beggar who was posing as a Czech and whom I met in the house on Daugavpils Street. Too bad about the young lad, now instead of a potato he'll receive a bullet.

I don't work for the *Judenrat* on Saturdays: that is my "day off." This Saturday I've decided to rest and not go anywhere.

I wanted to make a snowman with Dima, but the snow was too dry. We stayed home, I held him in my lap and read from "Uncle" Pushkin's "Tale About The Priest and His Worker Blockhead." This is Dima's favorite tale and he can listen to it again and again. Lidochka was romping on the floor.

There is no end to the rumors.

They say that only able-bodied men will remain in the ghetto and that the women and children will be sent to a camp, perhaps to Lublin. All this is very alarming, people are lost in conjectures and suppositions. It was only the other day that the *Judenrat* received an order to build a bathhouse; a whole building was made available for setting up various workshops. If the ghetto has been set up for only a few months, why was it necessary to move all the non-Jews out of it; why are we doing all this "construction"?

The Jewish doctors have supposedly received an order to take the lives of people who are dangerously ill. Rumors have it that in the hospitals in Germany all the seriously ill and frail people are being poisoned with something added to sweetened coffee.

People in the ghetto are extremely agitated. There is no noise, no shouting, no animated discussions. On the contrary, it is as quiet as a funeral. Everyone is waiting for something terrible; everyone feels as if a storm will vent itself with blood and tears.

Every minute we wait for a new order. The word "action" was heard. It somehow passed by us, we did not understand it. Soon blood would run cold from this little word. We did not have to wait long. Two orders were issued at once. Order number 1: on November 28, 1941 (maybe I am mistaken by a few days, I don't remember the exact date), all men 17 years old and older had to assemble at 7 o'clock in the morning on Sadovnikovskaya Street.

Order number 2: all men who were unable to work, as well as women and children, had to prepare for transfer to a camp. Each person had the right to take along belongings up to 20 kilograms in weight. The day and hour of the move would be announced separately.

After the second order, the first order somehow receded to the background. All the old men, without exception, understood that they had been sentenced to death. It was difficult to look at them — condemned men who had done nothing wrong. Alya's aunt, Sophia Osipovna, a very reserved old woman, came to see her. She seemed to be sitting calmly, but her tears flowed continuously. Besides a son in America, she had no one. She asked me and Alya, when the times were better, to send him her regards, but she asked us not to tell him how her life ended. Even at that moment the mother in her prevailed, and she was possessed by one thought — "Why should she cause her son unnecessary grief?"

All the neighbors are supplying each other with whatever they can. Warm things, shoes, food, everything has become common property. Today everyone is generous and is sharing everything sincerely. Today there is no more "mine" and "yours"; today there is only "ours."

I stopped by to see Magarik. His wife and I kiss like sister and brother. All the women have become dear and lovable to me. I feel so sorry for them — they are behaving so heroically. Women, I am convinced, are better able to withstand serious upsets.

The children instinctively sense their own destruction — they are quiet and dejected, and they display neither caprices, nor tears, nor nervousness. Mine too, like little mice, have hidden somewhere. Mama walks around with an expressionless look on her face. Alya is putting aside some warm things for me. It is evening now, tomorrow at daybreak I leave. Will I return, will I ever see my loved ones?. . . .

We know that this is our last night together. I don't know if I will see Alya again. I will never again spend a night under the same roof with Mama — I am convinced of this. My beloved, poor Mama, forgive me for being powerless to protect you in your old age.

The alarm clock ticks peacefully, the arrow mercilessly goes its way, the hours pass. Alya's head is on my shoulder, my shirt becomes wet there — silent, heavy tears. What is going on in her soul, in the souls of the thousands of women like her? No one can know because this can not be expressed in words. . . . The alarm clock keeps ticking.

People are already fussing about in the yard. They are standing in small groups. It is dark, their faces aren't visible.

The street is already full of people. I walk out of the ranks onto the porch of the .house to see how long the column is. What a strange and frightful sight! It reminds me of a grandiose funeral. Many of the old men are being led by the hand by young people. The column inches forward slowly and stops on Sadovnikovskaya Street. Apparently the authorities are afraid of a "slave uprising," because at every step there are groups of 4-5 Fascists armed to the teeth.

There is a severe frost; so as not to freeze, most of the people hop in place. If you didn't look at their faces, but only at their feet, you might think that these people were having a good time. Gradually the column loses its shape and turns into a big crowd. People change places. They are looking for acquaintances. From a distance I see my teacher Grigory Yakovlevich. He is standing, leaning on a stick. His eyes are swollen from tears and the cold and have turned into barely visible slits. He looks at me and his legs begin to tremble. For a long time his emotion keeps him from saying a word. He holds my hand and shakes it convulsively: "Farewell, Elik, it's the last time I'll see you. It's painful to know that I will soon be destroyed like an old, useless rag. My Fanny will also be killed. . . . See to it that you don't lose heart, you are still young, you will live to see brighter days. Remember your old teacher and friend some-times. Let me kiss you farewell."

At that moment a policeman walks by and shouts out an order that all invalids and those over sixty can go home.

The crowd comes alive and begins to buzz. In the distance one can hear the commands and loud voices of the Germans. Ap-proaching rapidly on the sidewalk are Stanke, Tuchel, and the others.

Stanke walks up and down the front of the column as if at a parade. His speech and order are laconic: "It is now two o'clock; run to your homes, pack your belongings, and by 2:30 gather by the gates of the Small Ghetto. March!"

Out of breath, I tumble into the house. It is already 2:10; in 20 minutes I have to be at the gates. The essential things I throw into a suitcase, my tools into a sack, and a blanket and pillow — into a bundle. For 10 minutes I can sit "quietly." I learn some news — Liza L. has given birth. The delivery was difficult, but both she and the baby are "out of danger."

Alya and I agree that no matter where we are sent, no matter what happens, the first chance we have we will let our friends in Sassenhof know about us. That way we will always be able to find each other. There is no such agreement with Mama — it isn't necessary. Mama's lips are cold, her face is like stone. Our little girl is sleeping, lying on her tummy; her rosy heel sticks out from under the blanket. I press close to it, tickling it with my mustache, and it disappears under the blanket. I hug Dima very, very firmly. But he does not shout. What will happen to him, what will they do with him? Why, for what? Hate, despair, hope fuse into one lump that presses and squeezes in my throat. We suffer most not from our own personal grief, but from that of our close friends and loved ones.

There is already a crowd by the gates of the "Small Ghetto." The guards keep order, sometimes using rifle butts. Near the gates, like a statue, stands a handsome officer, the new assistant to the commandant of the ghetto. He is handsome, one rarely sees eyes like his, but his are not human eyes; they are only organs of vision. They are like light, transparent glass, like a pretty, dead stone. They express neither spite, nor hate; they see, but they express nothing. To look for pity or mercy in these eyes is just as hopeless as forcing them to laugh. A good assistant to the commandant — no question about that.

Gertsmark met his friend S. Finkelstein. He lived on Liksnas Street, No. 26, and is trying to get to his apartment. He suggests that we settle there too. We hurry in order to get there before others. Only yesterday Finkelstein lived in this apartment with his family. He has a wife and a two-year-old daughter; at the moment it is harder for him than for us — we are in someone else's place. Every little thing in his apartment, each object reminds him of his wife and daughter. For a few minutes he tries to appear bold, then he is overcome with a wave of despair and throws himself down on his back, shaking with sobs.

Vilyanu Street (it is situated between Bolshaya Gornaya and Ludzas Streets) is short and wide like a square. At Bolshaya Gornaya Street there are new gates which lead from the ghetto to "freedom." The whole street is full of people. Here and there people are being formed into columns. Germans are strutting about, gathering people.

My comrades in misfortune, who know that this is extremely difficult work, look for a chance to slip away. Finally, a column of 120 people is formed. From Moscow Street we turn off onto a narrow by-street that leads past the Braun Factory, and we come to the Dvina River. There is a sawmill on the island and the island is connected to a coastal dam. In this dam, which is 200 to 300 meters long, they are laying that famous cable. It is an uncomfortable place to work in the winter — the wind whistles so, and the cold is severe.

At the factory office there is an awning, and under it are picks, shovels, and crowbars. The pits are being dug at a distance of approximately three and a half meters from one another; then the bottoms of the pits are connected by a tunnel. It is possible to dig only while lying on one's side or stomach. The most unpleasant and difficult thing is to reach soft sand. Without knowing earthwork and without knowing how to deal with frozen ground, this is just as difficult as trying to dig a pit in rock. I often had to install fence poles in the winter, and I dug ditches when I was in the military service, so it does not frighten me. For a physically weak person, of course, this work is too strenuous and torturous.

We have three bosses. The head engineer is a German — a big man with a red, wind-burned face, cold, tiny eyes, narrow lips and a broad chin. They say that in his youth he was an amateur boxer and now in conversations, to be more convincing, he likes to use his fists and sometimes his feet. Two people work on one pit. One of us chops off pieces of frozen earth with a crowbar, and the other throws it off to the side. You can't work on an empty stomach — you would freeze; the cold forces us to work faster. In the daytime we are allowed to gather in a small group for thirty minutes — we are considered to have had our lunch. We are not allowed inside, where the factory workers are and we are not allowed to talk to them. Some workers leave the factory to have lunch at home. One of them is a good friend of mine. We were very close when we were at the factory and worked together on various commissions and in MOPR.* I inconspicuously approach him on the road and for several minutes we walk together. He sticks a handful of cigarettes in my pocket. ". . . the front is drawing near, here's my address. . . . Maybe it will come in handy for you." We inconspicuously give each other a firm handshake.

The second half of the day passes just like the first, except that it is harder to work — it is very cold and we are hungry. It is getting dark, the Germans quickly count us, and we start back. There is the ghetto fence already, we can see the gates. A second later the word "action" spreads up and down the column. There was an "action" in the ghetto!

The last dozen meters we do not walk, but run. The guard at the gates does not recount us, there is no search. The sentry does not look at us; is it really possible that his conscience has begun to stir? While running, I find out that tonight part of the ghetto was led away and many were killed; workers on the unit for removal of corpses worked the whole day. Now people from the "Small Ghetto" are being admitted to the "Big Ghetto." I run to the gates. The guard, having turned his back to us, is looking somewhere in the other direction; now none of them can look us in the eyes.

*International Organization of Assistance to Revolutionaries.

Finally, I am on the other side of the gates, in the "Big Ghetto." The street is empty, the shutters are closed, many windows have become dark. On the edge of the sidewalk there are horseshoe tracks, horse dung, and puddles of blood. Puddles, stains, strips, individual drops. It is obvious that the street was cleaned up, but here and there are gloves and children's galoshes trampled down into the snow. Every now and then we step on small copper tubes — revolver cartridge shells. I step in some blood. Strangely, it is still sticky in spite of the cold.

Nothing has changed in our yard. It is still light outside, but the windows in our little house are dark. I knock two times at the window; that is our prearranged signal. Mama and Alya open up the door for me. Their faces are blank. There is unusual disarray in the apartment, the dishes are not washed, the beds are not made. They have not slept the whole night; they have been sitting without getting undressed — waiting for the Germans to come for them. The children went to sleep with their clothes on. In the evening they already learned that on Katolicheskaya, Sadovnikovskaya, and Moscow Streets — "it had begun."

The street is strewn with the corpses of old men. The Germans do not want to feed the old men for nothing, so to economize and for convenience they shoot them right in the ghetto.

That night many people committed suicide, including several doctors. Alya's cousin Lelya Bordo slit her own wrists as well as those of her five-year-old son, Zhorzhik. They were found in bed the next morning, covered with blood. Zhorzhik was already dead. His mother is now in the hospital; she was given a blood transfusion, and she will live. But why save Lelya? Try to think, to understand just for an instant what must be going on in the soul of a mother who has taken a razor and cut the arteries of the hands of her own beloved little son?

In one day puddles of blood have become an ordinary sight. We walk past them, step in them. On the corner of Daugavpils and Ludzas Streets we go into a house. The first thing that we see is that the front door has been smashed with an axe. The first apartment is wide open. The beds are torn asunder, there are pillows and clothes on the floor, everything is in a chaotic state. On the table there are various pieces of uneaten food and some unfinished tea. It is obvious that the people were driven out unexpectedly and in a hurry. The door is half open in the apartment to the left, and there is a strong draft. We pass through the kitchen into a room where a window is broken and the wind blows freely. Someone is lying on the bed. We come closer and look into the face of a dead man. It is an old man with a small gray beard, his eyes fixed upon the ceiling in a glassy stare.

I don't know why, but I cover him up again. I even make sure that I leave no tracks . . . after all, the window is knocked out. For a first impression this is enough. . . .

Mama, while letting me in, motions for me not to make any noise. In the untidy room, on an unmade bed, partially covered with a coat, Alya is sleeping. The children have also fallen asleep, although it is only seven o'clock. Mama will kiss Alya and the children for me, I must hurry.

Those who have lost their own, whose families have already been herded away, are convinced that the people remaining will also be taken away. They no longer have any hopes, and they look at things clearly; they are dead, but they are sober. Those of us whose relatives are still "at home" live with hope. We are still blind; we still do not understand the whole cruel consistency of the system of "actions."

Two residents of our apartment worked on the removal and burial of corpses. The number of dead inside the ghetto was either 500 or 600. As a rule, the Germans shot only the old and the sick. A few young people and children may have been killed accidentally. They shot people in the head — the famous *Kopfschuss*.

In the morning, at daybreak, we start out for the assembly place. I work the whole day at the harbor, loading coal. I was at the "Cable" again; I was chilled to the bone.

In the "Big Ghetto" we are no longer allowed to see our families, but the policemen assure us that everything is calm there. No one knows anything for certain about what became of the first group of people who were moved out. The most disparate rumors are circulating, the most incredible of which is that people are not being sent to any camp at all, but are being taken in groups to a nearby forest where all of them, without exception, are being massacred with machine guns.

We were told at the police station that we would be able to visit our families two or three times a week.

Today, when I was coming home from work, I found out that people are being let into the "Big Ghetto" — I had not seen my family in six days, and in our conditions, six days is an eternity.

Before going to my place, I ran to the gates. The sentry was warming himself by the fire and was not interested in anyone; I walked out onto Ludzas Street without any trouble. There has been a fresh snowfall the past few days and the street is covered with a white carpet which has hidden all traces of the recent tragedy. The desertedness of the ghetto is striking. After all, no one has been moved out from this area of the ghetto, the houses are packed full of people, but what a deserted street, what an ominous silence! I hurry so as not to lose precious moments. Our yard is covered over with snow, only narrow pathways lead from house to house. . . .

We say very little to each other; we just sit very close and look at each other's hands.

I chopped enough wood for a week, cleaned the pipe in the stove, ate a salted potato, and it was already time to say good-bye again. Good-bye Mama, good-bye children, good-bye my beloved Lenushka. Perhaps in a week I'll come again, and perhaps, we are parting forever!. . .

The door closes behind me. The first stars are in the sky, the snow crunches under my feet. I feel like inhaling the winter air with my whole being, but something inexpressibly heavy presses on my chest.

During my absence the number of people in our apartment has grown. A few quite elderly people have appeared. They have carefully shaved their beards, even their heads, so that their gray hair can not be seen. They are trying as hard as they can to appear young and "able-bodied."

Gradually they begin to settle down to rest. It is dark in our rooms, I can hear the whispering back and forth, individual words; then an oppressive silence ensues. But what is that? It sounds like people knocking somewhere, very close by, and suddenly the nocturnal silence is broken by wild shouting: *Aufmachen, Schweinehunde, oder wir schiessen!** We are at the window in a second. Thanks to the snow and the moon, everything is clearly visible. Opposite us, at a two-story house, a group of armed people are knocking at the door; and along the fence outside our house, there is a heavy soldier guard. Instantly the word "action" flies throughout the apartment. The shouting and the cursing intensify, a shot rings out, an axe flashes, the shutters over the cellar shatter. There is a

*German: "Open, you swine, or we shoot!"

342

light on in the cellar, and a soldier crawls through the window. A few seconds later the front doors are open. A woman with a travel bag on her back flashes by the open cellar window. One can hear isolated shots from inside the "Big Ghetto" — the same thing is happening there. Bent figures begin coming out of the house across the way. They are lined up, two in a row; many of the women have bags on their backs and children in their arms. Soldiers walk back and forth with cigarettes between their teeth. It is freezing outside, and the women just keep standing there with their children. Soon it is one o'clock in the morning. Finally, sometime after 1:30, an order is heard, and to the accompaniment of cheerful talk and abusive language, the column starts out in the direction of Ludzas Street. Shots ring out more and more frequently. Each shot means the end of someone's life. I lie on the bed; I can not feel my body. I can not feel my soul — it is as though I were made of wood. Could Mama, Alya, Dima and my little daughter have been driven from the house? Why, for what? No, this is not true, I'm just dreaming this. . . .

There is already some movement in the house, it is morning, but it is still dark outside. I am not going to work today, I have to find out what happened during the "action." So as not to be caught by one of the slave hunters, I walk with Gertsmark to the technical section. Everyone there already knows everything. Last night everyone who was left in the ghetto was herded away. There is great disarray on the streets; toward nine o'clock a work detail is supposed to assemble to clean up. The technical section is required to present people for work at the . . . cemetery. I join them. We drag out shovels, picks, and crowbars from a storehouse. On all the streets one can see the traces of a sleepless night. Everyone is gray and uncommunicative.

The sun has risen, a light morning has imperceptibly broken. The streets in the "Big Ghetto" are not recognizable. Where is yesterday's snow! It has disappeared, been kneaded, pressed down, dirtied. I have seen streets after the retreat of an army, with broken equipment and vehicles, the corpses of people and horses, all kinds of military debris, but they were traces of a battle, and these things here are traces of a slaughter. The street is covered with blood, and the white snow during the night has turned gray with red streaks. The corpses — old men, women, children! Trampled carriages, children's sleighs, purses, gloves and galoshes, bags with food, baby bottles filled with frozen oatmeal, children's overshoes. The corpses are still warm and soft, the faces are covered with blood, the eyes are open.

We have to deliver the corpses to the cemetery. We put two of them on each sleigh or cart. When we take them in a cart, they rock slightly, as though alive, and blood falls in lumps on the snow.

We take the corpses for the time being only beyond the gates of the cemetery, where we lay them out in rows — men and women separately. Members of the council search among the dead for documents. A boy about 12 years old is brought in — a lovely, handsome child in a gray coat with a fur collar, and wearing new boots. He is lying on his back with his blue eyes open wide. The bullet from a revolver landed in the back of his head and only part of the collar is covered with blood. He lies there like a doll, and somehow it is unbelievable that only recently he was still alive, probably, a happy child.

We are replaced by others and now we go to dig the graves. We dig a pit next to the burned-out cemetery synagogue. The ground is so frozen that we have to chip away pieces, as if from stone. I hardly notice the blood trickling from the lip I've bitten. There are no clear thoughts — only random fragments. I'm outwardly calm; I light up a cigarette, spit out some blood, and continue to bite my lips. Finally, we break through the frozen layer of earth, we cut out the roots and the pit begins — approximately two by five meters. We are already up to our chests in earth, we will dig one meter deeper and begin to bury the bodies. Some of the corpses have already arrived; for the meantime they have been piled up next to the walls of the synagogue that are still erect, some are leaning against the walls in a semi-sitting position.

A policeman approaches and warns us that now no one is to leave the cemetery or to come near the fence. It turns out that some streets — the last ones — could not be cleaned during the night, and now the last column is being brought through. The policeman warns that the curious will be shot. We listen intently and wait. We do not have to wait long — the familiar shouts ring out. The heads and shoulders of the mounted guards appear above the fence, beyond which can be heard the shuffling of many feet. The iron gates of the cemetery are 25-30 centimeters above the surface of the ground. Standing in the pit, one can see the endless number of feet. The feet move carefully, with small steps, as though afraid to slip. They are all women's feet, sometimes small children's feet flash by; someone feels the ground with a stick. In the small house across from the cemetery, in an attic room, the curtain is open; through it I can see the faces of several women. They are wearing an expression of horror, of mute reproach, of sympathy.

The feet of the victims and the heads of the horsemen say so much — how horrible these feet are, how much impudence and satisfaction in these heads and shoulders! We have no weapons — only hate and hunger for revenge, but this will not alleviate our grief. There is amazing silence beyond the fence; now and then one hears a child's crying or the shouts of the overseers. The feet are no longer visible, the horsemen move slowly into the distance. One of the women in the window brings a handkerchief to her eyes. The curtain is lowered. In front of us the corpses lie calmly in reclining or half-sitting positions. Their faces have not changed. . . .

The pit is ready, but a different shift will bury the corpses; it has already arrived, and we can rest. For some reason I remove my wedding ring from my finger and bury it in the bottom of the grave. With it I bury the past and hope.

We walk to the first gates, to take a look at the corpses which have just been brought; perhaps there are relatives among them. We walk along a narrow path in the snow which leads through the old graves. The sun is already setting and casts a long uneven shadow. My father is buried in this cemetery. It is an old cemetery, and no one has been buried here for many years. It did not expect such an influx of dead people. The rows of corpses near the gates are not getting any smaller: I walk in and look around. There are a few familiar faces — old men. Beyond some bushes, about 70 meters to the left of the gates, corpses are hurriedly being carried to the grave. The stretchers look as if they are painted red — so saturated are they with blood.

The sun is setting lower in the sky. The job has to be speeded up. The pits are quickly filled in with frozen dirt. The large light-yellow mound is growing. Everything is quiet; there is only some movement beyond the fence. The squeaking of the sleighs and carts which are moving toward the cemetery can be heard. And here as if by some unspoken agreement, 40-50 Jews stand facing east in a semicircle around the grave. Those who have just buried their mothers and fathers step forward. I do not pray — I do not know how, but I stand there as if in a trance, unable to feel my body, except that my heart is ready to leap from my chest, and I have a nervous shivery apprehension.

I do not understand the words of the prayer, and the meaning is not comprehensible to me. I only know that this picture has been burned into my memory as if with a red-hot iron.

Twilight. The street along which we are walking has not been cleaned up yet — there are no corpses, but stains remain in their places.

Our apartment is full of people. We try not to speak about what has happened — at least for now.

I lie down and fall asleep immediately without dreams or nightmares. I awake about ten o'clock. I come to slowly. Gertsmark is sitting opposite me on an ottoman, with his head pressed against his hands. His eyes are full of tears, but his face is dry. His lips just keep repeating the words: "poor people, poor people." It is as if my heart were slashed with a knife. Instantly everything appears in vivid and bright colors. I see the doors in our little house fly open, and people with green armbands rush in. Alya hurriedly wraps up Dima, snatches our sleepy little daughter from her bed. Mama helps with trembling hands. Alya, with a bag flung over her shoulders, pushes the carriage with our daughter, and Mama, also with a bag on her back, leads Dima by the hand. They get into the column; they wait, freeze, wait.

What happened inside of them, what did they feel? This secret they carried off with themselves. . . .

Prepared for publication by **V. Grossman** and **R. Kovnator.**

The Story of Syoma Shpungin

(Dvinsk)

I am 16 years old. When the Germans came, I was 12. I had just graduated to the fifth grade. We lived in Dvinsk, at 83/85 Rainis Street. My father, Ilya Shpungin, was a photographer. I also had a mother and a six-year-old sister, Roza.

When the Germans came, my whole family, along with many of our friends, left Dvinsk on foot. We walked while the bombing was going on. We walked all the way to Byelorussia, and there the Germans caught up with us. We knew we could go no farther and returned to Dvinsk.

The Jews in Dvinsk were seized on the streets and taken to prison, where they were tormented. They were forced to lie down on the ground and jump up again and again, and those who were unable to do this fast enough were shot. We did not return to our own home. It had burned down, so we stayed with grandma for awhile, and later we were taken to the ghetto. This was "good fortune," because many people were shot in the prison. They were killed in the yard and in the garden outside the railroad station.

On July 20 all the Jews who had thus far escaped death were in the ghetto. It was built on the far bank of the Dvina River, opposite the fortress, in an old building that the Germans themselves said was not suitable even for horses. Doctor Gurevich was with us. He said that the children would not live longer than two months there. But the children lived longer than that.

It was very crowded and dirty. And it was very cold. We lived without glass in the windows and the building was made of stone. Approximately two weeks later the Germans ordered all the old men (I think all men over 65, I do not remember exactly) to assemble in the yard and said that they would be transferred to a "second camp." Instead, the old men were shot. At the same time they shot everyone who came to Dvinsk from other places. The belongings of the victims were kept by the executioners for themselves.

Later the "selection" began. This was done almost every day.

People were assembled and divided into two groups. No one knew why he was being put in one group or the other, nor what would happen to his group — would it be sent to work or executed.

The butchers were very often drunk.

It was very cold. The Germans suddenly placed people in

"quarantine." During quarantine it was forbidden to go to the city even to work. And we were given 125 grams of horrible bread and water with rotten cabbage. People began to swell up from hunger. One woman by the name of Meyerovich, who had seven children, secretly tried to obtain bread from the workers who worked near the ghetto. She was caught and shot in front of everyone. Her children were killed on May 1, 1942.

I came down with typhus and was hidden inside the ghetto itself so that the Germans would not kill me; I recovered.

Our family was lucky up until November 6. We were even surprised that all four of us were still alive. Papa was working; he would secretly bring us a little food. He would eat only part of what he was given at work and secretly bring the rest of his food to the ghetto.

On November 6 a large "selection" began. One woman who was standing not far away from us took to her heels. She was not caught, so the Germans announced that because of her escape ten other people would be shot. My mother and sister had already been chosen, and they walked out of the ranks. I was supposed to go too. But I grabbed hold of Mama's hand, who was holding on to my sister, and I pulled them both back into the crowd. The crowd was dense, it would have taken a long time to find us, and the Germans did not take the trouble.

On November 9 the men who worked among the Germans, including my father, left the ghetto. And after their departure everyone was herded out into the yard. First an order was given for the members of the "committee" appointed by the Germans to step out of the crowd; then the medical workers and their families were ordered to line up. I do not know how I guessed that all the others would be killed. I rushed to the medical workers and began to pray that one of them would say that I was his son. A dentist named Magid who had a young daughter said to me: "okay." Then I left to find my mother and sister. But I could not find them. I went around all the people shouting "Mama! Roza!" No one responded. It turned out that the Germans had already taken one group away. Mama and Roza were probably in that group. And I remembered how I kept asking Mama when we were taken out into the yard: "Mama, where can we go?" And Roza also asked Mama where to go. We understood, as did Roza, that some people would be killed, and that the others would be left alone. But Mama answered: "I don't know." I wanted to take Roza and then Mama into the group of medical workers and beg someone to say that they were also members of his family. But I was too late.

In the evening Papa returned with the others with whom he worked. Papa already knew something. He immediately asked me: "Is Mama here? Is Roza here?"

The horrible sound of weeping was heard in the ghetto. Many of the men were unable to find any members of their families. Papa, too, cried awfully. The Germans said they would begin to shoot if the crying did not stop.

The killing continued throughout the winter. Papa and I remained alone. In case of a new "selection" we agreed that we would hide in the same hiding place. Once I did not have time to hide there and I spent the whole day in the outhouse up to my neck in excrement. They came into the outhouse but did not notice me.

In the winter a woman named Gitelson was hanged in the yard in front of everyone. She had been caught in the city. She had the right to be there, but she had not put on her Jewish badge and was walking on the sidewalk rather than in the street, as Jews were ordered to do. We did not have the right to step onto the sidewalk. And another girl was hanged. I do not remember her surname, but her first name was Masha. She had tried to conceal that she was a Jew. A Jewish man, whose name I did not know, was forced to hang her. He refused and was beaten. In the end, the Germans themselves fastened the noose around the girl's neck, but the man was forced, under the sight of an automatic rifle, to kick out the bench from under Masha's feet. Several Germans photographed this.

I remember also, how in the evening, some policemen came running and said that their car had broken down and they needed a rope. They were given a chain, but they said that a chain would not do. Then everyone knew that the rope was not needed for a car, and we told them that we had no rope. They swore at us for some time, then left. Later it turned out they had taken someone for execution and decided to hang him, but they did not have a rope.

The next big selection and attendant murders were on May 1, 1942. There were only a few of us left — perhaps one and a half thousand. After May 1 there were 375 people left, not counting those who worked for the Germans. People often said: "How are we better than our parents, our wives, brothers, sisters and children? How can we live when they have been killed?" There was nowhere to run to; our town was small, and it was impossible to hide. We did not know where the partisans were. Nevertheless, some people were armed. The weapons had been taken from German storehouses in the fortress where many of our people worked. I asked Papa if this wasn't stealing. Papa answered that the Germans had taken everything from us, had killed our relatives and close friends, were killing the entire Jewish people and so, anything that we could do against the Germans was not a criminal act, but an act of war. The Germans, he said, were not soldiers, but criminals.

Some of the young people were running away to join the partisans. For Papa and me, this was difficult to do. We did not have any weapons, it was difficult for Papa to leave the place where Mama and Roza had perished, and he was afraid for me. I was 13 then.

On September 23 during the night (almost at daybreak) secret sentries whom we ourselves had posted came running and shouted: "Jews! The situation looks very bad! The Gestapo has arrived!"

It turned out that the Gestapo men were already in the yard. They could have come only for murder. I shouted to Papa: "Papa, I'm going to the old place!" — that is, to our hiding place. And I took to my heels, thinking that my father was running behind me. He probably was, but it was already impossible to get to our place — the way was cut off. I rushed to hide under the stairway, then I jumped through a window onto the street. It was very dark. I waited a minute — my father was not there. . . . There was an exchange of fire between our people and the Gestapo. Later, those who survived told me that that night, in anticipation of death, many people poisoned themselves or hanged themselves so as not to be taken alive by the Gestapo. They say that Feigin, whose relatives had been shot by the Germans, had hidden a lot of rope and gave it to anyone who wanted to hang himself, and that he even helped people hang themselves, and in the end he hanged himself. Some of the people who escaped saw this themselves.

In the darkness I ran into two adults and one boy of my age who, like me, were running away. We started out on the road together. The adults soon felt behind: as a group of four, we were taking too great a risk of being noticed. Before evening the boy and I (I remember only that he was from Kreslav and that his name was Nosya) walked 25 kilometers. My feet were really sore. Whenever we met up with people I would shout: "Vanya, where's Papa?" or I would loudly sing Russian songs so that we would be taken for local Russians. Nosya was very frightened. We spent the night in a burned-out house. In the morning we realized that we would not reach Byelorussia; I decided to go to Poland. We were fed by a woman whom I told directly that we were running away from the Germans. Nosya said that we should surrender, that we would not be able to hide no matter what, but I encouraged him. A truck was driving down the road. I decided not to pay any attention to it, but Nosya stopped. I walked ahead and did not notice this, because I had decided not to look back. I heard someone shout in German. Then I turned off onto a path. Soon a bicyclist rode up to me and said that there were Gestapo men in the truck and that they had ordered me to go to the truck. I said: "I won't go." The bicyclist said: "As you wish. You'll be the one to pay the price." But he himself rode on — not back to the Germans. I hid in the bushes. I heard whistles; I heard the Germans asking someone if they had seen a boy. Nosya was caught then.

So I was completely alone. When everything quieted down, I started on my way. I decided to pass myself off as someone whom the Germans had transported out of the central regions of the U.S.S.R. But I had not had time to think what I would say, when I was already arrested. While I was being taken on the road to headquarters, I managed to throw out the small red star from my pocket — I had saved it from the ghetto. During the interrogation I declared that my name was Ivan Ostrovsky, that my father was a Tatar, and my mother was Russian. I thought I had to explain why I had thick black eyebrows so I added that my grandmother was a Gypsy. I did not know that the Germans exterminated all Gypsies. I knew that Moslem children underwent a rite of circumcision when they turned 13, which was just how old I was. I also said that my father had died when I was one in order to explain why I did not speak Tatar. Fortunately, the Germans knew as little about these things as I did. I made up the story that my mother was a laundress and worked for the "Collective of the Forestry Department" in Bryansk. All this was just the first things that came into my mind. I did not know the first thing about Bryansk, and when I was asked where my mother and I lived, I answered: "in the country, in a settlement, we had no address, people just wrote to us at '"Bryansk, KLD.'" I was unable to escape, and in the morning I was sent to Dvinsk. My feet hurt terribly, but I still tried to escape from the road because I knew that in Dvinsk I would, of course, be exposed or recognized. But I was caught, beaten, and taken on to Dvinsk.

At the Dvinsk police station I was beaten and continually badgered with questions: "Tell the truth, that you are a Jew, and nothing will happen to you, otherwise we will kill you." But I stood my ground. I was very lucky for several reasons. In the first place, the Germans in the place where I was arrested never forwarded my I.D., from which I had torn out the word "Jew," but from which I would have immediately been identified: after all, my real name appeared on it. In the second place, the doctor who was supposed to examine me to determine whether I was a Moslem or a Jew never showed up. Finally, in the accompanying document from the village it was written that a suspicious boy who was passing himself off as Ivan Ostrovsky was being sent to Dvinsk. And this was the name I was still using.

I was severely beaten at the police station. One time the police-man hit me in the face so hard that I fell head over heels: I did not get up when he walked into the cell. I already thought that I would die, but I decided not to surrender even if it meant the end. And suddenly I was sent to the *Arbeitsamt* (the labor exchange). In the paper it said the "boy posing as Ivan Ostrovsky" should be sent to work. Obviously, in the end they believed me. The *Arbeitsamt* gave me a travel pass to the village. In it it simply said: Ivan Ostrovsky. I spent almost nine months in the village until the Red Army arrived. I did not tell anyone there that I was a Jew. Only once while sleeping I began to shout in Yiddish. The landlord began to ques-tion me, but I was able to convince him that I was shouting in German. After that I slept very uneasily, fearing that I would again shout out.

When I returned to Dvinsk, the Jews whom I met and who escaped from the ghetto, told me that my father had hidden for three weeks in the city until he was found and killed.

I cannot say exactly how many of us there were in the ghetto. All together more than 30,000 Jews died in Dvinsk, and in the ghetto, I would say about 20,000. Here are the surnames of those who survived: men — the two Pokerman brothers, Motl Krom and his wife and child, Antikol the tailor, Lyak and his wife and child, Muler, Gallerman and two women: Olim and Zelikman. In all, 18 people were rescued, but I cannot remember the names of the others.

I left Dvinsk and would not want to return there because it is too painful for me to walk down the streets along which my parents, and so many Jews who died, walked; and it hurts me to walk past our burned-out house. Most of all I want to study and to find people whom I might grow to love and who might come to love me, so that I will not feel so lonesome in the world.

Prepared for publication by **O. Savich.**

THE SOVIET PEOPLE
ARE UNITED

A Letter of Officers Levchenko, Borisov, and Chesnokov

(Lopavshi, Rovno *Oblast*)

We dislodged the Germans from a commanding position and literally ran over the enemy to break through to a populated area. The Germans fled in panic.

The inhabitants welcomed us joyfully, crying with each other in telling us about the atrocities of the Fascists. Citizen Vera Iosifovna Krasov approached us and invited us to her place. We witnessed a horrible scene — there were six people sitting in a room. They were hardly recognizable as people; they looked more like shadows.

Vera Iosifovna, with tears in her eyes, began to tell her story: "I have kept these people from the Germans for a year and a half. When the Germans came, they began to round up the Jews; each Jew had to wear a badge on his sleeve. Then the commandant was replaced by another who ordered that a larger badge be worn so it could be seen from a distance. The next commandant changed the sleeve badge to a wide ribbon on the chest.

"Soon the mass extermination of the Jews began in the city of Dubno. They were herded together into a square where monstrous atrocities were committed — they were forced to run a gauntlet, the old men's beards were torn out, and then they were forced to dance, sing, and pray.

"After this the Jews were forced to dig graves and lie down in them in several rows, after which they were shot — many were buried alive. At first 90 people were shot. Children were seized by the feet and their heads were split open, or were drowned in bathtubs, and suffocated — all this was done by German women who, like their beast-like husbands, committed savage acts. Then the extermination of the Jews took on even more massive dimensions. . . .

"In the small town of Demiduvka a special camp was created; it was fenced in by barbed wire and as many as 3,700 Jews were herded there and exterminated each day. I had occasion to watch all this many times. Once I encountered Doctor Abram Emmanuilovich Grintsveyg, who had once treated me. I offered to help save his life. But he told me that he was not alone. And at night I transported them in a cart to my farm, where I hid them.

355

But it was difficult to conceal them so I decided to build an underground shelter. All night long, for days on end, secretly from everyone, I dug an underground shelter in which I hid everyone that I brought out from the death camp. No one knew about this except my daughter Irina. Several times the Germans rounded up the Jews, even searching homes, but my secret was not discovered. It was very difficult for me. During the night I would bring them food and let some fresh air into the shelter. All this entailed great danger. But my daughter and I kept our secret. We hoped that our people would come soon and that the Germans would no longer be able to live on our land. The lives of our Soviet people are very dear to us. And here you have come. These people are seeing daylight for the first time in a year and a half."

There are six people in the room — the Goringot sisters, Maria 21, Anna 18 years old. They do not look like girls in the full bloom of health — they are thin, black, hardly able to speak, there are tears of joy in their eyes. They still do not believe that they have been rescued. The Goringot sisters have no parents — they were shot by the Germans.

There is Michel Setz, 20, and his sisters, Ita, 14, Etl, 15 and his brother Yakov, 10. Their parents were shot by the Germans. Twenty-year-old Michel looks like an old man. He has trouble articulating his words. Little Yakov can not walk, he looks at us with a lost expression.

Our hearts after all this fill up with even more hatred for the thrice-cursed German.

Vera Iosifovna said:

"Comrades! These are not all the people whose lives I've saved. There are four more people in an underground shelter, but in a different one."

And the woman took us there. In the entrance hall we descended into a narrow well, passed through a dark, winding corridor, and in the dim light we saw four more people. They were Doctor Abram Emmanuilovich Grintsveyg of the Dubno Hospital, his 70-year-old father Emmanuil and his mother Anna Yakovlevna, and Anna Lvovna, the wife of the Dubno pharmacist, Oleynik.

We helped them climb out of their underground shelter. Their joy knew no limit; they cried with each other in thanking us and the woman who saved them.

Comrade Ehrenburg! We decided to write to you about this in

the hope that you would write about the heroic deed of Vera Iosifovna Krasov, resident of the village of Lopavshi, Demiduvka region, Rovno *Oblast*, and her 16-year-old daughter Irinka, so that our whole country will learn of it.

Field mail 39864. March 30, 1944.

With regards from the front,
Guards Captain **Levchenko**,
Guards Captain **Borisov**,
Guards Lieutenant **Chesnokov** . . .

The Peasant Woman Zinaida Bashtinin

(Dombrovitsy, Rovno *Oblast*)

Recently I was sent to carry out a special assignment. In one of the settlements of the area near the front where I stopped, the woman in whose hut I stayed received me very well. She told me about everything that peaceful people had been forced to endure during the years of the German occupation. While we were talking a young girl walked into the hut. She looked at me and ran off. I was surprised and asked who this girl was. The lady first told me that she was her daughter and then told me a terrible story that I will remember until the end of my days. This girl's nationality was Jewish. Her parents, sisters, and brothers were shot by the Germans. She was saved by a miracle. And this honest Russian woman had hidden her, even though the Germans could have killed her and her whole family for this. A modest Russian peasant woman had saved the girl, fed her, and clothed her just like one of her own five children. This old woman had done a tremendous deed. When I returned to my unit I told this story to my commander and all my fellow soldiers. They listened with emotion to my story.

The old woman's name is Zinaida Bashtinin. We took the girl into our unit, and she will live with us. Of course, it would be good to send her to the rear so she could study — she is only 14 years old. Her name is Feyga Fishman. Before the war she lived in the village

357

of Dombrovitsy in the Rovno *Oblast*. Please, describe the feat of Zinaida Bashtinin. Let the world know that the Russian people have never been hostile toward the Jews and that in these difficult times the Russian people have extended to the Jews a brotherly hand of friendship.

July 9, 1944.

With regards from the front,
R. Seltsavsky

Prepared for publication by **Ilya Ehrenburg**.

The Collective Farmer Julia Kukhta Saved Jewish Children

In the beginning of the war the surgeon of the First Soviet Hospital in Minsk, Sarra Borisovna Truskin, put her two sons — Mark, 7, and Alek, 11 months — into a cart together with their nannie Julia Kukhta and started out behind them on foot on the highway from Moscow to Minsk. During the bombing she lost sight of the cart. A stream of refugees carried it along behind them. She got as far as Chkalov, where she worked throughout the war, mourning the loss of her children.

A week after the liberation of Minsk her brother sent her a postcard he had received from Julia saying that the children were alive. Today the mother is living together with them in Minsk.

Here is the story told to Senior Lieutenant of Jurisprudence Mayakov by Julia Kukhta, a thirty-year-old collective farm worker from the village of Krivoye Selo, of the Veshenkovichesky region, Vitebsk *Oblast*:

"Beginning in 1934 I lived first as a housekeeper and then as a nannie in the family of Sarra Borisovna Truskin. I was present when both of her boys, Mark and Alek, were born. On June 24, 1941, when we left Minsk, I kept the children next to me in the cart and tried constantly not to lose sight of Sarra Borisovna. But the bombing began, and we lost each other. In the cart with us rode Sarra Borisovna's sister Anna Borisovna and her husband, as well as the boys' grandfather, Boris Lvovich. After traveling about 20 kilometers outside of Minsk, Felitsian Vladislavovich, Anna Borisovna's husband, said that it made no sense to keep going, and toward evening we returned to Minsk.

"At first we all lived together with the parents of Felitsian Vladislavovich. But when the grandfather and Anna Borisovna were taken by the Germans into the ghetto, the mother of Felitsian Vladislavovich, Polina Osipovna, began to insist that I take Mark to the ghetto too, because his face had Jewish features.

"'Because of him our whole family could perish, take him to the ghetto,' she repeated to me over and over again, and once she herself went with me and Mark in order to leave him with his grandfather.

"But after giving up the boy, I could not rest. 'He could die,' I

359

thought. Every day I went to the ghetto and behind the backs of the policemen I passed food through the wire. At that time I was able to register Alek in my name as my own child, and I never parted with him. Once I was dragged off to the police station, and they tried to find out how I had come to have a child.

"'You probably decided to hide the Jewish child for a great deal of money.'

"I continued to deny everything, even when they began to whip me with a lash. 'The child is mine — and that is all there is to it.' Fortunately, Alek became frightened when they began to beat me, grabbed hold of my dress, and started to shout: 'Mama, Mama.' They let me go.

"But then Polina Osipovna demanded that the boy and I leave. I rented a small room on a street far away, where I was not known.

"Meanwhile they had begun to shoot the Jews in the ghetto. I was terribly tormented by the thought of little Mark. I decided that what will be will be, but I had to get the boy out. And once during a meeting with Anna Borisovna, she was able to stealthily get Mark past the policemen and beyond the wire to me.

"Polina Osipovna used the neighbors several times to try to intimidate me by saying that I would do them in as well as myself. But I had firmly decided that it would be better to perish with the children than to give them up — and there was nowhere for them to go. Except for me, they had no one else in the whole world. Neither their grandfather nor Anna Borisovna came to the ghetto at that time — they had probably been shot like the others.

"Soon I was able to have Mark registered in my passport as my son.

"Of course, to do this I had to have both boys baptized. A priest in the next village performed the ceremony.

"From that point on I did not let the children go anywhere without me. When I went to work, I would lock them in my room, leave them food, and Mark, as the older one, looked after the baby; he understood that their lives depended on this.

"I had to change jobs several times as soon as the children roused suspicion. Every day I trembled with fear for their lives.

"But I knew that the Germans could not live among us forever, because sooner or later our people would come back. And I kept the children alive and well."

Report of Lieutenant of Jurisprudence **Mayakov**.

Prepared for publication by **Vasily Grossman**.

360

I Was Adopted by the Lukinsky Family

On June 21, 1941, I left Minsk, where I was in my second year of studies at the Medical Institute, for the city of Borisov in order to see my parents before I left to work at a Pioneer camp. I was supposed to leave for the camp on June 23, but I never left — on June 22 I heard over the radio that the Germans had invaded our homeland.

The Germans entered Borisov in the first days of July. I did not have time to evacuate. Frightened by stories about the atrocities of the Germans, I did not go out for two weeks. The Germans went from house to house, asked about the nationality of the people, and confiscated their best belongings. On July 25 the Germans began to create a ghetto. The Jewish people had to leave their homes and move to the outskirts of the city, to a section that had been fenced off by barbed wire and from which the Russian population had been evacuated earlier.

We were forbidden to communicate with the outside world — on every street and on the only entrance gate the Germans had hung the sign: "Jewish traffic forbidden." Each step we took was controlled by the police both outside and inside the ghetto. One could leave the ghetto only by having a special pass.

Everyone in the ghetto had to wear bright yellow badges on the left side of the chest and on the back. If the badge was not worn or if it was covered up with a kerchief, a person could be shot.

An order was issued for Russians: "Upon meeting a Jew, cross to the other side of the street, greetings are forbidden, as is exchanging things." For violating this order, Russians met the same fate as Jews.

Here is how a day passed ... All able-bodied people had to report to a specially designated square at six o'clock in the morning, then people were divided into groups and sent to work under guarded escort. When leaving for work, not one Jew knew whether he would return to the ghetto or not. The ration for all workers was 150 grams of bread. Hunger began. As a result of hunger, the hellish work, and the congested living conditions, people came down with infectious diseases, and many people died because of the lack of medicine.

The Germans ordered the people in the ghetto to surrender all their warm clothing — fur coats, felt boots, jumpers, gloves, sweaters, etc. Then came the order to turn in all items made of gold and silver. The Germans threatened to shoot 500 people for not turning in their warm clothing and 1,200 for not giving up their gold items. After this an order was issued to turn in all silk items, shorts, slips, knitted wear. When all the items had been taken away, the Germans imposed an indemnity of 300,000 rubles.

And then the mass extermination of the Jewish population began. All the Jews in the small towns and villages were exterminated.

On October 20 at six o'clock in the morning the ghetto in Borisov was surrounded by the police. I lived in the center of the ghetto and heard the shouts and children's crying all around. People were seized, loaded into vehicles, and taken away "to work" — that is, to be shot. At four o'clock in the afternoon on October 20 my father, mother, and other relatives were seized and taken away in vehicles. I heard my mother shout, plead for help. . . . But what could I do? I hid with my two little brothers (5 and 11 years old) in an attic, and from there I saw people being led away for execution. The shooting of the Jews continued for three days. The executioners tried to arrange this mass murder of people in such a way that it would remain secret. It was forbidden to walk on streets which were near the execution site; at the tannery directly adjacent to the ghetto, work was stopped for three days. Vehicles left the ghetto loaded with people and returned with the belongings of the dead victims. It was impossible to escape — policemen stood along the streets and would start shooting in a frenzy if someone tried to escape.

While sitting in the attic, I heard the drunken voices of the policemen who were searching our house for loot and dividing it up on the spot. A girl whom they were torturing for trying to escape shouted: "I'm Russian!" — but they killed her.

On the third day the police broke into the attic where we were hiding. Having ordered everyone to lie with their hands raised, they searched us, took all money and valuables, attached us to a group of about 60 people, and led us away to be shot. The sick who were unable to walk were shot on the spot.

We were taken to Razuvayevka, near the airport, two to three kilometers from the city. This is where the execution site was: the earth was freshly dug up, and we could even see human heads not covered with dirt. We were forced to undress, all photographs or documents found on us were torn up, and we were given shovels and ordered to dig pits. All you had to do was stop for a minute and a policeman would immediately smash you in the back with his rifle butt. I lagged behind the others because I had to dig a pit not only for myself, but also for my younger brother; I was often beaten for being slow about it, and the Germans who stood nearby with cameras just laughed.

When the pits were ready, we were lined up facing the pit, and I realized that we would be shot in the back. I was standing at the very end of the line, closest to a group of Germans. Among them was an Austrian, in whose unit I had worked as a cleaning woman. I looked at him, and he recognized me, motioned to me with his hand, and I, paying no attention to the policemen, ran to him. The chief of the police, Kovalevsky, demanded that I tell him my name, but the Austrian said that he knew I was Russian. He led me aside, put me in his car, and drove me to Minsk. While driving away, I heard the machine-gun fire — these were completely innocent people being massacred. In three days more than 10,000 Jews were killed.

About twenty kilometers from Minsk I was let out of the car and told: "Save yourself, however you can." I spent the night under the open sky and started at every rustling sound. "Where can I go?" — I thought. In the morning I set out for Minsk, where I had lived for two years — I had friends and relatives there. Minsk was badly destroyed, especially the center of the city. I had no documents, and I set out for the Minsk ghetto. There I related what had happened in Borisov. After spending one day, I decided to go farther to the east, closer to the front, so I could cross over into our land.

I used every means possible to enable me to reach Smolensk, a town with which I was not familiar. It was November 7 — the anniversary of the October Revolution. I stood on the bridge that crossed the Dnieper, not knowing where to take shelter. It was evening. The only thing left to do was to go to the Smolensk ghetto, which was located in Sadki. The front had moved far to the east, and I had no strength to go any further. I decided to remain for the meantime in Smolensk. Documents were checked very thoroughly in the city, and I had to look for refuge in the suburbs. I found out that in Serebryanka, two kilometers from Smolensk, there lived a Jewish family, the Morozovs, who had not yet landed in the ghetto, and so I set out to find them. But I spent only one day with the Morozovs, because a German translator from a flax plant was watching them. It was recommended that I go for help to a Russian family, the Lukinskys. I told the Lukinskys everything about myself, and they let me stay with them.

The Lukinskys risked their lives in offering me refuge, but that did not frighten them, and they treated me like their own daughter. It was necessary to get documents for me. The Lukinskys introduced me to some Russian girls, and one of them, Pechkurov, agreed to go to the passport table and get a passport for me in the name of her friend Olga Vasilyevna Khrapov. So began my new life under a new name. After receiving my documents, I got a job. I very quickly got used to my new family, and the Lukinskys became substitutes for my parents, who had been shot by the Germans.

On November 10 the Germans arrested the Morozovs. The Lukinskys managed to prevent the arrest of their children by sending them to a safe place. The Morozov family was shot by the Germans. In the spring of 1942 the Smolensk ghetto met the same sad fate as the Borisov ghetto — 2,000 people were executed. The Germans tried to find the Jews who were hiding under Russian names, and, when such people were found, they were shot along with the Russians who were sheltering them. My new parents, the Lukinskys, were very nervous about my fate. The Gestapo was seizing people in various places and murdering them.

I often became depressed, but my second father, E. P. Lukinsky, tried to keep up my spirits and my faith that the Red Army would come to save us from Fascist servitude. We read Soviet leaflets thrown from airplanes and learned that the Red Army was relentlessly moving west. We lived with the hope for speedy deliverance. The Germans herded off all the young people to dig trenches or to Germany. I was afraid of every policeman who walked past the house, but, fortunately, my turn never came, and we were liberated by the mighty Red Army. However, the very last days of the German occupation were very painful. I had just come out of the hospital and immediately went into the woods, because the Germans were evicting everyone from their houses; they were burning them.

There were quite a large number of us in the woods, and we spoke in whispers so that the Germans would not find us. On September 24, Soviet artillery shells began to fly over our heads and we applauded them. On September 25, 1943, we saw in the woods the first Red Army reconnaissance soldier. I kissed him with tears of joy in my eyes.

Olga Yevgenyevna Lukinsky
Polina Markovna Ausker

Information supplied by **Polina Ausker-Lukinsky**.

Prepared for publication by **V. Ilyenkov**.

The Russian Teachers Tolnev, Terekhov, Timofeyev

After graduating from the Smolensk Pedagogical Institute, I worked for three years in the Kasplyansky region of the Smolensk *Oblast*, first in Yenkov and later in Kasplyan. I devoted all my knowledge and energies to the children, and I enjoyed their love and the respect of their parents. When the Germans occupied the Smolensk *Oblast*, I was in the village Kasili, because I did not have enough time to leave with the evacuees. When the Germans began to register the Jews, I had to hide. Some of my colleagues and pupils helped me, especially Yekaterina Abramovna Tolnev and Anna Evseyevna Terekhov. For four months I wandered from place to place — in one place by day, in another by night. Finally, the teacher Aleksandra Stepanovna Timofeyev, with whom I had worked for two years in a school in Yenkov, gave me shelter in her home. I settled with her in the village of Babintsy, in a small house where Aleksandra Stepanovna's mother Domna Arsentyevna lived, as well as her married sister with two children. All of them were threatened with mortal danger, but Mrs. Timofeyev courageously helped me hide from the Germans. They hid me from the eyes of strangers — under pillows, above the stove. . . .

But then the Germans settled in the village, and I could no longer remain in Babintsy. Aleksandra Stepanovna arranged to have me stay with her aunt Yekaterina Yefimovna Ksendzov, who lived in the next village with her daughter Nina, a student at the Smolensk Pedagogical Institute. The Ksendzovs were already hiding a Jewish girl, Sarra Veniaminovna Vints, a girlfriend of Nina's from the institute. They lived in the school where Y. Y. Ksendzov had taught long before. And we built an underground passageway beneath the school and hid there with Sarra. I lived this way for six months — sometimes with the Timofeyevs, sometimes with the Ksendzovs. Sometimes I wanted to die; my situation seemed hopeless. But my friends the Timofeyevs and the Ksendzovs encouraged me and gave me the will to live. They also gave a great deal of help to the local partisans. The elderly Yekaterina Yefimovna Ksendzov would stand guard all night long so a partisan could get some sleep.

On May 8, 1942, Sarra and I went to join the partisans in the woods. There I met some familiar people: the secretary of the

Kasplyan district committee of the Communist Party, Volkov, who was the commander of the detachment, and the chairman of the district division of people's education, Goldnev, who was the commissar of the detachment. A little while later Ksendzov and her daughter came to the detachment. I was sent from the partisans to an area deep behind Soviet lines.

Soon after the Germans were driven from the Smolensk *Oblast*, I got the opportunity to embrace the fine Russian women who saved my life.

Report of **Anna Yefimovna Khodos**.
Prepared for publication by **Ilya Ehrenburg**.

The Bookkeeper Zirchenko

Seven Jewish families who lived in the city of Ordzhonikidze, Stalino *oblast*, were unable to be evacuated in time. The refugees went to the village of Blagodatnoye, of the Gulyaypole village Soviet, in Dnepropetrovsk *Oblast*.

The Germans executed people for sheltering Jews. This was known to the collective farm bookkeeper, Pavel Sergeyevich Zirchenko. However, he did not betray the Jews to the Germans. Jews worked on the collective farm, and on November 22, 1943, they were liberated along with all the residents of the village by the Red Army.

That is how the families of Trayberg, Nukhimovich, Babsky, Kuskovsky, Gontov, Peresedsky, and Shabis were saved — thirty people in all.

Prepared for publication by **Ilya Ehrenburg**.

The Story of F. M. Gontov

In October, 1941, I was living with my children in Yenakievo. My husband was in the Red Army. When the Germans began to approach our city, the children and I went to the Rostov *Oblast*. We lived there until June, 1942. But in June, the Germans came there too, and the village where I lived turned out to be in the middle of military activity. I went with several Jewish families to the steppe. We were able to hide the fact that we were Jews, and up until the fall, we moved from village to village in carts, under constant threat of death. By that time we were close to the village of Blagodatnoye, where one of our women had a friend, a veterinarian's assistant named G. I. Volkozub. He gave her a friendly welcome and helped us all find work and a place to live. We were given a great deal of help by a collective farm bookkeeper, P. S. Zirchenko. We told him about everything, and he, risking his life, helped us get settled.

We stayed in Blagodatnoye until the happy day when the German monsters retreated under the blows of the Red Army.

Prepared for publication by **G. Munblit**.

367

One Survived

On November 2, 1941 the Germans burst into Simferopol. All of them were clean-shaven and nicely dressed, as if they had come from a military parade, and not from nearby Perekop. These Germans were for show, for psychological effect on the Soviet people — a military unit transferred to the Crimea from behind the German lines. All shutters were closed tightly, the gates and doors in all courtyards and houses were locked. It was only toward the end of the day that fear compelled some people to come out of their homes. On street corners and in squares small groups of townspeople began to gather. Among them was 60-year-old Yevsey Yefimovich Gopstein, an old-timer and resident of Simferopol, an economist in the system of the People's Commissariat of the Municipal Economy. Gopstein's son, a pilot decorated three times, was at the front. His wife was a professor, a Russian by nationality who lived in Simferopol together with her two daughters. She had been evacuated from the Crimea back in August. She had persuaded her mother-in-law, the wife of Yevsey Yefimovich, to leave with her and her granddaughters. Old Gopstein remained in Simferopol alone, but before the arrival of the Germans, he had not felt lonely. His elderly sister, a chemist with a higher education, had remained in Simferopol working in one of the city's laboratories; and long-time friends of different nationalities were there too. Gopstein walked out into the street, depressed by the knowledge that the enemy had burst into the flourishing, fertile Crimea. He tells us:

"It was a sunny day, but the weather was not yet like in the autumn — just cool. I walked through the central streets, and took a look at Pushkin Street. There, near the theater in a bright red frame, hung the first order in three languages — Russian, Ukrainian and German. Several dozen people crowded near the order, and someone in a stentorian voice read it aloud. He read clearly, and I grasped the general sense, if not the full meaning of the order. It left a horrible, depressing impression — as if our former, Soviet life had been cut away with an axe. The population of Simferopol was multinational. People lived like brothers, in friendship. Half of the order applied to the Jews. The word "Jew" was not used in it. The word "Zhid" (kike) appeared repeatedly. It said that the filling-in of pits, the clean-up of Russian and German corpses, the collection of garbage and all kinds of sewage had to be

368

done by "Zhids." The responsibility for enlisting the Jewish population for these jobs was placed on elders who were appointed by the German command and partially elected by the population. I stopped listening and began to look into the faces of the crowd. It was mixed. There were Armenians, Tatars, Jews, and Russians there. And I am not mistaken, I remember exactly — not on one face did I see an expression of approval for the German order. People stood with their heads lowered. They listened silently and they silently walked off in different directions."

On the following days the German orders poured out on the residents of the city one after the other:

"1. Jews and Krimchaks* must report for registration. The penalty for evading the registration is execution.

"2. Jews and Krimchaks must wear identifying badges and hexagonal stars. The penalty for violation is execution.

"3. Russians, Tatars, and other inhabitants of the city must report for registration. The penalty for evading the registration is execution.

"4. After five o'clock in the evening walking in the city is forbidden. The penalty for violation is execution."

Simferopol turned into a complete torture chamber and loathsome slaughterhouse. On December 9, 1941, the Germans annihilated the oldest population of the Crimea — the Krimchaks. On December 11, 12, and 13 all the Jews were shot. The Germans had registered 14 thousands Jews in Simferopol, including about one and a half thousand Krimchaks. These were not the Jewish people who were living there before the war. During the war a large number of Jews were evacuated from Simferopol along with various institutions and enterprises, and a few left on an individual basis. In their place, however, Jews who had escaped from Kherson and Dnepropetrovsk settled there. The people from the Jewish villages of the Freidorf and Larindorf districts, as well as from Yevpatoria, rushed to Simferopol. There, in the heart of the large Jewish community, people thought they could find their salvation, but instead, they found death. The Krimchaks were massacred by the Hitlerites on November 9, and a day later they began to murder the other Jews by various methods and in many different places. Their death moan was heard for three days in a row in Simferopol and in the surrounding areas. V. Davydov, a Russian worker in the Simferopol mechanical plant, says: "I lived at

*Small group of Tatar-speaking Jews living in the Crimea.

Pushkin Street, not far from the stadium and I could see everything from the windows of my three-story building. Beginning early in the morning, thousands of Jewish families moved slowly into the square. Sanitarnaya, Gogol, Pushkin and Kooperativnaya Streets, along which the misfortunate people were herded, were cordoned off by SS men. The Germans were not certain that all the Jews had shown up, so they began to round them up in the city. They searched especially thoroughly in the Tatar district of Subri, near the cannery on Karl Marx Street. Many workers hid Jewish children and hospital patients in their own homes. Those who were caught were beaten with rifle butts and kicked by the German soldiers. By evening thousands of Jews had been herded into the area of the big city park. The park was well illuminated, music was playing. German officers and soldiers were amusing themselves. Around 10 o'clock the Germans began their monstrous slaughter. The old men were separated out into a special group — they were hanged on the balconies of nearby streets (Lenin Street, Salgyarnaya Street, Kirov Street, and Pochtovy Lane). The rest of the people were led to deep pits near the new bathhouse, where they were shot with automatic rifles. That night the world-famous Jewish psychiatrist Balaban and the Honored Actor of the Republic, the Jew Smolensky, were killed. The residents of this area told me afterwards that the Germans threw children into the pits alive, and that they cut off the breasts of young women.

Comrade Davydov finishes his story with these words: "Not a single Jew was left in Simferopol." Davydov was mistaken. One survived. Out of fourteen thousand people — one person. That was Yevsey Yefimovich Gopstein, who had listened to the first German order on Pushkin Street. Gopstein read no more of the German orders. He decided not to obey them. But it was impossible to hide from the malicious rumors which were heard everywhere. Here are five versions of these rumors:

1. The Jewish population would be sent as a covering detachment ahead of the German army which was moving against Sevastopol.

2. The Jews would be sent to work in Bessarabia.

3. They would be sent to do agricultural work in the colony of the Freidorf and Larindorf districts, where winter fields had not yet been sown.

4. All Jews would be deported to the U.S.S.R., to the front zone.

5. All Jews would be exterminated.

370

Not one Soviet person could believe the last rumor. Gopstein's sister was killed when she reported to the designated place for registration. All of his Jewish friends were shot as well — ranging from senile old men to infants. Then Russians of mixed marriages and their offspring were killed. It seemed that even the air had changed and was saturated with horror and blood. In January, 1942, mass roundups began. The Germans went from street to street, from house to house, from apartment to apartment, conducting their searches. When the registration first began, many Jews hid with relatives and friends. But in December, 1941, all the hideouts were uncovered; the people were caught like wild animals, rounded up during a hunt. Gopstein had lived for 28 years in the same house. Twenty apartments faced the courtyard. The people who lived in them were Russians, Jews, and Tatars. Not one of them betrayed Gopstein. A Russian teacher, a long-time friend of Gopstein's family, hid him in her own room in another house. He and his protectress experienced terrible days and nights. No one in the apartment knew that a Jew was hiding in the apartment of the lonely Russian teacher. When leaving, she would lock him in the apartment. And under no circumstances was Gopstein to make his presence known in the locked room — that would have been the undoing of the woman who was concealing him, as well as of himself. Once when the woman was not at home the Germans tried to open the room. The door was massive, with a strong American lock. It did not immediately give way to the blows and pushes from the outside. Suddenly Gopstein heard a dog scratching at the door. He stood perfectly still inside the room, the conversation on the other side of the door confirmed that a German officer had come with a German shepherd. It was impossible to conceal from the dog that a man was hiding behind the door, but another dog, which belonged to one of the former residents of the house, ran into the corridor. Usually the children played with it in the yard. It began to fight with the officer's German shepherd. The Germans rushed to pull them apart. Fearing for the safety of his dog, the officer pulled it back away from the door and led it out of the corridor. Next to the room where Gopstein was hiding, the Germans set up a dining room for their anti-aircraft gunners. The invaders were constantly scurrying back and forth in the corridor. The teacher had to move her boarder into the closet, and a few hours later she moved him back — to her room. At dawn, having heard a roundup beginning, the teacher led Gopstein to the closet which was crammed with cupboards, cluttered with geographical maps, suitcases and books; she locked the door and put the key in her pocket. But the owners of the house had a second key. Yevsey Yefimovich stood in the narrow space between two cupboards. When the Germans entered the closet Gopstein no longer had any fear. "I was reconciled with the thought," he says, "that this time I would not get away. I had to collect all my strength so that I could meet death with dignity, without humiliation."

But in the semi-darkness of the closet, cluttered with things, the Germans did not see the man who was hiding there. They went away, taking the key with them so that a short while later they could return there for the books. After they left, the teacher managed to seize the moment to return Gopstein to her room, which had already been searched. Other people in the house did not know that she had a second key to the closet door.

Gopstein lived in his hiding place for 23 months, until April 13, 1944. He was afraid he would lose his mind. He read, wrote. All this he had to do silently, so the neighbors did not hear him. There was hunger and cold — for the whole population in general, but for the woman who saved him, in particular. She divided up her meager supplies for two. And all they had was about 16 kilograms of flour, 24 kilograms of potatoes, a bottle of vegetable oil, a few kilograms of groats, and a started jar of lard. This jar was given to Gopstein back in the beginning of December, 1941, by a Russian carpenter he knew. At that time Yevsey Yefimovich was still going outside and one day near Feodosia Bridge he met his Russian carpenter friend. They spoke for only a short time. The Russian carpenter knew how hungry the Jews were and how difficult it was for them to live under the Germans. He simply said: "I can help you a little bit. I've slaughtered a sheep and I'll bring you a little lard." In the evening he, indeed, brought some meat and lard. He did not find Gopstein himself in the old apartment so he gave his gift, all that he was able to give, to other acquaintances to pass on to Gopstein. It was on these supplies that two people lived for three months, and then the teacher had to share her meager ration with Gopstein. That is how one of fourteen thousand Jews survived in Simferopol.

Story of **Yevsey Yefimovich Gopstein**.
Literary preparation by **Lidia Seyfullin**.

The Orthodox Priest Glagolev

On September 19, 1941, the German hordes entered Kiev. A horrible date! The following day I had to walk through Kreshchatik. This street, which I had known since I was a child, seemed ominously foreign. A doubled German guard stood outside some of the buildings (the post office and other places). I witnessed a German whipping a citizen who had dared to approach one of the buildings that was under guard.

On September 29 (i.e., nine days after the Nazi horde seized Kiev) the following order appeared in the Ukrainian language at intersections in the city, and on walls and fences: " . . . all Jews in the city of Kiev must report on September 29, beginning at eight o'clock in the morning on Dekhtyarivsky Street near the Jewish cemetery." They were to take along warm clothes, money, and valuables. The order threatened execution for any Jew who did not report and any non-Jew who dared to conceal Jews.

Terrible anxiety gripped not only the Jews, but every person who still had at least some human feelings.

Tormented by a foreboding of something horrible, people would either fall into utter despair, or, like a drowning person, they would grasp at a straw — the faint hope that the Jewish people would be taken somewhere outside the city (to the designated place, i.e., railroad tracks and stations).

The thought of violent, quick death, the death of one's relatives and close friends, but especially of little children, was so nightmarish that each person tried to drive it out of his mind. In all corners of the city one could hear the cries of agony. The horrible night gave way to an even more horrible morning. A continuous stream of tens of thousands of Jews moved slowly toward the place indicated in the order. All ages were represented in this human sea: blooming, healthy boys and girls, robust men, bent-over old men, and mothers with children, even infants.

There were professors, doctors, lawyers, office workers, artisans, and workers there. People gathered from various parts of the city. A sea of heads, tens of thousands of bundles and suitcases. The street was alive like never before, and at the same time the cold horror of death weighed heavily over everything. . . .

In the morning of September 29 my relatives started out (for the last time!). I walked with them for several blocks, and then, at their insistence, I went to find out whether my daughter and I also had to present ourselves. My husband was Russian. My relatives and I agreed that they would wait for me in one of the small public gardens near Dorogozhitskaya Street.

I went to various offices to try to get permission, as the wife of a Russian, to keep my residence in Kiev and to find out where the Jews were going. Of course, I received no "permission" and I learned nothing. The Germans everywhere told me with a threatening look: "Go to the cemetery."

I took my 10-year-old daughter to her grandmother's (my husband's mother) and took some of my belongings there as well.

That same day, September 29, around five o'clock in the afternoon, I set out for the Jewish cemetery. In the small public garden where we were supposed to meet, I found no one waiting — they had gone forever. I could not return home. I went to my husband's relatives and hid there for about a week in the storeroom, behind some firewood.

Very soon it became known that at Babi Yar, on September 29 and the days immediately following, more than 70 thousand Jews were brutally murdered.*

My relatives on my husband's side turned for help to the family of Priest Aleksey Aleksandrovich Glagolev. A. A. Glagolev was the son of a well-known professor of Hebraic studies from the Kiev Spiritual Academy, Aleksandr Aleksandrovich Glagolev, the former Father Superior of the Church of Nikola Dobry, in Podol. Professor Glagolev in his time had spoken out at Beylis's trial in his defense, trying to prove that there had been no ritual murders.

Aleksey's father went to take up my case with Professor Ogloblin, who was mayor at the time.

Ogloblin knew our family. He, in his turn, took up this question with the German commandant. Ogloblin left the commandant looking very troubled and pale. It turned out that the commandant had told him that the question of the Jews was within the exclusive authority of the Germans and they decided everything as they wished. My situation was hopeless. To hide with my husband's relatives meant to subject them to the threat of execution. Father Aleksey Glagolev's wife, Tatyana Pavlovna Glagolev, had a desperate idea — to give her passport and birth certificate of baptism to me,

*During the German occupation more than 100,000 persons, mainly Jews, were killed in Babi Yar.

374

Izabell Naumovna Yegorychev-Minkin. I was advised to go with these documents to some peasant acquaintances in a village.

Tatyana Glagolev, leaving herself without documents during such troubled times, subjected herself to great danger.

Moreover, it was necessary to replace her passport picture with my own. Fortunately, this operation was made easier by the fact that the edges of the passport had been burned and soaked with water while extinguishing a fire which had occurred in the Glagolevs' apartment. The seal on it was smudged and faded. The operation of changing the picture was successful. On the same day toward evening, with the passport and birth certificate of T. P. Glagolev, I set out for a suburb of the city — Stalinka (Demeyevka), and from there I went on to the village of Zlodievka (now called Ukrainka). I lived in the village for eight months under the name T. P. Glagolev with peasants whom I knew.

The Gestapo men who went from apartment to apartment in search of loot nearly took away T. P. Glagolev as a suspicious person without documents. It was only through the testimony of witnesses that she was saved.

As I have already said, I did not stay long in the village of Zlodievka. The local village authorities began to look at me with some suspicion. The fact is that partisans began to appear, and so any "stranger" began to seem suspicious. In the end I was summoned to the village authorities to establish my identity. Having somehow extricated myself from this trouble, I hurriedly fled to Kiev. Late in the evening of November 29 I arrived at the Glagolev home. From that time on I, and a little while later, my 10-year-old daughter, Ira, lived in the family of Father Glagolev as relatives. For two years we never left their side and wandered everywhere together with them.

We hid in the Glagolevs' apartment and in the church bell tower. Hiding was not an easy task, since I had to hide not only as a Jew, but also as a woman of an age subject to mobilization for various jobs, including being sent to Germany. I was known by quite a number of people in the city who could have given me away without even intending to do so.

In addition to my daughter and me, the Glagolevs helped several other Jews. Among them were Tatyana Davydovna Shevelev and her mother, Yevgenia Akimovna Shevelev. T. D. Shevelev, a 28-year-old woman, was the wife of a Ukrainian, D. L. Pasichny. They lived in a big house at No. 63 Saksagansky Street.

After becoming acquainted with the order of September 28, 1941, D. L. Pasichny decided that something bad was concealed in it. He locked his wife and mother-in-law in the apartment and set out to do some "intelligence work."

He showed up at the time that the Jews were supposed to report to Lukyanovka Street and he went so far in his investigation that he was detained and nearly perished himself along with the Jews (there were instances of non-Jews being killed with Jews). He barely managed to get himself out of there. It was completely obvious that for T. D. and Y. A. Shevelev to go to the cemetery meant that they would meet certain death. It would also spell their death if they stayed in his apartment. What could be done? While wandering through the city, D. L. Pasichny met a singer, M. I. Yegorychev, with whom he once worked. She recommended that he turn to Priest Glagolev for advice. Father Aleksey rummaged through all the papers of his dead father, among which were scraps of old church records. There he found several blanks which had long before been voided and had become invalid as certificates of baptism. On one of these blanks was written the birth record of the baptism of "Polina Danilovna Shevelev, born in 1913 in a Russian Orthodox family." Pasichny himself got the stamp for this certificate, having peeled it off some old document. With this document, which was highly questionable for any person competent in such matters, Polina Danilovna and her mother were secretly brought to the church estate and put up in a small house on Pokrovskaya Street, No. 6, which was under the authority of the church congregation. In all these matters Priest Glagolev received active assistance from a scholar at the Academy of Sciences, Aleksandr Grigoryevich Gorbovsky. He did not want to continue his work under the German occupation and "registered" as a manager of the church buildings of the Kiev-Podol-Pokrovskaya Church. On his "property" he hid not only Jews, but also many Russian youngsters who were threatened with being sent to Germany. He even managed to arrange for all his "tenants" to get bread tickets.

In order to escape from going to Germany, a number of people received certificates stating that they were choir boys, church officers, sextons, etc. If the Germans had figured out that at so small and poor a church there was such an enormous staff, the authors of those certificates would have been made to pay.

Pasichny's family, whom I have mentioned, hid in a small church building for approximately 10 months.

The Glagolev family expended a great deal of effort to save the family of Nikolay Georgievich Germayze. This family of Jewish descent was baptized back in pre-revolutionary times. According to their passports they were all Ukrainians. N. G. Germayze was a teacher of mathematics. His wife, Lyudmila Borisovna, was a housewife. Their adopted son, Yura, an exceptionally gifted, active 17-year-old, was a student at a pedagogical institute. If, by outward appearance, Yura could be taken for a Ukrainian, his parents had clearly recognizable Semitic features. And that was their undoing.

A few days after the events at Babi Yar it was announced that every man had to be registered. Yura went to the registration too. At the registration his surname drew attention. He was asked whether he was not of German descent. The boy's answer seemed unsatisfactory, and he was asked to summon his father. The appearance of the father instantly aroused suspicion and in the end, after a terrible beating, both the father and son were taken to the cemetery. Yura's comrade, who knew the Glagolevs, told them about everything when Yura was sent to get his father. The Glagolevs rushed to the school where Germayze taught, in order to get witnesses who could testify that Germayze was not a Jew. But before they could get the necessary papers, the tragedy had already taken place.

They had to at least try to save Lyudmila Borisovna. Her documents were lost along with husband and son. The unhappy, broken-hearted wife and mother (they very much loved their adopted son) endured some very painful times. The Glagolevs visited her all the time, although before this they had not even known the Germayze family. Once Lyudmila Borisovna's neighbors brought the terrible piece of news that she had been arrested and taken to the Gestapo, as a Jew. Tatyana Glagolev rushed to the Gestapo with a letter from Father Aleksey saying that Lyudmila Germayze was not a Jew, but she was received very sternly and was turned away without any results. Later it became known that the Germans starved Lyudmila Borisovna for five days, and on the sixth day, along with the other Jews who had been arrested throughout the city, they were getting ready to take her to Babi Yar. Among those arrested there were even children whom Russian relatives and neighbors had tried in vain to hide in their own homes.

Lyudmila Germayze was left with the Gestapo, and after a while an investigator went to Tatyana Glagolev to question her regarding Germayze's nationality — was she Ukrainian or not. Tatyana Glagolev was forced to sign a statement that said her testimony was truthful, and that in the event that Germayze proved to be Jewish, Glagolev would be shot along with Germayze. Tatyana Glagolev declared that she had known Germayze's family for a long time as parishioners of the church where her father and husband worked, and that there could be no room for doubt about Germayze's nationality. After that, Germayze was released.

A new blow awaited Lyudmila Borisovna at home. She found out that her 70-year-old mother had been found by the Germans and sent to Babi Yar. Three months later poor Lyudmila Borisovna was again taken to the Gestapo, where she perished.

In the fall of 1942 and the winter of 1942/43 I lived with the Glagolev family in villages on the other side of the Dnieper — first in the village of Tarasevichi, and later in the village of Nizhnyaya Dubechnya. By that time, i.e., beginning in the fall of 1942, beyond the Dnieper, especially in the wooded regions, partisan activity began to intensify. The partisans appeared during the night, and sometimes even in the middle of the day. They made short work of the oppressors and their lackey-policemen.

Since the Germans were unable to deal with the armed partisan force, they chose another path of struggle. They sent their punitive units to the villages which had "committed offenses" and these units would burn the villages, shoot, hang, and burn the peaceful inhabitants. Flourishing villages were completely reduced to ashes. That is how many villages near Kiev were burned: Piski, Novaya Visan, Novoselitsa, and later Oshitki, Dnieprovskie Novoselki, Zhukin, Chernin, and others. This wave rolled as far as Nizhnyaya Dubechnya, where we lived. Once the Glagolevs were summoned to the village authorities to have their passports inspected. There they were rudely informed in Ukrainian that the father, mother, and the children, as well as the deacon would be allowed to remain for the time being, but "the relatives and the girl (i.e., I and my daughter Ira) have nothing to do here, let them go to Kiev to work."

With considerable difficulty my daughter and I made it to the city and again found room in the bell tower of Pokrov Church. This was January 10, and by the end of the month Father Aleksey's whole family returned to Kiev. He himself stayed in Nizhnyaya Dubechnya. On January 31 a punitive unit arrived in the village to carry out reprisals for the fact that a partisan unit had passed through Nizhnyaya Dubechnya the night before. The Hitlerites caroused with the police throughout the night, and at dawn they committed monstrous atrocities. In one hut they locked three men, one woman, and a five-year-old boy, soaked the structure with kerosene, and set it on fire.

When he learned of what had happened, Priest Glagolev hurried to the place of the massacre, but except for the site of the fire and several weeping children, there was no one there. The following day (it was Sunday) he announced in church that after the usual service he would conduct a requiem for the innocent victims.

Two days later Father Aleksey buried the charred human remains in the cemetery. After that it was impossible for Father Aleksey to remain in the village, so he returned to his church in the city.

All this time I had been receiving certificates stating that I worked in the church as a maid and that I was financially supporting a young daughter. Bread cards were obtained for me. At that time all kinds of inspectors were searching for people, hunting up victims to be used for hard labor by the Germans. Fortunately, these inspectors never penetrated our "quiet cloister." The certificates that I mentioned, as well as the skillful maneuvering of A. G. Gorbovsky, saved us.

In the fall of 1943, when as a result of the approach of the Red Army, the Germans announced the evacuation of Podol, we all firmly decided to sit snug in Father Aleksey's apartment.

Ten days after Podol (part of Kiev) was declared a "restricted area," German gendarmes burst into our home and dragged out all of us, half undressed, to a nearby park, and then herded us to Lukyanovka, where people were still allowed to live. After that we moved from where we were staying three times, still not wanting to leave Kiev. The last place we stayed was in a church basement at the Pokrov women's monastery (Artem Street). From there the gendarmes herded us to a concentration camp on Lvov Street (a former military registration and enlistment office). Afterwards, having divided the men from the women, they herded us to the railroad station. In the process Father Aleksey's family got separated from us, and we lost track of each other.

My daughter and I, as well as A. G. Gorbovsky, his mother, and many other people were transported in closed traincars to Kazatin, where we were released (this was purely accidental). We were in

Kazatin when the Red Army arrived, and then we returned to Kiev. There we learned that Father Aleksey's family was in Kiev, but that he himself was very seriously ill. He had been severely beaten by the Germans for not wishing to leave Kiev. After that he became ill with a concussion of the brain and lay in the hospital for a long time.

All of us who were saved by Glagolev will forever be grateful to him.

The arrival of the Red Army returned us to life. It-was difficult to believe that we were once again freely living, feeling, walking.

Information supplied by **I. Minkin-Yegorychev**.

Prepared for publication by **R. Kovnator**.

The Catholic Priest Bronius Paukstis

Paukstis, a tall, stocky man about 40 years old, invited us to his study — the study of the oldest parish of the "Trinity" in Kaunas — and told us various details of his activity in helping to free and rescue the Jews during the time of the German occupation.

Paukstis established contact with a certain monk named Broliukas,* who supplied passports to save the Jews. Paukstis would often have to pay 500 marks from his own resources as the cost of obtaining a false passport.

As a priest, Paukstis himself wrote out birth certificates for children who had been abducted and rescued from the ghetto, and he personally helped to locate places for them to live. After he had found a home for the fourth Jewish girl, Vizgardiskaya, whom he had rescued, he was told that the Gestapo was interested in him. . . .

"What was there left for me to do?" says Paukstis. "I got on a train, and having said upon arriving that I was going to visit my colleague-priests, I went to see some peasants with whom I had found homes for my little Jewish 'daughters.' Thinking that I was traveling around to my various colleagues, the Gestapo was no longer suspicious of me."

In all, Paukstis gave out a hundred and twenty birth certificates to Jewish children.

But it was not only the children whom Paukstis helped. Twenty-five adults were hiding in his church. Among the people he saved or helped to save, we can mention Doctor Taft, lawyer Levitan, the daughters of the head of the Slobodsky Yeshiva, Grodzensky, Rachel Rozentsveyg, Kisenisky, lawyer Avram Golub and his family, Kapit, and others.

When someone he had saved fell into the hands of the authorities, Paukstis looked for ways to buy off the Gestapo and sometimes he was able to do so.

"You think," says Father Paukstis, "that I helped a great deal, but I think with sadness of how much more I could have done if I had been endowed with a greater understanding of concrete matters."

Paukstis showed us a letter from a Jewish girl, Rachel

---

*"Broliukas" is a Lithuanian nickname meaning "little brother." The real name is Bronius Gotautas. B. Gotautas died in a home for the aged in West Germany in 1973. S. Bindiene, *Ir be ginklo kariai*, "Mintis," Vilnius, 1967, p. 163 ("Warriors Even Without Weapons").

Rozentsveyg, whom he helped save and who is now attending Kaunas University.

The letter was written in Lithuanian. I'll translate a few of the beginning lines:

"Dear Father! Allow me to address you this way. Didn't you treat me the way a father would treat a daughter? Didn't you give me shelter when I came to you, so unhappy, after I had endured so much? Without questioning me or demanding anything of me, as if it were completely natural, you said: 'You will calm down here, my child, and you will stay with me a while. . . .'"

The letter was quite long. It is written with love and respect, and its entire content testifies to the fact that in the terrible conditions of the Nazi occupation in Soviet Lithuania there were kind, honest people who fulfilled their human duty calmly, as if this were only natural.

Author: **Girsh Osherovich**.

Translated from the Yiddish by **M. A. Shambadal**.

CAMPS OF DESTRUCTION

In the Khorol Camp

My name is Abram Reznichenko, and I am an artist. During the German occupation I hid under the name Arkady Ilyich Rezenko, a driver and native of the Kustanay *Oblast*.

During the retreat, in the fall of 1941, we were surrounded on the left bank of the Dnieper.

Wounded, separated from my own people, I wandered around Piryatin and for two weeks roamed through the woods, hiding in ravines. I was afraid to go into the city. Exhausted, hungry, weak, and infested with lice, I finally fell into the hands of the Germans. They imprisoned me in the Khorol camp.

Sixty thousand people languished in this small area fenced in by barbed wire. There were people there of all ages and professions — soldiers and civilians, old people and children of many nationalities.

For as long as I can remember, I have lived in the Soviet State. Of course, as a Soviet citizen, I never had to hide the fact that I was a Jew.

Early in October, 1941, in full view of many prisoners of war, a German soldier whipped a completely innocent man across the face and shouted at his bleeding victim: "You're going to die, Jew!" Then we were all lined up and this soldier, speaking through an interpreter, ordered all the Jews to step forward.

Thousands of people stood silently, no one budged.

The interpreter, a German from the Volga region, walked between the rows of people, carefully examining their faces.

"Jews, come forward," he said, "nothing will happen to you."

A few people took him at his word.

No sooner had they stepped forward than they were surrounded by a guard detachment and led off beyond some hills. We soon heard a volley of gun fire.

After the murder of these first victims, the camp commandant, the terror of Khorol, appeared before us.

The commandant addressed us:

"Prisoners of war," he said, "the war is over at last. A line of demarcation has been established. It runs along the ridge of the Ural mountains. . . . On one side of the ridge is mighty Germany, on the other side is mighty Japan. The Jewish commissars, as might have been expected, have run to America. But we Germans will find them, even in America. By the will of the Führer, you prisoners of war will be sent home tomorrow. First we will release Ukrainians, then Russians and Byelorussians."

In the Khorol camp, on the premises of a defunct brick factory, there was only one barracks, which was half-rotten and rested on posts that sank to one side. It was the only place to take cover, even partially, from the autumn rain and frost.

A few of us, sixty thousand prisoners, managed to cram in there. Once I made my way inside.

In the barracks the prisoners stood closely pressed against one another. They were gasping from the stench and the evaporation, steeped in perspiration. It took me only a minute to realize that it was better to go back out into the rain, better to grow numb in the autumn wind than to remain there. But how was I going to get out? Shouting, I started to climb over the backs and shoulders of those who stood in the direction of the only exit. I was pushed and thrown off to the side. With blind persistence, I crawled and crawled forward toward the others who wanted, no matter what, to get into the barracks. . . .

At five o'clock in the morning we were awakened for breakfast. Thousands of people immediately lined up in rows. The putrid liquid swill (in comparison with it the thin camp soup seemed tasty) was given out slowly. As a result, many had to eat "breakfast" late at night.

Almost every day, and sometimes several times a day, the camp commandant came to watch the food being dispensed. He would spur his horse and cut into the line. Many people were killed under the hooves of his horse.

Standing near the barrels filled with the hot swill were the German cooks, the Gestapos and their faithful assistants — the *folksdeutsche*.

"Jew?"

"No, no!"

"Kike."

And the poor man was pushed out of line.

Once a half-naked, shivering, dirty man covered with scabs, whom the Gestapo had found guilty of being a Jew, was lifted above the heads of the crowd, swung to and fro, and thrown head first into a barrel filled with hot swill.

They held him for several minutes by his legs. Then, when the poor soul had become still, the cooks overturned the barrel.

New groups of captured Jews were often brought to the Khorol camp. They were brought under heavy guard, and on their arms and backs were sewn identifying badges — hexagonal stars. Jews were persecuted throughout the whole camp, they were sent to do the most degrading jobs, and at the end of the day, before everyone's eyes, they were slaughtered.

There were various methods of execution in the Khorol camp. The Germans didn't confine themselves to shootings and hangings. They would set German shepherd dogs on the Jews. The dogs would chase the people, who ran in all directions, lunge at them, rip their throats open, and drag dead or near-dead victims to the commandant's feet. . . .

A soldier walked up to a young Jewish doctor, shouted *Jude*, and shot him point-blank. Bleeding profusely, the doctor fell; the bullet had shattered his jaw. The Germans picked him up, and holding him by his arms and legs, threw him into a pit. They began to fill in the pit on the spot. The doctor was still breathing, and the earth above his body stirred.

A dysentery epidemic broke out in camp. Thousands died each day.

The most fortunate among us were the ones who still had a pot to eat from; it could be loaned to someone else for a portion of the daily ration. People who didn't have a pot had to hold out an army cap or field shirt to the cook. . . .

People from neighboring villages tried to get some food to the prisoners. Once a wife brought a man from Zolotonosha a small bag of produce. She managed to throw this small bag over the wire fence. People clustered around the lucky man. He looked with frightened eyes at the people gathered around him.

"Brothers, people, there are thousands of you and only one of me," he whispered. "And I have only one small bag. . . . How could I possibly feed you with it?"

And he clenched a loaf of bread in his hands and pressed it to himself like a baby.

Three and a half months I spent in this camp; December was already coming to an end.

From time to time village elders from one area or another came to the Khorol camp. They came to arrange with the camp administration for the release of their fellow-villagers.

I watched with envy how they selected people: no one would be coming for me. I watched how these lucky people acted. One day when Lokhvitsa residents were called for I decided to test fate.

"Who is from Lokhvitsa?" the elder shouted. "Lokhvitsa residents, show yourselves!"

Some fellow responded, then two more walked up to the elder. And then I decided to be the fourth.

I was lucky: the elder "recognized" me as his fellow villager.

That is the way I got out of the camp at Khorol.

We went on foot to Lokhvitsa. It was a cold December. It was painfully difficult for me to walk because of a festering wound on my leg. But, still I walked. I was afraid to get separated from my "people," the residents of Lokhvitsa.

On the second day I came down with dysentery.

I stayed behind alone in the snow. Several hours passed. I got up, and began to drag myself along. By evening I reached a village and knocked on the door of a large hut. It turned out to be a school. I was given refuge and permitted to stay the night.

I lived there with a watchman's wife. I ate and warmed myself up. However, I couldn't stay with her for long. I didn't have any documents, and I could be spotted for a Jew. . . .

I decided to go to my native city of Kremenchug.

On the way to Kremenchug I stopped at the village of Pirogi and spent the night at the hut of a peasant woman from the village. I told her I was a prisoner of war, that I had been released from the camp, and she took me in.

In the morning a German suddenly burst into the hut. In the split second before he stepped across the threshold, my new friends — the housewife and her children — hid me on the stove.

The German acted as if he were the master in the hut. He sat at the table, gave orders, and ate everything that the woman had prepared for herself and her children.

Finally, he left and I continued on my way.

After a long, agonizing journey, I finally arrived in Kremenchug, and checked into the city hospital. My wounded leg was still festering.

I saw a lot of suffering in the Kremenchug hospital. I saw a gassing truck which carried off the sick and wounded Jews. I saw the death of Doctor Makson, a prominent specialist respected by everyone, an affectionate, sensitive, old man. In spite of his age, the doctor had continued to work in the hospital. He had remained at his post in the ward beside the hospital beds.

One day a German patrol appeared in the hospital building.

"Makson — the Jew. Give us this Jew."

Thousands of people from Kremenchug petitioned for Doctor Makson's release. The Germans gave in. The eighty-year-old man left the commandant's office surrounded by people and went home. The following morning the Germans broke into Makson's apartment, threw the old man into a cart, took him somewhere outside the city, and shot him. One of the patients, a shoemaker, heard about Makson's fate and tried to escape.

The shoemaker was caught, beaten unmercifully, tied up, and taken back to the hospital. During the night, he took a razor and slit his own throat.

In the morning a Gestapo man came over to the bed of the shoemaker, who was in agony. The Gestapo man put on a doctor's smock and white cap.

"Poor fellow," he said, sitting down on the edge of the bed.

"Look what your fear has led you to do."

He patted the shoemaker and repeated: "Poor man, poor thing."

Suddenly the German jumped up, raised his arm and punched the shoemaker in the face.

"You Jew! Jew! Jew!"

The shoemaker was shot outside the hospital gates. He was shot by the same Gestapo man; he didn't even . . .*

*At this point the text breaks off.

Report of **A. Reznichenko**
Prepared for publication by **Vasily Grossman**

The Camp in Klooga

(Estonia)

Editor's Note

The Red Army occupied the Estonian town of Klooga with such a swift attack that the bonfires of Jewish corpses shot by the Germans were still ablaze. The Germans didn't even have time to ignite one of the fires. Foreign correspondents who were there with the advance military units saw these fires. Their descriptions and photographs spread all over the world.

The speed of the Soviet offensive took the Germans by surprise. Otherwise they surely would have done away with their prisoners earlier and would have destroyed all traces of the shootings. But the surprise saved the lives of at least a few dozen prisoners in the camp. These fortunate few managed to hide and the Germans were not able to hunt them down.

The stories of a few survivors appear below.

* * *

Weintraub, a student of Vilnius University:

I was in the Vilnius ghetto. On September 23, 1943, we were awakened and ordered to prepare for evacuation. At five o'clock in the morning we were lined up in fives and under guard of a large detachment of storm troopers were led out of the ghetto. Near the fence of the ghetto stood forty to fifty people with their faces to the wall. These were people selected for execution. Why these particular people were singled out, I don't know.

We were taken to the area of Suboch (four kilometers from the ghetto). The ghetto, as well as the whole way to it, was under heavy guard by storm troopers.

In Suboch we were separated from the women and children. We found out later that the women and children were sent to Majdanek.

This "sorting" continued until ten o'clock in the morning. While this operation was going on, the Germans summoned Plaevsky. He wasn't there; he was hiding in the ghetto. Then Levin was summoned. He worked in Plaevsky's group. Levin, as well as Khvoynik, Bik, and Kaplan, the teacher, were taken away. Later we found that they were shot.

It wasn't until 16:00 o'clock that we were put into the heated boxcars. The windows and exits were enclosed with barbed wire.

The boxcars were locked, and the train, guarded by storm troopers, started off.

We took four days to arrive at the Vaivara camp. From there we were sent to the camp at Klooga.

At that time, there were four hundred men and one hundred fifty women there.

The first thing they did was search us. They took anything that had any value. A storm trooper found twenty rubles in Soviet currency on one of the prisoners and shot him on the spot.

We were put up in a demolished barracks and had to sleep on a cement floor. They divided us up into brigades and sent us to do various jobs. While on a job we answered to members of the organization, *Todt*. In the camp we were ordered about by the SS storm troopers. Both groups treated us the same way.

I belonged to a group of three hundred men who had to carry fifty-kilogram cement bags from the factory to the station (one hundred fifty meters).

We "porters" were followed by overseers. Anyone who did not show enough zeal was clubbed on the head by these overseers. As a result, we could not walk, but had to run with these heavy bags.

The other men worked at the cement factory, at the sawmill, in the mines and factory shops. The women worked in the quarries. They carried huge rocks from one place to another. They had to meet a quota of four tons a day.

Our daily routine was as follows: we got up at five o'clock in the morning, drank some tasteless coffee ersatz, went out for *Appell* (roll call); at six o'clock we began work; from 12:00 to 12:45 we ate lunch and then worked again until 18:00, after which followed the evening *Appell*. Lunch consisted of watery soup. There was no dinner.

During *Appell* we lined up in rows of one hundred people and had to wait until the overseer sent us to work or, in the evening, to the camp. Sometimes we had to stand for hours. Those who didn't stand at attention were punished.

Each group of one hundred people had its own torturer. Karel, Dybovsky, and particularly Steinberger, used unrestrained violence. Steinberger would club people or smash them on the head with a shovel. Dybovsky once broke the leg of a worker named Levi. Moreover, there was an *Obergruppenführer* in the camp, whose name I don't remember, but whom the prisoners called "Six-legs." He always had a huge wolf-hound with him, who would catch "criminals" — people who hid bread or sat down to rest for a minute. The dog would pounce on a "criminal," tear his clothes, bite him, and often cause severe wounds. Then "Six-legs" himself would give the "offender" twenty-five lashes with his whip.

There was another overseer named Daup. For no reason at all he shot Weinstein.

Bowing caused us a lot of grief. There was a standing order that Jews did not have the right to bow to Germans. However, when we did not bow, we were beaten for "rudeness." And when we did bow, we were beaten for "disobeying an order."

We were deprived of our names; everyone received a number which was attached to our clothes on the shoulder and knee. When an offense was committed, a German would write down this number, and during *Appell*, he would summon the offender for a beating.

They had a curved bench one meter long. They would tie an offender to it by his arms and legs. One of the butchers would sit on his head while another beat him. The offender had to count the lashes himself. If he lost count, the punishment would start again from the beginning. If he lost consciousness, he was doused with water, and the flogging continued. First he was beaten with a birch branch, then with a bull's penis which had steel wire drawn through it. The punishment was administered in front of all the prisoners.

There were other forms of punishment as well. People were tied to a tree and left in the sun or in the cold for several hours, without food, etc. The work was strenuous, the living conditions difficult and since we received nothing except coffee ersatz, watery soup and three hundred-forty grams of bread mixed with a touch of sand, many people became ill. Their stomachs swelled, and they grew weak and ended up in the hospital. The number of sick people grew with each day. But the Germans got rid of the severely ill by a simple method: they were poisoned and then cremated. No medical aid was administered.

The senior "sanitation officer" was Doctor Wodman. He was the one who decided who had to be poisoned, and he himself prepared the poison and prescribed it to a patient. Whenever he appeared before the patients, he would shout "*Achtung!*" (Attention). All the patients immediately had to fold their hands on top of their blankets. Those who were slow about it were beaten by the doctor with a stick.

We secretly organized evening get-togethers. The performers,

Blyakher, Rothstein, Rosenthal, Tumarkin, Fin, Poznansky, Motek, Krengel and others participated in them. We had discussions about the political situation, about the situation at the fronts, etc. In defiance of all the rules, we managed to get our hands on some newspapers and would discuss them. To find any grains of truth in the German newspapers, one had to be pretty sharp. We even had a circle of partisans. We secretly learned how to shoot in a cellar.

The women were kept separate from us. Their situation was even worse than ours. They did work that was beyond their physical strength and capabilities. They were whipped more often and were generally punished more frequently than the men. One of them tried to escape, but it was impossible to get away. The camp was too well guarded, and she was caught. It wasn't enough that they beat her unmercifully. The poor woman was forced to wear a sign on her chest that read: "Hurrah! Hurrah! I'm here again!"

Several children were born in the camp. By order of the camp commandant they were thrown into a furnace.

In August, 1944, most of the Estonian camps were liquidated, including Kivioli, Ereda, Ponar (Ponary) and Filipoki. We found out about this from the labels on the cement bags brought from those camps. That was the way prisoners corresponded with one another.

We knew that the Red Army was approaching and waited for it with bated breath. On the morning of September 19th, we were led out into a square where roll was being taken. The men were arranged in separate formation from the women. They called the names of three hundred of the healthiest men and announced that everyone was to be evacuated, but that these men were needed to carry firewood out of the camp. In light of the approach of the Red Army and the evacuation of other camps, all this seemed plausible to us. Moreover, the Germans gave an order for lunch to be prepared for everyone, including the three hundred men sent to carry the wood.

But at 13:30 we heard shots. At first we thought that these were Estonians having shooting practice, as they had done many times before. Soon, however, thirty armed Estonians showed up in the camp, selected thirty people, and took them away. Later, when we heard shots again, we realized that everyone would be killed. Many people began to flee. I hid in a cellar with about twenty others. A little while later we heard the Germans saying to each other: "Hurry up, hurry up! The Soviets are close by."

A few days later we heard above us the voices of Red Army soldiers. . . .

Anolik:

All together, there were twenty-three camps in Estonia. About twenty thousand people were held in them, half of whom were from Lithuania. The majority of the camps were located in eastern Estonia. There was a concentration camp in Vaivari. It was there that all the people from the different ghettos were sent, and it was there that people were assigned to other camps.

The camp at Klooga was surrounded by two rows of barbed wire. Between the rows were large balls of woven barbed wire. Along the fence stood tall towers from which the sentries watched us day and night.

Everyone was shaved. The women were shaved bald; a strip of hair five centimeters (two inches) wide was left on the men.

We were allowed only one shirt. If anyone was found wearing a second, he was whipped. If any amount of bread exceeding the regular ration was found on someone, they would punish all the prisoners in the cell. After April 1, we had to turn in our outer clothing and work without coats. We also had to stand for hours at *Appell* without the benefit of coats.

In some camps it was even worse. At Pifikoni the camp was illuminated by strong reflectors. Prisoners there huddled together in barracks that were built on a swamp. To reach this camp on foot, it was necessary to walk knee-deep through water. There was a special form of punishment in this camp: overseers would tie up prisoners and throw them in the swamp for several hours. Several people at Pifikoni were whipped to death. And in the Vaivara camp, of one thousand prisoners, six hundred died in a very short time.

In December 1943, a typhus epidemic broke out in the camps, and an enormous number of people died. Those who began to recover were sent back to work after only fourteen days. Of course, they could not withstand the work; they would collapse and then be shot. And then the Germans began to burn the corpses of the dead and the murdered in big bonfires.

At the camp at Kivioli prisoners worked in slate pits. In Zrite there was a camp for the sick. That's where I was. On February 1, 1944, the camp was evacuated. The sick had to walk one hundred eighty kilometers. Twenty-three people were so weak that they could not walk. The doctor who accompanied us ordered us to throw these people into the sea. This was near Evi. We flatly refused to carry out the order. So the SS men and the doctor himself threw these poor people into the sea.

In July, 1944, all the old men and the sick at the Kivioli camp were exterminated. This was called an "aktion." During this aktion, two Vilnius doctors, Volkovsky and Rudik, were killed. In July the camp at Laedi was evacuated, but the elderly and the sick were shot beforehand. The women had their dresses taken from them and were led off half-naked.

It wasn't until May, 1944, that I landed in Klooga, and, as a result, I didn't spend much time there. When the extermination of the prisoners began, I hid in the barracks and lay there under the blankets. I didn't move for five days until the Red Army arrived.

A. Yerushalmi:

As a former member of the *Judenrat* of Shavli (Shaulyai) ghetto, I can relate the following facts. In early February, 1944, a train passed through Shavli with women, children, and disabled people from Estonia. Throughout the trip (five days in Shavli alone), they were transported without food and water in sealed boxcars wrapped in barbed wire. In the train was a seventeen-year-old named Beker. He was suffering from typhus, but as soon as his temperature dropped, he was sent to work sixteen kilometers from the camp. His hands became frostbitten, he caught a cold in his kidneys, and he became an invalid — which is why he ended up in the train. At the station in Meshkuychay, he got permission from a convoy guard to get out of the boxcar for a drink of water. In the meantime the train left, and he was arrested.

Since he could hardly walk, he was sent to our ghetto and locked up with others who had been arrested. The commandant of our ghetto, *Obersturmführer* Schlef, asked Gekke, the man in charge of all the Jewish camps, what to do and Gekke issued an order: *Sonderkommando*. This meant that Beker had to be handed over to the *Sonderkommando*, which consisted of Estonians responsible for the extermination of the Jews. The *Judenrat* found out about this and tried to get permission from Schlef to poison Beker right in the ghetto. Schlef agreed and Beker was taken to the hospital, where for a whole month the execution of the sentence was delayed under all sorts of pretexts. Meanwhile, someone in the ghetto died and he was registered in the hospital records under the name of Beker.

Beker was then sent under the name of the dead man to another camp. We found out later that the train which had left Beker behind, had gone to Majdanek.

Vatsnik:

I was among the 301 people whom the Germans first led out of the camp to be shot, under the pretext of being used for gathering firewood. We put the wood on carts, and the carts were taken away. When the last cart had left, we were ordered to lie down on the ground. We lay there until 16:30. Then we were led back to the barracks. Armed Estonians were lined up along the way. We were ordered to walk "with our heads lowered" and with our hands behind our backs. They stopped us near one of the barracks. An Estonian walked up to me and ordered me to walk ahead to the barracks. I knew that death awaited me, and I began to tremble as I stepped through the barracks doorway. A German asked me very affectionately: "Why are you trembling, boy?" And in that very same second he shot me two times, in the neck and in the back. One bullet went right through me, the other lodged in my body. But I didn't lose consciousness. I fell and pretended I was dead. I heard the German walk out of the barracks and I wanted to get up. But at that moment the Germans brought in two more prisoners. Once again I pretended to be dead. The two were laid on top of me and shot. Then they brought in more and more prisoners, put them into one pile and shot them. They brought in a child. I heard him cry "Mama," and at that very moment a shot rang out. The dying people moaned and wheezed. Finally, the shots ceased.

I started to pull myself out from under the corpses. I was able to do so only with great effort. I had to step on the corpses in order to get to the door. Suddenly I noticed that my friend Lipengolts was still alive. I helped him to his feet. Jankel Libman was also alive. He said "Help me to stretch out my legs." We stretched him out, but he didn't have any strength left. We were both wounded. Libman soon became still. . . .

We smelled gasoline, and rushed to the doors and windows — they were nailed shut. I struck the window with all my might, broke it, and jumped out with Lipengolts behind me. We fell on the grass, jumped up and took to our heels. Without realizing it, we started to run toward the bonfires where the Germans were burning corpses. They fired at us, but we ran without turning our heads and fortunately, the bullets didn't reach us. We ran seven kilometers to a camp for Russian prisoners. The prisoners hid us in the hospital, and we waited there for the Red Army.

Anolik, Benjamin junior:

We were the first to see the captain of the Red Army. We asked for permission to touch him, because we just couldn't believe that we were free, that before us were Red Army soldiers. The captain embraced us and congratulated us on our liberation. And we, we just cried. And each of us wanted to touch the star on the captain's cap.

We led our liberators around the camp. There was the bench where they flogged us. The bloodied whip made out of a bull's penis lay on the ground. There were the trees they tied us to. And here was the block where the people lived. The captain took out his handkerchief; he could smell the corpses which the Germans had not had time to burn. There lay a dead three-month-old infant, its hands stretched toward its dead mother. I looked at the captain. Tears were streaming from his eyes, and he did not hide them. On his chest were medals and decorations for wounds he had received. He was Russian. He knew what death and suffering were. He kept crying. His tears meant more to us than anything on earth. . . .

And here stood an eight-room house that had been jammed with prisoners. All that was left of it were two chimney flues and piles of charred bones. And here were the bonfires. There were dresses, skirts and other things scattered around them. Three of the four fires still gave off smoke from the smoldering corpses. The Germans had not had time to ignite one of the fires. A layer of wood, a layer of corpses, a layer of wood, a layer of corpses. . . . When dying, the men covered their eyes with their caps, the women — with their hands. Here were two people in an embrace: they were brothers. And there was one fire with no corpses, just wood. This one had been prepared for us. If the Red Army had arrived a few days later, we survivors would probably be lying here burning. Miraculously, eighty-two of us survived.

But there were 2,500 in the fires. . . .

We begged the captain: "Take us with you! Take us into the army! We must have revenge."

Once again there were tears in the captain's eyes. "You are all sick," he said. "Wait. You have got to rest. We will take revenge for you. We'll go to Berlin and there we'll settle up with the Germans for you."

But one of our number joined the army right on the spot. He was healthier than the others. He was a poet whose name is familiar to every Jew: Beylis. He had the same surname as the Beylis, whom the tsarist authorities once put on trial as a suspect in a ritual murder, but who was later acquitted. The captain tried to persuade him to rest up and wait, too. But he pointed to the star on the captain's cap and said: "This is my only rest." And then he pointed to the west: "This is my only path." And then to the Red Army soldiers: "These are my brothers."

Prepared for publication by **O. Savich**

Treblinka

I

The terrain to the east of Warsaw along the Western Bug is an expanse of alternating sands and swamps interspersed with evergreen and deciduous forests. The landscape is dreary, and villages are rare. The narrow, sandy roads where wheels sink up to the axles and walking is difficult, are something for the traveler to avoid.

In the midst of this desolate country stands the small out-of-the-way station of Treblinka on the Siedlce railway branch line. It is some sixty kilometers from Warsaw and not far from the Małkinia station where lines leading to Warsaw, Bialystok, Siedlce and Lomza meet.

Many of those who were brought to Treblinka in 1942 may have had occasion to travel this way before the war. Staring out over the desolate landscape of pines, sand, more sand and again pines, scrubland, heather, unattractive station buildings and railway crossings, the prewar passenger might have allowed his bored gaze to pause for a moment on a single-track spur running for Treblinka station into the forest to disappear amid the pine thickets. This spur led to a pit where white sand was extracted for industrial purposes and urban construction.

The sand pit is situated about four kilometers from the station on an open stretch of country surrounded on all sides by pine woods. The soil here is miserly and sterile, and the peasants do not cultivate it. And so, the land is bare but for a few patches of moss and an occasional sickly pine. Now and then a jack-daw or a bright-combed hoopoe wings past.

This is the spot Heinrich Himmler, the SS *Reichsführer*, selected and approved for the site of a slaughterhouse the like of which the human race has not known from the age of primitive barbarism to these cruel days of ours.

There were two camps in Treblinka: labor camp No. 1 where prisoners of various nationalities, chiefly Poles, worked, and camp No. 2 for Jews.

Camp No. 1, of the labor or punitive type, was located in the immediate vicinity of the sand pits not far from the woods. It was

399

one of the hundreds and thousands of similar camps the Hitlerites had set up in the occupied countries of Eastern Europe. It came into being in 1941.

The thrift, accuracy, practicality and pedantic cleanliness common to many Germans are not bad traits in themselves. Applied to agriculture or to industry they produce laudable results. Hitlerism applied these traits to crime against mankind and the Reich's SS behaved in the Polish labor camp exactly as though they were raising cauliflower or potatoes.

The area of the camp was laid out in neat rectangles; the barracks stood in neat rows, the paths were lined with birches and covered with sand. There were concrete ponds for domestic fowl, pools for washing laundry with steps leading conveniently down, various services for the German personnel — a modern bakery, barbershop, garage, a gasoline-filling station, warehouses. Built on approximately the same principle — with the gardens, the drinking fountains, the concrete paths — was the Lublin camp at Majdanek and dozens of other labor camps in East-Poland where the Gestapo and the SS intended to settle for a long time. German accuracy, petty calculation, the pedantic fondness for orderliness, the German love for timetables and charts, for ticketing and docketing every detail were reflected in the layout of these camps.

People were brought to the labor camp for brief periods, sometimes no more than four, five or six months. They were Poles who had violated laws laid down by the governor-generalship — minor violations, as a rule, for the penalty for major violations was immediate death. A denunciation, a slip of the tongue, a chance word overheard on the street, failure to make some delivery, refusal to give a cart or a horse to a German, the harsh word of a girl declining the amorous advances of some SS man, not sabotage at factories but mere suspicion of the possibility of sabotage — these were the offenses that brought hundreds and thousands of Polish workers, peasants and intellectuals, men and girls, mothers of families, old people and juveniles, to this penal camp. Altogether about 50,000 people passed through its gates. Jews were sent there only if they happened to be skilled workers in their field — bakers, shoemakers, carpenters, stone-masons or tailors. The camp had all manner of workshops, including a substantial furniture factory which supplied armchairs, tables and chairs to German army headquarters.

Camp No. 1 existed from the autumn of 1941 until July 23rd,

1944. It was completely destroyed when the prisoners already heard the distant roll of the Soviet guns.

Early in the morning on July 23rd, the guards and SS men took a stiff drink and set to work to wipe all trace of the camp off the map. By evening all the inmates had been killed and buried. Only one man survived — Max Levit, a Warsaw carpenter, who was only wounded and lay beneath the bodies of his comrades until nightfall when he crawled off into the forest. He told us how as he lay there at the bottom of the pit he heard a group of some thirty young singing a popular Soviet song, "Vast Is My Native Land," before being shot down; heard one of the boys cry out: "Stalin will avenge us!"; heard the boys' leader, young Leyb, who had been everyone's favorite in the camp, scream after the first volley: "Panie Watchman, you didn't kill me! Shoot again, please! Shoot again!"

It is now possible to reconstruct the picture of the German regime in this labor camp from the accounts of dozens of witnesses — Polish men and women who escaped or were released from it at one time or another. We know how they worked the sand pits, we know that those who did not fulfill the work quota were pushed over the edge of a cliff into the abyss below. We know that the workers received a food ration of 170–200 grams of bread and a liter of some indescribable liquid which passed for soup; we know of the deaths from starvation, of the hunger-swollen wretches who were taken outside the camp on wheelbarrows and shot. We know of the savage orgies in which the Germans indulged; we know that they raped girls and shot them immediately afterwards; that they pushed people off a tower six meters high; that drunken Germans broke into the barracks at night, grabbed ten or fifteen prisoners and commenced calmly to demonstrate their adeptness in murdering their victims by shooting through the heart, the back of the head, the eye, the mouth or the temple. We know the names of the SS men in this camp, we know their characters and idiosyncrasies. We know about the chief of the camp, a Dutch-German named Van Eupen, an insatiable murderer and sex pervert who had a passion for good horses and reckless riding. We know about the massively-built young Stumpfe who was invariably overcome by a paroxysm of uncontrollable laughter whenever he killed anyone or when executions were carried out in his presence. "Laughing death" they called him, and Max Levit was the last to hear him laugh on July 23rd, 1944, when the boys were shot at Stumpfe's orders.

We know Svidersky, the one-eyed German from Odessa, known as the "hammer expert" because of his consummate skill at killing without firearms. Within the space of a few minutes he hammered to death fifteen children between the ages of eight and thirteen declared unfit for work. We know the skinny SS man known as "old Preifi," a gloomy and morose individual who looked like a Gypsy. "Old Preifi" amused himself by hunting down camp inmates who would steal to the garbage dump to pick up potato peelings. He would pounce on his victim and force his jaws apart so that he could shoot him in the mouth.

We know the names of the professional murderers Schwarz and Ledecke who relieved the monotony of their existence by shooting at prisoners returning from work. They killed twenty to forty people every day.

Such was routine in this camp, this lesser Majdanek. One might think that there could be nothing more terrible in all the world. Yet those who lived in Camp No. 1 knew very well that there was something a hundred times more ghastly than their camp.

Within three kilometers of the labor camp the Germans built a slaughterhouse for Jews. Construction was started in May, 1942, and proceeded at a rapid pace with more than a thousand workers on the job. Everything in this camp was adapted for death. It was Himmler's intention to keep this camp a dead secret. Anybody who chanced within a kilometer of the camp was shot at without warning. Luftwaffe craft were forbidden to fly over this area. The victims brought there by trainloads over a special branch line were ignorant of the fate awaiting them up to the last moment. The guards escorting the trains were not allowed inside the camp grounds; instead, SS men took over arriving trains. The trains, usually consisting of sixty cars, would be divided into three sections in the woods outside the camp, and the locomotive would haul twenty cars at a time up to the camp platform, shunting them from behind so as to stop outside the barbed-wire fence. Thus, neither an engineer nor a fireman ever crossed the boundary line. When one batch of cars had been unloaded, the non-commissioned SS officer on duty would signal for the next twenty cars. When all sixty cars were empty, the camp officials would telephone to the railway station for the next train, while the empty train would proceed farther up the line to the sand pit where it would load up with sand and pull out for Treblinka and Małkinia.

Treblinka was well located. Trainloads of victims came here from all the four points of the compass — West, East, North and South. Trains pulled in from the Polish cities of Warsaw, Międzyrzecz, Częstochowa, Siedlce, Radom; from Lomża, Białystok, Grodno and many Byelorussian towns; from Germany, Czechoslovakia, Austria, Bulgaria, and Bessarabia.

For thirteen months the trains rolled in to Treblinka. Each train consisted of sixty cars, and on each car were chalked the figures 150, 180, or 200, depending upon the number of people inside. Railway workers and peasants secretly kept count of these trains. Kazimierz Skarzyński, a sixty-eight-year-old peasant from the village of Wulka (the inhabited point nearest to the camp), told me that on some days as many as six trains would pass along the Siedlce line alone and hardly a day passed throughout these thirteen months without at least one train coming in. And yet the Siedlce line was but one of the four railways supplying Treblinka. Lucian Zukov, a railway section hand mobilized by the Germans to work on the line between Treblinka and Camp No. 2, said that from one to three trains were sent up to the camp from Treblinka every day throughout the period he worked there, which was from June 15th, 1942, until August, 1943. Each train had sixty cars, and in each car there were no less than one hundred and fifty people. We are in possession of dozens of like statements.

The fenced-in area of the camp with its warehouses for the belongings of the executed, platforms and other auxiliary premises occupied an insignificant area, 780 meters in length and 600 meters in width. If one were to entertain the slightest doubt as to the fate of the millions who were brought here, or to assume for a moment that they were not murdered immediately upon arrival, there arises the question: what became of all these people of whom there were enough to populate a small state or a large European capital? If their lives had been spared for only ten days, the human streams flowing here from all corners of Europe, from Poland and Byelorussia would have overflowed all barriers. For thirteen months or 396 days, the trains returned empty or loaded with sand; not a single one of those they brought to Camp No. 2 ever returned with them.

Everything recorded here has been compiled from the accounts of living witnesses, the testimony of people who worked in Treblinka from the first day of its existence until August 2nd, 1943, when the doomed people who made up its population rose up against their executioners, set fire to the camp and escaped into the woods, and from the testimony of apprehended guards who bit by bit confirmed and in many respects supplemented the stories of the eyewitnesses . I have seen these people and listened to them myself at great length, and I have their written testimony before me as I write this. All this voluminous evidence emanating from so many different sources dovetails in every respect, beginning with the description of the habits of Bari, the commandant's dog, and ending with the technology of murder and the mechanism of the death conveyor.

Let me conduct you through the circles of the Treblinka hell.

Who were the people brought here by the trainload? By the spring of 1942 the entire Jewish population of Poland, Germany and the western districts of Byelorussia had been rounded up in ghettos. Millions of Jewish workers, artisans, doctors, professors, architects, engineers, teachers, art workers and diverse other professions together with their wives and children, lived in the ghettos of Warsaw, Radom, Częstochowa, Lublin, Białystok, Grodno and dozens of other smaller towns. In the Warsaw ghetto alone there were about 500,000 people. Confinement to the ghetto was evidently the first, preparatory stage of the plan for the extermination of the Jews.

The summer of 1942 was chosen as the most suitable time to effect the second stage of the plan: physical extermination.

Himmler came to Warsaw and issued orders. Day and night work went on to prepare the Treblinka slaughterhouse for its gory work. In July, the first trainloads were on their way to Treblinka from Warsaw and Częstochowa. The victims were told that they were being taken to the Ukraine for farm work, and were permitted to take twenty kilograms of baggage and some food with them. In many cases the Germans forced their victims to purchase railway tickets to the station of Ober-Majdan, their code name for Treblinka, which soon acquired such fearful notoriety throughout Poland that the old name was dropped. The treatment of the victims, however, was such as to leave little doubt in their minds as to the fate in store for them. No less than 150 persons, and in most cases, 180 to 200, were crowded into each car. They were given nothing to drink throughout the journey, which sometimes lasted two or three days. People suffered so from thirst that many were reduced to drinking their own urine. The guards offered a mouthful of water for 100 zloty, but pocketed the money without giving anything in return. The prisoners were packed so tightly into the cars that each trip, especially in hot weather, usually took a toll of several old people and persons with heart ailments. Inasmuch as the doors were sealed throughout the journey, the bodies would begin to decompose, befouling the already nauseating air. It was enough for any of the prisoners to strike a match during the night for the guards to fire [through the walls of the car.] Abram Kohn, a barber, states that five persons in his car were killed and many wounded as a result of such shooting.

The trains that came to Treblinka from the Western-European countries — France, Belgium, Austria and others — were another matter entirely. These people had not heard of Treblinka and up to the last minute they believed they were being taken to work. The Germans painted alluring pictures of the pleasures and conveniences of the new life awaiting the settlers. Some trains brought people who thought they were being taken to some neutral country. Victims of a gruesome hoax, they had paid the German authorities large sums of money for foreign visas.

Once a train arrived in Treblinka filled with English, Canadian, American, and Australian citizens who had been stranded in Europe and Poland when the war broke out. After lengthy negotiations involving the payment of huge bribes, they had succeeded in gaining permission to travel to neutral countries.

All the trains from the Western-European countries were unguarded and provided with the normal sleepers and dining-cars. The passengers had large trunks and valises with them and abundant supplies of food, and when the trains stopped at stations the travelers' children would run out to ask how far it was to Ober-Majdan.

There were occasional trainloads of Gypsies from Bessarabia and elsewhere. Several trains brought young Polish peasants and workers who had taken part in uprisings and fought in partisan detachments.

It is hard to say what is worse: to ride to one's death in terrible agony knowing that the end is near, or to gaze calmly and unsuspectingly out of the window of a comfortable coach at the very moment when a phone call is being put through from Treblinka to the camp announcing the time the train is due to arrive and giving the number of people in it.

To keep up the farce at the expense of the people coming from Western Europe until the very last moment, the railhead at the death camp was got up to look like a railway station. The platform at which each batch of twenty cars was unloaded had a regular station building with ticket offices, luggage rooms, a restaurant and arrows pointing in all directions with the signs: "To Białystok," "To Baranowicze," "To Wołkowysk" etc. As the trains pulled in a band of neatly dressed musicians struck up a tune. A station guard in railway uniform collected the tickets from the passengers, letting them through to the square.

Thus three to four thousand people carrying suitcases, bags and bundles and supporting the aged and the weak, would find themselves on this square. Among them were mothers who carried infants in their arms while older children huddled against their skirts staring curiously at the strange surroundings. There was something frightening about this square which had been tamped down by so many millions of human feet. With growing dread the passengers became aware of alarming signs all around them: a bundle of clothing, an open valise, some shaving brushes and enameled kitchenware lying here and there on the square that had obviously been hastily swept a few minutes before their arrival. How had they come to be there? And why was it that just beyond the station the railway line ended and yellow grass grew and a three-meter barbed-wire fence obscured the view? Where were the railways to Białystok, to Siedlce, Warsaw and Wołkowysk? And what accounted for the strange smile on the faces of the new guards as they regarded the men straightening their ties, the neatly attired old ladies, young boys in sailor suits, slim girls who had miraculously contrived to look fresh and attractive after their long journey, young mothers who tenderly adjusted their infants' blankets?

All these guards in black uniforms and the SS non-commissioned officers looked and behaved like cattle drivers at the entrance to a slaughterhouse. For them the newly arrived group did not consist of living human beings and their lips curled at these manifestations of embarrassment, love, fear, solicitude for others and concern for the safety of belongings. It amused them to hear mothers scolding their children for running off for a few yards, to see the men pull out clean pocket handkerchiefs to wipe their perspiring brows and light cigarettes, and the girls adjusting their hair and holding down their skirts when a gust of wind blew. It struck them as funny that the old men tried to squat down on suitcases, that some carried books under their arms and wore mufflers and scarves around their throats.

As many as 20,000 people passed through Treblinka every day. Days when only six or seven thousand left the station building were rare. The square was filled with people four and five times a day. And all these thousands, tens of thousands, hundreds of thousands of people with the frightened, questioning eyes, all these young and old faces, these pretty dark-haired and light-haired girls, the bowed and baldheaded old men, the timid youths — all of them merged into a single flood that swept away reason, human knowledge, maidenly love, childish wonder, the coughing of old men and the throbbing hearts of living human beings.

The new arrivals trembled inwardly as they sensed the strangeness of that cool, smug leer on the faces of the Hitlerites watching them, the look of a live beast that feels its superiority over a dead man. In those brief moments on the square the newcomers found themselves noticing more and more alarming details.

What was behind that massive six-meter wall covered thickly with yellowing pine branches and blankets? The blankets too inspired fear: they were quilted and made of colored silk or calico exactly like those packed in the bedrolls of the travelers. How had they got there? Who had brought them? And where were their owners? Why had they no further use for their blankets? And who were these men with the blue bands on their arms? They began to recall all the stories they had heard recently, all the terrifying rumors that had been whispered back and forth. No, no, it could not be! They dismissed the fearful thought.

This feeling of alarm lasted for a few moments until all the passengers had emerged on the square. There was always a slight delay at this point for in every party there were crippled, lame, aged and sick people who had to be helped along.

But now the square was full. An *Unterscharführer* (noncommissioned SS officer) in a loud voice instructed the passengers to leave all their things on the square and prepare to go to the bathhouse, taking along only personal papers, valuables and toilet accessories. No doubt a dozen questions occurred to the people — should they take clean underwear, might they undo their bundles, would their belongings not get mixed up or lost if they did? But some mysterious, irresistible force compelled them to hurry forward in silence without asking questions or turning round, impelled them toward the opening in the six-meter barbed-wire fence camouflaged with boughs.

Inside they walked past tank obstacles, past the barbed-wire fence three times the height of man, past an anti-tank ditch three meters wide, past thin coils of steel wire strewn on the ground to trip up the fugitive and catch him like a fly in a spiderweb, and again past a barbed-wire fence, meters in height. A terrible sensation of despair, a feeling of utter helplessness would seize the newcomer. There could be no question of running away, of turning back, or fighting; from the low squat wooden towers the muzzles of heavy machine guns stared menacingly at them. Cry for help? What was the use with all these SS men and guards armed with tommy-guns, hand-grenades and pistols?

In the meantime two hundred workers with pale-blue armbands were busy on the station square untying bundles, opening suitcases and baskets, removing straps from bedrolls. The possessions of the new arrivals were being sorted out and appraised. Neatly packed darning sets flew on the ground, skeins of thread, children's panties, shirts, sheets, jumpers, pocket-knives, shaving sets, bundles of letters, photographs, thimbles, bottles of perfume, mirrors, nightcaps, shoes, ladies' slippers, stockings, lace, pajamas, parcels of butter, coffee, cans of cocoa, prayer robes, candlesticks, books, rusks, violins, children's blocks. It required considerable skill to sort out and classify within the space of a few minutes all these thousand and one articles, some for sending to Germany, the old and valueless to be laid aside for burning. Woe to the blundering worker who placed an old fiber suitcase on the pile of leather valises intended for shipment to Germany, or who threw a new pair of silk stockings with a Paris trademark on a heap of old mended socks! Such a blunder could be made only once. The workers were not allowed to make the same mistake twice.

Forty SS men and sixty guards worked on "transport," as the first stage of the Treblinka tragedy was called. Their work involved meeting the trains, leading the passengers out of the "station" to the square, and watching over the workers who sorted and classified the possessions. While they worked the men with the pale-blue armbands often popped into their mouths bits of bread, sugar or candies found in the baggage they were sorting, but they made sure that the guards did not see them for this was strictly forbidden. It was permitted, however, to wash up after the job was finished with eau de cologne and perfume, for there was a shortage of water in Treblinka and only the Germans and guards were permitted to use water for washing.

While the people were still preparing for their bath, the sorting of their possessions was being completed. The valuable articles were carried away to the warehouses, and the letters, photographs of newborn babies, brothers and brides, yellowed wedding announcements, all these precious bits of paper that had been treasured by their owners perhaps for years, were just so much trash for the Treblinka officials who collected them in a pile and carted them away to huge pits already partly filled with hundreds of thousands of similar letters, postcards, visiting cards, photographs, letters written in shaky childish handwriting and crude childish crayon drawings.

After a brief, hurried sweeping the square was ready to receive the next group of unfortunates.

Not always, however, did things go so smoothly. There were cases when prisoners who knew where they were being taken mutinied. A peasant by the name of Skarzynski saw people smash their way out of two trains, knock down the guards and run off into the forest. In both cases every one of the fugitives was killed. Four children between the ages of four and six were killed with them. Similar cases of skirmishes between the victims and the guards were described by a peasant woman named Marianna Kobus. Working in the fields one day she saw sixty people break away from a train and make for the forest.

By this time the group inside the camp had passed on to another square. On this square stood a huge barrack-like building, and to the right of it three other barracks, two for storing clothing and the third for footwear. On the west side of the camp were the buildings housing the SS men and guards, food stores, and automobiles, trucks, and armored cars. The general impression was that of the usual concentration camp.

In the south-eastern corner of the camp grounds, fenced off by branches, was a compound with a booth bearing the sign "Infirmary" in front. All the feeble and sick were separated from the crowd waiting for the bath and were carried off on the stretchers to this infirmary, where a man wearing the white doctor's smock and a red-cross band on his left arm met them. What happened inside the infirmary I shall describe later on.

The next step in handling the new arrivals was to break their will by barking curt rapidfire commands at them with the German "r" sounding like a whiplash, an accomplishment of which the German army is inordinately proud and which is regarded as one of the proofs that the Germans belong to the "master race."

409

"Achtung!" the command would ring over the crowd and in the leaden silence the voice of the *Scharführer* would repeat instructions repeated several times a day for many months on end:

"The men are to remain where they are. Women and children undress in the building on the left."

Here, according to witnesses, the heart-rending scenes usually began. The instinct of maternal, conjugal, filial love told the victims that they were seeing one another for the last time. Handshakes, kisses, blessings, tears, briefly murmured words invested with all the love, all the anguish, all the tenderness and despair that filled them were now exchanged. The SS psychiatrists of death knew that these emotions had to be stamped out at once. The psychiatrists of death were familiar with the primitive laws that operate in all the slaughterhouses of the world, laws which in Treblinka were applied by the cattle to the human beings. This was one of the most critical moments, the moment when daughters had to be separated from fathers, mothers from sons, grandmothers from grandsons, husbands from wives.

Again the words "Achtung! Achtung!" rent the air. This was precisely the moment when the minds of the victims had to be befuddled again, when a glimmer of hope had to be allowed to dawn, when death had to be made for a few moments to look like life.

"Women and children are to remove their footwear on entering the building," barks the same voice. "Stockings are to be placed inside shoes. Children's stockings inside children's sandals, boots and shoes. Be orderly."

And again: "On entering the bathhouse take with you valuables, documents, money, soap and towel. . . . I repeat . . ."

Inside the women's bathhouse was a hairdressers' department. As soon as they were undressed the women lined up to have their hair clipped off. Old women lost their wigs. For some inexplicable, psychological reason their final haircut, according to the testimony of the hairdressers themselves, had a reassuring effect on the women; it seemed to convince them that they really were about to take a bath. Young girls felt their close-cropped heads critically and asked the barber if he wouldn't please smooth out some of the uneven spots. The women usually calmed down after the haircut. Nearly all of them passed out of the dressing-room carrying a piece of soap and a folded towel. A few of the younger ones wept to part with their flowing tresses. Why were the women thus shorn? To

410

deceive them? No, the hair was needed in Germany. It was a raw material. . . .

I asked many people what the Germans did with all the hair they removed from the heads of these living corpses. According to all the witnesses, the huge mountains of black, golden, chestnut hair, straight, curly and braided, were first disinfected and then pressed into sacks and shipped to Germany. All the witnesses questioned confirmed that the sacks containing their hair had German addresses on them. What was it used for? According to the written testimony of one Kohn, the hair was used by the navy to fill mattresses, to make hausers for submarines and for other similar purposes. Other witnesses claim that the hair was used to pad saddles for the cavalry.

The men undressed in the yard. Of the first group of the morning arrivals some 150 to 300 would be selected for their physical strength to be used to bury the corpses. These would be killed the following day. The men were told to undress quickly, but were also warned to lay down their clothes neatly, shoes, socks, underwear, coats and trousers separately. These things were sorted out by another team of workmen wearing red armbands as distinct from the blue bands worn by the station team. Articles of clothing considered worthwhile sending to Germany were taken away at once to the warehouse. All metal and cloth labels were carefully removed. The rest of the clothing was burned or buried.

The feeling of alarm grew, heightened by a fearful stench mingled with the odor of lime that assailed the nostrils. What accounted for such huge swarms of fat and troublesome flies? Pine woods and paved ground did not usually breed flies. The men began to breathe heavily, they started at every sound and stared hard at every trifle in search of an explanation, a hint that would help them to unravel the mystery and gain an inkling of the fate in store for them. What, for instance, were those gigantic excavators doing over at the southern end of the camp grounds?

The next stage in the procedure began. The naked people were lined up at a window through which they were told to hand over their documents and valuables. And again the frightful, awe-inspiring voice seared their consciousness: "Achtung! Achtung! The penalty for hiding valuables is death! Achtung!"

A *Scharführer* sat in a small wooden booth. SS men and guards stood around him. Next to the booth were wooden boxes into which the valuables were thrown — one, for paper money, another for coins, a third for watches, rings, earrings and brooches with precious stones and bracelets. Documents were thrown on the ground, for no one on earth had any more use for these documents belonging to living corpses who within an hour would be lying stiff and dead in a pit. The gold and valuables, however, were carefully sorted out; dozens of jewelers were engaged in ascertaining the purity of the metal and the value of the stones and diamonds.

The spell of illusion was broken at this point. Here at the booth ended the anguish of uncertainty that had kept the people in a fever of anxiety causing them to pass within the space of a few minutes from hope to despair, from visions of life to visions of death. This torture by deception was part of the process at this slaughterhouse, it aided the SS men in their work. When the final act of robbing the living corpses was over, the attitude of the Germans to their victims underwent a sharp change. Rings were torn off unwilling fingers, and earrings wrenched out of ears.

At this final stage, speed was important for the smooth working of the death conveyor. Hence the word "Achtung" was replaced by another word, a hissing compelling word: "Schneller! Schneller! Schneller!" "Faster! Faster! Faster!"

Experience has shown that when stripped a man loses his power of resistance and ceases to resist his fate; having lost his clothes, he seems to lose his instinct of self-preservation and accepts what happens to him as the inevitable. He who a moment before wished passionately to live becomes passive and apathetic. In order to make doubly sure, however, the SS employed at the last stage of their gruesome death conveyor a monstrous method of stunning their victims, of reducing them to a state of complete mental paralysis.

How was this done?

By switching over suddenly to senseless and inexplicable brutality. These naked men and women who had been stripped of everything but who continued stubbornly to remain human, a thousand times more human than the creatures in German uniforms surrounding them, still breathed, still saw, still thought, their hearts still beat. Suddenly the soap and towels were knocked out of their hands. They were lined up five in a row and marched off to the accompaniment of rapped out commands:

"Hände hoch! Marsch! Schneller! Schneller!"

They were marched down a straight avenue about 120 meters

long and two wide, and lined with flowers and firs. This path led to the place of execution.

Wire was stretched along either side of the path which was lined by guards in black uniforms and SS men in gray standing shoulder to shoulder. The path was covered with white sand and as the victims marched forward with upraised arms they saw the fresh imprint of bare feet on the sand: the small footprints of women, the tiny footprints of children, the impress of heavy aged feet. These faint tracks on the sand were all that remained of the thousands of people who had recently passed down this path just as the present four thousand were passing now and as the next four thousand would pass two hours later and the thousands more waiting there on the railway track in the woods. Passed as they had the day before, ten days, a hundred days before, as they would pass tomorrow and fifty days hence, as they had passed throughout the thirteen months of the existence of the hell at Treblinka.

The Germans called it "the road from which there is no return."

Smirking and grimacing, a fiend in human shape whose name was Sukhomil ran alongside shouting in deliberately distorted German:

"Now then, lads, faster, faster! Your bath water is cooling. Schneller, Kinder, schneller!"

And bursting into loud guffaws, the creature danced in a frenzy of delight. The victims moved on in silence with upraised arms between the two rows of guards, who beat them with rifle butts and rubber truncheons as they went by. Children ran to keep up with the grownups.

The brutality of one of the fiends, an SS man called Sepp, especially impressed itself on all who witnessed this mournful procession. Sepp specialized in child-killing. Endowed with unusual physical strength, this creature would suddenly snatch a child from the ranks and either smash out his brains by flinging him against the ground or tear him in two.

The journey from the booth to the place of execution took between 120 and 180 seconds. Hurried forward by blows, deafened by shouts, the victims reached the third open lot and for a moment halted in astonishment.

Before them stood a handsome stone building surrounded by trees and built in the style of an ancient temple. Five broad concrete steps led to low, massive and handsomely decorated doors. Flowers grew at the entrance. For the rest, however, chaos reigned. There were mountains of fresh earth everywhere. A huge excavator clanked and rattled as it dug up tons of yellow sandy soil with its steel jaws, raising a cloud of dust that blotted out the sun. The roar of the machine digging huge graves from morning till night mingled with the wild barking of dozens of German shepherds.

On either side of the temple of death ran narrow-gauge lines over which people in loose overalls pushed small self-dumping waggonettes.

The wide door of the slaughterhouse opened slowly and two of the assistants of Schmidt, the chief of the death factory, appeared at the entrance. These were sadists and maniacs. One, about thirty years of age, was tall with massive shoulders, dark hair and a sallow-complexioned face beaming with excitement; the other, slightly younger, was short, brown-haired, with a pasty, jaundiced complexion, as if he had just taken quinacrine. We know the names of these traitors to humanity, to their homeland, to their oath of loyalty.

The tall one held a massive piece of gas piping about a meter long and a whip. The second carried a saber.

At this moment the SS men released the dogs who in obedience to careful training threw themselves on the crowd and dug their teeth into the bare flesh of the doomed people. With savage cries the SS men brought their rifle butts down on the women who stood rooted to the spot with terror.

Inside the building Schmidt's men drove the victims into the gas chambers.

At that moment Kurt Franz, one of the commandants of Treblinka, would appear leading his dog Bari by the leash. Bari had been trained by his master to tear the sex organs off the victims. Kurt Franz had made quite a career for himself in the camp. Beginning as a junior non-commissioned SS officer, he had been promoted to the rather high rank of an *Untersturmführer*. This tall, skinny thirty-five-year-old SS man not only displayed ability in organizing the death conveyor, not only did he love his work and could imagine no occupation for which he was more perfectly suited than the supervision of Treblinka but, in addition to all this, he was something of a theoretician and loved to generalize and explain the meaning or significance of his work.

One is shaken to the very depth of one's being by the stories of how the living corpses of Treblinka up to the last minute preserved

414

their human souls although they had lost everything else, how women tried to save their sons and for their sake accomplished feats of hopeless bravery, how young mothers tried to hide their infants under blankets. No one will ever know the names of these mothers. There are stories of little girls of ten who comforted their sobbing parents, of a little boy who on entering the gas chamber shouted: "The Russians will avenge us, mama, don't cry!" No one will ever know the names of these children. We were told about dozens of doomed people who fought against a legion of SS men armed with automatic weapons and grenades, and died standing up, their breasts riddled with bullets. We were told about the young man who stabbed an SS officer, about the lad who had taken part in the mutiny in the Warsaw ghetto and who by some miracle had managed to hide a grenade from the German and flung it into a group of executioners at the last moment. We heard about the battle that lasted all of one night between a group of the condemned and detachments of guards and SS men. The shooting and grenade explosions went on all night and when the sun rose the next morning the whole area was covered with the bodies of the fighters. Beside them lay their weapons — sticks wrenched out of the fence, a knife, a razor. Never on this earth will the names of these fallen fighters be known. We heard about the tall girl who tore a carbine out of the hands of a guard on the "road from which there is no return," and fought against dozens of SS men. Two beasts were killed in that fight, and a third lost his arm. Terrible were the tortures to which this brave girl was subjected before they finally put her to death. She, too, is nameless.

Yet is that quite true? Hitlerism robbed these people of their homes and their lives, Hitlerism sought to wipe their names out of living memory. Yet every one of them, the mothers who shielded their children with their bodies, the children who dried their fathers' tears, those who fought with knives and grenades and fell in the nocturnal massacre, and the naked girl who, like some ancient Greek goddess, fought alone against dozens — all of these people who have departed into the unknown have preserved forever the most splendid name of all, the name which the pack of Hitlerites and Himmlerites could not trample underfoot, the name of Man. History will inscribe on their tomb the epitaph: "They Died for Humanity."

Inhabitants of the village of Wulka, the settlement nearest to Treblinka, say that sometimes the shrieks of the women being murdered were so terrible that the whole village would run for miles into the forest to get away from the piercing cries that rent the air. Presently the screaming would subside only to break out again as terrible and soul-searing as before . . . This was repeated three or four times a day.

I asked one of the executioners who had been taken prisoner about the cries. He explained that the women usually screamed when the dogs were unleashed on them and the whole crowd of doomed people were driven into the death house. "They saw their end coming. Besides it was very crowded inside, they were beaten unmercifully and the dogs tore at them."

A sudden silence fell when the doors of the gas chambers closed. The screaming broke out again when a fresh group was brought. This occurred twice, three times, four times and sometimes five times a day. For Treblinka was not an ordinary slaughterhouse, it was run on the conveyor system, on the production line method copied from modern large-scale industry.

And like any industrial enterprise, Treblinka did not always work as efficiently as has been described above. It developed gradually as new equipment and new, more efficient methods were introduced. In the beginning there were three small gas chambers. While these were under construction several trainloads of victims arrived and the killing was done with axes, hammers and truncheons. This was done to prevent the surrounding population from suspecting the nature of the Treblinka work. The first three concrete chambers were 5×5 meters in size, i.e., with an area of 25 square meters each. The height was 190 cm. Each chamber had two doors, one to admit the living, the other to serve as an exit for the gassed corpses. This second door was very wide — nearly two and a half meters. The three chambers were erected on one foundation.

These three chambers did not have the capacity Berlin demanded. It was then that the construction of the building described above was begun. Treblinka officials took pride in the fact that their gas chambers surpassed those of all the other Gestapo death factories in Majdanek, Sobibór and Belżec for capacity and production floor space.

For five weeks 700 prisoners worked on the erection of the new death factory. When the work was at its height a foreman came from Germany with his crew and set about installing the equipment.

The new gas chambers, of which there were ten in all, were

416

symmetrically placed on the two sides of a wide concrete-floored corridor. Like the old three, they each had two doors, one from the corridor for the live victims, and another in the back wall to provide an outlet for the corpses. The latter led to platforms running on both sides of the building. Narrow-gauge tracks led up to the platforms. The corpses were first emptied out on the platforms and then loaded into waggonettes to be carried to the huge burial pits the excavators dug day and night. The floor of the gas chambers was laid at an incline toward the platforms to make it easier and faster to drag out the corpses. (This was a substantial improvement over the old chambers where the corpses had to be carried out on stretchers or dragged out with straps.)

Each new gas chamber was seven meters wide and eight long, fifty-six square meters in all. The total area of the ten made up 560 square meters, and the three old chambers which continued to operate when there were smaller groups to be wiped out brought the total production floor space of the Treblinka death factory up to 635 square meters. From 400 to 600 people at a time were herded into each lethal chamber, which means that working at capacity the ten new chambers could destroy an average of from 4,000 to 6,000 lives at once.

To snuff out life 10 to 25 minutes were required. In the early period after the starting of the new chambers when the executioners had not yet established the efficiency peak and were still experimenting, the victims were subjected to fearful torture lasting for two to three hours before life left their tormented bodies. During the very first days the intake and outlet installations worked badly and the victims writhed in agony for anything up to eight or ten hours.

Various means were employed to effect this mass slaughter. One of them was by forcing the exhaust fumes from the engine of a heavy tank that served as the Treblinka power station into the chambers. These fumes contained two to three per cent of carbon-monoxide, which has the property of combining when inhaled with the hemoglobin of the blood to form a stable combination known as carboxyhemoglobin. Carboxyhemoglobin is far more stable than the combination of oxygen and the hemoglobin of the blood formed in the course of the respiratory process. In some fifteen minutes the blood becomes saturated with carbon-monoxide to such an extent that the hemoglobin is no longer useful as an oxygen carrier. The victim begins gasping for air but no oxygen reaches the suffocating organism; the heart beats as if ready to burst, driving blood into the lungs, but the carbon-monoxide saturated blood can no longer combine with the oxygen in the air. Breathing grows hoarse, all the symptoms of painful strangulation appear, consciousness dims, and the victim perishes just as if he had been strangled.

The second method, and one that was the most widely used, was pumping air out of the chambers with suction pumps until the victims were dead. As in the case of the first method, death was caused by depriving the victims of oxygen.

The third method, used less but nevertheless used, was murder with steam. This method, too, aimed at depriving the organism of oxygen, for the steam was used to expel the air from the chambers.

Diverse poisons, too, were employed, but this was experimentation; the first two were the methods used for mass murder on industrial scale.

Can we overcome our horror and try to imagine how the victims felt during the last minutes of their lives? We know only that they were silent. . . . Packed so tightly that bones cracked and crushed lungs could scarcely breathe, they must have stood there, one mass of humanity, covered with the sticky sweat of imminent death. Someone, with the wisdom of age perhaps, may have conquered his own fear sufficiently to say to the others: "Take heart, this is the end." Someone no doubt shouted a terrible curse. . . . These sacred curses must come true! We can picture some mother making a superhuman effort to obtain a whit more breathing space for her child in order that his last anguished gasps might be alleviated if only by one-millionth by this last evidence of maternal solicitude. We can hear some young girl, her tongue turning to lead with horror, ask piteously: "Why are they suffocating me, why may I not live and have children?"

The brain swam, consciousness faded and the last moments of anguish seized the victim.

No, it is impossible to imagine what took place in that chamber. . . . The dead bodies stood pressed close together growing colder and colder. The children, witnesses maintain, clung to life longer than the adults. Within 20-25 minutes Schmidt's assistants would peep through openings. The time had come to open the doors to the platforms. Urged on by the SS men, prisoners in overalls set about emptying the chambers. Since the floor sloped toward the platforms, many of the corpses rolled out by themselves. People

the largest crematorium in the world could ever have handled such a gigantic number of corpses in so short a time as was required at Treblinka. The excavator dug a pit 250-300 meters long, 20-25 meters wide and 5 meters deep. Three rows of reinforced concrete pillars 100-20 cm. high were installed lengthwise in the pit to support steel beams that were laid along them.

Rails were then laid crosswise across these beams at intervals of five to seven centimeters. The result was the grating of a titanic firebox. A new narrow-gauge railway was laid from the burial pits to the furnace pit. Soon afterwards a second and then a third furnace of like dimensions were set up. Each of these furnaces took 3,500 to 4,000 corpses at a loading.

Another huge excavator arrived followed soon afterward by a third. Work went on day and night. People who took part in the cremation of the corpses say that the ovens resembled volcanoes; the frightful heat burned the faces of the workers, the flames leapt up to a height of eight to ten meters, clouds of thick black smoke reached the sky and hung in a heavy motionless blanket in the air. Inhabitants of villages in the neighborhood saw the flame at night from a distance of thirty and forty kilometers as it licked above the pine woods surrounding the camp. The stench of burning flesh poisoned the whole countryside. When the wind blew in the direction of the Polish camp three kilometers away, the people there were almost asphyxiated by the frightful odor. More than 800 prisoners (which is more than the number of workers in the blast-furnace or open-hearth departments of big iron and steel plants) were engaged in burning the corpses. This monster workshop operated day and night for eight months in succession without managing to handle the myriad of buried bodies. True, new batches of victims continued to arrive all the time which added to the load on the furnaces.

Trainloads were brought in from Bulgaria. The SS and guards were happy, for these people, deceived both by the Germans and the Bulgarian fascist government and totally unaware of the fate awaiting them, brought large quantities of vegetables, good food and white bread with them. Later trains came in from Grodno and Bialystok, from the rebellious Warsaw ghetto, trains of insurgent Polish peasants, workers and soldiers.

From Bessarabia came a group of Gypsies, 200 men and 800 women and children. They came on foot with their caravans; they too had been deceived and that is why two guards were able to bring 1,000 people, although even the guards had no idea they were leading them to their death. Witnesses say that the Gypsy women clapped their hands in delight at the sight of the handsome building of the death house and up to the last minute had no inkling of what awaited them, a fact which amused the Germans tremendously.

They had great sport too with a group of rebels from the Warsaw ghetto. They picked out the women and children and took them not to the gas chambers but to the cremation ovens. They forced the mothers, half crazed with terror, to lead their children between the red-hot bars on which thousands of dead bodies writhed and squirmed from the heat, twisting and turning as though alive; where the bellies of dead women with child burst open from the heat and still-born infants burned up inside rent wombs. This spectacle was enough to rob the strongest man of his reason, but the Germans knew that its effect on a mother would be a thousand times worse. Mothers tried to cover their children's eyes, but the children rushed to them with terrible screams: "Mama, what will happen to us? Will we be burned up?"

The infirmary was also rearranged. A round pit was dug and iron bars laid at the bottom for the burning of corpses. Around the pit were low benches like seats in a sports stadium, placed so close to the edge that anyone sitting on them was literally suspended over the edge of the pit. The sick and the feeble who were taken into the infirmary were led to these benches facing the bonfire built of human bodies. After enjoying the situation to the full, the Nazi barbarians then proceeded to shoot the gray heads and bent backs of the old people who fell, dead or wounded, into the blazing fire.

Can any human being on this earth picture to himself the humor of Treblinka, the amusements, the practical jokes of the SS?

The SS held football matches with teams made up of condemned men, forced the victims to play tag, organized a chorus of the doomed. Next to the Germans' dormitory was a ménagerie where wolves, foxes and other harmless beasts of the forests were kept in cages while the most terrible wild beasts the world has ever produced walked the earth freely, sat on benches and listened to music. They actually wrote a Treblinka hymn for the doomed unfortunates which included the following lines:

Für uns gibt's heute nur Treblinka
Das unser Schicksal ist.
For us today there is only Treblinka —
This is our fate.

Bleeding, tormented people were forced a few minutes before their death to sing idiotic German sentimental songs:
... Ich brach das Blümelein
Und schenkte es dem schönsten
Geliebten Mädlein.
I plucked a flower
and gave it to my beloved,
who is so beautiful ...
The camp's chief commandant selected a few children from one batch of prisoners, killed their parents, dressed up the children in fine clothes, fed them with sweets, played with them and a few days later when he was bored with them ordered them killed.

The Germans placed an old man in prayer clothing next to the outhouse and ordered him to make sure that no one spent more than three minutes inside. They hung an alarm clock around his neck and laughed when they looked at his clothes. Sometimes the Germans forced old Jews to perform prayer services, arrange funerals for individual murdered people. All the religious rituals were observed, gravestones were brought, and then — at some later time — these graves were dug up, the bodies thrown out, and the monuments disassembled.

One of the chief sources of entertainment were the night orgies of violence against young and beautiful women and girls who were selected from every group of victims. The next morning the rapers personally escorted their victims to the lethal chambers. This was how the SS, the bulwark of the Hitlerite regime, the pride of Fascist Germany, amused themselves at Treblinka.

It must be noted here that these creatures were by no means robots who mechanically carried out the wishes of others. All witnesses speak of a trait common to all of them, namely, a fondness for theoretical argument, a predilection for philosophizing. All of them had a weakness for delivering speeches to the doomed people, for boasting in front of their victims and explaining the "lofty" meaning and "importance" for the future of what was being done in Treblinka.

The summer of 1943 was exceptionally hot in these regions. There was not a drop of rain, not a cloud, not a puff of wind for many weeks. The burning of bodies proceeded at top speed. For nearly six months the furnaces had been going but little more than half of the dead had been cremated.

The fearful moral and physical suffering began to tell on the prisoners whose job it was to burn the corpses. Between fifteen and twenty of them committed suicide every day. Many deliberately courted death by violating disciplinary rules. "To get a bullet was a luxury," one baker from Kosów who had escaped from the camp told me. It was said that to be doomed to live in Treblinka was a hundred times worse than to be doomed to death.

Charred bones and ashes were carried outside the camp grounds. Peasants from the village of Wulka were mobilized by the Germans to load the stuff on carts and strew it along the roads leading from the death camp to the Polish labor camp. Child prisoners threw shovelfuls of ashes onto the road from the carts. Sometimes they would find melted gold coins or gold dental crowns among the ashes. These juvenile prisoners were called the "children from the black road" because the ashes made the road black as a funeral ribbon. Car wheels made a peculiar swishing sound as they rolled over this road. When I traveled this way I seemed to hear a sorrowful whisper issuing from beneath the wheels like a low, timid lament.

This black, funeral strip of ashes running between the woods and fields from the death camp to the Polish camp was like a tragic symbol of the terrible fate that had linked the nations who had fallen under the axe of Hitlerite Germany.

The peasants carted the charred bones and ashes from the spring of 1943 until the summer of 1944. Every day twenty carts were out each making six or eight trips in the course of the day. In every load went 100-125 kilograms or more of ashes and charred bones.

In the "Treblinka" song the Germans forced the 800 corpse-burners to sing were words exhorting the prisoners to obedience in reward for which they were promised "a tiny bit of happiness which passes in a flash." Surprisingly enough there actually was one happy day in the Treblinka inferno. The Germans, however, were mistaken: neither obedience nor submissiveness gave that day to the Treblinka doomed. It was the reckless courage of the brave that brought it into being.

The prisoners conceived the plan of a mutiny. They had nothing to lose. They were all doomed, every day of their lives was hell. Not one of the witnesses of the frightful crimes would have been spared. The gas chamber awaited them one and all; in fact most of them were killed after working for a few days and replaced by new workers from the current groups of victims. Only a few dozen men lived weeks and months instead of days and hours. These were skilled workers, carpenters, stone-masons, or the bakers, tailors and barbers who served the Germans. It was they who formed a committee of revolt. Only condemned men, only men possessed by an all-consuming hatred and a fierce thirst for revenge could have conceived such a mad plan of revolt. They did not want to escape before destroying Treblinka. And they destroyed it.

Weapons — axes, knives, truncheons — began to appear in the workers' barracks. At what a price, at what a tremendous risk was each axe and knife procured! What incredible patience, cunning and skill was required to hide all this from the Argus eyes of the guards! The workers laid in stocks of gasoline to use for setting fire to the camp buildings. How did this gasoline accumulate and how did it disappear without trace as if it had evaporated into thin air? By superhuman effort, tension of mind, will and incredible daring. A tunnel was dug underneath the German arsenal building. Here again sheer daring worked miracles; the god of courage was on their side. Twenty hand grenades, a machine gun, rifles and pistols were carried out of the arsenal and secreted in hiding places known to the conspirators alone. The latter divided themselves into groups of five. The extraordinarily complex plan for the uprising was worked out to the minutest detail. Every group had its definite assignment. Each of these mathematically perfect assignments was a piece of sheer madness in itself.

One group was given the task of storming the watchtowers where the guards sat behind machine guns. Other groups were to attack the sentries on duty at the entrances to the camp grounds. Others were to tackle the armored cars, to cut telephone communications, to attack the barracks, to cut passages through the barbed wire, to build a bridge across the anti-tank ditches, to pour gasoline on the camp buildings, set fire to them and to destroy everything that lent itself easily to destruction.

The plan even provided for the supply of money to the escaped prisoners. A Warsaw doctor who collected the money nearly gave the whole show away. One day a *Scharführer* noticed a fat bundle of banknotes sticking out of his pocket — it was the current sum the doctor had intended to hide. The *Scharführer* pretended not to have noticed and reported the matter to Franz. Franz decided to question the doctor himself. He suspected something immediately. Why should a doomed man need money? Franz proceeded to cross-examine his victim with calm deliberation. Franz prided himself on his ability to torture people. He was convinced no person on earth could stand the tortures known to Hauptmann Kurt Franz. The hell at Treblinka had its academicians of torture. But the Warsaw doctor outwitted the SS Hauptmann. He took poison. One of the participants in the uprising told me that never in Treblinka had such efforts been made to save a man's life. Evidently Franz sensed the dying doctor would carry his secret with him. But the German poison worked well and the secret remained unrevealed.

Toward the end of July the heat became unbearable. Steam issued from the graves as from gigantic boilers. The terrific stench and the heat of the furnaces killed men who toiled on the burning of the corpses. They dropped dead, falling headlong into the blazing furnace. Thousands of millions of fat-bellied flies crawled along the ground or filled the air with their monotonous drone. The last hundred thousand corpses were being burned.

The uprising was scheduled for August 2nd. A revolver shot was its signal. Fortune favored the sacred cause of the rebels. A new flame leapt skywards, not the thick heavy black smoke and flame of burning human bodies, but the bright, hot and dancing flame of a conflagration. The camp buildings burned and to the rebels it seemed that the sun had rent itself asunder and was burning over Treblinka, a symbol of the triumph of freedom and honor. Shots rang out and the machine guns on the towers captured by the rebels emitted a jubilant rat-tat-tat. The explosions of hand grenades sounded as triumphant as Truth itself. The air shook from the detonations, buildings came crashing down and the whistling of the bullets deadened the odious buzzing of the carrion flies. Axes dripping blood flashed in the clear, pure air. On this day, August 2nd, the soil of Treblinka hell was soaked with the evil blood of the SS men, and the radiant sky was tremulous with the triumph of this moment of vengeance.

As had happened in similar instances ever since the world began, the creatures who had strutted as members of a higher race, they who had thundered forth "Achtung, Mützen ab!", Attention! Remove caps! the creatures with the shattering compelling voices of masters "Alle r-r-r-aus!", Everyone out!, these creatures so confident of their power when it was a question of executing millions of women and children, showed themselves to be despicable cowards, miserable belly-crawling worms begging for mercy when it came to a real life-and-death struggle. They lost their heads, rushed back and forth like frightened rats; they forgot all about the ramified

426

system of defenses Treblinka boasted of, the all-consuming system of fire laid out in advance. They forgot their weapons. But is there really anything surprising about that, after all?

When Treblinka was enveloped in flames and the rebels, bidding a silent farewell to the ashes of their fellow prisoners, left the barbed-wire compound, SS and police units were sent in pursuit. Hundreds of police dogs were set on their trail. The Germans brought out their air force to hunt down the escaped prisoners. Battles were fought in the forests and marshes and few of the rebels lived to tell the tale. But they died in battle, they died fighting, arms in hand.

Treblinka ceased to exist on August 2nd. The Germans completed the burning of the remaining corpses, dismantled the brick buildings, removed the barbed wire, set fire to the wooden barracks that had survived the mutiny. The equipment of the death factory was blown up or dismantled and shipped away; the furnaces were destroyed, the excavators taken away and the huge innumerable ditches filled in with earth. The station building was razed to the last brick, the railway track and even the ties were removed. Lupine was planted on the site of the camp and a settler named Streben built himself a house there. The house is no longer there, for it has been burnt down since.

What was the object of all this destruction? The Germans wanted to hide the traces of the murder of millions of people in the hell of Treblinka. But how did they expect to do this? Did they really think it possible to force the thousands who had witnessed the death trains moving from all corners of Europe to the death conveyor to keep silent? Did they believe they could hide that deadly flame and the smoke which hung for eight months in the sky, visible by day and by night to the inhabitants of dozens of villages and small towns? Did they think they could make the peasants of the Wulka village forget the fearful shrieks of the women and children which lasted for thirteen long months and which seem to ring in their ears to this very day? Did they imagine they could compel the peasants who had strewn the road with human ashes for a whole year to keep silent? Did they imagine that they could compel to silence the survivors who had seen the Treblinka's slaughterhouse in operation from its launching until August 2nd, 1943, the last day of its existence; the witnesses who have given accurate and corroborated accounts of every SS man and guard; witnesses who, step by step, have helped to reproduce a faithful picture of life in Treblinka

427

from day to day? These can no longer be ordered: "Mützen ab!", these can no longer be led off to the lethal chamber. And Himmler no longer has power over these henchmen of his who with bowed heads and fingers that nervously tug at the edges of their jackets recount in dull toneless voices the delirium-like story of their crimes.

We arrived at the Treblinka camp early in September, i.e., thirteen months after the day of the uprising. For thirteen months the slaughterhouse had been in operation. For thirteen months the Germans had endeavored to hide the traces of its work.

It was quiet. The tips of the pines flanking the railway track barely moved. Millions of human eyes had stared out of the car windows at these pines, this sand, this old tree stump, as trains moved slowly up to the platform. Softly rustle the ashes and crushed slag on the dark road now covered in neat German fashion with white pebbles.

We enter the camp, we are treading the soil of Treblinka. The lupine pods burst open at the slightest touch, burst open by themselves with a faint popping sound; millions of tiny peas roll on the ground. The rattle of the falling peas, the popping sound of the bursting pods merge into a soft, mournful melody like a funeral dirge — faint, sorrowful, gentle — issuing from the bowels of the earth. The soil, rich and juicy as though linseed oil had been poured into it, the fathomless earth of Treblinka, as oozy as the sea bottom, gives under your feet. This plot of land fenced off with barbed wire has consumed more human lives than all the oceans and seas in the world ever since the birth of mankind.

The earth ejects the crushed bones, the teeth, bits of paper and clothing; it refuses to keep its awful secret. These things emerge from the unhealed wounds in the earth. There they are — the half-rotted shirts of the slain, the trousers, shoes, mouldy cigarette-cases, the tiny cog wheels of watches, penknives, shaving brushes, candlesticks, children's shoes with red pompons, towels with Ukrainian embroidery, lace underwear, scissors, thimbles, corsets, trusses. Out of another fissure in the earth emerge heaps of utensils: cups, pots, basins, tins, pans, aluminum mugs, bowls, children's bakelite cups. . . And beyond, out of the bottomless, swollen earth, as though pushed forward into the light of day by some invisible hand, emerge half-rotted Soviet passports, notebooks with Bulgarian writing, photographs of children from

Warsaw and Vienna, letters written in childish scrawl, a volume of poetry, a prayer copied on a yellowed fragment of paper, food ration cards from Germany. . . Hundreds of perfume bottles of all shapes and sizes, green, pink, blue. . . Pervading everything is the nauseating stench of corruption, a stench that neither fire nor sunshine, rain, snow or wind have been able to overcome. And hundreds of tiny forest flies swarm over the decaying fragments of clothing and paper.

We walk over the bottomless Treblinka earth and suddenly something causes us to halt in our tracks. It is the sight of a lock of hair gleaming like burnished copper, the soft lovely hair of a young girl trampled into the ground, and next to it a lock of light blonde hair, and farther on a thick dark braid gleaming against the light sand; and beyond that more and more. There are evidently the contents of one, but only one, of the sacks of hair the Germans had neglected to ship off.

Then it is all true! The last wild hope that it might be a ghastly nightmare has gone. The lupine pods pop open, the tiny peas beat a faint tattoo as though a myriad of tiny bells were ringing a funeral dirge deep down under the ground. And it seems the heart must surely burst under the weight of sorrow, grief and pain that is beyond human endurance.

Vasily Grossman

Children from the Black Road

We were walking through a field, densely overgrown with lupine. The sun beat down, the rustle of dry leaves and the crackle of pods blended inlo melancholy, almost melodious, sounds. Uncovering his gray quivering head, the old man who was our guide crossed himself and said: "You are walking on graves."

We were walking over the grounds of the Treblinka death camp where the Germans brought Jews from all corners of Europe and the occupied territories of the USSR.

Millions of people had been murdered here by the Germans. This dreadful black road cut through the Treblinka field. It was black because, for three kilometers, it was covered with human ashes. Tons of ashes had been brought here in carts. Eleven thirteen-year-old prisoners shoveled the ashes along the road. They were called "the children from the black road."

On a cold February day in 1943 an ordinary freight train delivered, along with its other "passengers," sixty boys to the Treblinka death camp. These were Jewish children from Warsaw, Vilnius, Grodno, Bialystok, and Brest. After getting off the train they were taken from their families. The adults were sent to the death camp, and the boys to the "labor camp." The chief of this camp, the *Hauptsturmführer*, a Dutch German whose name was Van-Eupen, decided that there was always time to kill the boys, but meanwhile, they could be put to work. He instructed the *Untersturmführer*, Fritz Preyfi, to take charge of the children.

The children were housed in the barracks. Their plank beds were bunks built three levels high. Preyfi ordered them to sleep on the rough-hewn planks. The tallest of the boys, fourteen-year-old Leyb., was appointed the *capo* (leader).

At five o'clock in the morning a detachment of children went to work. All day long they could hear the cries of thousands of men, women, and children who were being murdered by the Germans. The screams would die down and then start anew. These were cries of torment and torture. They made the blood run cold and filled the boys' souls with unspeakable suffering.

The adult prisoners in the barracks showed the boys the kind of tender affection that could only be shown by fathers who had lost their own children. These were Jews, highly skilled workers who were kept alive for labor. Their families had been exterminated.

Among them was an elderly foreman named Aaron from the Grodno meatpacking plant. No one knew his surname. (People in the camp were called by their first names or by nicknames.) He became friends with the children. They called him by the endearing name of Arli.

Arli was a good singer and even composed songs. In the evenings, to distract the children from depressing thoughts, he would teach them to sing. There was a red-haired boy who was nicknamed "Red." He had a soft treble voice and sang well. When Red sang, each of the adults thought of their own children. Aaron would cry and pat the boy on the back.

The Germans took everything away from the children who came from the Soviet territories. They took away their relatives, homes, schools. They took their joys, their dreams, their childhood. There was only one thing the Germans did not dare take — their songs. And the children sang about their homeland, about Moscow. Often in the dark, crowded barracks you could hear the song, "Vast is My Homeland."

The children's detachment tended geese and cows, cleaned potatoes in the kitchen, and sawed wood. The whole camp knew the children. On Preyfi's orders, the children had to dress in uniforms — blue linen jackets with metal buttons. Preyfi forced the children to march for hours and tried to get them to march in perfect ceremonial military step. He amused himself with the children as if they were living toys, breaking their formations when he felt like it. He would boastfully show off the marching of his "toys" to his boss, Van-Eupen.

Once Arli decided he would attempt to rouse in a German compassion for the children. He told the children to sing the saddest song they knew. The children's voices conveyed immeasurable bitterness.

At that time another boy came in carrying a skinny turnip for Arli. A German summoned a carpenter from Warsaw named Max Levit, gave him a stick, and ordered him to give the boy twenty-five blows. Levit hit the boy once lightly. Preyfi tore the stick away from him and, in a rage, began to beat the boy mercilessly. The boy was already dead by the time Preyfi delivered the last blows. After breaking his "toy," Preyfi said: "That's the way to beat someone."

One of the boys was named Isaac. He was a good dancer. Preyfi ordered him to dance on a table because all wind-up toys dance on tables. And Isaac danced on a square meter of the table with amazing speed, with dead mechanical rhythm, with a sad, waxen face that really was reminiscent of a wind-up toy.

There was another boy, an artist, named Yasha. He drew dismal pictures of camp life on pieces of plywood. Sometimes he drew a tank with a five-pointed star tearing up the barbed wire entanglement and crushing the *Wachmänner* (guards). Then he would erase the drawing.

Yasha and Red shared a bed. On cold nights the little singer and the little artist kept each other warm.

Preyfi was sent on business to the Cracow camp. The camp boss, Van-Eupen, appointed another *Untersturmführer*, Stumpfe, "guardian" of the children. Stumpfe was an extremely tall, fat, young SS soldier. According to the testimony of Polish and Jewish witnesses, he always laughed during the execution of prisoners and was nicknamed the "Laughing Death."

This "guardian" found a new job for the children. He ordered the detachment to arm itself with shovels and to spread human ashes trucked in from the death camp along the road.

July came, and the sun beat down mercilessly. The air was so hot that it was impossible to breathe. Suffocating from the heat and the stench, the weak, exhausted children, driven by the whips of the *Wachmänner*, fainted onto the ashes of their own mothers and fathers.

During evening inspection Stumpfe discovered that five boys were missing. Red's absence was particularly conspicuous.

"Where's Red?" roared the "guardian."

"I'm here," said a timid voice.

Stumpfe noticed a boy with black curly hair. It was Red covered with black dust. Stumpfe walked up to him, sank his fingers into the boy's thick curls, and with his powerful hand, lifted him up by the hair.

"Negrito," he said contemptuously, and released Red. Four others were missing. It turned out that two had died, unable to withstand the inhuman torment. Their small bodies lay on the black road among the ashes. Two had disappeared: quiet Misha and handsome Polyutek. The boys had run away.

The runaways were caught in a few days at the railroad station and were brought back to the camp.

The Germans had the detachment line up in front of the gallows. They brought out Misha and Polyutek. Their hands weren't tied. The *Untersturmführer*, Lants, said: "It's better this way. If his hands are free, the hanged man will wave them like a bird flapping its wings, and he'll fly straight to heaven."

"Laughing Death" Stumpfe burst out into loud laughter. The boys were hanged. Polyutek died quickly, almost without convulsions. Misha's rope turned out to be too long and he could touch the ground with his toes. He wheezed for a long time, quivering and rolling his frightened eyes in all directions. Lants cut the end of the rope from the branch, and with the boy still alive on the ground, he rested his foot on the boy's head, and firmly tightened the noose. He lifted Misha's skinny little body easily and hanged him again.

For the first time, the boys began to cry. The torments of comrades touched their hearts, which had turned to stone. Stasik started to feel sick. *Capo* Leyb held him up and said:

"Don't cry. Misha and Polyutek are okay now, they don't have to live any longer."

Hauptsturmführer Van-Eupen and *Untersturmführer* Stumpfe, Lants, Hagen, and Ledeke got on their bicycles, rode in a circle around the gallows and, merrily chatting, had their pictures taken.

In the evening the children sang a song which they called "We Lost." Arli composed it. Long and mournful, it depicted life in the camp and mourned over the boys who were still alive.

The song ended this way:

Roaring on the field of death is a fire,
The ashes of brothers and sisters burn the heart.
We've no more to live on this earth,
We've lived our short life.

That night, after the execution of their friends, the children could not sleep. The singer and the artist hugged each other and quietly wept.

On July 22, 1944, a detachment of children was sent with shovels, not to the black road, but to the edge of the forest. "We have to dig pits there for anti-aircraft emplacements," Stumpfe explained to them. But the *capo* noticed that the pit they were digging was not like an anti-aircraft emplacement. Soon everyone heard the distant rumble of guns. The front was drawing nearer. Red listened carefully to the noise and said: "The Germans are retreating, but we will remain here," and he knocked the shovel against the bottom of the pit.

The children realized that they were digging a grave. It had to happen sooner or later. They were doomed, but death did not frighten them. It had become a companion of their brief lives in the camp. Calmly Red said to his inseparable friend Yasha:

"When they kill us, let's lie down beside each other," he said. "We'll fall into the pit wherever we land."

"How in the world can dead people lie down next to each other?"

"They can. We'll stand up on the edge of the grave, give each other a hug, and fall down together. That's all there is to it."

And they both neatly evened off the edges of the grave.

Morning came. In the distance, beyond the fence, peasants were harvesting crops, storing up hay for the winter. You could hear the rumble of the guns more clearly. Whistling nervously, German railroad engines were rushing somewhere. The Germans hastily liquidated the Treblinka "labor camp" (the death camp had already been liquidated). The *Hauptunterführer* and other *Führers*, and *Wachmänner* drank up the remaining wine reserves. At seven o'clock in the morning shooting began. For security reasons, only ten people at a time were led to the graves. The "work" dragged out till evening. Then they brought the next-in-turn group of ten, including Arli and the carpenter Max Levit. Walking past the boys who were waiting for their own turn, Arli shouted:

"Farewell, my children!"

"Farewell," the boys answered.

"Good-bye, Arli, we'll soon be with you," said Leyba.

Red slipped past the *Wachmann*, hugged Arli tenaciously, pressing himself to him. Arli embraced his favorite.

"When did we last sing, was it on Wednesday? Remember? On Wednesday," he said to the boy.

Arli knew that he was going to be shot. He knew that they were going to kill the little singer, too. Why did he say "remember"? Before Red had time to ask the question, the *Wachmann* shoved him to the side.

When the *Wachmann* counted out ten boys, the whole detachment rose in objection.

"We all want to die together."

There were thirty of them. The *Wachmänner* were in a hurry, so they gave in. Leyb lined up his detachment and, lifting up his head, he led them in formation to the graves which they themselves had dug.

Max Levit was already lying in the pit. The drunken *Wachmänner* were not shooting straight. Max Levit wasn't harmed, but pretended to be dead. He could hear the harmonious voices of the children. On their way to their death the condemned young boys were singing a song about Moscow.

Closer, louder, closer. Levit heard the friendly patter of feet and the command of the German, Schwarz.

"Silence!"

"Long live Stalin!" the group answered. "He'll avenge us!"

The singer and the artist gave each other a firm embrace. A volley of shots rang out. Yasha was struck dead and when falling, he carried Red, wounded, into the pit. Red began to move, snuggled up closer to his friend, and glanced into the terrified face of Arli who was lying next to him. The boy closed his eyes, rested his forehead on Yasha's shoulder, and for a minute remained still. Then Red raised his head and said:

"*Wachmann*, sir, you missed, please, once more, once more."

The *Wachmann* swore. "Laughing Death," Stumpfe, broke out in a laugh. The *Wachmann* fired another shot. The copper-golden, curly, little head dropped and rose no more.

Twilight fell. The tired *Wachmänner* (during this day, July 23, 1944, they shot seven hundred Poles and Jews) decided to fill in the pits the next day, and left.

Max Levit crawled out from under the small corpses of the children and walked off into the forest.

We met the carpenter from Warsaw in the village of Vulka-Okronglik, two kilometers from the former camp at Treblinka. A sixty-two-year-old Pole from this village, Casimir Skarzynski, who worked with the children on the shoveling of the human ashes, came to see us. The carpenter Max Levit and the peasant Casimir Skarzynski told us the truth about the children from the black road.

By **V. Apresyan**

The Uprising at Sobibor

I

Like the camps at Majdanek, Treblinka, Belzec and Oswiecim, the death camp at Sobibor was created by the Germans for the organized mass extermination of the Jewish population of Europe. It was located in a huge area in the forest next to the small station of Sobibor. The railroad came to a dead-end, which was supposed to help keep the place a secret. As usual, the Germans guarded it thoroughly from the surrounding population; all criminals are afraid of witnesses.

The camp was surrounded by four rows of barbed wire, three meters high. The space between the third and fourth rows was mined. Guards patrolled between the second and third rows. Sentries were on duty day and night in the towers, from which they watched the whole barricade system.

The camp was divided into three basic parts, or subcamps, each having its own strictly defined purpose. The first contained the barracks, the carpentry, shoemaker and tailor shops, and two buildings for officers. The second contained the barbers' quarters, stores, and shops. In the third stood a brick building with iron gates; it was called the "bathhouse."

The camp at Sobibor began operation on May 15, 1942. The first groups of prisoners came from France, Holland, and Western Poland. Here is what a Dutch Jewish woman, Selma Weinberg, says about her stay in the camp:

"I was born in 1922 in the town of Evolle (Holland). In Holland there was no hostility between the Dutch and the Jews, and we lived in friendship, feeling no difference between our peoples. But the Germans came and the persecution began. In Westerbork, in 1941, they created a camp for Jews sent from Germany. When the persecution of the Jews began in the country and the Jews were forced to wear special badges, the Dutch welcomed the people who wore these badges. When they began to send the Jews to Poland (in 1941), a strike broke out in Amsterdam. Life in the city came to a standstill for three days. The Dutch hid the Jews from the Germans. Out of the two thousand Jews that were in Utrecht, only two hundred people went to Poland; the rest were hidden by the local population. There was a special organization operating in the

436

country to save the Jews, and it rendered a great deal of assistance to the people in the form of food and money. Many Jews were saved by the organization 'Free Holland.'

"My family and I ended up in the camp at Westerbork, which had been expanded by 1942. There were two thousand people in the camp, but the composition of the prisoners changed continually, since every Tuesday a train carried around one thousand people off to Poland. The German officer would tell the prisoners that they were going to work in Poland and the Ukraine. Many went willingly, taking along their clothes, shoes, and food. The fact was that letters were arriving from Wlodawa in which there was no clue that all this was a German provocation. People were being forced to sign postcards typed by the Germans. Sobibor was not mentioned in them.

"I did not want to leave Holland, so I ran away from Westerbork. I was taken in by a Dutch family. All of my relatives had been taken to Poland. A Dutch German ('folksdeutsche') betrayed me. I sat in a prison in Amsterdam for two months, then landed in the camp at Fichte, where there were both political prisoners and Jews. I worked in the laundry there.

"In March, 1943, we were taken to Poland. Many hoped that they would meet their relatives there. After all, sick Jews were first even given treatment in Dutch hospitals, and only afterwards were they sent to Poland. The Germans created the outward impression that the people were under no threat. When we traveled through Germany, German nurses came to our train cars and administered medical assistance to those who fell ill on the way.

"On April 9, 1943, I arrived in Sobibor. The men were ordered to undress and walk on, to a third camp. The women walked between two rows of pine trees to the barracks to undress and have their hair cut off. A German officer selected twenty-eight young women for work in the second camp. I spent five months in Sobibor."

The mass extermination of people presented a complicated task. Careful forethought, constant concern for all details of the trade, and shrewd practicality on the part of the executioners of long standing were all evident in the way that this task was carried out in Sobibor. People went to their execution completely naked. Their belongings, clothes, and shoes were sorted and sent to Germany. The women's hair was cut off. Human hair was used to make mattresses and saddles; a furniture workshop was located right in

437

the center of the camp so that the hair of those executed found an immediate use and ready market in the camp. Finally, the construction of the "bathhouse" itself, i.e., the main department in this monstrous death factory, was a complicated matter and demanded the attention and care of qualified technicians, furnacemen, guards, suppliers of gas, coffinmakers, and gravediggers.

At various stages the prisoners themselves had to perform this work under threat of immediate death.

One of the few survivors of Sobibor, a Warsaw barber, Ber Moiseyevich Freiberg, points out in his testimony of August 10, 1944, that about one hundred people worked in the first subcamp and one hundred and twenty men and eighty women worked in the second.

"I worked in the second camp," he writes, "where the stores and shops were. When the people who were about to be killed had undressed, we gathered all their things and distributed them to the stores: shoes went to one store, outer garments to another, etc. Once there, the things were sorted according to quality and packed up for shipment to Germany. Every day a train of ten cars loaded with these things left from Sobibor. Documents, photographs and papers, along with other things of little value, we burned in bonfires. Whenever possible, we threw into the fire money and other valuables found in pockets and suitcases so that the Germans could not lay their hands on any of these items.

"After a while I was transferred to another job. In the second camp they had built three barracks for the women. In the first, the women took off their shoes, in the second — their clothes, and in the third, their hair was cut off. I was made a barber in the third barracks. There were twenty of us barbers. We cut hair with scissors and put it in bags. The Germans told the women that their hair was being cut for cleanliness — 'to prevent lice.'

"While working in the second camp, in June, 1943, I inadvertently witnessed scenes of frightfully inhuman treatment of innocent people. I saw a train arrive from Bialystok crammed full of completely naked people. Apparently, the Germans were afraid the prisoners might try to escape. The half-dead on this train were mixed in with the dead. People were given nothing to drink or eat during the journey. Those who were still alive were doused with chloride of lime.

"The Gestapo men in the camp often threw children on the ground, kicked them with their boots, and split their skulls. They set dogs on defenseless people, and the dogs tore the people to shreds. Many could not bear up and committed suicide. The sick were put to death instantly by the Germans."

What happened in the third "subcamp" — in the brick building called the bathhouse? According to all testimony, the "bathhouse" area was surrounded by barbed wire. Entrance to this area was strictly forbidden to the workers in the first two "subcamps" and was punished with immediate death.

"When a group of eight hundred people entered the 'bathhouse,' the door closed tightly," writes the same Ber Freiberg.

In a separate building there was an electric machine which released deadly gas. Once released, the gas entered tanks, and from there, it came through hoses into the chamber. Usually it took fifteen minutes for everyone in the chamber to be asphyxiated. There were no windows in the building. A German, who was called the "bathhouse attendant," looked through a small glass opening on the roof to see if the killing process was completed. Upon his signal, the gas was shut off, the floor was mechanically drawn apart, and the corpses fell below. There were carts in the cellar, and a group of doomed men piled the corpses of the executed onto them. The carts were taken out of the cellar to the woods in the third camp. A huge ditch had been dug there, and the corpses were first thrown into it and then covered up with dirt. The people who delivered and disposed of the corpses were immediately shot.

The following incident occurred: A group of people was already in the "bathhouse" chamber, but the machine which released the gas unexpectedly broke down. The poor people forced open the door and tried to run in all directions. The Gestapo men killed many of them, and the rest were herded back. The mechanics quickly fixed the machine, and events took their regular course. One of the female prisoners who was tending the rabbits, which the Germans raised for themselves, saw, through the cracks of the rabbit hutch, a line of naked women and children. These people did not suspect anything and were talking peacefully among themselves in various European languages about the kind of life that awaited them in the camp.

Sometimes things were different too. An eighteen-year-old girl from Wlodawa, when walking to her death one summery, sunny day, shouted for all to hear: "They'll take vengeance on you for us. The Soviets will come and there'll be no mercy on you, criminals."

They beat her to death with their rifle butts.

Among the German troops of the third camp, there was a boxer from Berlin, Gomersky, a particularly dreadful man, who boasted that he could kill a man with one blow. But then there was another sentimental German who went around to all the naked children who were about to die, patted them on the head, slipped them candy and grunted:

"Hi, darling. Don't be afraid. You'll see, everything will be all right."

Once incredibly horrible screams were heard from the third camp. It turned out that women and children were being thrown alive into a fire. These were amusements — extra entertainment for the Gestapo men.

The reality of the camp abounded in grotesque dramas, before which any imagination pales. A Dutch boy who was sorting a delivery of prisoners' possessions, suddenly saw things belonging to his own parents. Beside himself, he ran out of the storehouse where he worked, and in a crowd of people walking to their execution, he recognized his whole family. Another boy found his father's body among the people who had been gassed. He tried to bury his poor father's body with his own hands. The Germans killed the son, too.

None of these details differ in any way from the terrifying and revolting stories of what happened at Majdanek or Treblinka. Perhaps, the only way in which the Sobibor butchers showed imagination and personal initiative was in the method they used to conceal their work from the surrounding population. They raised flocks of geese on farms in the camp, and whenever a massacre took place they would excite the geese and cause them to call. In this fashion, the Germans were able to drown out the moans and cries of their victims.

In the summer of 1943, in an effort to conceal all traces of their crimes, the Germans built stoves in the third "subcamp." A special earth-moving machine was delivered to Sobibor. The grave ditch was dug up, and the machine moved the unearthed corpses into fires located under the railroad tracks. On these days you could smell the corpses in and around the whole area of the camp.

No matter how well documented, this dreadful place still seems like the wild fiction of a sick mind. On October 14, 1943, in this small area of the earth defiled by the Germans, there was an uprising which ended in victory for the prisoners. During the uprising twelve of the most important German guard officers were killed, including the leaders of the camp and four rank-and-file guards. After the uprising the Sobibor camp was destroyed.

440

How did this happen? Whose human strength proved to be sufficiently tenacious and organized to counteract German hardware directed against unarmed people? Who in this frightful atmosphere of death and humiliation found the will, the cleverness, the foresight? On September 22, 1943, six hundred Jewish prisoners of war, officers, and Red Army men were brought from Minsk to Sobibor. Eighty of them were kept alive for work in the second "subcamp." The Germans gassed and burned the rest. Among those kept alive was Officer Aleksandr Aronovich Pechersky.

II

Pechersky was born in Kremenchug in 1909. Since 1915 he had been living in Rostov-on-the-Don. In the last years before the war his primary profession had been directing amateur performances. In the very first day of the Great Patriotic War Pechersky was drafted into the army and in September, 1941, he was recommended for technician and quartermaster, second class. In October his detachment was surrounded in an area near Smolensk and captured. While in captivity, he came down with typhus and lay ill in horrible conditions for seven months. It was only by a miracle that Pechersky survived after the typhus. Typhus victims were shot by the Germans. He was somehow able to conceal his illness. In May, 1942, Pechersky managed to escape, but he was caught on the same day along with four other escapees. The captured men were sent to a "penal" unit in Borisov, and from there to Minsk. It was not until the fall of 1942 that they arrived in Minsk. Here the new arrivals were faced with a medical examination. This is how it was discovered that Pechersky was a Jew.

He was called to an interrogation.

"Do you admit that you are a Jew?"

Pechersky admitted it. If he had not, he would have been mercilessly whipped. He was put with some other men into the "Jewish" cellar, where he spent about ten days. It was pitch dark in the cellar, and there was no escape. They were fed every other day: one hundred grams of bread and a mug of water.

On August 20, Pechersky was sent to the Minsk SS labor camp on Shirokaya Street. He stayed there until the middle of September. In this camp there were about five hundred Jewish specialists from the Minsk ghetto, as well as Jewish prisoners of war. There were also about two to three hundred Russians there. The Russians were put in the camp for having contacts with partisans, for not showing up for work, etc. In a word, these were people whom the Germans, in the end, considered "incorrigible." The people in the camp were only half-starved, mainly because they managed to steal from the Germans. They worked from dawn until dark. "The camp commandant Wachs," says Pechersky, "could not get through a day without killing somebody. If he didn't kill, he'd simply get sick. You had to look him in the face, this sadist — his fat, upper lip quivering, his left eye blood-shot. Always in a drunk, foul hangover. What didn't he do! At night someone went out to urinate. Wachs shot him from the window, and in the morning, with ecstasy, he showed his woman the dead man's body and said:

"'That's my work.'"

People would line up for bread. Wachs would come out, shout "attention," rest his automatic pistol on the shoulders of the man at the head of the line and shoot. Woe to the one who was even slightly "out of formation"; he would receive a bullet in the head or shoulder. Wachs's typical amusement was to set the dogs on the prisoners. And they were not allowed to defend themselves from the dogs, which were Wachs's favorites.

When the women were brought from the common ghetto to the bathhouse, Wachs would always be there to search them, naked, with his own hands.

There were attempts at mass escape from the camp. Next to the camp's food storehouse was the dormitory for the *Schutzpolizei*. Sometimes prisoners were able to steal weapons there. This is the way a group of fifty men who worked in the storehouse planned to get hold of some grenades, pistols, and cartridges. The day before the planned escape their scheme was discovered. They were betrayed by a driver who had agreed to drive them out of the camp area in exchange for twenty thousand marks.

The Germans herded the betrayed escapees into the cellar of a burned-out house, surrounded it with a heavy guard, and let the dogs loose. It was the Germans' intention that the prisoners would all survive this ordeal so that they could undergo further humiliation and torture. Afterward, the whole group was led through the city with their hands raised above their heads. In the camp the whole process started over again with merciless whippings and attacks by the dogs. All the Germans who "felt like it" took part. Each man was taken separately to the bathhouse, which had been heated to an extreme temperature. Inside the bathhouse there was a tub of hot water. The victim was pushed into the tub, dragged out again, and doused with cold water. After this, he was led out into the cold and, two hours later, shot.

This group of fifty men consisted exclusively of Jewish prisoners of war. Pechersky knew two of them personally: Boris Kogan from Tula and Arkady Orlov from Kiev.

In September, 1943, the Germans began to reduce the number of people in the camp. On September 18, Pechersky was put on a train headed for Sobibor.

The commandant of the Minsk camp, Wachs, told the prisoners that they were going "to work in Germany." They traveled for four days in cars with the windows nailed shut and without bread or water. On the fifth day the train arrived at the small station of Sobibor. The train was switched to the sidetrack and put in reverse; the engine pushed the cars to the gates on which hung a sign with the inscription: *Sonderkommando*. Pechersky arrived in Sobibor after two years in German captivity, having grown wise through the cruelest and most dreadful experiences, having seen and endured enough to orient himself immediately to the surroundings of the new camp now opening before his eyes.

Here is what Pechersky says about the first day of his stay in the camp:

"I was sitting on some logs near the barracks with Shleyma Leitman, who later became my chief assistant in organizing the uprising. A stranger of about forty walked up to us. I asked him what was burning in the distance, about five hundred meters from us, and what that unpleasant smell was that permeated the whole camp.

"'Don't look there, it's forbidden,' the stranger answered. 'They're burning the corpses of the comrades who arrived with you.'

"I didn't believe him. But he continued:

"'This camp has existed for more than a year now. There are five hundred Jews here — Polish, French, Dutch, Czech. This is the first time they've brought Russian Jews. Trains carrying two thousand new victims arrive here almost every day. They are exterminated in the course of an hour — no more. Here, on this little patch of land of ten hectares (twenty-five acres), five hundred thousand men, women, and children have been killed.'"

The appearance of war prisoners from the east — Red Army soldiers and officers — created a sensation in the camp. Eager, inquisitive eyes that seemed to be waiting for something were fixed upon the newcomers. The people from the east, "prisoners of war," seemed almost like "people from freedom" to the rest of the camp population.

From the first days of his stay in Sobibor, Pechersky pondered over the future. What could be done? Should he try to save himself from death which, here, was surely inevitable? Should he escape? But should he escape by himself or with only a small group of comrades, leaving all the others to torture and death? He rejected this idea.

From the very beginning his idea of escape was linked with the thought of revenge. To take revenge upon the butchers, to destroy them, to set the whole camp free, if possible, to find the partisans — this is how he pictured the plan for future action. The incredible difficulty of the task did not stop Pechersky.

First of all he had to learn the layout of the camp, the daily routine of the prisoners, officers, and guards. It was clear to Pechersky that everyone would want to escape from the camp. But how, among this mass of strangers, exhausted physically as well as perhaps morally, was he to find people upon whom he could rely? And did such people even exist?

Five days after his arrival at Sobibor, Pechersky was unexpectedly invited to the women's barracks. Awaiting him was an international group of prisoners, most of whom did not know Russian. They plied him with questions. The conversation amounted to a kind of political consultation. The situation was complicated by the fact that Pechersky did not know with whom he was dealing. Among those present there could have been a *capo*, that is, a prisoner who worked for the Germans, an informer. Pechersky spoke in Russian. The volunteer interpreters tried to make what sense they could of his evasive answers.

Pechersky told them about how the Germans were defeated near Moscow, surrounded and destroyed near Stalingrad, about how the Red Army was approaching the Dnieper. He told them that the hour was not far off when the army of liberation would march across the German border. Pechersky also talked about the partisan movement on the occupied territory of the Soviet Union. He was still in Minsk when he heard rumors of German trains being derailed by partisans and of terrorist acts in the city itself.

"Everyone listened intently, trying not to miss a word. Anyone who understood even a little Russian would immediately interpret to the person next to him. And these people, who were doomed to death, were sincerely moved by the story of the valor and struggle of others.

"'Tell me,' a weak voice said, 'if there are so many partisans, why don't they attack the camp?'

"'Why should they? To free you, me, him? The partisans have other things to do than worry about us. No one is going to do our work for us.'"

Turning around abruptly and slamming the door, Pechersky left the barracks. No one translated his last words. They were understood even without a translation.

In any event, all the prisoners were thinking about escaping from the camp. That was the impression Pechersky got from this first meeting. The task that he faced was to stop and reason with the most impatient —to persuade them that they needed thorough and well thought-out preparation before deciding to act.

Once some comrades, including Shleyma Leitman, came to see Pechersky.

"Sasha, we've decided to escape," he said. "There are only a few *Wachmänner* (guards). We'll kill them and go into the forest."

"That's easier said than done. While you're knocking off one of the sentries, another will open fire with a machine gun from up in the tower. But let's suppose you manage to eliminate the whole guard. What will you use to cut the wire? How will you get through the mine field? What will happen to the comrades who stay here? Do we have the right to forget about them? Escape if you want, I won't stop you, but I won't go with you."

And he left with one of the comrades who called himself Kalimali. The escape was canceled.

Right about then another incident occurred that greatly influenced Pechersky's decision. The elderly man with whom he had talked on his first day in Sobibor came to see him again. This old man was called Borukh. Later it turned out that he was a tailor. Borukh was in the women's barracks when Pechersky met with the camp prisoners. The man warned Pechersky that they had begun to watch him.

"Did you notice the tall thin man standing next to me yesterday in the barracks? That was *capo* Bzhetsky, a complete scoundrel. He understood everything."

"Wait a minute, what exactly are you worried about? Why should he spy on me? I'm not planning to do anything. It's hopeless to try to escape."

"You are afraid of me and you're right," he began. "It's only a few days since we first laid eyes on each other. But we have no alternative. You could leave suddenly and then everything would be over for us. Understand me," and he seized his arm. "There are many like me who would like to leave. But we need a man who will lead us and show us what to do. Trust us. We know a lot here and we can help you."

I looked at his kind, candid face and I thought: traitor or not, I'll have to risk it!

"How is the field mined beyond the wire? Do you understand my question?"

"Not quite."

"Usually mines are placed in a chessboard pattern."

"Oh, now I understand. That's exactly how the field is mined. The distance between the mines is one and a half — two meters.

"Thank you. And now here's what I want to ask you. Will you introduce me to a girl?"

Borukh was surprised:

"To a girl?"

"Yes. Yesterday standing to your right was a very young girl — Dutch, I think, chestnut-colored hair, cut short. Remember? She was smoking. She would do. She doesn't speak Russian, which is just what I want. It's not a good idea for you to meet with me again. Leitman and I sleep next to each other, so whatever you need to know, he will convey to you. Now let's go to the women's barracks and meet that girl."

A few days passed. Every evening Pechersky met with Lukke. That was the name of his new acquaintance, the young Dutch girl. They sat on some boards near the barracks. Now and again a prisoner would come up to Pechersky and start to talk to him about what seemed, at first glance, to be the most ordinary things. Then *capo* Bzhetsky would walk up to him and Pechersky would immediately become affectionate with the girl. Lukke had a vague idea from the very beginning that she had been drawn into some sort of serious game. Pechersky never so much as mentioned a thing to her. She silently went along with the conspiracy. Pechersky was an "Easterner," a Soviet man. That alone was enough to inspire Lukke's hope. She wanted to believe him. Pechersky was twice the age of this eighteen-year-old girl. But he became close to her. Lukke told him her story. Here, in the camp, she had to hide the fact that she was the daughter of a German communist who had

446

run away from Germany to Holland when the Hitlerites came to power. Her father managed to hide again a second time when the Germans occupied Holland. The mother and daughter were brought to Sobibor.

The relationship between Pechersky and Lukke remained friendly throughout the whole period of these tragic days. Lukke understood the meaning and purpose of their friendship. Being used from childhood to conspire, she didn't ask about a thing, realizing that Pechersky had serious reasons for not letting her in on his plans.

Thus, without arousing anyone's suspicions, Pechersky was establishing himself among a mass of people he didn't know and at the same time he was learning a thing or two about the layout of the camp, about people's moods, and about the guards.

On the seventh of November he again met with Borukh, this time over a game of chess.

"Here's the first plan," began Pechersky, "it's complicated and barely feasible, but listen anyway. The carpentry shop is located five meters from the wire. There are four meters between the rows of wire. The mine field is another fifteen meters wide. Add to this seven meters inside the carpentry shop, and that makes thirty-one. We have to dig a tunnel. I've calculated that we'll have to hide approximately twenty cubic meters deep under the floor and in the attic. We'll have to dig only at night. This plan has two negative aspects: six hundred people will hardly be able to crawl one after the other thirty-five meters in the course of one night. Besides that, if we do get out, then we'll leave without killing the Germans. Talk with your people about this plan. For now I won't say anything to you about the second plan.

"Why?"

"I need more information. But in the meantime, can you begin to get your hands on seventy knives or razors? I'll distribute them to the men."

"It'll be done," said Borukh. "But now I need your advice on a very important matter. Monya has come into our group. You know him. He's one of the young lads who are building the barracks. Yesterday *capo* Bzhetsky came up to him and said that he knew about the escape that was being planned. Of course Monya tried to tell him it wasn't so. Bzhetsky listened to everything and said that he would like to join us in the escape."

"I thought it over," writes Pechersky, "and although this did look like a provocation, the idea that the *capo* could help seemed extraordinarily tempting to me."

"Monya thinks," continued Borukh, "that no matter what kind of a scoundrel Bzhetsky has been, we can count on him now. Bzhetsky knows perfectly well that in the end, even the *capos* will be killed. They can't leave any living witnesses to their crimes."

"What did you answer Monya?"

"That alone, without you, I couldn't decide anything."

"Let's think about the *capos*. But now it's time to go."

Rayman, the blacksmith, secretly fulfilled Pechersky's order — he made the knives. The blacksmith shop was located next to the metal shop. On the evening of October 10, several people gathered at the blacksmith shop, including Bzhetsky. The German guards had sent a gramophone to the metal shop for repair. Pechersky and Leitman were invited "to listen to gramophone records."

The conversation began from afar. They wound up the gramophone. The blacksmith fried some pancakes with sugar. Bzhetsky explained that the flour and sugar had been stolen from the second storehouse during the sorting of things belonging to those who had been put to death. Pechersky says: "I refused the pancakes and began to talk about the records. Bzhetsky kept trying to change the conversation to the subject of the escape. I avoided it under various pretexts. Finally, he signaled to the blacksmith, who took the gramophone and went out into the metal shop. Everyone went out after him. I remained alone with Bzhetsky.

"'I want to talk to you,' he began. 'You know about what?'"

"'I don't understand German very well.'"

"'Okay, let's speak Russian. True, I speak Russian poorly, but if you're interested, we can manage. I'm asking you to hear me out. I know that you are preparing an escape.'"

"'Nonsense! It's impossible to escape from Sobibor.'

"'You are going about it very carefully. You are rarely in the barracks. You never talk with anyone except with Lukke. But Lukke, she's only a cover. Sasha, if I had wanted to betray you, I could have done it long ago. I know you consider me a base man. I have neither the time nor the desire now to convince you otherwise. You can think what you like. But I want to live. I don't believe Wagner (the camp boss) when he says they won't kill the *capos*. They'll kill us all right! When the Germans liquidate the camp, they'll exterminate us too.'

"'I can't help seeing what is going on. All the others are just

448

carrying out your orders. Shleyma Leitman talks to people on your behalf. Sasha, understand me. If the *capos* are together with you, it will be incomparably easier. The Germans trust us. . . . Each of us has the right to move freely around the whole camp. In short, we are offering you an alliance.'

"'Who is this we?'

"'Me and Chepik, a *capo* in the bathhouse unit.'

"I got up and paced back and forth across the blacksmith shop several times.

"'Bzhetsky,' I began, and looking him straight in the face. 'Could you kill a German?'

"He didn't answer right away.

"'If it were necessary for the good of the cause, I could.'

"'And if there were no benefit? Just exactly the way they have exterminated hundreds of thousands of our brothers. . . .'

"'I haven't thought about it that way. . . .'

"'Thank you for your frankness. It's time for us to go.'

"'Okay. But I ask you once more. Think about what I told you.'

"I answered that there was nothing for me to think about, said good-bye, and left. However, the very fact that Bzhetsky had to think before answering my question about murdering a German caused me to think that perhaps, in this instance, he really was not playing the role of a provocateur. A provocateur would have agreed immediately.

"The next day, October 11, while working in the north camp on the construction of barracks we heard screams and machine-gun fire. The Germans immediately herded people together into one place, forbade them to walk out of the workshops of the first camp, closed the gates, and posted an additional guard. It was not until five o'clock that the reason for all these extraordinary measures became clear. A regular train of condemned people had arrived. When they were divided up and led away, the people grasped the whole situation and took off in all directions. Stark naked, they were able to run only as far as the wire while the Germans opened fire with rifles and machine guns.

"The meeting at which the final escape plan was adopted took place on the next day, October 12, in the carpentry shop. Present at the meeting were Borukh, Leitman, Yanek, the foreman of the carpentry shop, Monya, Pechersky and a few other 'Easterners.' In the yard near the shop two men were calmly talking and near the gates of the first camp, two others. These were the lookouts.

"The meeting began with the question of what to do about Bzhetsky. It was decided that he should be invited to join. Monya left and a few minutes later returned with Bzhetsky.

"'We decided, Bzhetsky, to invite you,' I began, 'but by taking a man like you into our group, we are risking the fate of the whole camp. So remember, if there is the smallest failure, you'll die first.'

"'I know that.'

"'And so, comrades, here's the only plan which I consider feasible. We've got to kill all the German officers. One by one, of course, but all within a very short time. We'll have no more than an hour for this. Only the Eastern Jews, only the prisoners of war whom I know personally and on whom I can rely will kill the Germans. After lunch at 3:30, *capo* Bzhetsky under some pretext will take three men to the second camp. These people will kill four officers. At four o'clock the electricians must cut the telephone line that runs through the second camp to the reserve unit. At the same time we, in our camp, will start killing the Gestapo men. We have to see to it that we catch the Germans at different times and kill them one by one. At 4:30 Bzhetsky and Chepik will have the whole camp line up in a column as if for a work detail, and the column will start toward the exit. The 'Easterners' will be in the front ranks. On the way to the main gate they will have to seize the weapons depot — if possible, without making any noise. Remember that while the column is moving, people could easily panic. If that happens it will be all over; the Germans will realize it's an escape. If we manage to seize the depot, we'll fight. If we don't we'll have to break through. Not far from the carpentry shop, almost at the wire, is the officers' house. We can be sure that the Germans didn't dare mine the field next to it, but they may have planted a few signal mines. So we'll have to cut through the wire in just that spot. That's the whole plan. Think about it until tomorrow. Are there any objections?'

"Borukh answered for everyone that there were 'no objections.'"

III

This incredibly bold and courageous plan was devised by a man who burned with the desire for freedom and revenge. It goes without saying that the plan could work only if the strictest precision and secrecy were maintained.

It is no wonder that each hour of the next day, October 14, was marked off separately in Pechersky's diary.

He began work that morning in one of the barracks, from whose

450

windows he could see the whole camp. The seven men who worked alongside him that morning knew nothing of the escape. In the adjacent barracks twenty "Easterners" selected from a special list were building plank-beds under Leitman's supervision. At ten o'clock, Leitman called Pechersky and reported to him on the progress of the plan:

"At four o'clock *Untersturmführer* Ernest Berg will be invited to the tailor shop to be fitted for a coat. At 4:15 *Oberscharführer* Gettsinger (the boss of the third camp, the death camp) will arrive there. *Unterscharführer* Emil Schumacher is supposed to come to the shoemaker's shop at four o'clock. I'll take care of *Unterscharführer* Friedrich Gaulstich with my own hands. Four Germans will be killed in the second camp; the men will try to lure the rest of them somehow into the workshops."

"Good. Have the comrades who have taken the responsibility for killing the Germans come to see me one at a time."

"Five minutes later Kalimali stopped into the barracks where I was working.

"Today at three o'clock," I said to Kalimali, "you will go to the tailor shop. Take a plane, a chisel, and an axe. Watch out, Kalimali, if you miss your mark — we're dead. Understand?"

"Yes."

"Well, on your way now! Good luck."

"I gave him a firm handshake.

"A half hour later Boris Tsibulsky came to see me. He had been entrusted with killing the Gestapo men in the second camp.

"Boris," I said to him, "the time has come. I'm sending you to the most difficult area. Mikhail and Benya will go with you. Take two axes. Bzhetsky will lead you to the second camp. Remember, Boris, you will be the first. Your blow will inspire everyone. If the comrades going with you are afraid, replace them. Force won't do."

"Don't worry, Sasha, they're just waiting for the signal."

At two o'clock one of the Gestapo men suddenly appeared at the first camp, took *capo* Bzhetsky and three other men, and led them off somewhere. We were struck by a terrifying thought — "everything has been exposed!"

An hour later we learned that Bzhetsky had been taken to the North camp to stack wood. *Capo* Chepik took upon himself the task that had been given to Bzhetsky — he led people to the second camp to kill the Gestapo men.

The tension in the camp grew. The rebels' conspiracy was absolute. Very few of the camp prisoners knew about the impending escape, but many could sense a vague uneasiness. Almost everyone felt that they could trust those silent, sensible, gloomy people who had recently arrived at the camp and who were always discussing something among themselves. Two days before the escape was the Jewish holiday of Yom Kippur. There were devout persons in the camp. One of the "Easterners" turned to a cantor and asked:

"Why do you pray to God for his help? You should pray for Sashka" (Pechersky).

This was the answer he heard:

"We are praying to God that everything will turn out well for Sashka."

Hope filtered through the silence and through a general fear. Various rumors were spreading. The way was paved for the events which broke out on October 14.

* * *

The first one killed was *Untersturmführer* Ernest Berg, who came to the tailor shop twenty minutes earlier than anticipated. The minute that Berg removed the belt with his holster and pistol and began to try on the coat, Kalimali struck him on the head with his axe. The German's corpse was thrown on the bed and covered with a blanket. It is impossible to read Pechersky's diary without emotion:

"It wasn't yet four o'clock when Kalimali ran into the barracks and put the pistol in front of me. We embraced.

"'Now it's done,' I said. 'even if anyone felt like backing out, it's too late. Thank you, friend.'

"Kalimali left. Suddenly a Dutchman, who had gone deathly pale, got up and tried to walk out after Kalimali.

"'Where are you going?'

"'I want to urinate.'

"'Get back. You'll have to wait. Comrades, do you realize what's going on,' I said to everyone who was in the barracks. 'Watch this one, don't let him out.'"

At 4:10 in the same tailor shop Semyon Mazurkevich killed Michel, the chief of the guard for the whole camp. At the same time in the shoemaker's shop Arkady Weisspapier killed the boss of the death camp, *Oberscharführer* Gettsinger. At 4:15 Tsibulsky reported to Pechersky that he had carried out his task — the elimination of the Gestapo men in the second camp. Four Gestapo men were dead, the telephone line had been cut, the exits closed.

The time came to get the people in formation.

But Pechersky waited. He hoped to finish off one more German.

At this time Shleyma Leitman killed another Gestapo man (Friedrich Gaulstich).

At 4:30 *capo* Bzhetsky returned. This was very timely because only a *capo* could draw up a column without arousing suspicion.

There were only a few weapons in the hands of the rebels — eleven pistols taken from the dead Germans and six rifles which the tinsmiths had stored away long ago by hiding them in the drain-pipes. They had to make do with what they had.

At 4:45 Bzhetsky gave the signal to form the column. He gave a shrill whistle and people came running from all directions.

The chief of the sentries (a German from the Volga region) tried to force the people back to the barracks, but he was killed.

The crowd rushed toward the weapons depot. Heavy machine-gun fire blocked its way. Pechersky realized that he would not be able to seize the weapons. He shouted:

"Comrades, forward!"

People ran behind him toward the officers' house. Many ran in the other direction, to the central gate.

The sentry posts were overrun. People ran straight through the mine field toward the forest that was visible in the distance. Many of them were blown up by the mines. Of the six hundred who ran, four hundred nevertheless reached the forest.

Carpenter Khaim Povroznik, a resident of Chelm and a soldier in the Polish army who had been captured by the Germans back in 1939, talks about this day:

"A large group gathered in the camp. In the center stood our glorious leader, Sashka. (Earlier Povroznik calls Pechersky the 'glorious Rostov lad.' Sashka shouted:

"For Stalin, Hurrah!"

"After dividing up into small groups, we dispersed throughout the whole forest. The Germans tried to round us up. Airplanes fired at us with machine guns. A great many were killed. No more than fifty people survived. I managed to get to Chelm where I hid until the arrival of the Red Army. On that day life returned to me, a prisoner of Sobibor."

A Dutch girl, Selma Weinberg says:

"When the uprising occurred in the camp I managed to escape.

Two other girls ran away with me — Ketty Khokes from the Hague and Ursula Stern from Germany. Ketty later joined a partisan unit and died there from typhus. Ursula also fought in a partisan unit. She is now in Wlodawa. I was with Ursula in Westerbork and in the prison at Fichte. I lived through Sobibor with her and it was with her that I escaped."

The fate of Pechersky's friend, the Dutch girl Lukke, remains unknown, like her real name.

On October 22, Aleksandr Pechersky, after spending a long time wandering on the country roads of Poland, met up with a partisan unit which he joined with several of his comrades. At the present time he holds the rank of captain in the Red Army.

* * *

On ten hectares (twenty-five acres) of Polish land where the Sobibor death camp was located, the wind whistles through rusty barbed wire. The potato or cabbage field which the Germans planted here to hide the traces of their monstrous criminal work, has been dug up again. Underneath it have been found fragments of human bones, the pitiful debris of everyday life in the camp, odd pairs of shoes of all sizes and styles, a great number of bottles with labels from Warsaw, Prague, Berlin, children's feeding bottles and false teeth, Jewish prayer books and Polish novels, postcards with pictures of European cities, documents, photographs, a prayer tallith alongside a faded knit rag, boxes which had formerly contained tin cans and eyeglass cases, a child's doll with twisted hands. All these things are mute witnesses to the murder of hundreds of thousands of people brought to a death camp from all corners of Europe.

By **P. Antokolsky** and **V. Kaverin**

Ponary

(The story of engineer Yu. Farber)

I am an electrical engineer by profession. Before the war I lived in Moscow and worked in a communications research institute while completing graduate work.

Immediately after the war began I joined the Red Army.

In the fall of 1941, we were surrounded and after wandering through the woods, trying to make my way back to my unit, I was captured by the Germans.

One of the Germans looked at me and said: "This one won't have to suffer in captivity — he's a Jew and won't live to see today's sunset." Since I spoke German, I understood everything but did not let them know.

I was led, along with a large group of prisoners, to a knoll surrounded by barbed wire. We were lying on the ground under the open sky; machine guns stood on all sides of us. Three days later we were locked in freightcars and taken away. We were not given any food or water, and the doors were never opened. . . . On the sixth day we arrived in Vilnius. Many corpses were left behind in the train cars. Eight thousand captives were put into the camp at Novo-Vileyka, near Vilnius. People lived in what were once stables, without windows or doors, and with walls full of huge cracks. Winter was beginning.

The food ration was one kilogram of bread for seven people, but we were often not given even the bread. The Germans would bring in a block of icy potatoes frozen together with dirt, husks, and straw. This was thrown into a caldron and boiled down to a soft starchy consistency: a prisoner received half a liter of this soup.

Every morning dead people were pulled out of all the barracks. The corpses were dragged to a pit and sprinkled lightly with chloride of lime; but they were not buried because the next day a new group of corpses would be thrown into the same pit. There were days when the number of corpses exceeded a hundred and fifty and often, together with the corpses, they would throw in people who were still alive.

The Germans called us the dregs of humanity, the *Untermenschen* (subhumans). Once, for some minor offense, the Germans ordered two prisoners to lie face down in a puddle which was already covered with a thin sheet of ice.

They were left there for the night, and since they were forced to lie naked, they froze to death.

Two dates stand out in my mind — the night of December 5, 1941, and the night of December 6. I had a comrade, a young Ukrainian of twenty named Pavel Kirpolyansky. It was cold in our barracks and in order to warm up, we lay down on top of one overcoat, covered ourselves with another, and slept with our arms wrapped around each other. We were infested with parasites. Typhus was cutting people down. That night Pavel and I lay holding each other. Suddenly I was awakened by the feeling that he was going to try to pull free. I put my hand on his forehead and knew immediately what was wrong. Pavel had a burning fever, was delirious, and didn't recognize me. I could not leave him without an overcoat. I put my arms around him and held him tight until morning. . . . He died in the morning and he was dragged off to the pit. . . . However, I did not come down with typhus.

On the night of December 6 two Ukrainian lads lay on each side of me. We put our arms around each other; I was warm and slept soundly. At dawn the whistle sounded, and I began to waken my neighbor Andrey. He did not respond; he was dead. I tried to wake my second neighbor, Mikhaylichenko. He was dead, too. I had slept the night between two dead men.

The determination to stay alive and go back to Moscow never left me.

I forced myself to wash and even to shave. There was a barber in the barracks. Now and then he would shave the prisoners and as payment he would ask for a potato. On this day, October 7, a great piece of luck awaited me — a whole potato turned up in my watery soup. I decided to have a shave. When I offered the barber the potato which I fished out of my soup, he looked at me and said: "That's not necessary. . . ." I asked him: "Why?" He answered: "You're going to die this week just the same, eat it yourself."

A week passed. I again went to have a shave. The barber was amazed to see me: "How is it you're still alive? Well, all right, I'll shave you once more for free, you'll die soon all the same." However, when I came a third time, the barber said: "I'll shave you for free until you die."

By the new year, I could no longer walk — I was swollen from hunger. My toes began to turn black; then the flesh fell off, and you could see the bones.

An interpreter chosen from the prisoners, a Leningrad student named Igor Demenev (who later with some comrades killed the German guards and escaped), helped me to get into the camp infirmary. Among several wooden barracks in a small demolished brick house, the interpreter and a few doctors from among the prisoners of war had organized an infirmary. The doctors treated me very well.

The assistant to the chief doctor was Doctor Yevgeny Mikhaylovich Gunter, from Stalingrad. He treated me with brotherly sympathy and concern. By May I had learned to walk, and by June I was able to climb to the second floor. The infirmary was the only place in the camp the Germans did not enter because they were afraid of the typhus and tuberculosis. Instead of being kicked out of the infirmary, I was made a janitor. The number of deaths was enormous.

I lived in this infirmary until the end of 1943. The number of prisoners of war continually diminished. Of the eight thousand that were brought here only a small handful were still alive.

The Germans used the prisoners for work outside the camp. The local residents would give them food.

Military Doctor Sergey Fedorovich Martyshev took an enormous risk by trying to save as many people as possible. He kept people in the infirmary under every imaginable pretext and rendered them every assistance.

When we heard about Stalingrad, there was an enormous change in the mood of the prisoners and the civilian population, because everyone realized that the Germans had lost the war.

Cut off from the whole world, our little group also joined in the fight against the German invaders. Leaflets were written for the Germans. Even I wrote some of them in German. In one leaflet I wrote: "God, the Lord, gave the Germans three qualities: intelligence, decency, and National-Socialism, but no one has more than two virtues. If a German is intelligent and a National-Socialist, then he is indecent, but if he is intelligent and decent, then he isn't a National-Socialist."

Another leaflet simply said: "Hitler is kaput."

We wrote as many as twenty leaflets, and they had a considerable impact. We became bolder all the time. Often at twelve o'clock, as soon as the light would go out, we began to sing the *Internationale*. The Germans were furious and took all sorts of repressive measures; however, they were not able to find the "guilty ones."

457

My health became stronger little by little, even though Sergey Fedorovich considered this a miracle. I think the main reason was my internal conviction that I had to live until we were victorious. I mobilized all my physical and mental strength. I maintained the strictest self-discipline. I divided the bread ration of 150 grams into twenty slices, and later I learned to divide it into forty. These were small, oval-shaped loaves of German bread. The bread was made from a special flour — it contained a lot of sawdust. One little loaf was divided among seven people and from my own portion I made forty slices that were as thin as cigarette paper. We received the bread at five o'clock in the evening, and I made my portion last for five hours. I would take a slice, place it on a small wooden stick, hold it close to the stove, toast it, and eat it.

There was a small garden next to the infirmary; you couldn't find a blade of grass or the smallest leaf there. Even the bark from the trees had been eaten.

From time to time we were taken to the bathhouse, and that was where they would try to discover and catch the Jews. Once a German began harassing one of the prisoners, saying: "You Jew." The German wrote down the man's number so he could report it to the authorities. Vanya Nizhny, a prisoner of war, decided to save his comrade. When the German looked away, he managed to change the number on the note in a fraction of a second.

We washed in the bathhouse late in the evening, and the next morning the informer found himself in an embarrassing position. The fellow that was summoned turned out to be Russian and there was no way they could find fault with him.

At the end of 1943 new inspections began in an effort to catch the Jews. Everyone was lined up and forced to undress; our doctors were told to serve as the experts.

Sergey Fedorovich said categorically: "Kill me, do what you want, but I will not employ my expertise." He was threatened with all sorts of repressive measures; taking their cue from him, the other doctors also refused.

In the camp I was thought to be Yuri Dmitrievich Firsov, a Ukrainian.

Nevertheless, the Germans found out that I was a Jew. The Germans discovered six Jews; one of them turned out to be a Russian named Kostya Potanin from Kazan, who had never in his whole life even had any Jewish friends. But the Germans maintained that he had a big nose.

A memorable day arrived — January 29, 1944. A covered vehicle which was called the "Black Raven" arrived at the prisoner-of-war camp; the commandant led out the Jews who had been arrested (Kostya Potanin was among them). We were taken away. Suddenly the vehicle stopped, as we found out later, outside the Lukishskaya prison. Two Jews were led out; they had escaped from the ghetto, had hidden, were found and thrown into prison. A few minutes later, as soon as the vehicle had started off, these two began to cry. When we asked young David Kantorovich why they were crying, he said that the vehicle was going in the direction of Ponary, and from there there was no way back.

We were brought to Ponary. The place was fenced in by barbed wire. There was a sign on the gate: "Entry strictly forbidden, dangerous to life, mines." The vehicle drove through and in approximately three-hundred meters came to a second gate, behind which stood guards. Another group of guards emerged from the gate; neither those who were outside, nor those who came with us were allowed beyond the second wire. Procedure was strictly observed; Ponary was impenetrable.

The guards were strong, broad-shouldered, and stocky. The vehicle drove into the camp with a new guard. The barbed wire formed two walls, and as we found out later, there were mines in the space between them.

There was yet another small, narrow space in the wire. We were led through this passageway to the edge of an enormous pit which used to be the foundation area for an oil reservoir; its diameter measured twenty-four meters. The pit was four meters deep, and its walls were lined with concrete. Two-thirds of the pit were covered with wooden logs, and one third was open. I saw a woman at the bottom of the pit and realized that people were living there. There were two ladders on top. One ladder was considered "clean" and was used only by the Germans. They had us climb down the "unclean" ladder; the guard stayed above. From somewhere, they called out for the foreman; he was a Jew from Vilnius by the name of Abram Hamburg. The Germans called him Franz. They summoned another worker by the name of Motl, whom the Germans called Max. He was wearing shackles and was ordered to put us in irons too.

These were chains made of links that were almost as thick as a finger. They were put on the leg, slightly below the knee, roughly where boots end. The chain dangled to the ground, but we were allowed to tie half of the chain to the belt so that it did not prevent us from walking.

When all the newcomers had been put in chains, the chief appeared. He was a *Sturmführer*.

This man, a refined sadist, was about thirty years old. He was dressed like a dandy, wearing white suede gloves that came up to the elbow. His boots sparkled like a mirror. He smelled of very strong cologne. He behaved very arrogantly not only with us, but he also kept the German guards in incredible fear.

We were lined up, and he asked each of us where we were from. Kostya Potanin and I said that we did not understand him (I continued to conceal my knowledge of German), and foreman Franz translated. The *Sturmführer* spoke Yiddish and Polish and, with some difficulty, he could make himself understood in Russian.

When my turn came and he asked: "Where are you from?" I answered that I was from Moscow.

The *Sturmführer* said mockingly: "Moscow is a luxurious place" and stared at me. I answered: "What, you mean you don't like Moscow?" Franz, the interpreter, began to tremble and translated my words in a very softened form. The *Sturmführer* raised his hand threateningly, but did not touch me.

He said that we would be working on an important job of significance to the State: "Don't try to remove your shackles because they will be checked several times a day, and if there is the slightest attempt to escape, you will be shot. Don't think about escaping, because no one has ever left Ponary and no one ever will." Then the enumeration began: for the slightest attempt at escape — execution. We must obey every command of the bosses; for the slightest violation — execution. We must comply with all camp regulations; otherwise — execution. We must work diligently; if anyone is accused of laziness — execution. He spoke for a very long time and one thing became very clear to me: it was not difficult to die here. After this edifying speech, he left.

We stood at the bottom of the pit. There was one woman there, and from the depths of the pit came another. We began to talk with them.

We immediately asked a question: "Will they feed us?" They answered: "Don't worry about that, they'll feed you, but you won't get out alive."

We walked under a canopy. There was a wooden enclosure there, which was called the bunker, and a small kitchen. The women said that there were Jews from Vilnius and neighboring

460

villages living here. They had hidden outside the ghetto, but were found, put in prison, and — later — were brought here. Kantorovich, whom I've already mentioned (he was from Vilnius), exchanged a few phrases with the women. They became more candid and said that in Ponary not only Vilnius Jews were shot, but also Jews from Czechoslovakia and France. Our job would be to burn the corpses. This was kept in the strictest secrecy. The Germans thought that the women knew nothing, and we should not permit any slips of the tongue. When Germans were present we were to say that we cut timber. No sooner had we heard all this than a whistle sounded, and we had to climb up the ladder. We were paired off and led away.

The first thing that stunned us was the odor.

The S.D. (security forces) overseer said:

"Take shovels, remove the sand, and if you see a bone, throw it up."

I took a shovel, lowered it into the sand, and it immediately struck something hard. I dug away the sand and saw a corpse. The overseer said: "Never mind, it has to be that way." It was a huge pit which they had begun to fill as early as 1941. The people were not buried and were not even doused with chloride of lime. This was a conveyor which had operated uninterruptedly. The corpses fell in disarray, in various poses and positions. People killed in 1941 were dressed in outer garments. In 1942 and 1943 the so-called winter aid was organized — a campaign of "volunteer" donations of warm clothing for the German army. People who were herded to their deaths were forced by the Germans to undress to their underwear, and their clothes went into a fund of "volunteer" donations.

There was a technique for burning the corpses: on the edge of the pit was a small hearth, measuring 7 meters by 7 and built out of pine logs, a scaffold, one row of tree trunks stacked across other tree trunks, and in the middle was a chimney made from pine trunks. The first operation was to shovel the sand until a "figure" was uncovered; that is what the Germans ordered us to call the corpses.

The second operation was performed by the hook-man, which is what they called the worker who extracted the bodies from the pit with an iron hook. The bodies lay close together. Two hook-men, who were usually the strongest men from the work unit, would throw down a hook and pull out a corpse. In most cases the bodies came apart in pieces.

The third operation was done by the carriers — the *Träger*. They had to put a corpse on a stretcher, and the Germans made sure that they had a whole corpse on the stretcher, i.e., two legs, two arms, a head and torso.

The Germans kept a strict account of how many bodies had been removed. Our task was to burn eight hundred corpses a day; we worked from dawn to after dark. The *Träger* carried the bodies to the wooden hearth. There the figures were piled up in rows, one on top of the other. When one layer was stacked, spruce branches were put on top; a special worker, a *Häufenmeister*, looked after the fuel and added dry logs to the fires.

When the logs and branches had been piled on, black fuel oil was poured all over them, then a second layer was piled on, then a third, etc. In this way, the pyramid would reach four meters in height, sometimes even higher. A pyramid was considered ready when it contained three and a half thousand corpses. It was thoroughly soaked with fuel oil not only from above, but also from the sides; the sides were covered with special dry logs, which were amply soaked with gasoline, one or two thermite bombs were inserted, and the whole pyramid was set on fire. The Germans would stand around each of these fires very solemnly.

A pyramid usually burned for three days. It had a characteristically short flame; thick, black, heavy smoke containing large flakes of black soot would rise up, as if reluctantly.

A *Feuermeister* would stand nearby with a spade. He had to make sure that the fire did not die out.

After three days a heap of ashes would form, containing small bone fragments that had not burned through.

The very old men and people who were physically feeble were used to tramp down the ashes. The burned bones were shoveled onto a huge iron sheet where they were crushed by the stampers so that not a single piece of bone would remain.

The next operation was to shovel the ground bones through a fine-mesh metal net. This operation had a double purpose. If nothing was left in the net, it meant that the bones had been well ground; and secondly, this process uncovered metal objects such as gold coins and other valuable items which had not burned.

One more operation should be mentioned. When a corpse was lifted out of the pit, a special worker inserted a metal hook in the corpse's mouth, and if he discovered any gold crowns or bridges, he ripped them out and put them in a box.

There were pits that contained twenty thousand corpses each.

The stench literally turned one's insides out and brought on dizziness.

The pace of the work was such that it was not permitted to stop even for a second.

There were eighty of us workers. The guard consisted of sixty SS men. These were well-fed wolfhounds who were responsible for making sure that we did not escape. They stood in a chain around the pit and every fifteen minutes they would move from place to place. They had an abundance of everything: meat, wine, chocolate. But they could not go out beyond the limits of Ponary. They would either stand watch or stay in their own quarters.

Even more horrible than the SS men were the S.D. men. They were concerned with production and with keeping order. They would stand with their cudgels and often put them to use. We were constantly under their surveillance. Their vocabulary was very simple: they would either shout in German "*Renn, renn, renn,*" which means "run," "get going," "faster," or in Polish "*prendzej*" which means "quickly." They even used Russian swear words. They stood in positions from which they could see all areas of the pit. They would often use their cudgels, for any reason whatever. When we were carrying the bodies, the SS men would shout: "Carry them, carry them or soon you'll be carried like that."

On the first day the *Sturmführer* appeared, looked at the pit, and shouted: "Why is the one from Moscow working with a shovel, why can't he carry?" Immediately an S.D. man ran up to me and ordered me to take a stretcher.

We picked up a body and put it on a stretcher. It was very heavy, and my knees buckled. Suddenly the *Sturmführer* began to shout at the top of his voice: "He could carry one figure at a time in Moscow, let him carry two." I had to take a second body. Fortunately, I had a strong partner, Petya Zinin from the Mordovia Autonomous Republic of the USSR. We set off with two corpses. The *Sturmführer* shouted again: "They have a very light stretcher. Let them carry a third figure."

When the work day was over, we were counted again, all our chains were inspected, and we were ordered to go down to the bunker; when everyone had climbed down, the ladder was taken up. When we were brought here, we had to build a second bunker.

We couldn't complain about darkness; the pit had electric lighting.

When we came back from work, basins filled with a solution of manganese awaited us; we washed our hands with it thoroughly.

There were eighty of us in all — seventy-six men and four women. The men were in irons; the women did not wear them. Their duties were to clean up the living area, stock up on water and wood, and prepare the food. The oldest of the women was Basa — she was about thirty. She was an experienced woman and had a great deal of influence, because she had complete control over the foreman, Franz. The rest of them were very young girls of eighteen, nineteen, and twenty years. One of them, Susanna Bekker, came from a rich well-known family in Vilnius. It was typical that even there, in Ponary, some of the old men would take off their caps in front of her and say: "This is Bekker's daughter; how many stone houses he had!"

The third girl was called Genya. She was the daughter of a Vilnius artisan.

The fourth girl was Sonya Sheyndl. She was from a poor family, and was exceptionally hard-working and friendly. She tried to alleviate our existence in every way she could. For example, it was not part of her duties to wash our underwear, but she quite frequently did.

The men were mostly from Vilnius, and there wasn't one of them who did not find his family among the corpses.

A second group of workers, about fifteen men, were Soviet prisoners of war.

And a third group of men was from Iwie (Vevis), a small town between Vilnius and Kaunas.

The largest was the Vilnius group; it included people of various ages and social strata. They had known each other for many years, but quite often there was no friendship or unity between them. People would remind each other of misdeeds that had happened ten years previously. Isaac Dogim and David Kantorovich stand out among these people. Dogim, an energetic young worker from Vilnius, was a printer and electrician. He was born in 1914, and was an extremely unsociable person.

Kantorovich's story was unique. He was an active, sprightly fellow born in 1918. Before the war he worked as a clerk in a bookstore. The Germans killed his wife. He joined the partisans, but was captured.

Motl Zaydel was the son of poor parents from Sventsyany. His father and mother died; he lived in the ghetto. He was a nice-looking boy of nineteen; he had a fine voice and loved to sing.

Beginning in 1941, he was moved continuously from prison to prison. It was awful to listen to the stories about his endless sad wanderings.

We called him little Motl, "ingele," to distinguish him from the other Motl, with "vonses" (a mustache).

Leyzer Ber Ovseychik from Oszmiany and Matskin from Sventsiany were inseparable friends. Matskin was about thirty-five. He had been a rich man, a store owner. Ovseychik was a craftsman.

In spite of their social inequality, these two people were bound by close friendship. Instead of eating all his food, Ovseychik would give some to his comrade, and vice versa.

Shlema Gol was an interesting personality. He was a middle-aged man, extraordinarily kind, but extremely weak-willed. His wife, a communist and member of the Communist Party of Poland since 1933, was subjected to persecution and had been in the concentration camp at Bereza-Kartusska. During the Soviet period they both had positions of responsibility in Baranovichi.

Abram Zinger, a rather well-known composer, had conducted an orchestra before the war. He was an intelligent, educated man. He spoke good Yiddish, Russian, Polish, and German.

The foreman of the group, Franz, served as interpreter for the *Sturmführer*, but when the *Sturmführer* gave a particularly solemn speech, Zinger interpreted. Zinger would compose songs even in the horrible conditions which existed in the pit. He once composed a nice song in German, and we began to sing it in our pit. Unfortunately, the *Sturmführer* heard our song, wrote down the words, and typed it up under his own name; for this he gave Zinger one cigarette and one hundred grams of jam. Zinger was greatly upset by this; he poured his feelings out to me. He saw this plagiarism as a monstrous outrage upon his soul and said: "I don't sing songs for the Germans."

There were several clergymen in the pit. From time to time they would organize requiems in honor of the dead; the services were conducted solemnly and mournfully. . . . Everyone would wash up thoroughly and prepare for these prayer services. Ovseychik prayed twice a day, for two hours at a time, with great sincerity and enthusiasm.

I'll mention the prisoners of war. Aside from myself, there was Petya Zinin from Mordovia, a Russian paramedic by profession, born in 1922. After his escape he was with the partisans where he showed his greatest worth.

Miron Kalnitsky, a Jew from Odessa, was helpful because in his time he had worked near Ponary in a prisoner-of-war camp (not in a death camp), and he knew the area well. Among the prisoners there was also Veniamin Yulievich Yakobson from Leningrad, fifty-four years old, a pharmacist by profession. He was an extraordinarily good-natured man, who cared for the prisoners like a father. He always had some ointments, bandages, and powders in his pocket. He was greatly respected. If an argument arose, Yakobson would always reconcile the people who were at odds. But he was a little "off his rocker" and would say again and again that we would not be shot. "We are not guilty, why would they shoot us?"

The *Sturmführer* was a threat and a terror. Whenever he appeared at the edge of the pit, everyone knew that no good would come of it. People would strain themselves to the utmost, and the *Sturmführer* would stand there with his hands behind his back, look at us, and then say to someone (to certain people he gave contemptuous nicknames): "Why are you walking so slowly, are you sick?" The man would answer that he was well, not a thing was wrong with him. But the *Sturmführer* said to him: "Tomorrow you will go to the infirmary." Everyone knew that this meant he would be shot. That evening it was painfully difficult in the bunker. We felt terrible and ashamed that this old man would be taken to his death, and there was not a thing we could do to help. We tried to comfort "Feter." He said: "Why comfort me, I've lived my life."

Once when we came back from work, we had just reached the pit, when the *Sturmführer* suddenly appeared in a very malicious mood. He asked the question: "Who is sick?" Naturally, no one came forward. The *Sturmführer* lined everyone up in two ranks and said: "Now I'll find the sick ones." He approached each person and stared into his face, literally drilling each one with his eyes: "You're sick, step out," he said to one, then another.

But that did not seem sufficient for him. He approached a young, healthy man and asked: "Are you familiar with metalwork?" The young man answered: "I am." He too was taken out of the ranks and his irons removed. Everyone knew what that meant. Once a person's irons were removed, it meant he would be taken away and shot.

The *Sturmführer* went up to a fourth person and asked: "Are you familiar with metalwork?" The man answered: "No, I'm not." "Well, that's all right, you'll learn, step out." The fourth man's irons were also removed and he was taken above.

A few minutes later we heard four shots. The *Sturmführer* reprimanded our foreman: "What a disgrace, you can't wash people; you send them to the infirmary, and they're full of lice." This was the kind of method to which the *Sturmführer* resorted. He would walk around a row of people lined up in formation, peer into their eyes, and ask if anyone was not happy with his job. Everyone had to answer in unison that they were very happy. The *Sturmführer* turned to Zinger: "You are a musician, perhaps you don't enjoy working here?" The *Sturmführer* continued with his questions: "Perhaps one of the guards has been rude to you, has treated you badly?" We had to answer in unison that the guards treated us well. Then he ordered: "Sing songs." After a strenuous day we could barely stand on our feet, but we had to sing. Most often he ordered us to sing "Suliko," arias from the operetta "The Gypsy Baron," and a few other songs.

He would listen and then give an order to the sentry: "I'm leaving now, but have them sing until I return." There was no limit to the atrocities of the Germans.

Everything in me refused to accept this; it seemed unworthy to die a sheep's death. I was not the only one who felt this way. The thought of escape was everywhere.

Soon all this was translated into action. I was to play no small part in this whole affair. The fact that I was a Muscovite and that everyone saw me as an educated person, greatly strengthened my prestige.

I was brought to Ponary on January 29, and by February 1 we had already begun to construct a tunnel.

The people who were most actively involved in the tunnel were Petya Zinin, Isaak Dogim, and David Kantorovich. Shlema Gol also gave unsparingly of himself. If it was necessary, he would get up at four o'clock in the morning.

Ovseychik's expert hands proved very useful — whether it was a question of sawing or making some small adjustment, he was always right there. The Vilnius baker, Joseph Belets, was an illiterate, simple man but in working on the tunnel he proved to be very useful, because he had some experience in this area.

In regard to the tunnel, I should say a few words about two other people living in the pit.

Joseph Kagan (his real surname was Blazar) had previously spent time in prison for criminal acts. Kagan-Blazar is well known for having escaped twice from Ponary. In 1941 he was taken away and sent to Ponary, where he was lined up at the edge of the pit and "shot." He displayed amazing resourcefulness and self-control. Seeing that the line of machine-gun fire was drawing close to him, he was able, at just the right moment, to fall into the pit a split second before being shot. He survived. Corpses were falling on him from above, and some sand was poured over them. He lay like that until evening. When it grew dark, he climbed out of the pit and went back to the city. He hid in a conspiratorial apartment, but he was found and sent a second time to Ponary. He took part in a tunnel escape and thus escaped from Ponary a second time.

Franz (Abram) Hamburg was also in Ponary twice. The first time he was found in one of the conspiratorial apartments where seventeen people were hiding. They were all brought to Ponary; after being forced to strip naked, they were led to the edge of the pit. Contrary to the usual method, the people were shot one at a time. Hamburg stood seventeenth in line. He saw the Germans shooting point-blank in the back of the head and the people falling one after another. Sixteen people were shot that way. When his turn came he turned around and said that he had a lot of gold. "Don't shoot me, I'll give it to you." "Where is the gold?" asked the Germans. "It's hidden in the city." He was allowed to get dressed, was put in a car, and taken to Vilnius. In Vilnius he knew of a basement in which there were two thousand tons of potatoes. He took the Germans to this basement and said that the gold was there, under the potatoes, right in the corner. The Germans brought a large group of men who worked for several days removing the potatoes and clearing out the corner which Hamburg had indicated. He said they had to dig deep, since the gold was buried in the ground. They began to dig, but they did not find anything. The Germans gave him an awful beating but he insisted that the gold had been right there. To his surprise he was not shot, but instead was returned to Ponary and made chief "*Brenner*" (cremator).

On February 17, 1944, a new group of prisoners of war was brought in. Among them were two of my personal friends from a camp where I had been held previously.

Yury Gudkin, a civil engineer before the war, lived in *Elektrostal*, near Moscow. He had a wife and three-year-old daughter in Moscow. In the prisoner-of-war camp he took the most active part in putting out leaflets, he established connections with the partisans, etc. The second prisoner of war, Kostya Zharkov, a student of a Leningrad institute, was with me in the hospital and helped me a great deal. He was depressed. I tried to cheer him up. I showed Yuri our tunnel that very night. He thought it was well done and gave some valuable advice. I valued his opinion very highly. The next morning, we "old timers" were sent to work, and the newcomers were left in the pit. The women later told us that the *Sturmführer* came and lined everyone up and looked over the newcomers. If he asked us where we were from, the question he asked them was — what their profession was. I don't know how it happened that Yury Gudkin, a man who had been in difficult situations before, imprudently said that he was a civil engineer. It should be mentioned that the Germans exterminated educated people before anyone else. The *Sturmführer*'s mood became unusually cheerful. He rubbed his hands with joy. "Why were you sent here? We'll give you a job in your specialty. Remove his irons." He was led out of the pit. Kostya Zharkin and one other prisoner of war said that they were students. The *Sturmführer* was delighted. Saying that the Germans valued science very highly, he ordered that their irons be removed. They were all taken above and shot. The rest were sent to join us.

The provocativeness, sadism, and cynicism of the Germans were truly incredible.

Here is the story of Kozlovsky, who worked with us.

"On April 6, 1943, a trainload of women was brought to Ponary. The Germans started the provocative rumor that the ghetto in Vilnius would be liquidated, but that the ghetto in Kaunas would not be touched. The Germans selected two thousand five hundred of the prettiest and healthiest women and said that in a few days they would be going to Kaunas. They were given tags which were viewed as their right to live. People gave away everything they owned for these tags. When the train arrived at Ponary, the Germans entered the cars and told everyone to strip naked. The women refused, and for this they were beaten unmercifully. Then, under a strengthened, quadrupled escort, they were led to the pits. The persons responsible for checking made sure that not one rag, not one thread remained on them. . . . And, indeed, when we dug up that pit we discovered 2,500 well-preserved naked female corpses."

The man who ordered this slaughter was Weiss.

Kozlovsky, who was in the unit which picked up the clothes, told me of the following episode.

Weiss was rushing everyone; all you could hear was: "Faster, faster." The doors of one of the cars opened (Kozlovsky was next to them), and a woman who was coming out stumbled and fell. Then Weiss gave the sign for everyone to stop, gathered the men and women together, and delivered a speech to them: "How could it happen that a woman, getting off a traincar, could fall and find no one to help her up? Where is your gallantry, your gentlemanliness. After all, this woman may be a mother in the future." He lectured them like this for ten minutes, then gave the signal, and all the women, along with the one who had fallen, were taken away and shot.

There was a sixteen-year-old boy among us named Benya Vulf. Once a vehicle drove by, and Benya Vulf ran across the road in front of it. The *Sturmführer* was standing in the distance and saw this happen. He was very angry, blew the whistle, and ordered all the workers to gather at once. We stood there dirty, with shovels, while he gave Benya Vulf a reprimand: "How careless you are. You might have hurt your hand, which would have been very unfortunate. It's awful to think, you might have been killed; that would have been an irreparable catastrophe. Life is God's gift, no one has the right to infringe upon life. You are only sixteen years old, you have everything ahead of you." The *Sturmführer* considered this incident exceptionally important.

In one of the pits Isaak Dogim found his wife, mother, and two sisters. This affected him so much that he was close to insanity. Even before this he had been a gloomy, taciturn person. The Germans mocked and taunted him. . . . Motl found his own son in the pit. This day was the most difficult. When we came "home" to our pit, Isaak Dogim said that he had a knife, that he would sneak up to the *Sturmführer* and kill him. It took me a long time to persuade him not to do it, for it would have been the end for all of us. And in the meantime the tunnel was almost ready. I gave him my word of honor that he would be the first to go out to freedom.

How did we make the tunnel? We had a small storeroom for provisions. In this small storeroom we built a second, false wall. Two boards hung loosely on nails; if you gave them a tug, the nails would fall out, and it was possible to pass through. We found all the tools in the pits — the dead had helped us.

The soil was sandy, and the sand came out easily, but one difficulty arose — no sooner would we remove some sand, than it would slide off the roofing. We had to make supports, wooden props, for which we required boards. Ovseychik and Kantorovich were en-

470

listed for this job. When we were brought to Ponary, we had had to build a second bunker, since the first one was too crowded. We built the bunker and secretly removed some boards.

Once among the corpses, we managed to find a bread saw. It became our principal tool. We tempered it in fire; we also found a pack of small files. With these things we were able to make a real hand saw.

We worked on the tunnel after our daily work.

People would return from work, have dinner, and begin to sing. They sang the songs loudly, and the Germans were pleased with such merriment. I am a Soviet citizen, but I did not know as many Soviet songs as the Vilnius Jews. They knew all the Soviet motion pictures, the names of all the Soviet movie actors, and they knew all the songs from the movies by heart. They really liked the song, "Soviet Rifle": "Shoot, rifle, accurately, deftly."

Abram, as our foreman, rendered us assistance by making sure that dinner was left for us. We ate dinner later, separately from the others. Everyone rested and sang, and we immediately left for the storeroom and began to work on the tunnel. At first the work progressed slowly. In the first half of February, only Kagan and I were digging. Kostya and Ovseychik were busy preparing the boards. Matskin helped take the sand out of the tunnel and spread it over the field. The pit where we lived was four meters deep, but by the time our work was finished the pit was three meters and ninety centimeters deep, i.e., the layer of sand that we removed formed a layer ten centimeters thick on the floor. First we dug a shaft, and then we began to dig the tunnel — a gallery. We were making a passageway seventy centimeters wide and sixty-five centimeters high.

The work became more and more involved and required more effort. By then we had two bunkers; we arranged for the most reliable and active participants in the construction of the tunnel to be transferred to our bunker, while the people who were not involved were moved to the second bunker.

We had a system. First we installed two posts and upright supports — this part of the work had to be done by two people.

One person dug out the earth and put in the posts, the other handed him the boards and cleaned away the sand. This was extremely difficult work. Two people could work for an hour and a half to two hours and would come out of the tunnel completely exhausted. During these one and a half to two hours, four boards could be put in place. The difficulty was that there was not enough air, so matches and cigarette lighters would not burn. The question of installing electricity was raised.

Whenever two people who had been working crawled out (either Kagan and I, or Beletz and Kantorovich, or Shlema and his partner, whose surname I've forgotten), a brigade would crawl into the tunnel to throw out the sand. People lay with their chains to the side, took the sand near their heads by the handful and threw it to their feet. This was back-breaking work.

We managed to install electricity. The switch was in the girls' room, inside the bed. We left a man on duty in the kitchen to watch the top of the pit. If there were no Germans, then it was possible to work; as soon as the Germans showed up, the lookout would run to the switch and give the signal. We had to crawl out immediately. We would lie down and cover ourselves with our overcoats. One time, literally three seconds after we jumped out of the well and put the boards in place, an SS man appeared.

Many people refused to work in the tunnel, saying they did not believe it would be successful, but the main reason was that everyone was extremely tired after a day of hard labor. There were even those who did not want to leave Ponary. Some of the elderly, among whom was a rabbi, said: "My wife was killed here, my family was killed, where would I go?"

On April 9 we came upon the roots of tree stumps arranged in the shape of a triangle. We tried to fix it so that the tunnel would emerge on the surface between these stumps, since this spot was not watched by the sentries. When we stumbled on these roots I realized that we were on the right path, very close to the surface. We had an iron hook and we pushed it up through the ground. We felt a current of fresh air. I rejoiced with my comrades and was proud, as an engineer, that technically the problem had been solved correctly.

I had a compass and a ruler, and we made a level ourselves. It should be mentioned that in the beginning of April the people in the tunnel had to work to their utmost. One would hear voices say: "We've been digging for two months, and it hasn't done us any good." We probed the ground and it turned out that there was a pit full of corpses next to the tunnel. People were afraid that we might run into corpses. Some people began to reproach me, saying that I had incorrectly determined the direction of the tunnel. The last days were literally critical; only a small group of people still had faith in me. I had to show persistence and strength of mind, and my triumph was all the greater when on April 9, I stumbled on the roots and felt that we had found our way out. Now an extremely crucial question arose — how to organize our escape. We knew that the German guard was all around, but beyond that, everything was unknown. Were there partisans nearby? No one had the slightest idea about that either.

Zinger knew this locality. He told me that fourteen kilometers from Ponary was the famous Rudnitskaya Forest, near which he thought there was a river.

The Germans were extraordinarily thorough in guarding Ponary. Once there was a sudden moment of alarm. An SS man, dead drunk, lost his way and wandered into our area. The *Sturmführer* shot him on the spot. No one was supposed to discover the secret of Ponary.

We decided that we would all go together in a definite direction.

We divided up all the prisoners into eight groups of ten people. A commander was put in charge of each group. This commander knew the people in his group and gave them instructions. I put the problem this way: escape was possible only if we exercised iron discipline. I said: "Choose anyone you wish as your commander. I will carry out his orders unquestioningly."

I was instructed to make lists. I combined the first two groups into one. Among them I included the people who had done the most work on the tunnel and who, moreover, could later be of use to the partisans. Here, in order, is the list of people in the first group: 1-Dogim, 2-Farber, 3-Kostya Potanin, 4-Belets, 5-M. Zaydel, 6-Petya Zinin, 7-Ovseychik, 8-M. Kalnitsky, 9-Shlema Gol, 10-Kantorovich.

By April 9 everything was ready. I wanted to leave on April 12, because that was a significant date in my life — it was my brother's birthday.

But, unfortunately, on April 12 there was a bright moon; the rabbi gave us some useful advice at this point. Ovseychik had consulted with him, and the rabbi told him that April 15 would be the darkest night of the month.

On April 12 Belets and I went down into the tunnel. We had a small copper pipe with measurements marked off and we again made sure that there were ten centimeters left to the surface of the ground. We could already see the stars; we felt the fresh April air, and this gave us strength. We saw with our own eyes that freedom was near.

On April 15 we worked the whole day. That day a German,

whom we had nicknamed "the monkey," for no reason at all hit me on the shoulder with a stick.

At 11 o'clock in the evening Dogim and I got everyone together.

The first group had two knives and a large bottle of vinegar extract, which was poured into two bottles. We had taken all this from the corpses. In general, everything we had, we had gotten from the corpses. Before leaving I said: "Keep in mind that there is no way back under any circumstances. If we are discovered, we'll be shot anyway. Better to die fighting so just go forward."

We began to crawl. Dogim cleared away the last layer of earth; we were already breathing freely. The night really was very dark. There was absolute silence all around. When everything was ready Dogim and I removed our chains. Vulf was sent to give the signal that everything was ready and then, one at a time, the first twenty people went down into the tunnel. Kostya removed everyone's chains, and the people started to crawl out of the tunnel. We had to observe complete silence; even if they started shooting we had to maintain order and silence. We had to crawl about 200-250 meters from our pit, where there was a small grove. We made our way to the wire and cut it with pliers. There we hung two white rags so that the people who were following could see the passageway. I had figured that it was possible to walk fourteen kilometers in one night. The first to crawl was Dogim, I was second. I held him by his foot, we crawled out and, suddenly, I saw that Dogim was turning to the right. To the left, against the background of the sky, was the figure of a sentry. We crawled another twenty to thirty steps, but on this side too we could see the figure of a sentry. He was walking slowly. We had to turn again. While crawling, I experienced a completely inexpressible feeling. I was breathing with all the pores of my body.

I felt that our labor had not been wasted, and I rejoiced. Suddenly a shot rang out. Apparently, a twig had crackled under someone's hand. As soon as the first shot sounded, the shooting began from all sides. I looked around. Our entire path was filled with crawling people; some jumped up and ran in different directions. We crawled to the wire and cut it with the pliers, while the shots became louder and closer.

After two kilometers there was more barbed wire, which we also cut through; I saw that only five people were left around me. And the Germans were using mortar fire. This was the alarm signal for the whole garrison. We ran into the woods, but we had not taken into account that there were gun emplacements situated on all sides. We were being shot at from every direction. We reached the river. A new problem arose — not one of my five companions could swim. I had to ferry each person across the river one at a time. We walked the whole night, and during the day we took cover in the woods.

It took us a whole week to cover fourteen kilometers. By April 22 we had reached the heart of Rudnitskaya Forest and came to the forest village of Zhigariny. I asked some peasants whom I encountered: "Are there any Germans here?" They looked at me in surprise and said in Polish: "There are no Germans and there are no Poles." "And are there any Soviets?" "That I don't know, *prosze pana.*" In the evening we met three partisans, Soviet officers, among whom was a captain Vasilenko. I embraced and kissed him. "Where are you from?" he asked us.

"From the other world."

"Be more precise."

"From Ponary."

"From Ponary? Come with me."

I told him that I was a Muscovite. It turned out that he was a Muscovite too. Suddenly our conversation was interrupted — shooting broke out. There was heavy gunfire, but our lads made no move to hide. Captain Vasilenko asked them in amazement: "What's wrong, aren't you afraid of death?" "No," they replied.

We were taken to a partisan base; next to it was the base of the Jewish units "Death to Fascism" and "For Victory." My Vilnius companions found many acquaintances in these Jewish units. Isaak Dogim's cousin, Aba Kovner*, was the commander of the unit "Death to Fascism." The Jewish partisans knew perfectly well what Ponary was. No one could believe that we had returned from there alive; this made a tremendous impression. We were literally turned inside out with questions about everything and everyone. The order was given out to all partisan bases to look for escapees. On that same day a partisan reconnaissance party found five more people from our group.

Prepared for publication by **R. Kovnator.**

*Aba Kovner (born 1918), poet, writes in Hebrew. Lives in Israel and is a member of the Ein Ha-Horesh Kibbutz.

The Girl from Auschwitz*

(No 74233)

On August 16, 1943, the Germans finally liquidated the ghetto at Bialystok. All the survivors were assembled and taken to the prison at Grodno. We spent two days there and were then moved elsewhere. There were sixty people in each vehicle. My father died along the way and we, my relatives and I, took morphine which I had prepared long before. My brother gave his son, a thirteen-month-old child, the corresponding dosage of phenobarbital. Because of the jolting ride, the morphine did not take effect, and we arrived, exhausted, at Lomza prison. My brother's baby had died.

We were held in prison for three months. On November 18, 1943, we were led out into the yard, the surname and profession of each person was recorded, and we were driven to the railroad station.

We arrived in the area of Danzig and were taken off the traincars in a wooded area where SS men were waiting for us. Reflectors lighted the way to the camp. We were urged on by shouts. The men walked separately from the women. In the camp we were handed over to a senior woman official of the camps — a *capo*. As I approached the barracks. I smelled a strong odor of sulphur. It became clear to me that this would be the end of us. Nothing made any difference. The threat of death had hovered over our heads too often, and I thought: "If they would only hurry." The next morning we were taken to the bathhouse. All our things were taken away. We changed into camp clothes, were given numbers, and led back to the barracks. We received bread twice a day. A few people began to hope that we would be allowed to live — as proof that Hitler did not exterminate people. I should point out that people were not burned alive at Stutthof. But later, in Oswiecim, I learned from a woman prisoner who had come from Stutthof a half a year after me that even there they had begun to burn people alive.

Soon the rumor spread that we would be taken to another place, most likely to Oswiecim. We again endured difficult days.

On January 10, 1944, we were loaded into open trucks. From time to time I would look in the direction of the men, trying to find my brother. We rode for about three hours. We drove up to some

*Auschwitz — Polish: Oświęcim; Russian: Osventsim.

railroad station, and there we were herded into passenger train-cars. On January 12, we arrived in Oswiecim.

As we neared Auschwitz-Oswiecim, we saw a number of people working on the road. This raised our spirits a little: it meant that this was not a death factory and that people were living here. We had not yet learned that the Germans made special use of prisoners on back-breaking jobs, making conditions unbearable so that they would die faster. Getting off the train, I threw a final glance at my brother, who was herded off along with the other men. After an hour-long walk we reached the gates. The enormous camp, divided by wire into several fields, gave the impression of an entire city.

Near the gates, in a wooden house, was a kind of office. We were counted, and the gates closed behind us — forever. The barracks we were taken to for the night contained neither beds nor chairs. We had to sit on the bare ground. In the evening the *Obersturmführer* Hössler appeared with his right-hand man, Tauber. We were ordered to line up in fives; each of us was thoroughly examined and asked about our profession. The professions of some people, including my own, were written down. The next day the main executioner of the camp, Tauber, came again. Girls, prisoners of long standing, tattooed numbers on our left hands. We were no longer people. Toward evening we were taken to the bathhouse, undressed, and forced under a shower to wash. Before this our hair was removed with a machine. Those whose profession had been written down the day before by Hössler turned out to be the lucky ones. All the others looked horrible. The girls whose heads had been shaved were crying. A member of the camp personnel pointed to the flames of a large blaze rising up to the sky and said: "Do you know what that is? You'll be going there too. You won't need your hair or any of the things taken from you, there."

After bathing we were given old, dirty underwear and wooden shoes. On the outer garments there was a red stripe painted lengthwise, and numbers were sewn on; then we were directed to a room — the *Schreibstube* (office) located next to the bathhouse. Each of us received on a card index, besides our own name, the name "Sara." I did not understand what was going on and said that that was not my name; the person writing down the names grinned ironically and said that Hitler wanted it that way. We were taken to the so-called quarantine block. The block was divided into *Stuben* (barrack-rooms), and in each *Stube* there was a person on duty who was responsible for keeping order. We slept on plank-beds, five-six people crammed together in one bed; when we pointed to the empty beds and asked if we could move over to one of them, we were cursed and beaten. We were awakened at four o'clock in the morning, taken into the kitchen for tea, and roll was taken of everyone in the block. The roll call was called *Appell*, and it took place twice a day: in the morning and toward evening when people were returning to the camp from work. These roll calls lasted two to three hours each, regardless of rain, snow, or cold. We stood absolutely still, frozen through, and exhausted. Those who got sick were taken away to the hospital block, and there, they vanished.

On January 18 we suddenly heard whistles on the camp street and the shouts *Blocksperren!* (Lock up!). It was forbidden to leave the blocks. Only six days had passed since our arrival at Oswiecim. No one explained to us what was going on, but from the faces of the bosses we understood that something bad would happen. We were lined up, counted, and led to the bathhouse. There we were ordered to undress and had to parade before Hössler and a doctor. The names of some of the women, including my mother's, were written down. After we returned we found out that this sorting process was a "selection." This was the most terrifying word in the camp: it meant that people who were still alive today were condemned to burn. My situation was terrible — I knew that I would lose my mother, and I was unable to help her. My mother tried to comfort me, saying that she had already lived her life and that she was only sorry for us children. She knew that the same fate was awaiting us, too. Two days after the selection the condemned were still held in the block and fed like the rest of us, but on January 20, they were rounded up and taken to a special death block (block A25a). There these unfortunate people were gathered from all the blocks and carried off in vehicles to the crematorium. Many people from our block were missing that evening during *Appell*. The blaze and the smoke in the sky told us that on that day, January 20, many poor, innocent people had been burned; my mother was one of them. My only consolation was that I too would die, and that they were already rid of their suffering.

Those were difficult times. We were often beaten. It made no sense to complain. At best, there were new beatings, and we were forced to kneel for several hours in the block or in front of the block, regardless of the weather. The men in charge of the barrack rooms would force us unto the kitchen, and we had to haul heavy caldrons for them. This was very strenuous work even for strong men. We were given neither soap nor water, and there was simply no way to keep things clean. To wash up, we had to go to the so-called "bathroom": the whole block would be taken there at the same time and we had only 3-5 minutes to wash.

Usually people from the quarantine block were put to work after 5-6 weeks. We were put to work earlier. The majority of the girls who arrived in the same transport with me went to work at the "Union" factory (an artillery-shell factory). But since I was a pharmacist, I was sent to another block, and from there we were to be summoned again for work. That is how we came to be separated from the quarantine block. But it did not remain empty: every day new victims arrived from Poland, France, Belgium, Holland, and other countries. At the same time many people were dying. The death rate was as high as 300–350 people a day. Epidemics of typhus and dysentery raged, and lice swarmed over us.

The same order existed in the new block as in the old one. There were the same signs on the walls, the same demand for cleanliness; and the people in charge of the barrack rooms treated us the same way. When I got there, they began to ask me how it was that as a newcomer with such a high number, I had been allowed to keep my long hair. When I explained that the reason lay in my profession, I was told with irony: "Well now, just wait until you are called to do work in your profession." Later I found out what was meant by this. In order to get such a job, it was necessary to have protection, and this meant giving a bribe ("gift") to the people who provided the protection. To get a "gift" one had to know how "to organize," i.e., to steal. I did not know how to do this, and so I had to wait. We were not allowed to rest. . . . Carrying caldrons in and out and cleaning up the block became my responsibility. If I had objected, I would have wound up in the regular selection process. Since the block was supposed to be *rein* (clean), we would not be permitted in there for days on end, but instead were kept in a small unheated room. We were driven out of the block in the most bitter cold. Only after evening *Appell*, which lasted one and a half to two hours, were we permitted to go inside. We had to make sure that there were no traces of dirt on the "parquet" cement floor which we washed several times a day with freezing-cold hands while crying bitter tears. But even this was not enough. They did not like the fact that we had too little to keep us occupied, so it was decided to use us for hard labor. Four and five times a day we had to walk a distance of three kilometers and bring back heavy rocks which were used by the other women's units to pave the camp. Women from all the blocks who were not working in specific places were gathered together. We were counted at the gates, and there we were joined by a guard — a German and a dog, and under a shower of swearwords, we were herded to the place where the rocks were. Each person tried to find a small rock. But this did not work — we were checked and beaten. In addition to the guard, the women *Einweiser* watched over us. The *Einweiser* were German female prisoners, the majority of whom were prostitutes. An *Einweiser* could be bribed — a pack of cigarettes was enough; but to get this pack of cigarettes it was again necessary to know how "to organize." The work was very strenuous. I worked under these conditions for five weeks but could not continue; my legs were terribly swollen, and I simply could not walk. It was also impossible to remain in the block, because the Germans came to check to see if everyone had gone to work. Everyone was required to work — there was no room for the sick. They were sent to a special block — the *Revier* (sick bay). At that time the *Revier* meant death — it was rare for anyone to return from there. People became even more ill there; they would get infections from one another, grow weaker and would die. There was yet another danger in the *Revier* — selection. The people who were most liable to the danger of selection were the ones in the *Revier*. But I had no choice. Even though I knew everything that threatened me, I still asked the clerk in our block to send me to the *Revier*. These were new surroundings and new beasts. I was given a bed to share with another sick girl. Seeing that her whole body was covered with pimples and wounds, I burst into tears. I knew that under the same blanket with her, I would get infected. At that time people were stricken with mange. This condition, which under normal situation could be cured in two to three days, lasted forever here. Moreover, one could be burned for just having a few traces of this illness appear on the body during selection. I implored the nurse to give me another bed. She gave in only after I had pleaded for a long time. I lay in the *Revier* for three weeks. I washed my face and hands with the tea they gave us in the mornings. Twice a week I traded two portions of bread for hot water so I could wash myself better. I did this in the evenings. For two days I had to live completely without bread so that I could be comparatively clean. I cannot describe the surprise of my blockmates when they saw me again.

After I was released from the *Revier* I was taken to the bathhouse, washed, and given clothes — rags. Again it was necessary to begin "organizing" more decent clothes for myself. I had to deny myself bread so that with it I could "buy" myself clothes from people who worked on the sorting of the baggage from the trains which were continually arriving at Oswiecim. We had been in the same situation after the so-called *Entlausung* (disinfection of the block and the people against lice). We were then taken to the bathhouse to bathe, and our things were collected and disinfected in steam boilers. After this disinfection we received not our own things, but rags, and we had to acquire everything again from the beginning.

After the *Revier* I was put to work at the *Weberei* (weaving shop). I had to weave plaits from scraps of rags, leather, and rubber. We had to fulfill the norm no matter what, and for this an adequate amount of raw materials was required. But even for raw materials one had to "organize," i.e., give cigarettes or other things to the *Einweiser* who supervised the work. In addition to the *Einweiser*, we were watched by the women SS *Aufseher*, who also liked gifts. A number sewn poorly on a dress, or the absence of the red stripe (*Strich*) on the outer clothes were sufficient reasons for one of the *Aufseher* to write down the number of the "guilty one" and the number of the block where she lived. Numbers were also written down for conversing with the men or for being found with letters from them. The next day, those whose numbers had been taken down would be sent to a special block. People from this block wore a red circle on their backs and were sent to do even more strenuous jobs.

Here I should describe the circumstances in which we went to work. We got up at four o'clock in the morning. The regular woman on duty went to the kitchen to get the tea. After the beds had been made and the tea distributed, we were herded outside for *Appell*. There was no time to wash. After *Appell*, people who were going outside the camp to work lined up in fives on the camp street (*Lagerstrasse*). There we were counted again several times each by various *capos* and then we were led to the gates of the camp, where an orchestra of female prisoners played. When I first heard the music in the camp, I began to cry like a baby. Music and a blaze that streamed in the sky — who could have thought up such a thing? In the evening, when the people were returning from work they encountered the same orchestra. We were not allowed to rest. People had to stand one and a half to two hours more for *Appell*. From that time on, the evening *Appell* lasted a long time because almost every day there were escapes by the men — the ones who went outside the camp to work. We would learn of the escapes by the wailing of the siren. We would rejoice then, and although inspection lasted an especially long time on these days, we gladly stood for *Appell*. I worked only three days in the *Weberei* and then wound up working in the *Revier*. I ended up there, because I was listed in the card index as having had medical training. Without protection and a bribe this was an extremely rare bit of luck: hygienic conditions on this job were better and, besides that, it was not necessary to go outside the camp. In other words, we did not have to walk sixteen kilometers a day. But the main thing was that in the *Revier* I was working in the interests of unfortunate prisoners. Everyday we were visited by the camp doctor, Mengele. On this cutthroat's conscience were hundreds of thousands of people. The *Revier* was located in the camp, but isolated from it by barbed wire. The *Revier* occupied fifteen blocks. It was a kind of state within a state.

I began working there on April 21. A few days later, after the evening *Appell* whistles and shouts rang out: *Lagersperren!* — selection! Silence fell all around — the quiet before the storm. I already understood what it meant. I knew that the next morning I would not see many sick people in the block. With extraordinary punctuality, vehicles drove up and the people condemned to death were dragged out. The women in charge of the block and the night shift had to take an active part in this. There were shouts and cries. And suddenly I heard the Hebrew song "Hatikvah" (song of hope). Several more vehicles drove up, and silence reigned again. It was horrible to be so close, to hear everything, and not to be able to help! This selection was carried out just like the previous one. Several days before, Doctor Mengele had the doomed people's numbers written down.

After the selection, work continued as before. The most difficult days were drawing near. Every day large trainloads of Jews arrived from virtually all over Europe; at that time the greatest number of Jews were coming from Hungary. Previously the trains would stop at the station at Oswiecim. There they were unloaded, and it was there that the selection was made; the "lucky ones" entered the camp gates, and the rest, sentenced to death, were driven away directly to the crematorium. But this seemed wasteful to the Germans, so they had the prisoners build a side line which led directly to the ovens. The rails were laid parallel to the *Revier* blocks and were only 150–200 meters from us. We watched a continuous horrible spectacle: eight to nine trains arrived each day; they were unloaded, and the baggage remained lying near the rails; the poor people, who had no idea of what was going to happen to them, were selected by the chief butcher, Doctor Mengele. Mengele had a lot of work that summer. The people who came off the traincars could not even have imagined what awaited them. . . . Beyond the wire they could see girls in white aprons (that was us, the *Revier* workers); if they arrived in the morning they would hear the sounds of the orchestra, and see groups of girls walking to work outside the camps *(Aussenkommandos)*. The new arrivals could hardly understand where they were being taken. Meanwhile, they were taken to the crematorium. There they were undressed in a large hall, given a piece of soap and a towel and, although told they were going to the bathhouse, they were, in fact, herded into the gas chamber. There they were killed with gas and the bodies were burned. This task was carried out only by the men prisoners who belonged to the so-called *Sonderkommandos*. But they were not to work there for long: after one to two months these people were also burned and replaced by others who would meet the same fate. It was awful to watch the women, men, old people, and children walking endlessly in the direction of the crematorium. They understood so little of what awaited them that they were distressed about their baggage which had been left behind on the street. The trains at that time were arriving so frequently that there was not enough time to take away the baggage; the mountain of things grew bigger, but their owners were already dead. . . . During the period when the Hungarian trains were arriving Doctor Mengele, in his selection, spared the lives of twin children, regardless of their age. Mengele was also interested in dwarf families; they later even enjoyed his sympathy. It should be mentioned that in the *Revier* there were some abnormal people; twice a week they were taken to the men's camp at Buna, ten kilometers from our camp, where various experiments were performed on them. This was the work of Doctor Koenig. Even when people were no longer being burned in the crematorium, but were piled into ordinary ditches on logs

483

and soaked with kerosene, even then the sadists, Mengele and Koenig, were busy with their "scientific" experiments. The experiments were performed on prisoners too — men and women.

This was the terrible summer of 1944: endless trains arrived everyday. At the same time trainloads of men and women prisoners left Oswiecim for Germany to do various jobs. It was a "feverish" time — Germany needed people for its work force. Many people left gladly, running away from the hell that was Oswiecim. Our spirits were lifted by the fact that everyday now we were visited by "little birds" — Soviet airplanes. They did not drop bombs on the camp, but on two occasions bombs did fall on the SS barracks where, to our joy, there was a large number of casualties. We could feel the front approaching. Escapes became daily occurrences. Once the evening *Appell* lasted a very long time. The siren began to wail. At first we thought that it was an air raid, but the wailing was quite different — it was protracted. After a drawn-out count of the prisoners, it turned out that one of the female prisoners in our camp and a prisoner in the men's camp were missing. As we were to find out later, a Belgian Jewish girl, Malya, had escaped. She held an important position: she assigned jobs to those who came out of the *Revier*. She was a human being in the true and best sense of this word and went all out for everyone she was able to help. Malya escaped together with her friend who was a Pole. A few days later they were caught in Bielsk. They were dressed in SS uniforms and had weapons on them. They were brought to Oswiecim and put in the dungeon — a bunker. The Germans tried to get information out of them, but they refused to betray anyone. On August 21 we saw Malya, beaten, exhausted, and in rags, being brought to our camp by an SS man. She was to be hanged in front of the prisoners. She knew this. She also knew that her friend had already been hanged. Then she hit the Gestapo man who was accompanying her, snatched the razor blades she had hidden in her hair, and slit her own veins. . . . This was one heroic girl the Germans were not able to execute.

As the front drew closer, the Germans became increasingly nervous. People were no longer burned in the crematoriums. Moreover, in order not to leave any traces of their crimes, the Germans destroyed the death machines. They blew up one crematorium after another. It seemed that the barbarians were thinking about the inevitable day of reckoning. Even the conditions improved slightly. True, this was not reflected in our food. Our

Revier was transferred to the field at the Birkenau camp, where seventeen thousand Gypsies who had previously been held there, had been burned that summer. The positive aspect of our new place was that it was located between two men's camps. And it was nice, though at the same time cruel, when after work we would "meet" in the evening, separated by the wire, which had live current passing through it. What was even nicer was the fact that, of late, our evening encounters had come to be hampered by attacks from Soviet aircraft: the light on the wire would go out and we, with our hopes up, would go to our respective camps.

On January 17, we learned that the camp was being liquidated. That night all the hospital documents were destroyed. At ten o'clock in the morning Doctor Kit appeared and ordered the sick who were capable of marching and the personnel to be ready. He said that trains would be coming for those who were seriously ill. The evacuation was taking place on all the other fields of the camp as well. When Doctor Kit, in his selection on *Lagerstrasse*, assigned me to the group which was leaving the camp, I inconspicuously turned back and would not leave the barracks, despite the fact that I was told several more times to join the march. I lay down on a bed, reporting myself sick. Several thousand sick people along with the personnel remained in the *Revier*. Since the director of the pharmacy had also joined the group which left the camp, I was given a job in the pharmacy. On the days following, events developed very fast. On January 20, after a grandiose air raid, there was no electricity or water in the camp. The air raid, like all the others, was a great moral support for us. The camp was not bombed once. We were afraid that at the last minute the Germans would blow up our *Revier* camp in order to sweep away the traces of their crimes. This fear was the reason why the majority of people left on January 18. Those who left hoped that outside the camp, on the road, they would be able to escape. Many of them, in fact, managed to do this.

By January 21, there was already great disorder. Only a small number of SS men remained in the camp. Storehouses of bread, produce, and clothes were left open. The storehouses were filled with all kinds of good things. These barbarians had stocked up on everything in great quantities, but to us prisoners they gave the worst dirty underwear, rags instead of clothes, wooden shoes. Moreover, they fed us worse than pigs. About three o'clock in the afternoon the last SS men left, suggesting that anyone who wanted, except the Jews, could go with them. But no one went. The camp gates remained open. In the evening of the same day a fire broke out in the neighboring field of another camp (Birkenau), and that night the last crematorium was blown up. We were afraid that our camp would be dealt with in the same way as the crematoriums. We cut through the wire and joined the men who had stayed, like us, in the *Revier*. With them we felt much more confident. Many people had left the camp. January 23 was a very difficult day. In the morning several Germans appeared on bicycles. They spent several hours in the camp, trying to find anything of value for themselves, then left. On the morning of January 24, some more Germans showed up and shot five Russian prisoners in the men's camp. On the same day a vehicle arrived with a group of Gestapo men. They ordered all the Jews capable of walking to come out of the barracks. They lined up several hundreds of men and just as many women. Having learned from experience, I decided not to come out. A girlfriend and I made our way into a block that had been completely vacated. This was a block which contained bags of underwear and clothes. We hid under these bags, listening to what was happening in the camp. When it started to get dark, we came out from our hiding place. One by one, those who had not submitted to the Gestapo order began to show themselves. They, like us, had hidden wherever they could, and in this way, they saved themselves. All the Jews who had been lined up had been herded out of the camp and, obviously, shot.

We spent the night in the men's camp. We no longer had to hide. My girlfriend and I spent January 26 in the pharmacy of the men's camp where comrades, non-Jews, were building a hiding place for us under the ceiling. In case the Gestapo men appeared, they were supposed to hide us there. This was an exceptionally joyous day for us: Soviet artillery and aircraft were in operation and did not stop for a minute. The next day we heard no artillery fire and saw no airplanes. We decided that the front must have moved away from us. I was losing my nerve. When I thought that the Gestapo men might show up again, life seemed impossible. Suddenly, from the pharmacy window, I saw a silhouette in white and gray clothes on the road near the camp. This was approximately five o'clock in the afternoon. At first we thought that these were the people from the camp returning. I ran out of the pharmacy to see who was coming. What joy we felt when we saw that these were our saviors — Soviet soldiers. It was a reconnaissance party. There was no end to the kisses and the greetings. They tried to persuade us to leave, explaining to us that it was not possible to stay here because they had not yet determined where the enemy was. We stepped back several paces and then forward again to be closer to our liberators. Almost right up until evening we stayed near the gates. And when we returned to the camp, there too, we met our long-awaited and dear friends.

On January 28 many people who had been prisoners left the camp, having finally received their freedom. The commanders and soldiers visited with us in the pharmacy. We told them about our horrible life in the Oswiecim camp. On February 3, we left Birkenau behind us and went to the camp at Oswiecim. There we found many of our friends who, like us, had managed to save themselves. On February 4 we arrived in the city of Oswiecim. We could not believe that we were free. We looked with amazement at the people walking in the streets. On February 5, we started off toward Cracow. On one side of the road stretched gigantic factories built by prisoners who had died long ago from the exhausting work. On the other side was another big camp. We went in there and found sick people who, like us, were still alive only because they did not leave with the Germans on January 18. From there we went farther. We were followed for quite a while longer by the electric wires on stone poles, so well-known to us as the symbol of slavery and death. It seemed to us that we would never get out of the camp, but we finally reached the village of Wloseniuszcza. We spent the night there and the next day, February 6, we continued on. We were picked up by a vehicle and driven to Cracow. We were free, but we still could not rejoice for we had experienced too much and we had lost too many people.

Prepared for publication by **Osip Cherny**.

Twenty-Six Months in Auschwitz

(The Story of Mordekhay Tsirulnitsky, former prisoner No. 79414

1. In the Small Town of Ostrino

I was born in 1899 in the small town of Ostrino, which is now part of the Grodno *oblast*. I lived there with my family until the Hitler invasion. I had a large family — five children. My children were wonderful. They all studied. My oldest daughter Galya would have been twenty-two years old now. When the Soviet authorities came to power, she entered the Grodno technical school for civil engineering and in the spring of 1941, she entered her second year of study. My oldest boy, seventeen-year-old Yakov, was getting on-the-job training at a printing and publishing plant. The rest of my children were still in grade school: sixteen-year-old Joel had just entered the ninth grade; thirteen-year-old Vigdor was in the eighth grade; and the youngest, Lanya, who was only nine, would have already been in the fourth grade.

Ostrino was located close to the border. On June 23, 1941, the town was surrounded on all sides by the Germans, and those residents who tried to escape were forced to return. And on June 25, the Germans entered Ostrino.

Shootings began immediately after the Germans entered the town. The first victims were the people who had participated in the Soviet government and in the work of the Soviet in our area.

Our small town was part of the Shchuchinsky region. In the beginning of September a German Gestapo man was appointed commandant of our region. I can't remember his surname now — my memory has faded since my days in the camp. From the moment of his appointment shootings became common and frequent in our town. They were carried out for the most part on market days in order to frighten the surrounding peasant population. The commandant, who lived in the regional center of Shchuchino, often came to Ostrino, and on those occasions we already knew that there would be shootings. Among others, all teachers were shot: Miller with his wife and two daughters, Yelin, and others.

By order of the commandant, there was supposed to be a list of the tenants hung on the wall in every house. If the list were checked and someone was not found where he was supposed to be, the whole family would be shot. That is how the eight members of Osher Amstibovsky's family were killed.

The ghetto in Ostrino was organized in early December, 1941. Jews from all the villages in the *oblast* as well as from the small towns of Novy Dvor and Dzembrov were taken to our town. Those who came said that all the weak and sick people were killed on the way. When organizing the ghetto, about ten more people were shot. Then new orders and new shootings followed. Leyb Mikhelevich and his sister Feyge-Sore were shot because they furtively brought a little grain into the ghetto. Osher Boyarsky was caught grinding some grain — he was shot. One simply can't remember it all!

In January, 1942, it was announced that Ostrino, along with the whole Grodno region was being annexed by the *Reich*.

Everyday the ghetto population was herded into the woods to work. The men cut timber and collected tar. The overseers would beat these people within an inch of their lives, and the ones who fell behind in the work or were weak would be killed right on the spot. It often happened that people accused of sabotage were sent to prison, and once a Jew landed in prison, he lived only until the next Friday. On Fridays there were executions of inmates in the prison, including all the Jews.

2. In the Kelbasino Camp

On November 2, 1942, the entire Jewish population of the town of Ostrino was moved to the camp at Kelbasino, near Grodno. Before that, it had been a camp for Soviet prisoners of war. By the time we arrived at Kelbasino there were no longer any prisoners of war there. Jews from every city and small town of the Grodno region were gradually being brought there. People were put in small dugouts, which had up to three hundred people in each one. You could forget about lying down — at times there was no room to stand. The cramped conditions, the stench, and the dirt were unbelievable. People were forced into the swamps to do difficult work. One hundred fifty grams (one third of a pound) of bread per person was given out daily, and even that was completely inedible, as were the one or two frozen potatoes given out. The *Lagerführer* Insul would beat people unmercifully with a heavy stick for the slightest offense — he would strike them on the head until they were completely unconscious.

Hunger and typhus raged in the camp. There was not a dugout

in which several people would not die in a single day; they would die at work, too. And even now it makes me shudder to think of the so-called hospital, that is, the dugout into which the typhus victims were thrown. None of the sick people who landed there could even hope to survive, despite all the efforts of Doctor Gordon, a most noble man who did everything he could to save the sick, doomed people.

We later met this Doctor Gordon in the Auschwitz camp. He was one of the most active members in our resistance organization. I don't know if he managed to survive.

The bodies of the dead were not even buried at the Kelbasino camp. On the grounds of the camp, at some distance from the inhabited dugouts, there was an enormous pit which always remained uncovered. The dead people were thrown into this pit, sprinkled from above with a thin layer of lime, and on top of them were thrown more and more new corpses. It is difficult even to imagine how many human bodies were devoured by this fraternal grave.

3. The First Months at Auschwitz

We spent a month at the Kelbasino camp.

On December 1, 1942, we received the order to prepare for departure. We were instructed to pack our belongings and to sign our first names and surnames on them; we were promised that they would be sent after us to our new place of residence. On December 2 all of us, along with our families, were loaded into uncovered boxcars. We received neither bread nor water. People suffered most of all from thirst — especially the children. While the train was moving we tried all sorts of ways to get even a few drops of moisture: we lowered a tin can on a string, trying to catch a little snow so we could at least moisten the lips of the children who were burning with thirst; we lowered rags, pieces of paper — a rag would get wet in the snow, and then it was possible to squeeze out a few drops of water.

In spite of the very heavy guard, I managed to lower two of my boys out of the car — Yakov and Joel. Maybe, I thought, they would somehow save themselves. But they did not. . . . Yakov decided to run into the woods to find the partisans. Only now, after the war, while at home, I learned that he died before reaching the partisans. Joel managed to get to Grodno where my sister was living in the ghetto. He was brought to Auschwitz several months later together with my sister's whole family and sent directly from the train to be gassed. And my wife Sarra and I and our three children were brought to Auschwitz on December 5, 1942.

Our train stopped at a small platform in the middle of a field. As I later found out, this platform was built specially between Auschwitz and Birkenau. . . . Not far off, a shed could be seen. Farther on there was an endless line of barbed-wire obstructions.

Near the platform stood a small group of people in civilian clothes. And the first thing I saw was a man, bent over, being beaten with a stick by a fat SS man. How many times afterwards I had to witness similar scenes, but I will never forget this brutal impression of my first minutes at Auschwitz.

The *Lagerführer* Schwartz drove up to our group in a car bearing the signs of the Red Cross (incidentally, boxes of poison for "gassing" people in the camp were always carried in a car with Red Cross signs). We were surrounded by SS men. Our belongings were unloaded from the traincars, but we were not allowed to go near them. The bodies of the people who had died on the way were immediately pulled off the traincars and piled up to the side. A unit of prisoners in striped uniforms approached; they were directed toward our belongings.

The selection began. The sick and the weak were led off to where the bodies of the dead were. The men who looked healthy were put into a special group. All the rest — the women, the elderly, the children — were put into vehicles and taken away. That is the way I parted with my wife and children forever, without saying good-bye, without realizing that they were being taken to their deaths.

I wound up among the 189 men who had been selected. We were taken to the central camp — Oswiecim [Auschwitz]. Near the entrance we saw an arch. There was a sign on top: "*Arbeit macht frei*" (Labor makes you free). In the bathhouse each of us had a number and a triangle tattooed on the left hand. My number, as you see, is 79414. Numbers and triangles were tattooed only on the Jews — on the ones who were kept alive for awhile to work. Moreover, all prisoners were required to wear identification badges on their clothes, on the left side of the chest: the Jews had to wear a red triangle with a yellow one superimposed on it so that the two formed a hexagonal star (later this badge was replaced by a red triangle with a yellow strip above it). Political prisoners wore a red triangle, criminals wore a green one.

491

Anyone who showed himself on the grounds of the camp without his identification badge or who wore it in the wrong place would meet certain death. The first SS man to come along could detain you, knock you down on the ground, kick you in the face and chest with his boots, and then send you to the gas chamber.

Our whole group spent the first night together in one of the barracks. The next morning there was a new selection. All the men younger than forty were separated out and sent to the camp at Buna — the third largest camp after Auschwitz and Birkenau. One hundred forty of these men were collected. The remaining forty-nine of us were housed in the fourth block (barracks). I was assigned to a work detail whose task was to level the Sola River (*Solodurchstich*). Roll call (*Appell*) lasted two-three hours in the morning, before work, and the same amount of time in the evening. We had to walk three kilometers to work. The work was strenuous, exhausting. We were accompanied by a special unit of SS men who watched us while we worked. There are no words to describe the sadism of the SS men, who tormented and beat us for the slightest reason, often for no reason at all.

A guard would come up. The command would ring out: "Bend over!" and right on the spot he would count out twenty-five or fifty blows with his stick. All thoughts at this time are concentrated on one thing: how to remain on your feet, not to fall; otherwise, a bullet would be waiting.

At the end of December a "sanitary" campaign was conducted (*Entlausung*). All our clothes were taken from us, we were locked up completely naked, then we were herded stark naked into the bathhouse.

On January 2, 1943, I was assigned to the unit which sorted the belongings of the prisoners arriving in the camp. In this same unit with me was a group of Jews from France. Among them was a Jewish actor, Blyumenzon, my cousin Aaron Leyzerovich, and others. Part of us worked on unpacking the newcomers' belongings, others — on sorting them, and a third group — on packing them for shipment to Germany. Everyday seven-eight traincars filled with these things were sent to various cities in Germany. The old, shabby things were sent for processing to Memel (Klaypeda) and Lodz.

The work went on uninterruptedly round the clock, day and night, and still it was impossible to handle it all — there were so many things.

Here, in a bundle of children's coats, I once found the coat belonging to my youngest daughter — Lanya.

Soon after I began working in this unit I found out about the gas chambers, about the crematoriums where everyday thousands of people were burned; I found out about the fate of all those people who were not lucky enough to wind up in the work units, and I understood that the very same fate had befallen my family. People who grew weak, tired, sick, unsuitable for the work units, were inevitably "gassed," and in their place others were sent. Once, in freezing cold weather, SS men forced a whole group to work unclothed. In two hours people were completely frost-bitten. The work stopped. The SS men beat the people with sticks. Those who could not withstand the punishment and fell down were sent to be "gassed."

To report sick and wind up in the out-patient clinic was tantamount to volunteering to be sent to the gas chamber. We learned this very quickly. My oldest brother Mikhl, who was with me in Auschwitz, had trouble with swollen legs. He went to the clinic and never returned. That's the way many of my other countrymen from Ostrino died: Moyshe-Yankel Kamionsky, Shloyme-Girsh Shilkovsky, Motl Krinsky, and others.

I felt my strength decline with each day, and I could barely stand on my feet. But my comrades in the work unit supported me and helped me conceal my ill health from the guards. If it had not been for their help, I would not have escaped the "gas."

On January 12, 1943, our unit was transferred to Birkenau.

The Germans tried to give Auschwitz the outward appearance of a labor camp. It was rare to see a corpse of a prisoner on the grounds of the camp.

The situation looked completely different at Birkenau. Here everything testified to the fact that we were in a death factory. Everywhere near the blocks lay dead or dying people. There was indescribable dirt in the barracks. On freezing, wintery days people were sent to cold bathhouses and doused with icy water. Those who became ill were sent to the gas chambers. At first people were sent there once a week, later it became more and more often. The weak, emaciated people could barely pull their feet out of the dirt which covered the whole area of the camp. And the SS men, amusing themselves, tripped them with sticks. If a person fell, he would not get up again. One evening, while going out to work, I saw two trucks with trailers full of corpses.

No less violent were the overseers of the individual barracks, the majority of whom were recruited from the criminals. The German overseer of our block once killed fourteen people right before my eyes. The situation in other barracks was no better, if it was not worse.

We would get up at four o'clock in the morning. *Appell* in the morning and evening lasted three hours. It was conducted in the yard. The evening *Appell* was particularly agonizing. Right there, in front of the formation, people who had committed some offense at work would be flogged. In addition to beatings which they received from the guards while still at work, during *Appell* they would be beaten again. And sometimes a person would be sent directly to the gas chamber. *Appell* was especially violent if someone was missing. On those occasions *Appell* would last forever. Everyone who worked with the escapee would be made to pay.

I remember once in the summer of 1943 eight Russian prisoners from an agricultural unit drove out of camp with a load of manure. They remained working outside the camp for several hours. Three of them managed to escape. The guard shot the other five prisoners several times in the face. Their bodies were brought back to the camp and laid out on tables near the gates in order to frighten the rest of the prisoners. They lay there for two days.

If someone was unable to go to work, he would be sent to the seventh barracks. That was the place where all the sick people were concentrated. When the barracks filled up, they would all be sent to the gas chambers.

Not even two months had gone by since the moment of our arrival at Auschwitz and of our whole group of forty-nine people there were only four or five left. All the others had been gradually killed off or sent to be gassed.

Part of our people from Ostrino worked in the forest, in a unit that cut timber for the crematoriums or for burning corpses in the ditches. I found out from one of them, Fishel Lyubetsky, that Leyb Bril, Yakov Slatsnik and Leyb Slatsnik were hanged in the forest by SS men. Lyubetsky himself had bruises over his entire body as a result of the beatings he had received, but he was a strong lad — he held up and was with me in the camp right up until the last days.

In February, I saw my own nephew among the newcomers. He was the son of my sister from Grodno — Joel Kamionsky. From him I learned of the fate of my boy Joel, whom I had tried to save on the way. He did not escape Auschwitz either. He was brought here together with my sister's entire family, and of the whole family only Joel Kamionsky got into a work brigade. The fate of the others was already clear to me — they had been gassed.

Before the spring of 1943 trainloads of people were coming primarily from Polish areas annexed by the Hitlerites to the Third Reich, but also partially from the "general-government." Then the first trainloads began to arrive from Greece, Czechoslovakia, Germany, and France.

Once a train arrived from the city of Pruzhany. One of the newcomers, after seeing the people in our unit, asked: "Tell me, what kind of death are we condemned to die?"

I felt my strength fade with each day. No matter how my comrades in the unit tried to shield me from the gazes of the guards, I began to land frequently under the blows of their sticks. To this day the command still rings in my ears: "Bend over!" In the things which we sorted, we would sometimes come across something edible. We would try to hide it from the guards, but if the SS men ever found any food on our persons or noticed us eating something, they would beat us without mercy. I once received twenty-five blows with the stick for handing my nephew Joel Kamionsky a piece of stale bread that I had found. Life was becoming unbearable. But my comrades tried in every way to raise my spirits and to convince me that I should guard my life — that it might still prove useful.

I now recall my comrades with special gratitude: Albert (who came from France) and Kabachnikov. They wound up in Auschwitz even earlier than I — their identification numbers were in the forty thousands.

The Jews who were brought from Greece were primarily residents of Salonika. Before being sent from Greece they had been told that they were going to work in Poland. The people had believed this and were stunned when, upon arriving at Auschwitz, they were immediately taken off the train and the Germans began to separate the healthier men from the women, children, and the elderly. *"Wie so, Frauen separat?"* (Why is it that the women are being separated?) a young man, speaking in German, asked in amazement when he was separated from his family.

Three rabbis were among the first trainloads of Greeks delivered to Birkenau. They were forced to sign a letter which said that all the people were alive, working, and doing fine. Then they suffered the common fate.

In the fall of 1943 about four thousand Jewish prisoners, primarily from Greece, were singled out in the camp. They were taken to Warsaw to clean up the ruins of the ghetto. A small number of these people were able to escape, but the majority were later taken back and burned in the Auschwitz crematoriums.

Children from an orphanage were brought here on one of the trains from Greece. On the railroad platform the SS men wanted to separate the teacher from the children with whom she had arrived: She categorically refused to leave the children alone and, instead, she walked off with them to the gas chamber.

We were amazed once when several Jewish families from Germany, including the wives and children, were brought to the men's camp. Our bewilderment quickly cleared up. The gas chambers and crematoriums could not immediately handle the enormous number of victims delivered to Auschwitz. It was necessary to detain them for a while. A day or two later all of these people were sent to the crematorium.

Somewhat later, near our barracks, there was a family camp in which were kept Jews brought from Theresienstadt in Czechoslovakia. This camp existed for about a half a year, after which all of its inhabitants were sent to their deaths.

I saw a family camp for Gypsies, too. They occupied two large blocks. There were more than one thousand of them there. They were all killed — to a man.

That is the way we lived, seeing death each minute before our eyes. Only the support of my comrades enabled me to live through those times, in spite of it all. With the onset of spring I came to my senses somewhat and felt better. And in the summer my life in the camp changed.

4. At the Factory

In June, 1943, I was assigned as a mechanic to a factory located seven-eight kilometers from Auschwitz. All together, there were two thousand six hundred prisoners working at the factory, and of them approximately one thousand three hundred were men; the rest were women.

At one time the factory had belonged to the Krupp firm. Some of the machines and tools that were brought here were new, others were mutilated, charred, obviously damaged from bombings. The sight of these machines truly brought us satisfaction. A short while later all the Krupp equipment was hauled out and the factory was transferred to the "Union" firm which brought here equipment bearing Soviet trade marks from Zaporozhye.

The shop foreman where I wound up was a Czech named Kotšeba. He and I soon began making pots, pans, etc. The Germans were pleased about this. The demand for pans was growing every day. Sometimes an extra piece of bread came our way for our pans. Incidents of people dying right there at a machine in the factory were rather frequent.

Beatings of prisoners in the factory were regular occurrences. An especially violent person was the *Obermeister* Stratman, a scoundrel who had few equals. He would walk up to his victim slowly, talk with a smile, and then end up giving the man a savage beating.

Once it seemed to us that the gassing and burning of people had abated somewhat. Even the following incident occurred: four hundred people who had been picked to be sent to the gas chambers were returned to the barracks. *Lagerführer* Hofmann, declared that no one else, especially non-Jews, would be gassed. But that was only for the sake of outward appearance. In fact the gas chambers and crematoriums continued to devour tens of thousands of victims every day. On the very next day after Hofmann's "solemn" promise several thousand people were sent to the gas chambers from the smaller camps: Jaworzno, Buna, Janina-Gruben and others. Previously, people who had become exhausted from the work in these smaller camps were brought to Birkenau or Auschwitz, and from there they would be sent to the gas chambers. Now the procedure was shortened — people were being taken to the crematoriums directly from these camps. Often, even people from our factory were sent to be gassed.

The summer of 1944 was particularly horrible with regard to the number of people exterminated in the Auschwitz camps. At that time they burned people who had been brought from the Theresienstadt camp, as well as Gypsies who had occupied two large blocks for a while at Auschwitz.

In the winter of 1943-1944 several trainloads of people were delivered from Bialystok — participants in the uprising of the Bialystok ghetto. Many of them were shot by the SS men immediately upon exiting the traincars; this was the first incident of a mass shooting on a railroad platform. The rest were sent to the gas chambers. Of all these trainloads of people there was not one person who was actually delivered to the camp.

In the summer of 1944 a large group of men and women from

Majdanek were brought in. A violent epidemic of dysentery broke out among them, and every morning hundreds of people were sent off to the gas chambers.

At the end of June to the beginning of July, 1944, people sensed that the Germans were urgently preparing to receive and exterminate a large number of people. In spite of the uninterrupted operation of all the ovens in the crematoriums, ditch diggers began to dig large pits, and wood cutters — to cut timber. Soon trainloads of Hungarian Jews began to arrive. Throughout the course of July and August no less than five hundred thousand of them were delivered.

The first groups of Hungarian Jews were brought to the camp. They were forced to write letters home saying that they were in the Waldsee region, near Vienna, and that they were doing fine. Soon, however, these groups began to be taken directly to the gas chambers. The people were convinced that they were being taken to the bathhouse and stood quietly outside the chambers, waiting for their turn.

The gas chambers at that time "processed" between twenty and twenty-six thousand people every day. The crematoriums could not handle such an enormous number of corpses and so fires burned around the camp day and night. It seemed that the whole place was enveloped in flames, and the smell of burning human flesh was everywhere. Clouds of smoke spread over the ground. We inhaled this odor, this smoke — it made us choke, drove us mad.

At the very height of the annihilation of the Hungarian Jews, one Sunday the *Lagerführer* decided to amuse himself a little. We were all driven out of the barracks into the camp yard where an orchestra played uninterruptedly, and Hössler himself, dressed in a Tyrolese outfit, in short leather pants and a feathered hat, strolled about the camp admiring the crimson-colored sky produced by the flames.

It was about this time that a large group of Jewish women and children from Yugoslavia were brought to Auschwitz. Soon afterwards, a group of sixty-five thousand people from the Lodz ghetto was brought there.

In 1944 "medical" experiments on people became particularly widespread. As early as 1943 children younger than sixteen were selected from a number of trains. For awhile there were some sort of experiments conducted on them, and then they were all injected with poison. Subsequently, the victims for these experiments were selected from each of the groups brought to the camp. In the spring of 1944 the women set aside for experiments were transferred to a separate barracks (the second barracks in the new building). A fence of barbed wire was erected around it, and a guard was posted.

In just this way they fenced in the eighth, ninth, and tenth barracks, where "experimental" women were also kept.

Almost all of them were gradually sent to the gas chambers. Those who survived until the camp had to be liquidated were exterminated during the evacuation.

The men were castrated: some of them had one testicle cut off, others — both.

Isolated incidents of resistance and attempts to escape from the camp were rather frequent. As early as the summer of 1943 a Polish engineer escaped, having taken with him the building plans for the camp. In revenge for this escape twelve Poles who worked with him were hanged. It was announced that in the future, for each person who escaped, one hundred would be executed. This, however, did not stop people. Escape attempts continued. In the summer of 1944 Henach Gromp from Warsaw tried to escape with his brother and a Czechoslovak Jew. They were caught. Henach was sent to the camp at Janina-Gruben, the other two were put in the "bunker" (prison) at Birkenau. At Janina-Gruben Henach tried to build a tunnel but was caught again. He was taken to Birkenau and was hanged there.

The camp prison, the bunker, was located in the eleventh barracks. The fate of the people who ended up in the bunker was known in advance. A comedy of justice occurred every ten days. There was only one sentence handed out — the death penalty. The wall against which the shootings took place was called the "Black Wall." Among those executed in the bunker were many Polish partisans — men and women. And it was here that the Jews who tried to escape the ghetto were executed, too. Once a young Jewish woman and her two children were shot against the "Black Wall."

In 1944 shootings at the "Black Wall" were replaced by a mobile gas chamber. The mobile gas chamber operated right up until the last day of the camp.

Often, when returning from work, we would see on the ground traces of human blood that had not yet congealed. Once, when entering a fenced-off area, we came upon a truck which was leaking streams of blood from its bed. The vehicle was loaded with bodies of murdered people.

In the winter, early in 1944, returning from work late one night when *Appell* should have been completed long before, we found the whole camp in the yard. We knew from the general mood that something serious had happened. And in fact, it turned out that something had occurred that was very alarming to the Hitlerites. In one of the trainloads of people brought in from France there was a young Jewish woman. When she, already naked, was led to the gas chamber, she started to plead with *Raportführer* Schillinger, who was in charge of the gassing, to let her live. Schillinger stood there with his hands in his pockets and, rocking on his feet, he laughed in her face. With a strong punch to the nose, she knocked Schillinger to the ground, grabbed his revolver and got off several shots, killing him and an SS man on the spot, and wounding another.

The following incident also occurred. A Jew from Yugoslavia who had been assigned to a *Sonderkommando*, while burning corpses, threw himself into the fire, dragging an SS man along with him.

At the end of 1943 a resistance organization sprang up in the camp. There were people of different nationalities both in the organization itself, as well as in its leadership. At first the work was conducted among each nationality separately. We knew that Communists were at the head of the organization.

I was engulfed in the organization by Gutman, a participant in the Warsaw ghetto uprising. Later it was I who enlisted other comrades: Alberstat, Robert (he was from Belgium, I don't remember his surname). In general we were organized in groups, and each of us knew only his own group — those people from whom he received assignments and those to whom he was supposed to give assignments. We managed to establish contact with the women's barracks, with the workers of the *Sonderkommando*, even with the prisoners from the small camps.

At first the organization's main task was to render assistance to the comrades who needed it most. Then the transmission of information was arranged. Through comrades who worked in the radio shop, it became possible to listen with more or less regularity to Soviet broadcasts. Information about the victories of the Red Army was passed on by word of mouth and gave us courage and faith that the hour of reckoning with the Hitlerite cannibals was drawing near. At the factory we secretly made snips in preparation for the right moment to cut the wire entanglements around the camp.

We began to commit acts of sabotage in the factory: we slowed down the work pace and damaged the machines.

In May, 1944, upon the suggestion of the organization, I managed to transfer to the night shift so I could establish connections and set up the work of the organization in this shift. Our activity, undoubtedly, produced results. Little by little we began to steal gunpowder from the factory and give it to the members of the organization who were in the *Sonderkommando*.

At the end of August the Hitlerites began to exterminate the *Sonderkommando* whose job was to burn the corpses of the Hungarian Jews. Several hundreds of people from these units were suffocated at Auschwitz in the disinfection chambers. The others quickly found out about this. One hundred twenty people from the *Sonderkommando* attacked their guards and killed them. The boss of the one of the crematoriums was burned in an oven, the crematorium was blown up, and the prisoners ran off. A group of soldiers was sent out after them, many of the escapees were killed, but as we were told, thirty-six of them still got away.

After this, indiscriminate searches and repressive measures began in the camp. Even a German was arrested — the *capo* in our night shift, Schultz. A letter was found on a girl from Cracow, and as a result of this letter, three more girls were arrested. All four of them were hanged in front of the factory building — two during the day shift, and two during the night shift. *Lagerführer* Hössler supervised the executions.

Five members of the organization decided to escape from the camp to establish contacts with the outside world and to prepare for action on a broader scale. They were put in boxes, which were used to haul things out of the camp. But the driver noticed them and turned them in. They were all brought back to the camp and hanged "for attempting to escape and blow up the camp."

The mood in the camp became extremely tense. Construction was begun on a special road fenced off by barbed wire and leading from the factory to the camp.

In December of 1944 we began to sense that the Germans were preparing to liquidate the camp. Rumors started going around that all the prisoners were about to be executed.

In early January, air attacks on Auschwitz by Soviet aircraft intensified considerably. On the night of January 12, we had hardly begun the night shift when a deafening explosion was heard. The light went out. We soon learned that a bomb had fallen on a section of the camp where the apartments of the SS stood, and that it had inflicted heavy casualties.

During the bombing, people prayed to God that they be killed by the bombs and not at the hands of the Hitlerites.

The Hitlerites were in a complete panic. One could feel that the end was drawing closer. But what would the end be for us? We were very uneasy.

The evacuation of the camp began. First, all the Poles were taken out. On the night of January 18 our factory was still working. But on January 18 we were herded in a westernly direction. There was an SS man posted for every five prisoners. We were taken on foot for seventy kilometers. Those who fell behind were shot — during two days of the journey as many as five hundred people were killed that way.

On January 20 we were brought to a small station. The corpses of those who had been shot were everywhere. They shot every person who tried to leave the ranks by even one step. There we were put into open freight cars and taken away.

During the night, at a small station fifteen kilometers from Neisse River, I managed to escape. I lay in the forest for nine days, then tried to leave, was arrested, escaped again, got into a group of German refugees and along with them I made it to Falkenberg. There I was arrested again and sentenced to be shot. But I was able to escape again, and after long and trying ordeals, on February 3, I crossed the line of the front. After being checked out, I had the honor to be enlisted into the ranks of the Red Army. I was happy to be able to take part in several battles against the Hitlerites. On May 7 I was wounded and spent two months in the hospital.

I am discharged now. I am home in Ostrino. Life in the city is being restored. But at the moment, it is too difficult for me to live here. The wounds in my heart bleed. Everything reminds me of my family, and my dear friends. So I've decided to live in another town. The Soviet motherland has given me this opportunity. I am not a bad craftsman, I'll work. One must live! We will live!

Literary preparation by **L. Goldberg.**

The Story of M. Sheynman, Former Prisoner of War

During the first days of the war I joined the National Guard and tried quickly to join the active army. In early October, 1941, the unit in which I was serving was surrounded near Vyazma. We immediately found ourselves deep behind the German lines. On October 12 I was wounded in the leg during an attack. The winter of 1941 came early. I had to ford a small river, and both my legs became frostbitten. On October 19 I could no longer walk and was left in the village of Levinka in the Temninsky region of Smolensk *oblast*. It was there, on October 27, that the Germans found me. From that day on I began my ordeal through the Fascist camps.

As a Soviet citizen, battalion commissar, and a Jew as well, my position was that of a prisoner condemned to death, a sentence which could have been carried out at any moment, had the Germans found out something about me. Captured Soviet citizens perished in multitudes from hunger and cold, from the unbearable living conditions in the camps, in the camp "hospitals," and in the so-called "work units." The Germans shot prisoners by the thousands while transporting them. The wounded were often killed off on the field of battle. The Germans developed and methodically and persistently implemented a whole system of measures directed toward the extermination of as large a number of their prisoners as was possible.

In the first period of the war the Germans did not even try to conceal the fact that they were premeditatedly murdering their prisoners, so convinced were they of victory and that their deeds would go unpunished. The extermination of prisoners of war continued right up until the last day of the war. But towards the end the Germans tried to disguise their deeds.

I will mention some facts about the camps where I have been as well as facts related to me by my comrades in captivity.

From November, 1941, through February 12, 1942, I was in the Vyazma hospital for prisoners of war. According to the testimony of the doctors who worked in the hospital and the camp at that time, during the winter of 1941–1942 as many as seventy thousand people died in the Vyazma camp. People were put in half-demolished buildings without roofs, windows, or doors. Often, many people who went to sleep would not wake up — they froze to

503

death. At Vyazma, the exhausted and the ragged, people who could barely drag themselves along — Soviet prisoners of war, were forced by the Germans to do back-breaking jobs that were beyond their strength. A few wound up in the hospital; the majority perished in the camp.

In February, 1942, I was transferred from Vyazma to the camp at Molodechno (Byelorussia). There, according to the testimony of doctors and medical orderlies, by this time as many as forty-three thousand people had died, primarily from starvation and typhus, since the beginning of the war.

From December to August, 1944, I was in the camp at Czenstochowa (Poland). Tens of thousands of prisoners of war either died or were shot by the Germans in this camp. Everyday those who had died of hunger and tuberculosis were taken out in a covered car to the cemetery. The paramedic who went to bury the dead told me that there were several cemeteries in Czenstochowa where Soviet prisoners of war were buried. They were buried in two or three layers: the corpses were put one on top of the other in enormous pits, approximately ten thousand people in each pit. In 1942–1943, there were systematic shootings in Czenstochowa of prisoners of war — political workers, Jews, officers and educated people.

Many thousands of Soviet prisoners of war were tortured by the Germans in camps in Germany. Not far from the last camp I was in — "Wesuwe" (near Meppen on the Ems, on the Holland border), was a small camp of Russian prisoners of war — Dalium. In June of 1945, after being liberated from captivity, our comrades who lived long enough to be liberated, erected a monument in the Dalium cemetery to the thirty-four thousand Russian prisoners of war who had been murdered by the Germans. In camp No. 326, not far from Padeborn and Bielefeld, a monument was built after the liberation to the sixty-five thousand Soviet prisoners of war who had been murdered in that camp.

M. V. Sutugin is a former commissar in an infantry regiment of the Moscow guard division who, like me, was captured near Vyazma. He testified that, in December of 1941, four to five-hundred people died every day in the camp at Gomel, where he was.

My comrade-in-captivity, Colonel A. G. Molev (a former division commander), was in the camp at Demblin (Poland). From September 1941 through March 1942, out of the one hundred six thousand prisoners in that camp, as many as one hundred thousand had died. At Zamostye, in a camp for officers, according to the testimony of my comrade-in-captivity, Lieutenant D. V. Shuturov (Dnepropetrovsk), out of twelve thousand people only two and one half thousand were still alive by the end of March, 1942. The rest had died from starvation and the cold.

According to the testimony of military physician V. A. Sayko, in the camp at Zhitomir from 1941 through May, 1943, about sixty thousand people died; and in the camp at Suvalki — from the beginning of the war until May 1, 1944 (according to data from the German commandant's office), fifty-four thousand prisoners of war died.

Engineer V. V. Fokin, who was the chief of medical services for a period at the end of 1941 at the Mogilev camp for prisoners of war, and with whom I spent time in the Kalvaria camp in 1943, told me that at Mogilev more than one hundred thousand people were tormented by the Germans and finally died from starvation and exposure during the winter of 1941–42. As many as seven hundred fifty people died each day. There was not enough time to bury the dead.

According to the testimony of S. P. Doroshenko, military doctor second class, who worked in the Minsk hospital for prisoners of war, one hundred ten thousand people died at the Minsk forest camp from July 1941 through March 1942. Four to five hundred people died each day.

During the fall and winter of 1941–1942 the Germans, in a number of places, set up camps for prisoners of war under the open sky. These camps were in Zamostye, Sukhozhebrovo (near Siedlce), in Minsk and in other places. As a result, almost everyone in those camps died. In a camp for the rank and file at Zamostye at the end of 1941 prisoners lived under the open sky. In October there was a snow fall. In two days two thousand people froze to death.

In the winter of 1941–1942 the Germans would force the prisoners out of the camp barracks in the morning and would not let them back inside until night. The people froze to death. Food was also distributed in the cold. In the winter of 1941 in the Mogilev camp people had to stand in the cold for two-three hours to receive lunch. Several thousand died each day while they waited.

Thousands of prisoners of war died at transit points and while being transported by train. Groups of prisoners were often transported on foot. Those who lagged behind were shot, and this was practiced until the last days of the war. The escort guards would often shoot into the columns of soldiers just for the sake of amusement. In the winter of 1941 there were instances when a column of six thousand people would leave a camp, and only two to three thousand would arrive at the designated destination. The rest either froze to death along the way or were killed by the Germans.

Prisoners were transported by train either in freight cars (without heaters), or in open flat cars. In each car there were as many as one hundred people. People froze to death and suffocated from lack of air. In February, 1942, the hospital for prisoners of war was transferred from Vyazma to Molodechno. At each stop along the way the people who had died from exhaustion or who froze to death were carried off the traincars.

Lieutenant-major D. S. Filkin was in Grodno camp No. 3 in the winter of 1941–1942. He says that in January 1942 a train arrived from Bobruysk carrying one thousand two hundred prisoners of war. When the cars opened it turned out that eight hundred people had frozen to death or suffocated en route. By July, 1942, out of that entire trainload of people only sixty were still alive.

In December, 1941, a train arrived at Vyazma with prisoners sent by the Germans from the Shakhovskaya station. A considerable number of people had frozen to death en route. I was told this by the doctor who was sent to the station to meet the train. The corpses were carried off the traincars and stacked. Some of them still showed signs of life, tried to raise their arms, moaned. The Germans would walk up to these people and shoot them.

In the camps for prisoners of war, in both penal and work units, the cruelty of the Germans and their ingenuity in the matter of murder knew no limits.

In 1941–1943, during the first five-seven days in captivity, people were not, as a rule, given anything to eat. The Germans cynically maintained that this was done so that people would grow weak and be unable to escape. In January and February, 1942, hospital patients were allowed seventy grams of unground rye a day. From this grain, "soup" was prepared two times a day — each time a person received a half liter. It is not surprising that people grew feeble and died off like flies.

In the summers of 1941 and 1943 people in the camps ate all the grass in the yards, the leaves from the trees, and if a frog came their way, they would eat it too. They would also roast horse hide in a fire and eat it, if they could obtain it. Salt was an unobtainable luxury.

The maximum caloric content of the daily ration for Soviet prisoners in the German camps, according to the calculations of the doctors, was 1,300–1,400 calories, while a person who is in a state of rest needs 2,400 calories, and one who is doing physical labor requires 3,400–3,600 calories. There were adults in the camps whose weight had dropped to as low as thirty to thirty-two kilograms (sixty-six to seventy pounds). That is the weight of a child.

The Germans prevented in every way possible the serious organization of medical assistance in the camps. For the most part they did not give out medicines at all. In the hospitals the wounded would go for weeks without having their wounds redressed, because there were no bandages. The Germans did not make available any surgical instruments. Many thousands of Soviet citizens died in hospitals from wounds, blood poisoning, and still more from exhaustion, dysentery, typhus, and tuberculosis.

As a prisoner I was in hospitals for prisoners of war in Vyazma, Molodechno, Kalvaria, Czenstochowa and Ebelsbach. The word "hospital" is in no way appropriate as a name for these institutions. In Vyazma the hospital was housed on the outskirts of the city in small, half-destroyed buildings that had been abandoned by their residents, and in the ruins of a creamery. It was always cold and dark in these small buildings. The wounded lay on the bare floor. There was not even any straw for bedding. Only toward the end of my stay in Vyazma did they build plank-beds in the buildings, but even on these the patients had to lie without straw, on the bare boards. There was no medicine. The lice infestation was incredible. For the three and a half months I was in Vyazma I did not take one bath.

It was the same in the Molodechno hospital. On the bare floor, in every ward, eighty people lay in four rows, closely pressed against one another. Typhus was rampant. For the whole floor (eight to ten wards) there was only one thermometer. I came down with typhus. During the whole time I was sick the paramedic was able to take my temperature only once. It was obligatory that the lice be removed three to four times a day. People stripped naked and examined everything. Each time as many as three or four hundred large lice would be collected, the small ones were gathered up by the handfuls. The Germans did nothing to combat the lice prob-

507

lem. The doctors told me about incidents when the Germans came up with the fundamental solution to the problem of typhus — they set fire to the typhoid barracks along with all the sick people who were inside them.

The Germans developed a whole system of specific punishments which were calculated to inflict physical suffering on the prisoners of war and to humiliate them. Flogging, beatings, confinement in punishment cells and bunkers — all these things were employed in the camps. People were tortured, hanged, and shot without the slightest cause.

At the Molodechno camp (later at Kalvaria too) many times we saw prisoners flogged in the yard. They were beaten by policemen, but German officers often supervised the whole procedure. Once I saw an officer grab a whip from a policeman and begin with all his might to beat the naked body of a man spread out on a bench. After he had finished his beating, the officer threatened the policeman, saying that if he was going to be compassionate and use the whip lightly, then the policeman himself would be flogged.

Only the perverted mind of a sadist could have thought up a system of tortures such as existed in the camps, especially for the political workers and the Jews.

This is what junior political instructor Melnikov (a native of the village of Rogachevo, Stalingrad *oblast*, Berezov region) told me: He was captured near Kerch in May, 1942. He was betrayed, and the Germans were told that he was a political worker. The Germans sent him to camp No. 326 (near the village of Augustdorf, not far from Padeborn and Bielefeld). There was a special "SS block" there where they put political workers, Jews, and others who were particularly suspect.

Comrade Melnikov wound up in this block. During the interrogation the Germans were most interested in his ancestors — whether there were any Jews among them. While interrogating him they pistol-whipped him in the face and knocked out a tooth. Then they beat him with a rubber club, trying to get him to confess that he was a political instructor. At the interrogations in this block people were beaten until they lost consciousness. When a person lost consciousness, he was doused with cold water, would come to, and then would be beaten again. They would put a person's fingers in the crack of an open door, close the door, and break the fingers in the process. They would submerge a person's head in a pail of

508

water. Sometimes they held the head in the water until the person choked.

After two hours of this torture comrade Melnikov was taken out to "tactics"; in a gutter, into which the urine from the bathroom flowed, he had to crawl on his stomach (half undressed) fifteen-twenty meters, then in the same gutter he had to crawl this distance on his back.

The procedure for obtaining lunch in this block was as follows: soup was poured into mess tins and the people were formed into lines twenty to thirty meters long. They had to crawl on their bellies, to the mess tins, take them, and quickly eat the soup. Those who fell behind or crawled out ahead were beaten or set upon by the dogs. A half a tin of camp soup (turnips and water), and one hundred grams of bread were given out in the day, and in the evening, boiled water was distributed. After lunch, from 12:30–14:30, people were led out to do "physical exercise" — endless running around the barracks. Those who could not keep up the pace or who fell were beaten and punished: they were forced to stand motionless for two hours with their hands tied behind them and with a stone hanging from their neck. After running, people were forced to dig a ditch fifty by fifty centimeters big. One of the prisoners had to climb into the ditch, and his comrades had to cover him up to the chest with dirt. After this the person would be dug up and the same procedure would be applied to the others. Then water was poured into the pit from a pail that was full of holes, only so that it could be scooped out afterwards with the same holey pail. Towards evening everyone in the block (at that time there were eighty people) upon command had to quickly climb up to the top of the three-tiered bunk beds, lie down, jump down to the ground, and climb up again. The ones who could not keep up were set upon by the dogs. This continued until seven to eight o'clock in the evening. Then the prisoners were forced to scoop out the urine from the bathroom with their mess tins (they had to eat from these same tins). Then people were taken to the bathhouse and washed down with water from a fire-hose with hot and then cold water, alternately. At nine o'clock in the evening the prisoners were given boiled water — "tea." From 9:30 to 11:00 there was "physical exercise" again: these exhausted people had to run continuously around the barracks. From eleven to twelve o'clock at night — they had to do the "goose step" around the barracks. At twelve o'clock at night the signal was given to return to the barracks. A day of torture began again at three o'clock in the morning. After these agonizing tortures, the Jews would be killed. But there were few among the Russians comrades who could withstand these inhuman tortures. The end for everyone was the same.

The Germans tormented and killed prisoners at hard labor — in factories, mines, and quarries. From December, 1944, until the end of my captivity I was in the death camp at Wesuwe. Soviet prisoners of war who had worked for a period of time in German factories were sent there to die. There were many camps like this for people who were dying. Not far from the camp at Wesuwe were similar camps for condemned prisoners: Dalium, Witmarschen, Aleksis, and others. They were all part of one camp organization — the so-called "*Stalag* VI S."

After we were liberated from captivity, English and Canadian officers and soldiers came to the camp at Wesuwe. The doctors among them asked the people who were dying of tuberculosis how they had become so sick. They heard shocking stories about how the Germans had sent young and healthy people, captured soldiers and officers of the Red Army, to the mines and factories; how they were forced to work fourteen and sixteen hours a day and were given, for one work day, one or two liters of camp soup made from grass and turnips. People were subjected to unheard-of humiliations and beatings. Even the healthiest people would contract tuberculosis in four-five months, and then the Germans sent them to a death camp. Specially selected healthy people were sent from other camps to take their place, only so that in four-six months they too would be worn out. That is how the German death conveyer worked. But even in the death camps people were not allowed to die peacefully. Right up until the last minute of life the Germans tormented people with hunger, cold, beatings, and atrocities.

From the first minute of captivity the Germans removed the prisoners' clothing and shoes and dressed them in rags. In this way they not only condemned the prisoners to the tortures of the cold, but also debased their human dignity. In early January, 1942, a group of recently captured Red-Army officers arrived at the Vyazma hospital. The majority of them had come with frost-bitten feet. Instead of shoes, they had rags on their feet. As these comrades told me, when they were captured the first thing the Germans did was to take all their warm winter clothes and shoes, and then they were herded barefoot in groups out into the cold of winter. In

February, 1942, on the way from Vyazma to Molodechno, I saw the Germans remove the footwear from prisoners, taking their warm felt boots from them, and right then and there, they put them on their own feet.

It is no wonder that, given these conditions and the savage treatment received as prisoners of the Germans, hundreds of thousands of Soviet people perished. They were literally tortured to death by the Germans.

The Germans did not spare any nationality, be they Russians, Ukrainians, Byelorussians, Armenians, Georgians, Tatars, Jews, Uzbeks, or Kazakhs. And at the same time they tried to stir up national differences among the prisoners in order to divide the Soviet people, to set one national group against another and in this way to facilitate their vile plans. In their newspapers they set the Russians against the Ukrainians, and the Ukrainians against the Russians and Byelorussians. In cheap newspapers which the Germans distributed in the Ukrainian language Pushkin, Belinsky, and other outstanding Russian people were portrayed in the crudest terms. In the Byelorussian newspapers the Germans cursed the Russians, Ukrainians, and others. Here and there in the camps the guard was "Ukrainian." All the dregs, nationalists, and hooligans were selected for this guard. They would beat the prisoners — the Russians, Ukrainians, Byelorussians, Tatars, and others, and they handed over the Jews. In this way the Germans kindled national hostilities.

The Germans tried to rouse an especially savage hostility toward the Jews. The Fascists carried on unprecedented anti-Semitic propaganda.

Every Soviet citizen who was captured by the Germans was a doomed person, regardless of his nationality. But still, the position of the Jews was even more horrible. The hunt for the Jews and the political workers did not stop even for one day. Jews were captured just as were Russians, Ukrainians, Byelorussians, Armenians, Georgians, and others — either their units had been surrounded, or they had been wounded. Among the few Jews whom I met in captivity, there were doctors who had been surrounded along with the hospitals and the wounded. Some of them, when captured, were seriously wounded — bleeding heavily on the field of battle. Jewish soldiers knew that an agonizing death awaited them among the Germans. And if, nevertheless, they were captured, it was only because of extraordinary circumstances.

511

At the end of 1941, I was at Vyazma in a "hospital" for prisoners of war. Once in December a medic walked down into our ward and said: "The Germans are looking for Jews." Not far from me lying on a plank-bed was Doctor S. Labkovsky, a military physician who, before the war, had been the head of a railroad outpatient clinic in Kaluga. His unit had gotten surrounded, and while escaping the Germans, both his feet became so badly frostbitten that his toes fell off. His feet were bloody stumps. He was not able to walk even with crutches. The Germans learned that he was a Jew. In the evening six Germans came and ordered him to prepare to leave immediately. Seriously ill, he was taken away. That day all the sick people whom the Germans suspected of being Jews were taken away. Also arrested and taken were the Jewish doctors, paramedics, and nurses. They all knew what awaited them — torture, suffering and death.

In the camp at Roslavl in the Smolensk *oblast*, according to the stories of people who were there in 1941, the Germans set dogs upon the Jewish prisoners of war; they led the people out into the camp yard and set the dogs loose. Those who tried to defend themselves or drive off the dogs were beaten by the Germans, who were amused by the sight.

Jews and political workers surrounded in the area of Vyazma in October, 1941, were thrown alive down well shafts. While in the Vyazma and Molodechno camps, I heard many stories about this from witnesses. Those who were surrounded were picked up in the woods and villages and delivered to collecting points. There the Jews were picked out on the basis of external appearances and killed. At the Baranovichi penal camp (the so-called *Ostlager*) there were systematic shootings of Jewish prisoners of war, including women nurses and doctors. At the Brest-Litovsk camp there was a special penal company (it had a more intense regimen) which consisted of political workers and Jews. From time to time people from this company would be taken away and shot.

In many camps the Germans arranged a general examination of the prisoners to discover who the Jews were. The German doctors disgraced themselves with their base roles as servants to Hitler and his gang. At the Slavutsky camp the Germans lined up each group of new prisoners and ordered them to uncover their penises. The Gestapo men would walk up and down the rows and select those who they suspected of being Jews. They were taken away and shot. The same thing went on in camp No. 326. There, in addition to the

Jews, the Germans caught political workers, officers, and educated people.

Captain K. Ya. Manushin (a resident of Simferopol) told me that in February 1942, in the camp hospital at Bogunya (near Zhitomir), the Germans held a general physical examination of all the sick and wounded (four thousand people). The sick who were able to walk were lined up in the camp yard. A commission consisting of the commandant, a sergeant major, and two doctors examined each person individually. Thirty-three suspects were selected and separated from the other prisoners. The Germans and the policemen began to beat them right on the spot. After examining the sick who could walk, the commission went to examine those who were sick in bed. The seriously ill and wounded who were suspected of being Jews were dragged out of their beds, beaten, and sent in carts to the general camp. At five o'clock in the morning all those who had been selected — forty people — were taken in their underwear beyond the camp fence and shot. The same thing was done in the camp at Zhitomir.

The Jews were systematically rounded up in the camp at Czenstochowa: a "commission" consisting of the commandant, sergeant major, and a doctor picked out, by examination, the Jews from a group of new prisoners. The people who had been picked out were then shot.

Commander V. A. Pshenitsyn, who was captured in September, 1941, to the east of Piryatin, told me that from the first day of his captivity he had observed the Jews being hunted out while being transported, at assembly points, and in the camps. At an assembly point in the village of Kovali a column of prisoners was lined up, and the Jews were picked out on the basis of external appearance. Germans from the Volga region and traitors, Ukrainian nationalists, helped in the selection. Those selected were led off in groups outside the village, forced to dig graves, and were shot on the spot. At all subsequent transit points, at stops, the Germans announced: "Jews and political workers, step out." At a stop at Khorol four Jewish doctors stepped out. The Germans taunted them and later, in Vinnitsa, shot them. In the camp at Vinnitsa during the first days of October, 1941, the Germans shot 378 Jews. At the end of September, 1941, V. A. Pshenitsyn saw Jewish prisoners of war being taken away for execution in the camp at Kremenchug. The wounded who were unable to walk were carried on stretchers to be shot. The Germans committed a similar massacre in the Vladimir-Volynsky camp, as well. On March 2, 1942, two hundred twenty political workers and Jews, including doctors, were led out beyond the wire and shot. The seriously ill and typhus victims were shot, too. They were carried out unconscious with a temperature of 40° Centigrade (104° Fahrenheit) on stretchers to be shot. Among others who perished were Commander Shilkrot, Zinger, Doctor Greenberg from Kiev, and others.

The comrades who in the summer of 1942 ended up in the camp at Czenstochowa say that after newcomers were put into the barracks the policemen began to hunt for the Jews and political workers. The Jews were picked out on the basis of external appearance. They were taken out and shot on October 5, 1942, and the political workers — ten days later.

In the camp at Zhitomir, the Germans tried to exterminate Jews and political workers first so that then they could slowly and methodically exterminate the thousands of prisoners of other nationalities. Everyone who entered the camp had to be passed by a special "commission." Those identified as Jews were handed over to the SS. They were housed separately from the other prisoners and were forced to perform the dirtiest and most difficult tasks. They were fed once every three days. Every evening they would be visited by the Gestapo men and their dogs. The dogs would lunge at people, bite, and tear at them. After lengthy humiliation, they would be taken out of the city and shot.

Senior Lieutenant D. S. Filkin has reported that on July 9, 1942, two SS men arrived at camp No. 3 at Grodno. There was a "special" room in the camp where one hundred and six people were kept — wounded Jews and political workers. All night long the German beasts beat these armless, legless, and seriously wounded people. In the morning of January 12 a vehicle with a trailer drove up to the camp and fifty people from the "special" room wearing only shorts were put into the vehicle, taken away, and shot. A little while later the vehicle returned and took away another fifty people to be shot. Six people remained alive.

Mayor Tikhonenko, who in 1941-1942 was in the prisoner-of-war camp at Mitava, says that all the political workers and Jews were uncovered by the Germans through their agents, after which these prisoners disappeared without a trace.

Here is what Commander L. B. Berlin told me: In September, 1941, a group of prisoners of war were brought to the camp at Zhitomir. They were gathered up in the yard, and a German interpreter who accompanied a camp officer addressed them with a speech: "By order of camp headquarters, Ukrainians may go home tomorrow. But we can not release you, because among you there are commissars and Jews. Give them up to us, and we will let you go home." These exhausted people were offered freedom at the price of betrayal.

In February, 1942, I was transferred to the camp for prisoners of war at Molodechno. By this time there were as many as eight thousand people in the camp, and in the hospital — as many as two thousand. The prisoners lived in barracks. It was unbearably cold in them. The amount of food given out in the camp bordered on the starvation level. In December, 1941, the Germans lined up everyone living in the barracks and counted out every tenth person. There were fifty of them. They were led off to the side and before the eyes of the whole camp were fired on with machine guns. Only a small number of them saved themselves by mixing in with the crowd of prisoners after the first shots were fired.

The camp had a cruel regimen: people were publicly whipped. As a form of punishment, people were held in a cage for several hours in the freezing cold.

The Germans did not allow the Jewish doctors to work. There wece isolated exceptions, but even these were temporary. Doctor Kopylovich (formerly head of an outpatient clinic in the city of Shakhty) worked as a physician in the camp hospital at Molodechno. He was allowed to work only because he was an excellent surgeon. I heard from many comrades that even in the difficult conditions of German captivity this doctor fulfilled his medical duties honestly and saved many Soviet people from death. He himself was sent from Molodechno to the Baranovichi penal camp "Ost," where the Germans sent the political workers and Jews and from which there was no return.

Military doctor S. P. Doroshenko, who in 1941 was in the Minsk camp, told me that at the end of 1941 the Germans forbade the Jewish doctors to work in the hospital. The hospital at one time was headed by Doctor Feldman (who was said to have been the former chief of the Mogilev *oblast* hospital). At the end of November he was summoned to the German commandant's office and was not seen in the camp again. Jewish women-doctors were also taken away and were sometimes starved, sometimes shot. Wounded and sick Jews were put in the typhus section, although they were not sick with typhus. Later they were all sent to a special Jewish section of the

Minsk forest camp. There was a severe regimen in effect there: food was given out every other day, and it was of very poor quality. By spring all the Jews in this camp had been killed or had died of starvation or disease. In this same Minsk camp, according to the testimony of officer I. K. Deryugin, the Jews were put in a cellar, from which they were regularly taken out in groups and shot. Typhus was rampant in this cellar. Corpses of the dead were carried out once a week.

In June, 1942, all the officers from the Molodechno camp were taken to Kalvaria (Lithuania). Along with the hospital, I was among the patients who ended up in this camp. A regimen of brutal arbitrariness reigned here as well.

The situation was especially difficult for a small group of about twenty Jewish doctors who were among the prisoners of war who had come from Molodechno. They included Belenky, Gordon, Krup (from Moscow), Kleyner (from Kaluga), and others. Before Kalvaria they had already experienced many terrible things. In Kalvaria they and a small group of political workers were isolated from the other prisoners. No matter what happened in the camp, the Germans would first vent their anger on the Jews. Doctor Gordon, an old man, surgeon, and experienced doctor (he said he had performed more than ten thousand operations), was seriously ill. He was swollen from hunger, and he was in the hospital. By order of the German Doctor Breuer, he, being a Jew, was expelled from the hospital and, while seriously ill, had to stand for hours at roll calls and suffer unheard-of indignities.

The hospital was supervised by a German paramedic, a barber by profession, who was a young man, but what a scoundrel! He treated all Soviet people with malicious contempt. He once stopped by the barracks. Doctor Gordon, who was then sitting on a plank-bed, was not able to stand up on time. So this fascist degenerate beat him without mercy. Living under the constant threat of death, persecuted and victimized, Doctor Gordon still found the strength to conduct discussions on medicine with his circle of comrade-doctors and to secretly consult with the young Russian doctors in the hospital on cases involving complex illnesses.

Another doctor, a specialist on children's illnesses, Doctor Belenky, was beaten by the same German barber "paramedic." He died in the fall of 1942.

The hunt for Jews and political workers in the camp did not stop even for a single day. By spring of 1942 about twenty-five Jews had been discovered; they had arrived with groups of prisoners at different times, had earlier concealed their nationality, and miraculously had escaped death. The German commandant ordered them to sew on their outer clothes — on the chest and back — white quadrangular scraps — "a sign of disgrace." In the summer of 1943 they, along with a group of political workers, were taken out of the camp.

The Soviet people who had the misfortune to find themselves in German captivity and who remained faithful to their homeland understood perfectly the goals of the foul policy of the Germans and did what was in their power to counteract it. Many Soviet doctors who worked in hospitals of prisoner-of-war camps hid Jews and political workers in the hospitals, as well as those officers and rank-and-file soldiers who were especially threatened with the danger of being torn to pieces. Many thousands of prisoners passed through distributive camp No. 326, where a thorough examination of all new arrivals was conducted to identify Jews. There was a group of Russian doctors and paramedics who set themselves the task of saving the political workers and the Jews, as well as those military workers whom, for one reason or another, the Germans were trying to hunt down. These people were given a place in the hospital, "underwent" fictitious operations, had their names changed, and were transferred to a camp for invalids.

I know of instances when Russian comrades went to the physical examination in place of Jews and thereby saved their lives.

I was personally saved thanks to my Russian comrades — officers and doctors.

At Vyazma, Doctors Redkin and Sobstel hid me, wounded and sick, from the German police dogs. In Kalvaria, at the urgent request of some comrades (in particular Lieutenant-Colonel S. P. Proskurin) the doctors kept me in the hospital. When in February 1943 I was discharged to the camp and there was a real danger of being discovered by the Germans, Doctor Kuropatenkov (from Leningrad) put me in the hospital's isolation ward. Afterwards, along with a number of other comrades I was hidden in the hospital by Doctor B. P. Yevseyev (from Moscow) until the end of 1943. In Kalvaria, where Gestapo espionage was particularly widespread, the doctors (especially Doctor N. M. Tsvetayev from Kizlyar) hid me in the hospital among the tuberculosis patients and thereby saved me from being shot.

A considerable number of the officers and soldiers of the Red

Army who had the misfortune, through the uncertainties of war, to be captured by the Germans, perished in the camps from unheard-of persecution, starvation, unbearably horrible daily conditions, and diseases. In Germany today there is almost no city without a Russian cemetery. And if among those who survived there is a small group of Jews, they survived only because of the support of their Russian, Ukrainian, and Byelorussian comrades.

ADDENDA

The Racial Policy of Hitlerism and Anti-Semitism

The history of civilized peoples has not known a war more barbarous and predatory than the one which the Hitlerites waged against the peoples of the Soviet land.

The "racial policy" of the Hitlerite mechanism of state from the very first days of its inception was meant not only to instill into the consciousness of a German his "right" to supremacy over other peoples, but also in fact to "train" him for this goal.

The target of this "training" in the *beginning* was the Jewish population of Germany, and the ground had already been prepared in this regard.

Beginning in the last quarter of the nineteenth century the most reactionary elements in Germany (like Treitschke, like Wilhelm's court preacher Stöcker, and various Junker circles) had used anti-Semitism even before Hitler to distract the attention of the discontented masses from the real culprits responsible for their miserable situation.

The Jews, who made up less than one percent of the population of Germany, were made the scapegoat for all the ills of the masses. Social problems, which derived from exploitation by the nobility and prominent financial and industrial cliques, were substituted by questions of religion, race, and nationality. Furthermore, anti-Semitism was embellished with "social" nuances, being presented as "real German and Christian socialism." The old August Bebel already called German anti-Semitism "the socialism of fools."

The "racial training" of the Germans began the moment the Hitlerites came to power. It began with Jewish pogroms, beatings, murders, and pillaging of the Jewish population. The pogroms were directed by the Hitlerite storm troopers and the police apparatus, which was filled with Hitlerite cadres.

The Jewish population was placed "outside the law." Jews were expelled from state, public, and other institutions. Jews were deprived of German citizenship — a fact which was formally confirmed by the so-called "Nuremberg laws of 1935."

The criminal laws of civilized states usually make provision for the serious punishment of murderers, robbers, their inspirers and accomplices. It was in Germany, with the rise of the Hitlerites to power, that it was openly preached in the schools and universities, in books and in the daily press, that for Germans, the "higher race," anything was permitted — that they could build their own prosperity and well-being on the bones of other peoples.

This was not a state apparatus in the conventional sense. This was a weapon in the hands of political gangsters, who, in using the power of the state (the police, officialdom, the army), directed this power for the purpose of political plunder and pillage punishable by the legal codes of all civilized states.

* * *

Hitler taught: "If we want to create our great German Empire, then we must first expel and exterminate the Slavic peoples — the Russians, Poles, Czechs, Slovaks, Bulgarians, Ukrainians, and Byelorussians."

This was *fundamental* in the plans of the Hitlerites. As early as several years before the war, Hitler, in an effort to stir up predatory instincts at a congress of the Fascist rabble in Nuremberg, said: "When the Urals with their immeasurable wealth of raw materials, the innumerable forests of Siberia, and the endless fields of the Ukraine are in German hands, our people will be assured of everything essential."

The greedy and presumptuous Germans during the first year after their attack on the Soviet land triumphantly declared that henceforth, Ukrainian wheat, Ukrainian lard, and Donets-Basin coal would be in German hands. Hitler's henchman, the "Reich Commissar of the Ukraine" Erich Koch, wrote that the Ukraine must "support and provide the German military command with the extraordinarily large quantities of raw materials and wheat products of the country so that Germany and Europe could wage war for as long as they wished."

The Hitlerites thought that they would facilitate the implementation of their "new order" by creating hostilities between the Soviet peoples. Goering's "Green Folder," which contained the instructions for German agents in the temporarily-occupied Soviet regions, stated directly that it was necessary to create conflict and animosity between the peoples of the U.S.S.R. so as to weaken their resistance.

Thus, for example, the Hitlerites established good relations with a small group of Ukrainian nationalists (the Bendera group and others), with whose help they enslaved the Ukrainian people and tried to set the Ukrainians against the Russians and Jews. And at the same time in a secret circular dated July 18, 1942 (No. 5771/ 564/42 — secret), from the commander of the German army, Kinzinger, it was emphasized: "The Ukrainian was and remains alien to us. Each simple, trusting expression of interest in Ukrainians and their cultural existence is harmful and weakens those essential traits to which Germany is committed with its might and grandeur."

The leaders created a system by which it was possible to advance professionally and rise up the fascist hierarchical ladder only after becoming skilled in murder and brutality against the peaceful population of the occupied regions and against unarmed people in concentration camps.

In their instructions the leaders constantly reminded their subordinates of the necessity to play off one nationality against the other.

In accordance with the directions in Goering's "Green Folder" the German commandant of the city of Borisov told his superiors: "I am trying to create antagonism between Byelorussians and Russians and to set both groups together against the Jews."

With the arrival of the German armies a nightmare of blood and plundering began everywhere, the victims of which were primarily the Jews. After the armies came the Gestapo men and the "specialists" on the occupational policies.

A special "Jewish apparatus" was created to specialize in the plundering and murdering of the Jews. The Hitlerites threatened all Russians, Ukrainians, Byelorussians, etc., with death if they tried to conceal Jews.

The cities of Lvov, Kiev, Kharkov, Minsk, Gomel, Riga, as well as many other cities of the Soviet land, were witnesses to the almost total extermination of Jewish working people and their families.

* * *

The closer the end of the war came, all the greater was the madness of the Hitlerite monsters. In all the vassal states (in Italy, Rumania, Hungary) Hitler's henchmen introduced "racial legislation." The Jews from all the occupied regions were transported to Maidanek and Auschwitz for extermination.

In December, 1942, the governments of Belgium, Great Britain, Holland, Greece, Luxemburg, Norway, Poland, the U.S.A., the U.S.S.R., Czechoslovakia, Yugoslavia, and the French National Committee pointed out in a declaration that the German-Fascist invaders were "implementing Hitler's often stated intention to exterminate the Jewish people in Europe."

The governments reaffirmed "their solemn commitment to ensure jointly with the entire United Nations that the people responsible for these crimes not escape their deserved punishment."

The report published subsequently by the Information Bureau of the People's Commissariat of Foreign Affairs of the U.S.S.R. "On the Hitlerite Government's Implementation of its Plan for the Annihilation of the Jewish Population of Europe" (*Izvestia*, December 19, 1942) produced concrete materials concerning Hitler's annihilation policy. This report, incidentally, pointed out: "Through such atrocities against the Jews and with its barbarous anti-Semitic propaganda the Hitlerites are trying to divert the attention of the German people from the catastrophes which are obviously becoming imminent for Fascist Germany. Only the doomed adventurists in Hitler's gang who have become entangled in their own lies could be so fanatical as to think it possible to drown in the blood of many hundreds of thousands of completely innocent Jews their innumerable crimes against the peoples of Europe who have been plunged into war by insatiable German imperialism."

Now all of this is in the past. Hitler's armies have been crushed, his plundering machinery has been liquidated. Now the main perpetrators of the crimes, those who inspired and carried out these mass murders and tortures stand before the International Military Tribunal. Thus far there are twenty-four of them in all. Among them is the "specialist" on anti-Semitism, Hitler's close friend and associate — Julius Streicher. It was he who was the main editor of the detestable sheet *Der Stürmer*, which while pandering to obscurantists and sadists, combined pornographic amusement with anti-Semitism. Streicher received the title of general of the SS troops. He became the *Gauleiter* (area commander) of Franconia. Ahead of him as defendants before the International Military Tribunal come Goering, Ribbentrop, Hess, Kaltenbrunner, Rosenberg, Frank, and others who supervised military pillage on a governmental scale.

In Europe, now liberated from the German-Fascist invaders, all racial and nationalistic discrimination has been liquidated, including discrimination with regard to the Jewish population.

But is it possible to say that with the liquidation of Hitlerite gangsterism and the Hitlerite state, the struggle is over with Fascism, with its misanthropic "ideology," including anti-Semitism?

Of course not! This is obvious from how serious a struggle is still being waged with Hitlerite lackeys in the liberated countries, with pro-Fascists who, for now, have gone underground, but take every opportunity to crawl up to the surface — to once again begin their barbarous "work."

Even in England it has proven possible for a reactionary (conservative) member of Parliament, Captain Ramsey (who was held in prison from May 1940 through September, 1944, under the law on State Security), to openly introduce a proposal from the rostrum of Parliament which demanded that the British government "reintroduce the Jewish statute and bring its points into practice."*

In Rumania, where General Radescu has become the head of the government, in a struggle against democratic reforms, the General tried in February, 1945, to provoke a civil war. To achieve this end, he came out with anti-Semitic attacks against individual participants in the democratic front.

In Poland, now liberated from the German-Fascist invaders, anti-Semitism is still a weapon in the arsenal of the adherents of the former "government-in-exile" which, in an alliance with former Gestapo men, is trying even now to stir up nationalistic dissension. As early as August 1945 in Cracow, former Gestapo men tried to provoke a Jewish pogrom but were suppressed by military force and the organized democratic public.

The struggle against anti-Semitism, therefore, can not be successful without an active struggle for democracy and for a close alliance of democratic elements in all countries. The stronger and more consistently democracy develops, the more firmly the alliance and the cooperation of all nations and races will strengthen, and the sooner there will be an end to anti-Semitism.

An example is the U.S.S.R. where, on the basis of the Soviet Constitution, any encroachment on the equality of nations and races, or propagation which has the character of nationalistic persecution, is punished with all the severity of the Soviet criminal code.

Academician I. P. Trainin.

---

*The Jewish statute was adopted in England in 1290 and was abolished in 1846 during the reign of Queen Victoria.

Testimony of Germans and Documents from Materials of the Extraordinary State Commission

1. Himmler's Order. Report of Major Bernhard Bechler, member of the Board of the Union of German Officers.*

Excerpt

In executing the order in the army group of the Center in November, 1941, the head of the intelligence division of the group expressed an urgent desire to talk with my general. For the reasons mentioned above, I took part in the discussion. On the instructions of Field Marshal von Bock, the head of the intelligence division told us the following: Every army group has a high ranking SS *Führer*. Three days ago SS *Reichsführer* Himmler visited the SS *Führer* of the given army group and, in passing, asked how many Jews were being shot daily as per his order. After a certain quantity was named, Himmler shouted: "What swinishness. Follow the example of your colleague in the army group *Nord*, who has ordered five times as many shot as you have!"

2. Text of a German dispatch found in the area of Rossoshi among the staff documents of the Fifteenth German Police Regiment.**

Concluding Report

After the order to march immediately was canceled, the company, on October 27, 1942, received another order: arrive on October 28, 1942, at 21:00 in Kobrin. In accordance with the order, the company arrived by vehicle at Kobrin, and from there it marched to Pinsk. The company reported at the western approach to Pinsk on October 29, 1942, at 4:00 A.M.

At the meeting held on October 28, 1942, in Pinsk with the regiment commander, Colonel Kurske, it was decided that two battalions, namely, the Second Battalion of the Fifteenth Police Regiment and the Second Cavalry Division, would form an outer

*The Newspaper, *Freies Deutschland*, No. 23, Sept. 19, 1943.

**The text has been compared with the publication "The Documents Accuse: A Collection of Documents About the Monstrous Crimes of the German-Fascist Occupants on Soviet Territory," Edition II (Moscow), 1945, where it was published under the title "Report of Captain Saur on the Mass Murder of the Jewish Population in the City of Pinsk," pp. 34-36.

cordon, while the Tenth Company of the Fifteenth Police Regiment and the Eleventh Company of the Eleventh Field Regiment, minus two platoons, were assigned to comb the ghetto. The Eleventh Company of the Eleventh Police Regiment minus one platoon, which had been released in the evening from combing the ghetto, was assigned to the guard at the assembly point; this was the guard for the individual transportation of prisoners to the place of execution which was located four kilometers outside of Pinsk, and for the cordon around the place of execution. For the latter assignment, cavalrymen were subsequently used at times. This measure proved its value brilliantly, because when one hundred and fifty Jews tried to escape they were all caught again, although a few of them managed to go a few kilometers.

The cordon was set for 4:30 A.M., and it turned out that thanks to the previous personal reconnaissance of the leaders and to maintenance of secrecy, the cordon was completed at a very early date and the Jews were unable to get away. The combing of the ghetto was supposed to begin, according to the order, at 6:00 A.M. But due to darkness, it began a half hour later. The Jews who were paying attention to what was going on began for the most part to gather voluntarily for roll call on all the streets; with the help of two cavalry sergeant majors it was possible in the very first hour to bring several thousand people to the assembly point; when the rest of the Jews saw what was going on, they joined the column so that the roll call, which had been planned by the police guard at the collecting point, did not have to take place, thanks to the enormous unexpected gathering of people. (On the first day of combing the city they counted on only one to two thousand people.) The first search ended at 17:00 and passed without incident. On the first day about ten thousand people were executed. That night the company was ready for action at the soldiers' club.

On October 30, 1942, the ghetto was combed for a second time; on October 31 — for a third time; and on November 1 — for a fourth time. In total, about fifteen thousand Jews were herded to the assembly point. The sick Jews and the children who had been left in the houses were executed right there in the ghetto yard. About twelve hundred Jews were executed in the ghetto. With one exception, there were no incidents. The Jews had been promised that they would be spared if they would reveal where they had hidden their gold belongings. So one Jew appeared saying that he had hidden a lot of gold. A cavalry sergeant major went with him.

But since the Jew kept delaying and asked the officer to come up to the attic with him, the officer took him back to the assembly point in the ghetto. There the Jew refused, like all the other Jews, to sit down on the ground. Suddenly he rushed toward a mounted cavalry trooper, seized his rifle and stick and began to beat the horseman. It was only due to the assistance of the soldiers in the company that this attack did not succeed. Since the use of firearms was forbidden, the Jew engaged in the fight was struck so hard in the head with an axe that he fell and did not get up. He was executed immediately.

On November 1 at 17:00 the company was assigned to the outer cordon, and the second cavalry unit started out for its post. There were no unusual events.

On November 2 at 8:00 A.M. the company was released from Pinsk and started marching to its post. The company reached Kobrin at 13:00 and by 17:00 it again reached its bases.

Results:

1. The units involved in combing the ghetto must definitely have axes, pole-axes, and other instruments, since it turned out that almost all the doors were locked or bolted and could be opened only through force.

2. Even when no internal entrances to the attic are visible, it nevertheless should be assumed that there are people there. Attics should therefore be searched with extreme care from the outside.

3. Even when there are no basements, a considerable number of people can hide in a small space underground. These places should be broken in from the outside or searched by police dogs (in Pinsk the police dog "Asta" really proved its value in this task), or a hand grenade should be tossed in, after which the Jews always come out immediately.

4. It is necessary to probe the ground around the house, since countless numbers of people hide in well camouflaged ditches.

5. It is recommended that the young Jews be enlisted to point out these hiding places, promising them in return that they will be spared.

Captain of the police guard and commander of the company Saur.

3. From the testimony of the commander of the police squad, Captain Salog, an active participant in the crimes of the Germans in Kamenets-Podolsky.

. . . The preparation for the shooting of the Jewish population, without a doubt, was done ahead of time. And, as I later learned, it consisted of the following:

1. The concentration of the Jewish population.
2. The designation of the Jewish apartments (houses).
3. A compilation of precise lists.
4. The assembling of Jews from the different populated areas.
5. The selection of the day and place of the shooting.

Clearly visible hexagonal stars were to mark Jewish houses.

The place of the shooting was selected jointly by the chief of the S.D. (the main executioner), the chief of the gendarmery, and the regional chief. How many days prior to the shooting the place was chosen, I do not know. Judging by when the chief of the gendarmery left for Staraya Ushitsa, it was probably three to four days. The S.D. chief left for Staraya Ushitsa on the same day. Then the question was worked out together with the district commissar.

I know from personal observations that right before such events the chief of the gendarmery very often would spend hours with the district commissar and the chief of the S.D., that the chief of the S.D. more often than usual would stop by to see the chief of the gendarmery, and that there were more frequent telephone discussions between the district commissar and the chief of the S.D. In such cases, the doors which lead from the room where the sergeant majors and I were to the general office of the chief of the gendarmery, where the telephone was, were closed more carefully. An office worker stood guard at the doors, warning gendarmes that the chief of the gendarmery was not to be disturbed.

Saturday was always the day chosen for shootings. Why, I can not say. I always got evasive answers to that question.

I am not familiar with the first shootings which were carried out in Kamenets-Podolsky in 1941 and the beginning of 1942.

I do know the following from conversations with others about one of the biggest mass shootings of the Jewish population:

During the first days of the occupation of Kamenets-Podolsky, Jews began to arrive there from the Western Ukraine, Bessarabia, and Northern Bukovina. For various reasons they had not been evacuated deeper inside the country in time and found themselves on occupied territory. These Jews were arrested right in Kamenets-Podolsky or back at the border and then delivered to Kamenets-Podolsky. Later, I was told, they were joined by a larger group of Jews from Czechoslovakia, and they were shot there in Kamenets. The figures mentioned for the number of people shot are conflicting — eight, ten, and twelve thousand. Whether this figure included the Jewish residents of Kamenets-Podolsky, I can not say.

Of the mass shootings of the Jewish population of citizens of the U.S.S.R. at Kamenets-Podolsky, which occurred in 1942, I am personally aware of two.

While serving with the gendarmery in Kamenets-Podolsky as company commander of the police squad, I participated with my subordinates for the first time in the mass shooting of the Jewish population of the cities of Staraya Ushitsa and Studenitsa in August-September, 1942, and a second time in Kamenets-Podolsky. A mass shooting was carried out in the area of the Cossack barracks (the training Battalion) in November, 1942.

As the company commander, on the evening preceding the day of the shooting, I was ordered by the chief of the gendarmery, Lieutenant Reich, through the commander of the first company, Krubasik, to call out about fifty policemen from my company. At the same time I was ordered to call the commander of the troops at Staraya Ushitsa and find out from him whether he had received the order sent through the chief of the gendarme post of Staraya Ushitsa about forming a police staff from among his troops. The troop commander told me that he understood everything and that he had given the necessary orders, having coordinated them with the chief of the gendarme post, with the cavalry sergeant major Kunde and with the district chief of Staraya Ushitsa.

He was not able to explain the matter to me over the telephone, just as I was not able to ask him, both of us having been warned: he — by the chief of the gendarme post, and I — by the chief of the gendarmery. To my question about what we would be doing, company commander Krubasik answered that we would know about that tomorrow.

The order was given to take ten cartridges for each rifle plus a machine-gun cartridge belt in reserve. In addition, a portable machine gun and three automatic rifles were taken. About ten to twelve gendarmes and about fifty policemen, some from Krubasik's company, part from mine, drove out. Members of the S.D. and of the criminal police drove out independently.

Upon arriving at the village of Grushka, we found there the policemen from the districts of Zelenye Kurilovtsy and Privorottya all assembled.

Lieutenant Reich drove out to Staraya Ushitsa in an automobile with three gendarmes; four members of the S.D., led by the chief of the S.D., drove out in a second automobile. They issued an order to the rest of the gendarmes and policemen to go to sleep.

At dawn, after getting up, we all drove out in two consecutive groups to Staraya Ushitsa. About one to one-and-one-half kilometers before Staraya Ushitsa the vehicles were stopped, and the policemen were lined up. There Lieutenant Reich announced the purpose of the trip and its mission — to assemble the entire Jewish population of Staraya Ushitsa and Studenitsa and to deliver the Jews to a place of execution which was there, not far from the highway.

The place of execution had been agreed upon ahead of time by the chiefs of the SS, the gendarmery, and the district chief during one of the trips of the chief of the S.D., and also the chief of the gendarmery to Staraya Ushitsa.

The entire Jewish population of Staraya Ushitsa was assembled in a square which was cordoned off by gendarmes and the police staff. All the males (adults and children, except for infants) were separated from the women, right there on the square. They were all ordered to sit down on the ground and not to speak to one another.

Attempts at conversation were stopped by a peremptory shout and a blow with a rifle butt or club.

The chief of the S.D. and the chief of the gendarmery announced to the Jews that they were going to Kamenets-Podolsky. In some instances the women were permitted to take clothing for themselves and their children, since many came out of their apartments barefoot and with scarcely any time to throw on a dress after the order to come out into the square.

In the process of assembling the Jewish population many people were found hiding in their apartments. Cellars and attics served as hideouts, having been prepared in advance for this purpose with a supply of food and clothing.

Everyone who was found was beaten with rifle butts and clubs.

There was one incident when a Jew who was hiding in the attic was shot and killed right on the spot by a policeman.

The sick old men and women who were not able to walk to the square were led or carried in the arms of their relatives, and if there were no relatives, then we gave the order for other Jews to carry them.

One sixty to seventy-year-old woman, who walked very slowly out of the room, was forced out into the street by the blows of rifle butts to her back.

After this incident and the sound of shots, crying and screams broke out among the women and children. The screams and the crying were stopped only with great difficulty, and with the help of blows from rifle butts and clubs.

The chief of the SS and the chief of the gendarmery issued orders and drove out in their automobiles to the place of execution. The orders were as follows:

1. Send vehicles to the village of Studenitsa of the Staraya Ushitsa region for Jews living there.

To the village of Studenitsa were sent three or four vehicles with a police unit of fifteen to twenty men headed by a representative of the S.D., whose rank and surname I do not remember, and by the *Hauptwachmeister* of the gendarmery, Peucker. Toward the end of the shooting of the residents of Staraya Ushitsa they brought about eighty to one hundred residents of Studenitsa. The convoy guard was strengthened by eight border guards.

2. Organize a guard for all of the apartments vacated by the Jews.

I delegated the responsibility for organizing this guard to the troop commander of the police, who, after seeing to it that the guard was organized, came to the place of the shooting.

3. The district chief was ordered to have lunch prepared for fifty to sixty men from the police staff and for the gendarmes. Lunch was supposed to be ready at noon.

The column's guard was organized this way: in front walked two gendarmes, five to seven steps from the first row of the column of Jews, on the sides there were about thirty to thirty-five policemen (three to four steps away from the column), and the task of those who brought up the rear was to urge on any people who fell behind. This was accomplished with the help of shouts and blows from rifle butts or clubs which they thought to take along when they left Staraya Ushitsa. I walked in the rear, behind the carts, with one gendarme, a *Wachmeister* radio operator, and a policeman.

The whole route through the city of Staraya Ushitsa, from the square to the outskirts, went more or less smoothly and without any incidents. But as soon as the column passed the outskirts of the city, one could hear first the quiet, then continually louder crying of children, and then of the women. It did not stop for almost the whole stretch of the way. In spite of all the measures for restoring silence — kicks, blows from rifle butts, threats of immediate execution — the crying and screams stopped for a short while, only to begin again with greater force. The women and the old men whispered prayers; some people, whispering quietly to one another, spoke about something to their relatives or to the person walking next to them. Some people threw the bundles containing their belongings on the road, but they were picked up by a policeman and tossed into a cart. The false claim that the Jews were being taken to Kamenets-Podolsky was repeated several times throughout the journey.

About one to one-and-a-half kilometers past Staraya Ushitsa I saw automobiles parked on the road. I later found out that they carried the district commissar Reindl and his men. They were talking with the chief of the S.D. and the chief of the gendarmery.

When the column had almost reached the automobiles and the gendarme walking in front reported to the district commissar, the chief of the S.D. pointed out the direction for the column to take, i.e., he pointed in the direction of the pit, toward which the whole column turned.

The moment the column turned toward the pit there was a general outcry. No shouts, rifle-butting, or kicks could stop these cries. The penetrating, shrill cries of the women were interwoven with the children's crying and the requests of the children for their mothers to take them in their arms. The crying gradually died down, then began again with growing force. It continued for one to two hundred meters, until they reached the place of the execution — a dug-up pit.

The pit was approximately twelve by six meters and about one-and-a-half meters deep. On the side that was closer to Kamenets-Podolsky, the pit's entrance was about two meters wide, with a slope to the bottom, along which the condemned walked.

At this last part of their journey, the Jews, seeing that the order to send them to Kamenets-Podolsky was a deception, began to throw out cigarette cases, rings, and earrings. They ripped up documents, photographs, letters, papers with notes, and other things.

In the event that a Jew tried to escape the execution, it was not permitted to open fire inside the cordon; but once he was out beyond the cordon, one was to turn, facing him, and open fire. In order to make it possible to open fire from the pit, the two people closest to the escapee were supposed to run away from him, thereby clearing an area in which to shoot.

A second, inner ring of the cordon was formed directly around the Jews who were thus squeezed extremely close together in a single group. However, the former arrangement was maintained, i.e. the men stood in front, the women behind. This ring was closed at the pit in which the executioner stood with a machine gun.

The process of the execution consisted of the following, if one can say this, elements:

Fifteen to twenty meters from the pit, as I have already said, stood the closely packed mass of people who were condemned to death. Everyone, including the women and children, were stripped naked. Urged on by blows, five people at a time were directed to the pit.

Near the pit also stood several gendarmes who, in their turn, prodded the people with blows from their clubs or rifle butts into the pit toward the executioner. The executioner, whose first name was Paul (I don't know his surname), drank a fair amount of schnapps and ordered the victims to lie face down at the side of the pit opposite the entrance. The victims were killed with a point-blank shot in the back of the head. The following group of five lay down with their heads on the corpses of their fellow-Jews and were killed the same way, having received, as they said there, "one coffee bean." Standing over the top of the pit was a "marker," a member of the criminal police; he marked off each group of five with a small cross.

The truth is that there were often instances when instead of five people, a family of six to eight people, in spite of orders to the contrary, and of being beaten half to death for a distance of fifteen to twenty meters, would nevertheless walk to the pit together; but the same small cross was written down just as if there had been only five people.

Not far from the pit stood the chief of the gendarmery, Lieutenant Reich, the chief of the S.D., whose surname I do not know, and commissar Reindl; during the course of the executions they would issue commands. In the intervals between commands they encouraged their subordinates, sometimes laughing at successful blows which landed in great numbers on the heads and backs of the Jews who were already dazed; otherwise they just stood stonefaced, silently watching the picture of the extermination. Sometimes they would turn away from the pit, put their hands in their pockets, and talk quietly about something among themselves.

Reindl, who had spent about two hours at the pit, shook hands with the supervisors, saluted all the others, smiled, said something again, got into his automobile, and drove off to Kamenets-Podolsky.

The execution continued.

The picture would not be complete if I did not speak in more detail about the condition of the condemned people.

After the first shots of the executioner the whole crowd quieted down for a few seconds and then, after realizing the horror of the situation, the voices of the crowd erupted in such an outcry that the heart stopped beating and blood ran cold.

There were many threats about retribution, curses. The old ones called to God and asked him to take revenge.

The men, under the blows of rifle butts and clubs, shouted on the way to the pit and inside the pit itself: "Long live the leader of all peoples — Stalin!" "Long live the homeland of all peoples — the Soviet Union!"

There were also shouts against the Germans: "Death to the one-eyed wolf — Adolph."

Among the old men and women there were some who lost their senses. These people with wide-open, crazed eyes, paying no attention to the blows, walked on slowly, with their arms hanging at the side, stumbled, fell, got up again and reaching the executioner, then stopped, stood stupefied, without saying a word or making a single movement. Only a forceful push from an automatic rifle or a kick from the executioner would get one of these victims to the bottom of the pit.

The small children, who were forcibly separated from their mothers, were thrown into the pit by the gendarmes up above. A child of three or four years of age took off all his clothes and walked up to the pit himself. A gendarme grabbed him by the arm and, after warning the executioner, threw the child into the pit. The executioner shot the child while he was still in the air. Many women, trying to cover their nakedness, had not removed their slips. Their slips were torn from them and they were beaten. A few young women and girls suffered especially. They spit in the face and eyes of an SS man and several gendarmes. They were beaten on the face and breasts and were kicked with boots in the genital area.

The stockings or socks were ripped from the legs of the women and children with the muzzle of a rifle or a stick.

Many women begged for the lives of their small children.

Many ripped their clothes to shreds, tore out their hair, bit their arms.

Some of the men tried to run. A middle-aged man, already completely naked, started to run in zigzags toward some bushes which were north-west of the execution site. He ran seventy to one-hundred meters beyond the second ring of the cordon and was killed by combined submachine-gun and rifle fire.

A second man took off his outer clothes and shoes and started to run in approximately the same direction, but he did not make it through the second ring and was killed, too.

I saw the same thing happen during the mass execution in Kamenets-Podolsky in November, 1942, where an escapee was also killed.

Among the women there were no attempts to escape. While undressing, the condemned Jews ripped their good shoes and clothes to pieces and hid their valuables in the ground. The experienced members of the S.D., however, were on the alert for this and stopped the attempts to destroy valuables. The valuables covered up with soil or grass were handed over to a special "collector" — one of the S.D. persons.

Families, relatives, even acquaintances, when saying good-bye, shook each other's hands and kissed. Sometimes people, having embraced in a farewell kiss, stood several seconds under a shower of blows and pressed tightly one against the other, the whole family, carrying the children in their arms, walked to the pit.

By the end of the execution the bottom of the pit was already full. The executioner standing in the passageway, ordered a victim to run along the corpses and then shot him in motion. If the shot was not successful and the man was still alive, rifle and pistol shots from above would finish him off.

There were instances when a person who had been shot still

moved for fifteen to twenty minutes underneath the corpses of his brothers.

Under the supervision of an S.D. man, the policemen began to shake and examine the clothes and shoes of those who had been shot. The clothes were examined with particular care. This was done because in the pleats of the clothes, in the linings, in the waist-bands of trousers they hoped to find valuables.

All valuables were put in a sack which was kept by an S.D. man. That is where they put cigarette lighters, penknives, leather brief-cases, cigarette cases, and wallets.

New articles — dresses, kerchiefs, boots, shoes, coats as well as unfinished garments — were taken by the people who participated in the execution. Sometimes they tore things from each other's hands and argued violently.

Thus, on this day about four hundred citizens of the Soviet Union were shot — men and women of all ages, as well as children. The execution continued for approximately four hours (from 7:00 or 8:00 to 11:00 or 12:00).

The second mass execution of the Jewish population of the city of Kamenets-Podolsky took place at approximately the end of November or in December, 1942. I know this because I participated in this execution along with my subordinates in the second ring of the cordon.

At this time, the ghetto, which was in the vicinity of Svyato-Yurskaya and Zelenaya streets, contained about forty-eight hundred Jews, the overwhelming majority of whom were specialists in various professions, including doctors and nurses.

I learned about this execution from the chief of the gendarmery, Lieutenant Reich, the preceding morning. Through the commander of the first police company, *Wachmeister* Krubasik, Reich ordered me, by evening, to summon from the stations the staff of the second police company, which I commanded. The process of this mass murder was the same as in Staraya Ushitsa; it differed only in certain details, of which I will speak below.

As soon as the cordon had been set up (five to ten minutes after Reich arrived), three trucks drove up with Jews from the ghetto. The vehicles were covered with tarpaulins and from them, accompanied by gendarmes and S.D. men, emerged about fifty to sixty people. They were directed to the execution site, where they had to undress. That's the way it continued for the whole length of the execution, approximately until 17:00-18:00, i.e., about twelve hours. The Jews were brought in groups of forty to sixty people.

As I later learned and personally witnessed, soldiers from the Kamenets-Podolsky garrison were drilling in small groups as large as a platoon throughout the city — in parks, squares, at the stadium, at the market square, and in villages near the place of execution.

During this period the German garrison at Kamenets-Podolsky consisted of about two to three thousand young soldiers. They were undergoing training and were later sent to the front.

The people who dug the pits were led behind the barracks.

Two executioners from the S.D. "worked" there in turns — when one of them got tired, he would rest in an automobile where a snack and vodka had been prepared ahead of time. His place was taken by the other. They took turns like that for the whole period of the execution. It was not only the executioners who fortified themselves with vodka. From time to time one or another of the people participating in the execution would walk up to a vehicle (a gendarme — to a gendarme vehicle, an S.D. man — to a Gestapo vehicle), climb in, eat a sandwich, drink some vodka, light up a cigarette, and return again "to work."

As I said earlier, there was only one instance of an attempted escape. A middle-aged man, having run seventy to one hundred meters beyond the second ring of the cordon, was shot while running.

I learned from conversations that during the night before the day of the execution about five hundred people ran away from the ghetto. Apparently, the Jews learned about the impending execution the day before. Later more than two hundred people were found in buildings. This group of Jews was also executed a short time afterwards. When, where — I do not know.

How many of the people who escaped were caught again, I also do not know. In 1943 about six to eight Jews were brought to the gendarmery. I saw one of them — an agronomist called Gartman. He was brought in in the summer of 1943 from the village of Lyantskorun in the Chemerovetsky region, where he was hidden in an attic by a local peasant woman. I don't remember her surname. By order of Captain Otto he was handed over to the S.D.

Belongings and valuables, as in the first case, were collected: the valuables went to the S.D., and the new things — to the participants in the execution.

This time about four thousand citizens of the Soviet Union were annihilated: old men and women, the sick and the invalids, men and women, specialists, young children, even infants.

In this number about twenty to thirty Russians from the prison were shot. I can't be sure of the exact figure, because I left the city four times; they were brought in on a truck and were shot, along with the Jews, in groups of six to eight people.
Kamenets-Podolsky, 5/25/44

4. Excerpts from the diary of the prisoner of war Karl Johannes Drexel, Lance Corporal of the 513th Reserve Battalion, "Lublin" Regiment, "G.G." Division.

April 1, 1942 — Promoted to private first class.

September 25, 1942 — Assigned to the second company of the 513th reserve battalion in Chelm and housed in the barracks for military preparation.

October 15-30, 1942 — On leave.

November 1, 1942 — Campaign against the Jews. Ten thousand Jews shot — from the oldest man to the tiniest child. All of them were thrown into carts and taken to mass graves. A horrible sight.

November 3, 1942. The Jews are rounded up. Three to four thousand Jews are annihilated each day. They are herded in columns on their last journey. With tearful eyes they enter the other world. If they fall behind, it means immediate death. They are being gassed and electrocuted with high voltage current. Ninety thousand Russians have died from typhus and from bloody diarrhea. They are wrapped in barbed wire and dragged through the swamp.

November 6, 1942. Morning. Three and a half thousand Jews. Grenades are strung together and thrown into apartment houses. Day and night. Five Jews. A heart-rending and unnerving experience. A cold night.

November 8, 1942. A mother with a child in her arms, unprotected by the law, are killed by the blows from a rifle butt.

November 12, 1942. I was in the ghetto, and later at the sight of the mass graves. Pillage of the living and the dead. Four days in a row there has been inhuman treatment of the Jews. They gave us vinegar to smell.

539

Women who had just given birth, children, and old men were forced to kneel and barely alive, like skeletons, were dragged out and shot indiscriminately. People died while suffering cruelties worse than any mankind had known. Houses were ravaged. Corpses lay in houses for six days. Both men and women were unclothed. It was a horrible sight. In spite of all this, I stealthily made my way into the houses. I looked for people whom, with a shot, I could put out of misery. Not one soldier went into the ghetto on his own. The doors and windows creak.

November 20, 1942. Forty Jews were dragged out from hiding places. No girls were found.

December 4, 1942. The dead are lying all around. The houses are demolished. An epidemic of bloody diarrhea and typhus broke out.

December 10, 1942. A partisan shot at our company commander.

May 12, 1943. We set out to fight the partisans.

June 4, 1943. A battle with bandits in Zamostye. We marched on Whitsunday.

March 12, 1943. Assigned as a guard at Lublin.

December 11, 1943. At the base in Ulanov.

January 16, 1944. At the base in Krasnikhin.

5. From the Testimony of Private-First-Class Christian Farber

Last year before I was captured (on November 3, 1942) I was a witness to a horrible atrocity committed in a large village near Chelm.

One SS sub-unit cruelly murdered about three hundred people — men, women, and children — mostly Jews. The men stood in small groups in a single row in front of a pit which they had dug for themselves. They were gunned down with machine-gun fire. The same fate befell the others. There were moans and cries all around, because not everyone had been mortally wounded by the burst of machine-gun fire. These seriously wounded people were buried alive. Among the SS men, Sergeant Major Joseph Schmidt from Freiburg was particularly distinguished as a murderer. If one of the men or women tried to escape, they would be chased and shot at like rabbits. Little children were picked up by their feet and their heads smashed against a rock.

One young girl had hidden in a barn behind a beam. When the SS men found her there, one of them climbed up into the loft, while others formed a circle below with fixed bayonets. The girl was stabbed with a bayonet until she had no choice but to jump down. She was literally run through with bayonets. When I asked Lieutenant Carl Dehr (from Ludwingshafen, near Mannheim; he was the SS man in charge) why such horrible things were being done, he said: "We kicked the Jews out of Germany, and now we have to do away with them here too." Toward the end all the livestock from the village was herded together and driven off, and the village was burned to the last house.

Christian Farber, private-first-class, shoemaker, 3rd company,
347 infantry regiment (Schwitzingen, near Mannheim).
Case No. 43, pg. 231.

6. Excerpt from the Examination Record of Private First Class Erich Heubaum from the 1st company of the 173rd infantry regiment, 87th infantry division.

Atrocities Against a Peaceful Population

In April, 1942, I came to the city of Lvov and worked there as a driver. My car serviced the railroad administration in Lvov.

In May and June of 1942, articles appeared in all the Fascist newspapers of Lvov calling for the annihilation of the sixty thousand Jews remaining in Lvov. By that time ninety thousand Jews had already been taken away and shot.

In June the order to annihilate the remnants of the Jewish population was received. At first, part of the city was allotted for a ghetto. Then in a small wooded area near the railroad station a camp was built, to which large groups of one thousand people were taken from the ghetto to be shot. In the beginning the condemned were taken from the ghetto to the camp in the daytime. But since this roused the indignation of the rest of the population, as well as some soldiers and army officers, they began to take people to be shot at night. Those who were unable to walk — the sick, old men, children — were thrown down onto the railroad platforms and taken to the camp. At night all of them would be shot with machine guns.

Many of the condemned hid in the ghetto area and did not want to come out. So the SS men cordoned off the ghetto and set fire to it. I saw this. I saw people running out of burning houses, jumping out of windows. The SS men shot all of them with submachine guns. The whole street, for three hundred meters, was covered with corpses. The dead lay in piles, one on top of the other.

When I saw a young mother with a little child in her arms jump through a window of a burning house and then saw them begin to shoot at her, I had to turn away — I felt awful and I decided to go home. . . .

After this the smell of burned corpses lingered in the city for several days.

In addition, I saw peaceful residents exterminated with gas. I would drive telephone operators to a small station located twenty kilometers from the city of Rava Russkaya. An underground barracks had been built at this station in the woods. Once when I was at the station a group of Jews was brought in. The traincars were closed and the people, with their hands stretched out the windows, pleaded for some water, but no one was allowed to go near them. In the evening these people were herded into the woods. All the strangers were forced into the station. The woods were surrounded by S.D. units.

There these people, regardless of sex and age, men and women, the elderly and the children, were stripped naked and herded into the underground barracks. Three quarters of an hour later men from another group were sent in there to carry out the corpses. Then the next group was herded into the barracks. . . . This is the way three hundred people were exterminated every evening.

I saw this go on for eight days. That people were being gassed there I learned from an SS man, Carl Horst from Saxony. He took part in it. The executions were supervised by *Sturmbannführer* (SS Major) Herbst, from the city of Breslau.
Fund No. 1 Case 37, Sheet 7.

7. From the written testimony of prisoner of war, Corporal Michael Wennrich, of the 54th Field-Engineer Battalion, tank grenadier SS division "Netherland," regarding atrocities committed by the German-Fascist invaders in the Ukraine.

(From December 1941 to March 18, 1942)

At that time I was serving in the Rumanian army, in the gendarmery. We were attached to a group consisting of a company of field police and a unit for keeping order.

We were assigned to the occupied area stretching from Rybnitsa on the Dniester to Golta on the Bug. There were already units there who were going on leave, and we were supposed to replace them. The troops. under the command of a lieutenant, were put up in the small town of Kruty. The troops were active in an area including the populated points of Semenovka, Moyna, Labushna, Frantsyushka, Kodyma, Aleksandrovka, and others.

The Jewish population, including women and children, in all these places was uprooted from its apartments and housed in barracks which had neither windows nor doors. All property was taken away from the Jews. They were given no food, they went hungry, and many died of starvation.

An order came from the military authorities to send the Jews on foot to another region under very heavy guard. It was freezing cold, but all warm things, even shoes, were taken away from them, so that the majority walked barefoot.

There were three hundred and fifty people in all. A Rumanian corporal Gavrila commanded the convoy. He boasted that he would torment three hundred people to death, and then he would be able to transfer to another job.

Mothers walked along the road carrying their children in their arms. When they became completely exhausted and were unable to go any further, Gavrila would shoot them. He did the same thing with the old men and the weak. The Jews were locked up in barns for the night. As a rule, by morning, we would find thirty to forty people who were frostbitten. They were immediately shot. When the group arrived in Birzuli, it was scarcely half its original size.

Typhus broke out, since there were many corpses lying on the village streets. An order was given to bury all corpses, not to leave them in the streets. The Russian population was assembled and ordered to dig pits, each one big enough for a hundred people. Executed Jews were thrown into these pits, although often, along with the dead, the living were buried as well. One of these graves is located on the road leading from the village of Kruty to Budai. Another one of these graves which I know of is near Kodyma. . . .

I personally shot, upon the order of the troop commander, a woman who was fifty or sixty years old. I did not know the reason for her execution.

As far as I know, in the area in which our unit operated, not one Jew was spared. Some were shot where they lived, others in the camp.

SS Corporal Michael Wennrich

July 30, 1944

8. From the testimony of Wolfgang Janiko, 1/3rd Company, 368th Infantry Regiment, 122nd Infantry Division.

(Draftsman, from Leipzig)

Koburgerstrasse, 91.

When I was with headquarter's 281st guard division in July 1941 in the city of Rechekus (Latvia), I was a witness to the execution of Jews. There were approximately seven thousand Jews in the city; they were all arrested and systematically "liquidated" (about three hundred people a day).

Once I was a witness to one of these executions. And what I saw there was horrible. The place where this atrocity occurred was not far from the city. A large, very long and deep canal had been dug there. Latvian auxiliary troops under German command ordered thirty or thirty-five poor victims to stand at the edge of the canal (there were people there of all ages, from children to old men). I heard the order: "Fire!" And the first victims fell into the canal (they were shot in the back of the head).

The next group arranged the corpses in piles and sprinkled them with chloride of lime, and then they themselves walked up to the edge of the canal to be shot. One of our comrades even took a photograph, but the others saw this and from that time on the troops were forbidden to watch the executions.

This experience left us with an impression that no words can express and which to this day has not been blotted out by any other

544

scenes of the war. At that time the commander of the division was Lieutenant-General Bayer. It should also be mentioned that all valuable belongings were taken from the victims and confiscated before they were taken from prison to the place of execution. This execution of Jews was in Rechekus (now called Rzitten). I do not know the surname of the commandant in charge of the execution.

W. Janiko

Wolfgang Janiko wrote and signed this report in my presence after a conversation with him.

E.S. Fabri
Instructor of Political Section No. 27

Translation by Stern
April 14, 1943

9. Excerpt from the record of the political interrogation of the prisoner Private First Class Albert Endersch from the 14th Company of the 195th Assault Regiment, 78th Assault Division.

I know that the German army committed a number of crimes on Russian land.

In Kirovograd in the fall of 1941 all Jews received an order to take one day's ration with them and report to the regional commissar. When they had all gathered there, they were taken to the antitank ditches and shot. There were not only Jews there, but Russians too. They say that the number of people killed was about thirty-five thousand. Many were hanged with the sign "Thief." I saw this myself. Sometimes six, eight, or ten people were hanged at once, and this happened very often. All this was done by the SS.

We saw the same scene at Dnepropetrovsk.

At Uman I lived with a Jewish woman. At four o'clock in the morning the SS arrived, took the woman, and told me that she was being liquidated. She never returned.

In Krasnodar and Tikhoretsk in the summer of 1942 I saw posters announcing that Jews who did not report to the regional commissar would be shot immediately. The civilian population would sometimes ask us why the Jews were being killed. Rank and file soldiers, in response, could only make a helpless gesture.

2673

September 24, 1944

10. Record of the interrogation of Wilhelm Sudbrack:

1. Surname, first name — Wilhelm Sudbrack
2. Date of birth — 1905
3. Place of birth — Aikel, area of Wanne-Aikel (Westfalen)
4. Nationality — German
5. Education — higher
6. Party membership — non-party man
7. Affiliation — soldier of the 15th Company, 195th Assault Regiment, 78th Assault Division
8. Time and place of capture — surrendered voluntarily on 6/24/44 in the area of Bryukhovtsy
9. Marital status — married

I have been warned about the responsibility for giving false testimony and for the refusal to give testimony according to statutes 92 and 95 of the Criminal Code of the RSFSR.

(signature)

Testimony:

From the beginning of the German-Soviet war until May, 1943, I served in the administration of a camp for Russian prisoners of war (Starlag), which was located in the Ukraine. From one to five thousand prisoners passed through this camp.

From our camp, as from other camps (for example from the Slavutsky camp), captive political workers and Jews were turned over to units of the "SS Police." Formally, the "SS Police" took commissars and Jews under their protection, but in fact these people were killed. All our people knew about this, although it was done very secretly and no one had the right to divulge the facts about the killing of prisoners. The translator of our camp, *Sonderführer* Fastl, who told me over the telephone that seventeen Jews had been killed by the SS, was immediately taken somewhere. The rumor was that he was arrested.

In the Kovel camp for Russian prisoners of war in the winter of 1941-1942 there were twelve or thirteen thousand Russian prisoners. As a result of the fact that prisoners were herded several hundred kilometers to the camp on foot, that they were poorly fed, that no sanitary measures were taken, the prisoners who entered the camp died in great numbers from exhaustion and typhus. At that time the boss of the camp was Major Otto. The same situation was true for Vladimir-Volynsky (an officer camp) and for other

The Hitlerites considered the destruction of the Jews to be the most easily realizable goal, since the Jews were scattered among the rest of the population. In the Ukraine and in Byelorussia the young men were in the ranks of the Red Army. Everyone who was able to had evacuated, so that the Hitlerites were able to wreck their violence only upon the elderly, the ill, and women burdened with children.

The Fascists' attempt to sow discord among the peoples of the Soviet Union was in vain. With the exception of a handful of traitors, Soviet citizens who fell into the paws of the invaders remained true to the ideals of Stalin's constitution. Risking their own lives, Russians, Byelorussians, and Ukrainians hid Jews in their homes. I am compelled to mention the heroism of Pavel Sergeyevich Zinchenko, a bookkeeper in the collective farm in the village of Blagodatnoye, Gulyaypolsky rural *Soviet*, Dnepropetrovskaya *oblast*. In spite of the threat of execution, he saved from death thirty Soviet citizens of Jewish nationality — old people and women with children.

I offer to the attention of the readers two letters, the story of a girl, and the testimony which I have collected of atrocities committed by the Hitlerites in Rostov and Morozovsk. This is not literature, but a dry report.

I have heard many stories of mass executions. I have read hundreds of letters written in blood and, like the girl from Ozyr, I can say: the groan of the earth under which the old people were buried alive keeps me from sleeping. In Kiev a small girl whom the Germans had thrown into a grave shouted: "Why are you throwing sand in my eyes?" At nights I hear the cry of this child. All our people hear it. Our conscience is indignant and does not permit us rest. It demands — death to the murderers of peoples!

Days have ensued which Russia and all of humanity have long awaited — days of judgement. In the Ukraine, in Byelorussia, near Leningrad — thousands of these henchmen have found their deaths. They have perished at the hands of their judges, the people, the Red Army. Its highest feelings of love for man and justice offended, our people has sworn an oath to destroy Fascism, and it will be true to its word. The unprecedented advance of the Red Army is our assurance of that.

High ideals have inspired all the children of our Soviet Homeland — Russian and Ukrainian, Byelorussian and Kazakh, Georgian and Armenian, Uzbek and Jew. The Germans courageously murdered old women and children, but now they are retreating under the blows of the Red Army. Before us are henchmen, murderers of the helpless — not soldiers. And who, having read the story of Zmievskaya Ravine or the tractor factory, will not exclaim: "Death to the murderers of peoples!"

Ilya Ehrenburg

A Letter from Kramatorsk

My dear aunts,

Yesterday we received your letter with the photographs, and I can't tell you how happy we are. Your photographs have remained at home; they are buried in the yard together with my high-school certificate and mama's diploma. Perhaps we will find them when we return to Kramatorsk.

It seems to me that I have become very mean. I have had to experience many things in these sixteen months, and my heart is silent. Can it be that it has become so hardened? Only when I first saw the Germans did it beat very strongly and also when they said "Get ready to be deported to Palestine." After that nothing affected me — neither the rifle pointed at me by a Rumanian, nor the police interrogations, nor sudden visits by soldiers from the "Death's Head" division. Perhaps my heart decided that this was all trivia? But then, there is no use philosophizing. I had best tell you what we experienced, beginning in September, 1941. It was raining, muddy, and the general mood was terrible. Shapiro left with the hospital, and mama remained to run the dispensary. The town began to be evacuated. Mina was bitten by a dog that tore off her finger. She could not leave alone, and they would not let mama go. The last train left, the rails were blown up, and of the Jews were left we, Grisha and his family, Lazar and his family, and 69 other families — the elderly, the ill, children.

German scouts appeared on October 20. On the twenty-first the first Italian units entered town. The commandant appointed a "mayor," and a registration of all Jews and horses was announced. There were yellow armbands with the Star of David.

In early November I was standing by the window, when suddenly I saw Busya. I ran out. He was with a comrade from the same unit as he. They had been captured in Popovka, near Mariupol. At night, while being taken to a camp, they escaped. They had managed to obtain new clothing. We let them wash up and washed their underwear. That night the Germans came to our home and "bought" three blankets and a gramophone for ten rubles. We asked Busya to stay for a while longer, but he did not want to. They were going to Voroshilovgrad. He was in an excellent mood and said he would reach our people. I don't know what happened to him later.

Every day things became worse and worse. First the Germans took our beds, couch, and table. Then they began to come for little things — a bucket, a tooth brush. They took my dresses and mama's old stockings. When they came through the front entrance, I ran away through the back door, and vice versa. I believe I have the architect of our house to thank for the fact that the Germans did not beat me much. A portrait of grandmother hung on the wall; mama wanted to take it down, but I wouldn't let her — "Let grandmother watch as they take from the house everything that she acquired." (I am thinking now of the poor censor who will read this letter. Let him know that "life is a great thing," as Kirov said, but at the same time life is not worth a kopeck, and it is not at all terrible to know that in a few minutes you will no longer exist. . . .)

January 20 arrived. It is -30° Celsius (-22° Fahrenheit)"Deportation to Palestine." Mama and I ran through other people's backyards to the outskirts of town. Women were walking down the street with their belongings. Then they were put in cars and taken outside of town to the antitank trench. Among them were Mina, Grisha and his family, Schneider's family, the wives of the Brailovsky brothers and their children, Reizen and Polina. (At least before death he had his own way, and she went with him — not with Kuznetsov.)

That's enough! I only want to know if you despise us for having abandoned Mina? I won't make excuses. I don't know anything, and I can't understand anything. After the police left, I said to mama: "Do whatever you want, but I'm getting out of here." I started to put on my coat. How could I have said something like that to mama? Not to anyone else, but to my poor old mama? Probably you don't think at moments like those. She went with me, but several times she wanted to return and go with the others to the execution. She kept speaking of her duty. I remember as if it were yesterday — snow, snow, and more snow. The houses were shut up, and no one would let us in to get warm. Going back meant death — simple and plain. No, we would go forward even if we froze to death or died from hunger. They could catch us and hang us, but we would not go ourselves to our deaths. And we went on. Judge us for everything. And if you judge us guilty, then let it be as you have said. Don't consider me your "favorite niece" any more. That would be terrible, but I would know it was a correct judgment of me and my acts. And I will endure this, as I have endured much (as, surely, I will yet endure many unexpected and terrible things).

Busya

July 26, 1943

PHOTODOCUMENTS

О П И С Ь   Ф О Т О
К
" Ч Е Р Н О Й   К Н И Г Е "

О ЗЛОДЕЙСКОМ, ПОВСЕМЕСТНОМ УБИЙСТВЕ ЕВРЕЕВ
НЕМЕЦКО-ФАШИСТСКИМИ ЗАХВАТЧИКАМИ ВО ВРЕМЕННО-
ОККУПИРОВАННЫХ РАЙОНАХ СОВЕТСКОГО СОЮЗА И В
ЛАГЕРЯХ УНИЧТОЖЕНИЯ ПОЛЬШИ ВО ВРЕМЯ ВОЙНЫ
1941 - 1945 г.г.

Составлена под редакцией:

Василия Гроссмана
Ильи Эренбурга.

Faximile of the first page of list of photographs in *The Black Book*

IN THE GHETTO.

Signs sewn on the clothing of Jews

Signs denying admission to Jews.

556

In the ghetto hospital.

An SS man cuts off a Jew's beard
with a knife.

A notice posted by the
German-Fascist
authorities.

At the announcement
board.

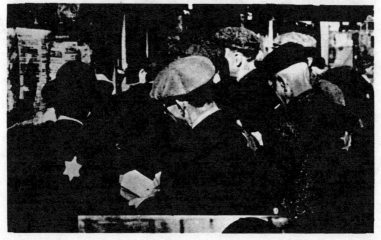

THE TREBLINKA DEATH CAMP (POLAND).

General appearance of the camp.

Slag formed while burning corpses.

A child's shoe and a nipple found among the belongings of the murdered people.

AUSCHWITZ (POLAND)

Oswiecim (Auschwitz) prisoners tormented to death by the Germans

KAUNAS

Fort of death.

A wall used for mass executions by shooting.

Preparation for
execution and the
execution.

Photographed by
SS officers.

The doomed dig a grave.

The bodies of murdered children.

Doctor Pochter with his wife and daughter. Their bodies were found in a mass grave.

A mass grave (photograph taken by an SS officer).

A murdered old Jew.

Letters written by Z. Wiszniacki and her daughter before their death.

Notes of the Vilnius Jews.

Horror . . . vengeance. . . . I kiss you fervently. . . . I bid farewell to all of you before we die. . . . Z.

Dear father, In bidding you farewell before we die, we very much want to live, but our hearts are heavy. They won't let us live. I am so afraid of this death, because little children are thrown alive in the grave. I bid you farewell forever and kiss you fervently.

Your I.
A kiss from G.

"All husbands are leaving on September 24 for Estonia from the Vilnius ghetto, which was liquidated yesterday. They are going without their wives and children."

"Another train with our wives and children is supposed to follow ours. . . . In a few days. . . ."

"The Vilnius ghetto has been liquidated. We are going to Estonia, separately from our wives. . . ."

"September 25. Shavli. We are leaving Vilnius. . . . separate from our wives. . . . We are moving on . . . to Estonia."

"September 29. Jews of Shavli! As of September 23 the Vilnius ghetto has ceased to exist. Most of the Jews from the Vilnius ghetto are being sent through Shavli to forced labor in Estonia. . . . The men passed through today — approximately 1,600 people. The women — about 6,000 — will pass through tomorrow or the day after tomorrow."

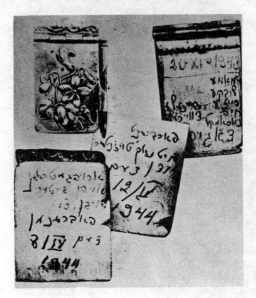

November 20, 1943
Mother
Liubka
Reize-Sheinele
Khaya-Dveirele
Nekhamka

Dogim

Burned together with
thousands of Jews
April 12, 1944

Put in a bonfire
April 8, 1944 .

Isaak Dogim was brought by the Germans to Ponary, where he
and other shackled prisoners were forced to burn the bodies of
murdered Jews. In one of the graves he found the bodies of his
friends and relatives. Dogim recorded this in a notebook which
he found in the common grave.

**Polya Medvetsky and
Shurik Milner, whom she
saved.**

Itsik Vitenberg, leader of the United Partisan Organization of the Vilnius ghetto. Tormented to death in the Gestapo dungeon.

Khaim Yelin, leader of the resistance organization of the Kaunas ghetto. Died a hero's death.

Mikhl Gebelev, leader of the underground Bolshevik organization in the Minsk ghetto. Died a hero's death.

Aleksandr Pechersky, leader of the uprising in the Sobibor death camp.

567

Boris Shereshnevsky, secretary of the underground Bolshevik committee in the Vilnius ghetto. Later a political commissar in the partisan unit "Death to Fascism."

OATH OF THE KAUNAS PARTISANS

I enter the struggle against Fascism and join the ranks of the Red partisans.

I promise to unflaggingly struggle against the Fascist invaders, threaten the areas where they reside, interfere with transportation, commit arson, blow up bridges, destroy railroad beds, and organize acts of sabotage under any conditions.

I promise to fight until the total victory of the Red Army without regard for my health and even sacrificing my life, if necessary.

At the same time, I promise to be a conscientious, disciplined soldier, to precisely, courageously, and unreservedly carry out the orders of my senior comrades, to strictly keep all secrets entrusted to me as well as everything communicated to me in the course of my work, and to concern myself with keeping the conspiracy.

I am aware that those who violate discipline and the conspiracy are declared to be provocateurs and are condemned to death.

(Signature)

569

Ilya Ehrenburg among the Jewish partisans who succeeded in breaking out of the Vilnius ghetto.
This photograph was not among the photographic documents attached to the manuscript of *The Black Book*. Ilya Ehrenburg sent this photograph to Joseph Guri, who works in Yad Vashem. The picture was accompanied by the following letter:

Sept. 6, 1963
Moscow

Dear Mr. Guri,

At your request I am sending to you the photograph which I mention in my memoirs. This is a Soviet partisan unit which consisted of Jews who succeeded in escaping from the Vilnius ghetto. The unit took part in battles during the liberation of the city.

I have the Ivrith translation of the first and second part of my book. Thank you for your attention.

Respectfully yours,
Ilya Ehrenburg

ABOUT THE AUTHORS

Aliger, Margarita Iosifovna (1915) — poet and translator. Author of well known works: *To the Memory of the Brave* (1942), *Zoya* (1942), *Lyrical Poems* (1943), *From a Notebook 1946–1956* (1957). In some of her writings Aliger attempted to philosophically fathom Jewish problematics — *Your Victory* (1945) and a cycle of poems about Germany.

Antokolsky, Pavel Grigorievich (1896-1978) — poet and translator. A war correspondent during the war years. His most famous works are: *The West* (1926), *Robespierre and Gorgonne* (1928), *François Villon* (1934), *Pushkin's Year* (1938), *In a Lane Beyond the Arbat* (1954), *The Shop* (1958). During the war Antokolsky created works dedicated to the tragedy and heroism of the Jewish people: *Son* (1943), *Camp of Destruction* (1945), *Uprising in Sobibor* (co-authored with V. Kaverin — 1945), *A Non-Eternal Memory* (1946).

Apresyan, Vagram Zakharovich — prose writer and essayist, military correspondent during World War II.

Cherny, Osip Evseyevich (1899) — writer, art historian, musical director. Main works: *Musicians* (1940), *Snegin's Opera* (1953), *Paths of Creativity* (1957), *Franz Shubert* (1941), *Musorgsky* (1956), *Rimsky-Korsakov* (1959).

Derman, Abram Borisovich (1880-1952) — literary scholar, prose writer. Main works: *Mikhail Semenovich Shchepkin* (1937), *Anton Pavlovich Chekhov* (1939), *The Case of Father-Superior Parfeny* (1941), *The Life of V. G. Korolenko* (1946), *On the Art of Chekhov* (1953).

Ehrenburg, Ilya Grigoryevich (1891-1967) — prose writer, poet, publicist; during the years of World War II a military correspondent. A portion of Ehrenburg's anti-Fascist articles and pamphlets written during World War II was published in a three-volume set of his publicistic writings — *War* (Moscow, 1942-1944); *The Chronicle of Heroism* (Moscow, 1974) is a collection of publicistic writings from the war period written for overseas news agencies and newspapers. He was a member of the Jewish Anti-Fascist Committee and was published in *Einikeit*. Main works: *The Face of War* (1920), *The Extraordinary Adventures of Julio Jurenito and His Pupils* (1922), *Six Tales About Easy Endings* (1922), *The Life and Tragic Death of Nikolay Kurbov* (1923), *The Trust D.E.* (1923), *Thirteen Pipes* (1923), *The Love of Jeanne Ney*

(1924), *The Tumultuous Life of Lazik Roytshvanets* (1928), *Visa of Time* (1929), *Spain* (1932), *The Second Day* (1934), *A Book for Adults* (1936), *The Fall of Paris* (1941), *Tree* (1946), *The Storm* (1948), *The Thaw* (1954), *People, Years, Life* — 3 volumes, (1961-1966).

Frayerman, Ruvim Isayevich (1892-1972) — prose writer and journalist; in 1941 joined the ranks of the National Guard; worked in army publications. Main works: *The Snowstorm* (1926), *Vaska-Gilyak* (1929), *The Spy* (1937), *The Wild Dog Dingo, or a Story of First Love* (1938), *Distant Voyage* (1946).

Gekhtman, Yefim — journalist, publicist. A war correspondent for the newspaper *Krasnaya Zvezda* during the war.

Gerasimov, Valeria Anatolyevna — prose writer. Worked in a military publishing house during the war.

Goldberg, Leyb (1892-1955) — prose writer, translator, journalist; wrote in Yiddish and translated Sholom Aleichem into Russian. During the war years he participated in the work of the Jewish Anti-Fascist Committee and published in *Einikeit* ("Unity").

Grossman, Vasily Semenovich (Iosif Solomonovich, 1905-1964) — prose writer. A correspondent of *Krasnaya Zvezda* during the war. His main works are: *Gliukauf* (1934), *Stepan Kolchugin* (1937-1940), *A People Is Immortal* (1942), *The Direction of the Primary Blow* (1943), *The War Years* (1945), *For a Just Cause* (1952), *All Is Flux* (1970). A number of Grossman's essays and stories is dedicated to the Jewish catastrophe: *The Old Teacher* (1942), *The Ukraine Without Jews* (*Einikeit*, Nov. 11 and Dec. 2, 1943), *The Hell of Treblinka* (1945).

Ilyenkov, Vasily Pavlovich (1897) — prose writer, became famous during the war years as an essayist, publicist, and journalist. Main works: *Leading Axle* (1931), *City of the Sun* (1935), *Home* (1942), *To the Other Shore* (1945), *The Highway* (1949).

Inber, Vera Mikhailovna (1890-1972) — poet, prose writer, became famous during the war years as an essayist, publicist, and journalist. Main works: *Sad Wine* (1914), *To a Son Who Is No Longer* (1927), *A Place in the Sun* (1928), *At Half Voice* (1932), *Ovid* (1939), *The Soul of Leningrad* (1942), *The Pulkovo Meridian* (1943), *Almost Three Years* (1946).

Ivanov, Vsevolod Vyacheslavovich (1895-1963) — prose writer and playwright, wrote publicistic articles and stories on military topics during the war. His main works are: *Armored Train 14-69* (1922), *Hills: Partisan Tales* (1923), *Khabu* (1925), *The Mansion* (1928), *Adventures of a Fakir* (1935), *We Are Going to India*.

Kaverin (Zilber), Veniamin Akeksandrovich (1902) — prose writer, during the war was a military correspondent for TASS and *Izvestia*. Was a member of the Jewish Anti-Fascist Committee. Main works: *The End of Khaza* (1926), *Baron Brambeus* (1929), *Two Captains* (1944), *The Open Book* (1956), *Seven Unclean Pairs* (1962), *The Slanted Rain* (1962). A number of the writer's works are devoted to the heroism of Jews during the years of World War II: an essay about the captain of a submarine, Izrail Fisanovich, Hero of the Soviet Union; *Uprising in Sobibor* (co-authored with P. Antokolsky).

Kovnator, Rakhil — journalist, worked in the Jewish Anti-Fascist Committee during the war. Wrote for the newspaper *Einikeit*.

Kvitko, Leyb (Lev Moiseyevich, 1890-1952) — poet, founder of poems for children in Yiddish in the Soviet Union. During the war he was a member of the Jewish Anti-Fascist Committee. Author of publicistic articles in the newspaper *Einikeit*. In the beginning of 1949, after the liquidation of the Jewish Anti-Fascist Committee, he was arrested and shot on August 12, 1952, together with a large group of Jewish writers and cultural figures. Main works: *Steps* (1919), *Green Grass* (1922), *1919* (1929), *Struggle* (1929), *Songs and Poems* (1933), *New Poems* (1939), *The Song of My Mind* (1947), *Selected Works* (1948).

Lidin (Gomberg), Vladimir Germanovich (1894-1979) — prose writer, a war correspondent for *Izvestia* and army newspapers during the war. Main works: *Mouse Work Days* (1923), *North Wind* (1925), *The Heretic* (1927), *The Grave of the Unknown Soldier* (1932), *Exile* (1947).

Munblit, Georgy Nikolayevich (1904) — prose writer, critic, scenario writer; a journalist-publicist during the war. Main works: scenarios of the films *A Musical Story* (1940, co-authored with E. Petrov), *The Restless Man* (1940, co-authored with E. Petrov), *Anton Ivanovich Is Angry* (1941, co-authored with E. Petrov), *The Situation Requires* (co-authored with A. Galich); *Stories About Writers* (1962).

Osherovich, Girsh (1908) — poet, writes in Yiddish. During the years of World War II he published his work on anti-Fascist topics in publications of the Jewish Anti-Fascist Committee. He was a correspondent for *Einikeit*. In 1949, after the liquidation of the Jewish Anti-Fascist Committee, he was arrested. He was released in 1956 and repatriated to Israel in 1971. Main works: *Dawn* (1941), *Out of the Plight* (1947), *Holy Weekdays* (1968), *Sunset*

(1969), *Between Lightning and Thunder* (1973), *My Ponieviezh (1974)*, *In the World of Sacrifices* (1975), *Song in the Labyrinth* (1977), *Biblical Poems* (1979), *Blue Boomerangs* (1979).

Ozerov, Lev Adolfovich (Goldberg, Lev Ayzikovich, 1914) — poet, translator, critic. During the war a correspondent of the military newspaper *Victory Is Ours*. Main works: *Near the Dniester* (1940), *The Downpour* (1947), *Chiaroscuro* (1961), *A Poet's Work* (1963), *Lyrics* (1966). His large poem *Babi Yar* is dedicated to the catastrophe of the Jewish people.

Savich, Ovady Gertsevich (1896-1967) — prose writer, poet, publicist, journalist. During the war years a war correspondent. Main works: *An Imagined Interlocutor* (1928), *People of the International Brigades* (1938), *Two Years in Spain 1937–1938, Essays and Stories* (1961).

Seyfullin, Lidia Nikolayevna (1889-1954) — prose writer, playwright; worked in newspapers and on the radio during the war years. Main works: *Virineya* (1924), *Kain-Kabak* (1926), *On My Own Land* (1946), *Son* (1959).

Shklovsky, Viktor Borisovich (1893) — prose writer, literary scholar, critic, movie-scenario writer. Main works: *Sentimental Journeys* (1923), *The Zoo: Letters Not About Love* (1923), *The Third Factory* (1926), *The Hamburg Bill* (1928), *Marco Polo* (1936), *Tale of the Artist Fedorov* (1955), *Once Upon a Time* (1962), *Leo Tolstoy* (1963).

Trainin, Ilya Pavlovich (1887-1949) — lawyer, full member of the Academy of Sciences of the U.S.S.R. During the war, as director of the Institute of Law of the Academy of Sciences of the U.S.S.R., he did a great deal of work in collecting documents on Nazi crimes committed on occupied Soviet territories. He cooperated with the Jewish Anti-Fascist Committee and was one of the members of the Special Government Committee for the Investigation and Verification of Crimes Committed by the German-Fascist Invaders and Their Accomplices. Main works: *The U.S.S.R. and the National Problem* (1924), *The State and Communism* (1940), *The Mechanism of the German-Fascist Dictatorship* (1942), *Questions of Territory in Governmental Law* (1947).

INDEX OF NAMES

L., 325
L., Liza, 337
Labkovsky, S., 512
Lakhman, 203
Landau, Lipa, 190
Lange, 313, 319
Langman, Lyubov Mikhailovna, 27
Lants, 432, 433
Lantsman, E., 27
Lapchinsky, Khaim, 232
Lapidus, 162
Lapin, Andrey Ivanovich, 90
Lapin, Varvara Andreyevna, 90
Laun, A., 116
Ledek, 402, 433
Leenzon, I. M., 83
Lef, Abram, 245
Leger, 103
Leger, Tamara, 103
Leibl, Dina, 135
Leitish, 229
Leitman, Shleyma, 443, 445, 446, 448,
    449, 451, 453
Lenard, 122
Lerner, 32
Lerner, 42
Lerner, David, 103
Lerner, Khana, 69
Lev (Dr.), 175
Lev, Ayzik, 200
Levchenko, 355, 357
Levi, 391
Levin, 390
Levin, 155
Levin (Bersarin), 158
Levin, Ruvim, 231
Levit, Max, 401, 431, 434, 435
Levitan, 381
Levkovets, Andrey Ivanovich, 218
Lev-Mlynsky (Dr.), 175
Lex, 110
Leyb, 401, 430, 433, 434
Leyzerovich, Aaron, 492
Liaks, Kveta, 228
Liberman, 18, 23
Liberman, David (Rabbi), 39
Liberman, V., 3
Libman, B. A., 5
Libman, Jankel, 396
Lichter, 300
Lichter, Jurek, 123
Lidin, Vladimir, xii, 26
Lifschits, 162
Lindvor, Rosa, 136
Lipengolts, 396

Lipets, 245
Lipke, Jan (Janis), 322
Lipmanovich, 322
Liskovsky, Anya, 229
Liss, Nina, 157, 159
Litoshchenko, 10
Litoshchenko, Yevgenia, 3
Livshits (Dr.), 272
Lorenzen, 302
Lourié, 257
Lozovsky, S[olomon], xxii
Lukinsky, E. P., 364
Lukinskys, the, 361, 363, 364
Lukke, 446, 448, 454
Lumer, 42
Lupescu, 86
Lyak, 352
Lyarek, 229
Lysy (Dr.), 272
Lyubetsky, Fishel, 494

Machiz, A., 181
Magarik, 336
Magat, Regina Lazarevna, 6
Magid, 348
Maindl (overseer), 104, 105, 106
Maizels, 156
Makhol, 242, 243, 245
Makson, 388, 389
Malkin, 36
Malkin, 203
Malkin Mrs., 313
Malmed, 231, 232
Malya, 484
Malyavsky, 203
Mandel, 116
Mandelblat, Leybush, 229, 232
Manke, 322
Mannskeit, Hans, 302
Manushin, K. Ya., 513
Manzon, 219
Marenes (Dr.), 268
Margolin, Esfir (Dr.), 148, 156
Margulis, Anna, 81
Marinescu, 98
Markewicz, 233
Markushevich, 327
Martyshev, Sergey Fedorovich, 457,
    458
Masha, 349
Matskin, 465, 471
Mayakov, 359, 360
Mayzel, 164
Mazovsky, Sima, 35
Mazurkevich, Semyon, 452

INDEX OF GEOGRAPHICAL NAMES